# ESSAYS IN SHAKESPEAREAN CRITICISM

# ESSAYS IN SHAKESPEAREAN CRITICISM

*edited by*

James L. Calderwood

Harold E. Toliver

*University of California, Irvine*
*Irvine, California*

PRENTICE-HALL, INC.
*Englewood Cliffs, New Jersey*

13–283655–6
Library of Congress Catalogue Card No.: 70–100590
Printed in the United States of America
Current printing (last digit):
10 9 8 7 6 5 4 3 2 1

PRENTICE-HALL INTERNATIONAL, INC., *London*
PRENTICE-HALL OF JAPAN, INC., *Tokyo*
PRENTICE-HALL OF AUSTRALIA, PTY. LTD., *Sydney*
PRENTICE-HALL OF CANADA, LTD., *Toronto*
PRENTICE-HALL OF INDIA PRIVATE LTD., *New Delhi*

# Preface

When Bottom the weaver returns to reality after consorting with the dainty Queen Titania in fairyland, his dimly flickering wit tells him that he has "had a dream past the wit of man to say what dream it was" and that "man is but an ass if he go about to expound this dream." Bottom's remarks are hardly designed to embolden professional expounders of Shakespeare's dramatic dreams. Nevertheless, shakespeare critics since the seventeenth century have been risking long ears and hairy cheeks with growing frequency, apparently less impressed by Bottom's warning than by Falstaff's reply when accused by Prince Hal of being a pickpocket: "Why, Hal, 'tis my vocation, Hal. 'Tis no sin for a man to labour in his vocation." As the critical vocation has become increasingly popular, the labors of the general student have grown increasingly difficult. In 1964 alone, for instance, the annual bibliography of the *Shakespeare Quarterly* ran to well over 3,200 items—a forbidding number to even the most passionate of bardolaters and sufficient proof to most students that Shakespeare has indeed had a dream past the wit of man to say what dream it was.

In the face of an ever-multiplying number of books and articles, however, the reasonably serious student of Shakespeare may take some comfort from the thought that not everything in print merits reading and that by a process of natural, or perhaps unnatural, selection the best criticism gradually comes into prominence. To help accelerate that process for the criticism of the last twenty odd years, when much of the finest scholarship and most perceptive analysis of Shakespeare has been done, is the purpose of this collcetion of mid-twentieth century essays. Not, of course, that Shakespeare critics of this period have been gracious enough to restrict their finest statements to some thirty-five or so articles and chapters that have patiently awaited our discovery and reprinting here. There are naturally many essays that we should have liked to include but could not because of space, and no doubt many others that should appear but do not because of editorial ignorance (we cannot claim to have read even those 3,200 items of 1964). Still, we have read fairly widely and selected wiht as much care as we could, trying to include only those pieces that manage in one way or another to open up, suggest, clarify, illuminate, and occasionally pin down something distinctively Shakespearean.

The "something" of the last sentence is intentionally imprecise, for if the study of Shakespeare teaches us anything it is that critics of Shakespeare must rest content with limited perspectives and partial truths. Nowhere more conspicuously than in Shakespeare criticism has the assumption of twentieth century aesthetics been borne out that the work of literary art is polysemous and hospitable to a variety of interpretations. "I can call spirits from the vasty deep," Owen Glendower proclaims to Harry Hotspur, and receives a dry reply: "Why, so can I, or so can any man; / But will they come when you do call for them?" Infinitely generous, Shakespeare makes successful Glendowers of us all, sending forth reasonably substantial spirits in response to the most diverse kinds of critical summons. (Indeed the cry of "appearance and reality," or "nature," or "time and eternity," or any of a dozen others has started ghostly legions from the Shakespearean deep, and the cry keeps echoing in article after article, term paper after term paper.) Which of the various critical methods calls forth the most meaningful and enduring responses from Shakespeare it would be difficult, and not especially profitable, to establish, since it has become abundantly clear that Shakespeare has more answers in supply than we have questions to ask. Surely it would be premature at this point and unShakespearean in spirit to jettison diversity in the interests of unity.

The virtues of such diversity have perhaps become most evident in criticism of the past twenty or so years. However a brief sketch of the major positions of earlier tewntieth century critics will suggest the ways in which that diversity was prepared for. We might begin by mentioning the fine English critic A. C. Bradley, who in *Shakespearean Tragedy* (1904) brilliantly explored the interpenetration of character and action in the tragedies, giving special emphasis to the attitudes, motives, and feelings of the "personages." If Bradley made too little distinction between drama and life, compensatory reactions were quick to develop in the work of Harley Granville-Barker (*Prefaces to Shakespeare,* 1927–1947) and of E. E. Stoll (*Art and Artifice in Shakespeare,* 1933), both of whom analyzed the plays as works of theatrical art divorced from life and governed by the conventions and conditions of the stage. And if Bradley disregarded the poetic language of Shakespearean drama, one aspect of that language began to come to the fore with Caroline Spurgeon's seminal though somewhat indiscriminately statistical study, *Shakespeare's Imagery and What It Tells Us* (1935). Interest in Shakespeare's imagery was given more significant focus by G. Wilson Knight, who around 1930 began to develop the view that the plays are complex orchestrations of symbolic themes (life and death, good and evil, order and disorder, etc.) expressing a somewhat mystical vision of human experience. Meanwhile, historically oriented critics like Lily B. Campbell, E. M. W. Tillyard, Hardin Craig, and E. K. Chambers, to mention merely a few, continued to reconstruct the general cultural milieu of the age in which and beyond which Shakespeare wrote and to interpret the plays as reflections of the issues, traditions, and values of that age. Finally, and often in opposition to historical criticism, the New Critics of the thirties and forties—for instance, Cleanth Brooks, Robert Penn Warren, and Robert B. Heilman in America and William Empson, F. R. Leavis, and Derek Traversi in England—contributed to a sophistication of analytic technique that enabled a close and careful scrutiny of the local texture and formal structure of individual plays.

Thus criticism since about 1950 has been able to draw on rich methodological reserves built up in the past while investing in its own portfolio of interests. We have not tried systematically to represent the full range of these methods or to include all the topics of Shakespeare criticism, but the student will find a reasonably various sampling nonetheless: for instance, history of ideas (Theodore Spencer), theater (J. L. Styan), genre (Northrop Frye, Maynard Mack, R. G. Hunter), sources (A. P. Rossiter, Sigurd Burckhardt), structure (David Young), language (Murray Krieger), style (Joan Webber, Arnold Stein), myth and ritual (C. L. Barber, Francis Fergusson, John Holloway), theme (Winifred Nowottny), imagery (M. M. Mahood), form (Kenneth Burke), and so on. Such designations, however, do scant justice to the flexibility and quick responsiveness with which these critics adapt their methods to the complexities of the plays they treat. Rather than force essays into groupings based on method, which would imply the division of criticism into certain well defined sects, we have thought it better to let the organization of the selections derive from the plays themselves, bginning with essays on some general issues, then focusing on the natural unit of Shakespearean criticism, the individual play. Each of the major comedies, tragedies, and histories is represented by at least one essay, often by two; and an occasional article links plays that are closely associated by genre, theme, or serial continuity. With this organization we hope to have made this a broadly serviceable as well as readable collection, one that should go at least part way toward relieving the despair of the Shakespeare student rummaging wearily through the card catalog or shuffling from journal to journal in the stacks.

*University of California, Irvine*

JAMES L. CALDERWOOD
HAROLD E. TOLIVER

# Contents

## GENERAL

## COMEDIES

# TRAGEDIES

# ESSAYS IN SHAKESPEAREAN CRITICISM

# GENERAL

# 1

# Staging and Acting Conventions

*J. L. Styan*

## Convention in Shakespeare's Theatre

An efficient staging convention is properly something that the spectator forgets as soon as the processes of theatre are under way. The Elizabethan spectator took for granted matters of symbolism in character or dress and ignored the play's elasticity of place and time. Dr. Johnson testified to Shakespeare's practical art which required that the rules of neo-classical criticism be amended before the plays should be censured and that the spectators in the theatre should be the judges of the merit of Shakespeare's rejection of the unities. Johnson's famous dictum, "The truth is, that the spectators are always in their senses, and know, from the first act to the last, that the stage is only a stage, and that the players are only players," for all it needs judicious qualification, might have been a piece of post-Brechtian criticism. The spectators know that it is theatre, not life, but they choose not to know. When Coleridge pursued the case further, he observed that "The very nakedness of the stage was advantageous,—for the drama thence became something between recitation and a re-presentation." He

*Reprinted from J. L. Styan,* Shakespeare's Stagecraft, *pp. 28–50 by permission of Cambridge University Press.*

recognized more particularly in these words the framework of convention within which Elizabethan drama worked, one which allowed it to range between symbolism and naturalism.

When in *Macbeth,* I, v, Shakespeare's audience saw Lady Macbeth reading the letter from her husband, they did not pause to consider that now, suddenly, the scene had changed from Forres to Inverness, from Duncan's palace to Macbeth's castle. The change had been accomplished before Lady Macbeth made her entrance. The audience had heard Macbeth say to the King,

> I'll be myself the harbinger, and make joyful
> The hearing of my wife with your approach, (I, iv, 45–6)

and the playwright would have upset them had the first lady to enter reading a letter *not* been Macbeth's wife, although they would justly have been surprised at the kind of joy they saw her exhibit. Speech and context of situation were imaginatively one whole. It is a modern habit to query the place of the action, here an irrelevance for which Shakespeare cared nothing. He wrote a drama that created its own atmosphere and identified its own locality, if it needed to.

He mocked the exertions of both silly realism and fatuous symbolism in his burlesque of the preparations for "Pyramus and Thisbe." Peter Quince needs moonlight for his lovers, so Bottom, keen amateur student of the drama that he is, calls for the real thing:

> A calendar, a calendar...look in the almanac...find out moonshine, find out moonshine. (*A Midsummer Night's Dream,* III, i, 48–9)

Quince has a second problem, to provide a wall with a chink for the lovers to talk through. Again Bottom is quick with a ridiculous solution, although this time a symbolic one:

> Some man or other must present wall: and let him have some plaster, or some loam, or some rough-cast about him, to signify wall; and let him hold his fingers thus... (62–5)

To see Robin Starveling or Tom Snout smothered in real plaster is to understand the muddle of ideas in Bottom's head.

In holding his mirror up to nature, Shakespeare was reflecting general truths for his audience to recognize with the minimum of imaginative acrobatics and distracting obstacles. When he wanted to show actuality, he did so with that compulsive particularity found so often in his work: to measure cruelty and pain, blood must spill when Gloucester's eyes are put out; for Rosalind to enact a girl in love, she must see Orlando's verses pinned to a tree. Having caught the spectator's attention by particularities, he swiftly shows him human responses in their general image. The detail of verisimilitude in Shakespeare is not an obstacle but a directive for the imagination.

The simple sweep of the Elizabethan platform not only lent the playwright the freedom he wanted, but also cleared the mind of the spectator for conjuring up visions. By its nature Shakespeare's was a stage which invited the spectator to "play with his fancies," as the Prologue to *Henry V* puts it. It is when the imagination is unrestricted that the playwright's skill in curbing and directing it takes on qualities of magic. The actor's convention and the poetic drama are in this way joined; the playwright is the go-between diligently arranging the match, exploiting first the actor, then the spectator; first the wooer, then the wooed.

"It is essential that a work of art should be self-consistent, that an artist should consciously or unconsciously draw a circle beyond which he does not trespass: on the one hand actual life is always the material, and on the other hand an abstraction from actual life is a necessary condition to the creation of the work of art." So wrote T. S. Eliot in criticism of the conventions in Elizabethan drama. "An actor in an Elizabethan play is either too realistic or too abstract in his treatment."[1] Nevertheless, the freedom of Shakespeare's stage and his lack of consistency, in Eliot's sense, permitted his play to pass between particularity and generality, between the real and the abstract, building an experience measurable against the detail of real life, yet finally moving into those areas which constitute good theatre.

## Properties and Symbols

This flexibility is seen at its simplest in Shakespeare's handling of two less abstract elements of theatrical convention, properties and costume. No theatre has done without properties, whether scenic set-pieces or devices to help the actor create the action. The Elizabethan theatre was no exception. Shakespeare inherited a lively tradition of using scenic emblems which he used like other conventional equipment, both as adjuncts to acting and aids to the imagination. When he wanted, even a hand property could have its significance intensified to point his theme, the spectator's attention being drawn to it until the object acquired formidable moral or political qualities.

Glynne Wickham suggests[2] that a tent used emblematically in the medieval way could be transformed into a throne, a pavilion, a house, a palace, a temple, a castle or a city by some decorative device like a vane or a shield. Mansion staging (the setting of localized stations upon the same stage) along such easy lines would be in keeping with our image of the fluidity of the Elizabethan stage: it permitted the kind of real-and-unreal

---

[1] *Selected Essays,* pp. 111–12.

[2] *Early English Stages,* vol. II, part 1, p. 298.

setting of the stage and released the platform for simultaneous scene playing without crushing it with the weight of carpentry; it enabled stagehands to shift a property while the players were still on and kept the mechanics of production and décor light and mobile. The traditional thinking behind mansion staging, which permitted the arena to represent parts of the globe or the Kingdom of God, was readily assimilable to the planning for the formal outlines of the platform. With its symmetrical doors and permanent balcony, the platform supplied a spacious neutral acting space over which the actors could pass, freely creating meaningfully localized areas. The Elizabethan stage could embrace effects of simultaneous staging, linking all its scenes without changing the formal appearance of the platform and the façade behind it.

It was also traditional to introduce scenic tokens convenient to the stage: trees, arbours, pavilions, monuments and thrones, as well as many others found in Henslowe's inventory of the properties he kept in his Rose Theatre in 1598 and in the Revels Office books, those accounts of costumes and properties supplied by the Master of the Queen's Revels for performances at Court. The solidity of these properties need not be doubted: a tree and an arbour had to be substantial enough to seem to bear a hanging man (as in *The Spanish Tragedy* and *Every Man Out of His Humour*), and strong enough to climb (Berowne in *Love's Labour's Lost,* IV, iii). The box-tree in *Twelfth Night,* II, v, was probably sizable enough to conceal Toby, Andrew and Fabian, all three.

Yet in Shakespeare's hands the objective limitations of the properties are transcended, and as symbols their meaning grows. His was the same theatrical imagination as Christopher Marlowe's, whose Fautus hears the striking of a clock while in imagination he counts the minutes of an eternity in hell. So for Shakespeare a property was a dramatic opportunity—think only of Macbeth's dagger, the real weapon slung at his waist, the "air-drawn" fantasy a chance to plumb his mind and compel us to visualize the murder we do not actually see.

*Richard II,* IV, i, is a scene in which Shakespeare seems to be experimenting with his properties as cues for poetry. Thus the King's business with the mirror:

> Give me that glass, and therein will I read...
> No deeper wrinkles yet? hath sorrow struck
> So many blows upon this face of mine,
> And made no deeper wounds? O, flatt'ring glass,
> Like to my followers in prosperity,
> Thou dost beguile me!...
> A brittle glory shineth in this face,
> As brittle as the glory is the face,
> For there it is, cracked in a hundred shivers. (276–89)

Here he dashes the glass to the ground. This is an actor's piece, climactic with the rhetorical repetitions characteristic of Richard, and the property mirror is a first-rate aid to him. Yet for the sense, the property is especially apt: the speech is of self-scrutiny, and Shakespeare supplies a visible symbol for a self-conscious and oversensitive man. Later, other sensitive men, like Cassius and Hamlet, speak also of the glass with which to "see the inmost part," but for them Shakespeare is content with verbal imagery. For Richard he has made the feeling of the actor and the point of the speech theatrically objective.

The royal crown of the King of England was an early and obvious symbolic property, both for Richard in his contest with Bolingbroke (*Richard II,* IV, i, 181 ff.) and for Prince Henry. Hal moralizes upon it in the presence of his dying father, for whom it is the "troublesome bedfellow," a "polished perturbation," the "golden care" (*2 Henry IV,* IV, v, 21 ff.). Its momentary theft starts that great discussion between monarch and heir apparent on the responsibilities of rule.

*Hamlet* is a play imbued with the imagery of mortality, and this is pointed by the Clowns who dig Ophelia's grave. The property skulls prompt Hamlet's comments, first cynical, then of feeling and understanding, as he fingers all that is left of Yorick. When he realizes it is Ophelia's grave, he speaks with genuine sorrow, in his anger modulating into a parody of Laertes's high-flown expression of grief. The acting, the illustration of a theme, the development of the action and the particularizing of the character, first in his intimate relationship with Yorick and then by reflection with Ophelia, whose remains would match his and lie in the same place, are married in the scene by the use of the properties.

The mature plays are mature in their handling of such objective emblems, and the control of the handkerchief and the taper in *Othello* is particularly sure. Coming at the right moment in Othello's progress to corruption, the handkerchief, that "trifle light as air" and one so casually dropped, is magnified fantastically by the tortured mind. Its meaning is reinforced by the exotic poetry that seems to weave the magic in its web. It obsesses Othello to the last, while its triviality increasingly belittles the nobility of the soldier we first met. Again, the actor takes up the taper which is at once to mark the dead of night and the Moor's impulse to offer prayer, and its visual suggestion of light and darkness becomes associated with the issue of the life and death of a Christian soul and the murder of a young woman in her vital beauty:

But once put out thy light,
Thou cunning'st pattern of excelling nature,
I know not where is that Promethean heat
That can thy light relume. (V, ii, 10–14)

This taper makes of her deathbed a sacrificial altar, one upon which man's love of life and hope of heaven are annihilated.

## A Wardrobe for Scene and Symbol

No theatre has ignored the contribution to mood and meaning that costume can make, and in Elizabeth's time the actor's wardrobe was lavish. A rich tradition of splendour of costume had been handed down through Tudor times, deriving from the pride in presentation belonging to the craft guild players of the Mystery Cycles. Nor could there be amateurishness in an intimate theatre: conviction of authenticity prevailed.

However, enough is known from Henslowe, the Revels Office, contemporary German accounts of English tours and from internal evidence for it to be said that while the players cared much for magnificence, historical or national accuracy did not bother them. Hamlet wore doublet and hose, and Cleopatra dressed like a wealthy Elizabethan lady. Although for mockery a particularly topical note might be introduced, as for Le Beau and Osric, a non-committal contemporary dress stressed both the relevance and the timelessness of the subjects.

Where a play or a scene is distinguished by straightforward contrasts of attitude, costume underlines the differences for immediate apprehension by the spectator. *The Merchant of Venice* hints at the Elizabethan view of Venetian luxury which the gentile merchants displayed; and set against them are the sombre gaberdines of Shylock, Tubal and the Jewish community. Shakespeare marks the contrast at the Battle of Agincourt in *Henry V* between the tired English in their "war-worn coats" and "the confident and over-lusty French" boasting of their splendid armour, a familiar theatrical preliminary to the ironic victory of the Englishmen. A visual contrast between opposing forces was a commonplace in the chronicle plays, as also between the Scots and English in *Macbeth,* the Romans and the Volsces in *Coriolanus* and the Romans and the British in *Cymbeline. Antony and Cleopatra* offers an interesting extension of this principle. Costume reminds the spectator constantly of the play's seesaw issues when the formal Roman soldiery is visually opposed to the colourful Egyptians. Dress is a visible reminder throughout the play of a masculine Rome at discord with a feminine Egypt.

The playwright probably had less control over this selection of costume than the wardrobe master, but in particular matters of dress Shakespeare revealed his eye for the effect that colour and cut can imply. There is no forgetting the comic entrance of Juliet's Nurse to the cries of the young gallants, "Here's goodly gear! A sail, a sail!" (*Romeo and Juliet,* II, iv, 98). In visually conceived scenes he demonstrates his flair for using costume to dramatic ends. King Henry V strikes a note of personal distinction from both the English and the gaudy French when he borrows Sir Thomas Erpingham's cloak (*Henry V,* IV, i) to humble himself and his thoughts with the prosaic soldiers round the campfire. The colossus Caesar shows himself subject to human weakness when he appears clad in a nightgown to hear of Calpurnia's nightmare (*Julius Caesar,* II, ii). He is seen following a scene of conspiracy made sinister by thunder and lightning and dangerous men with hats "plucked about their ears,/And half their faces buried in their cloaks" (II, i, 73–4). In another vein, Malvolio cuts a wildly comic figure in his nightgown when he bursts upon Sir Toby's drinking party in the middle of the night (*Twelfth Night,* II, iii).

The situation at the court of Elsinore is immediately apparent as Hamlet sits apart in his "inky cloak," the mourning of his "nighted colour" making its persistent rebuke to the showy, oblivious court that lives "too much in the sun" (*Hamlet,* I, ii). Moreover, when the Prince adopts the undress of his antic disposition, as described by Ophelia (II, i, 74 ff.), both words and dress mock the proprieties of Polonius. Isabella in the white habit of a novice confronts Angelo in the black robes of a judge (*Measure for Measure,* II, ii). Othello the Moor visually denies Iago's cynical description of the "black ram...tupping your white ewe" when he makes his entrance into a familiar setting dressed like a prince from a remote sun-scorched country (*Othello,* I, ii). Cleopatra robes herself for the stroke of death and her noblest gesture (*Antony and Cleopatra,* V, ii), and both outwits and outshines her enemy. Coriolanus, previously seen only in military finery, must stand proud and angry before the citizens in his despised "gown of humility"; the incongruity between his soldierly presence and the costume itself is a neat stroke for drama as he stands alone to face an ordeal he loathes (*Coriolanus,* II, iii).

Shakespeare takes the conventional equipment of property and costume and uses them as a way of speaking to the audience. Their strength is sustained for as long as they are displayed on the stage.

## Ranging Between Naturalism and Ritual

The mixing of naturalism and ritual is also to be seen in the acting conventions. It was typical of the traditional pattern to break through convention altogether. In the Mystery Plays the amateur actors not only addressed the spectators but played among them and spoke for them. In Henry Medwall's highly formal disputation *Fulgens and Lucrece* (1497), a naturalistic link with the real audience is made by the presence of two youths "A" and "B," who at the beginning of the play emerge from the crowd of guests at an imaginary banquet, and like the real audience discuss the play about to be seen. In the role of comic servants to the noble suitors wooing

Lucrece, their task is to burlesque their masters. This is a descent to naturalism and a manner of burlesque that extends in Shakespeare himself from the drunken presence of Christopher Sly throughout *The Taming of the Shrew* to Falstaff's intimate parodies of warfare, which establish a similarly close link with the spectator.

In the compact Elizabethan theatre this link was always potentially present, and Shakespeare regularly stresses the actuality of the play's experience by naturalistic means. An aside to the audience, a sudden allusion to some topic of the moment, a chance for the company's clown to extemporize, the courteous appeals of Prologue and Epilogue for attention or applause—these bear witness to the direct contact between player and spectator.

Naturalism and intimacy are not interchangeable elements, but the history of the theatre has indicated their interdependence. The physical nearness of the street audiences of the Mystery Plays encouraged a homely and often incongruous demonstration of the Scriptures, as well as a streak of farce. At another extreme, the impact Shakespeare has on television audiences derives from those moments of familiar speech and conduct scattered through his work. Television, from one view the most intimate dramatic medium, cannot accommodate the delivery of ritualistic speech and the photographic representation of formal battle scenes, but the balance has often been redressed by a soliloquy spoken quietly and naturalistically into the camera's eye.

A theatre which could permit both the rant and the whisper encouraged Shakespeare to develop a structural technique which exploited both: early in his career he applied astringent touches to romantic comedy, introducing unsophisticated workmen, for example, into the moonlight of *A Midsummer Night's Dream*. It was predictable that Falstaff and the companions of The Boar's Head should supply the "control group" of normality for his social study of politics and politicians in *I Henry IV*. In his early tragedies he learned with what effect simplicity of utterance or silence could mark moments of emotion:

> *Juliet.* Romeo!
> *Romeo.* My niëss!
> *Juliet.* What o'clock tomorrow
> Shall I send to thee?
> *Romeo.* By the hour of nine.
> *Juliet.* I will not fail. 'Tis twenty year till then.
> I have forgot why I did call thee back.
> (*Romeo and Juliet,* II, ii, 167–70)

The actress's exercise is to place the pauses in this reproduction of a shy girl's inability to leave her lover. The lyricism had lifted the balcony scene into a region where now these commonplace lines reflect a natural human beauty.

On the other hand, the ritualistic tradition of Shakespeare's forerunners and contemporaries was the Elizabethans' special delight and Shakespeare's forte. He knew how to have his actor strike an attitude: a speech from the throne by Henry V or Caesar, or in comedy a fairy tale ceremony like choosing a husband by casket as Portia does in *The Merchant of Venice* or by dance as Helena does in *All's Well That Ends Well*; or in tragedy a ritualistic end for Macbeth or Hamlet, where pageantry lends that sense of finality long after the real crisis has passed:

> Let four captains
> Bear Hamlet like a soldier to the stage,
> For he was likely, had he been put on,
> To have proved most royal. (*Hamlet,* V, ii, 393–6)

So speaks Fortinbras, and "*Exeunt marching: after the which, a peal of ordnance are shot off.*" The dead must be carried off the Elizabethan stage; an added dignity is given to Hamlet's death by the practice of a stage ritual.

## Actor and Atmosphere on a Neutral Stage

Whether in naturalistic or ritualistic terms, Shakespeare is quick to anticipate his scene's mood and atmosphere, and for this reason it is difficult to separate descriptive effects from acting opportunities. Every actor must be ready to pass temporarily outside the action of the story. He has to do more than play in character: he has also to play as if he were a chorus, setting and lighting the stage and prompting a response to it. Any character may be called upon to report the place and the time, and even a major character may find himself made the excuse for a word-picture. This convention has the effect of bringing together the action on the stage, the thoughts of the character and the spirit of the scene, ensuring that the final image is received as it was conceived—as a whole.

Shakespeare practises this technique from his earliest plays. *Titus Andronicus,* II, iii, is a scene depicting the adulterous love of Tamora, the revengeful murder of Bassianus and the rape of Lavinia, but these horrors are prepared with simple irony by Titus' incongruous woodland sketch:

> The hunt is up, the morn is bright and grey,
> The fields are fragrant, and the woods are green... (II, ii, 1–2)

This is echoed and enhanced by Tamora herself:

> The birds chaunt melody in every bush,
> The snake lies rollèd in the cheerful sun... (II, iii, 12–13)

A generation later he opens *The Tempest* with an enacted shipwreck, but a minute later is still filling out the impression by choric speech:

> The sky, it seems, would pour down stinking pitch,
> But that the sea, mounting to th'welkin's cheek,
> Dashes the fire out... (I, ii, 3–5)

Words here take precedence over action, but the supernatural quality of the storm poetry is also a calculated prelude to the island's magic and is the more fearsome on the lips of Miranda in her pity for those aboard the ship. Word-scenery, character and situation are integrated.

The visualizing power of language is rarely absent, but Shakespeare knows to inform it with a strength drawn from the dramatic situation. A static line of description from Arthur Brooke's *The Tragical History of Romeus and Juliet* reports the dawn thus:

> As yet he saw no day, ne could he call it night,
> With equal force decreasing dark fought with increasing light.

Shakespeare seizes upon this and charges it with urgency. He stresses the conflict of night and day by associating it with the opposing attitudes of a reluctant Juliet and an anxious Romeo, while making more particular the twilit colour of the original:

> *Juliet.* Wilt thou be gone? It is not yet near day.
> It was the nightingale, and not the lark,
> That pierced the fearful hollow of thine ear...
> *Romeo.* It was the lark, the herald of the morn;
> No nightingale. Look, love, what envious streaks
> Do lace the severing clouds in yonder east.
> (*Romeo and Juliet,* III, v, i ff.)

He puts the moon in the sky at the beginning of *A Midsummer Night's Dream* and sustains its presence by some eighteen reminders throughout the play, incidentally indicating its importance by playing variations upon its range of associations from chastity to romance. By skilful implication the forest in *As You Like It* is represented as a different kind of place from the wood near Athens. It becomes a "desert inaccessible,/Under the shade of melancholy boughs" (II, vii, 110–11), suiting the mood of a lovelorn Orlando and creating an Arden that is ambivalently civil and uncivil.

The mature tragedies are more particular in their atmospheric effects, as befits their specific patterns of emotion. The "civil strife in Heaven" prepares the audience for the civil strife of the politicians in *Julius Caesar,* and this storm is pursued through the night of the conspiracy, to be sharply contrasted with the quiet of Brutus' meditations in his orchard and the dawning of the Ides of March with its reiterated warnings by Artemidorus and the Soothsayer. The preparation for the events of *Macbeth* is scarcely less striking. In supernatural colours the Witches paint and enact the thunder and lightning, the rain and the fog, and make the heath their own. As in *King Lear* many of the play's characters serve its atmosphere. Through Banquo,

> There's husbandry in heaven,
> Their candles are all out. (II, i, 4–5)

or Macbeth,

> Now o'er the one half-world
> Nature seems dead. (II, i, 49–50)

or Lady Macbeth,

> It was the owl that shrieked, the fatal bellman. (II, ii, 3)

or through the Porter, Lennox, Macduff, the Old Man, Ross, and later through the Murderers themselves, Shakespeare repeatedly strikes the same note, until darkness, evil and the unnatural night impregnate the theatre.

## A Note on Sex and the Boy Actor

Not unrelated to Shakespeare's way of identifying the spirit of a scene is his handling of women's parts, since he must make a like effort of suggestion to accentuate their femininity. With boys playing the major roles of his heroines—and Rosalind and Cleopatra are as demanding in point of complexity of speaking and acting as any male character he drew—he sought to seduce the spectator with oblique impressions of their sex. He uses, as might be expected, poetry as commentary. The spectator's image of Imogen is seen through Iachimo's sensuality:

> How bravely thou becomest thy bed! fresh lily,
> And whiter than the sheets!... (*Cymbeline,* II, ii, 15 ff.)

To give the opposite effect, he will drench a character in repulsive sexuality, as he does Gertrude on Hamlet's tongue:

> Nay, but to live
> In the rank sweat of an enseamèd bed
> Stewed in corruption, honeying, and making love
> Over the nasty sty. (*Hamlet,* III, iv, 91–4)

The femininity of some of the ladies of the comedies—Portia, Beatrice, Rosalind—is given wings by their buoyant repartee. He will point a few particulars of their sexual individuality, like Juliet's innocent pertness or Lady Macbeth's negative sexuality, and write on as if there were never a doubt that they are women, as modern actresses can verify.

Nevertheless, all the women have to play out their parts with warmth, and sometimes with coquetry. Kisses abound. For the sexual relationship is repeatedly Shakespeare's concern, and it is a Victorian myth that the boy actors were not centrally involved in a sexual situation. Isabella's forbidding habit in the presence of Angelo's lust hardly suppressed the fact of her sex; Desdemona's whiter skin than snow, so admired by black Othello, unquestionably stressed the theme of miscegenation; Cleopatra with her reputation as a bewitcher of emperors, Marina in the loathsome brothel, Imogen in imminent danger of rape, Miranda seeing a young man for the first time—these instances suggest that conveying sexual attractiveness was a condition of the boy player's art.

Here again is Shakespeare substituting for the actuality a broad theatrical symbolism. The transvestism of the "breeches parts" in Restoration times and after offered the actresses merely an opportunity to reveal their legs, which were otherwise draped. Shakespeare's transvestism, on the other hand, revealed femininity by emphasizing the differences of mind and behaviour between man and woman, helping us to see something as familiar as sex in a fresh light, through Portia's delight in tricking Bassanio, Rosalind wooing circuitously or Viola pathetically frustrated.

## The Daylight Convention

In the public theatre Shakespeare's drama was played in afternoon daylight, the theatre open to the sky. Yet it is curious to recall that a high proportion of his scenes are set at night time, whether indoors or out. The whole of *Macbeth* is characteristically a play of shadow and night. Such an effect might seem reasonable had the playwright been able to call upon the skills of the lighting engineer in the modern theatre, but a perverse *tour de force* when it had to be played on a possibly sunlit stage.

The justification is not far to seek. In the terms of the theatrical experience, the overall lighting of an open-air theatre is equivalent to its unlocalized setting. It could suggest everything or nothing and equally freed the visual imagination of the spectator. Just as radio drama engages the helpful blindness of the listener, so daylight was a challenge to the poet to conjure special illusions. Moreover, if his play was performed indoors, as at Court, the stage and the auditorium were again lit overall, and the same brush which painted Macbeth's "black and midnight hags" would serve him as well.

A careful use of candles, lanterns and torches assists the verbal creation of the night scenes. These properties would in addition draw attention to the important entrance: Romeo into the vault, Brutus in his orchard, Iago rousing Brabantio from his sleep, Othello approaching Desdemona's bed with the light on his black face, Banquo and Fleance walking into their ambush, Lady Macbeth in her sleepwalking, Gloucester's discovery of Lear on the heath and Iachimo's sly invasion of Imogen's chamber where

> The flame o'th'taper
> Bows toward her and would under-peep her lids...
> (*Cymbeline,* II, ii, 19–20)

Shakespeare may also introduce sounds offstage, owls and clocks, bells and cocks, to strengthen the scene's impression, but he never relies upon realistic properties and effects alone.

His ability to call up darkness displays itself from the outset, and it is worth remarking that several of these scenes in the early plays create the night in order to achieve a subsequent contrast of light or day. Richard III's nightmare before Bosworth is built up by many calculated references. The mood of a tormented night prepares the spectator for the appearance of the Ghosts, but it especially creates an ironic tension before the activity of the dawn:

> *Norfolk.* Arm, arm, my lord; the foe vaunts in the field.
> *Richard.* Come, bustle, bustle. Caparison my horse...
> (*Richard* III, v ,iii, 288–9)

He so accustoms the spectator to the nocturnal mood in *A Midsummer Night's Dream* that the dawn of the May morning arrives in IV, i with a winding of horns as a surprise and a revelation. In *Henry V,* "the foul womb of night," as evoked by Chorus and character and campfire, creates a quiet suspense before the battle and provides an apt setting for the King's heart-searchings and his prayer to God; but again the audience is roused with the shock of

> *Orleans.* The sun doth gild our armour. Up, my lords!
> *Dauphin.* Montez à cheval! My horse! varlet! laquais! ha!
> (IV, ii, 1–2)

So completely may Shakespeare conceive a scene in terms of light and dark, that in *Hamlet* he marks a critical moment in the unmasking of Claudius by his cry, "Give me some light—away!" echoed by Polonius's "Lights, lights, lights!" (III, ii, 269–70). The confusion of the court and the scurrying of torchbearers have deluded the audience into accepting that nature is subject to the whim of the poet. After the scene in *Macbeth* in which bells and shouts and bold movement stir Macbeth's castle, Shakespeare practises another risky device. He has Ross remind the audience of the daylight convention with the words

> Thou seest the heavens, as troubled with man's act
> Threatens his bloody stage: by th'clock 'tis day,
> And yet dark night strangles the travelling lamp:
> Is't night's predominance, or the day's shame,
> That darkness does the face of earth entomb,
> When living light should kiss it? (II, iv, 5–10)

This would be overweening did Shakespeare not feel in command of his theatre. His skill here again is a visualizing one, and such chiaroscuro effects are his response to the challenge of writing for the daylight convention.

## The Localizing Convention

When Shakespeare makes no localizing suggestion in his lines, it is because he requires his arena to remain neutral for dramatic or symbolic reasons. The general emphasis is on costume rather than scenery, on actor rather than setting. The players can quickly create and dismiss the background, so that the spectator may feel directly the confidence between the actor and himself or apprehend an essential relationship between two or more characters.

Any player is used to place a scene instantly:

> *Rosalind.* Well, this is the forest of Arden!
> (*As You Like It,* II, iv, 14)

Often, however, setting and place are indicated economically in the bearing and language of the player in his character: for all that *Antony and Cleopatra* chops between Egypt and Rome, there is never any doubt where the scene is, even if dress did not show it. Antony embraces his mistress with

> Let Rome in Tiber melt, and the wide arch
> Of the ranged empire fall! Here is my space. (I, i, 33–4)

and Octavius Caesar greets the spectator with

> From Alexandria
> This is the news: he fishes, drinks and wastes
> The lamps of night in revel. (I, iv, 3–5)

Location is implicit. A fairy embodies in his voice and movement the nature of the lovers' moonlit wood:

> Over hill, over dale,
> Thorough bush, thorough briar...
> (*A Midsummer Night's Dream,* II, i, 2–3)

and by similarly immediate means Ariel captures the spirit of Prospero's island:

> I come
> To answer thy best pleasure; be't to fly
> To swim, to dive into the fire...to ride
> On the curled clouds... (*The Tempest,* I, ii, 189–92)

Nor in our admiration for the way Lear conjures up his heath in the storm should it be forgotten that others have their share, particularly in such physically racing lines as Edgar's

> Away! The foul fiend follows me!
> Through the sharp hawthorn blow the cold winds...
> (*King Lear,* III, iv, 45–6)

Under the fluid conditions of the Elizabethan stage, to change an imaginary location presented no problem, and players pass without fuss from the "inside" to the "outside" of a building (as in *The Merchant of Venice,* IV, i–ii), or from the "outside" to the "inside" (as in *Romeo and Juliet,* I, iv–v), from a "street" to "the Capitol" (as in *Julius Caesar,* III, i), or from a "bedroom" to a "street" (as in *Othello,* iv, ii). Representational drama must account for the place where actors find themselves. Presentational drama asks only that the actors adjust their relationships with each other; the stage they stand on remains the same. Romeo departs, and Juliet's orchard goes with him; Lady Capulet enters, is joined by Juliet, and Juliet's chamber has passed from the balcony to the platform (*Romeo and Juliet,* III, v).

The stage is as empty or as full, as anchored or as shifting, as particular or as anonymous, as our fancies make it. When Claudius greets his Council of State, actors and costumes display the pomp of Elsinore, and words supply the formal speech for the occasion; but with "*Exeunt all but Hamlet,*" the Prince is alone, and where is he then but in a world of obsessive brooding? Again, for how long in the central scenes of *King Lear* does the King remain on a particularized heath before we have been caught up in his despair?

As a problem the convention of place seems hardly to have entered Shakespeare's conscious mind. That relationships and not localities matter is well illustrated by the scene in which Othello accuses Desdemona of being a whore (*Othello,* IV, ii). The text may suggest that this scene must be acted in some private room, until it is found that it seems to end inappropriately with an exchange between the conspirators Iago and Roderigo. They are joined by Othello, Lodovico, Desdemona and Emilia, and then Desdemona is left to undress for bed (IV, iii). What were Iago and Roderigo doing in her bedroom? By the power of his imagery Shakespeare had translated the platform into a room in hell into which Iago fits exactly, and it is in a kind of hell that the innocent wife is unpinned. There is no change of place and no pause in the playing.

There are scenes when Shakespeare's impressionistic localizing puts setting and atmosphere at odds with character and situation, the poet painting his scene in incongruous detail. Thus, by his instruction to his Page, the County Paris prepares the gruesome place in which Juliet's beauty is to shine:

> Under yond yew-trees lay thee all along,
> Holding thine ear close to the hollow ground;
> So shall no foot upon the churchyard tread,
> Being loose, unfirm with digging up of graves,
> But thou shalt hear it. (*Romeo and Juliet,* V, iii, 3–7)

Whether it is the romantic Rosalind restless in the restricting court, or the courtiers incongruously disporting themselves in Arden; whether the inflexible Octavius Caesar caught awkwardly in the exotic world of Cleopatra and Egypt, or Cleopatra visualizing her humiliation in the streets of Rome; whether Polixenes and old Camillo bemused by the youth of the Bohemian country-side in *The Winter's Tale*; whether the chaste Marina trapped in the sordid Metaline brothel in *Pericles*—contrast nourishes the drama, and place and setting are its servants.

Shakespeare's localizing exists for the life of the drama. The spirit of place invades Hamlet's Denmark, or Macbeth's Scotland, or the Vienna of *Measure for Measure*; but in these, Denmark, Scotland or Vienna are used to point the play, dealing in corruption or violence or licentiousness. This is not unity of place, but unity of atmosphere.

## Dramatizing Time

For Shakespeare a theoretical "convention of time" would have had little meaning, and only on a few, careful occasions is time required to enter the conscious mind of his audience. It is a modern habit for an audience to fasten a time pattern upon a play. If a scene is localized and if it is set up with the details of actuality, automatically the drama assumes a chronological time-scheme. Naturalistic presentation thus controls the action in a way which the Elizabethans would have found intolerable. Shakespeare's plays are long one-act plays, and time exists in them only for exploiting. Tempo matters because plays are written in the fourth dimension, and the speed with which the action passes before the eyes is important, but the clock and the calendar are there only when needed.

A facility for suggesting the mere passage of time was always his. The night passes to the horrors of *Richard III* or the chase of *A Midsummer Night's Dream* by the pointing of a few lines. Even in this early drama, however, such pointing, whether Radcliff's

> The early village cock
> Hath twice done salutation to the morn.
> (*Richard III,* V, iii, 209–10)

or Puck's

> night's swift dragons cut the clouds full fast,
> And yonder shines Aurora's harbinger.
> (*A Midsummer Night's Dream,* III, ii, 379–80)

is also always to direct the audience toward the dénouement to come: Richard's fate at the hands of Richmond, or the hasty pairing of the Athenian lovers. Even such time effects as these are not there for their own sake.

A straightforward temporal pressure is exerted in *Romeo and Juliet,* in which Shakespeare displays his early skill. Arthur Brooke's *Tragical History* dealt in a leisurely narrative covering nine months; Shakespeare's play has its lovers assaulted by time, and its audience with them. Three days are all that Romeo and Juliet are granted, while Juliet's father jocularly fires her suitor's ardours:

> *Capulet.* . . .bid her, mark you me, on Wednesday next—
> But soft, what day is this?
> *Paris.* Monday, my lord.
> *Capulet.* Monday, ha, ha; well, Wednesday is too soon;
> O'Thursday let it be—o'Thursday, tell her,
> She shall be married to this noble earl. (III, iv, 17–21)

Subject to a grim irony, a confident daughter asks her father's pardon, only to find that he lops off a further precious day, one which proves fatal:

> Send for the County: go tell him of this.
> I'll have this knot knit up tomorrow morning.
> (IV, ii, 23–4)

Shakespeare continues to press the point with repeated reminders: "we'll to church tomorrow"—"prepare up him/Against tomorrow," while the Friar vainly tries to warn Romeo in time. Chance will blast the fortunes of the lovers, although time has been tightening the net since the Prince banished Romeo in III, i. It seems not a moment before the wedding morning is upon them, and old Capulet bustles in to rouse the family with

> Come, stir, stir, stir! The second cock hath crowed.
> (IV, iv, 3)

until the stage is alive with the servants of an excited household. All this in twenty minutes' playing time.

Time becomes an instrument of Shakespeare's theatre, and its passing is regularly linked with the emotion of his scenes. By hints and suggestions the night passes in the scene of Cassio's undoing (*Othello,* II, iii), but a scene which begins lightly with dancing, sport and the celebration of Othello's nuptials grows swiftly to a crisis of drunkenness, brawling and the ringing of bells; its mood changes with the anger of an Othello brought from his bed,

> My blood begins my safer guides to rule. (201)

until Iago, his design accomplished, is left with Roderigo his agent upon a quiet and sinister stage, hugging himself:

> By th'mass, 'tis morning;
> Pleasure and action make the hours seem short. (370–1)

Freedom with time lends freedom for symbolism. In *Antony and Cleopatra* suspense is prolonged and the battles are clocked by the passage of two unusual nights. In the first (IV, iii) Antony "drowns consideration," while the soldiers who guard him guide the audience's appropriate response to the eery noise-off indicated in the direction, "*Music of the hoboys is under the stage*:" this prelude to the fighting is marked by its sly presage of Antony's fate. The second (IV, ix) interrupts the fluctuations of battle, and "the hand of death" is vividly present in the melancholy Enobarbus, who takes his own life while all except sentries are asleep.

Shakespeare measures the hours by the needs of his drama, matching the tempo of a sequence with a chronology of the imagination, catching a symbolism of life in its flux and flow, as in *The Winter's Tale,* whose seasonal sheep-shearing scene suggests the progress of the natural world as Perdita suggests the progress of the human, making of "Time, the Chorus" a protagonist who has only to "turn his glass." This kind of time will be anarchical, especially in the Elizabethan theatre, unless its meaning is stressed. It is delicately manipulated in *Othello*. That here it is "contracted and expanded like a concertina"[3] gives the lie to those who feel that its twenty-four hours between marriage and murder makes it the most formally classical play in Shakespeare's repertoire. The telescoping of the action after the happy arrival in Cyprus is used to make the spectator sense the contraction of the horizons of the jealous mind, suggesting the swift development of Othello's passions when once strongly roused, and that he had little time to check and prove Iago's hints. The Moor's downfall is accomplished with rare speed as Iago's poison does its work so that neither he nor the audience stops to consider that Desdemona and Cassio had no opportunity to commit adultery in any case. Yet this play also introduces a new trick of the clock: time is

---

[3] H. Granville-Barker, *Prefaces to Shakespeare, Fourth Series,* p. 11.

used to cheat the spectator. Upon Othello's decisive words,

> Strumpet, I come!
> Forth of my heart, those charms, thine eyes, are blotted;
> Thy bed lust-stained shall with lust's blood be spotted. (V, i, 34–6)

Shakespeare appears to stretch time. A short sequence of spectacular action, which includes the stabbing of Roderigo and the wounding of Cassio, tautens the suspense before Othello's next entrance to his defenceless wife and puts the defenceless spectator under the strain of anticipation.

# 2

# The Jacobean Shakespeare: Some Observations on the Construction of the Tragedies

*Maynard Mack*

This chapter aims at being a modest supplement (I cannot too much stress the adjective) to A. C. Bradley's pioneering analysis of the construction of Shakespearean tragedy, the second of his famous lectures, published some fifty-five years ago. Bradley's concern was with what would probably today be called the clearer outlines of Shakespearean practice —the management of exposition, conflict, crisis, catastrophe; the contrasts of pace and scene; the over-all patterns of rise-and-fall, variously modulated; the slackened tension after the crisis and Shakespeare's devices for countering this; and the faults.

Bradley is quite detailed about the faults. Sometimes, he says, there are too rapid shiftings of scene and *dramatis personae,* as in the middle section of *Antony and Cleopatra.* Sometimes there is extraneous matter, not required for plot or character development, like the player's speech in *Hamlet* about the murder of Priam, or Hamlet's advice later to the same player on speaking in the theater. Sometimes there are soliloquies too obviously

*From* Stratford-upon-Avon Studies: Jacobean Theatre *(Vol. I), ed. John Russell Brown and Bernard Harris, London: Edward Arnold (Publishers) Ltd., 1960; New York: St. Martin's Press, Inc., 1961.* 

expositional, as when Edgar disguises to become Poor Tom in *King Lear*. Or there is contradiction and inconsistency, as the double time in *Othello*. Or flatulent writing: "obscure, inflated, tasteless," or "pestered with metaphors." Or "gnomic" insertions, like the Duke's couplet interchange with Brabantio in *Othello,* used "more freely than, I suppose, a good playwright now would care to do." And finally, to make an end, there is too often sacrificing of dramatic appropriateness to get something said that the author wants said. Thus the comments of the Player King and Claudius on the instability of human purpose arise because Shakespeare "wishes in part simply to write poetry, and partly to impress on the audience thoughts which will help them to understand, not the player-king nor yet King Claudius, but Hamlet himself." These failings, Bradley concludes, belong to an art of drama imperfectly developed, which Shakespeare inherited from his predecessors and acquiesced in, on occasion, from "indifference or want of care."

Though Bradley's analysis is still the best account we have of the outward shape of Shakespearean tragedy, a glance at his list of faults and especially his examples reminds us that a vast deal of water has got itself under the critical bridges since 1904. It is not simply that most of the faults he enumerates would no longer be regarded as such, but would instead be numbered among the characteristic practices of Shakespearean dramaturgy, even at its most triumphant. Still more striking is the extent to which our conception of the "construction" of the tragedies has itself changed. The matters Bradley described have not ceased to be important—far from it: several of our current interpreters, one feels, would benefit if, like Bottom of Master Mustardseed, they were to desire him "of more acquaintance." Still, it is impossible not to feel that Bradley missed something—that there is another kind of construction in Shakespeare's tragedies than the one he designates, more inward, more difficult to define, but not less significant. This other structure is not, like his, generated entirely by the interplay of plot and character. Nor is it, on the other hand, though it is fashionable nowadays to suppose so, ultimately a verbal matter. It is poetic, but it goes well beyond what in certain quarters today is called (with something like a lump in the throat) "the poetry." Some of its elements arise from the playwright's visualizing imagination, the consciousness of groupings, gestures, entrances, exits. Others may even be prior to language, in the sense that they appear to belong to a paradigm of tragic "form" that was consciously or unconsciously part of Shakespeare's inheritance and intuition as he worked.

At any rate, it is into this comparatively untraveled and uncharted territory of inward structure that I should like to launch a few tentative explorations. I shall occasionally look backward as far as *Julius Caesar* (1599), *Richard II* (1595–1600), and even *Romeo and Juliet* (1595–6); but in the main I shall be concerned with the tragedies of Shakespeare's prime, from *Hamlet* (1600–1) to *Coriolanus* (1607–8). In these seven or eight years, Shakespeare's golden period, he consolidated a species of tragic structure that for suggestiveness and flexibility has never been matched.[1] I do not anticipate being able to return with a map of this obscure terrain. I hope only to convince better travelers that there is something out there to be known.

First, the hero. The Shakespearean tragic hero, as everybody knows, is an overstater. His individual accent will vary with his personality, but there is always a residue of hyperbole. This, it would seem, is for Shakespeare the authentic tragic music, mark of a world where a man's reach must always exceed his grasp and everything costs not less than everything.

Wert thou as far
As that vast shore wash'd with the farthest sea,
I would adventure for such merchandise. (*Romeo,* II, ii, 82)

'Swounds, show me what thou'lt do:
Woo't weep? woo't fight? woo't fast? woo't tear thyself?
Woo't drink up eisel? eat a crocodile
I'll do't. (*Hamlet,* V, i, 297)

Nay, had she been true,
If heaven would make me such another world
Of one entire and perfect chrysolite,
I'ld not have sold her for it. (*Othello,* V, ii, 140)

Death, traitor! nothing could have subdued nature
To such a lowness but his unkind daughters. (*Lear,* III, iv, 72)

Will all great Neptune's ocean wash this blood
Clean from my hand? (*Macbeth,* II, ii, 60)

Quarter'd the world, and o'er green Neptune's back
With ships made cities, . . . (*Antony,* IV, xiv, 57)

I go alone,
Like to a lonely dragon, that his fen
Makes fear'd and talk'd of more than seen.
(*Coriolanus,* IV, i, 29)

This idiom is not, of course, used by the hero only. It is the language he is dressed in by all who love him and often by those who do not:

This was the noblest Roman of them all: . . .
His life was gentle, and the elements
So mix'd in him that Nature might stand up
And say to all the world "This was a man!" (*Caesar,* V, v, 68)

The courtier's soldier's, scholar's, eye, tongue, sword;
The expectancy and rose of the fair state,

[1] The flexibility of the structure is witnessed by the amazing differences between the tragedies, of which it is, however, the lowest common multiple. In my discussion, I shall necessarily take the differences between the tragedies for granted and stress simply the vertebrate characteristics they share.

> The glass of fashion and the mold of form,
> The observed of all observers, . . . (*Hamlet,* III, i, 159)

> Can he be angry? I have seen the cannon,
> When it hath blown his ranks into the air,
> And, like the devil, from his very arm
> Puff'd his own brother:—and can he be angry?
> (*Othello,* III, iv, 134)

> On the Alps
> It is reported thou didst eat strange flesh,
> Which some did die to look on. (*Antony,* I, iv, 66)

> Let me twine
> Mine arms about that body, where against
> My grainèd ash an hundred times hath broke,
> And scarr'd the moon with splinters.
> (*Coriolanus,* IV, v, 112)

But by whomever used, it is a language that depends for its vindication —for the redemption of its paper promises into gold—upon the hero, and any who stand, heroically, where he does. It is the mark of his, and their, commitment to something beyond "the vast waters Of the petrel and the porpoise," as Mr. Eliot has it in *East Coker,* a commitment to something—not merely death—which shackles accidents and bolts up change and palates no dung whatever.

Thus the hyperbole of tragedy stands at the opposite end of a tonal scale from the hyperbole of comedy which springs from and nourishes detachment:

> When I was about thy years, Hal, I was not an eagle's talon in the waist; I could have crept into any alderman's thumb-ring.
> (*I Henry IV,* II, iv, 362)

> O, she misused me past the endurance of a block! an oak but with one green leaf on it would have answered her; my very visor began to assume life, and scold with her. (*Much Ado,* II, i, 246)

> He has a son, who shall be flayed alive; then 'nointed over with honey, set on the head of a wasp's nest; then stand till he be three quarters and a dram dead; then recovered again with aqua-vitae or some other hot infusion; then, raw as he is, and in the hottest day prognostication proclaims, shall he be set against a brick-wall, the sun looking with a southward eye upon his, where he is to behold him with flies blown to death.
> (*Winter's Tale,* IV, iv, 811)

Comic overstatement aims at being preposterous. Until it becomes so, it remains flat. Tragic overstatement, on the other hand, aspires to be believed, and unless in some sense it is so, remains bombast.

Besides the hyperbolist, in Shakespeare's scheme of things, there is always the opposing voice, which belongs to the hero's foil. As the night the day, the idiom of absoluteness demands a vocabulary of a different intensity, a different rhetorical and moral wave length, to set it off. This other idiom is not necessarily understatement, though it often takes the form of a deflating accent and very often involves colloquialism—or perhaps merely a middling sort of speech—expressive of a suppler outlook than the hero's and of other and less upsetting ways of encountering experience than his hyperbolic, not to say intransigent, rigorism. "'Twere to consider too curiously to consider so," says Horatio of Hamlet's equation between the dust of Alexander and a bunghole, and this enunciates perfectly the foil's role. There is no tragedy in him because he does not consider "curiously;" there are always more things in earth and heaven than are dreamt of in his philosophy.

Each of the Shakespearean tragedies contains at least one personage to speak this part, which is regularly assigned to someone in the hero's immediate entourage—servitor, wife, friend. In *Romeo and Juliet* it is of course Mercutio, with his witty resolution of all love into sex. In *Julius Caesar* it is Cassius, whose restless urgent rhythms, full of flashing images, swirl about Brutus's rounder and abstracter speech, like dogs that bay the moon:

> *Brutus.* I do believe that these applauses are
> For some new honors that are heap'd on Caesar.
> *Cassius.* Why, man, he doth bestride the narrow world
> Like a Colossus, and we petty men
> Walk under his huge legs and peep about
> To find ourselves dishonorable graves. (I, ii, 133)

In the famous forum speeches this second voice is taken over temporarily by Antony, and there emerges a similar but yet more powerful contrast between them. Brutus' prose—in which the actuality of the assassination is intellectualized and held at bay by the strict patterns of an obtrusively formal rhetoric, almost as though corporal death were transubstantiated to "a ballet of bloodless categories"—gives way to Antony's sinewy verse about the "honorable men," which draws the deed, and its consequence, the dead Caesar, ever closer till his own vengeful emotions are kindled in the mob.

In *Hamlet* the relation of foil to hero undergoes an unusual adaptation. Here, since the raciest idiom of the play belongs to the hero himself, the foil, Horatio, is given a quite conventional speech, and, to make the contrast sharper (Hamlet being of all the heroes the most voluble), as little speech as may be. Like his stoicism, like his "blood and judgment"—

> so well commingled,
> That they are not a pipe for fortune's finger
> To sound what stop she please— (III, ii, 74)

Horatio's "Here, sweet lord," "O, my dear lord," "Well, my lord" are, presumably (as the gentleman in *Lear* says of Cordelia's tears), "a better way" than Hamlet's self-lacerating virtuosities and verbosities. But of course we do not believe this and are not meant to: who would be Horatio if he could be Hamlet?

Plainly, this is one of the two questions that all the tragic foils exist to make us ask (the other we shall come to presently). Who, for instance, would be Enobarbus, clear-sighted as he is, in preference to Antony? His brilliant sardonic speech, so useful while he can hold his own career and all about him in the comic focus of detachment, withers in the face of his engagement to ultimate issues, and he dies speaking with imagery, accent, and feeling which are surely meant to identify him at the last with the absoluteness of the heroic world, the more so since his last syllables anticipate Cleopatra's:

> Throw my heart
> Against the flint and hardness of my fault;
> Which, being dried with grief, will break to powder,
> And finish all foul thoughts. O Antony,
> Nobler than my revolt is infamous,
> Forgive me in thine own particular;
> But let the world rank me in register
> A master-leaver and a fugitive:
> O Antony! O Antony! (IV, ix, 15)

Such unequivocal judgments are a change indeed on the part of one who could earlier rally cynically with Menas about "two thieves kissing" when their hands meet.

King Lear is given two foils. The primary one is obviously the Fool, whose rhymes and riddles and jets of humor in the first two acts set off both the old king's brooding silences and his massively articulated longer speeches when aroused. But in the storm scenes, and occasionally elsewhere, one is almost as keenly conscious of the relief into which Lear's outrageous imprecations are thrown by the mute devoted patience of his servant Kent. For both foils—and this of course is their most prominent function as representatives of the opposing voice—the storm itself is only a storm, to be stoically endured, in the one case, and, in the other, if his master would but hear reason, eschewed:

> O nuncle, court holy-water in a dry house is better than this rainwater out o' door. Good nuncle, in, ask thy daughters' blessing:... (III, ii, 10)

Doubtless the Fool does not wish to be taken quite *au pied de la lettre* in this—his talk is always in the vein of the false daughters', his action quite other. But neither for him nor for Kent does facing the thunder have any kind of transcendent meaning. In Lear's case, it has; the thunder he hears is like the thunder heard over Himavant in *The Waste Land*; it has what the anthropologists call "mana"; and his (and our) consuming questions are what it means—and if it means—and whose side it is on.

In my view, the most interesting uses of the opposing voice occur in *Macbeth* and *Othello*. In *Macbeth* Shakespeare gives it to Lady Macbeth, and there was never, I think, a more thrilling tragic counterpoint set down for the stage than that in the scene following the murder of Duncan, when her purely physical reading of what has happened to them both is met by his metaphysical intuitions. His "noise" to her is just the owl screaming and the crickets' cry. The voice of one crying "sleep no more" is only his "brain-sickly" fear. The blood on his hands is what "a little water clears us of." "Consider it not so deeply," she says at one point, with an echo of Horatio in the graveyard. "These deeds must not be thought After these ways." But in the tragic world which always opens on transcendence, they must; and this she herself finds before she dies, a prisoner to the deed, endlessly washing the damned spot that will not out. "What's done cannot be undone" is a language that like Enobarbus she has to learn.

Othello's foil of course is Iago, about whose imagery and speech there hangs, as recent commentators have pointed out, a constructed air, an ingenious, hyperconscious, generalizing air, essentially suited to one who, as W. H. Clemen has said, "seeks to poison. . .others with his images."[2] Yet Iago's poison does not work more powerfully through his images than through a corrosive habit of abstraction applied in those unique relations of love and faith where abstraction is most irrelevant and most destructive. Iago has learned to "sickly o'er" the central and irreducible individual with the pale cast of class and kind:

> Blessed fig's end! The wine she drinks is made of grapes. . . . (II, i, 251)
>
> These Moors are changeable in their wills. . . . If sanctimony and a frail vow betwixt an erring barbarian and a supersubtle Venetian be not too hard for my wits . . . (I, iii, 342–43, 350–53)
>
> Come on, come on; you are pictures out of doors,
> Bells in your parlors, wildcats in your kitchens,
> Saints in your injuries, devils being offended,
> Players in your housewifery, and housewives in your beds.
> (II, i, 108)
>
> I know our country disposition well;
> In Venice they do let heaven see the pranks
> They dare not show their husbands. (III, iii, 201)

Othello's downfall is signaled quite as clearly when he drifts into this rationalized dimension—

> O curse of marriage,
> That we can call these delicate creatures ours,
> And not their appetites— (III, iii, 267)

2 *The Development of Shakespeare's Imagery*, p. 122.

leaving behind his true vernacular, the idiom of "My life upon her faith!" as when his mind fills with Iago's copulative imagery. Shakespeare seems to have been well aware that love (especially such love as can be reflected only in the union of a black man with a white woman, East with West) is the mutual knowing of uniqueness:

> Reason, in itself confounded,
> Saw division grow together,
> To themselves yet either neither,
> Simple were so well compounded,
>
> That it cried, How true a twain
> Seemeth this concordant one!
> Love hath reason, reason none,
> If what parts can so remain.
>
> Whereupon it made this threne
> To the phoenix and the dove,
> Co-supremes and stars of love,
> As chorus to their tragic scene.
>
> (*The Phoenix and the Turtle,* 41)

And also that there are areas of experience where, as a great saint once said, one must first believe in order that one may know.

To one who should ask why these paired voices seem to be essential ingredients of Shakespearean tragedy, no single answer can, I think, be given. They occur partly, no doubt, because of their structural utility, the value of complementary personalities in a work of fiction being roughly analogous to the value of thesis and antithesis in a discursive work. Partly too, no doubt, because in stage performance the antiphonal effects of the two main vocabularies, strengthened by diversity in manner, costume, placing on the stage, supply variety of mood and gratify the eye and ear. But these are superficial considerations. Perhaps we come to something more satisfactory when we consider that these two voices apparently answer to reverberations which reach far back in the human past. *Mutatis mutandis,* Coriolanus and Menenius, Antony and Enobarbus, Macbeth and Lady Macbeth, Lear and his Fool, Othello and Iago, Hamlet and Horatio, Brutus and Cassius, Romeo and Mercutio exhibit a kind of duality that is also exhibited in Oedipus and Jocasta (as well as Creon), Antigone and Ismene, Prometheus and Oceanus, Phaedra and her nurse—and also, in many instances in Greek tragedy, by the protagonist and the chorus.

If it is true, as can be argued, that the Greek chorus functions in large measure as spokesman for the values of the community, and the first actor in large measure for the passionate life of the individual, we can perhaps see a philosophical basis for the long succession of opposing voices. What matters to the community is obviously accommodation—all those adjustments and resiliences that enable it to survive; whereas what matters to the individual, at least in his heroic mood, is just as obviously integrity—all that enables him to remain an *individual,* one thing not many. The confrontation of these two outlooks is therefore a confrontation of two of our most cherished instincts, the instinct to be resolute, autonomous, free, and the instinct to be "realistic," adaptable, secure. If it is also true, as I think most of us believe, that tragic drama is in one way or other a record of man's affair with transcendence (whether this be defined as gods, God, or, as by Malraux, the human "fate," which men must "question" even if they cannot control), we can see further why the hero must have an idiom—such as hyperbole—that establishes him as moving to measures played above or outside our normal space and time. For the *reductio ad absurdum* of the tragic confrontation is the comic one, exemplified in Don Quixote and his Sancho, where the comedy arises precisely from the fact that the hero only *imagines* he moves to measures above and outside our normal world; and where, to the extent that we come to identify with his faith, the comedy slides towards pathos and even the tragic absolute.

These considerations, however, remain speculative. What is not in doubt is that dramaturgically the antiphony of two voices and two vocabularies serves Shakespeare well, and in one of its extensions gives rise to a phenomenon as peculiar and personal to him as his signature. Towards the close of a tragic play, or if not towards the close, at the climax, will normally appear a short scene or episode (sometimes more than one) of spiritual cross purposes: a scene in which the line of tragic speech and feeling generated by commitment is crossed by an alien speech and feeling very much detached. Bradley, noting such of these episodes as are "humorous or semi-humorous," places them among Shakespeare's devices for sustaining interest after the crisis, since their introduction "affords variety and relief, and also heightens by contrast the tragic feelings." Another perceptive critic has noted that though such scenes afford "relief," it is not by laughter. "We return for a moment to simple people, a gravedigger, a porter, a countryman, and to the goings on of every day, the feeling for bread and cheese, and when we go back to the high tragic mood we do so with a heightened sense that we are moving in a world fully realized."[3] To such comments we must add another. For the whole effect of these episodes does not come simply from variety or from the juxtaposition of bread and cheese with the high tragic mood; though these elements are certainly present in it.

It arises, in the main, I think, from the fact that Shakespeare here lays open to us, in an especially poignant form, what I take to be the central dialogue of tragic experience. It is a dialogue of which the Greek dialogue of individual with community, the seventeenth-century dialogue of soul with

[3] F. P. Wilson, *Elizabethan and Jacobean,* p. 122.

body, the twentieth-century dialogue of self with soul are perhaps all versions in their different ways: a dialogue in which each party makes its case in its own tongue, incapable of wholly comprehending what the other means. And Shakespeare objectifies it for us on his stage by the encounter of those by whom, "changed, changed utterly," a terrible beauty has been born, with those who are still players in life's casual comedy. Hamlet and the grave-diggers, Desdemona and Emilia, Cleopatra and the clown afford particularly fine examples of Shakespeare's technique in this respect.

In the first instance, the mixture of profoundly imaginative feelings contained in Hamlet's epitaph for Yorick—

> I knew him, Horatio: a fellow of infinite jest, of most excellent fancy; he hath borne me on his back a thousand times; and now, how abhorred in my imagination it is! my gorge rises at it. Here hung those lips that I have kissed I know not how oft. Where be your gibes now? your gambols? your songs? your flashes of merriment, that were wont to set the table on a roar? Not one now, to mock your own grinning? quite chap-fallen? Now get you to my lady's chamber, and tell her, let her paint an inch thick, to this favor she must come; make her laugh at that— (V, i, 203)

is weighed over against the buffoon literalism of the clown—

> *Hamlet.* What man dost thou dig it for?
> *First Clown.* For no man, sir.
> *Hamlet.* What woman, then?
> *First Clown.* For none, neither.
> *Hamlet.* Who is to be buried in 't?
> *First Clown.* One that was a woman, sir; but, rest her soul, she's dead—
> (V, i, 141)

and against his uncompromising factualism too, his hard dry vocabulary of detachment, without overtones, by which he cuts his métier down to a size that can be lived with:

> I'faith, if he be not rotten before he die, . . . he will last you some eight year or nine year: a tanner will last you nine year. (V, i, 180)

But in this scene Hamlet's macabre thoughts are not allowed to outweigh the clown. A case is made for factualism and literalism. Horatio is seen to have a point in saying it is to consider too curiously to consider as Hamlet does. A man must come to terms with the graveyard; but how long may he linger in it with impunity or allow it to linger in him? Such reckonings the opposing voice, whether spoken by the primary foil or by another, is calculated to awake in us: this is the second kind of question that it exists to make us ask.

In a sense, then, the implicit subject of all these episodes is the predicament of being human. They bring before us the grandeur of man's nature, which contains, potentially, both voices, both ends of the moral and psychic spectrum. They bring before us the necessity of his choice, because it is rarely given to him to go through any door without closing the rest. And they bring before us the sadness, the infinite sadness of his lot, because, short of the "certain certainties" that tragedy does not deal with, he has no sublunar way of knowing whether defiant "heroism" is really more to be desired than suppler "wisdom." The alabaster innocence of Desdemona's world shines out beside the crumpled bedsitters of Emilia's—

> *Desdemona.* Wouldst thou do such a deed for all the world?
> *Emilia.* Why, would not you?
> *Desdemona.* No, by this heavenly light!
> *Emilia.* Nor I neither by this heavenly light;
> I might do't as well i' the dark.
> *Desdemona.* Wouldst thou do such a deed for all the world?
> *Emilia.* The world's a huge thing: it is a great price
> For a small vice.
> *Desdemona.* In troth, I think thou wouldst not.
> *Emilia.* In troth, I think I should...who would not make her husband a cuckold to make him a monarch? I should venture purgatory for 't.
> *Desdemona.* Beshrew me, if I would do such a wrong
> For the whole world.
> *Emilia.* Why, the wrong is but a wrong i' the world; and having the world for your labor, 'tis a wrong in your own world, and you might quickly make it right.
> *Desdemona.* I do not think there is any such woman— (IV, iii, 65)

but the two languages never, essentially, commune—and for this reason the dialogue they hold can never be finally adjudicated.

The same effect may be noted in Cleopatra's scene with the countryman who brings her the asps. Her exultation casts a glow over the whole scene of her death. But her language when the countryman has gone would not have the tragic resonance it has if we could not hear echoing between the lines the gritty accents of the opposing voice:

> Give me my robe, put on my crown; I have
> Immortal longings in me.
>
> Truly, I have him: but I would not be the party that should desire you to touch him, for his biting is immortal; those that do die of it do seldom or never recover.
>
> The stroke of death is as a lover's pinch,
> Which hurts, and is desired.
>
> I heard of one of them no longer than yesterday: a very honest woman, but something given to lie; as a woman should not do, but in the way of honesty: how she died of the biting of it, what pain she felt.

peace, peace!
Dost thou not see my baby at my breast,
That sucks the nurse asleep? (V, ii, 283–313)

Give it nothing, I pray you, for it is not worth the feeding.
(V, ii, 245–71)

The "worm"—or "my baby"; the Antony Demetrius and Philo see—or the Antony whose face is as the heavens; the "small vice" of Emilia—or the deed one would not do for the whole world; the skull knocked about the mazzard by a sexton's spade—or the skull which "had a tongue in it and could sing once": these are incommensurables which human nature nevertheless must somehow measure, reconcile and enclose.

We move now from "character" to "action," and to the question: what happens in a Shakespearean tragedy? Bradley's traditional categories—exposition, conflict, crisis, catastrophe, etc.—give us one side of this, but as we noticed earlier, largely the external side, and are in any case rather too clumsy for the job we try to do with them. They apply as well to potboilers of the commercial theater as to serious works of art, to prose as well as poetic drama. What is worse, they are unable to register the unique capacity of Shakespearean dramaturgy to hint, evoke, imply, and, in short, by indirections find directions out. The nature of some of Shakespeare's "indirections" is a topic we must explore before we can hope to confront the question posed above with other terms than Bradley's.

To clarify what I mean by indirection, let me cite an instance from *King Lear*. Everybody has noticed, no doubt, that Lear's Fool (apart from being the King's primary foil) gives voice during the first two acts to notations of topsiturviness that are not, one feels, simply his own responses to the inversions of order that have occurred in family and state, but a reflection of the King's; or to put the matter another way, the situation is so arranged by Shakespeare that we are invited to apply the Fool's comments to Lear's inner experience, and I suspect that most of us do so. The Fool thus serves, to some extent, as a screen on which Shakespeare flashes, as it were, readings from the psychic life of the protagonist, possibly even his subconscious life, which could not otherwise be conveyed in drama at all. Likewise, the Fool's *idée fixe* in this matter, his apparent obsession with one idea (often a clinical symptom of incipient insanity) is perhaps dramatic shorthand, and even sleight-of-hand for goings-on in the King's brain that only occasionally bubble to the surface in the form of conscious apprehensions: "O let me not be mad, not mad sweet heaven." "O fool, I shall go mad." Conceivably, there may even be significance in the circumstance that the Fool does not enter the play as a speaking character till after King Lear has behaved like a fool and leaves it before he is cured.

Whatever the truth of this last point, the example of the Fool in Lear introduces us to devices of play construction and ways of recording the progress of inward "action," which, though the traditional categories say nothing about them, are a basic resource of Shakespeare's playwriting, and nowhere more so than in the tragedies. We may now consider a few of them in turn.

First, there are the figures, like the Fool, some part of whose consciousness, as conveyed to us at particular moments, seems to be doing double duty, filling our minds with impressions analogous to those which we may presume to be occupying the conscious or unconscious mind of the hero, whether he is before us on the stage or not. A possible example may be Lady Macbeth's sleepwalking scene. Macbeth is absent at this juncture, has gone "into the field"—has not in fact been visible during two long scenes and will not be visible again till the next scene after this. In the interval, the slaying at Macduff's castle and the conversations between Malcolm and Macduff keep him before us in his capacity as tyrant, murderer, "Hell-kite," seen from the outside. But Lady Macbeth's sleepwalking is, I think, Shakespeare's device for keeping him before us in his capacity as tragic hero and sufferer. The "great perturbation in nature" of which the doctor whispers ("to receive at once the benefit of sleep, and do the effects of watching"), the "slumbery agitation," the "thick-coming fancies That keep her from her rest": these, by a kind of poetical displacement, we may apply to him as well as to her; and we are invited to do so by the fact that from the moment of the first murder all the play's references to sleep and its destruction have had reference to Macbeth himself. We are, of course, conscious as we watch the scene that this is Lady Macbeth suffering the metaphysical aspects of murder that she did not believe in; we may also be conscious that the remorse pictured here tends to distinguish her from her husband, who for some time has been giving his "initiate fear" the "hard use" he said it lacked, with dehumanizing consequences. Yet in some way the pity of this situation suffuses him as well as her, the more so because in every word she utters his presence beside her is supposed; and if we allow this to be true, not only will Menteith's comment in the following scene—

> Who then shall blame
> His pester'd senses to recoil and start,
> When all that is within him does condemn
> Itself for being there— (V, ii, *22*)

evoke an image of suffering as well as retribution, but we shall better understand Macbeth's striking expression, at his next appearance, in words that we are almost bound to feel have some reference to himself, of corrosive griefs haunting below the conscious levels of the mind:

> Canst thou not minister to a mind diseased,
> Pluck from the memory a rooted sorrow,
> Raze out the written troubles of the brain
> And with some sweet oblivious antidote
> Cleanse the stuff'd bosom of that perilous stuff
> Which weighs upon the heart? (V, iii, 40)

Such speeches as this and as Lady Macbeth's while sleepwalking—which we might call umbrella speeches, since more than one consciousness may shelter under them—are not uncommon in Shakespeare's dramaturgy, as many critics have pointed out. *Lear* affords the classic examples: in the Fool, as we have seen, and also in Edgar. Edgar's speech during the storm scenes projects in part his role of Poor Tom, the eternal outcast; in part, Edmund (and also Oswald), the vicious servant, self-seeking, with heart set on lust and proud array; possibly in part, Gloucester, whose arrival with a torch the Fool appropriately announces (without knowing it) in terms related to Edgar's themes: "Now a little fire in a wide field were like an old lecher's heart"; and surely, in some part too, the King, for the chips and tag-ends of Edgar's speech reflect, as if from Lear's own mind, not simply mental disintegration, but a strong sense of a fragmented moral order: "Obey thy parents; keep thy word justly; swear not; commit not with man's sworn spouse. . . ."

But in my view, the most interesting of all the umbrella speeches in the tragedies is Enobarbus's famous description of Cleopatra in her barge. The triumvirs have gone offstage, Antony to have his first view of Octavia. When we see him again, his union with Octavia will have been agreed on all parts (though not yet celebrated), and he will be saying to her, with what can hardly be supposed to be insincerity:

> My Octavia,
> Read not my blemishes in the world's report:
> I have not kept my square; but that to come
> Shall all be done by the rule. Good night, dear lady. (II, iii, 4)

Then the soothsayer appears, reminds Antony that his guardian angel will always be overpowered when Caesar's is by, urges him to return to Egypt; and Antony, left alone after the soothsayer has gone, meditates a moment on the truth of the pronouncement and then says abruptly:

> I will to Egypt:
> And though I make this marriage for my peace,
> I' the east my pleasure lies. (II, iii, 38)

There is plainly a piece of prestidigitation here. It is performed in part by means of the soothsayer's entry, which is evidently a kind of visual surrogate for Antony's own personal intuition. ("I see it in my motion, have it not in my tongue," the soothsayer says, when asked for the reasons he wishes Antony to return; and that is presumably the way Antony sees it too: in his "motion," i.e., involuntarily, intuitively.) But a larger part is played by Enobarbus' account of Cleopatra. Between the exit of the triumvirs and the reappearance of Antony making unsolicited promises to Octavia, this is the one thing that intervenes. And it is the only thing that needs to. Shakespeare has made it so powerful, so colored our imaginations with it, that we understand the promises of Antony, not in the light in which he understands them as he makes them, but in the riotous brilliance of Enobarbus's evocation of Cleopatra. The psychic gap in Antony between "My Octavia" and "Good night, dear lady," on the one hand, and "I will to Egypt," on the other, is filled by a vision, given to us, of irresistible and indeed quasi-unearthly power of which the soothsayer's intuition is simply a more abstract formulation. Here again, by indirection, Shakespeare finds direction out.

Not all mirror situations in the tragedies involve reflection of another consciousness. Some, as is well known, emphasize the outlines of an action by recapitulating it, as when Edgar's descent to Poor Tom and subsequent gradual re-ascent to support the gored state echoes the downward and upward movement in the lives of both King Lear and Gloucester; or as when Enobarbus's defection to, and again from, the bidding of his practical reason repeats that which Antony has already experienced, and Cleopatra will experience (at least in one way of understanding Act V) between Antony's death and her own. *Hamlet,* complex in all respects, offers an unusually complex form of this. The three sons, who are, in various senses, all avengers of dead fathers, are all deflected temporarily from their designs by the maneuvers of an elder (Claudius for Laertes and Hamlet; the King of Norway, inspired by Claudius, for Fortinbras), who in two cases is the young man's uncle. There are of course important differences between these three young men which we are not to forget; but with respect to structure, the images in the mirror are chiefly likenesses. Hamlet, outmaneuvered by Claudius, off to England to be executed, crosses the path of Fortinbras, who has also been outmaneuvered by Claudius (working through his uncle) and is off to Poland to make mouths at the invisible event, while at the same moment Laertes, clamoring for immediate satisfaction in the King's palace, is outmaneuvered in his turn. Likewise, at the play's end, all three young men are "victorious," in ways they could hardly have foreseen. The return of Fortinbras, having achieved his objective in Poland, to find his "rights" in Denmark achieved without a blow, is timed to coincide with Hamlet's achieving his objective in exposing and killing the King and Laertes' achieving his objective of avenging his father's death on Hamlet. When this episode is played before us in the theater there is little question, to my way of thinking, but that something of the glow and martial upsurge dramatized in Fortinbras's entrance associates itself to Hamlet, even as Fortinbras's words associate Hamlet to a soldier's death. Meantime, Laertes, who has been trapped by the King and has paid with his life for it, gives us an alternative reflection of the Prince, which is equally a part of the truth.

Fortinbras's arrival at the close of *Hamlet* is an instance of an especially interesting type of mirroring to be found everywhere in Shakespeare's work—the emblematic entrance, and exit. Sometimes such exits occur by death, as the death of Gaunt, who takes a sacramental view of kingship and nation in *Richard II*, at the instant when Richard has destroyed, by his personal conduct and by "farming" his realm, the sacramental relationships which make such a view possible to maintain. Gaunt has to die, we might say, before a usurpation like his son's can even be imagined; and it is, I take it, not without significance that the first word of Bolingbroke's return comes a few seconds after we have heard (from the same speaker, Northumberland) that Gaunt's tongue "is now a stringless instrument." Something similar, it seems clear, occurs with the death of Mamillius in *The Winter's Tale*. Sickening with his father's sickening mind, Mamillius dies in the instant that his father repudiates the message of the oracle; and though in the end, all else is restored to Leontes, Mamillius is not.

In the tragedies emblematic entrances and exits assume a variety of forms, ranging from those whose significance is obvious to those where it is uncertain, controversial and perhaps simply a mirage. One entrance whose significance is unmistakable occurs in the first act of *Macbeth*, when Duncan, speaking of the traitor Cawdor, whom he has slain, laments that there is no art to find the mind's construction in the face, just as the new Cawdor, traitor-to-be, appears before him. Equally unmistakable is the significance of the King's exit, in the first scene of *Lear,* with the man who like himself has put externals first. "Come, noble Burgundy," he says, and in a pairing that can be made profoundly moving on the stage, the two men go out together.

But what are we to say of Antony's freedman Eros, who enters for the first time (at least by name) just before his master's suicide and kills himself rather than kill Antony. This is all from his source, Plutarch's life of Antony; but why did Shakespeare include it? Did Eros's name mean something to him? Are we to see here a shadowing of the other deaths for love, or not? And the carrying off of Lepidus, drunk, from the feast aboard Pompey's galley. Does this anticipate his subsequent fate? and if it does, what does the intoxication signify which in this scene all the great men are subject to in their degree. Is it ordinary drunkenness; or is it, like the drunkenness that afflicts Caliban, Trinculo, and Stephano in *The Tempest,* a species of self-intoxication, Shakespeare's subdued comment on the thrust to worldly power? Or again, what of the arrival of the players in *Hamlet?* Granted their role in the plot, does Shakespeare make no other profit from them? Are such matters as the speech on Priam's murder and the advice on acting interesting excrescences, as Bradley thought, or does each mirror something that we are to appropriate to our understanding of the play: in the first instance, the strange confederacy of passion and paralysis in the hero's mind,[4] in the second, the question that tolls on all sides through the castle at Elsinore: when is an act not an "act"?[5]

These are questions to which it is not always easy to give a sound answer. The ground becomes somewhat firmer underfoot, I think, if we turn for a concluding instance to Bianca's pat appearances in *Othello.* R. B. Heilman suggests that in rushing to the scene of the night assault on Cassio, when she might have stayed safely within doors, and so exposing herself to vilification as a "notable strumpet," Bianca acts in a manner "thematically relevant, because Othello has just been attacking Desdemona as a strumpet" —both "strumpets," in other words, are faithful (*Magic in the Web,* p. 180). Whether this is true or not, Bianca makes two very striking entrances earlier, when in each case she may be thought to supply in living form on the stage the prostitute figure that Desdemona has become in Othello's mind. Her second entrance is notably expressive. Othello here is partially overhearing while Iago rallies Cassio about Bianca, Othello being under the delusion that the talk is of Desdemona. At the point when, in Othello's mental imagery, Desdemona becomes the soliciting whore —"she tells him how she plucked him to my chamber"—Bianca enters in the flesh, and not only enters but flourishes the magic handkerchief, now degenerated, like the love it was to ensure, to some "minx's," some "hobbyhorse's" token, the subject of jealous bickering. In the theater, the emblematic effect of this can hardly be ignored.[6]

Further types of mirroring will spring to every reader's mind. The recapitulation of a motif, for instance, as in the poisoning episodes in *Hamlet. Hamlet* criticism has too much ignored, I think, the fact that a story of poisoning forms the climax of the first act, a mime and "play" of poisoning the climax of the third, and actual poisoning, on a wide scale, the climax of the fifth. Surely this repetition was calculated to keep steady for Shakespeare's Elizabethan audiences the political and moral bearings of the play? We may say what we like about Hamlet's frailties which are real, but we can hardly ignore the fact that in each of the poisoning episodes the poisoner is the King. The King, who ought to be like the sun, giving warmth, radiance and

---

[4] See an important comment on this by H. Levin, in *Kenyon Review* (1950), pp. 273–96.

[5] I have touched on this point in *Tragic Themes in Western Literature,* ed. C. Brooks (1953).

[6] Another emblematic entrance is the first entrance of the soothsayer in *Julius Caesar;* see "The Teaching of Drama," *Essays on the Teaching of English,* ed. E. J. Gordon and E. S. Noyes (1960).

fertility to his kingdom, is actually its destroyer. The "leperous distilment" he pours into Hamlet's father's ear, which courses through his body with such despatch, has coursed just as swiftly through the body politic, and what we see in Denmark as a result is a poisoned kingdom, containing one corruption upon another of Renaissance ideals: the "wise councilor," who is instead a tedious windbag; the young "man of honor," who has no trust in another's honor, as his advice to his sister shows, and none of his own, as his own treachery to Hamlet shows; the "friends," who are not friends but spies; the loved one, the "mistress," who proves disloyal (a decoy, however reluctant, for villainy), and goes mad—through poison also, "the poison of deep grief"; the mother and Queen, who instead of being the guardian of the kingdom's matronly virtues has set a harlot's blister on love's forehead and made marriage vows "as false as dicers' oaths"; and the Prince, the "ideal courtier," the Renaissance man—once active, energetic, now reduced to anguished introspection; a glass of fashion, now a sloven in antic disarray; a noble mind, now partly unhinged, in fact as well as seeming; the observed of all observers, now observed in a more sinister sense; the mold of form, now capable of obscenities, cruelty, even treachery, mining below the mines of his school friends to hoist them with their own petard. All this in one way or another is the poison of the King, and in the last scene, lest we miss the point, we are made to see the spiritual poison become literal and seize on all those whom it has not already destroyed.

> a Prince's Court
> Is like a common Fountaine, whence should flow
> Pure silver-droppes in generall: But if't chance
> Some curs'd example poyson't neere the head,
> Death, and diseases through the whole land spread.

The lines are Webster's, but they state with precision one of the themes of Shakespeare's play.

Finally, in the tragedies as elsewhere in Shakespeare, we have the kinds of replication that have been specifically called "mirror scenes,"[7] or (more in Ercles' vein) scenes of "analogical probability."[8] The most impressive examples here are frequently the opening scenes and episodes. The witches of *Macbeth,* whose "foul is fair" and battle that is "won *and* lost" anticipate so much to come. The "great debate" in *Antony and Cleopatra,* initiated in the comments of Philo and the posturings of the lovers, and reverberating thereafter within, as well as around, the lovers till they die. The watchmen on the platform in *Hamlet,* feeling out a mystery—an image that will re-form

---

[7] By H. T. Price, in *Joseph Quincy Adams Memorial Studies,* ed. J. McManaway (1948), pp. 101 ff.

[8] See P. J. Aldus, *Shakespeare Quarterly* (1955), pp. 397 ff. Aldus deals suggestively with the opening scene of *Julius Caesar.*

in our minds again and again as we watch almost every member of the *dramatis personae* engage in similar activity later on. The technique of manipulation established at the outset of *Othello,* the persuading of someone to believe something he is reluctant to believe and which is not true in the sense presented—exemplified in Iago's management of both Roderigo and Brabantio, and prefiguring later developments even to the detail that the manipulator operates by preference through an instrument.

*Lear* offers perhaps the best of all these instances. Here the "Nature" of which the play is to make so much, ambiguous, double-barreled, is represented in its normative aspect in the hierarchies on the stage before us—a whole political society from its *primum mobile,* the great King, down to lowliest attendant, a whole family society from father down through married daughters and sons-in-law to a third daughter with her wooers—and, in its appetitive aspect, which Edmund will formulate in a few moments, in the overt self-will of the old King and the hidden self-will, the "plighted cunning," of the false daughters. As the scene progresses, in fact, we can see these hierarchies of the normative nature, which at first looked so formidable and solid, crumble away in the repudiation of Cordelia, the banishment of Kent, the exit of Lear and Burgundy, till nothing is left standing on the stage but Nature red in tooth and claw as the false daughters lay their heads together.

I have dwelt a little on these effects of "indirection" in the tragedies because I believe that most of us as playgoers are keenly conscious of their presence. I have perhaps described them badly, in some instances possibly misconceived them; but they are not my invention; this kind of thing has been pointed to more and more widely during the past fifty years by reputable observers. In short, these effects, in some important sense, are "there." And if they are, the question we must ask is, Why? What are they for? How are they used?

I return then to the query with which this section began: what *does* happen in a Shakespearean tragedy? Is it possible to formulate an answer that will, while not repudiating the traditional categories so far as they are useful, take into account the matters we have been examining? In the present state of our knowledge I am not convinced that this is possible: we have been too much concerned in this century with the verbal, which is only part of the picture. Nevertheless, I should like to make a few exploratory gestures.

Obviously the most important thing that happens in a Shakespearean tragedy is that the hero follows a cycle of change which is, in part, psychic change. And this seems generally to be constituted in three phases. During the first phase, corresponding roughly to Bradley's exposition, the hero is delineated. Among other things he is placed in positions that enable him to sound the particular timbre of his tragic music:

Not so, my lord; I am too much i' the sun. (*Hamlet,* I, ii, 67)

Seems, madam! nay, it is; I know not "seems." (I, ii, 76)

My father's brother, but no more like my father
Than I to Hercules. (I, ii, 152)

My fate cries out,
And makes each petty artery in this body
As hardy as the Nemean lion's nerve. (I, iv, 81)

Chiming against this we are also permitted to hear the particular timbre of the opposing voice, spoken by the foil as well as others:

If it be,
Why seems it so particular with thee? (I, ii, 74)

For what we know must be and is as common
As any the most vulgar thing to sense,
Why should we in our peevish opposition
Take it to heart? (I, ii, 98)

What if it tempt you toward the flood, my lord,
Or to the dreadful summit of the cliff
That beetles o'er his base into the sea,
And there assume some other horrible form,
Which might deprive your sovereignty of reason
And draw you into madness? (I, iv, 69)

From now on, as we saw, these are the differing attitudes towards experience that will supply the essential dialogue of the play.

The second phase is much more comprehensive. It contains the conflict, crisis, and falling action—in short, the heart of the matter. Here several interesting developments occur. The one certain over-all development in this phase is that the hero tends to become his own antithesis. We touched on this earlier in the case of Hamlet, in whom "the courtier's, soldier's, scholar's, eye, tongue, sword" suffer some rather savage violations before the play is done. Likewise, Othello the unshakable, whose original composure under the most trying insults and misrepresentations almost takes the breath away, breaks in this phase into furies, grovels on the floor in a trance, strikes his wife publicly. King Lear, "the great image of authority" both by temperament and position, becomes a helpless crazed old man crying in a storm, destitute of everything but one servant and his Fool. Macbeth, who would have "holily" what he would have "highly," who is too full of the milk of human kindness to catch the nearest way, whose whole being revolts with every step he takes in his own revolt—his hair standing on end, his imagination filling with angels "trumpet-tongued," his hands (after the deed) threatening to pluck out his own eyes—turns into the numbed usurper, "supped full with horrors," who is hardly capable of responding even to his wife's death. The development is equally plain in Antony and Coriolanus.

"The greatest prince o' th' world, The noblest," finds his greatness slipped from him, and his nobility debased to the ignominy of having helpless emissaries whipped. The proud and upright Coriolanus, patriot soldier, truckles in the market place for votes, revolts to the enemy he has vanquished, carries war against his own flesh and blood.

This manner of delineating tragic "action," though it may be traced here and there in other drama, seems to be on the whole a property of the Elizabethans and Jacobeans. Possibly it springs from their concern with "whole" personalities on the tragic stage, rather than as so often with the ancients and Racine, just those aspects of personality that guarantee the *dénouement*. In any case, it seems to have become a consistent feature of Shakespeare's dramaturgy and beautifully defines the sense of psychological alienation and uprootedness that tragic experience in the Elizabethan and Jacobean theater generally seems to embrace. Its distinctively tragic implications stand out the more when we reflect that psychic change in comedy (if indeed comedy can be said to concern itself with psychic change at all) consists in making, or in showing, the protagonist to be more and more what he always was.[9]

In this second phase too, either as an outward manifestation of inward change, or as a shorthand indication that such change is about to begin or end, belong the tragic journeys. Romeo is off to Mantua, Brutus to the Eastern end of the Roman world, Hamlet to England, Othello to Cyprus, Lear and Gloucester to Dover, Timon to the cave, Macbeth to the heath to revisit the witches, Antony to Rome and Athens, Coriolanus to Antium.[10] Such journeys, we rightly say, are called for by the plots. But perhaps we should not be wrong if we added that Shakespearean plotting tends to call for journeys, conceivably for discernible reasons. For one thing, journeys can enhance our impression that psychological changes are taking place, either by emphasizing a lapse of time, or by taking us to new settings, or by both. I suspect we register such effects subconsciously more often than we think.

Furthermore, though it would be foolish to assign to any of the journeys in Shakespeare's tragedies a precise symbolic meaning, several of them have vaguely symbolic overtones—serving as surrogates either for what can never be exhibited on the stage, as the mysterious processes leading to psychic change, which cannot be articulated into speech, even soliloquy, without losing their formless instinctive character; or for the processes of self-discovery, the learning processes—a function journeys fulfill in many of the world's best-known stories (the *Aeneid,* the *Divine Comedy, Tom Jones,* etc.) and in some of Shakespeare's comedies. Hamlet's abortive journey

[9] I have elaborated this point in an introduction to Fielding's *Joseph Andrews* (1948).

[10] These are merely samples; other journeys occur that I have not named here.

to England is possibly an instance of the first category. After his return, and particularly after what he tells us of his actions while at sea, we are not surprised if he appears, spiritually, a changed man. Lear's and Gloucester's journey to Dover is perhaps an instance of the second category, leading as it does through suffering to insight and reconciliation.

During the hero's journey, or at any rate during his over-all progress in the second phase, he will normally pass through a variety of mirroring situations of the sort formerly discussed (though it will be by us and not him that the likeness in the mirror is seen). In some of these, the hero will be confronted, so to speak, with a version of his own situation, and his failure to recognize it may be a measure of the nature of the disaster to ensue. Coriolanus, revolted from Rome and now its enemy, meets himself in Aufidius's embrace in Antium. Hamlet meets himself in Fortinbras as the latter marches to Poland but does not see the likeness—only the differences. Lear goes to Goneril's and there meets, as everyone remembers, images of his own behavior to Cordelia. Thrust into the night he meets his own defenselessness in Edgar and is impelled to pray. Encountering in Dover fields, both Lear and Gloucester confront in each other an extension of their own experience: blindness that sees and madness that is wise. Macbeth revisits the witches on the heath and finds there (without recognizing them) not only the emblems of his death and downfall to come but his speciousness and duplicity. Antony encounters in Enobarbus's defection his own, and possibly, in Pompey, his own later muddled indecision between "honor" and *Realpolitik*. Othello hears the innocent Cassio set upon in the dark, then goes to re-enact that scene in a more figurative darkness in Desdemona's bedroom. Sometimes, alternatively or additionally, the hero's way will lie through quasi-symbolic settings or situations. The heath in both *Macbeth* and *King Lear* is infinitely suggestive, even if like all good symbols it refuses to dissipate its *Dinglichkeit* in meaning. The same is true of the dark castle platform in Hamlet, and the graveyard; of the cliff at Dover and Gloucester's leap; of the "monument," where both Antony and Cleopatra die; and of course, as many have pointed out, of the night scenes, the storm, the music, the changes of clothing, the banquets. So much in Shakespeare's tragedies stands on the brink of symbol that for this reason, if no other, the usual terms for describing their construction and mode of action need reinforcement.

After the hero has reached and passed through his own antithesis, there comes a third phase in his development that is extremely difficult to define. It represents a recovery of sorts—in some cases, perhaps even a species of synthesis. The once powerful, now powerless king, will have power again, but of another kind—the kind suggested in his reconciliation with Cordelia and his speech beginning "Come, let's away to prison"; and he will have sanity again, but in a mode not dreamed of at the beginning of the play. Or, to take Othello's case, it will be given the hero to recapture the faith he lost,[11] to learn that the pearl really was richer than all his tribe and to execute quite another order of justice than the blinkered justice meted out to Cassio and the blind injustice meted out to Desdemona. Or again, to shift to Antony, the man who has so long been thrown into storms of rage and recrimination by the caprices of his unstable mistress receives the last of them without a murmur of reproach, though it has led directly to his death, and dies in greater unison with her than we have ever seen him live.

I believe that some mark of this nature is visible in all the tragedies. Coriolanus, "boy" though he is and in some ways remains, makes a triumphant choice (detract from his motives as we may), and he knows what it is likely to cost. Moreover, he refuses the way of escape that lies open if he should return now with Volumnia and Vergilia to Rome. "I'll not to Rome, I'll back with you," he tells Aufidius, "and pray you Stand to me in this cause." The young man who after this dies accused of treachery—by Aufidius's treachery and the suggestibility of the crowd, as slippery in Corioli as Rome—cannot be thought identical in all respects with the young man who joined Menenius in the play's opening scene. He is that young man but with the notable difference of his triumphant choice behind him; and there is bound to be more than a military association in our minds when the Second Lord of the Volscians, seeking to quell the mob, cries, "The man is noble, and his fame folds in This orb o' th' earth"; and again too when the First Lord exclaims over his body, "Let him be regarded As the most noble corse that ever herald Did follow to his urn." Even the monster Macbeth is so handled by Shakespeare, as has been often enough observed, that he seems to regain something at the close—if nothing more, at least some of that *élan* which made him the all-praised Bellona's bridegroom of the play's second scene; and everything Macbeth says, following Duncan's death, about the emptiness of the achievement, the lack of posterity, the sear, the yellow leaf, deprived of "that which should accompany old age, As honor, love, obedience, troops of friends," affords evidence that the meaning of his experience has not been lost on him.

To say this, I wish to make it clear, is not to say that the Shakespearean tragic hero undergoes an "illumination," or, to use the third term of Kenneth Burke's sequence, a Mathema or perception.[12] This is a terminology that seems to me not very useful to the discussion of tragedy as Shakespeare presents it. It is sufficient for my purposes to say simply that the phase in which we are conscious of the hero as approaching his opposite is followed by a final phase in which we are conscious of him as exhibiting one or more aspects of his original, or—since these may not coincide—his better self: as in the case of Antony's final reunion with Cleopatra, and

[11] This point is well made in Helen Gardner's *The Noble Moor* (1956).
[12] *A Grammar of Motives* (1945), pp. 38 ff.

Coriolanus's decision not to sack Rome. Whether we then go on to give this phenomenon a specific spiritual significance, seeing in it the objective correlative of "perception" or "illumination," is a question that depends, obviously, on a great many factors, more of them perhaps situated in our own individual philosophies than in the text, and so, likely to lead us away from Shakespeare rather than towards him. Clearly if Shakespeare wished us to engage in this activity, he was remiss in the provision of clues. Even in *King Lear,* the one play where some sort of regeneration or new insight in the hero has been universally acknowledged, the man before us in the last scene—who sweeps Kent aside, rakes all who have helped him with grapeshot ("A plague upon you, murderers, traitors all. I might have saved her..."), exults in the revenge he has exacted for Cordelia's death, and dies self-deceived in the thought she still lives—this man is one of the most profoundly human figures ever created in a play; but he is not, certainly, the Platonic idea laid up in heaven, or in critical schemes, of regenerate man.

I have kept to the end, and out of proper order, the most interesting of all the symbolic elements in the hero's second phase. This is his experience of madness. One discovers with some surprise, I think, how many of Shakespeare's heroes are associated with this disease. Only Titus, Hamlet, Lear, and Timon, in various senses, actually go mad; but Iago boasts that he will make Othello mad and in a way succeeds; Antony, after the second defeat at sea, is said by Cleopatra to be

> more mad,
> Than Telamon for his shield; the boar of Thessaly
> Was never so emboss'd; (IV, xiii, 2)

Caithness in *Macbeth* tells us that some say the king is mad, while "others, that lesser hate him, Do call it valiant fury"; Romeo, rather oddly, enjoins Paris at Juliet's tomb to

> be gone; live, and hereafter say,
> A madman's mercy bade thee run away. (V, iii, 66)

Even Brutus, by the Antony of *Antony and Cleopatra,* is said to have been "mad."

What, if anything, one wonders, may this mean? Doubtless a sort of explanation can be found in Elizabethan psychological lore, which held that the excess of any passion approached madness, and in the general prevalence, through Seneca and other sources, of the adage: *Quos vult perdere Jupiter dementat prius.*[13] Furthermore, madness, when actually exhibited, was dra-

13 "Whom God wishes to destroy he first makes mad."

matically useful, as Kyd had shown. It was arresting in itself, and it allowed the combination in a single figure of tragic hero and buffoon, to whom could be accorded the license of the allowed fool in speech and action.

Just possibly, however, there was yet more to it than this, if we may judge by Shakespeare's sketches of madness in Hamlet and King Lear. In both these, madness is to some degree a punishment or doom, corresponding to the adage. Lear prays to the heavens that he may not suffer madness, and Hamlet asks Laertes in his apology before the duel to overlook his conduct, since "you must needs have heard, how I am punish'd With a sore distraction." It is equally obvious, however, that in both instances the madness has a further dimension, as insight, and this is true also of Ophelia. Ophelia, mad, is able to make awards of flowers to the King and Queen which are appropriate to frailties of which she cannot be supposed to have conscious knowledge. For the same reason, I suspect we do not need Dover Wilson's radical displacement of Hamlet's entry in II, ii, so as to enable him to overhear Polonius.[14] It is enough that Hamlet wears, even if it is for the moment self-assumed, the guise of the madman. As such, he can be presumed to have intuitive unformulated awarenesses that reach the surface in free (yet relevant) associations, like those of Polonius with a fishmonger, Ophelia with carrion. Lear likewise is allowed free yet relevant associations. His great speech in Dover fields on the lust of women derives from the designs of Goneril and Regan on Edmund, of which he consciously knows nothing. Moreover, both he and Hamlet can be privileged in madness to say things—Hamlet about the corruption of human nature, and Lear about the corruption of the Jacobean social system (and by extension about all social systems whatever)—which Shakespeare could hardly have risked apart from this license. Doubtless one of the anguishes of being a great artist is that you cannot tell people what they and you and your common institutions are really like—when viewed absolutely—without being dismissed as insane. To communicate at all, you must acknowledge the opposing voice; for there always is an opposing voice, and it is as deeply rooted in your own nature as in your audience's.

Just possibly, therefore, the meaning of tragic madness for Shakespeare approximated the meaning that the legendary figure of Cassandra (whom Shakespeare had in fact put briefly on his stage in the second act of *Troilus and Cressida*) has held for so many artists since his time. Cassandra's madness, like Lear's and Hamlet's—possibly, also, like the madness *verbally* assigned to other Shakespearean tragic heroes—contains both punishment and insight. She is doomed to know, by a consciousness that moves to measures outside our normal space and time; she is doomed never to be believed, because those to whom she speaks can hear only the opposing voice. With

[14] *What Happens in "Hamlet"* (1935), pp. 103 ff.

the language of the god Apollo sounding in her brain, and the incredulity of her fellow mortals ringing in her ears, she makes an ideal emblem of the predicament of the Shakespearean tragic hero, caught as he is between the absolute and the expedient. And by the same token, of the predicament of the artist—Shakespeare himself, perhaps—who, having been given the power to see the "truth," can convey it only through poetry—what we commonly call a "fiction" and dismiss.

In all these matters, let me add in parenthesis, we would do well to extend more generously our inferences about Shakespeare to the Jacobean playwrights as a group. Some of us have been overlong content with a view of Jacobean tragedy as naïve as those formerly entertained of Restoration comedy, eighteenth-century literature, and modern poetry. But a whole generation of writers does not become obsessed by the sexual feuding of cavalier and citizen, or rhetorical "rules" and social norms, or abrupt images and catapulting rhythms, or outrageous stories of incest, madness, brutality and lust, because the poetic imagination has suddenly gone "frivolous," or "cold," or "eccentric," or "corrupt." Such concerns respond to spiritual needs, however dimly apprehended, and one of the prime needs of Jacobean writers, as the intelligible and on the whole friendly universe of the Middle Ages failed around them, was quite evidently to face up to what men are or may be when stripped to their naked humanity and mortality and torn loose from accustomed moorings. Flamineo's phrase in *The White Devil*—"this busy trade of life"—offered as a passing summary of the play's monstrous burden of blood and madness:

> This busy trade of life appears most vain,
> Since rest breeds rest, where all seek pain by pain—

is characteristically understated and ironic, like Iago's "Pleasure and action make the hours seem short." The creators of Iago and Flamineo, and all the responsible writers of Jacobean tragedy along with them, knew perfectly well that it was not in fact the "trade," or habitude, of life to which they held up art's mirror, but life "on the stretch," nature at its farthest reach of possibility. They were fascinated by violence because they were fascinated by the potencies of the human will: its weaknesses, triumphs, delusions, corruptions, its capacities for destruction and regeneration, its residual dignity when, all else removed, man stood at his being's limit; and because they knew that in violence lay the will's supreme test, for aggressor and sufferer alike.

Whatever the themes of individual plays, therefore, the one pervasive Jacobean theme tends to be the undertaking and working out of acts of will, and especially (in that strongly Calvinistic age) of acts of self-will. This is surely the reason why, in Clifford Leech's happy phrase, these writers know so little of heaven, so much of hell, and why, to one conversant with their work, so many products of the century to come seem like fulfillments of ancient prophecy: Milton's Satan and his "God"—the philosophy embodied in *Leviathan*—even, perhaps, the clash of the Civil Wars and the cleavage in the English spirit reaching from Cavalier and Puritan to Jacobite and Whig and well beyond. At the very beginning of the century, these writers had got hold of the theme that was to exercise it in all departments, political, economic, religious, cultural, till past its close, the problem of anarchic will; and so decisive, so many-sided is their treatment of this problem that even in Milton's massive recapitulation of it in *Paradise Lost* the issue seems sometimes to be losing in vitality what it has gained in clarity, to be fossilizing and becoming formula. The utterances of *his* white devil have more resonance but less complexity and immediacy of feeling than those of Vittoria Corombona, Bosola, Macbeth, or Beatrice Vermandero, and some of them bear a perilous resemblance to the posturings of Restoration heroic tragedy, where the old agonies are heard from still, but now clogged, and put through paces like captive giants in a raree show.

However this may be, I return at the end to the proposition I set out with: there is a lot about the construction of a Shakespearean tragic "action" that we still do not know. My own attempts to get towards it in this chapter are fumbling and may be preposterous: even to myself they sound a little like Bottom's dream. But the interesting thing about Bottom's dream, from my point of view, is that, though he found he was an ass all right, the Titania he tried to tell about was real.

3

# The Argument of Comedy

*Northrop Frye*

The Greeks produced two kinds of comedy, Old Comedy, represented by the eleven extant plays of Aristophanes, and New Comedy, of which the best known exponent is Menander. About two dozen New Comedies survive in the work of Plautus and Terence. Old Comedy, however, was out of date before Aristophanes himself was dead; and today, when we speak of comedy, we normally think of something that derives from the Menandrine tradition.

New Comedy unfolds from what may be described as a comic Oedipus situation. Its main theme is the successful effort of a young man to outwit an opponent and possess the girl of his choice. The opponent is usually the father (*senex*), and the psychological descent of the heroine from the mother is also sometimes hinted at. The father frequently wants the same girl and is cheated out of her by the son, the mother thus becoming the son's ally. The girl is usually a slave or courtesan, and the plot turns on a *cognitio* or discovery of birth which makes her marriageable. Thus it turns out that she is not under an insuperable taboo after all but is an accessible object of desire, so that the plot follows the regular wish-fulfillment pattern. Often

*From* English Institute Essays, *1948, 1949, pp. 58–73. Copyright 1949 by Columbia University Press. Reprinted by permission of the publisher.*

the central Oedipus situation is thinly concealed by surrogates or doubles of the main characters, as when the heroine is discovered to be the hero's sister and has to be married off to his best friend. In Congreve's *Love for Love,* to take a modern instance well within the Menandrine tradition, there are two Oedipus themes in counterpoint: the hero cheats his father out of the heroine, and his best friend violates the wife of an impotent old man who is the heroine's guardian. Whether this analysis is sound or not, New Comedy is certainly concerned with the maneuvering of a young man toward a young woman, and marriage is the tonic chord on which it ends. The normal comic resolution is the surrender of the *senex* to the hero, never the reverse. Shakespeare tried to reverse the pattern in *All's Well That Ends Well,* where the king of France forces Bertram to marry Helena, and the critics have not yet stopped making faces over it.

New Comedy has the blessing of Aristotle, who greatly preferred it to its predecessor, and it exhibits the general pattern of Aristotelian causation. It has a material cause in the young man's sexual desire and a formal cause in the social order represented by the *senex,* with which the hero comes to terms when he gratifies his desire. It has an efficient cause in the character who brings about the final situation. In classical times this character is a tricky slave; Renaissance dramatists often use some adaptation of the medieval "vice"; modern writers generally like to pretend that nature or at least the natural course of events is the efficient cause. The final cause is the audience, which is expected by its applause to take part in the comic resolution. All this takes place on a single order of existence. The action of New Comedy tends to become probable rather than fantastic, and it moves toward realism and away from myth and romance. The one romantic (originally mythical) feature in it, the fact that the hero or heroine turns out to be freeborn or someone's heir, is precisely the feature that trained New Comedy audiences tire of most quickly.

The conventions of New Comedy are the conventions of Jonson and Molière, and a fortiori of the English Restoration and the French rococo. When Ibsen started giving ironic twists to the same formulas, his startled hearers took them for portents of a social revolution. Even the old chestnut about the heroine's being really the hero's sister turns up in *Ghosts* and *Little Eyolf*. The average movie of today is a rigidly conventionalized New Comedy proceeding toward an act which, like death in Greek tragedy, takes place offstage and is symbolized by the final embrace.

In all good New Comedy there is a social as well as an individual theme which must be sought in the general atmosphere of reconciliation that makes the final marriage possible. As the hero gets closer to the heroine and opposition is overcome, all the right-thinking people come over to his side. Thus a new social unit is formed on the stage, and the moment that this social unit crystallizes is the moment of the comic resolution. In the last scene when he dramatist usually tries to get all his characters on the stage at once, the audience witnesses the birth of a renewed sense of social integration. In comedy as in life the regular expression of this is a festival, whether a marriage, dance, or a feast. Old Comedy has, besides a marriage, a *komos,* the processional dance from which comedy derives its name; and the masque, which is a by-form of comedy, also ends in a dance.

This new social integration may be called, first, a kind of moral norm and, second, the pattern of a free society. We can see this more clearly if we look at the sort of characters who impede the progress of the comedy toward the hero's victory. These are always people who are in some kind of mental bondage, who are helplessly driven by ruling passions, neurotic compulsions, social rituals, and selfishness. The miser, the hypochondriac, the hypocrite, the pedant, the snob: these are humors, people who do not fully know what they are doing, who are slaves to a predictable self-imposed pattern of behavior. What we call the moral norm is, then, not morality but deliverance from moral bondage. Comedy is designed not to condemn evil, but to ridicule a lack of self-knowledge. It finds the virtues of Malvolio and Angelo as comic as the vices of Shylock.

The essential comic resolution, therefore, is an individual release which is also a social reconciliation. The normal individual is freed from the bonds of a humorous society, and a normal society is freed from the bonds imposed on it by humorous individuals. The Oedipus pattern we noted in New Comedy belongs to the individual side of this, and the sense of the ridiculousness of the humor to the social side. But all real comedy is based on the principle that these two forms of release are ultimately the same: this principle may be seen at its most concentrated in *The Tempest.* The rule holds whether the resolution is expressed in social terms, as in *The Merchant of Venice,* or in individual terms, as in Ibsen's *An Enemy of the People.*

The freer the society, the greater the variety of individuals it can tolerate, and the natural tendency of comedy is to include as many as possible in its final festival. The motto of comedy is Terence's "Nothing human is alien to me." This may be one reason for the traditional comic importance of the parasite, who has no business to be at the festival but is nevertheless there. The spirit of reconciliation which pervades the comedies of Shakespeare is not to be ascribed to a personal attitude of his own, about which we know nothing whatever, but to his impersonal concentration on the laws of comic form.

Hence the moral quality of the society presented is not the point of the comic resolution. In Jonson's *Volpone* the final assertion of the moral norm takes the form of a social revenge on Volpone, and the play ends with a great bustle of sentences to penal servitude and the galleys. One feels perhaps that the audience's sense of the moral norm does not need so much hard labor. In *The Alchemist,* when Lovewit returns to his house, the virtuous characters have proved so weak and the rascals so ingenious that the action dissolves in laughter. Whichever is morally the better ending, that of *The Alchemist* is more concentrated comedy. *Volpone* is starting to move toward tragedy, toward the vision of a greatness which develops *hybris* and catastrophe.

The same principle is even clearer in Aristophanes. Aristophanes is the most personal of writers: his opinions on every subject are written all over his plays, and we have no doubt of his moral attitude. We know that he wanted peace with Sparta and that he hated Cleon, and when his comedy depicts the attaining of peace and the defeat of Cleon we know that he approved and wanted his audience to approve. But in *Ecclesiazusae* a band of women in disguise railroad a communistic scheme through the Assembly, which is a horrid parody of Plato's *Republic,* and proceed to inaugurate Plato's sexual communism with some astonishing improvements. Presumably Aristophanes did not applaud this, yet the comedy follows the same pattern and the same resolution. In *The Birds* the Peisthetairos who defies Zeus and blocks out Olympus with his Cloud-Cuckoo-Land is accorded the same triumph that is given to the Trygaeus of the *Peace* who flies to heaven and brings a golden age back to Athens.

Comedy, then, may show virtue her own feature and scorn her own image—for Hamlet's famous definition of drama was originally a definition of comedy. It may emphasize the birth of an ideal society as you like it, or the tawdriness of the sham society which is the way of the world. There is an important parallel here with tragedy. Tragedy, we are told, is expected to raise but not ultimately to accept the emotions of pity and terror. These I take to be the sense of moral good and evil, respectively, which we attach to the tragic hero. He may be as good as Caesar, and so appeal to our pity, or as bad as Macbeth, and so appeal to terror, but the particular thing called tragedy that happens to him does not depend on his moral status. The tragic catharsis passes beyond moral judgment, and while it is quite possible to construct a moral tragedy, what tragedy gains in morality it loses in cathartic power. The same is true of the comic catharsis, which raises sympathy and ridicule on a moral basis but passes beyond both.

Many things are involved in the tragic catharsis, but one of them is a mental or imaginative form of the sacrificial ritual out of which tragedy arose. This is the ritual of the struggle, death, and rebirth of a God-Man, which is linked to the yearly triumph of spring over winter. The tragic hero is not really killed, and the audience no longer eats his body and drinks his blood, but the corresponding thing in art still takes place. The audience enters into communion with the body of the hero, becoming thereby a single body itself. Comedy grows out of the same ritual, for in the ritual the tragic story has a comic sequel. Divine men do not die: they die and rise again. The ritual pattern behind the catharsis of comedy is the resurrection that follows the death, the epiphany or manifestation of the risen hero. This is clear enough in Aristophanes, where the hero is treated as a risen God-Man, led in triumph with the divine honors of the Olympic victor, rejuvenated or hailed as a new Zeus. In New Comedy the new human body is, as we have seen, both a hero and a social group. Aristophanes is not only closer to the ritual pattern, but contemporary with Plato; and his comedy, unlike Menander's, is Platonic and dialectic: it seeks not the entelechy of the soul but the Form of the Good and finds it in the resurrection of the soul from the world of the cave to the sunlight. The audience gains a vision of that resurrection whether the conclusion is joyful or ironic, just as in tragedy it gains a vision of a heroic death whether the hero is morally innocent or guilty.

Two things follow from this: first, that tragedy is really implicit or uncompleted comedy; second, that comedy contains a potential tragedy within itself. With regard to the latter, Aristophanes is full of traces of the original death of the hero which preceded his resurrection in the ritual. Even in New Comedy the dramatist usually tries to bring his action as close to a tragic overthrow of the hero as he can get it and reverses this movement as suddenly as possible. In Plautus the tricky slave is often forgiven or even freed after having been threatened with all the brutalities that a very brutal dramatist can think of, including crucifixion. Thus the resolution of New Comedy seems to be a realistic foreshortening of a death-and-resurrection pattern, in which the struggle and rebirth of a divine hero has shrunk into a marriage, the freeing of a slave, and the trimph of a young man over an older one.

As for the conception of tragedy as implicit comedy, we may notice how often tragedy closes on the major chord of comedy: the Aeschylean trilogy, for instance, proceeds to what is really a comic resolution, and so do many tragedies of Euripides. From the point of view of Christianity, too, tragedy is an episode in that larger scheme of redemption and resurrection to which Dante gave the name of *commedia*. This conception of *commedia* enters drama with the miracle-play cycles, where such tragedies as the Fall and the Crucifixion are episodes of a dramatic scheme in which the divine comedy has the last word. The sense of tragedy as a prelude to comedy is hardly separable from anything explicitly Christian. The serenity of the final double chorus in the St. Matthew Passion would hardly be attainable if composer and audience did not know that there was more to the story. Nor would the death of Samson lead to "calm of mind all passion spent" if Samson were not a prototype of the rising Christ.

New Comedy is thus contained, so to speak, within the symbolic structure of Old Comedy, which in its turn is contained within the Christian conception of *commedia*. This sounds like a logically exhaustive classification, but we have still not caught Shakespeare in it.

It is only in Jonson and the Restoration writers that English comedy can be called a form of New Comedy. The earlier tradition established by Peele and developed by Lyly, Greene, and the masque writers, which uses themes from romance and folklore and avoids the comedy of manners, is the one followed by Shakespeare. These themes are largely medieval in origin and derive, not from the mysteries or the moralities or the interludes, but from a fourth dramatic tradition. This is the drama of folk ritual, of the St. George play and the mummers' play, of the feast of the ass and the Boy Bishop, and of all the dramatic activity that punctuated the Christian calendar with the rituals of an immemorial paganism. We may call this the drama of the green world, and its theme is once again the triumph of life over the waste land, the death and revival of the year impersonated by figures still human, and once divine as well.

When Shakespeare began to study Plautus and Terence, his dramatic instinct, stimulated by his predecessors, divined that there was a profounder pattern in the argument of comedy than appears in either of them. At once—for the process is beginning in *The Comedy of Errors*—he started groping toward that profounder pattern, the ritual of death and revival that also underlies Aristophanes, of which an exact equivalent lay ready to hand in the drama of the green world. This parallelism largely accounts for the resemblances to Greek ritual which Colin Still has pointed out in *The Tempest*.

*The Two Gentlemen of Verona* is an orthodox New Comedy except for one thing. The hero Valentine becomes captain of a band of outlaws in a forest, and all the other characters are gathered into this forest and become converted. Thus the action of the comedy begins in a world represented as a normal world, moves into the green world, goes into a metamorphosis there in which the comic resolution is achieved, and returns to the normal world. The forest in this play is the embryonic form of the fairy world of *A Midsummer Night's Dream,* the Forest of Arden in *As You Like It,* Windsor Forest in *The Merry Wives of Windsor,* and the pastoral world of the mythical sea-coasted Bohemia in *The Winter's Tale.* In all these comedies there is the same rhythmic movement from normal world to green world and back again. Nor is this second world confined to the forest comedies. In *The Merchant of Venice* the two worlds are a little harder to see, yet Venice is clearly not the same world as that of Portia's mysterious house in Belmont, where there are caskets teaching that gold and silver are corruptible goods and from whence proceed the wonderful cosmological harmonies of the fifth act. In *The Tempest* the entire action takes place in the second world, and the same may be said of *Twelfth Night,* which, as its title implies, presents a carnival society, not so much a green world as an evergreen one. The second world is absent from the so-called problem comedies, which is one of the things that makes them problem comedies.

The green world charges the comedies with a symbolism in which the comic resolution contains a suggestion of the old ritual pattern of the victory of summer over winter. This is explicit in *Love's Labour's Lost*. In this very masque-like play, the comic contest takes the form of the medieval debate of winter and spring. In *The Merry Wives of Windsor* there is an elaborate ritual of the defeat of winter, known to folklorists as "carrying out Death," of which Falstaff is the victim; and Falstaff must have felt that after being thrown into the water, dressed up as a witch and beaten out of a house with curses, and finally supplied with a beast's head and singed with candles while he said, "Divide me like a brib'd buck, each a haunch," he had done about all that could reasonably be asked of any fertility spirit.

The association of this symbolism with the death and revival of human beings is more elusive but still perceptible. The fact that the heroine often brings about the comic resolution by disguising herself as a boy is familiar enough. In the Hero of *Much Ado About Nothing* and the Helena of *All's Well That Ends Well,* this theme of the withdrawal and return of the heroine comes as close to a death and revival as Elizabethan conventions will allow. The Thaisa of *Pericles* and the Fidele of *Cymbeline* are beginning to crack the conventions, and with the disappearance and revival of Hermione in *The Winter's Tale,* who actually returns once as a ghost in a dream, the original nature-myth of Demeter and Proserpine is openly established. The fact that the dying and reviving character is usually female strengthens the feeling that there is something maternal about the green world, in which the new order of the comic resolution is nourished and brought to birth. However, a similar theme which is very like the rejuvenation of the *senex* so frequent in Aristophanes occurs in the folklore motif of the healing of the impotent king on which *All's Well That Ends Well* is based, and this theme is probably involved in the symbolism of Prospero.

The conception of a second world bursts the boundaries of Menandrine comedy; yet it is clear that the world of Puck is no world of eternal forms or divine revelation. Shakespeare's comedy is not Aristotelian and realistic like Menander's, nor Platonic and dialectic like Aristophanes', nor Thomist and sacramental like Dante's, but a fourth kind. It is an Elizabethan kind and is not confined either to Shakespeare or to the drama. Spenser's epic is a wonderful contrapuntal intermingling of two orders of existence, one the red and white world of English history, the other the green world of the Faerie Queene. The latter is a world of crusading virtues proceeding from the Faerie Queene's court and designed to return to that court when the destiny of the other world is fulfilled. The fact that the Faerie Queene's knights are sent out during the twelve days of the Christmas festival suggests our next point.

Shakespeare too has his green world of comedy and his red and white world of history. The story of the latter is at one point interrupted by an invasion from the comic world, when Falstaff *senex et parasitus* throws his gigantic shadow over Prince Henry, assuming on one occasion the role of his father. Clearly, if the Prince is ever to conquer France he must reassert the moral norm. The moral norm is duly reasserted, but the rejection of Falstaff is not a comic resolution. In comedy the moral norm is not morality but deliverance, and we certainly do not feel delivered from Falstaff as we feel delivered from Shylock with his absurd and vicious bond. The moral norm does not carry with it the vision of a free society: Falstaff will always keep a bit of that in his tavern.

Falstaff is a mock king, a lord of misrule, and his tavern is a Saturnalia. Yet we are reminded of the original meaning of the Saturnalia, as a rite intended to recall the golden age of Saturn. Falstaff's world is not a golden world, but as long as we remember it we cannot forget that the world of *Henry V* is an iron one. We are reminded too of another traditional denizen of the green world, Robin Hood, the outlaw who manages to suggest a better kind of society than those who make him an outlaw can produce. The outlaws in *The Two Gentlemen of Verona* compare themselves, in spite of the Italian setting, to Robin Hood, and in *As You Like It* Charles the wrestler says of Duke Senior's followers: "There they live like the old Robin Hood of England: they say many young gentlemen flock to him every day, and fleet the time carelessly, as they did in the golden world."

In the histories, therefore, the comic Saturnalia is a temporary reversal of normal standards, comic "relief" as it is called, which subsides and allows the history to continue. In the comedies the green world suggests an original golden age which the normal world has usurped and which makes us wonder if it is not the normal world that is the real Saturnalia. In *Cymbeline* the green world finally triumphs over a historical theme; the reason being perhaps that in that play the incarnation of Christ, which is contemporary with Cymbeline, takes place offstage, and accounts for the halcyon peace with which the play concludes. From then on in Shakespeare's plays, the green world has it all its own way, and both in *Cymbeline* and in *Henry VIII* there may be suggestions that Shakespeare, like Spencer, is moving toward a synthesis of the two worlds, a wedding of Prince Arthur and the Faerie Queene.

This world of fairies, dreams, disembodied souls, and pastoral lovers may not be a "real" world, but, if not, there is something equally illusory in the stumbling and blinded follies of the "normal" world, of Theseus' Athens with its idiotic marriage law, of Duke Frederick and his melancholy tyranny, of Leontes and his mad jealousy, of the Court Party with their plots and intrigues. The famous speech of Prospero about the dream nature of reality applies equally to Milan and the enchanted island. We spend our lives partly in a waking world we call normal and partly in a dream world which we create out of our own desires. Shakespeare endows both worlds with equal imaginative power, brings them opposite one another, and makes each world seem unreal when seen by the light of the other. He uses freely both the heroic triumph of New Comedy and the ritual resurrection of its predecessor, but his distinctive comic resolution is different from either: it is a detachment of the spirit born of this reciprocal reflection of two illusory realities. We need not ask whether this brings us into a higher order of existence or not, for the question of existence is not relevant to poetry.

We have spoken of New Comedy as Aristotelian, Old Comedy as Platonic and Dante's *commedia* as Thomist, but it is difficult to suggest a philosophical spokesman for the form of Shakespeare's comedy. For Shakespeare, the subject matter of poetry is not life, or nature, or reality, or revelation, or anything else that the philosopher builds on, but poetry itself, a verbal universe. That is one reason why he is both the most elusive and the most substantial of poets.

# 4

# Shakespeare's Kingship: Institution and Dramatic Form

*Harold E. Toliver*

The playwright's privileged disregard of whatever does not fit his dramatic plan gives him an incalculable advantage over historians, who as Sidney points out, are responsible to real events and people. But even the playwright is obliged to concede something to history's shapelessness: he takes images and conventions from the public stock, and these bring with them something of the same confusing forces and daily acts that we try to control in our institutions, codes, statutes, grammars, and dictionaries. In Shakespeare, the king is both a central dramatic control and a way of incorporating into drama large segments of national history, often in its most turbulent moments. Hence in the king we can often see clearly a critical tension between the raw materials of art and the finished work and can trace the transformation of one into the other. But the king is also a very special kind of raw material: he comes to the playwright already well-disciplined by society's formalistic patterns. He is something of a work of art even before he gains admission to the cast of a play, especially if he has undergone the editing and mythic heightening of a Tudor chronicle. He is ready to become part of an organic system of symbols and signs that can make good use of a central figure of such promising stature, sure to be in on all major plots and to provide dramatic flare and eloquence.

The mere presence of a king does not legislate the attitude, tone, or genre of a work, of course: A king is obviously fair game for comedy as well as tragedy, for fairy tales, comic strips, and sonnets as well as for panegyrics, royal masques, and feudal romances. But he does have predispositions somewhat stronger and more complex than many of the raw materials that the imagination has to work with. The idea of a king, Jack Cade's liberties with it in *2 Henry VI* notwithstanding, is potentially a dramatic idea of a definite style, formal leaning, and majestic proportion. The mythic extensions, insignia, gestures, regalia, and formal movement of kingly ceremonies both draw upon the dramatic imagination in their real historical staging and provide models of structural progression that theatrical productions in turn may exploit in accommodating *mimesis* to dramatic formality.[1] As a highly visible symbol, a king is eminently stageable in a medium so dependent upon pageantry as drama.

Beyond that, the monarch in Shakespeare is often assumed to represent a natural and providential order that transcends normal politics. He is the manifest of providence in whom we can gauge the working of inscrutable forces upon the body politic. As an archetypal symbol, he stands in a closed and articulate universe whose divine and cosmic influences converge in the action he performs. Though Shakespeare is seldom unequivocal about links between that broader order and politics, what society does is seldom

---

1 Stripped of political realism, the ceremonies of kingship are better material for masques, royalist panegyric and court entertainment than for drama—for Inigo Jones and Jonson than for Shakespeare. In *Oberon the Fairy Prince,* for instance, Jonson associates King James with the presiding powers of nature and has him establish majesty by pure magic and masquelike display. The king preserves others in "their being" so that "they live/ Sustained in form, fame, and felicity" (332–33). In a panegyric that Marvell appears to have had in mind in the opening lines of "The First Anniversary," Jonson writes of the king's power of yearly renewal,

> 'Tis he, that stays the time from turning old,
> And keeps the age up in a head of gold,
> That in his own true circle, still doth run;
> And holds his course, as certain as the sun.
> He makes it ever day, and ever spring,
> Where he doth shine, and quickens every thing
> Like a new nature: so, that true to call
> Him, by his title, is to say, Hee's all. (350–57)

It might be profitable to juxtapose the dramatic situations peculiar to kingship with more general situations such as George Polti's *Les trente-six situations dramatique,* but I have chosen what seems a prior matter: ways in which an institution leans toward certain literary embodiments and affects them, and ways, in turn, in which literary form reaches out to incorporate subjects cohesive enough to retain something of their original shapes in the work. Kingship is not the only institution with which an institutional-generic criticism might concern itself, of course: the army, the city, the courtroom (with its interrogations, reversals, and recognitions), the corporation, or the university also apply certain pressures to whatever literary forms try to deal with them. In "Property and Value: the Genre of the Country-House Poem in the Seventeenth Century" in *Genre,* I (1968), 141–57, Charles Molesworth's assessment of the impact of the country house on several poems illustrates a similar approach.

completely dissociated from what the signs and portents of nature indicate are the higher purposes of providence, which alter the course of society and enter into the shaping of the play. These purposes are secrets to be probed in dramatic agon and clarified in disclosure and recognition scenes: They may reinforce the benevolent finality of comedy or the mystery of tragedy to which the tragic hero resigns himself with a sense of exalted inevitability; or they may play through the complex business of rights and royal succession in the histories. Because of their telic nature, they tend to give a play formal enclosure. But on the other hand, they are also veiled in political negotiations that have their own more evident causes, in a world of historical circumstances that in Shakespeare inclines toward realism rather than toward myth and ritual. The king himself may fail to uphold the office that tries to shape him as a majestic symbol, and weak or villainous kings resist the coherent work that the imagination likes to practice on them. An unkingly Richard II or a calculating Henry IV would rather take his own way than play by the rules of his inherited role. They unleash formless intrigues against the masquelike pageantry and majestic controls that a king should command and allow historical circumstance to impinge upon the stable appointments of the institution. Whereas pre-Shakespearean morality kingship plays tend to make all periods of history variants of the soul's typical rituals, Shakespearean drama pins its magistrates to definite eras, social disorders and personal whims, which require constant adjustment between the formal office and individuating circumstances, and between dramatic form and social realism.

Though Shakespeare normally begins with a kingship that has lost some of its prerogatives and lapsed into political entanglements, however, intrusions of realism and individual motives are not allowed to erase entirely the play's sense of underlying social form and ritual. Most of the plays eventually reinstate the kingship and the ceremonial decorum it prefers: The institution is patched up and perhaps inoculated, for a time, against similar trials, often with a harmonious reintegration of social ranks. Thus in *The Winter's Tale,* hereditary succession is reestablished and the peasants of Bohemia pay tribute to it. Where the restoration of social decorum coincides with the play's need for formality in this way, we may find it difficult to distinguish between a real *destiny* that satisfies our sense of *justice* and a *well-made work* that satisfies our sense of *dramatic rightness*. The mode of imitation and the thing imitated run together. (If good theater and a well-run kingdom both call for the ceremonial elevation of honor and justice in *2 Henry IV*, for instance, which gets credit for preventing Falstaff from spoiling the coronation of Henry V?) But therein lies part of the king's usefulness to dramatic form: As an institutionalized man, he fuses statecraft and stagecraft; he enables us to think that an image of order in the play reflects a real order in history—that plays may have their formal shapes and remain true to reality as well. The king is thus not only the manifest of providence but a demonstration of divine artistry. Some effort may be required even of the best of kings to gather his people into the cast of his majestic enactment, but with the help of Shakespeare's stagecraft, he succeeds. Prince Hal, for instance, performs in a variety of small scenes preparatory to the coronation: He plays roguish colleague with Falstaff; reveals another face to Poins in their mutual plot; offers a more definitive and predictive view of his plans to the audience in soliloquy; plays prince to Falstaff's king and king to Falstaff's prince in practicing for later interviews with his father; mimics Hotspur and then captures his honors in a battlefield performance partly in the manner of Hotspur; and finally, having practiced in all these corners of the kingdom, assigns proper subordinate places to everyone in a central disclosure of the new king. He manages to pull both history and the series of plays into shape at the same time.

The central moments of dramatic integration and public renewal in Shakespeare's kingship plays are normally moments when the king's procedure—his mode and style—becomes theatrically effective and his power is solidified in some equivalent to a coronation. As dreams and illusions are banished in the final processes of dramatic unfolding and enlightenment, Henry V, the true Lear, the new Leontes, or equivalents to the king like Duke Senior, Theseus and Prospero stand revealed on stage, fully defined in relation to the society reordered around them and its natural context.

For the moment, however, I wish to set aside these areas of special coincidence between the form of a kingdom and the form of a play and concentrate on tensions within the institution itself, especially between social kings and kings by nature.

A clear sense of these tensions can sometimes be gained from conflicts waged on the borders of the kingdom and in the transitions that take place at its edges. By juxtaposition to a wilderness, for instance (a place of dislocation, bewilderment, untamed animals or *wild-deor,* and confusion), a well-mapped kingdom gives every address a measured distance from the palace or some crossroad, every position reasonable definition, and every event a date by which it is placed in the chronology that makes up the history of the realm. In a complete wilderness, strength is always on trial, and standards of fair play, pieties, applause, chivalry, categories, genres, styles, and even history are lacking because the wilderness has no order within which symbols can be united in connected plots—and by which, in passing from mind to mind, events may become part of an enduring and remembering public. A kingdom on the other hand has inherent standards of judgment and form that define social stations and provide standards that tragedy and comedy can use in representing the "rise" and "fall" of great men, the buffoonery of lesser men, or the incongruous folly of those who should be and try to be majestic but are not.

It is typical of Shakespeare's dramatic technique to expose the kingship to radical opposites of this kind as part of its difficult synchronization with the greater nature around it. As in ancient kingships, the state's periodic transfers of power and calendar of events must be aligned with the greater periodicity of day and night, sun, moon, birth and death, planting and harvesting; and though kings may be forced to bear witness to the intent of the gods merely in dark signs and portents, they assume that they enjoy special favor in imposing social form on the wildness of their people and nature. They are the gods' instruments of recurrence and renewal. Thus above the complexities of social motives, the monarch seeks to establish a social dignity based on high-pageant symbolism; and among the difficulties of an unfinished nature, he establishes a sense of purposeful economy in which nature is induced to make regular offerings to the commonwealth. Consulting a vizier of practical affairs on his right and a soothsayer on his left, he becomes a message center of sorts, attuned both to the daily communiques of the economy and to the augury of the gods—and perhaps symbolically attuned to an original creative dominion exercised by the gods, as an imitator of divine authority wresting order from chaos. All subordinate labors of the kingdom are thereby given their own quota of symbols and quota of piety as they share in the labor of controlling the wilderness. Marks of veneration as well as reminders of practical jobs are inscribed on the peasant's calendar; the alchemist's pot holds mysteries as well as herbs and metals—and therefore requires incantation as well as exactness of measurement and industry in stirring. This piety registers in Shakespearean drama as a sense of outrage and fear when the kingship is violated and as solemn enclosure when kingly order is reestablished against the threat of chaos. It unites politics, nature and religious ritual. Insofar as the kingdom masters *social* diversity and factions, it does so by the exertion of a form and style whose strongest model is, ideally, the manner and bearing of the prince. Insofar as it masters stars, sun, rain and hail, it does so by an exercise of piety in the charms and pageantry by which it participates in and celebrates the cyclical order of the seasons.

Because he is given pragmatic dominion over the tangible elements of government and at the same time holds an invisible order in stewardship, a monarch can be expected in his effective dramatic moments both to initiate actions and define their ultimate meanings. He *knows* and *does* and thus causes others to know and do in ways keyed to his central management; executive power and intelligence are united in him. This double function is evident especially in the coronation, the dramatic potential of which we would expect Shakespeare to exploit to its fullest in plays in which institutional form and dramatic form reinforce each other. At a time of stress and transition when historical forces have a chance to break into the kingship, the coronation locks all elements into place *as* a system—like a center pole establishing tension with the pinned sides of a tent. If it succeeds, word and deed subsequently issue directly from center stage, and the symbolic order of the pageant is communicated directly to the body politic. "Plot lines" are thereafter conveyed by messengers, heralded by trumpets, and adorned by the masquelike increments of the kingship's visible style. As both *As You Like It* and *The Tempest* illustrate, Shakespeare likes to reinforce the seating of civil power in this way with the promise of natural renewal and continuity in the marriage ceremony.[2] In several tragedies he combines the coronation (or an equivalent) with elegies for the dead king as an image of cathartic calm after the purging of ailing elements. Whatever its special functions, however, the coronation is merely one stage in the processes of kingship and can never cure political factions permanently. It is characteristic of Shakespeare's moments of settlement to make a gesture towards other moments when circumstance and the interplay of personal wills will resume their war against the kingship. The crowning of Henry V completes a violent period of weakened authority but also leads forward to more trouble to come, hinted even in the final solemnities of *Henry V*. Still less effective is the crowning of Bolingbroke in *Richard II,* which leads to the troubled reign of Henry IV and the crowning of York in *3 Henry VI,* which mocks the ceremony itself as all solemnities are drowned in a riotous bloodbath. Thus in unprotected moments Shakespeare's kings are forced to confront rabble, counter-kingdoms of madness, fury and mockery without sufficient assistance from formal rites, and the king himself may become a mock figure who fosters intrigue and counter-intrigue, debasement of language and the abridgment of normal standards.

The nature of kingship and the formal ceremony it encourages is evident in these moments of enshrinement because we can then see clearly the possibility of the submergence of the system in the wildness of history, nature and the disrespect of a people following their individual wills into chaos. The failure to found social dignity in the greater will of the gods and nature calls the entire pageant into question and suggests that it is an invented and hollow show incapable of controlling the forces it is asked to.

The king's participation in mockery is not necessarily destructive to the formal influence of the office and its sanctification in the coronation, however. Mockery may itself be a kind of ritual that borrows the style of the institution that it undermines and proves friendly to what it mocks—if it gives vent to the disbelief and resistance that all systems generate. It is true that to carry mockery too far is to threaten the kingdom with a mad

---

[2] In other Elizabethans as well, nuptial and coronation rites are often linked: order and festivity, the seating of royalty and the marriages of a new generation, the ring and the crown reinforce each other. In Jonson's *Hymenaei,* for instance, the king and queen of peace preside over the mysteries of nature as illustrated by the divine conjunction of male and female. Cf. also *Pan's Anniversary*.

carnival of confusion and bloodshed that converts the normal piety of the coronation into saturnalian debauchery. On some levels its improvised comedy gives way to the inflated styles of warriors and false claimants to the crown who noisely forget that their true archetype is Jack Cade; and a York who considers himself beyond comedy is much more dangerous than the comic rebels that implicitly stand as his reproach. In the case of Richard II, mockery ends in a kind of decoronation pageant of persecution and ridicule, the king's attitude toward himself having spread through the entire social body:

> *Duch.* Alack, poor Richard! Where rode he the whilst?
> *York.* As in a theater the eyes of men
> After a well-graced actor leaves the stage
> Are idly bent on him that enters next,
> Think his prattle to be tedious,
> Even so, or with much more contempt, men's eyes
> Did scowl on gentle Richard. No man cried "God save him!"
> No joyful tongue gave him his welcome home.
> But dust was thrown upon his sacred head. (V, ii, 22–30)

Mockery never proceeds further than in Cade's battery of commands and messengers, in government by capricious whim: "Away, burn all the records of the realm," he orders, "my mouth shall be parliament of England" (*2 Henry VI*, IX, vii, 16). Destroying the records and scrolls that assign legitimate parts to the social cast (as records of the constitutional framework), Cade has heads installed on pikes merely that he may turn a pun in the sentencing. Though behind the whimsy of his most arbitrary command is a policy of sorts ("spare none but such as go in clouted shoon"), he improvises parts with each new cue.

But mockery is parasitic: its very sense of incongruity implies the standards it feeds upon. Cade needs authentic social ranks to exercise his wit against as badly as a York or Clifford needs them for his honor and high-toned style. The comedy of mock coronations reminds us that it is not far from Cade to the common man's playful participation in the coronation game and other rites of the folklore kingdom. If the kingship is to spread its influence into the ranks, it must have parts for everyone and at some point embrace irony in order to be translated, by various stylistic modulations, into the comedy of the rustics. Falstaffian parody of royalty is one such translation, the folklore kingdom another. Both extend ritual form into broadened areas of social concern where realism is more appropriate than heroic myth. Like all kingdoms, the folklore kingdom has its orthodoxies and its court, whether composed of Peaseblossoms and Cobwebs or satyrs and nymphs. In effect it permits a fusion of seriousness and mockery and replaces institutional ceremonies with pastoral ceremonies—crownings of kings with folk dances and the beflowered crownings of the May Queen. Thus we may move into the forest and the wilderness without totally sacrificing the kingship. Cade's closest kin is perhaps not Falstaff, who is potentially more dangerous, but Bottom, whose desire to play roles beyond his range is rendered harmless by his own lack of ambition and by Oberon's and society's firm control over casting procedures. Cade himself is puffed over by the first breath of serious opposition (plucked like a weed from the garden of Iden) because he has so clearly miscast himself: though murderous he can never be more than a buffoon whose mockery of justice turns against him.

In each of these encroachments against it, when it is required to confront the complex stuff of history and the alien forces of nature, the kingship resists change and tries to encompass the wilderness with its own periodic renewal of form. As a conservative force it lays bare the twist of mind of those who run against it and converts their efforts to change the social order into a dramatic trauma that only its own restoration—often liberalized and cured of arbitrary exercises of will—can lay to rest. But because civil and natural law differ so basically in Shakeaspeare at times, one can run against the bias of nature as well as against the social proprieties of the institution, and social propriety itself may be unnatural. The clash between civil polity and nature, rather than allowing a modulated transition of styles and ceremonial forms through the ranks to craftsmen and fairies, then splits the kingdom into two factions, the civil kingship operating under the rule of jurisprudence, inheritance and custom, and the folklore kingship under the aegis of forests, dreams, love, fairies, intuition, witches and imagination. One realm links human with divine forces (if at all) through visible public institutions and rationally decipherable symbols, the other through mysterious bonds that loosen the rational controls of the institution. Each kingdom fosters different principles of dramatic interrogation, ceremony and language and establishes different links among the contending elements of its structure. In effect, then, Shakespeare bases one kind of dramatic imitation on the king as a public spectacle and another upon the king as an archetypal power ruling by magic and poetry. Messengers and courtiers are the arm of one, Puck and Ariel of the other. Ironic cross-references between the two indicate how difficult it is to conceive of a single effective ruling instrument. I will return to that difficulty later in an examination of *King Lear* and *The Tempest*; but more immediately I wish to examine the king's role in both spheres as the visible symbol of the public welfare and the index of nature—and therefore as the play's central instrument in making its dramatic disclosures.

## Shakespeare's Two Kingdoms and the King's Visibility

In romance comedy these realms eventually find a workable compromise: the exile of representatives from the court proves therapeutic, as magic and nature restore their psychological balance and reintegrate human polity and nature's greater periodicity. A pervasive benevolence in the atmosphere asserts its own dominion and allows the king to shrink into a cooperative paternal duke. (In other respects we can treat dukes and kings as much the same.) In the histories, the social kingship predominates, but through frequent imagistic excursions into witchcraft and the idealized archetype of the garden kingdom both demonic and divine elements of nature are brought to bear upon society. In several tragedies the two realms are drawn apart more disastrously, and monarchical dominion is reestablished only after a severe lesson on the misdirection and limits of free will. In *Macbeth* and *King Lear* the two kingdoms interact with maximum disturbance, with witches and omens substituting for fairies and divine powers, and political ambition and greed for legal order and custom. Macbeth's witches set him on, firing his desire with an apparently free unleashing of will—only to reveal finally a predestined end. All the frantic action he conceives and pursues cannot prevent the execution that destiny and Shakespeare's sense of dramatic rightness have in store for him. In other plays, the king's willed independence carries him outside the intent of the office until some form of Nemesis, operating as a concealed strand of the plot, overrides him and draws the kingdom back to its accustomed patterns. That a Claudius cannot pray, a Richard III is tormented by ghosts, a Lear is exposed to nature's uncultic fury, and a Macbeth is mistaken about oracles indicates an unbridgeable gap between realms.

But Shakespeare's places of exile are never complete wildernesses, and as I suggested they may harbor kingdoms as orderly in their way as the civil court. Under the influence of what he supposes to be a wilderness, Orlando walks with sword drawn into Duke Senior's forest court and is reminded of the chivalric standard he has momentarily forgotten; what sets out to be a crude contest of strength turns quickly into a ceremonial greeting in the style of royalty. Moreover, the dangers of the wilderness often lie concealed in the court itself, as in the initial societies of *As You Like It* and *The Winter's Tale,* which contain a primitive viciousness behind legal authority. Perdita in Bohemia is naturally regal, whereas her father in court is merely tyrannical. Behind Perdita is the truth of Apollo's oracle; behind Leontes is blind authority. The king's exposure to nature often reveals to him the principles of nature inherent in the social office he fills. We come to realize that the artifice of his position and its stagecraft are justified only by the authentic power that stems from the natural context.[3]

[3] The last plays tend to expand the rule of art and nature until many of the offices of government pass into the command inherent in its discovery and subjects' reactions to it. The recognition scene of *The Winter's Tale,* for instance, produces an enlivened statue, as though art could pass from its frozen symbolism into the living world of nature: the image of a queen *becomes* queen, while Perdita as queen of the May brings to court a sense of nature and art united.

Yet the civil and the folklore kingdoms often stage quite different kinds of spectacle, and their union even in romance comedy takes place only after Shakespeare has explored their incongruities. The civil king puts on royalty like a costume and sanctions his command with official-sounding oaths of office. He operates from within the social fictions that a people assume in order to coordinate their functions, and these fictions tend to bury the natural man: they are too often a strategic rather than a genuinely symbolic pageantry. Thus Falconbridge advises King John in a tight moment to play an epic part:

> Be great in act, as you have been in thought.
> Let not the world see fear and sad distrust
> Govern the motion of a kingly eye.
> Be stirring as the time. Be fire with fire.
> Threaten the threatener, and outface the brow
> Of bragging Horror. So shall inferior eyes,
> That borrow their behaviors from the great,
> Grow great by our example and put on
> The dauntless spirit of resolution.
> Away and glister like the God of War. (V, i, 45–54)

John is to encourage his subjects by a visual dignity that they in turn may imitate in their own styles. In a similar reliance on display, Richard comes forth on the walls of Flint Castle determined to give his crown away in splendor:

> *York.* Yet looks he like a king. Behold, his eye,
> As bright as is the eagle's, lightens forth
> Controlling majesty. Alack, alack, for woe,
> That any harm should stain so fair a show! (III, iii, 68–71)

But a manifestation of power without execution is obviously inadequate. When his reign fails and his former royalty shrinks to mortal clay, John discovers that "all this thou seest is but a clod/ And module of confounded royalty" (V, vii, 57). Thinking of the costume changes and stage props forced upon him, Richard intones,

> I'll give my jewels for a set of beads,
> My gorgeous palace for a hermitage,
> My gay apparel for an almsman's gown,
> My figured goblets for a dish of wood,
> My scepter for a palmer's walking-staff,
> My subjects for a pair of carved saints,
> And my large kingdom for a little grave,
> A little little grave, an obscure grave.
> Or I'll be buried in the King's highway,
> Some way of common trade, where subjects' feet
> May hourly trample on their sovereign's head. (III, iii, 146–57)

These icons and fictions of the king may thus either conceal or give visible form to the king's natural condition and personal make-up. Regal display is an expression of genuine majesty in *Henry V* but a form of propaganda to Claudius, King John and Richard III. The difference is hard to see for characters on stage because kings adept in the arts of staging use those arts to test the theories they have about others. Richard II in several scenes prearranges what he hopes will seem improvisation; Lear carefully prepares a setting for his daughter's initial speeches in order to fix them in the new social contract he has in mind; Claudius is both a victim of shows that extract the truth from behind his facade and a stager of his own tests designed to expose Hamlet's craft.

The folklore kingdom also relies on controlled staging and spectacle, but it has quite different aims in doing so. Controllers of charms, illusions and stage-machinery such as Oberon and Puck or Prospero and Ariel possess the infallible powers of the playwright himself in manipulating the imaginations of the audience. Though Prospero may eventually set aside the theatrical instruments by which he commands illusions, he derives his power from something beyond mere costume and political craft, and he controls more than the political order. Indeed, in one sense he places illusion on the same footing as all substantial reality since from the perspectives of nature's ageless vistas both eventually dissolve, one merely sooner than the other. All the world is pageant and each member of the cast its unwitting instrument. Hence the real controller is a kind of king-poet combination who manages to fuse manifestation and executive power, symbolic display and politics: manifestation *becomes* power. (We are tempted to think that in one corner of his mind Shakespeare entertained a wish for such an equation of kingdoms and the stage, where human intelligence and imagination could command the ensemble and create its brave world—if not as naive as Miranda's, at least as musical and intelligible.) In double kingdom plays a fusion of seer and executive is impeded by basic contrasts between the two kingdoms as the social kingdom and the natural kingdom begin unknown to the other. But the action progresses as their mutual disclosure to each other, while the audience from its privileged perspective anticipates what each party will bring to the other. Realizing that Bottom and Titania belong to entirely different orders and speak radically different styles, for instance, we are alerted to their impact upon each other under the spell of Oberon's potions and are conditioned to see the difficulty of integrating ranks of society, styles of performance, levels of mind, modes of government.

A limited exposure of the same kind occurs in plays lacking a fully articulated second kingdom, which may be present in an extended metaphor, as in the garden scene of *Richard II* (III, iv, 29ff.), or suggested by a piece of augury from some portent or dream. Ultimately, as Richard II realizes, the civil king must convince his subjects that politics is a kind of providential pageantry and history a sacred representation of the larger configurations that might normally be read in nature, and to make such claims he must demonstrate correspondences between his reign and a healthy cosmos. In doing so, Shakespeare's kings instinctively call upon folklore elements and edge toward the magician-poet who wields illusions in marshalling factions toward a recognition of his special influence. When Richard returns to the coast of Wales to resist the invasion of Bolingbroke, he momentarily finds himself, in imagination, on the borders of the kingdom of fairies where by magical incantation he may conjure spirits of the air to administer his part of the national drama:

> Dear earth, I do salute thee with my hand...
> let thy spiders, that suck up thy venom,
> And heavy-gaited toads lie in their way,
> Doing annoyance to the treacherous feet
> Which with usurping steps do trample thee.
> Yield stinging nettles to mine enemies,
> And when they from thy bosom pluck a flower,
> Guard it, I pray thee, with a lurking adder. (III, ii, 6–20)

If political force submits to magic and the hidden power of fairyland, he may well end the plot against him effortlessly by the mere pageantry of his own visibility:

> when this thief, this traitor, Bolingbroke,
> Who all this while hath reveled in the night
> Whilst we were wandering with the Antipodes,
> Shall see us rising in our throne, the east,
> His treasons will sit blushing in his face,
> Not able to endure the sight of day,
> But self-affrighted tremble at his sin. (III, ii, 47–57)

We never discover if Richard's faith in the king's manifestation is justified because of two deficiencies in the dramatic plan: his own behavior, clearly visible on other occasions to his subjects, has separated king from kingship; and he himself, after losing faith in the magic of his association with cosmic powers, inconsistently decides upon tragedy in preference to a symbolic masque that can exercise its influence by pure manifestation.

In his dependence upon dramatic improvisation, Richard is not unique in Shakespeare, of course. Whenever accustomed roles are disturbed, inventive characters, cut adrift from the internal commands of their own natures, create new roles to counter the improvisations they meet in those equally inventive standing before them in their social disguises. Their new styles are likely to be a patchwork put together from the styles of other roles they have observed, because if majesty is *preservable* in the symbols and common language the kingship provides it is also *transferable:* one may lay false claim to it. Unsure of his office, Richard II plunges into the roles that he invents with each new message that comes to him: He redefines the kingship in the light of each additional scrap of evidence. His difficulty lies in distinguishing between the general providence, granted to every man in the laws of nature and requiring no special adjustment, and the particular providence assigned to each social position and requiring a suitable style and language. He finally accepts the assault of nature upon the king's body as the most drastic evidence of the fiction of regal dignity and therefore feels constrained to play the fall of majesty, the only role within the range allotted to the fallibility of men. The particular role of the king is thereby swallowed by the general role (as Jacques insists in the seven ages speech in *As You Like It* that all special roles be). His histrionic sense argues that if he seeks accord with inevitability, then, he must play victim: Is it not the basic worm that destroys all "respect,/Tradition, form, and ceremonious duty"?

> For within the hollow crown
> That rounds the mortal temples of a king
> Keeps Death his Court, and there the antic sits,
> Scoffing his state and grinning at his pomp,
> Allowing him a breath, a little scene,
> To monarchize, be feared, and kill with looks,
> Infusing him with self and vain conceit,
> As if this flesh which walls about our life
> Were brass impregnable, and humored thus
> Comes at the last and with a little pin
> Bores through his castle wall, and farewell King!
> Cover your heads and mock not flesh and blood
> With solemn reverence. (III, ii, 160–72)

But the fact remains that if a king's dignity fails so easily, all representation and pomp become mere pretence whether crowns pass on to successors or not. Having found nature personified in the unceremonious worm rather than in the greater designs of fertility and renewal, Richard loses the concept of periodicity upon which monarchical symbolism and display depend; and he further undercuts the possibility of staging successfully the potential of his office by the antic quality of his improvisation. Genuine tragedy depends upon the inevitable destruction of an authentic dignity arising from the most inescapable drives of the hero's nature. Richard's misfortune is twisted by the irony that he has after all chosen the part himself and it may be merely a bizarre mistake in casting. Whatever dignity he might have gained from nature's inevitability he undermines in the relish with which he takes up the role—making truth appear fictional and what is unavoidable seem merely a whimsical choice.

What happens on the other hand when the king tries to function with a minimum of dramatic machinery, keeping himself out of sight, is revealed in Richard's opponent, Bolingbroke. Richard's determination to bring Bolingbroke into his version of the fall of kings is matched only by Bolingbroke's determination to resist making any public display at all. Their confrontations are studies in contrasting procedures, and on another level contrasts between the punctual operations of practical intrigue and Richard's initial assumption of the king's archetypal role in the cosmic pageantry. One of the ironies of *Richard II* is that the failing king initially claims to be a deputy of providence but has no program or policy to allow the people to assume their subordinate positions in such a government, whereas the rising king, a punctual intriguer, plans every move politically but makes no serious claim to being a deputized administrator of higher purposes. In neither case is manifestation wedded to power, as an ordering of subjects by the vision of a greater scheme instrumented in the king. If we discount Bolingbroke's early challenge to Mowbray (which though couched in terms of divine purpose is obviously rote conduct in a style demanded by the occasion), only after he has become king does he begin searching for a rhetoric to weave his momentary purposes into larger configurations; he never grasps the potential mythic and ritual dimensions of the office.

Henry V is clearly less inadequate than Richard and Henry IV in making the king's visibility both political and symbolic of the greater dominion he is presumed to represent; but despite the commendation that Canterbury and others give Prince Hal's theatrical effectiveness, critics have rightly felt that something is lacking in the king that he becomes—that somehow in passing from the festive and loose plotting of his youth to the strict accountability of the office he leaves too much behind. The folklore kingdom reminds us that partly what he lacks is again natural, mythic and poetic dimensions—perhaps much the same thing finally as human dimensions of a certain kind. That such a figure—the subject of Shakespeare's most pronounced choral approval and the wielder of an effective public rhetoric—would be better for an exposure to witches and fairies perhaps stretches credibility, but it is an intriguing possibility when we consider what such exposure adds to Theseus, Macbeth and Prospero—and what exposure of another kind, to a different world of enigma and mystery, means to the complexity and range of Hamlet and Lear.

The forms of address that subjects may make to a king who is primarily a warrior and an instrument of justice, though they may have a certain enthusiasm, fall short of venerable ceremony. Throughout the series of plays from *Richard II* to *Henry V* royal ceremonies never quite escape the "calculated neutrality" (in Leonard Dean's phrase) so prominent in the initial ordeal by combat:

> We sense at once that the king and the nobles are reading lines, that their social behavior is play-acting. Our subsequent judgment that the ceremony is a hypocritical disguise, that it will not cure the disorder which it is momentarily suppressing, is the product both of the glib ritualistic styles

> and of those few lines in which contrary emotions come to the surface and announce themselves through a complication of the normally neutral and ceremonial tone.[4]

In these "abortive or perverted"[5] ceremonies, appellants are squeezed by their quasi-legalistic roles, and their appeals are frozen into unresponsive formulas. At its best, political ceremony is a stately ranking of people in positions of relative and perhaps merited status: If the monarch who believes himself to be a god could in fact be held to godlike behavior, the ranks of his people might in turn resemble ranks of angels celebrating his epiphany with hymnal responses, and the natural environment might coalesce around him like the obedient elements of paradise. But in their lesser moments kings are sorry figures of the reality they seek to manifest, and ceremonial chivalry is merely masked warfare, burdened with self-assertion and appeals to high principle. Incantation brings to the rites no sense of animation, either natural or supernatural.

If Shakespeare's fairy kings and magicians sometimes command a fuller and more poetic language, it is partly because they reinforce pageantry with dream-associations. The position and identity of the participants melt and are transformed. Whereas disguise in court is a sign of intrigue and usually has for its goal a transfer of power, disguises in the fairy court are symbolic play that distort apparent truths only in order to expose something vital that lies concealed. Improvised display tends to reveal a deeper bent of some kind—as Bottom exposes something more or at least something different in the unrehearsed role that Oberon gives him than in the role he chooses for himself to play before the court. What a natural king makes visible finally is a spectacle of deepest motives becoming reconciled to their natural context, a context that argues in part that growth and ripeness, youth and senescence, romantic love and inexplicable hate are as much part of the social covenant as edicts and statecraft.

---

[4] Leonard F. Dean, "*Richard II:* The State and the Image of the Theater," *PMLA,* LXVII (1952), 211–18, quoted from *Shakespeare: Modern Essays in Criticism* (New York: Oxford University Press, 1957), p. 162. Cf. Joan Webber, "The Renewal of the King's Symbolic Role: from *Richard II* to *Henry V,*" below pp. 193–203.

The movement of the series from *Richard II* to *Henry V* is from a use of ritual as concealment, through upheaveals governed by false report and rumor, to the open coronation and policies of the new king. The movement of the Henry VI series is nearly opposite: the series begins with a death march for Henry V, "a king blessed of the King of kings," who, lacking a coronation to heal the sickness of the realm, plunges into the chaos of a nearly kingless state in the hands of warriors, a lord protector, courtiers, a domineering queen and untamed subjects. As J. P. Brockbank points out below, the death of Gloucester releases a strong urge of disorder centralized in Jack Cade, to whom lawyers, scholars courtiers, gentlemen and kings are mere "false caterpillars."

[5] See C. L. Barber, "Saturnalia in the Henriad," Dean, *Shakespeare: Modern Essays,* p. 170.

## Policy, Courtship, and the Social Contract

Revealing the true king is a common goal of Shakespeare's plots, perhaps as common as returning the king from exile and often much the same in creating a social order. Control of rabble and nature's demons attends upon the disclosure of the king's operative, visible policy.[6] For sooner or later an institution must apply itself through policy, the punctual instrument of its enduring form. The king's improvised plotting must be based on a comparatively long-ranged plan of enactment in which power, showmanship and intelligence conspire to weld the kingdom together. Hence as Henry V emerges as the queller of rumor and riot he corrects the false rumor of the thing he was and exposes the falsity of the dream Falstaff has had of himself as Chief Justice: Putting an end to surmise, mockery and the confusion of identities, he extends his hand to Chief Justice and *institutionalizes* the policy of his own development—so shadowy and uncertain up to now to observers within the play:

> You shall be as a father to my youth,
> My voice shall sound as you do prompt mine ear,
> And I will stoop and humble my intents
> To your well-practis'd wise directions.
> And Princes all, believe me, I beseech you,
> My father is gone wild into his grave,
> For in his tomb lie my affections;
> And with his spirits sadly I survive
> To mock the expectation of the world,
> To frustrate prophecies, and to raize out
> Rotten opinion, who hath writ me down
> After my seeming. The tide of blood in me
> Hath proudly flow'd in vanity till now.
> Now doth it turn, and ebb back to the sea,
> Where it shall mingle with the state of floods,
> And flow henceforth in formal majesty. (V, ii, 118–32)

Policy applies the form of kingship to its passing details as plot imposes centrality and dramatic coherence on miscellaneous characters and motives.

---

[6] Jonson associates false rumor with the misleading prediction of witches and black magic and opposes both to good fame and proper social identification. The witches' vat is "delirium," and hags of ill-fame are like evil spirits released from matter by the disintegrating structure of things turning to fumes—like the bristling needles, blood and dung of *Lumpenwelt*. True fame is salvageable by a queen whose glory retrieves the age of gold; with her mere appearance profane rites, owlish charms, sulphurous scourges and curses give way to panegyric and messages of divine import brought down by Hermes (the *Masque of Queens, for Queen Anne,* 1609).

The policy that most strengthens the social bond concerns not merely obedience and justice, however, but also the continuity that stems from filial devotion and bonds of love. It requires as its instrument a flexible courtship and poetic language capable of encompassing a range of social relations from the affairs of statesmen and generals to the propitiation of nature and the wooing of gods and lovers. In *The Winter's Tale* the perversion of all forms of courtship in the opening act leads to a miscarriage of justice and the substitution of accusations and condemnation for what should have been a model of courtliness in the king and queen. Exposure to the pronouncements of the oracles and the pastoral rites of a simpler and more humane society in Bohemia is proper therapy, and when a new order replaces Leontes' tyrannical and arbitrary kingship, the central recognition brings with it a restoration of both authority and the love of lost heirs, now ready to initiate a new cycle and extend a new policy. Dramatic message-bearing spreads the new bond into the social ranks, whose former division is healed by the manifestation not merely of new royalty but of the plan and continuity time and nature have unfolded:

> *Sec. Gent.* How goes it now sir? This news, which is called true, is so like an old tale that the verity of it is in strong suspicion. Has the king found his heir?
>
> *Third Gent.* Most true, if ever truth were pregnant by circumstance: that which you hear you'll swear you see, there is such unity in the proofs. The mantle of Queen Hermione's, her jewel about the neck of it, the letters of Antigonus found with it, which they know to be his character; the majesty of the creature in resemblance of the mother, the affection of nobleness which nature shows above her breeding, and many other evidences proclaim her, with all certainty, to be the king's daughter.
>
> (V, ii, 27–40)

With public vows and proclamations, art and the circumstances of the majestic show—the costume, the countenances, the handwriting and letters—*verify* nature, whose affections and natural likenesses require these dramatic acts of publication. At the same time they verify the dramatic procedures and forecasts of the play. All bonds are sealed by a public love and recognition of true, published identities.

For even love proceeds by policy, manifestation, and plot—often against parental authority and system and therefore by counterplot and intrigue. (Perdita returns home thinking that she is running away from authority and problems of social class.) Eventually it seeks social recognition —the blessings of a Leontes or a Prospero—and like politics follows the channels of communication laid out for it by the social structure: Only the old king, finally, can really sanctify it. These contracts of the new society are based on personal feeling displayed at large in public speech and spread by normal dramatic processes of exchange and clarification. The courtship of both kings and private parties depends upon the durability of the terms of appeal and contractual agreements and upon the nuances of a poetic medium capable of rendering the twists and turns of personal relations and bringing them to light. If the public order is slighted on behalf of private courtship, as in *Antony and Cleopatra* and *Romeo and Juliet,* the results are disastrous for the lovers, and society tends to harden.

The king may himself confuse public acknowledgment of his authority *with* love, as Lear does when obliterating the finer dimensions of courtship in the interests of the official and blunt declarations that he coerces from his daughters—in payment for equally blunt and exactly answerable transfers of power and goods. But though a king may squeeze love to feed power, he *can* legitimately command that love and private language be brought to bear upon public ceremony. As a propitiator of the gods and coordinator of social elements, the king links the local to the general, punctual and private acts to cyclical duration and the public welfare. If he does so successfully, his ceremonies elevate those who pay court to him: The best of one's private moments are given public dignity and permanence by association with him, by incorporation into the joint "plot." (To socialize love and courtship in this way is a recurrent goal of knowledgeable lovers in Shakespeare from the sonnets and early comedies to the last romances.) Thus in its attenuated forms courtship is a branch of diplomatic policy by which one party establishes agreements with another and defines each of their relative positions. As a dramatic extension of policy, it is a means for individuals to keep pace with the changing relations of the ensemble and participate in the enduring form of the social order. Kings, especially, depend upon it to urge the business of the kingdom onward—by the hints and innuendoes of courtly language as well as by direct command and public displays of favor. Through stylistic proprieties and a range of manners that matches style to social rank, it mortars the social structure and governs the decorum of dramatic dialogue.

Courtship is central to several of the king-centered plays but to none more than to *King Lear,* which is especially useful in gauging the impact on dramatic form of the king's visibility, secrecy, mockery, the division between civil and natural kingdoms, and the strain on courtship that a problem king creates. Critics have recently become more willing to concede some justification for Lear's initial demand for acknowledgment from his daughters, and indeed, from one viewpoint, he is not only justified but without choice: Given his age and the certainty that nature will soon transfer the crown, open declarations of loyalty and love are his best weapon against future division. He emphasizes the public saying of love and its bondage to the king in order to establish positions for each daughter that they will feel constrained to observe later:

> Tell me, my daughters,
> Since now we will divest us both of rule,
> Interest of territory, cares of state
> Which of you shall we say doth love us most?

> That we our largest bounty may extend
> Where nature doth with merit challenge. (I, i, 49–55)

The difficulty with his plan is that it offers maximum opportunity for deception and presupposes a mutual reinforcement between love (or its speeches) and politics. Each adjective and stylistic felicity presumably wins a jewel or a piece of land.

In this contest, Cordelia's plain statement "I love your Majesty/ According to my bond, nor more nor less" (I,i,94–95) is correct in pinning love to degree and custom, and it implicitly acknowledges that the majesty she loves is both father and king. However, it is obviously too clipped in style and fails to take notice of the source of the bonds, which derive from more than mere duty. It also lacks the range of metaphoric association and feeling that would indicate awareness of the quasi-sacredness of the bond and the presence in human relations of manifold forces very difficult to institutionalize. In this respect, Lear's response is still worse: It collapses all courtly style into flattery in order to yoke the wills of subjects to the king's will. Failing to receive the commitment he expects, he shatters the decorum he has himself initiated, though ironically his reply is also cast in the arch and formal language of an inverted charm or fairy curse:

> By the sacred radiance of the sun,
> The mysteries of Hecate, and the night,
> By all the operation of the orbs
> From whom we do exist and cease to be,
> Here I disclaim all my paternal care,
> Propinquity, and property of blood,
> And as a stranger to my heart and me
> Hold thee from this forever. The barbarous Scythian,
> Or he that makes his generation messes
> To gorge his appetite shall to my bosom
> Be as well neighbored, pitied, and relieved
> As thou my sometime daughter. (I, i, 110–22)

Rather than linking the diurnal and annual recurrences of nature to paternal inheritance, he swears by their constancy to be himself inconstant, to break the continuity of blood's natural and inherent "property." In effect, despite the stylization of the speech, he devours his generation as crudely as "the barbarous Scythian." Courtship, which is a way of respecting the status of the party with whom one is establishing bonds, gives way to the personal and wolfish act of swallowing the other party.

In Goneril and Regan's cases as well as Cordelia's, Lear eventually calls for a suspension of natural law on behalf of his own preemptive and consuming will and breaks the continuity of the generations:

> Here, Nature, hear, dear goddess, hear!
> Suspend thy purpose if thou didst intend

To make this creature fruitful.
Into her womb convey sterility.
Dry up in her the organs of increase,
And from her derogate body never spring
A babe to honor her! If she must teem,
Create her child of spleen, that it may live
And be a thwart disnatured torment to her.
Let it stamp wrinkles in her brow of youth,
With cadent tears fret channels in her cheeks,
Turn all her mother's pains and benefits
To laughter and contempts. (I, iv, 296–304)

"Blast and fogs upon thee," he adds for good measure. And as for Regan:

All the stored vengeances of Heaven fall
On her ingrateful top! Strike her young bones,
You taking airs, with lameness. . . .
You nimble lightnings, dart your blinding flames
Into her scornful eyes. Infect her beauty,
You fen-sucked fogs, drawn by the powerful sun
To fall and blast her pride. (I, iv, 164–70)

The object of a kingly vow is to secure a people against mutability and sudden changes of mind; but Lear's vow calls down nature's assorted weapons in onrushing ruin.

Such inverted fairy curses have a way of rebounding upon the invoker. Once love, law, and knowledge are forced apart, we realize how they depend upon one another and upon the king as the center of both courtly negotiations and nature's abundance. Love without the other two becomes poisonous lust and self-seeking, making its links in secret messages and intrigues, broken off from its anchor in reverence and from the courtly modes by which self-seeking is altered and made socially acceptable. Law in turn becomes an arbitrary assignment of rewards and punishments beyond all decencies and pleadings for mercy: the just and true-speaking are blinded, imprisoned in stocks, and ridiculed; the vicious gain in the equipage and visible aspects of glory. Deprived of public trust that is enshrined in law and love, knowledge is twisted by false evidence, rumor, disguise and by the incredible transformation of kings and courtiers into unrecognizable beggars and madmen. In the cursed kingdom of Lear's exile, what one puts on his back and into his mouth is tangibly close, yet beyond all propriety. Unlike things are yoked together without the sanction of natural propinquity or the ceremonies of courtly introduction. The moment-by-moment experience of those cast loose on the heath is a styleless and uncovenanted violence. For once in Shakespeare the kingship very nearly *is* lost to the wilderness. As Edgar remarks, the beggar is both consumed and consumer: All manner of odd creatures must pass under his power if he is to survive. Poor Tom

> eats the swimming frog, the toad, the tadpole, the wall newt, and the water; that in the fury of his heart, when the foul fiend rages, eats cow dung for sallets; swallows the old rat and the ditch dog; drinks the green mantle of the standing pool. . . . "But mice and rats and such small deer/Have been Tom's food for seven long year." (III, iv, 134 ff.)

The king in exile in this upside-down fairyland is an image not of royalty returning to the green world for naturalization but of cosmos sinking into chaos, of social and natural forms at the mercy of degrading circumstance. But as he passes into the language of witches and demonology, Lear also reaches for a new union of regal dignity and poetic incantation, as though in the unseating of forms new principles of order were released, founded in a courtship that manages, somehow, profounder links among its parties. Love formerly known by the *propriety* of its rendering comes to be known paradoxically, by acts that appear to be puzzling and veiled but render genuine service and respect. Everyone who enters the wasteland with good will, in fact, discovers or brings with him a natural charity that could not find expression in the court's initial manner of paying tribute or bespeaking love:

> Poor naked wretches, wheresoe'er you are,
> That bide the pelting of this pitiless storm,
> How shall your houseless heads and unfed sides,
> Your looped and windowed raggedness, defend you
> From seasons such as these? Oh, I have ta'en
> Too little care of this! Take physic, pomp.
> Expose thyself to feel what wretches feel,
> That thou mayst shake the superflux to them
> And show the Heavens more just. (III, iv, 28–36)

Heaven's justice depends upon human justice, and justice in turn on love and knowledge borne home to the king by his own unceremonious exposure to wretches. Gloucester in turn says to Lear, "I ventured to come seek you out/ And bring you where both fire and food is ready" (III,iv,156–57). Cordelia recognizes that Lear's kingdom is now the kingdom of weeds: he is

> Crowned with rank fumiter and furrow weeds,
> With burdocks, hemlock, nettles, cuckoo flowers,
> Darnel, and all the idle weeds that grow
> In our sustaining corn. (IV, iv, 3–6)

But she too brings about a discovery of bonds of a more profound kind and a more flexible poetry responsive to them. Lear's description of their new courtship appropriately concludes with an awareness of their transcendence of nature—not by setting aside its laws or by mastering them with the magic, merely by enduring them:

We two alone will sing like birds i' the cage.
When thou dost ask me blessing, I'll kneel down
And ask of thee forgiveness. So we'll live,
And pray, and sing, and tell old tales, and laugh
At gilded butterflies, and hear poor rogues
Talk of Court news. And we'll talk with them too,
Who loses and who wins, who's in, who's out,
And take upon's the mystery of things
As if we were God's spies. And we'll wear out,
In a walled prison, packs and sects of great ones
That ebb and flow by the moon. (V, iii, 9–19)

As an intelligence-gathering messenger for the gods overseeing the trauma of social change from the safety of one to whom rising and falling are irrelevant, Lear encompasses and in some respects goes beyond the language of the fool, whose weedy disorder defies logic and normal expectation. Fleetingly visible in his speech is a stability that does not depend upon negotiation and diplomacy, as pacts and sects of great ones do. Lear replaces the court's exchanges of verbal oaths for blessings of quite another kind. They resemble pageantlike courtship in the kneeling and beseeching, but are liberated from the worst requirements of negotiation and self-interested action. Having initially subordinated love to political maneuvering, Lear would now use the style of politics as a vehicle for a reverence that in its highest range touches upon "the mystery of things."

It is also true, however, that Lear's imagined pageant is that of a father and daughter in private; though it would make use of familiar forms of appeal it would also assume exile from society. The unfortunate truth is that the eminence and centrality of the king cannot be combined with these natural ceremonies of love; the king exposed to the wilderness is destroyed *as* king of the general body politic. As the Lear of the last act transcends the limits of the political office, then, the levels of the social spectrum separate. On one hand, normal contractual relations are restored through the authority of Albany, a substitute king who speaks in the original language of imperative moods and openly declared intent:

For us, we will resign,
During the life of this old Majesty,
To him our absolute power.
[To Edgar and Kent] You, to your rights,
With boot, and such addition as your honors
Have more than merited. All friends shall taste
The wages of their virtue, and all foes
The cup of their deservings. (V, iii, 298–304)

The various contracts here sealed are the product of a dramatic process in which inner merit, as laid bare by the abrasives of circumstance and manners of courtship, is exactly matched to the king's gifts, the "boot" and "addition" of courtly position. It is the language of justice tempered by love and informed by the knowledge of character that the king discovers from his reading of the action. But on the other hand the mad poetry of Lear stretches common sense with its odd concatenations of objects and animals, its personal courtesies, its incantational calls to nature, and its gesture towards mysteries beyond institutional containment. Lear ends merely by pointing at Cordelia, like a stager of harrowing knowledge for an audience that can only know, not enact or react.

This separation points up a central concern in all Shakespeare's double kingdom plays: What courtship is to the civil king, incantation and charm are to the folklore king, one belonging to the realm of dramatic negotiation where speeches lead to action, the other to the realm of poetry where speech propitiates and charms nature or the gods. Ideally, as we have seen, the speech of the king should be the speech of the poet as well as the magistrate, and what moves the gods should also move society. But if *King Lear* suggests a periodic renewal of social forms as recapitulated in the new king, it also exposes the impossibility of individual renewal and of complete harmony between natural, individual motives and social motives. Sooner or later each subject drops out of the order that has harbored him. (Kent desires to do so immediately: "I have a journey, sir, shortly to go./ My master calls me, I must not say no," V, iii, 321. His refusal to live underlines the chasm between the dead king and the formalities of a surviving society that does not attract him.)

The basic difficulty of uniting the social king with the controller of nature and the imagination proves unsolvable not only here but in Shakespeare generally. Correspondingly, there always remains some incapacity in art as well to incorporate history into poetry or dramatic pageantry, some recalcitrant, unaesthetic set of facts inhospitable to coherent meaning and ceremony. A civil king cannot move too far toward the poet without leaving behind the *Realpolitik,* any more than Theseus can adopt the charms and poetic incantation of Oberon and Puck without ceasing to be quite the same governor of Athens—or from another direction, any more than Prospero can return as duke of Milan without breaking his staff and leaving behind his magical and poetic transactions with nature. In retrospect it appears that Shakespeare avoided an irreparable division between the two kingships in the earlier plays by exhibiting the king or duke in a natural setting that has its own atmospheric magic apart from them. In effect, it is Arden and not Duke Senior that cures those who enter the forest: While magic brings about its cure of the social order, the onstage manipulators need only be masters of ceremony. Though a Jaques and an Oliver, by retreating to holy orders beyond the reach of civil power, suggest a breach between spiritual and civil affairs, Shakespeare reduces the importance of their segregation by making them self-willed outcasts. He emphasizes the sacred quality of the marriages that fall within the province of the restored society so that even the trip home to the social polis is not divisive.

The gap between the kingdoms is destructive in *Lear,* however, and wide enough in *The Tempest* to modify seriously the play's comic effect. Prospero must set aside the deeper layers of his nature as decisively as we would imagine Lear doing if he resumed his role as king—or as Antony if he were committed to Rome rather than to Egypt. In contrast to Lear's personal loss, Prospero has his sweeping and more distant vision of the world's dissolution in which, perhaps, some final king or playwright—some center of knowledge and power unavailable even to magicians—will end the spectacle as he chooses. As it is, only on an island where the poet-stager is in control can all levels unite in a single action and the courtship of poetry and song be used to beckon culprits to their political-psychological awakening. It is true that Prospero's therapy will probably be lasting, without being particularly harrowing: His patients pass from terror to wonder, and as the fumes dissolve from their minds he stands before them as the power to which they have been unwittingly submitting—the source of all the visions and songs that have led them onward. For a final time, to complete their illumination, he commands elves and demipuppets (his true but temporary subjects) to work for him:

> A solemn air, and the best comforter
> To an unsettled fancy, cure thy brains,
> Now useless, boiled within thy skull! There stand,
> For you are spell-stopped.
> Holy Gonzalo, honorable man,
> Mine eyes, even sociable to the show of thine,
> Fall fellowly drops. The charm dissolves apace,
> And as the morning steals upon the night,
> Melting the darkness, so their rising senses
> Begin to chase the ignorant fumes that mantle
> Their clearer reason. (V, i, 58–63)

Nonetheless, Prospero cannot manifest all the secrets of nature that he has commanded. Realizing that in this role he will still be unrecognizable to the island's visitors, he puts on a more readily identifiable costume:

> Not one of them
> That yet looks on me, or would know me. Ariel,
> Fetch me the hat and rapier in my cell.
> I will discase me, and myself present
> As I was sometime Milan. (V, i, 82–86)

Even then Gonzalo awakens in amazement and asks heavenly powers to guide them out of this bewitched country, and Alonzo, though assured that he confronts a living prince, is still afraid that he sees ghosts. Dream and social reality, the powers of imagination and the powers of legal and reasonable identification, fail to coincide because no public power is fully informed by all the elements from within the complex heart or from the cosmos at large. No means of courtship or theatrical display is effective in discovering or manifesting the place of the social kingdom in nature. Though Prospero does what he can to unite wonder and tangibility (V,i,153–62), Alonzo continues to look for "some oracle" to "rectify our knowledge," and we are left wondering how Prospero will explain Ariel to the Milanese. The affairs on the island and on stage far exceed in coherence and beauty any ceremony we can imagine among historical kings, however expert in royal display they may be.

# SONNETS

# 5

# The Structure of Figurative Language in Shakespeare's Sonnets

*Arthur Mizener*

In *The World's Body* Mr. John Crowe Ransom has an essay that is pretty severe on Shakespeare's sonnets; Mr. Ransom's strategy is to set Shakespeare up as a metaphysical poet and then to assail his metaphysical weaknesses. The late Shakespeare—the Shakespeare of *Measure for Measure, Antony and Cleopatra,* and the romances—had a good deal more in common with Donne than may sometimes be recognized, but even this Shakespeare was not, I believe, a metaphysical poet in Mr. Ransom's sense of the term. But whether Mr. Ransom is right or wrong, he has done the sonnets a good turn by raising in a serious way, for the first time since the eighteenth century, the problem of their figurative language.

In those distant days, some severe strictures were passed on this aspect of Shakespeare. Dr. Johnson remarked that "a quibble was to him the fatal Cleopatra for which he lost the world and was content to lose it"; Warburton laboriously explained that "he took up (as he was hurried on by the torrent of his matter) with the first words that lay in his way; and if, amongst these, there were two mixed modes that had a principal idea in com-

*The original version of this essay appeared in* The Southern Review, *V (1940), 730–747. It is here reprinted, with the author's revisions, by permission of Louisiana State University Press.*

mon, it was enough for him"; Steevens roundly declared that "such labored perplexities of language, and such studied deformities of style, prevail throughout these sonnets" that he saw no reason to print them in 1793, since "the strongest act of parliament that could be framed would fail to compel readers into their service." These eighteenth-century critics were never answered. The usual remarks about this aspect of the sonnets ("An average Shakespeare sonnet comes dancing in, as it were, with the effortless grace of a bird, etc.") are not answers but ways of filling an embarrassing pause.

Mr. Ransom, however, is not Steevens or another of those outspoken and outmoded eighteenth-century gentlemen, but a contemporary critic, less outspoken and as a consequence in some ways more devastating, and very far indeed from being outmoded. One can of course say that if we distill off the poetry of Shakespeare's sonnets, leaving in the flask only the bare "idea," that "idea" will be found not only familiar but, indeed, trite. Even the most ardent advocate of this view, however, usually gives his case away before he is through with some reference to the mystery of Shakespeare's language. Nor does this view meet Mr. Ransom's argument. The only way that argument can be met is by a description of the structure of the sonnets' figurative language which accounts for that structure without damning Shakespeare as, at his best, a metaphysical poet who lacks the courage of his convictions, and, at his worst, a manufacturer of trifles. If Shakespeare's sonnets are really metaphysical, then they are bad in the way and to the extent Mr. Ransom says they are.

Mr. Ransom's argument is that good poetry is always airtight extensively (to borrow a term from Mr. Allen Tate). He is willing to allow it to function intensively only within the limits set by a vehicle that is described with logical consistency. A poet, that is, must never be more in earnest about the tenor of his metaphor than about the vehicle, must never be willing to sacrifice the strict logic of his vehicle in order to imply something further about the tenor. This is a seductive definition of good poetry but an arbitrary one, which, if strictly applied, excludes from the category of good poetry all nonmetaphysical poetry. In the present state of our knowledge of the way language works, this consideration alone is enough to cast serious doubt on such a definition. It produces, in addition, some curious results. For instance, Mr. Ransom says of the opening quatrain of sonnet LXXIII ("That time of year thou may'st in me behold") that the metaphor here is compounded and that "the two images cannot, in logical rigor, co-exist." It is true that *choirs* can be looked on as a metaphorical extension of *boughs,*[1] but it is only by a

[1] By taking the boughs as the choirs and the trees as the cathedral. But "in logical rigor" Mr. Ransom's definition will not permit this ingenuity of Steevens; no metaphor is strictly logical—certainly this one is not—and the metaphorical extension of a metaphor's vehicle is therefore illegal.

pun that this extension can be maintained in the phrase "sweet birds," and Mr. Ransom cannot allow puns. Not even a pun, moreover, will bring "shake against the cold" within the limits of the figure, since by no stretch of the imagination can ruined cathedrals be thought of as shaking against the cold.

But it is plain before one reaches the end of this analysis that the success of Shakespeare's compound metaphor does not depend on the strict logic of its vehicle. His purpose is apparently to relate to his time of life, by some other means than the strictly logical elaboration of vehicle, both the boughs which shake against the cold and the bare ruined choirs. The age of Shakespeare's love, which is his life, is like the autumnal decline of nature, and thus natural, inevitable and, perhaps, only the prelude to a winter sleep rather than death; it is at the same time like the destruction of an artificial and man-made thing by man's wilful violence, and thus not inevitable, save as evil is inevitable, but regrettable as is the destruction of a building beautiful not only in itself but as a symbolic act. The fusion of these two meanings brought about by the compound metaphor is richer and finer than the sum of them which would be all the poem could offer if the two metaphors did not coexist.

The fusion is brought about by Shakespeare's slurring up from *boughs* to *choirs* and then down again. He gets up to choirs with the adjectival sequence "bare ruin'd"; "bare" modifies, primarily, *boughs,* and it is only through the diplomatic mediation of "ruin'd," primarily the modifier of *choirs*, that "bare" becomes intimate with *choirs*. He gets down again to *boughs* with the pun on "sweet birds"; in the phrase's secondary, euphemistic sense these are the choristers, but in its primary sense they are the quondam occupants of the now shaking boughs. The fact that this fusion gives the vehicle, not logic, but an ingeniously devised air of being logical really deceives no one (least of all, I suspect, Mr. Ransom) into supposing that Shakespeare's lines do rely for their power on the rigorous logical coherence of the metaphor's vehicle. Mr. Ransom's real point is not that he believes Shakespeare *did* intend them to, but that he believes Shakespeare *ought* to have intended them to.

Shakespeare's method is, then, fundamentally different from the metaphysical method: Where Donne, for example, surprises you with an apparently illogical vehicle which can be understood only if its logic is followed, Shakespeare surprises you with an apparently logical vehicle which is understandable only if taken figuratively.

The position taken by critics like Mr. Ransom thus forces them to write down as a blunder one of the most essential features of Shakespeare's kind of poetry. A critic is of course free to dislike Shakespeare's kind of poetry, and I imagine Mr. Ransom does not mean to express admiration when he describes Shakespeare's poetry as the kind "which we sometimes dispose of a little distastefully as 'romantic.' " Probably a great many more people than profess to would dislike it were they not bullied by Shakespeare's name into accepting it. But the critic has not the right to treat this poetry as if it were of another kind, as Mr. Ransom does in discussing what he calls Shakespeare's "metaphysical" sonnets.

The characteristic feature of Shakespeare's kind of poetry at its best is a soft focus; a metaphysical poem is in perfect focus, perhaps more than perfect focus (like those paintings in which every detail is drawn with microscopic perfection). In a good metaphysical poem each figurative detail may be examined in isolation and the poem as a whole presents itself to us as a neatly integrated hierarchy of such details. Mr. Ransom suggests that the metaphysical poet shows a special kind of courage in committing his feelings in this way "to their determination within the elected figure"; probably no one will question this claim, or the implication that the special intensity of good metaphysical poetry derives from this self-imposed restriction. But the metaphysical poet shows also a special kind of perversity. He achieves a logical form at the expense of richness and verisimilitude; for the more ingeniously he elaborates his elected figure, the more apparent will it be that it is either distorting or excluding the nonlogical aspects of his awareness of the object.

Mr. Ransom, however, believes that the business of the poem is to express not the poet but the object, and draws a distinction between the poetry of knowledge and the poetry of feelings. This is a useful distinction, particularly in dealing with nineteenth-century poetry of the kind from which Mr. Ransom is such an expert in selecting horrible examples; but it does not go all the way. For whether or not the object has an existence independent of our awareness of it is for poetry an academic question; so far as poetry is concerned its existence is our awareness of it. That awareness may be more or less disciplined by what it thinks things actually are, more or less in control of its tendency to see them as it wishes them to be. But in either case, it remains an awareness. This awareness is what the poem presents; it never presents actual objects (even if poets could somehow present collages or *objets trouvés* the very process of selection itself would color the objects in such a way as to destroy their objectivity: objects are never just found; someone finds them). Expressing an object, giving to it, in Mr. Ransom's phrase, "public value," consists in "publishing" our awareness of it; and feelings are no less feelings for being a publishable, a communicable, part of that awareness. Mr. Ransom's very proper distaste for a poetry which presents a gross awareness, one which includes undistinguished or ill-distinguished feelings about the object, seems to have led him to try to eliminate the concept "feeling" from his definition of the best poetry. But to say that the best poetry expresses the object is to use a figure of speech which only apparently allows you to escape the fact that "speech as behavior is a wonderfully complex blend of two pattern systems, the symbolic and the expressive, neither of which could have developed to its present perfection without the interference of the other."[2]

Since poetry is not the world's body but a verbal construct between which and the world-as-object the poet's awareness mediates, there are bound to be disadvantages to any kind of poetry which requires a definite distortion of that awareness for its intensity. It is this price which Shakespeare's poetry does not have to pay. There is, certainly, much to be said against his kind of poetry too. It is, for one thing, always wantoning on the verge of anarchy; and I think Mr. Ransom is right as to the unhappy effect of Shakespeare's example on such poets as Matthew Arnold, who brought himself to announce of Shakespeare's receding hairline that an assorted collection of painful sensations "find their sole speech in that victorious brow." But whatever may be said against it, much, too, must be said in favor of a poetic method which made possible the richness and verisimilitude of the best of Shakespeare's sonnets.

## II

The only way to particularize this description of Shakespeare's method is to examine one of the sonnets in some detail. I have chosen for this purpose CXXIV (I have modernized the spelling but kept the punctuation of the 1609 edition):

> If my dear love were but the child of state,
> It might for fortune's bastard be unfathered,
> As subject to time's love, or to time's hate,
> Weeds among weeds, or flowers with flowers gathered.
> No it was builded far from accident,
> It suffers not in smiling pomp, nor falls
> Under the blow of thralled discontent,
> Whereto the inviting time our fashion calls:
> It fears not policy that heretic,
> Which works on leases of short numbered hours,
> But all alone stands hugely politic,
> That it nor grows with heat, nor drowns with showers.
> To this I witness call the fools of time,
> Which die for goodness, who have lived for crime.

This sonnet has at least two advantages in this connection: it is obviously a serious effort, and it is not likely therefore that its consequences are

[2] Edward Sapir, "Language," *The Encyclopedia of the Social Sciences.*

unintentional; and it has that "excessive dispersion in the matter of figures" which seems to be characteristic of Shakespeare at his most serious and has annoyed others besides Mr. Ransom.

"If my dear love were but the child of state." The difficulty here is with *state,* which has a very complex meaning. It covers, in its general sense, the condition of those who live in this world and in time; in its specific senses, it includes most of the particular aspects of life which are touched on in the rest of the sonnet. I begin with the general sense. If Shakespeare's love were the product of, had been generated by, the combination of circumstances and attributes belonging to the young man addressed and to the age, it might, as a subject of the kingdom of time and consequently "subject to" the whimsical decrees of Time's perverse rule,[3] at any time be "unfathered." The more specific sense of *state*—the metaphorical father of which Shakespeare's love would risk being deprived—touched on in the rest of the sonnets are: (1) Fortune, the deity who rules worldly affairs; (2) status; (3) wealth; (4) natural endowment (talent, beauty); (5) authority, pomp, display, the more obvious of the secondary characteristics of *state* in the previous senses; (6) the body politic; (7) statesmanship, "policy," the kind of maneuvering by which all earthly results, good or bad, are achieved. Of this complex father Shakespeare's love, were it the child of state, would run the constant risk of being deprived, either as the bastard of state in sense (1) or in order to make way for some other bastard of state as Fortune. In either case, Shakespeare's love, as a child of state, would be a bastard.[4]

Nothing, I think, could show more clearly than these three lines the difference between Shakespeare's figurative language and that of a metaphysical poem. For no single one of the meanings of *state* will these lines work out completely, nor will the language allow any one of the several emergent figures to usurp our attention; it thus becomes impossible to read the lines at all without making an effort to keep all the meanings of *state,* all the emergent figures, in view at once. That is, the purpose is to make the reader see them all, simultaneously, in soft focus; and the method is to give the reader just enough of each figure for this purpose. The figure of state as Fortune, for example, emerges just far enough to make it possible for the

---

[3] The figure at this point is tending, on the one hand, toward a comparison to the court of an omnipotent prince, perverse, moody, shrewd, as Queen Elizabeth was; it is tending, on the other hand, toward the essentially medieval idea of Fortune, who rules everything on this side of the moon, and whose rule is wholly without order or meaning.

[4] There seems to have been a close connection in Shakespeare's mind between bastardy and Machiavellian, policy-breeding, anarchic cynicism, as if this cynicism presented itself to his mind as the bastard of Time. See, for example, Edmund and Thersites ("I am a bastard begot, bastard instructed, bastard in mind, bastard in valor, in everything illegitimate"), or the cynicism of that strangely unfathered child of state, Hamlet.

reader to see what this figure would have come to had it been worked out completely; and the figure of state as the body politic within which Shakespeare's love would be subject to Time just far enough to suggest what that figure would have come to. And so of the rest. If any one of these emergent figures had been realized in full, all the rest would necessarily have been excluded. They must then have been developed separately, and Shakespeare would have written a poem in which each of these figures appeared seriatim, perhaps a figure to a stanza, as in Donne's "Valediction; of the booke," which Mr. Ransom offers as an illustration of metaphysical structure.[5]

It is difficult to say how daring a venture "Weeds among weeds, or flowers with flowers gathered" is; it all depends on how familiar in Shakespeare's day were the associations of weeds and flowers he is using here. It is easy enough to show that they were familiar to Shakespeare, but I suspect they were also peculiar to him. Fortunately the line is carefully paralleled with l.12; indeed, the primary sense-connection of l. 12 is to l.4. From this parallel I think l.4 gains enough support so that it will serve simply in its general sense: if Shakespeare's love were the child of state, so long as Fortune favored it, its every aspect would be a flower gathered with all the other flowers blossoming in the sunshine of Time's love; if Fortune ceased to favor it, its every aspect would be a weed, gathered with all the other weeds which rot noisomely in the damp of Time's hate. *Gather'd* carries out the personifications of the first three lines and hints at a new one, Father Time (cp., the scythe in the final line of CXXIII); the flowers and weeds represent the specific consequences of Time's love and Time's hate.

But the particular value of this line as a summing up of the whole quatrain depends on our familiarity with Shakespeare's usual use of weeds and flowers; and it is not quite fair therefore to say that this value is communicated as well as expressed. In Shakespeare the contrast between weeds and flowers is most frequently applied to court life, society, problems of state, this-worldly affairs; figures of this kind are frequent in the history plays and in *Hamlet*. Weeds, particularly in their rankness (vigorousness, grossness, rancidity, indecency), are among the strongest of Shakespeare's

---

[5] There is an interesting parallel between Donne's poem and the present sonnet which not only demonstrates the commonness of the "ideas" treated in both poems but also allows the very different methods of the two poems to be compared. Donne starts his sixth stanza as if he were going to take the other side of the argument from Shakespeare. Statesmen, he says, can learn much useful "policy" by studying the annals of his love, since in both love and statecraft "they doe excell/Who the present governe well/ Whose weaknesse none doth, or dares tell"; but then, just as Shakespeare implies that the "policy" of love is of a very different order from that of statement, so Donne adds that any statesman who fancies he finds love's methods like his is comparable to the alchemist who believes he finds authority for his art in the Bible.

images for evil.[6] Thus the gardener in *Richard II* ends his elaborate comparison of his garden to a commonwealth by saying:

> I will go root away
> The noisome weeds, which without profit suck
> The soil's fertility from wholesome flowers.[7]

Hamlet finds the world

> an unweeded garden,
> That grows to seed; things rank and gross in nature
> Possess it merely.

This sense of evil is primarily a result of his mother's sins; these are for Hamlet both weeds on which she is in danger of spreading compost "to make them ranker" and an "ulcerous place," the rank corruption of which may infect all within unseen. But Hamlet's sense of evil is not limited to its immediate cause; it is *all* the uses of this world which seem to him weary, stale, flat, and unprofitable, just as in the present sonnet Shakespeare distrusts Time's love as much as its hate. The "facts" of both the play and the sonnet are the vehicle for a feeling about the world as a whole. It is the essence of Shakespeare's success with this kind of figurative language that he never loses the individual "facts" in the perilously extended feeling.

With the association of rank weeds and spiritual corruption goes quite naturally the association of physical and spiritual decay which appears in Hamlet's "ulcerous place" figure. The ease with which Shakespeare bridged what may seem to the reader the considerable gap between the imagery of flowers and weeds and the imagery of disease can be demonstrated from a simple narrative passage in *Macbeth:*

> *Caithness.* Well, march we on,
> To give obedience where 'tis truly ow'd:
> Meet we the medicine of the sickly weal;
> And with him pour we, in our country's purge,
> Each drop of us.

[6] Caroline F. E. Spurgeon, *Shakespeare's Imagery,* pp. 154–155, 220–223.

[7] There is the implication here and throughout *Richard II* that a proper gardener can put things right. The gardener himself specifically adds that "The weeds...are pluck'd up root and all by Bolingbroke," and it is only at the end and only from Richard that we hear:

> Nor I nor any man that but man is
> With nothing shall be pleas'd till he be eas'd
> With being nothing.

It is a very different matter in *Hamlet*—and in the present sonnet—where all the authority of Hamlet is behind the belief in the incurable weediness of this world and where the mere easement of death has become the only "felicity." Hamlet's authority is not of course complete. but the king is a distinctly lighter weight in the scale against him than Bolingbroke is against Richard.

> *Lenox.* Or so much as it needs
> To dew the sovereign flower, and drown the weeds.

Here, quite characteristically, their blood, in Caithness's speech a medicine with which to purge the sick society, becomes the dew which makes the sovereign flower grow and drowns the weed. And, precisely as in the present sonnet, the fact that the ultimate referent of weeds is a group of human beings leads Shakespeare to use a verb (*drown*) which is more immediately applicable to persons than to weeds.[8]

The physical decay of this imagery may be either that of disease or that of death. It is the special horror of this aspect of life that the sun's breeding maggots in a dead dog and the son's breeding sinners in that living variety of good kissing carrion, Ophelia, are scarcely distinguishable. Both kinds of physical decay appear frequently in connection with the evils of human life, especially the evils of power and passion. Hamlet's mind is haunted by the smell of rotting flesh as well as by the imposthume that inward breaks. The king will be able to nose the corpse of Polonius as he goes up the stairs into the lobby; and Hamlet's final comment on the humiliating futility of Yorick's life is: "and smelt so? Pah!" But perhaps the most perfect collocation of all these images and their association is the close of sonnet XCIV:

> The summer's flower is to the summer sweet,
> Though to itself, it only live and die,
> But if that flower with base infection meet,
> The basest weed outbraves his dignity,
>   For sweetest things turn sourest by their deeds:
>   Lilies that fester, smell far worse than weeds.

Rain is closely connected with these images of corruption, too, for though it causes flowers as well as weeds to grow (but "sweet flowers are slow and weeds make haste"), it is also the cause of weeds' and flesh's rotting and stinking. The first gravedigger, after observing that "we have many pocky corpses now-a-days, that will scarcely hold the laying in," remarks that a tanner's corpse will last the longest because "'a will keep out water a great while, and your water is a sore decayer of your whoreson dead body." And it is the rankness of nettles which lends the terrible dramatic irony to Cressida's reply to Pandarus:

---

[8] In the present sonnet, of course, Shakespeare is dealing directly with the mystery of loyalty and sovereignty which gave such limited perfection as it possessed to government, whereas in *Macbeth* that mystery is incarnate in the royal family and its loyal followers. Hence, in *Macbeth* the sovereign flower is ultimate earthly good, whereas, in the sonnet, it is only smiling Fortune. The overriding metaphor in *Macbeth* is such as to eliminate those impediments to the marriage of true minds the tragic reality of which so haunts Hamlet, Troilus, Othello, Lear, and the present sonnet. But apart from this distinction, the use of weeds and flowers is the same in *Macbeth* and the sonnet.

> *Pandarus.* I'll be sworn 'tis true: he will weep you,
> and 'twere a man born in April.
> *Cressida.* And I'll spring up in his tears, an 'twere a
> nettle against May.

It is these associations of weeds and flowers (and of heat and showers too) which give such great force to l. 4.

## III

With the second quatrain Shakespeare starts another of his great metaphors for the destructive power of time, that of a building: "No it was builded far from accident" (where "waterdrops have worn the stones of Troy,/ And blind oblivion swallow'd cities up,/ And mighty states characterless are grated/ To dusty nothing"). This metaphor is then compounded in much the same way that the opening metaphor of sonnet LXXIII is; that is, the building is personified: "It suffers not in smiling pomp, nor falls/ Under the blow of thralled discontent." The figurative significances which may be derived from this compounded metaphor, taken in connection with the two metaphors of the first quatrain, are so many and so shaded into each other that a listing of them is neither possible nor desirable. The effect here, as in the first quatrain, depends on our being conscious of as many of these figurative significances as possible without bringing any of them exclusively into focus. They resist any effort to separate them one from the other; if the reader nevertheless insists on trying to force the lines to work for any one meaning alone, they will appear hopelessly defective. If this were not the case, they would be unable to function for all their meanings simultaneously.

The disadvantages of trying to bring any one implication of this complex of interacting metaphors into sharp focus are manifold. If the reader will oversimplify the problem by ignoring the metaphor of a building which intervenes between Shakespeare's love and the personification which suffers in smiling pomp and falls under the blow of thralled discontent, he will discover that there is a variation of meaning in these lines for every variation of meaning to be found in the first quatrain as a result of the multiple signification of *state*. But if he tries to bring each of these possible meanings of the second quatrain successively into focus he will find not only that the lines will not support any one of them alone, but that each of them tends to shade off into every other, till the possibility of bringing any one into focus becomes remote. There are certainly very real differences between *state* as status, as wealth, and as physical beauty, and it is certain, too, that one can associate a different kind of pomp and a different kind of discontent with each of them. But if the reader attempts to elaborate in detail each of these combinations, he finds in the first place that *suffer* and *fall* range from merely awkward to downright impossible, and in the second that the pomp of the young man's status and the pomp of his wealth begin to fade into each other, that the thralled discontent of status unrecognized, of talent unrealized, of policy unsuccessful begin to merge; and so it is with the rest of these distinctions which are perfectly satisfactory in a general focus.

But the reader cannot afford to ignore the fact that the *it* of l.6 refers quite as clearly to that which was builded far from accident as to "my dear love." For unless he realizes that ll. 6–7 retain the metaphor of the building he will miss the delicacy with which Shakespeare carries out the irony, obvious enough, in a general way, in the implications of the negatives. (*Unless* the young gentleman possesses all this state and is at least conceivably within danger of being victimized by it, and *unless* Shakespeare is capable of being hurt by such a development, it would never occur to Shakespeare to protest that his love is not the child of state.) Shakespeare does not say that the young man is tossed from success to failure and from discontent to satisfaction on the whirligig of time and that, in spite of this, Shakespeare's love remains unchanging. What he does say is that his love is like a building, a building which may be thought of most significantly as not like a courtier riding such a whirligig. The delicacy of the irony thus depends on the fact that this comparison is ostensibly chosen as the perfect description of the building and on the implication that Shakespeare would be surprised and dismayed were he to discover the young man taking it as a reference to himself. Shakespeare, that is, ostensibly and indeed ostentatiously disowns any responsibility for the coincidence of the young man's state and this figurative courtier's.

The insistence of Shakespeare's sonnet on generalizing the focus of the reader's attention will be quite clear, I think, if he will work out the simplest meaning for ll. 6–7 at each of the three levels, without considering either the remoter figurative significances, or the interaction of the various levels of meaning, or the interrelations of these lines with other lines. A courtier may be said to go about smiling and pompous in the conceit of his success; he may not be said to "suffer smiling and pompous." He may be described as wholly enslaved by discontent but only by some stretching of the figure as falling under the blow of his discontent. A building may be described as rich and elegant; it can scarcely be said to "suffer rich and elegant." It may fall under the blows of rebelling slaves; one blow, however, seems a little inadequate.[9] Finally, Shakespeare's love, not having been generated by anything that dwells in Time's kingdom, is beyond the power

9 My implication of dislike for richness and success and of sympathy for the discontented is, I think, in the lines. Notice that l. 8 tends to attach itself exclusively to "thralled discontent." This implication places Shakespeare, for all his brave show of living in the light, not of this world but of eternity, among the discontented and even, perhaps, among the approvers of violence. This implication may be a deliberate preparation for the irony of the final couplet.

of either Time's love or Time's hate, both of which are spoken of in 1. 6 as disastrous (the first causing suffering and the second discontent). The language of 11. 6–7 is directed just sufficiently toward each of these meanings to make it impossible for the reader to ignore any one of them. In no instance is it directed toward any one of them sufficiently to make it possible for the reader to contemplate that meaning to the exclusion of the others. The reader is thus forced to try to contemplate them all simultaneously. This procedure obviously permits an immense concentration of meaning within the particular passage. It has the further effect of almost forcing the poet to use the multitude of interrelations between the various passages which suggest themselves. This is, of course, the great danger of Shakespeare's kind of poetry. It is a danger over which Shakespeare at his best always triumphed but which has pretty consistently defeated his imitators.

"Whereto the inviting time our fashion calls." To such an existence this encouraging age calls us to fashion our lives as nobles, our relatively more permanent structures (both physical and social), our lives. (There is an ominous quality in "inviting" not represented by "encouraging." Perhaps, therefore, a less literal paraphrase would be more accurate; for example, "a way of life in which this easy age encourages us." But the point here is to bring out the metaphorical richness of the line.) But there is another important meaning here. It is impossible to keep this *time* from establishing relations with the *time* that loves and hates in 1. 3; thus Time in its local and temporary manifestation, this age, calls on our fashion to become subject to King Time and thus calls on us to expose ourselves to its love and hate (smiling pomp and thralled discontent being the results of accepting).

## IV

In the final quatrain Shakespeare draws together all his metaphorical themes. His love "fears not policy" since it is no child of state but was born in another kingdom than that of Time, in which policy operates.[10] Policy is a heretic by the familiar trick of transferring the vocabulary of the Christian worship of God to the lover's worship of the loved one. But it is also a heretic ("an indifferentist in religion, a worldly-wise man")

[10] "Policy" here is a kind of metonym. That is, the figurative courtier of ll. 6–7 is a politic fellow. The substitution has the advantage of allowing the meaning of ll. 9–11 to extend beyond the courtier to the general philosophic attitude of shrewd, ambitious, and worldly people. The linking of this line to the figurative courtier of ll. 6–7 thus makes it an extension of the statement that Shakespeare's love, since it is not a child of state, is like a building built far from the kingdom of accident and chance and thus not subject to the alternate pomp and discontent of all which is subject to Time: not only does this love know nothing of the maneuvering of courtiers; it knows nothing of worldly policy in any form. It may be worth noting, as a part of the link, the very specific senses of "an indifferentist in religion, a worldly-wise man" which was given the noun *politic* in Shakespeare's days: "A carnal fellow, a mere politic." (N.E.D.)

because it is a child of state, worshipping the god of Time rather than the God of eternity. *Policy* is then said to be able to work only within the limits of human foresight, which is a space of short numbered hours compared to the eternity in terms of which those work who are subjects of God's kingdom. The line in question (10) is another one of those which says several things and works out without defect for none of them alone. That is, policy, personified as a heretic, may be said to work, but scarcely on a lease of any kind; on the other hand this same policy may *have* a lease on life of short numbered hours. A building in Time's world will presumably be held on a short lease, the duration of which is carefully measured; it can hardly, however, be described as *working* on that lease.

"But all alone stands hugely politic." With a slight stretching of "hugely politic" this line will work for the two immediate meanings involved, those of the previous line. That is, Shakespeare's love, as a building, stands all alone, perhaps like New Place with its orchards and gardens rather than like one of those speculative structures in London, crowded between other buildings, which were giving the authorities so much to worry about. It stands "far from accident," incredibly old and wise, (This is the stretching of "hugely politic." The Elizabethans used *politic* in this good sense regularly; as in the phrase "theyr polytycke wyt and learnyng in Physicke." [N.E.D.]) representing, as it were, the good old certainties of faith rather than the new-fangled values of shrewdness and calculation. Shakespeare's love, as person, stands apart from the human world of petty policy, dependent on no earthly devices, politic only in the infinite's craft, learned not in Machiavelli's but in God's book.

Thus Shakespeare's love is unlike the blooming favorites of Time's love and the rank and weedy creatures of Time's hate; it is unlike the worldly courtier who flourishes in the sun of prosperity ("For if the sun breed maggots in a dead dog...Let her not walk i' th' sun") and goes down in the floods of adversity ("Pulled the poor wretch from her melodious lay/ To muddy death");[11] it is unlike the house built upon the sand which shows in

[11] The richness of Shakespeare's flood imagery has been emphasized by Mr. G. Wilson Knight, but the significance of his sun and light imagery seems to have been unduly neglected. Richard uses it in describing his earthly glory and ends with talk of the "brittle glory [which] shineth in this face" and of melting "before the sun of Bolingbroke." Hal, warning the audience that presently he will emerge as the perfect king, says that "herein will I imitate the sun...." Juliet associates the "garish sun" with ordinary, worldly, daily living; it is the light by which Capulet and the nurse live; but the face of Juliet's heaven is made bright by the starlight of her love. For Hamlet Juliet's sun is not merely garish but a breeder of maggots, as Richard's garden is for him weedy not merely through carelessness but by nature, incurable. Angelo combines the sun imagery with that of flowers and weeds: "but it is I/That, lying by the violet in the sun,/Do as the carrion does, not as the flower,/Corrupt with virtuous season." This whole complex of weeds, flowers, carrion, sun and rain, seems, as the Variorum points out, to be derived ultimately from a speech in *Edward III,* but the beautiful and complex use of it in the plays and sonnets is Shakespeare's own.

pomp in the sun and sinks to ruin in storms. "It nor grows with heat, nor drowns with showers."

Shakespeare calls to witness the truth of this statement those people who are made fools of by Time. In general in Shakespeare everyone is in one way or another made a fool of by Time; those who know enough try to escape its tyranny most tragically of all. For these discover, as Troilus did, that their fears are only too well grounded:

> What will it be
> When that the watery palate tastes indeed
> Love's thrice repured nectar! Death, I fear me,
> Sounding destruction, or some joy too fine,
> Too subtle potent, tun'd too sharp in sweetness
> For the capacity of my ruder powers:
> I fear it much;...

Troilus, Hamlet, Isabella, all in their ways tried to escape from the life of this world, and all discovered that they could not escape the human consequences of the fact that they were living in it. "Does your worship mean to geld and splay all the youth of the city?"[12]

I think these facts are necessary to an understanding of the amazing inclusiveness of Shakespeare's description of the fools of time. At the most obvious level this line (14) makes a distinction between martyrs and worldly-wise men. (*Crime,* not ordinarily a very strong word among the Elizabethans, is here roughly equivalent to "worldly success.") For though *who* certainly modifies *which,* the change of relatives tends to divide those which die for goodness from those who have lived for crime. And this division is reënforced by the ambiguity of *goodness,* which may mean what Shakespeare takes to be good or what the criminals take to be good. Those who die for goodness in this second, ironic sense may, like "Pitiful thrivers in their gazing spent," (Cp. the second quatrain of Sonnet CXXV) die physically for the sake of the "compound sweet" which they, "dwellers on form and favour," have devoted their worldly lives to seeking; it may be that they also die eternally, are damned, for lack of goodness in the serious sense and for living sinful lives. Those who die for goodness in the serious sense, who are martyrs, may die physically, because, like Richard, they failed to give enough attention to the worldly-wise man's kind of good, after living

---

[12] The thought is developed as early as *Richard II;* cp., 5.5. 45–49, where Richard, having mentally escaped from his prison into the timeless world of ideals, is reminded by the imperfect beat of the music that he still lives in this world:

> And here have I the daintiness of ear
> To check time broke in a disordered string;
> But for the concord of my state and time
> Had not an ear to hear my true time broke.
> I wasted time, and now doth time waste me....

A moment later Richard, who has lived for crime, dies for goodness.

lives which, even at their best, were not without sin ("in the course of justice, none of us/ Should see salvation") and, at their troubled worst, offended against more than one of the world's canons, to say nothing of the Everlasting's.[13]

The most astonishing consequence of this line is its inclusion among the fools of Time of the speaker of this sonnet, so that by a terrifying twist of irony Shakespeare offers his own failure—the unavoidable fact that for all he has been saying about it, his love cannot escape the consequences of his being human and not divine—as part of the evidence for the truth of his contention that his love is not "the child of state."

## V

The pattern which one of Shakespeare's sonnets aims to establish in the reader's mind is not the pattern of logic aimed at by the metaphysical poem; his typical sonnet is rather a formal effort to create in the reader's mind a pattern, externally controlled, very like the pattern of the mind when it contemplates, with full attention but for no immediately practical purpose, an object in nature. Such a pattern is not built simply of logical relations nor does it consist simply of what is in perfect focus; it is built for all the kinds of relations known to the mind, as a result of its verbal conditioning or for other reasons, which can be invoked verbally. The building of a verbal construct calculated to invoke such a pattern requires the use of every resource language as a social instrument possesses, and it involves a structure of figurative language which at least approaches, in its own verbal terms, the richness, the density, the logical incompleteness of the mind.

No one can say how much the effect which a poem may fairly be said to produce can in the ordinary sense have been intended by the poet; apparently a good deal it does is not consciously intended. But unless the best of Shakespeare's sonnets are to be passed off as miraculous accidents, it is difficult to see what grounds there are for supposing that they are the result of following the path of least resistance in contrast to Donne's poems, which Mr. Ransom quite justly claims must be the result of stern intellectual labors. If the structure of figurative language in Shakespeare's sonnets is not an accident, and if its consequences are calculated, in so far as the consequences of any poem may be said to be calculated, then it seems more than probable that their making involved at least as great an effort of the intellect and imagination as the making of Donne's poems.

---

[13] I omit the significance which may be derived from taking *die* less literally (i.e., desire deeply) which several editors have noticed, perhaps because they are so prominent in sonnet CXXV; they are remoter in this sonnet, and my paraphrase is already overburdened.

Mr. Ransom has it that in a formal lyric "the poetic object is elected by a free choice from all objects in the world, and this object, deliberately elected and worked up by the adult poet, becomes his microcosm. . . . It is as ranging and comprehensive an action as the mind has ever tried." It seems to me that Shakespeare's serious sonnets fail, as they do sometimes fail, not because they do not live up to this admirable description of the formal lyric but because they have tried to live up to it altogether too well.

# 6

# The Innocent Insinuations of Wit: The Strategy of Language in Shakespeare's *Sonnets*

*Murray Krieger*

This essay is intended as a postscript to my book *A Window to Criticism: Shakespeare's* Sonnets *and Modern Poetics* (Princeton, 1964). There I tried to maneuver Shakespeare's language in the *Sonnets* into a typological system of metaphor, a system that would express the substantive union of discrete entities made possible first by love and then by poetry as love's unique discourse. But in my pursuit of the direction and constellation of the metaphors, I did not generalize upon the strategy in accordance with which these manipulations of metaphor were managed, the method—the unique syntactical dispositions—which controlled their farthest reaches. I propose here to stand aside from my more substantive work and to try to do just this. In the course of this essay I shall occasionally have to echo a few observations on individual sonnets from my book and make some fresh ones. But here these observations are to serve a totally different purpose since, I repeat, it is the method or strategy, and not the substance or thematic range, of Shakespeare's language that concerns me.

If I were to use a single phrase to characterize Shakespeare's strategy at its best, I would term it "the innocent insinuations of wit"—and if "inno-

*Reprinted from Murray Krieger,* The Play and Place of Criticism *(Baltimore: The Johns Hopkins Press, 1967), pp. 19–36 by permission of the publisher.*

cent insinuations" suggests an oxymoron, this is precisely to my purpose. The "innocent" is apparent only: on the face of it there is no guile in the words as they marshal themselves into syntax. But at their best the undercurrents in the sonnets seem to wind themselves about into unforeseen unions of meaning that create constant surprises for us and—we almost allow ourselves to believe—for their poet. What artfulness there is, is artless, though its subtlety demands our endless search—and admiration. For, as the word *wit* assures us, everything has been under a shrewd aesthetic control all along.

This strategy is perhaps best seen by contrast to another, and my use of the overused term *wit* permits me to draw this contrast. Some time back my friend and former colleague Leonard Unger, borrowing terms from Freud, proposed to establish a scale along which poetry could be measured, a scale extending from the extreme of "dream-work" to the extreme of "wit-work."[1] As I understood it, at the "wit" end of the scale he would place the self-consciously metaphysical poem, whose metaphorical development is traceably explicit in a strategy that borders on the exhibitionist. Whatever unpredictable accretions the dialectic may achieve, it achieves through a mastery of manipulation that is everywhere observable—indeed that shouts to be observed. At the "dream" end of the scale he would place the poem that appears to be controlled by little more than random association. If a poem by John Donne reflects the "wit" strategy, the Shakespearean sonnet reflects the "dream" strategy. But the word *strategy* is all-important, as is the word *appears* in the claim that the "dream-work" "*appears* to be controlled by little more than random association." For surely Unger did not mean that the one kind had art while the other left all to chance. It is not a choice between strategy and no strategy but a choice between strategies, between a strategy of explicit wit and an apparent strategy of dream which, after all, has its own wit, however innocently it seems to insinuate it and, thus, to entwine and capture, as it enraptures, us.

This contrast between the strategies of Donne and Shakespeare is not dissimilar to an earlier one drawn by John Crowe Ransom, except that Ransom's was far less sympathetic—indeed it was positively disrespectful—to Shakespeare. In his by now nearly infamous "Shakespeare at Sonnets"[2] Ransom accuses Shakespeare of having, in effect, insufficient strategy, of failing to have what Ransom elsewhere terms "the courage of [his] metaphors"—which is the very courage that he sees Donne as having. For Ransom seems to have fallen into the error—which I have rejected—of claiming that the metaphysical is the only strategy that wit may employ, so that if the poet does not indulge it, he is turning from wit altogether: he is giving over

---

1 To my knowledge he has never developed this proposal in his published writings beyond the epigraph to, and the hints lurking in the background of, his essay "Deception and Self-Deception in Shakespeare's *Henry IV,*" *The Man in the Name* (Minneapolis, 1956), pp. 3–17.

2 *The World's Body* (New York, 1938), pp. 270–303.

the reins from the intellect, which critics in the line from Eliot have assured us is the ruling faculty for poetry as wit, to mere emotion ruled by little more than the rushes of chance. And heaven pity the clumsy, inconsistent structure of language, little better than careless prose, that arises from such indulgence, such abdication of rule. Heaven pity it, for the Ransomian critic will not!

It is by reason of the multiple strategies allowed by the Unger formulation that I prefer it and see it as a capacious alternative to Ransom's. (So, I suspect, would Ransom for many years now—indeed from a period not long after his early and narrowly polemic, if then necessary, way of positing his doctrine.) It was in part for this reason also that I saw in the subtler, dreamlike play of wit of poems like Shakespeare's *Sonnets* challenges to critical method in the Renaissance lyric far more pressing than the intricate, but more clearly patterned, lines of the metaphysicals. Between the golden and the drab poets that C. S. Lewis too conveniently speaks of in his history of sixteenth-century literature in England are poets whose wit need not lead to the open skepticism, open paradox, and open cacophony that deny the golden voice of poetry, poets who produce not the shock of open clash, but the ever-renewed wonder at the surprises to which soft and cherished words can—almost on their own and by accident—lead us. But only *almost,* of course. And of no poet more than Shakespeare in his *Sonnets* can we make this claim. This is why he becomes the greatest challenge, and the delineation of his strategy the greatest necessity, to a disciplined criticism of the lyric.

## I

I shall propose here just two of the ways in which Shakespeare produces his deceptive effects, ways in which a seeming looseness works its dialectical path into the tightest of aesthetic traps. The first I term association as dialectic. Instead of the common metaphysical tactic of working carefully through an image, allowing it to expand into the constitutive symbol that becomes the poem, the poet shifts rapidly and with a seeming abandon from image to image. Yet there seems to be no way of our justifying the selections and movements aesthetically; that is, we can neither claim a principle in terms of which they are exhaustive possibilities that together comprehend a whole, nor can we even justify a principle of inclusion for those we have or of exclusion for those we have not. The choice rather seems quite arbitrary: the poet seems to choose those that occur to him as they occur to him, and he stops when he has enough to satisfy the externally imposed limits of the sonnet form. The individual image is hardly developed but is mentioned and dropped, and the next one picked up with no sense of inevitability even tried for.

We can relate this habit causally to the commonly acknowledged weakness of the Shakespearean sonnet form, in contrast to the Italian: That three prosodically independent quatrains and the epigrammatic couplet are too many semi-autonomous units for so brief and powerful a lyric as the sonnet. And in making this relation a general observation, we have further struck at the aesthetic firmness of Shakespeare's frequent practice. We seem to be taking dead aim at the "when...when...then" sonnet as typically unsatisfying. The poet chooses at random two or three examples—just about any two or three will do—in the natural and the human world of some universal process, say mutability, devoting a couple of lines or at most a quatrain, beginning with "When," to each example; he adds, for contrast, the painful consequence of these observations, prefixed by an expressed or implied "Then"; and he closes with a generalizing couplet that expresses the poet's sadness at, and struggle against, the inevitability as it touches him and his love. Here is hardly a formula that promises much more than the obvious, though prettily and wistfully dressed up, hardly a formula that can hope to transform conventional materials into a unique aesthetic form and symbolic statement. Nor was it, in the hands of many lesser poets.

How does Shakespeare, despite this seeming relaxedness of attitude toward his materials, subdue the passivity of dream through the strategy of wit? Sonnet 12 would seem to be a typically uncontrolled example of this flabby form—and typically devoted to the poet's sentimental regrets at the ruinous passage of time. Possible instances of the universal process are everywhere, to be found as soon as looked for; nor do the ones chosen at first appear especially ingenious in their selection or combination.

> When I do count the clock that tells the time,
> And see the brave day sunk in hideous night;
> When I behold the violet past prime,
> And sable curls all silver'd o'er with white;
> When lofty trees I see barren of leaves
> Which erst from heat did canopy the herd,
> And summer's green, all girded up in sheaves,
> Borne on the bier with white and bristly beard;
> Then of thy beauty do I question make,
> That thou among the wastes of time must go,
> Since sweets and beauties do themselves forsake
> And die as fast as they see others grow;
>    And nothing 'gainst Time's scythe can make defence
>    Save breed, to brave him when he takes thee hence.

The octave begins with the painfully simple reference to the clock, which is further weakened by the redundancy of the first line and the obvious opposition of "brave day" and "hideous night." Then the symbols of summer's death: the fading flower of line 3 juxtaposed to the fading hair of line

4, followed by the leafless trees of lines 5–6 and "summer's green" which has been cut down (lines 7–8). These are the random examples cited in the octave from which the personal application of the sestet is to follow.

But is there not a structure to these as Shakespeare deploys them? There is—and, as is often the case in these sonnets, it arises out of the way in which he builds, gradually and almost imperceptibly, to the finally total union of nature and man, out of the metaphorical reduction of the human world to the natural or rather the reading of the natural world in terms of its human consequences. The violets and the human hair are juxtaposed, as if by association; they are analogous coordinates, but only that, since no relation between them is suggested. But in the next two lines nature is brought into explicit relation with animal life. The trees are related to the herd as its former protector from summer's heat. Or is the herd human too by extension, the humanity of pastoral convention, humanity in its natural—its communal, its herd—aspect? And is this not the herd which *is* under nature's protection, the nature in whose fruitfulness, mirror of its own, it must trust? But this is only the merest suggestion, only the faint glimpse of possibility—we can hardly be sure. The two lines that follow make us certain, even as they make the union of man and nature total—which is to say, substantive: "And summer's green all girded up in sheaves/ Borne on the bier with white and bristly beard." The funeral of "summer's green" is transformed as we watch from merely personified nature to the literally human in nature. It is, of course, the "bier" and its crucial echo in "beard" which manage this utter transformation. Unquestionably "beard" is brilliant: in its vegetative meaning it is true to the grain, the now lifeless "green," even as, in combination with the almost homonymous "bier" which makes it possible for "beard" to work its double way, it humanizes the ritual procession. "Borne on the bier with white and bristly beard." *Exeunt* as natural man is inevitably borne from the stage.

In three two-line units, then, we have moved from analogy to relation to identity between nature and man. Although this poem, as a "when... when...then" sonnet, seems to promise only a series of undeveloped, alternative analogies drawn from an apparently random association and designed to illustrate a single general claim, it has gradually grown into a full, total, and even substantive union of its varied elements. For it has been a seemingly random movement from chance analogy to a two-faced, single-bodied metaphor.

How proper that only now has Shakespeare earned his logical conclusion beginning on line 9; only now can be justly say that consequential word "then": "Then of thy beauty do I question make/That thou among the wastes of time must go." The vision to which he has built in the octave has been too inclusive and conclusive for anything less mandatory than "*must* go"—even for nature's fairest flower, the loveliest of men. And the generality with which the couplet begins ("And nothing 'gainst Time's scythe can make defence") is given fearful specificity as "Time's scythe" returns us to the earlier described harvest that awaits us all as we move toward the "white and bristly beard" that will place us, like spent grain, on the bier to be borne as all *exeunt*. "Time's scythe" cuts several precise ways by cutting its one universal way in line 13. How fully Shakespeare has refreshed, has given new substance to, the conceit of the grim reaper that grows naturally out of the analogy of the life of man to the seasons of vegetable life.

Still there is more than this. For the escape from the scythe that cuts at all levels must spring from the poem, whose materials seem to build toward a destruction that is escape-proof. And, as if by accident, these materials will provide the poet-Monte Cristo the tools he needs, even out of the carelessly weak opening two lines we have observed ("When I do count the clock that tells the time/And see the brave day sunk in hideous night"). For in the couplet the hopelessness of the penultimate line ("And nothing 'gainst Time's scythe can make defence") is taken back at the last moment by that remarkably polysemous word—here a mere preposition (or is it?)—"Save" ("Save breed, to brave him when he takes thee hence"). The way to resurrection is the universal way that is the way of "breed," always the answer to the "barren," the always newly won "canopy" for "the herd." But why, in terms of the poem? Because this way is the "brave" way. We recall that in line 2 it was the "brave day" that was lost as symbol for all that time destroys ("When I do count the clock that tells the time/And see the brave day sunk in hideous night"). This phrase, "brave day," reasserts itself in the "brave" of the last line ("Save breed, to brave him when he takes thee hence"). In this line "brave" is an echo, a reflection of the "breed" with which it alliterates: it is the breeding which is the braving of time. But as an echo also of line 2, "brave" is at the same a kind of equivalent for day, that which the "hideous night" has replaced. By braving time through breed, the friend in effect restores the bravery which is day, overcoming night (and the destructive cycle of the natural process), which is hideous in the extinction it threatens.

In the octave, in the relation of the octave to the conclusive third quatrain, and in the relation of all these to the couplet, to the stopping short of total defeat, the naiveté of apparent association has become the witty strategy of dialectic. The poet has (I shall not say unwittingly) made available to himself the very materials he needs. The very process of the poem has seemed to be a dreamlike search that has led us (and, the illusion persuades us, has led the poet) to discover, to come upon, almost to trip upon an aesthetically sound resolution whose inevitability has been fed by all that he has uttered.

Let me cite more briefly several other examples of association become dialectic. We can observe a similar movement to a similar fusion of man and nature in the considerably more brilliant "when" sonnet, Sonnet 64:

> When I have seen by Time's fell hand defaced
> The rich proud cost of outworn buried age;
> When sometime lofty towers I see down-razed,
> And brass eternal slave to mortal rage:
> When I have seen the hungry ocean gain
> Advantage on the kingdom of the shore,
> And the firm soil win of the watery main,
> Increasing store with loss and loss with store:
> When I have seen such interchange of state,
> Or state itself confounded to decay;
> Ruin hath taught me thus to ruminate—
> That Time will come and take my love away.
>   This thought is as a death, which cannot choose
>   But weep to have that which it fears to lose.

In moving from the first to the second quatrain, we move from the world of man to the world of nature, from the succession of political states to the succession of unending cycles in the rhythmic heart of the universe. Shakespeare begins by observing the destruction of the noblest and most ambitious of human productions, with the ironic use of "eternal" ("brass eternal") the clue to his scornful view of human claims to immortality. Even more insulting to the "eternal" is its being at the mercy of a rage that is itself "mortal." Thus the contrast between these "mortal agents," in the first quatrain, who have undone their victims, the would-be "eternal" who are thesmelves to be undone in turn, and the natural, seemingly immortal agents who face a mutual undoing in the second quatrain. As if to prove the claim that the human political state is a microcosmic reflection of the universal state under time, the antagonists of the second quatrain, the ocean and the shore, are rendered totally in human terms, as they act in accordance with political motives. Thus the apparent distinction between the human and the natural in the two quatrains comes to be methodically blurred. All the realms of "state" have been identified and reduced to the extreme consequences of its narrowest meaning, that of human politics. The word "state," despite its range of meanings, from narrow to broad, from politics to the general condition of being (or rather of becoming), is shown to be a single reductive entity that can contain and unite them all even within its narrowest confines. For these confines can be extended unlimitedly without losing their more precise limitations. The ocean, seen as "hungry" for the acquisition of another's, reduces "the kingdom of the shore," only later to be forced to give back what it has gained along with some of its own. Thus the inconclusive (even as it is the most conclusive and inclusive) "interchange of state" or, in terms that suggest the first quatrain, "state itself confounded to decay," as the political sense of state achieves its universal sway under time, incorporating the other senses. The many politic antagonists can only interchange their states, as his metaphor enables Shakespeare's human and natural antagonists to interchange *their* states. And all, mutually aided or mutually impeded, must eventually face the reduction to identity, the obliteration of "state" itself as an entity, as a static concept. (The redundancy is intended.)

A similar reduction to the indifferent sameness of mutability and decline is emphasized as the uniting force of yet another "when...when... then" sonnet, Sonnet 15.

> When I consider everything that grows
> Holds in perfection but a little moment,
> That this huge stage presenteth naught but shows
> Whereon the stars in secret influence comment;
> When I perceive that men as plants increase,
> Cheered and check'd even by the self-same sky,
> Vaunt in their youthful sap, at height decrease,
> And wear their brave state out of memory;
> Then the conceit of this inconstant stay
> Sets you most rich in youth before my sight,
> Where wasteful Time debateth with Decay,
> To change your day of youth to sullied night;
> And, all in war with Time for love of you,
> As he takes from you, I engraft you new.

The universality of time's process begins in the first line with the "everything" that permits of no exceptions. Its all-inclusiveness is echoed by the unqualified "naught but" of line 3, the "selfsame" of line 6; and as a most constant "conceit" it sharply underlines the "inconstant stay" (line 9) which characterizes man's feeble role in the natural process. It is the utterly contingent, "inconstant stay" of man, thrown against the "conceit" of the uncontingent single law of time, that justifies the use of the theatrical figure that reduces "everything" to helpless, insubstantial puppetry. An indifferent, pagan nature that is pure process and thus absolute in its transience controls completely. It is the nature of the influencing stars and the maddeningly "selfsame sky" that equally *cheer* and *check* (and how effective the alliteration that proves the identity, from the perspective of nature's indifference, of blessing and curse). Further, they indifferently cheer and check men and plants, or rather, more extremely, "men *as* plants." In the face of his nature, what hope can there be for man to command his "brave state" (the state associated with day, we recall from Sonnet 12) but most inconstantly? The total leveling in the sonnet is impressive. It reminds us that the "when...

when...then" poem, as we saw with Sonnet 12, moves in its seemingly random way from example to example in part to show the unrestricted universality—indeed the absolute oneness, whether in nature or in man—of the process.

Sonnet 73, though not a "when" sonnet, has the same quatrain organization as the "when" sonnets we have examined, and again the movement is from annual ruin in nature to permanent death in man.

> That time of year thou mayst in me behold
> When yellow leaves, or none, or few, do hang
> Upon those boughs which shake against the cold,
> Bare ruin'd choirs where late the sweet birds sang.
> In me thou see'st the twilight of such day
> As after sunset fadeth in the west,
> Which by and by black night doth take away,
> Death's second self, that seals up all in rest.
> In me thou see'st the glowing of such fire
> That on the ashes of his youth doth lie,
> As the death-bed whereon it must expire,
> Consum'd with that which it was nourish'd by.
>   This thou perceiv'st, which makes thy love more strong,
>   To love that well which thou must leave ere long.

Each of the metaphors is seen as if occurring *in* the poet, but how much less metaphorical (or rather, how much more than just metaphorical, how substantive) they become: from the bare boughs, the "sweet birds' " "ruin'd choirs," with their many subtly probing implications for the aging poet, to the twilight and its bleak promise of darkness. But in this second quatrain a metaphor within metaphor carries us closer to what most concerns the poet, even as we remain with nature; for "black night," which overcomes the last of twilight, is "death's second self, that seals up all in rest." It is for the third quatrain to bring us to death's *first* self, now seen in the expiring of another fire than the sun's, the modest flame of life in its last glow:

> In me thou see'st the glowing of such fire
> That on the ashes of his youth doth lie,
> As the death-bed whereon it must expire,
> Consum'd with that which is was nourish'd by.

We can use the three-quatrain arrangement of Sonnet 60 as a grand reprise to all these poems, as the total (and totally brilliant) confounding of nature and man: the endless fluidity of tides and the immeasurable flux of human time, the beauties of human features transformed to nature's plowed and blooming field awaiting the reaper.

Like as the waves make towards the pebbled shore,
So do our minutes hasten to their end,
Each changing place with that which goes before,
In sequent toil all forwards do contend.
Nativity, once in the main of light,
Crawls to maturity, wherewith being crown'd,
Crooked eclipses 'gainst his glory fight,
And Time that gave, doth now his gift confound.
Time doth transfix the flourish set on youth
And delves the parallels in beauty's brow,
Feeds on the rarities of nature's truth,
And nothing stands but for his scythe to mow;
  And yet to times in hope my verse shall stand
  Praising thy worth, despite his cruel hand.

Once more, and perhaps with the most impressive maestro flourishes yet, the several, seemingly parallel and coordinate images fuse into one. Still the synthesis, as it is won, is subtly won, is won in the process of winning it without seeming to.

There is yet another purpose which this unmethodical method, in the hands of Shakespeare, can serve: the solving of an insoluble problem at the end of a search for a metaphorical way out. There is a throwing up of metaphors that will not quite work on the path to one that will. But again the path is less random than the projected psychology of the speaker would suggest. Sonnet 34, the second in a sequence of sonnets on guilt and innocence in the poet and his beloved friend, is a helpful example. After a quatrain that summarizes the effect upon him of his awareness of the friend's guilty act dwelt upon in Sonnet 33, the rest of the poem seeks a way for the poet to excuse an irrevocable, seemingly inexcusable act. With the friend seen in Sonnet 33 and the first quatrain of Sonnet 34 as the heavily clouded sun, the poet must in the next two quatrains reject several metaphorical ways to dissolve the offense:

'Tis not enough that through the cloud thou break,
To dry the rain on my storm-beaten face,
For no man well of such a salve can speak
That heals the wound and cures not the disgrace.
Nor can thy shame give physic to my grief;
Though thou repent, yet I have still the loss:
Th' offender's sorrow lends but weak relief
To him that bears the strong offence's cross.

From the rain as "salve" to heal the "wound" to "shame" as "physic" for "grief" to repentance as relief for the poet's burden, none will work. But the last may open the way for the poet—or rather the friend—to find an escape: "Th' offender's sorrow lends but weak relief/To him that bears the strong offence's cross." The final word, "cross," promises more than we should have expected from the negative force of these lines which in this seem to resemble those that preceded it. With this word we have not only the prospect of the poet, as innocent, taking the sin upon himself, but also the introduction of hope, of the chance for ransom, for redemption. We are ready for the couplet which fulfills that hope, if with too much abandon and too little resistance: "Ah, but those tears are pearl which thy love sheds/And they are rich and ransom all ill deeds." Finally this metaphor works the trick, if only by fiat. The "ah" suggests the sudden, surprising discovery of the specious opening that the metaphor in the couplet offers him. The poet leaps to grasp the unearned transfer from "tears" to "pearl" to "ransom" which appears to solve his problem at an unsubstantive level of language only. Are we to see him as permitting himself to be deceived by his language in his desperation to exonerate his friend? May this not be the poet's sin whose consequences he willingly accepts in the following sonnets? And is this not the "ransom" which does fulfill the expectations of "cross"? The poet has ended by joining the friend in a search to evade the consequences of sin. The parade of rejected metaphors has not after all been pointless, has finally led to one which has worked at least verbally as the poet, in grasping at it as a miraculous transformation—"tears" into "pearl"—opens himself to the ransom that he, in taking on the sin, must pay. Thus the weaving dialectic and its further unpredictable consequences.

In Sonnet 65 a more desperate search for escape from a more inescapable trap leads to a less affirmative consequence, one that keeps us still in the box. The universal and indifferent reduction to "ruin" which we witnessed in Sonnet 64 ("When I have seen by Time's fell hand defaced") has been dramatically extended to the small helplessness of the poet's love in 65. If not the mightiest and most powerful, human or natural, can retain its "state," what chance for the poet's love? The poet searches for a metaphor:

> O fearful meditation! Where, alack,
> Shall Time's best jewel from Time's chest lie hid?
> Or what strong hand can hold his swift foot back?
> Or who his spoil of beauty can forbid?

But this time the poet seems to give up: "O, none!" He seems not to have come upon his discovery. Still, however it may appear, the dialectic is not really done with. For immediately after "O, none!" the poet takes it back with "unless": "O, none! *unless* this miracle have might/That in black ink my love may still shine bright." So the impossibilities have led to affirmation after all, through the bold appeal to miracle where less daring metaphors failed. But what is this miracle ("that in black ink my love may still shine bright") except a yet more daring metaphor, one which discards the material and worldly character of the rejected metaphors for the spiritual motive of the appeal to miracle, an appeal which is given to us in the absurd, even impossible, paradox of its material reflection—the brightness of love in the blackness of ink. Thus the rejection not only of the discarded metaphors but of the very strategy of making the desperate attempt in this futile direction, in accepting Time and his material world on his own terms. And again the dialectic has tightly controlled, even where it seems to have been ignored for less planned, more emotionally spontaneous methods.

In all poetic dialectic we are surprised. In the dialectic of wit we expect eventual surprise. We feel it has been well plotted in the very tissue of the seeming logic—very like the Aristotelian peripety in drama, distinguished by its combining of surprise with probability. But in the deceptive sort I am tracing here, the apparent dreamlike association suddenly become dialectic, we are surprised to be surprised; and so is the poet, we are convinced during our own double surprise, even if this conviction only attests to the greater perfection of the illusion of artlessness.

## II

The second of the devices I shall mention of Shakespeare's deceptive dialectic, of the casual procedure turned inevitable, we have already observed repeatedly in passing. We may term it pun as argument, using *pun* most broadly as coincidence of meaning and seeing it as the ground for the self-effacing, smuggled conceit. Not only does Shakespeare use his extra dimensions of meaning where he finds them ready-made in certain words, he also creates unique semantic dimensions for his language out of his construction of a unique syntax. And the critic working with this language must create—out of its internal relations—a special glossary for it.

We have repeatedly observed Shakespeare creating the added dimensions that make a word a nucleus of meanings from which his special dialectic can emerge. Remember what happened to "brave" in Sonnet 12 as it was used, first to characterize "day" in opposition to "hideous night," then in an alliterative relation to "breed" to borrow some of breed's strength in its heroic struggle with death's night. This combination of juxtapositions gives it a union of meanings which it can carry to its use in Sonnet 15 (man's "brave state") or even to Sonnet 33 (day's "bravery"). We have seen similar phonetic borrowings of meaning in Sonnet 12 in "bier" and "beard" and in "*ch*eer'd and *ch*eck'd even by the self-same sky" in Sonnet 15. And we may find these borrowings at the two ends of the climactic line of Sonnet 64, "Ruin hath taught me thus to ruminate": "ruin," echoed in "ruminate," is *in* the rumination, becomes its cause and its subject, its formative principle, even as its continuous process keeps the rumination from ever being complete. Or in Sonnet 6 the "self-kill'd" friend who refuses marriage becomes the "self-will'd" friend, as the rhyme allows identity to arise in the verbs despite the transfer of initial consonants—and of crucial meanings.

There are also many other juxtapositions that create new accretions of meaning as Shakespeare works up his unique glossary. We can look briefly and inadequately at the complex relations between "world" and "worms" in several sonnets, especially 71.

> No longer mourn for me when I am dead
> Than you shall hear the surly sullen bell
> Give warning to the world that I am fled
> From this vile world with vilest worms to dwell.
> Nay, if you read this line, remember not
> The hand that writ it, for I love you so
> That I in your sweet thoughts would be forgot
> If thinking on me then should make you woe.
> O if, I say, you look upon this verse
> When I perhaps compounded am with clay,
> Do not so much as my poor name rehearse,
> But let your love even with my life decay,
> Lest the wise world should look into your moan
> And mock you with me after I am gone.

The poet, looking toward his death, asks his friend to be a wise enough worldling not to mourn him. But notice: he speaks, not of his death, but of his fleeing from this vile world to dwell with vilest worms, "vile world" and "vilest worms" occurring as echoes in one line. And in the couplet the friend is warned that if he insists on honoring dead love, he risks the scorn of the "*wise* world." Here once more is a remarkable collision of juxtapositions, of worms and world and their adjectives, "vile," "vilest," and "wise." The movement from the positive to the superlative degree of the adjective, "vile" to "vilest," in moving from "world" to "worms," is crucial: the worms are the furthest extension of the very tendency that makes the world "vile." The world as practical time-server that takes material truth as its total reality has the quality that is most purely represented in the activity of the worms. The vile world is a lesser worm. The friend's love, then, is to be permitted to "decay" even as the poet's "life" does; he is to feed on the body of love as the worms do on the body of life, since he is to see both bodies as suffering the identical limitation of the flesh. And the shift from the "vile world" of line 4 to the "wise world" of line 13 is the final evidence of Shakespeare's irony. For this world is wise—that is, shrewd, prudential—only as it is vile, only as it exercises those characteristics which ape the destructive perfection, the absolute cooperation with time, of the "vilest worms." The human impact Shakespeare packs into the earthy gluttony of the worms gives new force to their use elsewhere: in Sonnet 74 ("So then thou hast but lost the dregs of life,/The prey of worms, my body being dead"), in the anti-material address to the soul in 146 ("Shall worms, inheritors of this excess,/Eat up thy charge? Is this thy body's end?"), in Sonnet 6 ("...thou art much too fair/To be death's conquest and make worms thine heir"), and, by implication, in the marriage plea to the narcissistic friend in Sonnet 1 ("Pity the world, or else this glutton be,/To eat the world's due, by the grave and thee") and in the "all-eating shame" that follows in Sonnet 2. The same charges and pleas fill Sonnet 9, although wormy self-consumption is related more insistently to the "world," a word that occurs with increasing force four times.

Sonnet 9 also marks the climactic joining of the several senses given the words "use" and "unuse" as a consequence of their earlier connection with "abuse" and "usury" in Sonnets 4 and 6. In Sonnet 4 ("Then, beauteous niggard, why dost thou *abuse*/The bounteous largess.../Profitless *usurer,* why dost thou *use*/So great a sum of sums.../Thy *unus'd* beauty must be tomb'd with thee,/Which, *us'd,* lives th' executor to be"), in Sonnet 6 ("That *use* is not forbidden *usury*"), and in the climactic Sonnet 9 (beauty "kept *unus'd,* the *user* so destroys it"). In these Shakespeare creates new possibilities for punning—creating the paradoxical possibility of a use that is a saving with interest and an unuse that is a using up—by forcing the relation of "use" to "usury," of finding "use" *in* "usury." Here we move toward his creation of a new semantic out of already existing coincidences of sound and meaning. There are innumerable examples of the use of double meaning to enclose narrow dimensions within broad, all-inclusive ones. We have observed in Sonnet 64 the effective manipulation of "state" that unites the narrowly political condition with the universal human condition, which proves in the end, alas, to be no more than political. Sonnet 124 ("If my true love were but the child of state") is an even more dramatic use of this maneuver, with its shockingly paradoxical turn, in which the great affirmation is that the poet's uncontingent, unpolitical love "all alone stands hugely politic," that is, as its own body politic. I could point also to the implicit reference to biblical typology under the more obvious uses of *figure* in Sonnet 6 ("Ten times thyself were happier than thou art,/If ten of thine ten times refigur'd thee") and 106, in which the praises of historical personages become "but prophecies/Of this our time, all you prefiguring" (and we can note the alliterative echoes as well among "praises," "prophecies," "prefiguring"). I could point to the forced union of three worlds in one by the pun on *husband* in Sonnet 3 ("For where is she so fair whose unear'd womb/Disdains the tillage of thy husbandry")—the pastoral, the domestic, and the world of proper management and conservation. Only by accepting the need to act as pastoral husband encouraging nature's yield and as sexual husband in the home can he husband—that is, conserve, keep from expending—the value that is himself. But, as I have said, the examples seem innumerable.

A more clustered use of the double meaning in a single poem leads to the kind of conceit that Shakespeare manages most effectively in the *Sonnets,* what I have called the smuggled conceit. It is not, of course, the self-conscious, witty sort that calls attention to itself as the organizing principle of the poem. Rather it arises, seemingly without pressure or even guidance, under our very eyes. It grows, in the background, out of the narrow range within which the secondary meanings are contained. Sonnet 30 is a splendid, if obvious, example.

When to the sessions of sweet silent thought
I summon up remembrance of things past,
I sigh the lack of many a thing I sought,
And with old woes new wail my dear time's waste:
Then can I drown an eye, unus'd to flow,
For precious friends hid in death's dateless night,
And weep afresh love's long since cancell'd woe,
And moan the expense of many a vanish'd sight:
Than can I grieve at grievances foregone,
And heavily from woe to woe tell o'er
The sad account of fore-bemoaned moan,
Which I new pay as if not paid before.
  But if the while I think on thee, dear friend,
  All losses are restor'd and sorrows end.

As in many of the sonnets, the protestations of love come strangely trailing the language of crass finance. Such bits of soft sentiment as "sweet silent thought," sighs, wails, drowning eyes, grievings and moans, are held in the businesslike framework of "sessions," to which one is harshly summoned up, of woes that are "cancell'd," of "expense," accounts, and payments. We must be puzzled by "precious friends" or by "losses," which can be read into either world, or both; or by the telling over the "sad account," which can refer to the narrating of his sentimental tale or to the "telling" activity of the auditor. But it is just this language which has a foot in both worlds that seems to prove how thoroughly the poet has proved their union. Yet this union should be a shocking one, a yoking of elements that are surely most heterogeneous. And it is this union that aggravates the poet's losses since it emphasizes their immeasurability, their resistance to being balanced out, cancelled. It calls for nothing less than the total leap of love in the couplet.

Sonnet 87 is a more spectacular example of the effective mingling of matters of money and affection.

Farewell! thou art too dear for my possessing,
And like enough thou know'st thy estimate.
The charter of thy worth gives thee releasing;
My bonds in thee are all determinate.
For how do I hold thee but by thy granting?
And for that riches where is my deserving?
The cause of this fair gift in me is wanting,
And so my patent back again is swerving.
Thyself thou gav'st, thy own worth then not knowing,
Or me, to whom thou gav'st it, else mistaking;
So thy great gift, upon misprision growing,

> Comes home again, on better judgment making.
> Thus have I had thee, as a dream doth flatter,
> In sleep a king, but waking no such matter.

With the word "dear" in the first line, and the related "possessing" ("thou art too dear for my possessing"), the two poles of meaning that create the dialectic and the unity of the poem are sent forth. The unbroken multiplication of legal and financial terms shouts almost too loudly the poet's bitterness at having love's "dear" reduced to the merchant's "dear," to mere price. But the poem does so reduce it. Material reality will not permit love to be assigned where worths are so unequal. Only in the dream, from which the poet has been rudely awakened, can the beggar deserve a kingly love. This would appear to be an indictment of the shrewdness of the intellect, of the rational judgment of equivalence. But may we not see in this indictment a defense of the very strategy of language I have been tracing here? It is the controlled wit, under the service of the directing intelligence, that is being disdained for the seeming abandonment to an almost dreamlike associationism, with the bizarre equations and identities it produces. Why not, then, beggar and king in defiance of the world's rational denial?

## III

There are, to be sure, sonnets in the sequence which do tumble in a more orderly manner out of an initially proposed and imposed conceit, whether it be the four elements in Sonnets 44–45 ("If the dull substance of my flesh were thought") or the careful comparison of love to food in 75 ("So are you to my thoughts as food to life"). How different this latter from the juxtapositions which we witnessed earlier, which, in discovering themselves, discovered the oneness of worminess and gluttony. The predetermined wit of the more obviously planned conceits is not the strategy Shakespeare handles well—or characteristically. It is rather out of the seeming abandonment to dream that, as in dream, unexpected, even unaccounted for, identities may arise—out of the accidents and miracles of a language that has been newly, and fully, empowered, even if by a masterful control that everywhere disguises itself as chance. The meanderings of dream, with the impossible reappearances, disappearances, and unions of contradictory identities, these meanderings at last discover themselves under the firm direction of art. The dream is yielded to as it is captured, flows even as it is frozen.[3] Caprice is transformed, while indulging its capriciousness, into the inevitability of pattern. The *logos* affirms its hegemony by absorbing all that is wayward into the firm teleology of the word.

---

[3] I call attention to the extensive development of this metaphor in "The Ekphrastic Principle and the Still Movement of Poetry."

We have seen the double-reaching language of Sonnet 87 destroying the very judgment it seems intent on making, as the final lines establish the richness and beauty that, as dream, have been exploded ("Thus have I had thee as a dream doth flatter,/In sleep a king, but waking no such matter"), richness and beauty established only in the act of their vanishing, existing only in the discovery of their impossibility. We are reminded of the stubborn, if desperate, postulation of love's and poetry's miracle at the close of the universal ruin of Sonnets 64–65 (What chance? "O, none! unless this miracle have might,/That in black ink my love may still shine bright"), miracle in the teeth of rational impossibility. Without impossibility, no miracle; without reality, no awareness of the magic unreality of dream. The miracle, then, as dream, and poetry and love as the mutually enabling agents of both miracle and dream, in the teeth of the wise world's prose. We are beyond the limiting and limited world of wit—but not beyond the world of art and its breakthrough. We are rather following the words of Theseus, in the play appropriately for us called *A Midsummer Night's Dream,* who appreciates the "shaping fantasies" in which "the lunatic, the lover, and the poet/Are of imagination all compact." We follow his words to Prospero, that magician-poet-god of *The Tempest,* who transforms reality and knows of the dreamlike "stuff" of man. And we have a new sense of Prospero as Shakespeare's archetypal poet-as-maker—vision of his own best self; a new sense of Prospero's magical metaphysic as Shakespeare's magical poetic. In no one more than Shakespeare, and nowhere more than in his *Sonnets,* can we know and cherish the magic unpredictability of poetry's spell. The wisely sensitive critic can try only to pass it on as a noble contagion; he must treat it tentatively; he dare not try to capture it lest he loosen its hold on him.

# HISTORIES

# 7

# The Frame of Disorder—*Henry VI*

*J. P. Brockbank*

The four plays about the Wars of the Roses were staged fully and in sequence, probably for the first time, in 1953. The experience was arresting and moving, testifying to the continuity of our own preoccupations with those of Tudor England; here, it seemed, was yet another historical instance of anarchy owed to innocence and order won by atrocity. The three parts of *Henry VI* express the plight of individuals caught up in a cataclysmic movement of events for which responsibility is communal and historical, not personal and immediate, and they reveal the genesis out of prolonged violence of two figures representing the ultimate predicament of man as a political animal—Henry and Richard, martyr and machiavel. But one would not wish to over-stress whatever analogues there may be between the fifteenth century and the twentieth, since these might be proved quite as striking for ages other than our own. If we are now more sympathetically disposed towards Shakespeare's history plays than were the readers and audiences of

*Reprinted from* Early Shakespeare, *ed. John R. Brown and Bernard Harris,* Stratford-Upon-Avon Studies, *III (London: Edward Arnold, Ltd., 1961), pp. 73–75, 81–90, and 93–99 by permission of the author and Edward Arnold (Publishers) Ltd. A section on* Part 1 *of* Henry VI *and a portion at the beginning of the section on* Part 3 *have been omitted.*

seventy years ago, it is largely because we have more flexible ideas about the many possible forms that history might take. We are less dominated by the Positivist view that the truth is co-extensive with, and not merely consistent with, the facts. Contemporaries of Boswell-Stone were reluctant to take seriously a vision of the past that made free with the data for purposes they took to be simply dramatic. Following the lead of Richard Simpson, critics began to read Shakespeare's histories as documents of Tudor England, addressed primarily to contemporary problems and not fundamentally curious about the pastness of the past.[1] Now we are better placed to see them from the point of view represented, for instance, by R. G. Collingwood's *The Idea of History* and Herbert Butterfield's *Christianity and History,* putting a less exclusive stress on facts and looking harder at the myths and hypotheses used to interpret them—at ideas of providence, historical process, personal responsibility and the role of the hero. These are precisely the ideas that the playwright is fitted to explore and clarify, and Shakespeare's treatment of them is the most searching our literature has to offer. For Shakespeare was peculiarly sensitive to the subtle analogues between the world and the stage, between the shape of events and the shape of a play, between the relationship of historical process to individuals and that of the playwright to his characters. He tried from the beginning to meet the urgent and practical problem of finding dramatic forms and conventions that would express whatever coherence and order could be found in the "plots" of chronicle history. Where narrative and play are incompatible, it may be the record and it may be the art that is defective as an image of human life, and in the plays framed from English and Roman history it is possible to trace subtle modulations of spectacle, structure and dialogue as they seek to express and elucidate the full potential of the source material. A full account would take in *The Tempest,* which is the last of Shakespeare's plays to be made out of historical documents and which has much to do with the rule of providence over the political activities of man. But from these early plays alone there is much to be learned about the vision and technique of historical drama, and these are the plays that are submitted most rigorously to the test of allegiance to historical record.

We might begin by taking a famous passage of Nashe as the earliest surviving critical comment on *Part 1*:[2]

> How would it have joyed brave *Talbot* (the terror of the French) to think that after he had lyne two hundred yeares in his Tombe, hee should triumphe againe on the Stage, and have his bones new embalmed with the teares of ten thousand spectators at least, (at severall times) who, in the Tragedian that represents his person, imagine they behold him fresh bleeding.

---

[1] Richard Simpson, 'The Politics of Shakespeare's History Plays', in *Trans. New Sh. Soc.* (1874). A similar approach is made by L. B. Campbell.

[2] Quoted in E. K. Chambers, *Shakespeare* (1930), II, p. 188.

This, primarily, is the ritual experience Shakespeare sought and won. He transposed the past of the tombs, the "rusty brass" and the "worm-eaten books" into living spectacle. Whatever else must be said about all three plays, they keep this quality of epic mime and with it an elementary power to move large audiences. There is, too, something in Nashe's glance at those early performances that chimes with Coleridge's observation that "in order that a drama may be properly historical, it is necessary that it should be the history of the people to whom it is addressed."[3] Shakespeare's early histories are addressed primarily to the audience's heroic sense of community, to its readiness to belong to an England represented by its court and its army, to its eagerness to enjoy a public show celebrating the continuing history of its prestige and power. This does not mean, however, that we must surrender these early plays to Joyce's remark that Shakespeare's "pageants, the histories, sail full-bellied on a tide of Mafeking enthusiasm." In the more mature plays of *Henry IV* the heroic sense of community will be challenged by the unheroic—by that range of allegiances which binds us less to authority and the King than to each other and to Falstaff; and the death of Hotspur is a more complicated theatrical experience than that of Talbot in Nashe's description. But the early histories too express stresses and ironies, complexities and intricate perspectives beyond the reach of the condescensions usually allowed them. . . .

[An analysis of *Part 1* is here omitted.]

*Part 2: the Sacrifice of Gloster and the Dissolution of Law*

There is much in *Part 2* to remind us that we are witnessing the education of a tragic playwright. Shakespeare assimilates and puts to the test theological, political and moral outlooks which, however ugly and pitiless, seem to meet with unsentimental honesty the recorded facts of human experience. *Part 1* could not end in the manner of an heroic tragedy, for the history confronted Shakespeare with the fact that society somehow survives the deaths of its heroes and the conditions for its survival must go on being renewed—a point that tells again in *Julius Caesar. Part 1* concludes by establishing the minimal and provisional terms of survival—the death of Joan and the marriage bargain, but the historical facts allow no revival in *Part 2* of the austere, soldierly virtues that supply the moral positives of the first part—Talbot will be displaced by Gloster.

From one point of view the second and third plays share the same structural frame, supplied by Holinshed in passages such as this:

> But most of all it would seeme, that God was displeased with this marriage: for after the confirmation thereof, the kings freends fell from him, both in

[3] T. M. Raysor (ed.), *Coleridge's Shakespeare Criticism* (1930) I, p. 138.

> England and in France, the lords of his realme fell at division, and the commons rebelled in such sort, that finallie after manie fields foughten, and manie thousands of men slaine, the king at length was deposed, and his sonne killed, and this queene sent home againe, with as much miserie and sorrow as she was received with pompe and triumphe: such is the instabilitie of worldlie felicitie, and so wavering is false flattering fortune. Which mutation and change of the better for the worse could not but nettle and sting hir with pensiveness, yea and any other person whatsoever, that having beene in good estate, falleth into the contrarie. (*Hol.,* p. 208)

In their unabashed drift from God's displeasure to the waverings of fortune Holinshed's pieties are characteristic of chronicle theology. The subtler medieval distinctions between the will of God and the waywardness of Fortune are lost, but the dominant ideas remain, and they are crucial to an understanding of Shakespeare's tetralogy, and more particularly, of the role of Queen Margaret. The chronicle is enlisting Old Testament theology to rationalize the processes of history: when the land is sinful, God's judgment recoils upon it, and evil must be atoned by blood sacrifice. Shakespeare makes fullest use of Margaret to exemplify this moral order; through the span of the plays she is in turn its agent, victim and oracle. It is in *Richard III* that Shakespeare's ironic questioning of the chronicle providence is most telling, when Margaret, disengaged from the action but brought to the court in the teeth of historical fact, is made the malignant prophetess of God's displeasure, and Clarence is allowed to protest with humane eloquence against the theology of his murderers (I, iv, 171–265). In the *Henry VI* plays the chronicle theology is exposed to a different kind of test—that of the chronicle's own political ideology.

The chronicles were more ready to accept the tragic-religious solution of social disorder as a past and finished process than as an omnipresent law. They wrote in a tradition which had quietly assimilated the mundane, realistic attitudes for which Machiavelli was to become the most persuasive apologist; and whenever they write with an eye on the prospect of Tudor security, they show themselves sympathetic to the "machiavellian" solution—stability imposed by the strong authority. Hence their strictures on the "overmuch mildness" of a Henry found "too soft for governor of a kingdom," and hence the coolness with which they recognize the peace and prosperity of the later part of Edward IV's reign,[4] which owed more to the King's military ability and popularity (however limited) with nobility and commons, than to his integrity as Rightful King and Servant of God. Shakespeare's most decisive criticism of the chronicle is his virtual suppression of the temporary recovery under Edward, thus making his moral of peace at the end of *Richard III* distinctly less "machiavellian" than it appears in Holinshed—peace returns

[4] Hall's titles pass from the "troublesome season" of Henry VI to the "prosperous reign" of Edward IV. Shakespeare's judgment of Edward is harsher than that of any of the chroniclers.

by God's ordinance only when the forces of evil are quite expended. The kind of dramatic thinking about history that makes Shakespeare's plays does not prove hospitable to the kind of uncritical good sense that allows the chroniclers to shift from one scale of values to another. In *Henry VI* the sacrificial idea, which makes catastrophe a consequence of sin, is sharply challenged by the "machiavellian" idea that makes it a consequence of weakness.

While this range of problems is entertained in *Part 2* about the plight of the King himself, the unique form of the play is yielded by the martyrdom of Gloster. The play climbs to one crisis—a central point in the third act where the killing of Gloster calls out the strongest statement of the moral-political positives; and it falls to a second—where the battle of St. Albans occasions the most powerful poetry of negation.

It opens with a "Flourish of Trumpets: Then Hoboyes" announcing Margaret with chronicled "pompe and triumph," but almost at once, as he lets the paper fall and addresses his "peroration with such circumstance" to the assembled peers, it is Gloster who dominates the theatre, assuming his representative and symbolic role. Like Gaunt in *Richard II,* he recollects the chivalry of the past and epitomizes a political wisdom alienated in the dramatic "present." But there is none of the spiritual and physical malaise that complicates the figure of Gaunt, no sterility or decay. Gaunt's prophecy is the "ague's privilege"—his approaching death calls out his honesty; but Gloster is vigorous and defiant, and his honesty brings about his death. If the Gaunt study is the more penetrating exploration of the relation of moral strength to political impotence, this version of Gloster is the shrewder study of heroic virtue.

Holinshed says that Gloster's praise should be undertaken by writers of "large discourse," and notes (as he takes over the Tudor legend) the "ornaments of his mind," his "feats of chivalry," "gravity in counsell" and "soundness of policy" (*Hol.,* p. 211; *Stone,* pp. 250, 265). Together with his magnanimity Holinshed finds a love of the commons and a devotion to the public good. With so strong a lead from the chronicle Shakespeare makes Gloster's qualities both personal and symbolic. In the first two acts he comes to stand for the rule of law and for the integrity of nobility and commons—the conditions of social order that cease to prevail the moment he is murdered. Holinshed is outspoken about the destruction of the rule of law: "while the one partie sought to destroie the other, all care of the common-wealth was set aside, and justice and equitie clearelie exiled" (*Hol.,* p. 237). But his moral is untied to any single incident, and Shakespeare gives it greater dramatic force by linking it specifically with the destiny of Gloster. The chronicle supplied hint enough:

> Suerlie the duke, verie well learned in the law civill, detesting malefactors, and punishing offenses in severitie of justice, gat him hatred of such as

> feared condigne reward for their wicked dooings. And although the duke sufficientlie answered to all things against him objected; yet, because his death was determined, his wisedome and innocencie nothing availed.
>
> (*Hol.*, p. 211; *Stone*, pp. 250, 265)

In the chronicle Gloster's learning in civil law takes the form of a wearisome passion for litigation. In the play he is first the severe executor of Justice and then its patient, vicarious victim.

As Protector he prescribes the judicial combat between Horner and his prentice, and replaces York by Somerset in France: "This is the Law, and this Duke Humfreyes doom" (I, iii, 208). When Eleanor is banished he again speaks the formal language of his office: "the Law thou seest hath judged thee, I cannot justifie whom the Law condemnes" (II, iii, 16). Too much in this manner would have been wearing, but Shakespeare traces in Gloster the humane impulses from which and for which the Law should speak. His practical genius for improvising justice is exemplified in the mock-miracle of St. Albans (II, i), it delights the dramatic townsmen as much as the theatre audience, making Humphrey the shrewd, popular hero respected and "beloved of the commons." The King's piety gives place to laughter, displaying his curiously mixed qualities of ingenuousness and insight; and the scene concludes with an elegant exchange of sarcasms, a timely reminder that Suffolk and Beaufort are jealous of Gloster's public virtues.

Shakespeare makes less use in *Part 2* of the heraldic and pageant devices which accent the pattern of *Part 1,* and fuller use of the specifically dramatic techniques of the Morality-play and English Seneca. Borrowing as much of the chronicle language as he can, he illuminates the historical event by casting it into a Morality perspective:

> Ah, gracious lord, these days are dangerous:
> Virtue is choked with foul ambition
> And charity chased hence by rancour's hand;
> Foul subornation is predominant
> And equity exiled your highness' land. (III, i, 142)

"Justice and equitie clearelie exiled," says Holinshed (p. 237). But the Morality abstractions are in their turn tempered by the immediate interest in people that Shakespeare learned from his attempts to make historical facts dramatically convincing.

The private man is never for long masked by the public figure. Gloster speaks of his condemned Duchess in tones admirably poised between personal feeling and the decorum of his office (II, i, 185), and he speaks from his office unequivocally when she is led from the court (II, iii, 16). But as soon as she is gone, his eyes "full of teares," he asks the King's permission to leave, and for the first time we learn that Shakespeare's Gloster (not the chroniclers') is an old man; the personal pathos is heightened, and we are reminded that honour is the prerogative of a fading generation. When he next appears, as looker-on at Eleanor's penance, the scene enlarges into a mutability threnody, including the conventional *Mirror for Magistrates* image of summer giving place to barren winter, and the chronicle sentiment about the irony of personal misfortune—"To think upon my pomp, shall be my hell" (II, iv, 41). But it remains an event in the London streets. The picture of Eleanor's humiliation (however deserved) confesses the cruelty of,

> The abject people gazing on thy face,
> With envious looks, laughing at thy shame. (II, iv, 11)

The intensely passive philosophy of Gloster meeting the frustrated malice of his Duchess foreshadows the second scene of *Richard II,* but Gaunt puts jaded faith in the principle of non-resistance to an anointed king, while Gloster's more naïve faith is in the integrity of the law: "I must offend, before I be attainted" (II, iv, 59). His trial scene (III, i) takes on a symbolic quality. Henry's reaction to it, undescribed in the chronicles, is used in the play to disclose the natural sympathy between the King's impotent saintliness and Gloster's political and personal integrity:

> Ah, uncle Humphrey! in thy face I see
> The map of honour, truth, and loyalty...
> And as the butcher takes away the calf,
> And binds the wretch and beats it when it strays,
> Bearing it to the bloody slaughter-house;
> Even so remorseless have they borne him hence. (III, i, 202)

Gloster's murder is a piece of politic butchery at the centre of the "plotted tragedy" of the conspirators who are credited with a perverse skill in making an unnatural offence taste of expediency and practical wisdom: "But yet we want a Colour for his death," and "'Tis meet he be condemned by course of Law" (III, i, 234).

We are not made witnesses to the actual murder, but Gloster's strangled body is exhibited in a sort of verbal close-up, a remarkable passage, which throws an unusual stress on physical horror (III, ii, 160 ff.). By this device a frightening spectacular force is given to the dominant historical and tragic idea of the play. By a staged metaphor now, "Virtue is choked with foul ambition," and the play's mime displays the historical cause-and-effect, by which the murder of Gloster issues in the Cade rebellion. The strangled body lies on the stage while the commons "like an angry hive of bees" beat upon the doors.

But this death, as Gloster says himself, is but the prologue to the plotted tragedy. Shakespeare is exposing a period of English history when atrocities became part of the routine of public life and stayed so for some twenty years.

Hence his knowledge, if not experience, of the arts of English Seneca becomes relevant to his own art as dramatic historian. It is perhaps no accident that at this point of the narrative Holinshed refers us to "maister Foxe's book of acts and monuments" (*Hol.*, p. 212). No reader of Foxe could be easily startled by the *Thyestes*, the *Troades*, or *Titus Andronicus*. And in the central acts of *Part 2* we can observe the confluence of the Senecal dramatic tradition, with its ruthless retributive morality, and the Christian (or Hebraic) cult of *Vindicta Dei*. These acts present not only what Foxe calls "the cruel death or martyrdom of the Good Duke of Gloccster" but also "the judgement of God upon them which persecuted the Duke" (*Foxe* (1583), p. 706). But Shakespeare is not uncritical of the myth behind the grim theocratic drama that features the deaths of Suffolk and Winchester. Although he allows some of his characters to enjoy a complacent relish in witnessing or executing the interventions of the wrath of God, the audience is not allowed to share it. All the acts of retribution in this play and the next are invested in an atmosphere of evil—the images sickening and grotesque:

> And thou that smiledst at good Duke Humphrey's death
> Against the senseless winds shall grin in vain. (IV, i, 76)

Suffolk's death is an act of lynch law, and one of several similar happenings which is at once a satisfying act of retribution and therefore a recognition of the chronicle "Providence"; and "a barbarous and bloody spectacle" (IV, i, 174) and therefore a moral and aesthetic challenge to the validity of that Providence. In his presentation of the Cardinal's death (III, iii), however, and in his insinuations of the causal chain of prophecy, omen, curse, imprecation and dream, Shakespeare does stage the pitiless pageant of Holinshed and Foxe—*Vindicta Dei* works through revenge figures, through the worm of conscience (as plastic as a tape-worm) and through "chance" contingencies. But so much (were it not for the tightness of the organization) might have been within the range of Peele or Greene. Shakespeare's play is distinguished by its understanding of the tragic rhythm of political history.

At first glance it might seem that Shakespeare's treatment of the Cade rebels is less sympathetic than Holinshed's. The chronicle Cade is "of goodlie stature and right pregnant wit"; his "fair promises of reformation" and his "Complaint of the Commons of Kent" are responsible and sensible (*Hol.*, p. 222); and his tactics at the start are admirably humane. Why then the comic but bloody spectacle of the fourth act of *Part 2*? Brents Stirling[5] suggests that Shakespeare was aligning himself with those who most severely judged the rioting Brownists and Anabaptists of his own day, and claims a specific parallel between the dramatic Cade and Hacket, a riot leader convicted in 1591. But Hacket was a far grosser fanatic than the Cade of the

---

[5] *The Populace in Shakespeare* (1949), pp. 101 ff.

play (out of spiritual zeal he bit off a man's nose and swallowed it), and in any case there is evidence that Shakespeare deliberately avoided giving any religious savour to the rebellion; it might have been quite otherwise had he delayed the Cardinal's death for a scene or two. It has been said too that Shakespeare coarsened his stage mobs from personal antipathy, and no doubt he had an eye for outrages in the London streets, a nose for the sour breath of the plebeians and an ear for riotous chop-logic; but at no point in any play do they pervert Shakespeare's objectivity of judgment or his rich human sympathies.

To understand the Cade scenes we must recognize that Shakespeare distorts Holinshed's account of the rebellion itself merely in order to emphasize its place in a larger and more significant movement of historical cause and effect. The rebellion is offered as an evil consequence of misrule, specifically of the misrule of Suffolk. The fuse is touched early, when Suffolk tears the petitions of the innocent, conscientious citizens (I, iii, 37). But the petitioners, voicing their bewildered, nervous protests, the apprentices of the Peter Thump scenes, and the crowd at St. Albans, while they make up the "populace" are not yet the "mob." The mob emerges at the moment of Gloster's death, when the people are compelled, through lack of a law-giver, through the total breakdown of the constitutional rule of order, to take the law into their own hands. The "populace" with a just grievance is by the exercise of violence transformed into the "mob," executors of lynch law. At first they are free from a "stubborn opposite intent" (III, ii, 251), but finally, "thirsting after prey" (IV, iv, 51), they are capable of a full range of atrocities.

The violence is not merely self-generated; all that York stands for in the way of destructive political purpose is right behind the reprisals of Smithfield. Nor are the reprisals quite arbitrary. Since Gloster is the dramatic symbol of regular administration of the law, and unquestioning faith in its authority, it is no accident that Shakespeare focused the iconoclasm of the rioters upon the agents and monuments of the civil law. To do so he turned back in the chronicle to the Tyler rebellion in the reign of *Richard II* and borrowed just those touches which furthered his purpose—the killing of the lawyers, the destruction of the Savoy and the Inns of Court, and the burning of the records of the realm.[6] It is significant too that Lord Say, the "treasurer of England" in 1450, is merged with the Lord Chief Justice beheaded by Tyler in 1381; his stage martyrdom (IV, vii) is that of a humane judge—thus obliquely repeating the point about Gloster.

Holinshed tells how the rising was subdued by Canterbury and Winchester bringing to Southwark a pardon from the King (*Hol.*, p. 226; *Stone*, p. 280). In the play the bishops figure only momentarily, in a soft-

---

[6] See Stone, 271, 277–8, for the relevant chronicle passages.

hearted plan of Henry's (V, iv, 9), and Shakespeare abstains from giving to Lord Say the role he allows Sir Thomas in comparable circumstances in *Sir Thomas More,* quietening the people by authoritative eloquence (II, iv, 62–177). Although Lord Say has a comparable dignity,

> The trust I have is in mine innocence,
> And therefore am I bold and resolute, (IV, iv, 59)

he shares the vulnerability of Gloster as well as his integrity, and his head soon dances on a pole. Stafford tries abuse (IV, ii, 117), but that fails too, and it is left to Buckingham and Clifford to restore their version of "order" (IV, viii). In place of the leisured approach of two prelates, gathering exhausted citizens about them, Shakespeare offers the murderous rabblement, their full cry silenced by a trumpet and by the appearance of two leading soldiers with their body-guards. The pardon, garbled by Buckingham (IV, viii, 8), is not made a factor in the peace. Clifford steps in with a sharply different appeal, invocating, as Shakespeare puts it elsewhere, the ghost of Henry V. Cade brutally reminds the people that they have still to recover their "ancient freedom," but his brand of demagoguery is surpassed by the fine irrelevance of Clifford's patriotic exhortation—as from soldier to soldiers, from one Englishman to another. The oratory is not endorsed by the situation in the play (no French invasion threatens), but its effect is to canalize destructive energy along a track less threatening to the Nobles of England—profitable indeed, and as Shakespeare shows in *Henry V,* even glorious in its own way. But *Henry V* touches the heroic through its setting of a tiny group of English against terrible odds; here the mob yell of "A Clifford! A Clifford! We'll follow the King and Clifford" (IV, viii, 53), is ironically close in spirit to the "Kill and knock down" of the scene's opening. The true interpretation of these events is voiced by the only figure on the stage who is not implicated any longer, in Cade's: "Was ever feather so lightly blown to and fro, as this multitude? The name of Henry the Fifth hales them to an hundred mischiefs and makes them leave me desolate" (IV, viii, 54). Cade is seen for what he is, but when he is chased off stage by his followers, there is a strong impression that he is victimized. The blood-lust of the mob has been diverted but not sublimated.

In accents reminiscent of his apostrophe on Horner's death (II, iii, 99), Henry acknowledges the gruesome gift of Cade's head: "The head of *Cade*? Great God, how just art thou?" (V, i, 68). There is this recognition that God's spirit showed itself in the dispersal of the rebels, not in the tide of rebellion; in the killing of Cade, not in his subornation. But Henry's outlook is of a piece with his isolation and impotence. Cade's death is not much more than a marginal note (IV, x); it occurs when he is alone and starving and cannot have the central significance that Henry's piety attributes to it. Iden, the yeoman in the garden and Cade's killer, is (as E. M. W. Tillyard puts it) a "symbol of degree," one who "seeks not to wax great by others' waning"; but he is a formal symbol, mechanically put together out of the chronicle, and can only appear as a "representative figure" to King Henry himself in a scene which Shakespeare is careful not to put last. As it is, the silence of the stage garden is not allowed to still the audience's memory of the clamour of Southwark; the internecine violence of the rebellion is carried through, across the recessed interludes, to the battlefield of St. Albans, where Clifford himself speaks the most terrible of Shakespeare's pronouncements about war (V, ii, 31 ff.).

Thus the moral of the last part of the play is not the simple-minded one of the *Mirror for Magistrates* which tells "How Jack Cade traitorously rebelling against his King, was for his treasons and cruel doings worthily punished."[7] It is assimilated into a firm comprehensive structure, a version of political and historical tragedy that will serve later as the ground of *Julius Caesar*—another play which moves through the plotting and execution of an assassination, through the generation of lynch-law in the streets, to the deflection of that violence into civil war.

*Part 3 and the Shape of Anarchy*

. . . For the greater part of the third play Shakespeare is content to follow Holinshed in making his characters public masks, without intimately felt life, and therefore hardly seeming responsible for what they do. He tightens the sequence of atrocities, telescopes time, and eliminates all rituals of government, until the stage action and reaction appear yet more savagely mechanical than in the chronicle. So long as the characterization is neutral the first tetralogy displays a barbarous providence ruling murderous automatons whose reactions are predictable in terms of certain quasi-Hobbesian assumptions about human nature: when argument fails men resort to force; when an oath is inconvenient they break it; their power challenged, they retort with violence; their power subdued they resort to lies, murder or suicide; their honour impugned, they look for revenge; their enemies at their mercy, they torture and kill them; and if a clash of loyalties occurs they resolve it in the interest of their own survival. Such might be the vision of the play's pantomime, but its dimensions are not confined to its pantomime and to its shallower rhetoric. The anarchic, egocentric impulses are not presented as the inescapable laws of human nature; they are at most manifestations of forces that automatically take over when the constraints of government are withheld. Law and order cease to prevail when men cease to believe in them, and the process by which this comes about is explored in the play's dominant characters.

---

7 *Mirror,* ed. L. B. Campbell (1938), p. 171.

The figures of Clifford and York who, in *Part 2,* personalize two kinds of anarchic scepticism—the soldier's nihilism and the politician's realism—are displaced in *Part 3* by the more significant contrast between Richard of Gloster and King Henry. With obvious propriety these are chosen to characterize the moral tensions which give meaning to the deep chaos of the last phase of the reign. But the crimes of the Roses Wars are so multiple and their agents so numerous, that Shakespeare could not attempt, even if at this early date it were within his power, the comprehensively intimate exploration of evil he undertakes in *Macbeth,* and he allows himself only that measure of intimate soliloquy and address which will accord with the conventions of historical pageant.

In the first two plays the chronicle myth of a King absurdly and irrelevantly virtuous can just about pass muster, and in the first scene of *Part 3,* Henry's virtue is still associated with impotence; his war of "frowns, words, and threats" is disarmed by his readiness to concede the Yorkist claims, by the wry defection of Exeter (unwarranted by the history), and by the Robin Hood trickery of Warwick; his conscience-stricken asides carry as little conviction as his military posturing, and one feels the *gaucherie* is the playwright's as well as the character's. In the next phase, however, Shakespeare's tragic art wins distinction from the ferocity of the material and Henry assumes a stature outside the chronicle compass.

Both the finer qualities of Henry's virtue and the intensity of Richard of Gloster's virulence spring from Shakespeare's treatment of the Battle of Wakefield. Conventional heroic ideals cannot survive the battle which turns on two blasphemies of chivalry—the killing of the prince and the degradation of the mock-king. Clifford's slaughter of Rutland (I, iii), in calculated contempt of the Priest and the law of arms, is a repudiation of the myth that expects from every "gentleman" in battle the virtues of the lion. The values apt to an heroic battle play are displaced by those prevailing in parts of English Seneca; in Heywood's *Thyestes,* for example, where "ire thinks nought unlawful to be done," "Babes be murdered ill" and "bloodshed lies the land about" (I, i, 79–89). Shakespeare gives the revenge motive a great political significance by relating it to the dynastic feud for which Clifford is not alone responsible.

Anarchism, Shakespeare had learned from the Cade scenes, is more dramatic when it is iconoclastic, and the next Wakefield outrage, the paper crowning (I, iv), mutilates the idols of Knighthood, Kingship, Womanhood and Fatherhood. In making a ritual of the atrocity Shakespeare imitates the history—the scene is a formal set-piece because it was so staged by its historical performers. Holinshed tells how the Lancastrians made obeisance and cried, "Haile, king without rule"—"as the Jewes did unto Christ" (*Hol.* p. 269; *Stone,* p. 299). Although Shakespeare suppresses the open blasphemy, he keeps the crucifixion parallel with the line, "Now looks he like a King"

(I, iv, 96), and, more significantly, by combining the mockery reported in one of a choice of chronicle accounts with the paper-coronation in another (*Hol.,* p. 268; *Stone,* p. 299). He takes little liberty with the chronicle, moreover, when he makes the stage-managed historical ceremony into an ordered, antiphonal combat of words, with Northumberland presiding, as it were, in the rhetorical lists. In spite of the controlling formality the language moves on several planes between gnomic generalization, " 'Tis government that makes them seem divine, The want thereof makes thee abnominable" (I, iv, 132); stylized feeling, "Oh tiger's heart wrapt in a woman's hide! How could'st thou drain the life-blood of the child" (I, iv, 137); plain, personal pathos, "This cloth thou dip'dst in blood of my sweet boy" (I, iv, 157); and colloquial venom, "And where's that valiant crook-back prodigy, Dicky, your boy, that with his grumbling voice Was wont to cheer his dad in mutinies?" In the blinding scene of *King Lear* the same changes will be rung in a richer peal, but there is enough in the Wakefield scene's counterpoint of reflection and feeling to tax the resources of its actors.

Henry is not made witness to the event. He is allowed the dignity of total isolation, and when he comes to the stage molehill at Towton (II, v), it is to speak the most moving of Shakespeare's comments on the civil wars. Shakespeare is less fully engaged when he writes about the objectives of the battle as seen by the participants than by its futility as it appears to a suffering observer. Hall had felt a similar need to withdraw into reflection:

> This conflict was in maner unnaturall, for in it the sonne fought agaynst the father, the brother agaynst the brother, the Nephew agaynst the Uncle, and the tenaunt agaynst hys Lorde, which slaughter did sore and much weaken the puyssance of this realme. (1548/1809, p. 256)

In *Gorboduc* and in Daniel's *Civil Wars* the commonplace is retailed with a complacent omniscience damaging to living language.[8] But by attributing it to the King in the course of battle Shakespeare is able to quicken it with personal feeling; beneath the ceremonious surface we again sense the pulse and surge of events.

The hint for the opening lines is one of Hall's "ebb and flow of battle" clichés (*Stone,* p. 306), but Shakespeare insinuates rarer images of the peaceful, symmetrical rhythms of nature—"the morning's war" and "the shepheard blowing of his nails," and after touching the conflicts inherent in nature, arrests the movement of battle in that of the sea—"the equal poise of this fell war." A glance at the humour and pathos of Henry's isolation (Margaret and Clifford have chid him from the battle), with a touch of wry exhaustion ("Would I were dead, if God's good will were so"), offers assur-

[8] The peroration of *Gorboduc* and the first stanza of *The Civil Wars.*

ance of Shakespeare's gift for "re-living the past," and the sequent lines of exquisite pastoral seem to recreate the convention out of the kind of human experience which underlies it. An alarum returns us to the battle and to a glimpse of its victims in another statuesque mirror-scene in which blood and pallor are made heraldic (II, v, 97 ff.). Once again the feeling for the past is the cathedral-pavement sort, not the chronicle sort; it is at once a refreshing and a potentially devitalizing mood, and after a hundred and twenty lines Shakespeare pulls us out of it and lets the pantomime get under way again.

The authority of Henry's commentary on Towton is sufficiently memorable to help vindicate the innocence of the speech he makes before the keepers arrest him: "My pity hath been balm to heal their wounds. My mildness hath allay'd their swelling griefs, My mercy dry'd their water-flowing tears" (IV, viii, 41 ff.). From this and a few other passages in the plays it would be possible to present Henry as the centre of a moral parable whose lineaments are traced in Thomas Elyot's *The Governour.* The King, says Elyot, must be merciful, but too much *Clementia* is a sickness of mind; as soon as any offend him the King should "immediately strike him with his most terrible dart of vengeance." But the occasions when Henry seems guilty of an excess of virtue are rare, and he is at his most impressive when he is martyred in his last scene of *Part 3,* not when he tries to throw his weight about in the first. The Wakefield battle once fought, moreover, "the terrible dart of vengeance" is lost to the armoury of virtue. Henry's bemused and disappointed faith in the political efficacy of mercy, pity, peace and love does not deserve the editorial mockery it has received—"characteristically effeminate" and "smug complacency."[9] Henry's virtue may be defective but Shakespeare commands from his audience a full reverence for it when, at the moment of his extermination, the King confronts his ultimate antagonist, Richard of Gloster.

Richard is introduced as York's heroic soldier son, but in his first characteristic speech of length (II, i, 79 ff.) he becomes the bitter, unchivalrous avenger—a reaction to the Messenger's report of Wakefield which seems instinctive and inevitable. But Richard not only reacts to events (all the barons do that) he also becomes the conscious embodiment of all the drives—moral, intellectual and physical—that elsewhere show themselves only in the puppetry. Translating into theatrical terms, we might say that when he takes the stage for his first exercise of the soliloquy-prerogative he inherits from York (at the end of III, ii), his language shows him capable of playing the parts of York, Clifford, Edward, Margaret or Warwick. All their energies are made articulate: the doggedness of York "that reaches at moon" and the same eye for the glitter of the Marlovian crown; the dedication to evil

[9] See notes to IV, viii, 38–50 in Hart's Arden and Wilson's New Cambridge Editions.

which characterizes Clifford; the prurience of Edward; the decorated and ruthless rhetoric of Margaret; and Warwick's gifts of king-maker, resolute "to command, to check, to overbear." Shakespeare has him use the fantastic lore about his birth to admirable effect: it strengthens the impression of blasphemy against love and fertility, makes deformity license depravity and, most important, allegorizes the birth of a political monster in the present by recalling that of a physical monster in the past, "like to a chaos or an unlick'd bear-whelp." But it is not all specifically birth-imagery—about Richard having teeth and the dogs howling. The sense of violent struggle, of unnatural energies breaking free, is best caught in lines that are not explicitly about birth at all:

> And I—like one lost in a thorny wood,
> That rends the thorns and is rent with the thorns,
> Seeking a way and straying from the way;
> Not knowing how to find the open air,
> But toiling desperately to find it out—
> Torment myself to catch the English crown:
> And from that torment I will free myself,
> Or hew my way out with a bloody axe. (III, ii, 174)

It is from the kennel of England's womb that this hell-hound is to bite itself free. At the end of the soliloquy Richard promises the audience a performance more entertaining than any heroic fantasy or medieval Trojan legend; he will outplay all politic dissemblers, "add colours to the camelion," "change shapes with Proteus" and "set the *murtherous* Machivill to school." The ground is prepared for *Richard III*, where for three acts the comic idiom will dominate the tragic, with politics a kings' game best played by cunning actors.

But the continuity with the mood of *Richard III* is deliberately fractured and the tragic mode made to dominate the comic in the scene of Henry's death. The King opposes Richard's tongue and sword with a moral force that Shakespeare makes all but transcendent and the "scene of death" that "Roscius"—the actor and devil Richard—performs at last, comes near to a tragic consummation. Yet the qualifications "all but" and "comes near" are, after all, necessary. The brute facts of history will not allow a satisfying tragic outcome; Shakespeare cannot pretend that the martyrdom of an innocent king appeased the appetite of providence or exhausted the sophisticated savagery that Richard stands for.

Nor can Hall's dynastic myth be enlisted to reassure us that all will be well when the White Rose is wedded to the Red—that will only be possible at the end of *Richard III* when, in a kind of postscript to the complete tetralogy, Richmond will step into the Elizabethan present and address an audience sufficiently remote from Henry's reign. As it is, the plays of *Henry VI* are not, as it were, haunted by the ghost of Richard II, and the catastrophes of the civil wars are not laid to Bolingbroke's charge; the catastrophic virtue of Henry and the catastrophic evil of Richard are not an inescapable inheritance from the distant past but are generated by the happenings we are made to witness.

The questioning of the ways of God and the roles of good and evil in English history will be re-opened in *Richard III*, but in the interim *Part 3* ends, as tragedies remotely derived from fertility rites of course should, with some elaborate imagery of autumn reaping. It is fitting that Richard should be standing by to blast the harvest and to boast himself a Judas.

# 8

# Satiety and Conscience: Aspects of *Richard III*

*Robert B. Heilman*

Perhaps one would do best to think of Richard III as simply another machiavel, under Shakespeare's direction most amply fulfilling the role long before assigned him by the chroniclers. Though an easy way of placing him, it would not be an erroneous start. One could then seek out his individuality by endeavoring to distinguish him from other products of the same mould—Aaron, Iago, Edmund. If Richard does not quite equal Aaron in pure ferocity, he also lacks the touches of parental feeling in Aaron; if he has something of Iago's ability to charm, he does not have, as an inaugural motive, Iago's single-minded destructiveness; if he shares Edmund's resentment at disabilities dating from birth, nevertheless his sense of being "cheated. . . by dissembling nature" is in contrast with Edmund's embracing Nature as "my goddess." Such comparisons would make clear that one may be more or less a machiavel, this or that kind of machiavel.

The pursuit of Richard, however, takes us outside the familiar category. For Richard has resemblances to the great figure of Macbeth: he snatches a throne that brings no certainty or contentment, he recklessly disposes of other claimants in a reign of terror springing from and yet increasing his own

*Reprinted from* Antioch Review, *XXIV (1964) No. 1, pp. 57–73 by permission of the publisher.*

insecurity, and he dies in a battle furiously fought. Hence we see that he might have been, not a diamond-like scoundrel of extraordinary hardness and sparkle, but a tragic hero. In the dozen or so years between *Richard III* and *Macbeth* Shakespeare learned to regard self-enthronement by murder, not simply as a bloody melodrama of unmixed evil, but as the tragedy of a man who chooses evil instead of good. In that sense Richard III seems like a preparatory sketch for a major portrait. Yet the familiar comparison has a special utility: in Macbeth Shakespeare catches a powerful aspiration to be like Richard III.

Macbeth craves, struggles to escape knowing what he is and does, and he becomes increasingly addicted to the narcotic of action. Could he be like Richard, he would be, if not a happy man, at least a less painfully torn man. It took Shakespeare some years to work into and develop fully the drama of anguished self-confrontation. In the earlier tragedies the probing or facing of self does not become an important action; then in the major tragedies self-examination and self-understanding assume major dramatic importance. They are treated not only with utmost variety but with a sense that beneath the variety there is one unvarying constant: all the tragic heroes resist self-knowledge. This resistance is at the heart of *Macbeth*; Macbeth is the one protagonist who knows the moral truth at the beginning and has to spend all the rest of his life trying not to know it. So he takes us back to Richard, who manages not to know without trying. Either Richard lacks moral self-knowledge or, when he uses a vocabulary that implies such knowledge, he seems immune to the pain and shock that afflict the knower. Such a character might be the creation of a not-yet-mature artist who cannot depict evil without creating an all-black devil, or on the other hand of a disillusioned older man taught by experience to think human depravity unlimited. If we did not know that the play is early, we could, on some grounds, think of it as late. The fact is that *Richard III* has in it something more than youthful simplicity; in his first few years of writing Shakespeare gives some novel turns to melodramatic character.

The problem is: what else is there in Richard besides the murderous revengefulness of a bully boy come to manhood? We take it for granted that if there is to be a human significance beyond the pathological, the basic need is the sentience of one who does, or can, or must struggle not to, see himself in the perspective of moral order; without this we have merely a monster of rather limited interest. Richard has something that looks like this sentience: a factual kind of self-knowledge. His soliloquy that opens the play is full of it—"rudely stamp'd," "want love's majesty," "deform'd, unfinish'd." Richard keeps grinding on the thought of his deformity; his resentment is understandable; initially we hardly look for counterbalancing movements within the personality. Yet we miss them; the logic of his nature is too simple. His "I am determined to prove a villain" and "I am subtle, false, and treacherous" are too explicit, and we scent the thinned-out, allegorical air of the morality play. A conventionalized unfelt self-definition, it appears, will have to do in place of the self-knowledge in which a moral vocabulary is used with moral feeling.

So, emphatically labeled "villain," Richard shows one face to Clarence and another in soliloquy; likewise with Hastings. The pattern continues in scene after scene; Shakespeare develops at insistent length the business of successful false appearance that in Edmund he would manage subordinately and casually. But the hypocrisy that deludes is joined with an effrontery that renders ineffectual, at least for a time, those who are undeceived; one cannot gasp and attack simultaneously. If he is a coarser Edmund, Richard is also a coarser Iago. (His malice is that of the physical cripple, Iago's that of the spiritual cripple.) He has less of the charm, of the style of easy geniality, that flows from Iago. On the other hand, he has Iago's zest in his role, a lively glee in the triumph of his histrionic art. He relishes the sense of a force emanating from himself: not only in getting what he wants, but in putting something over on others.

In sum, Richard has elements of the picaresque hero, and this is a notable alteration of the mere villain. Ordinarily the picaro is a sterilized criminal; he turns cleverness, not evil, against his victims. He must outwit, not outrage. By definition, the picaro is all operative mind; he simply does not have the ordinary component of human feeling. To say that he is "without feeling" may seem to describe Richard adequately: the phrase ordinarily means pitilessness. But the picaro acts in a vacuum of feeling, and there is never an inrush of events creating a pressure of feeling; the situations maintain emotional neutrality except for the transitory fun of trickery. Now, Richard is pitiless but not without feeling; he derives his power from profound surges of envy and hatred. This is not picaresque; it is criminality unsterilized. Yet it is combined with a certain gamesomeness, a certain friskiness in tactics, a quickwitted sizing up of weaknesses and openings, a virtuosity in role that we can ordinarily enjoy for their own sake; they seem innocuous forms of aesthetic play and permit our enjoyment of a morally inexpensive triumph. But suddenly give the almost amiable trickster ruthlessness and treachery, and we find ourselves, if not painfully trapped, at least thrust into an ambiguity of response that betokens the dramatist's escape from stereotyped situation. If Shakespeare does not actually shock by giving a con man a dagger, he plays a hard game by giving a murderer the air of a con man. To the melodrama of pure villainy he has added some ambitious complications.

Quite aside from craving power in, and seeking revenge on, the world, Richard needs also the kind of triumph that belongs to the con man: the histrionic triumph, the mastery through role. The picaro is an actor in life, and the actor in turn needs hard roles to satisfy himself. Shakespeare finds in Richard an extraordinary passion for the taxing role, the impossible part, the unique tour de force. Throughout, this side of Richard is no less evident than his executive ruthlessness; it emphatically dominates three scenes—those in which Richard makes love to Anne, lets himself be coaxed into accepting the throne, and tries to persuade Queen Elizabeth to approve him as lover of her daughter. The excessive length of these scenes betrays Shakespeare's fascination with aspects of personality that make Richard something different from the ruthless villain that he is a good deal of the time, and the scenes themselves reveal some significant complications of his nature.

In making his suit to Anne (I, ii), Richard picks an incredibly difficult moment: he stops the funeral procession of Henry VI in which Anne is a mourner. Shakespeare may simply have opted for the bald theatricality of it, but the action conforms to Richard's bravado in brazenness. His discipline is immense; he endures protracted abuse as if the words meant nothing. He picks up Anne's words in logical games (I "am no beast" because I "know [no pity]"), says he can "excuse" himself as a murderer, bases quips on Christian doctrine (he cannot hang himself, since despair is a sin; he deserves thanks for sending Henry to the Heaven for which he is suited). Amid her very condemnations he proposes; her beauty, he insists, drove him to crime; if he killed her husband, it was to help her to a "better" one; he lavishes Petrarchan oxymoron on her eyes, "which kill me with a living death"; finally he gives her his sword and invites her to kill him. If these machinations in the realm of emotion are somewhat coarse-fibered, still Shakespeare tops it off with a subtle stroke: after putting a ring on Anne's finger, Richard promises "repentant tears" for the dead king and thus hands Anne the very blinders she now needs for the self-deception without which the already accomplished seduction could not be ratified. If cynicism of thought and impudence of style keep Richard still further away from being a tragic hero, they also reveal a singularity of being rather different from the predictableness of the vindictive man or of the politician without ruth or scruple.

Indeed, the political ends seem almost by-products or after-thoughts when Richard undertakes to enthral an audience with a chosen role, to gull the upright by thrusting ceaselessly at tiny areas of vulnerability. Not that this is not a form of vengeance, but it takes somewhat more effort and skill than arranging drownings in a butt of malmsey or smotherings in the Tower; besides, the drama is focused, not on the end, but on the process. Richard's histrionic imperturbability in the face of Anne's revilement is paralleled, three acts later, by his demeanor, only a little less self-contained, when he is verbally attacked by his mother, the Duchess of York, and his sister-in-law, Queen Elizabeth (IV, iv). As before, he seizes an unlikely moment for an incredibly unlikely suit: this time to Queen Elizabeth for the hand of her daughter Elizabeth, his niece. Again he endures the most bitingly truthful replies, the naming of his savagery and his treachery, as if self-assurance alone could survive any attack and win any heart. Let's not cry over spilt blood, he says, with a precocious touch of modernity; if I've done away with some of your children I'll marry another and make it all up to you. "Again you shall be mother to a king." Richard does capers on a tenuous middle ground between vulgar obtuseness and daring cynicism; Shakespeare seems always to be risking the former yet in the end presenting moral imperceptiveness as a bold strategy. Pushed far enough, insensitivity becomes a masterfulness that, through legalistic defenses and the dangling of rewards, breaks down all resistance before it. An apparent parody of the self-confident lover turns into a portrayal of a gross actuality we had not believed in. Richard finally calls the Queen "dear mother," and she goes out as if to arrange matters[1] so that he can "bury" her murdered children "in [her] daughter's womb." It is the last we see of her or any other female character; the scene leads nowhere, but its own long life testifies to Shakespeare's absorption in the character of the con man, the actor who takes on an utterly unsympathetic role and believes that in it he can hypnotize his audience.

Between these two "love"-making scenes stands another that, with roles reversed, exhibits Richard's histrionic personality again savoring its special triumph: the scene, again conspicuously long, in which Richard, with cool persistence aping the "holy man," appears stubbornly to resist the throne that, under the pressure of a ventriloquist's *vox populi,* is relentlessly seeking him out (III, vii). Richard must especially relish the tactics of Buckingham when, apparently faced by insuperable reluctance, he alludes to Richard's "conscience" and its danger of becoming too "nice and trivial" and, even more deadpan, compliments Richard's "gentle, kind, effeminate remorse,/Which we have noted in you to your kindred." Yet Richard's ironic sense, which is seldom less than sardonic, finds largest gratification in the style of his own surrender: his final triumph is to lay on others the blame for all that he may do because they have forced him to do that which he was determined to do.

It is a high spot in the scenes dominated by the picaresque Richard, the man who loves to seduce and bamboozle (as if he were an actor playing Richard and enduing him with a magnetic charm irresistible even to audi-

---

[1] The director, Stuart Vaughan, argues that Elizabeth "only pretends to acquiesce." See "A Director's Comments" in the Laurel edition of *Richard III,* ed. Francis Fergusson (New York, 1958), p. 28. See also E. K. Chambers, *Shakespeare: A Survey* (New York, 1958), p. 19. It seems to be possible to believe that Elizabeth actually yielded to Richard and only later, when free of Richard's influence, "heartily consented" that Richmond "should espouse Elizabeth."

ences who know that he is to be shunned but whose ready hisses are forced back and given issue only as gasps of admiration). But on top of this, Shakespeare has caught a further development that shows a very keen sense of personality. In those who triumph by a tour de force we expect a magnification of victory by a magnification of the enemy: he is the toughest man I ever faced. Not so Richard; on the contrary. What stands out boldly is his contempt for the person who has yielded to his blandishments; this comes out most fully and directly when, just after Anne has accepted him, Richard speaks his second-longest soliloquy (I, ii). True, there is plenty of ego-balm in the speech; Richard rehearses all the reasons why Anne should have remained faithful to her memory of Edward and spurned him; he works up to a mock-admiration of himself, and thus savors triumph. But all the explicit and implicit self-praise ("to win her, all the world to nothing!") never really cancels his first spontaneous sense of her folly: "Was ever woman in this humour won?/I'll have her, but I will not keep her long." There will be no glory in possessing her, parading her. The winning is the thing; the winnings are worthless. The contempt for the gull appears even more sharply when Queen Elizabeth apparently agrees to "win my daughter to thy will." She may be gulling the con man and thus contributing to an ironic effect. However that may be, Richard's response to what he believes is a triumph is unmistakable. He sneers, "Relenting fool, and shallow changing woman!" The contempt borders on disgust; we sense a reaction of unusual intensity, and it even seems likely that Shakespeare has imagined an analogous revulsion after Richard's theatrical exploit of appearing to reject, and then accepting, the crown.

These three scenes have in common, it appears, something more than the con man's tireless gamesmanship. The scenes are long drawn out; the expenditure of psychic energy is followed by a reaction, of lassitude or something stronger. In two of the scenes, Richard is a wooer; in the third, he is wooed (he literally does, in Buckingham's words, "Play the maid's part"—III, vii).[2] After the extended erotic engagement he is something of the

---

[2] Since Richard does "play the maid's part," it is interesting that in his final acquiescence to Buckingham and the others who "would...heap this care on me"—Richard uses language that might be used by a woman coyly yielding to seduction:

> I must have patience to endure the load.
> But if black scandal or foul-fac'd reproach
> Attend the sequel of your imposition,
> Your mere enforcement shall acquittance me
> From all the impure blots and stains thereof;
> For God doth know, and you may partly see,
> How far I am from the desire of this.

The style resembles that which Restoration comedy liked to attribute to the Puritan woman willing to be seduced but intent on avoiding responsibility.

*animal post coitum triste,* though *triste* less after coitus than after consent. He is a voluptuary of the approach and the attack, a tireless lover of receding prizes; craving challenge, difficulty, novelty; finding excitement in resistance to his will. Ennui follows, and disgust with the creature used. We need not press the erotic analogy unduly, but it does have some illustrative usefulness. We have seen the revulsion with both Anne and Elizabeth as persons; we will come in a minute to that which follows the acceptance of kingship.

The life of these three "wooing" scenes extends, in a special way beyond that of ordinary dramatic continuity, into the succeeding actions. Though Richard is ready to cast off Anne in disgust, his hypnotizing of her has exhilarated him and actually released a new store of psychic energy. In part, however, the discovery of this energy is a response to the total context: so much is yet to be done that the over-all situation is stimulating rather than relaxing. The obstacle course ahead is still a harsh challenge to initiative and ingenuity. After the soliloquy in which he sneers at Anne, Richard charges headlong into one character after another at the palace, trades diatribes with old Queen Margaret, arranges the death of Clarence (I, iii), plays the hypocrite at court (II, i), exchanges amenities or quips with the young princes while steering them to the Tower and revealing his designs in heavy asides (III, i), and finally by arrests, threats, executions, false alarms (Buckingham responds to a scheme of Richard's, "Tut, I can counterfeit the deep tragedian"—III, v), and rumor-mongering advances toward the throne. But once he has the throne, and the long tension of the assault is gone, he tends somewhat toward hysteroid conduct, discontent, and even lack of direction; toward an odd union of languor and petulance, as of one deprived of a spur and resentful of the loss. Satiety begets a kind of revengefulness, a random striking out from an unforeseen and nauseous weariness; by indecency and random cruelty, ennui tries to set in motion a cure for itself.

This mode of response is especially evident after Richard's tremendous outpouring of energy in endeavoring to seduce Queen Elizabeth, to win her support for his suit to her daughter. His immediate disgust with her we have noted. But what follows is a larger aftermath of that exhausting love-making. He snaps at Catesby for not carrying out a command that he has not yet given (IV, iv); he gives a command to Ratcliff, is quarrelsome when Ratcliff asks for necessary details, and, with a burst of feeling wholly unsuited to his executive role, cuts him off with, "My mind is chang'd." He is ungracious and rude to Stanley, accuses him of disloyalty, censures him for not carrying out a command not given, demands his son as a hostage. Then he strikes a messenger. Though this last act of royal self-indulgence is a familiar one, the scene as a whole cannot be attributed only to the strains of a shaky throne. The significant thing is this: for almost three hundred lines Richard has remained imperturbable under the diatribes of his mother and Queen Elizabeth and has found immense resources for his "wooing" of the latter. Under great pressure he showed no irritability or irascibility. Then, the impossible conquest seemingly achieved, he feels not only disgust for the victim but a general dullness and dissatisfaction. This new state leads him, within seventy-five lines, not only to hit a messenger but, by a spontaneous voiding of post-climactic ill-being, to risk pointlessly the alienation of followers he can ill afford to displease.

Pointlessly: the sense of program, ordinarily strong in Richard, is overcome by malaise of spirit, by emptiness after victory, by spitefulness that is half punishment of the world and half effort to relight the flame of passionate action. Insofar as it is disgust with the instrument of lust, it appears most plainly in the casting-off of Anne almost as soon as she has said yes—a casting-off whose intensity is easily distinguishable from the indifference of the cool calculation of advantage that a little later is plainly present in his treatment of her. But the revulsion against Anne and the comparable revulsion against Elizabeth throw Richard's sudden rejection of Buckingham into a very interesting perspective. The easiest explanation of this rejection is that, having snatched the throne by evil means, Richard is desperately anxious to secure it by having the young "bastards dead," that anxiety makes him monstrously impatient, that his paranoid streak makes him suspect even Buckingham and test him by an ultimately brutal assignment. No doubt there is much here of the tough usurper's palace politics amid dangers realistically perceived. Yet two facts stand out. One is that when Buckingham hesitates to kill "those bastards in the Tower," Richard has no difficulty at all in finding a substitute executioner, Tyrrel; that is, Buckingham's reluctance is not a disaster or anything like it. Even more important, Richard seems in haste to shift to a substitute: in a mere twenty-five lines he has given up on Buckingham, his right-hand man. What is more, from the beginning of the scene he has been chill and curt with Buckingham, as if he expected a break. His style with a man without whom he could hardly have got the throne is incredible; and his urgency is incredible in a man who has shown a great capacity for waiting, for patience, for putting up with what had to be put up with on the road to the throne.

We can consider this an inconsistency of pace in a young playwright whose dramaturgy is still often gauche. But there is an explanation which does not have to rely on inconsistency. For what is entirely consistent in Richard is the sudden aversion to someone whom he has used, and used in a relationship of wooer and wooed. Richard's style with Buckingham is plain enough if we see it as essentially his style with Anne and Elizabeth. Here the situation is subtler because it is not literal; the wooing is political, and Richard, the real seducer, plays the reluctant virgin ("the maid's part"). Buckingham, we should note, is the instrument of Richard's passion, as

Anne was and Elizabeth is to be; they are not objects in themselves, not partners in a mutual enterprise, but contributors to another's satisfaction. It is instruments that most easily arouse disgust. With them, post-coital lethargy slips into nausea and ill will; the source of satiety must be blamed and cast off. In this view, Buckingham was doomed when he became Richard's cool servitor in political lust. If this reading is valid, the first twenty-five lines of IV, ii constitute a terse psychological drama, for they portray Richard taking steps to get rid of a Buckingham of whom he is tired and sick: he is not disappointed in a request, but makes a demand that he knows will compel a break. He demands a final perverse service which even the most pliant prostitute cannot stomach. Had Buckingham given in, we can anticipate that afterwards Richard would have felt an even greater aversion and need for restorative violence.

The unusual complication of the wooing scenes modifies the bare melodrama; a similar variation of the melodramatic pattern is achieved, as we have seen, by the partial treatment of Richard as picaresque hero. To combine the man who lives by his wits and the man of limited but strong passions that, after his long-savored climbs to triumph, plunge him into despair and strangely-directed malice—into a perverse need to get even with those who have given in to him—is to innovate impressively in portraying the villain. It is in that sense that *Richard III,* if not mature, still has in it much more than a beginner's conventionality and naivete. Still, as we have seen, Richard remains limited, and that is the deeper source of immaturity in the play. His shrewdness is never a full-bodied intelligence. Even his operative acumen is finally undercut by his emotional disturbances. He has ups and downs that interfere with his purely practical sense of the motives and needs of others. But his worldly sharpness, such as it is, is not matched by an acute vision of himself, though at one time anxiety pushes him awkwardly in that direction. He can say perceptive things about himself, but they are rarely touched by the moral feeling and perspective that give depth to self-knowledge. Hence when he says, in one way or another, "I am a villain," he names himself to the audience rather than identifies himself to himself. This is what he does in his opening soliloquy, and it is about all he does in his second longest soliloquy, which follows his amatory conquest of Anne. Just before talking to the Murderers (I, iii) he does a fifteen-line self-description, but here his words are palpably no more than a cue for anyone in the audience who needs help: "And thus I clothe my naked villainy/With odd old ends stol'n forth of holy writ." Three acts pass before Shakespeare again thinks of involving Richard in self-comment: when he plans to get rid of Anne and marry his niece (IV, ii), he acknowledges that the tactic is risky but that when one is in as deep as he is, "sin will pluck on sin." "Sin" is a surprising word to find in his mouth, yet one quickly realizes that it does not come out of moral perception but that Richard is again speaking to the audience: "See, one villainy after another, but I am smart enough to know that the game is getting tighter." But even in that sense the word does not occur to him in the next scene when he lists his more recent evil deeds and then thinks of the young Elizabeth: "To her I go, a jolly thriving wooer."

Then, just before the end of the play, Shakespeare slips—one is almost inclined to say *drifts*—into an unexpected deepening of Richard's character. On the night before the final battle (V, iii) the ghosts of Richard's victims rise up, one after another, and threaten the sleeping Richard (while encouraging the sleeping Richmond). Out of this mechanical scene, with its heavy touch of the allegorical that always hovers over the play, a surprising psychological action emerges. The scene has been prepared for: Margaret's curse on Richard has included the "tormenting dream," and Anne has reported on Richard's uneasy nights with "timorous dreams." Hence it is not surprising that the vision of revengeful ghosts should affect Richard as nothing else has done: he can admit "terror" and urge himself, "Let not our babbling dreams affright our souls." What is surprising is that beneath the premonitions and sense of a danger that perhaps even physical courage in battle cannot master, Richard has the first touches of that serious inward-looking which was to be much more highly developed in later tragic heroes. In his last soliloquy—longer again: thirty lines—there is a kind of moral self-knowledge trying to break through. The speech catches our eye because in it we see Shakespeare getting a glimpse of an inner incoherence rarely presented in the early plays, and indeed quite new in Richard himself. This seems almost an inadvertent by-product of the drama of fear, as if Shakespeare were examining fear and discovering that, even in unlikely souls, its implied source is not only physical danger but moral retribution. He sees that Richard's initial problem is to master an anxiety created by the apparitions, and so to restore to himself the undividedness necessary for the crucial battle ahead. But the anxiety persists in being more than a sense of lurking defeat and death, in including a sense of moral being; hence Richard must push it back, down, and under (thus the scene is a brief sketch for the kind of moral action that is at the dramatic center of *Macbeth*). Fright is partly transmuted into an intimation of guilt, and words like "murder" and "villain" take on an emotional resonance wholly new in Richard.

So he is farthest both from the picaresque hero that he has been part of the time and from the monster of ambition and perversity that he has been most of the time. Some new force runs athwart the old energy, and he shifts back and forth uncertainly, as if Shakespeare did not quite have a sure grasp on his motives. Yet the leaps that make up the soliloquy find a partial form through the love-hate counterpoint in the soliloquy. As reassurance against inner accusations trying to erupt, Richard relies on self-devotion:

"Richard loves Richard; that is, I am I," and, with a touch of the old self-irony, "Alack, I love myself." He cannot sustain it: "O, no! alas, I rather hate myself"; but the potential force of this is cut down by the somewhat mechanical rhetoric of the context. He catalogues his evil deeds but shifts naturally from the possible vision of self to the world's vision of self: "There is no creature loves me,/And if I die no soul shall pity me." The awareness of how others respond comes from his theatrical side, from his instinct for observing the impact he has on others; hence it is possible that noting the absence of love in others may be the most penetrating self-judgment of which he is capable. He may slip into a more direct self-judgment in the sardonic pull-back of the next two lines: "Nay, wherefore should they, since that I myself/Find in myself no pity to myself?" but the sense is equivocal. He may mean, "Away with self-pity"; he may mean, "The pitilessness that I have shown others extends to myself"; he may mean, "I deserve no pity." The very ambiguity evidences Shakespeare's instinctive pulling away from a stereotype.

Richard's last-minute ruminations of this kind give him momentary, if unwilling, contact with a world in which self-judgments are so frequent as to be almost mechanical. After bad dreams in the Tower, Clarence acknowledges, "I have done these things," and prays, "O God! if...thou wilt be aveng'd on my misdeeds,/Yet execute thy wrath on me alone!" (I, iv). After the murder of Clarence, King Edward recalls in painful detail all the reasons he had to be generous to Clarence: "All this from my remembrance brutish wrath/Sinfully pluck'd..."; "...for my brother not a man would speak,/Nor I, ungracious, speak unto myself/For him, poor soul" (II, i). Suddenly condemned to death by Richard, Hastings acknowledges, "...I, too fond, might have prevented this," and

> I now repent I told the pursuivant,
> As too triumphing, how mine enemies
> To-day at Pomfret bloodily were butcher'd
> And I myself secure in grace and favour. (III, iv)

Anne, now Richard's miserable wife, blames herself, not him: "Within so small a time, my woman's heart/Grossly grew captive to his honey words" (IV, i). En route to execution, Buckingham remembers all the victims whom he helped treat unjustly, acknowledges the "wrongs" he has done, recognizes that "That high All-Seer, which I dallied with" is now, ironically, punishing him, and concludes, "Come, lead me, officers, to the block of shame;/Wrong had but wrong, and blame the due of blame" (V, i).

There is something pat about these self-judgments, however; like other elements in *Richard III* they remind us of the morality play. There is an overly symmetrical balance between Richard's customary defect of moral sensitivity and the sudden restoration of it in his victims after disaster has come upon them. Nevertheless there is no doubt that Shakespeare is aware of a new sense of self and of deed as a dramatic possibility of consciousness, and he explores it even in unlikely places. With Tyrrel he does it awkwardly; with the murderers of Clarence, at tedious length. Tyrrel, who undertook to murder Edward's young sons for Richard, reports on the "tyrannous and bloody act," the "most arch deed of piteous massacre," and on the guilt and grief of Dighton and Forrest, "who I did suborn/To do this piece of ruthless butchery" (IV, iii). But Tyrrel, though he provides another contrast with insentient Richard, is still the messenger rather than the doer of the deed, so that we do not have here an immediate drama of self-judgment. Shakespeare came closer to such a drama in the dialogue between Clarence's Murderers, which suffers both from the extensiveness that we see several times in the play when Shakespeare's interest in a subject outweighs his dramatic judgment, and from the allegorical danger that is also recurrent. There is too neat a balance between the First Murderer, who wants to get the job done, and the Second Murderer, who has qualms. Yet Shakespeare does give us more than abstractions. Repeatedly the First Murderer expresses the view that to hesitate or to relent is "cowardly and womanish" (I, iv); the drama is enhanced by the play of an idea, the primitive concept of manliness that Shakespeare was often to explore in later plays and to place in tension with alternative concepts of the manly. More important, the Second Murderer is not all of a piece; his hesitancy to kill conflicts with his itch for the reward, and his stichomythic responses have a strong comic side. Yet beforehand he acknowledges "a kind of remorse"; afterwards he would "like Pilate,... wash my hands/Of this most grievous murder," and he certifies his verbal repentance by relinquishing the reward.

These various appraisals of oneself and one's actions are the means by which Shakespeare creates a sense of a human world from which Richard is almost wholly cut off, a world which, for all of its widespread corruption, still retains some grip of the means to know and save itself. In presenting this negative relationship Shakespeare makes a key word of "conscience," which, by an irony of the creative process, is used more frequently in *Richard III* than in any other play except *Henry VIII*. The word is dinned into our awareness in the dialogue of the Murderers. The Second Murderer feels some "dregs of conscience" but does not deny his colleague's sardonic view that, when Richard "opens his purse...thy conscience flies out." But then he comes up with the extended definition of conscience which combines ironic wit, tour de force, and moral realism:

> ...it makes a man a coward. A man cannot steal but it accuseth him; a man cannot swear but it checks him; a man cannot lie with his neighbour's wife but it detects him. 'Tis a blushing shamefac'd spirit that mutinies in a man's bosom. It fills a man full of obstacles. It made me once restore a

> purse of gold that by chance I found. It beggars any man that keeps it. It is turn'd out of towns and cities for a dangerous thing; and every man that means to live well endeavours to trust to himself and live without it.

After this we cannot forget *conscience,* and we see how steadily it is present in Shakespeare's imagination throughout the play, and how heavily he relies on it in crucial passages near the end. Richard has already observed that Anne's "conscience" had to be against him (I, ii); in one of her tirades Queen Margaret has exclaimed to him, "The worm of conscience still begnaw thy soul" (I, iii). Buckingham and Richard exchange deadpan jokes when Buckingham, urging the throne on Richard, warns him against a "conscience. . .nice and trivial" and Richard yields "against my conscience" (III, vii). Against these Tartuffian ironies there is Tyrrel's report that the Princes' murderers "are gone with conscience and remorse" (IV, iii). Then the Richard who could look with scorn at the operation of Anne's conscience and make gags about his own finds Margaret's curse ironically come true: after his terrifying dream he exclaims, "O coward conscience, how dost thou afflict me!" and "My conscience hath a thousand several tongues" (V, iii). If this is questionable in itself, what Shakespeare does with it is very effective; it reveals him feeling his way toward the ideas and values that define the evil men of his mature period. In these the identifying mark is the conviction that all sanctions lie in the self—in its desires and powers—and that no outer authority can constrain the will. This is essentially what Richard believes, though he has not articulated it; then his frightening dreams of hostile spirits suddenly give him a vision of supernatural sanctions. It is these that he must deny; he must find a rationale of conduct true to his own being. This is what he does:

> Let not our babbling dreams affright our souls,
> For conscience is a word that cowards use,
> Devis'd at first to keep the strong in awe.
> Our strong arms be our conscience, swords our law!

His one attack of anxiety and guilt has led him to a theoretical formulation of what has always been his implied position, and in this he looks forward to Edmund, Goneril, and Iago. Shakespeare uses his key word to connect the passage with the related one that expresses the counter view. The words are Oxford's: "Every man's conscience is a thousand men/To fight against this guilty homicide" (V, ii).

Insofar as Richard identifies conscience with cowardice, he adopts the First Murderer's primitive conception of manliness. Insofar as he has some difficulty with his conscience, he resembles the Second Murderer. That Richard permits some comparison with both Murderers shows Shakespeare endeavoring, even though somewhat artificially, to bring together in one character conflicting elements initially represented in two characters: that is, he has taken a small step from allegory toward tragedy. *Richard III* illustrates with considerable clarity some of the steps that have to be taken: the significant fact is that they all have to do with remedying mechanical separations like that between the two Murderers (or like that between Tyrrel and the men who murdered the princes, which results in a narrated rather than a presented remorse). Queen Margaret rants on tirelessly, driven by a rancor separated out from all other elements of personality. A half-dozen characters for a time act confidently as their passions dictate and then suddenly, when disasters strike, break into condemnatory self-knowledge; their ordinary lives and their consciences are separated in allegorical fashion. In no later drama do so many characters end in self-reproof; the later Shakespeare brings knowing and doing together in complexer mixtures that do not so easily permit separate action by one or the other. Finally, all those who acknowledge their misdeeds are separated from a Richard who for the most part seems to have no capacity for such action. At the end, true, Shakespeare finds some hint of it in him, and that is, for the history of Shakespeare the dramatist, a very interesting moment. But this early experiment in bringing together conflicting tendencies creates at least some awkwardness in the portrait of Richard, who, despite recurrent trouble with dreams, has had a rather magnificent freedom from inner brakes upon total action toward a chosen end.

Hence his demonic energy, which ought to succeed. In some men it would go all for nought because of self-doubt or self-criticism or an intelligence too gross or too finicky; in Richard it goes all for nought because his deficiencies of feeling alienate him beyond survival. If Richard, compared with the later tragic heroes, is too simple a figure, still Shakespeare has managed a psychic portrait that has unexpected variety. There are of course the elements of the player, the jester, the picaro, the self-ironist that Shakespeare would more than once discover in villains. But perhaps the greatest originality is in the conception of Richard's deficiency of feeling: it is not only that he loves no one and feels no obligations, but that he cannot really relish a triumph and hence ease the men around him and reduce their fears. The trouble is not altogether that the precariousness of his perch begets incurable tension. Rather the successful striving renders the success tasteless. Above all, the person striven for or through, subdued or used, loses savor; he must be blamed for an acquiescence that in the end is revolting. It leaves one with too much, that is, with nothing to lust for. Satiety begets contempt and indecency, and these may flame out even against bystanders. Richard's nausea is not with himself, as in tragedy; not with deadly enemies, as in pure melodrama; but with his victims and tools. His knowledge is not of a flaw in himself but of the flaws that one has surmised in others, teased into efficacy, and made serviceable beyond endurance. His satiety simulates conscience, for both declare "enough"; but one calls for penance, the other for meting out penalties.

I have used the erotic analogy as a tool to define a singular malaise of the summit, a distemper of success. In detecting it Shakespeare was obviously not writing tragedy; but he was giving a new hue to melodrama. For while melodrama can accommodate despair and hatred, it rarely derives the one from triumph, the other from pampered self-love.

# 9

# Richard's Divided Heritage in *King John*

*William H. Matchett*

In 'Commodity and Honour in *King John*' (*University of Toronto Quarterly,* April, 1960, 341–56) Mr. James Calderwood demonstrates the essential role of those themes in Shakespeare's play. I should like to confirm, strengthen and extend his perceptive analysis through a discussion of structure. In brief, my argument is as follows: The plot of *King John* is built around the question of who should be King of England and thus of what constitutes a "right" to the throne. In the first act, three characters are shown to have particular claims to the crown. With the death of Arthur, the failure and eventual collapse of John and, through the course of the play, the growth of the Bastard in his perception of the distinction between commodity and true honour, it would appear that the Bastard is being groomed to take over as the rightful king. The final scenes, however, with their surprising introduction of a new claimant of unknown character and ability, defeat this expectation and shift the emphasis from the original question to a deeper consideration of the requirements of honour. The very qualities which constitute the Bastard's claim to the throne lead to his repudiation of personal ambition and his kneeling to Prince Henry. True

*Reprinted from* Essays in Criticism, *XII (July 1962) No. 3 by permission of the publisher.*

honour, a matter not of prestige and power but of duty, is decided, in this play, upon the basis of what is best for England. The Bastard, in kneeling, renounces his recently established "right" to the throne and thus ensures his already suffering country against civil war. True honour makes him the best of subjects in a unified England and this, in the logic of the play, is more important than the character of the King.

A crux in this reading of the play, as it is in Calderwood's discussion of the central themes, is the weight of meaning it finds in the Bastard's kneeling to Prince Henry. Speeches at that place, as critics will point out, do not sustain the argument that the Bastard, in kneeling, is renouncing a personal claim to the crown. Similarly, both Calderwood and I interpret V, vi, as a scene in which Hubert is inviting the Bastard to seize the throne, while critics may claim that the text of that scene does not justify such a reading. I would agree that the speeches in these two key scenes do not deal explicitly with the issue as I see it, but I hope to demonstrate that Shakespeare is working by means of dramatic implication. The speeches are understatements (not, it is worth pointing out, contradictions) of the issue, while the main weight of meaning in the actions and speeches is carried by their relationship to the inevitable expectations aroused by the structure of the play.

# I

King John enters his play as a usurper. Unlike his mother, he offers no objection to Chatillon's reference to his "borrow'd majesty" (4),[1] and even Eleanor's objection is a political gesture, not an assertion of principle, as is clear as soon as Chatillon has left the stage. When Chatillon urges Arthur's right to the throne (based, of course, upon primogeniture), John's response is not an argument but the cold question "What follows if we disallow of this?" (16). The dramatic image is unmistakable. Chatillon three times uses the word "right" for Arthur's claim; John's only rebuttal is force, "war for war and blood for blood" (19). Eleanor also, though she disapproves of "ambitious Constance" (32), speaks of "the right and party of her son" (34). Finally, when John couples "Our strong possession and our right" (39), Eleanor immediately distinguishes them, leaving John's position dependent upon "Your strong possession much more than your right" (40). John is king *de facto* but not *de jure*.

It is necessary to insist upon this initial image in the play because

[1] All citations are from the Arden edition, edited by E. A. J. Honigmann (London, 1954), because I am convinced by his arrangement of the act- and scene-divisions. Where these differ from the traditional arrangement, I give a second reference to that, as found in J. D. Wilson's Cambridge edition (1936).

critics, pointing to Holinished and Richard I's will, have shown that John had in fact a legitimate claim to the throne. Historically perhaps, but not here. John's claim to the throne is his presence on it, and the issue raised is one of possession vs. right.

The remainder of the act, devoted to introducing the Bastard, repeats the national situation on a domestic scale. The Bastard is also in possession of an estate to which another, his half-brother Robert, is the rightful heir. Our sympathies, like John's, are of course with the "good blunt fellow" (71); under the influence of these sympathies, however, both "right" and "honour" begin to twist in our hands. Robert's assumed moral right to his inheritance is denied by John in the name of another right, the legal fiction of the Bastard's legitimacy. Everyone concerned knows that Robert, for lack of sufficient proof, like Arthur, for lack of sufficient power, is being "legally" cheated. Though he happens to have truth on his side and to be fighting for his right, Robert is, dramatically, a deserving victim both because of his unprepossessing appearance, especially in comparison with the Bastard, and his willingness to sacrifice his mother's good name, however undeserved, for his own gain.

But the Bastard, unlike John, is not permitted to enjoy his dishonourably held possessions. To save him for his later role in the play, he is presented with a choice between "honour" and possessions. He chooses "honour" (here merely "reputation"), and his ambitious choice immediately pays off, for John knights him—"Arise Sir Richard, and Plantagenet" (162). There is in his response an impetuous decisiveness, uncalculating, heedless of consequences, a little naïve. He is not one to ask "What follows if we disallow of this?" but says at once, "I'll take my chance" (151). In appearance already judged "perfect Richard" (90), the image of his father, he further convinces his grandmother of his parentage by his blunt, bawdy and attractive enthusiasm:

> *Bast.* [to Robert] Brother by th' mother's side, give me your hand:
> My father gave me honour, yours gave land.
> Now blessed be the hour [punning with *whore*], by night or day,
> When I was got, Sir Robert was away!
> *Elea.* The very spirit of Plantagenet! (163–7)

Though we have not yet seen Arthur, it is clear that the first act has set up three characters as each being in a special relation to kingship through his share in Richard's heritage: the nephew, Arthur, the throneless rightful king; the brother, John, who has usurped the throne; and the bastard son, who, with neither right to nor possession of the throne, has nevertheless inherited the self-reliant decisiveness of a true king. For the memory of Coeur-de-lion haunts this play as the mythically heightened image of a good and heroic king. A little cuckolding on the side merely proved his manliness, and it is the manliness of "this same lusty gentleman" (108), his son, that is played off against the debility of Sir Robert's son by the same mother. Coeur-de-lion triumphantly combined what has now been divided, his right going to the child, Arthur, his throne to the man, John, and his personal qualities to the youth, Sir Richard, the son who now has his name. The division is an imbalance demanding resolution: which—right, possession, or character—is the essential ingredient for a king? Arthur has been denied his right and John's possession is threatened; only the Bastard cannot be alienated from his inheritance, for it is intrinsic and he can boast, "I am I, howe'er I was begot" (175).

There would seem to be a contradiction, then, between the Bastard's self-sufficient character and his pursuit of an honour which is merely reputation. So there is. His discovery and handling of this contradiction is a primary development in the play. But the reputation he has chosen is one to which he has in fact a right: gambling on future "chance," he trades his spurious respectability for an honest reputation as a royal bastard. He has made the right choice for the wrong reason; he has yet to add insight to the character which is already his. It is safe to say that the first act leaves the audience more interested in what will happen to the Bastard than in the immediate challenge to John, which, in the absence of Arthur, has as yet been somewhat abstract.

## II

The second act, however, is concerned almost completely with the dynastic struggle, and the Bastard, though he attempts once, unsuccessfully, to control the action, serves primarily as an observant commentator. His simple presence as an observer needs to be stressed since, in the shade of his lively comments, one might overlook its importance: his political education is beginning and he has much to learn. By the end of the act the once naïve young man has found the proper name for the political motivation he observes.

The point at issue between John and Arthur, so clearly stated in the first act, becomes more ambiguous when looked at more closely in the second; we meet Arthur in circumstances which overshadow his right. While his immaturity and weakness may attract some personal sympathy, sympathy for his cause is dissipated as we observe the company he keeps. King Richard's rightful heir is first seen agreeing to "Embrace," "love," "welcome" and "forgive" (11–12) Austria, the man who killed King Richard. Instead of avenging England's honour, which he is of course too weak to do, Arthur—or Constance through Arthur—is seeking to further his cause and to force his way into Angiers by embracing England's enemies. The patriotic determination to "follow arms" till England, "That water-walled bulwark, still secure/And confident from foreign purposes. . . Salute thee for her king" (27–31) rings falsely from the tongue of one who is not merely a foreigner but the very foreigner who wears the lion-skin of England's last rightful king. After his first brief, formal (and no doubt prompted) speech, Arthur speaks only twice more in the act, both times in brief and vain attempt to pacify his mother, who does his fighting and decision-making for him. He is too retiring, but Constance—especially since she is not above the suspicion that she fights primarily for personal power—is overbearing. Arthur is a pawn surrounded by an unscrupulous, self-seeking league. Were he to gain his right and become king, the results would presumably be disastrous for England.

For, though the word "right" is used sixteen times in the act,[2] it is eclipsed by the recurring threat of the bloodshed to which the issue is leading: "blood" and its cognates ("bleed," "bleeding," "bloody"), used only four times in the first act's foreshadowing of this result, appear in the second act no less than twenty-six times.[3] While the issue of dynastic "right" is being shown to be far from simple, its very existence unresolved is being shown to invite, or indeed ordain, carnage.

But the attack on Angiers is interrupted by the arrival of John and the English forces. The first battle is verbal, with the opponents paired: John vs. France, Eleanor vs. Constance, and the Bastard vs. Austria. Opposed to France—" 'Tis France, for England"—John appears in a new light—"England, for itself" (202). We realise again—especially now that we have seen poor Arthur—that, usurper or not, John *is* the King. The meeting of the two rulers, each backed by an army and mouthing "Peace," is, however, a bit of political farce, no less so for being true to the life of power politics: each subverts the peace he claims to desire, since each will have it only on his own terms. John's self-righteous claim is no criterion; "God" is a mere political gambit, one which can be used equally by France in citing Arthur's right: "In the name of God,/How comes it then that thou art call'd a king" (106–7). (And Hubert, demurring from both positions, will claim, "A greater power than we denies all this" [368].)

The women's exchange is close to hair-pulling, especially Eleanor's unjustified slur on Arthur as "thy bastard" (122) and her witty play on Constance's desire to be "queen" (123)—*royal queen,* and *chess queen* ("check the world")—which oversteps any pretence of royal dignity in its

---

[2] Nine times as Arthur's; once—"God and our right!" (299)—the French king, in Arthur's name, claiming for himself in English what English kings are supposed to claim in French; once (548) Arthur's right given to Constance; once (335) John claiming right for himself; and twice (139 and 236) with a different meaning altogether.

[3] Four times, it is true, in reference to lineage; five times, with greater richness of connotation, in reference to vital existence; but the remaining seventeen times in reference to the butchery of war.

third significance, *quean*. Constance, with Arthur's right on her side, is nevertheless forced onto the defensive and, frustrated, becomes increasingly violent. First Austria—"Peace!" (134)—then Arthur—"Good my mother, peace!" (163)—then John "Bedlam, have done" (183)—and finally France —"Peace, lady!" (195)—seek to quiet her, her three allies using the same maligned word in the attempt to reconcile her to the etiquette of political duplicity.

The Bastard's immediate antipathy to Austria, motivated of course by the lion-skin, contrasts his sense of honour directly with Arthur's and, by extension, with John's. Whatever the moral masquerades of the others, the Bastard, as Richard's son, has a legitimate personal grudge against Austria.

France brings the general verbal violence back to the practical here-and-now of Angiers and suggests discovering "Whose title they admit, Arthur's or John's" (200). The decision of the men of Angiers then, though not necessarily a final resolution of the main issue, has its dramatic importance as a test case. Hubert—for, though as yet unnamed, it is he who is the citizen-spokesman for Angiers (as Wilson first made clear and Honigmann has adopted)—gives an answer that has all the appearance of eminent sense: "we are the king of England's subjects. . .he that proves the king,/To him will we prove loyal" (267–71). John, after an exasperated appeal to his simple logic—"Doth not the crown of England prove the king?" (273)—adduces the thirty thousand Englishmen who accompany him. It is, of course, a double argument: that so many Englishmen follow him attests his moral right to the English throne; that so many men follow him attests his threat to Angiers. France cannot match the moral half of this claim though he can match the threat with "As many and as well-born bloods" (278). But Hubert remains adamant: "Till you compound whose right is worthiest,/ We for the worthiest hold the right from both" (281–2). After the frustrated kings indulge in a brief and bloody, but fruitless skirmish, Hubert for a third time maintains his seemingly sensible neutrality: "One must prove greatest: while they weigh so even/We hold our town for neither, yet for both" (332–3).

But, however sound the arguments which might convince a modern man of the virtues of neutrality, Hubert's position is unacceptable in *King John*. This is not the moral superiority of "A plague o' both your houses!" with which Mercutio, "the prince's near ally," rejects the parochial quarrel that has caused his death (*R. & J.*, III, i, 105–8); this is the willingness of common citizens to accept either of two contradictory national loyalties. It has the sound sense of self-preservation—and perhaps today that seems enough—but it is meant to have little else; as comes increasingly clear in Hubert's progressive responses, it is not a moral position at all, but a refusal to face the issue. (That the issue is not resolvable in the terms in which it has been set does not, apparently, excuse a man from involvement.) At no time is Hubert concerned with Arthur's rights. He faces the straight power politics of England and France. His first response sounds fine till probed: "he that proves the king,/To him will we prove loyal." What kind of loyalty is this?" Like "honour" in the first act, it is not the real article, but a calculated substitute; what ought to be the warm and total response of a committed man is here the small change of a self-indulgent apathy. What "proves the king" is precisely the issue that Hubert avoids, and his restatements, "the worthiest" or "greatest," are equally hollow, assuming only that might makes right. Hubert abdicates the citizen's duty to act according to his best moral lights and, selfishly holding himself aloof, leaves the decision to naked force.

It is in contrast with Hubert that one is to understand the Bastard's behaviour. Loyally (he declared his loyalty to John with his entering line in the first act), unselfishly and also, one must add, unthinkingly, he urges on the battle which seems to him the sole way of settling the issue: "Cry 'havoc' kings; back to the stained field, ... Then let confusion of one part confirm/The other's peace; till then, blows, blood, and death!" (357–60). But, though superior to Hubert here in his loyalty and his freedom from selfish calculation, the Bastard is not himself facing any moral issues. His response is warm and total, but it is not yet what one would call perceptive. He, no less than Hubert, leaves the decision to naked force; the difference is his willingness to involve himself on the side to which he is loyal. After Hubert's fourth refusal, the Bastard, unable to stomach men who can stand coldly before "industrious scenes and acts of death" (376), makes his "wild" (395) suggestion that the kings join forces against Angiers before turning back to their own quarrel. It is his first venture into political strategy, and his "smacks it not something of the policy?" (396) shows his naïve pride in what he is pleased to consider his approach to political wisdom.

But what is the rash response of naïve loyalty in the Bastard as an individual becomes insane ruthlessness when it is accepted and given royal authority by John:

> France, shall we knit our powers
> And lay this Angiers even with the ground;
> Then after fight who shall be king of it? (398–400)

To such inhuman nonsense has the political stalemate led.

Hubert, fortunately for Angiers, has another suggestion: the marriage of John's niece, Blanche, to the Dauphin, Lewis. The Bastard reacts with disgust to Hubert's rhetoric, which has usurped the place of his own strategy, but both kings see in the plan a way of saving face while abandoning their sterile enmity. With the few gestures owed to respectability, the political match is arranged. Lewis plays the game with a will and his ability to switch so rapidly from enemy to lover, patently insincere, gilding his political opportunism with the language of a sonneteer, is in sharp contrast not only with the Bastard's disgusted and less-flexible sincerity, but with the honesty of his bride-to-be. Blanche plays only a brief role in the play, but it is a crucial one for, though she is almost as much as Arthur a political pawn, she has something to teach the Bastard. Without loss of dignity or femine propriety, she is hardly less plain-spoken—when called upon to speak—than he is:

> My uncle's will in this respect is mine:...
> Further I will not flatter you, my lord,
> That all I see in you is worthy love,
> Than this: that nothing do I see in you...
> That I can find should merit any hate. (510–20)

To marry Lewis is her duty, and therefore she will marry Lewis. When John asks for formal assent, she pronounces herself "bound in honour still to do/What you in wisdom still vouchsafe to say" (522–3). This is the only appearance of the word "honour" in the second act, and its first appearance in the play as a high-minded sense of personal obligation, a trait of character rather than a mere claim for public approval. Blanche is controlled by her honour, whatever the personal consequences. The Bastard is silent but his education has now truly begun, as comes clear when he is left alone at the end of the scene.

In his well-known soliloquy—"Mad world! mad kings! mad composition!" (561)—with new insight, he gives the name, missing so far in the play, to the primary motivating force behind what we have seen: "Commodity, the bias of the world" (574), commodity, the unprincipled self-interest which perverts "all indifferency, ...direction, purpose, course, intent" (579–80), and brings the noblest-sounding resolutions to the most ignominous results. This speech is clearly crucial in the play, as others before Calderwood have recognised, but there has been much disagreement as to what it is meant to imply. Though the Bastard is disgusted by commodity, he has been thought to advocate it, and, indeed, his final words are: "Gain, be my lord, for I will worship thee!" (598).

Many of the problems commentators have with this speech seem to me to arise from attempts to make of it a summation of the Bastard's character, a final position rather than a stage in his development. He is not static, and it is enough in the second act that he has begun to consider where he is. What was blind loyalty now sees madness on both sides. For the first time he is critical of John. Though he is wrong in his estimate of King Philip's original motive, accepting the public declaration for the fact, the important point is that he is beginning to judge for himself, and no longer just following chance. The word "honourable" in the Bastard's mouth now, though we may demur from "honourable war," is not what it was in the first act, but what he has learned from Blanche.

After this insight into the kings, there is surely a hesitation (between lines 586 and 587) while, in his honesty, the Bastard recognises its application to himself: "And why rail I on this commodity?/But for because he hath not woo'd me yet" (587–8). Must we demand conversion at the very incipience of self-knowledge? The Bastard, realising that he has been living in the very spirit he has condemned in the kings, concludes most humanly by reversing his complaint and turning their conduct into a rationalisation for his own. But he has found a name for such conduct; he has seen "commodity" and its opposite. Never again can he remain unconscious in following chance. It is enough for now. It is a place to end a scene but not a play.

The brief scene which follows and concludes the act (traditionally III, i, 1–74) brings Constance the news of her loss of support. "I have a king's oath," she insists (10), but we have seen what such an oath is worth. Arthur has only a single line: "I do beseech you, madam, be content" (42). His cause would appear to be lost; the act thus ends with John's possession of the throne apparently secure and the primary suspense once again is that of what is likely to happen next to the Bastard.

## III

The third act, however, quickly introduces a new challenge to John. Pandulph's entry is abrupt, but John's response is even more so. To the legate's greeting—"Hail, you anointed deputies of heaven!" (62 [136]), clearly meant as an immediate assertion of the Pope's claim to superior authority—John returns his thoroughly and anachronistically Protestant answer. Having just won his victory over Arthur, John is carried away into attempting to brazen out another which, could he win it, would leave him even stronger. The stakes are high. John must carry France with him in this reckless rebellion or suffer not only excommunication but, what makes it a political threat, loss of the very support which he has just purchased to seal the possession of his kingdom against the threat of Arthur's right. The ensuing struggle is not spiritual, but political jockeying, with Pandulph merely another power politician, his weapons excommunication and incitement to political purge of the excommunicant.

When Pandulph can argue that "indirection...grows direct,/And falsehood falsehood cures" (202–3 [276–7]), he is a master politician at the furthest remove from the Bastard. But the Bastard has been presented with no special problem by all this. Remaining loyal to John, he has been more concerned with his animosity for Austria, whom he continues to bait, than with Pandulph. Blanche, however, is trapped between her loyalty to her uncle and her new loyalty to her husband. She is hardly more in this scene than a formalised image of the dilemma of loyalties; her having acted honourably has not protected her from subsequent suffering.

Two brief images of importance must emerge from the chaos of the staged battle: the Bastard enters with Austria's head, having achieved his revenge; and Hubert is entrusted by John with the custody of their prisoner, Arthur. There are no speeches to explain Hubert's presence as John's follower; we can only look for the implications. France having broken the league, Hubert has apparently remained loyal to the injured party. A possible further implication of the entry with Arthur is that Hubert himself has been responsible for Arthur's capture. The battle over, these same characters return to the stage. John commissions the Bastard to precede him to England and "shake the bags/Of hoarding abbots" (ii, 17–18 [iii, 7–8]). More attention has gone to debating the degree of Protestantism of this commission—which is hardly a remarkable one, given John's defiance of the Pope—than in recognising its obvious structural function. For the sake of his dramatic development, the Bastard cannot be permitted to witness John's charge to Hubert. Sending him to England gets him off the stage; sending him to rob the monastaries adds another touch to John's defiance and to the Bastard's own character. Clearly the issue between Church and Crown has not touched him. He is still John's loyal follower with a responsible commission—one from which he presumably stands to gain a percentage for himself. Thus his earlier choice has begun to pay off in cash as well as title.

The Bastard gone and Eleanor claiming Arthur's attention, John turns and fawns on Hubert. The warmth of his approach—"O my gentle Hubert,/We owe thee much!" (ii, 29–30 [iii, 19–20])—has, I believe, a double motivation. John is not merely flattering Hubert in order to bring him to murder Arthur, but indeed owes Hubert much, just as he says—owes him the very capture of Arthur, as the former appearance implied. John is promising a reward already due and hinting for just one further service. Hubert's response, moving from his noncommittal "I am much bounden to your majesty" (39 [29]) to his more fervent declaration of love, is not unclouded. Whatever the circumstances that determined him, he is no longer in a position to maintain his neutrality; he has made, or been forced to make, his choice, and the loyalty then so coldly promised to the stronger must now be delivered. After a number of false starts, John finally manages the most pointed of commissions, as though his will were less tainted through showing naked so briefly:

*K. John.* Death.
*Hub.* My lord?
*K. John.* A grave.
*Hub.* He shall not live.
*K. John.* Enough.
(76 [65–6]

John leaves the promised reward unspecified, but the more significant ambiguity lies in the sinister irony of his final statement to Arthur that

Hubert will attend on him "With all true duty" (83 [73]). True to whom? to what? and in what sense? The nature of "true duty"—whether Hubert's, John's, the Bastard's, Blanche's, King Philip's, Pandulph's, Lady Faulconbridge's, or that of other yet to appear—is precisely what is at issue in this play, whether we call it that, or loyalty, or honour.

In the final scene of the third act, Pandulph, the master strategist, shows the defeated French how they yet stand to win. John, he points out, cannot rest while Arthur lives. Arthur is John's prisoner, and John must kill him; thus freeing Lewis to claim the English throne through Blanche and simultaneously driving the English to revolt. John, as we know, has already headed directly into the trap Pandulph has described, but, should John eliminate himself along with Arthur, we are left with a claimant whom Pandulph has not imagined: The English Bastard will be on hand to contest the issue, and he, we feel, should take precedence over the foreigner. As though to heighten the developing contrast, the final comment of the willing Lewis—"Strong reasons makes strange actions" (182)—is a direct affirmation of commodity.

## IV

The fourth act closes the trap, with complications no one could have foreseen. However unexpected, and even illogical, the shift in intent from murder to blinding—or, more likely, to murder as an "accident" during blinding—the resultant stage business is an image of the moral situation, an image which is echoed and reëchoed in the lines. The dilemma of conflicting loyalties is here most acute, with Hubert, the very man who thought he could hold himself aloof from commitment, now caught between the claims of political allegiance and those of simple compassion. It is his "duty" that is iron:

> *Arth.* Must you with hot irons burn out both mine eyes?
> *Hub.* Young boy, I must.
> *Arth.* And will you?
> *Hub.* And I will. (39–40)

Human sympathy is the living eye that Hubert must put out. Hubert, with his irons and backed by two burly accomplices, concealed but at hand, is brute power; the child Arthur is powerless innocence, wronged right.

Arthur's insistence upon his own innocence and upon his loving attendance when Hubert's head once ached drives the scene dangerously close to the sentimental. To maintain his helplessness, there can be no one else to defend him, and, in the economy of the play, there has been no time for a scene demonstrating the attendance he is forced to cite, a bit priggishly, in his own behalf. In the difficulty of putting goodness on the stage, Shakespeare makes of Arthur, as he did of Blanche, a formal image of victimised virtue, Arthur the image of suffering innocence as Blanche was of suffering integrity. Perhaps the ultimate horror in the viciousness of "this iron age" (60) is the recognition by innocence that its own appearance must be suspect: "Nay, you may think my love was crafty love,/And call it cunning" (53–4). But Hubert is unable to proceed and, surprising no one more than himself—"Yet am I sworn" (123)—he spares Arthur. His choice of a higher duty over a lower creates no moral millenium; it involves him immediately in duplicity—he must lie to John—and in "Much danger" (133).

In the second scene, the English lords, who have formed John's silent retinue throughout the play, now first have a hand in the action, detaching themselves from John as Pandulph foretold. They are ostensibly objecting to the "wasteful and ridiculous excess" (16) of a second coronation which John has just staged. (The unspoken implication is that John has been reasserting his authority after the excommunication, enforcing a new oath of allegiance to counteract Pandulph's having freed his followers from their former oaths.) Behind their cold acceptance, however, lies an obvious discontent. Their very worry about John's "safety" (50), in requesting freedom for Arthur, has about it more of threat than of concern. Hubert's entrance before John's reply (as the Folio has it, rather than following that reply, where most editors have seen fit to place it) plainly implies, as Honigmann points out, that John grants their request as a matter of hypocritical policy, assured by Hubert's appearance that Arthur is dead. The nobles' well-justified suspicion leads them to depart with all the dignity of outraged principle. But, as Calderwood demonstrates, it becomes clear in the next scene that this apparent dependence upon principle has been the commodity of traitors.

Before we see them again, however, we have a new view of the Bastard. His increasing maturity is evident. He is no less open, no less loyal, but he makes his decisions more slowly, suspending judgment without hiding his grounds for suspicion. He is more critical. He speaks to John with more than a hint of annoyance—"if you be afeard to hear the worst,/Then let the worst unheard fall on your head" (135–6)—an annoyance which must arise from his close inspection of John and his disappointment with what he sees. He has met the lords "going to seek the grave/Of Arthur, whom they say is kill'd tonight/On your suggestion" (164–6). This report clearly invites denial from John, and the Bastard's suspicions cannot but increase when the invitation is not accepted. John instead claims ambiguously, "I have a way to win their loves again" (168), and sends the Bastard to bring them back. His first response is merely a sober acceptance of the charge—"I will seek them out" (169)—quite unlike his earlier enthusiasm, but John's reminder of the need to reconcile "subject enemies" (171) in the face of a French invasion restores his usual zeal. His loyalty to England takes precedence over any doubts he is feeling about John.

John's "way to win their loves again" is presumably explained in his immediate attempt to put the blame for Arthur's supposed death upon Hubert. Even while struggling to clear himself of the responsibility, John, with no sympathy for the boy, shows merely his own dismay at the outcome. Learning that Arthur lives, he expresses no joy, but thinks only of his own advantage: "Doth Arthur live? O' haste thee to the peers' (260). It is obvious, however, that Hubert has best served his king, both morally and politically, by disobeying him.

What John wanted was Arthur's death without the responsibity for it. The consequences of the alleged death have no sooner forced him to welcome the news that Arthur is yet alive than Fate gives him exactly what he first wanted: the third scene begins with Arthur's accidental death while leaping from the wall to escape. But it is too late and the thing John wanted becomes its own opposite. Though, as it turned out, he lacked the power, he is left with the responsibility—or at least the alleged responsibility, which is equally harmful.[4]

Arthur's body lies unfound on the stage, however, while the skein is tangled still further. The lords, who appeared to be leaving the king on the basis of outraged principle, turn out to have been already in correspondence with Pandulph. They know the French plans and are deserting John to save their skins; Arthur's supposed death was a pretext for treason, not a cause of revulsion. The justice of their pretext cannot excuse such hypocrisy. They have just renewed their oaths to the king they are deserting. In contrast, though he shares the same suspicions, the Bastard puts his duty to England first: "Whate'er you think, good words, I think, were best" (28). Given England's danger and the absence of evidence that Arthur is dead, "there is little reason in your grief" (30).

Discovery of Arthur's body will confirm all suspicions, and the audience waits in suspense for the Bastard's reaction while the lords indulge in self-justifying superlatives of horror. "Sir Richard, what think you?" Salisbury asks (41), but he and Pembroke both favour him with their own I-told-you-so's before—following surely a lengthy pause—he answers, simply and directly:

> It is a damned and a bloody work;
> The graceless action of a heavy hand,
> If that it be the work of any hand. (57–9)

His conditional conclusion, which in John would be but a final attempt to protect his own false position, is in the Bastard a sign of his increasing wisdom. It is under-girded for the audience by their knowledge that he is

---

[4] Th moral responsibility may, of course, be disputed, with the emphasis either on the accident or on the justified fear of John which forced Arthur to take the chance.

right to withhold final judgment, for the death was in fact accidental. But this rational contingency can only strike the eager lords as pussy-footing, and Salisbury returns the Bastard's "If" with indignant scorn. The lords, carried away by their own performance, join in a "holy vow" (67) for revenge. In spite of the evidence, they are mistaken; whatever John's unsuitability, they are taking a vow that can only be seen as traitorous.

Hubert's untimely message that Authur lives can hardly be expected to convince them of their error. The Bastard is forced to defend Hubert from their wrath, though his "If" is still unresolved. Shown Arthur's body, Hubert weeps, which the hypocrites naturally take for hypocrisy, but, held off by the Bastard, they cannot attack him, and they leave to join the Dauphin at Saint Edmundsbury.

Though willing to defend Hubert from attack while the facts are unclear, the Bastard has not abandoned his own strong suspicions. Hubert, in spite of his choice of a higher duty, is entangled in circumstantial evidence. The Bastard demands a direct answer—"Knew you of this fair work?" (116)—indicates both his stand if the answer is *yes*—"There is not yet so ugly a fiend of hell/As thou shalt be, if thou didst kill this child" (123–4)—and his honest opinion—"I do suspect thee very grievously" (134). This is the new, more thoughtful, less hot-headed but no less forthright man that the Bastard has grown to be, a far cry from the unthinking enthusiast he was in the first act. Having accepted Hubert's protestation of innocence, however, he is left with his suspicions of John. The issues surrounding Arthur's death are more complex, more confused and human, than most critics have been willing to allow, and the Bastard's reaction is the appropriate one for any conscientious man: "I am amaz'd, methinks, and lose my way/Among the thorns and dangers of this world" (140–41). The moral life is never, for a perceptive man, a simple choice between black and white, but life in a maze. The ambiguity of the Bastard's ensuing soliloquy reflects the ambiguity of the issues themselves, and his conclusion the neccessity to act in spite of it. He recognises both Arthur's right to the throne and the fact that the very question of right is now irrelevant; that "England" is dead, but that England remains to suffer, and "vast confusion waits,/As doth a raven on a sick-fall'n beast,/The imminent decay of wrested pomp" (152–4). This is what commodity has cost England. But, though he realises now that John's pomp was wrested, the Bastard sees no choice but continuing loyalty: "I'll to the King" (157).

## V

The fifth act begins with the king reduced to a most unkingly posture, however, yielding his crown to Pandulph. True, he receives it back at once, but only as the Pope's vassal, and we cannot fail to realise how far he has fallen from his earlier proud defiance. There is no religious issue here, but once again a simple political bargain, a yielding to force: John's immediate response to the brief ceremony is "Now keep your holy word: go meet the French" (5). He sees himself as re-establishing his own rule in his kingdom, where his people have been "Swearing allegiance . . . To stranger blood" (10–11), but, remembering his assurance that "No Italian priest/ Shall tithe or toll in our dominions" (III, i, 79–80), we realise that we have witnessed him doing precisely what he blames in his subjects.

The Bastard, upon his arrival with bad news, is again closely observing John and controlling his disgust only with difficulty. After mentioning military reversals and the nobles' treachery, he concludes, "And wild amazement hurries up and down/The little number of your doubtful friends" (35–6). He is reporting not merely a general but a pointedly personal condition ("I am amaz'd"), and though others may be "doubtful friends" because they are both fearful and untrusting, he is a trustworthy and fearless friend tormented by doubt. John's assumption that Arthur yet lives sounds to the Bastard like the sheerest hypocrisy and almost leads to a break. Given the Bastard's suspicions, "some damn'd hand" (41) is dangerously blunt, backing down no whit before John's face from the firm position already taken (IV, iii, 57–9). There is a crescendo of excitement, with John, in horror and guilt, attempting again to put the blame on Hubert, and the Bastard, having accepted Hubert's innocence, responding with a direct insinuation of John's responsibility for murder:

> *K. John.* That villain Hubert told me he did live.
> *Bast.* So, on my soul, he did, for aught he knew. (42–3)

The final pronoun, clearing Hubert, accuses John. This exchange, in which tempers have risen on both sides, must be followed by a long, electric silence, while John cringes and the Bastard cools to consider what he is doing. England must again be uppermost in his thoughts, for he stops, as it were, in mid-stream in his attack and turns to rallying John's spirits for the battle with the invaders. This self-control, this ability to quell his passionate outrage in order to undertake what is required by a higher loyalty, demonstrates the maturity the Bastard has reached. His moral superiority to John is clear; it is one of his glorious moments and prepares us to accept what follows.

Though he has, technically, misjudged the detail of Arthur's death, he has not in fact misjudged John. He pleads now only that the man act with outer semblance of the king in order to inspire his followers. But John has abandoned his authority to Pandulph and, pleased merely to have retained his throne, considers it a "happy peace" (63). Such peace with an invading army horrifies the Bastard—"O inglorious league!" (65)—and leads to so overwhelming a remonstrance that John, having just yielded to Pandulph, yields again, this time to the Bastard. John, a king incapable of kingship, is finally replaced in action by the man most capable of it.

The little ceremony by which John and Pandulph exchanged oaths is succeeded in the second scene by another little ceremony in which the Dauphin and the traitorous nobles do the same. These are the formalisations of allegiance, the hollow rites which political practice substitutes for the living loyalty exemplified by such a man as the Bastard.

The Bastard's new role is mirrored in the stage direction: always before he has been on his own, but now, as Regent, he enters "attended." Though he speaks of "the scope/And warrant limited unto my tongue" (122–3), it is but a way of postponing action until he learns how things stand; once he knows the situation, he assumes full authority. The King of and for whom he speaks—who "is prepar'd" (130), who "doth smile" (134) at the invasion, "the gallant monarch" (148), "warlike John" (176) —is of course not the man John but a verbal image of the king England needs at the moment. The image is not a mere fiction, however, for it is personified in the Bastard himself; though not the King, he wields the King's authority and speaks for England.

As though to ensure this distinction, the brief third scene shows us, in direct contrast to "warlike John," the utter impotence of the man beneath the public image. Ill with a fever, he is ordered off the field by the Bastard lest his very appearance dishearten the soldiers. The kingly role has been entirely transferred. The Bastard "alone upholds the day" (V, iv, 5).

The fourth scene twists the ironic complications of meaningless oaths and meaningful loyalty about as far as they can go. The dying Melun, breaking an oath (his to the Dauphin) which broke an oath (the Dauphin's and his to the English nobles) which broke an oath (theirs to John) reveals to the nobles that the Dauphin intends to execute them as soon as the battle is over. Abandoning their "holy vow," they hasten to return to John. Who is to disentangle true honour from such a skein as this? But Melun, saving their lives, says that he does so for the love of "one Hubert" (40), and because he himself had an English grandfather. This personal loyalty stands out above the meaningless oaths as a return to sanity and honour. The men saved by his love for Hubert are, however, the very men who misjudged and misused Hubert for their own selfish ends. They are saved by love for the man they scorned; the cutting of the skein carries overtones of Christian forgiveness.

Hubert it is who brings to the Bastard the news that John is dying. No time is wasted in the play on the mechanics of John's death; poisoning by a monk is supplied by history as Shakespeare knew it; his attention, however, is not on John but on the effect of John's approaching death on the Bastard. As they meet in the night, Hubert's "Who art thou?" (vi, 9) is precisely the question which remains to be settled, and the Bastard's "Who thou wilt" (9), coupled with the reminder of his Plantagenet blood, stresses the possibility toward which the play has apparently been aiming. We have seen Hubert grow from his attempt at a coldly rational avoidance of the problem of choice between loyalties to a realisation that a man is forced to commit himself and can only hope to do so honourably. We have seen the Bastard grow from a naïve enthusiast following chance to a man of mature insight and ability. What Hubert brings the Bastard now is, in effect, an invitation to take the throne, to assume the role he has in fact been filling and for which the character he inherited from his father has proven so eminently fitted. It is all understated, but the implications are clear: "I left him almost speechless; and broke out/To acquaint you with this evil, that you might/The better arm you to the sudden time" (24–6). Hubert foresees a struggle, and he wants the Bastard to have the throne. A struggle with whom? "The lords are all come back" (33). Clearly they must not gain control. But then a new complication is introduced: "And brought Prince Henry in their company" (34). This is the first mention in the play that John has a son and heir; the Bastard is (and many in the audience are) presumably reminded; dramatically it is startling news, further snarling the problem of moral choice.[5]

Prince Henry is apparently, like Arthur earlier, a young successor surrounded by a self-seeking league.[6] The Bastard is in the identical situation which faced John upon the death of Richard and the question is, will he, like John, usurp the throne? However self-seeking such a move might appear, it could clearly be considered also, given the Bastard's truly kingly character, to be for England's own good. The Bastard's immediate response is a prayer, as much for England as for himself: "Withhold thine indignation, mighty heaven,/And tempt us not to bear above our power!" (37–8). It is not a decision, but it is surely an aspiration not to be misled by the temptations of commodity. He is, in fact, not even willing at the moment to entertain the possibility. His immediate revelation that he has lost "half my power this night" (39), half of his army having been wiped out by a perverse tide, has been taken as showing that he is forced to his dynastic

[5] The structure of the play is not affected by whether or not the audience "knows all the time" that John must, historically, be followed on the throne by his son Henry. Whether or not the audience is surprised by the conclusion, the fact remains that the play, in its original division of claimants to the throne and its eventual elimination of two of them, seems to be moving toward the coronation of the third and only frustrates that expectation at the last minute by introducing the hitherto unmentioned heir.

[6] Where, when and how the lords made contact with the Prince is unmentioned. It would not be out of line with their duplicity and the complications of V, iv, to think of them as having been holding him in reserve as a future resource against Lewis.

decision only by his inability to muster sufficient strength to seize the throne from the combined forces of the returning noblemen. It is rather the explanation to Hubert of his prayer that heaven withhold its indignation. His worry is, as always, for England, facing the invader now with decimated forces. The invasion, not the succession, is his business at the moment. And the question is doubly untimely, for John is still "the king" (43).

But the audience knows, as the Bastard does not, that Lewis also has suffered grievous losses quite apart from the battle. Structurally, it remains only for John to die and the Bastard to reach his decision. Shakespeare first shows us Prince Henry, however, though the lines give us almost no clue as to how the author directed his company to have that part played. Prince Henry's few speeches leave him sounding a sensitive enough young man facing the death of his father, but it would be equally possible to play him as a weakling reminiscent of Arthur or as a young man of promising strength of character. And the effect he creates will naturally cast its light on the Bastard's decision. I think director and actor are called upon to attempt a compromise: Henry must be kept young enough to underline the similarity between the Bastard's choice and that which originally faced John; at the same time he must show some vitality and promise, for a suggestion of his complete dominance by the former traitors would be out of key with the generally hopeful conclusion of the play. This ambiguity of effect in the Prince's role is in part indicative of the fact that our attention is no longer on the question of what a king ought to be but has shifted over to that of how, given this situation, the Bastard ought to act.

John, who commenced the play as a successful usurper, dies miserably as he listens to the Bastard's news of England's losses. Even as John lies dying, his faithful follower pays him the compliment of not tempering the truth. And, though "God He knows how we shall answer" Lewis (60), John is no sooner dead than the Bastard turns to rallying the defence. But defence is not necessary, for the others know that Lewis has already sued for peace. There remains then but the single question, and it is quickly settled: The Bastard turns and kneels to Prince Henry. Whether the Prince combines the true kingly character with the possession and right here acknowledged, we are given little chance of knowing. That, however, is not the point. The very strength of character which made the Bastard the most worthy of Richard's heirs leads him to relinquish any devisive personal ambitions and to acknowledge a true duty to support the new king. This is the heir who alone remains of those who were established in the first act as having a share in Richard's heritage; this is the young man who once said "Gain, be my lord, for I will worship thee!"; this is the efficient commander who, as John failed, has actually been wielding the royal power. In spite of all these indications of a contrary denouement, he kneels to Prince Henry. In a world of self-seekers, his conception of honour has grown until he is capable of this self-denying loyalty to England. It is, of course, one of the tragic ironies of politics that a man may be cut off from authority by the very act which best demonstrates his worthiness to wield it.

Though it takes a paragraph—and could take more—to sketch the implications of the Bastard's kneeling, he is not to be seen as one who has thought it all through. He is impulsive at the close as he was at the beginning, but his impulses now are those of one whose original promise has come to maturity. His closing speech, with its ringing final couplet—"Nought shall make us rue/If England to itself do rest but true!"—has sometimes been dismissed as a platitudinous set piece. It is so only if we cannot see that the play has demonstrated the moral complexity of the problem of loyalty while the Bastard (and to a lesser extent Hubert) has shown us the self-denying acceptance of a higher duty which true loyalty demands from the man of honour.

# 10

# *Richard II*

*A. P. Rossiter*

The ancients had a thrifty habit of scrubbing parchments and using them again: these written-over documents are called palimpsests. It is a pity that frugal Elizabethan dramatists did not use parchments for play-books: we should not then need to rely on the hazardous ultraviolet of interpretative criticism or the infrared of critical bibliography, to decide whether to treat a play as a palimpsest or some other kind of problem, such as lack of coherence in its author's mind, divided aims, and the like. We only want to know things like this where immediate or considered subjective reaction makes us feel some kind of discontinuity, or inconsistency, in the *stuff* (a vague term, used deliberately: ultimately, the arrangements of words and their effects).

Over *Richard II* most critics have felt this. Pater is an exception: for him it does possess "like a musical composition . . . a certain concentration of all its parts, a simple continuity, an evenness in execution, which are rare in the great dramatist".[1] Dover Wilson echoes this; but elsewhere

*Reprinted from A. P. Rossiter,* Angel With Horns, *ed. Graham Storey (London: Longmans, Green & Co. Ltd., 1961) pp. 23–39 by permission of the publisher.*

[1] *Appreciations,* p. 210.

excludes the Fifth Act, which he wants blamed on to one of his "old plays": the lucubrations of that Master William Hypothesis, energetic researcher but no poet, who "assembled" Shakespeare's plots. Other commentators are bothered by inconsistencies or discontinuities; and I share their view. Whether you approach *Richard II* from the angle of the texture of the verse, the verse-styles, character, plot or theme, you encounter what geologists call "unconformities": The strata right of the "dyke" are said to be "unconformable"; and as geology has an overriding time-scheme, the dykes and upper layers are "later" than the rest. Applied to a play, it is only a rough analogy; although "old play" and "revisionist" theories will accept it as descriptively diagrammatic, I only use it to clarify the word "unconformable": implying "the whole *may* be consistent; but only if we have a theory of derangements or interruptions."

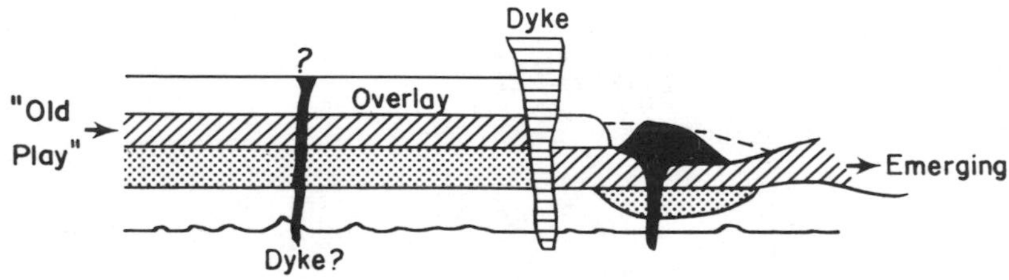


If ours is the character-approach, we find a lack of continuity between the Richard of Acts I and II and the melancholy introvert re-imported from Ireland. Those who praise the play as character-piece most highly, seem to *begin* their reading with Act III; and to "explain" the autocratic, capricious Richard of the first two acts as an imperious adolescent play-acting. This does not cover up the *lack of inside* in the early Richard; and when Coleridge remarks on "a constant flow of emotions from a total incapability of controlling them . . . a waste of that energy which should have been reserved for action," he as clearly labels the *second* Richard as he misses the *first*, who shows uncontrolled *action* and a lack of *feeling*. He makes him a Hamlet of the sentiments: i.e. what Coleridge thought "thought" was to Hamlet, he made emotion to Richard.

Dowden, in a study mainly very sound in what it points to, leaves him as sentimentalist, dreamer and dilettante; with a wistful charm, but condemned morally for want of what Newman called "seriousness of the intellect: the adult mind." That at any rate gives a firm line. There is something in Richard which calls out the latent homosexuality of critics; and I am gratified to find Dowden resisting it. Pater[2] is all the other way: Richard is "an exquisite poet. . . from first to last, in light and gloom alike, able to

---

[2] *Appreciations: Shakespeare's English Kings.*

see all things poetically, to give a poetic turn to his conduct of them" (and so on, to be softly echoed in a dozen school editions). "What a garden of words!" as Pater says. Others take the diametrically opposite view of exactly the same matter: plainly more from moral than dramatic reasons. And for all but the stern moralists, Richard's physical beauty is almost a main characteristic. You can dodge all contradictions by taking Aristotle's ὁμαλῶς ἀνώμαλον;[3] but, despite Aristotle, I think that such a character cannot be tragic: it surely lacks the perspicuity which makes logic of the tragic action.

About the other characters the critics are fairly agreed. Bolingbroke is an outline—a strong one; Gaunt is made rather too much of, considering he is gone by Act III; the Favourites are zeros; York "an incomparable, an incredible, an unintelligible and a monstrous nullity" (Swinburne) or (G. M. Young) "the first civil servant in our literature."[4] (I do not offer these as synonyms.) In short, they are mainly orchestra: Gaunt, the woodwind Queen, Messengers, marches and noises-off.

If we consider the play's themes, we find that although political approaches—making the play historical-epical-moral—do something to smooth-in the Duchess of Gloucester (I, ii), the omens, the Gardener and the substance of Gaunt, they cannot make the beginning unragged, nor the rumpus in Westminster Hall (the second Quarrel-scene) clearly relevant; nor do anything to put the York-Aumerle scenes into any sort of order or "degree". To generalize, most commentators direct attention to parts of the play which they *can* manage, and tacitly divert it from "misfits" they cannot; and in this there is no great critical difference between "character" and "thematic" approaches. Both do vaguely agree in taking measures to smooth over a kind of "fold" between Acts II and III; and both, in different ways, have difficulties over Shakespeare's not very pellucid method of presenting some of the essentials of the story, over the awkward way in which he leaves us to guess here and there, mainly in, or as a result of, Acts I and II. This also applies to his artistic intentions. The view of the play as "ceremonial";Dover Wilson's contention that "it ought to be played throughout as ritual...it stands far closer to the Catholic service of the Mass than to Ibsen's *Brand* or...St. *Joan*"; the lyrical-tragedy view,[5] the poet-king view: All show a similar smoothing-over of unconformities, once taken back to the text.

If we look at the verse, it is a crude discrimination to say there are three styles: rhyme (mainly couplets) and two sorts of blank verse—that

---

3 "consistently inconsistent."

4 In a private letter to Dover Wilson quoted in the *New Cambridge* edition of *Richard II,* p. iv.

5 If this is what Dover Wilson's relation of it to *Love's Labour's Lost* means (op. cit., p. xi).

of the Deposition, say, and an "earlier" kind. The "early" type in fact ranges from a flattish competence (Act I, or Bolingbroke at V, iii, 1–12, "Can no man tell me of my unthrifty son?...") to a jumbled incompetence, aptly described by York's comment on the state of England at II, ii, 121–2:

> All is uneven,
> And everything is left at six and seven.

The couplets vary as much, although this is less striking, as Shakespeare wrote within a convention that did not *hear* bad couplets as we hear them; and in Acts I and II especially they pop in and out most disconcertingly. The worst in both kinds, rhyme and blank verse, is distressingly or comically bad. As a *formal* type of play in what Dover Wilson[6] calls "deliberately patterned speech", it contrasts strikingly with the operatic consistency of *Richard III*.

Examine the texture of the verse, and Eliot's "patterned speech" *is* there; mainly in the "early" type of verse, but also in some of the other. It is easiest seen where not very good: where it represents the heavily over-written Elizabethan High-Renaissance manner, over-ingenious with a mainly *verbal* wit, and obtrusive. It is obtrusive, I mean, in Keats's sense: "Poetry should be great and *unobtrusive*, a thing which enters into one's soul and does not startle or amaze it with itself, but with its subject." e.g.

> The setting sun, and music at the close,
> As the last taste of sweets, is sweetest last,
> Writ in remembrance more than things long past. (II, i, 12–14)

There is a marked degree of what Keats would call "obtrusiveness" in such writing. Frigid ingenuities accompany it, such as this from Northumberland:

> And hope to joy, is little less in joy
> Than hope enjoy'd. (II, iii, 15)

or the Queen's tortuous lines where she has conceived a grief, and wrenches her imagination to find out what has caused it:

> *Bushy.* 'Tis nothing but conceit, my gracious lady.
> *Queen.* 'Tis nothing less: conceit is still deriv'd
> From some forefather grief; mine is not so,
> For nothing hath begot my something grief,
> Or something hath the nothing that I grieve;
> 'Tis in reversion that I do possess—
> But what it is that is not yet known what,
> I cannot name; 'tis nameless woe, I wot. (II, ii, 33–40)

---

6 *Ibid.*, p. xii.

That is really far worse than York's simple Kyd-pattern:

> Grace me no grace, nor uncle me no uncle.
> I am no traitor's uncle; and that word 'grace'
> In an ungracious mouth is but profane. (II, iii, 87–9)

lines all right as patterned, although what follows—"Why have those banish'd and forbidden legs..."—is not easily taken seriously.[7]

It is not only that there is more wit in the word-connections than in the thought (and the "wit," even when called "metaphysical," is always rather shallow); it is that these "formal" tricks, like the eruptions of couplets, upset and confuse the *tone* both for reader and actor. Take, for instance, Bolingbroke's lines in III, i, "Bring forth these men...": blank verse in neither the "early" nor the "more mature" style, but extremely fluent, very competent, totally without flourish. He has a statement of a heart-felt grievance to make, and he makes it: with force, clarity and cool dignity. Look back at Bolingbroke's lines in Act I, and you see at once how difficult two such disparate manners are for the best of actors.

The result tends to be recitation in a pageant, where dress and décor are everything (bar, of course, Richard). Once again, there is a kind of fold (or "fault") in the play: Acts I and II are on one side of it, III and IV on the other; and in Act V something comes up to the surface which one is very strongly tempted to call "half-revised Old Play." I cannot pretend that the division in verse-texture is as sharp as all that; but the view of the play as "ceremonial" rests heavily on the Quarrel, the Lists and the "patriotic" oration of Gaunt; and in Act III there does come a marked change. Richard's

> Well you deserve. They well deserve to have
> That know the strong'st and surest way to get (III, iii, 200–1)

has, for example, in context, a sinewy force, an essential *unobtusive* poetry, which is totally absent in Acts I and II (say what you will of Gaunt's melodious lamentation on England gone to the dogs).

It is on the assumption of that unconformity of Acts I and II that I shall rest my further examination of the play: accepting, that is, a discontinuity in character; some marked incoherences and dubieties in the story; a related uncertainty in the theme (tragic or political); and more than one kind of inconsistency in the texture of the verse. In so doing, I shall seem to be quarrelling with the "political" view of the play: that

[7] York's lines embarrass most Yorks; and so much of him is a fussy, incompetent old gentleman, that I wonder whether he always *was* a bit of a joke: a mild one, and perhaps poorly and misguidedly imitated from the comical side of Woodstock.

here we have the fall of a rightful king, brought about by wilful rebellion, the lifting of "an angry arm against God's minister," his Deputy; and that the curse that this brings on Lancaster and England is the uniting theme of an English dramatic-epic, in Shakespeare's peculiar double tetralogy. I am not really refuting the political pattern, although it has been given too much emphasis, and also, I think, made too *simple*. What I really question is the *unity,* the integral quality of the sequence.

*Richard II,* as the first play, seems to me to have no real beginning; a coherent middle; and a ragged, muddled end, only some of which can be explained as a Shakespearian parallel to the famous "end-links" of Chaucer. Taken by itself, if we stand back far enough, it does look like the Aristotelean "simple" tragedy: The sort he thought inferior, having neither *peripeteia* nor any real *anagnorisis*. Richard seems to slip steadily into calamity, mainly through "force of circumstances"; and his *hamartia* (unless we accept all the Bradleyan critics tell us) is a fatal step, a *blunder,* the mishandling of a quarrel between two violent noblemen. But go near enough to grasp the *action,* sticking tight to the text, and you will find that this alleged first term in a coherently planned series is thoroughly uncertain about its own start, and uncertain at the simplest level of the story, as well as on the major matter of essential (or political) rights and wrongs.

From now on, I shall dogmatize: state my case and leave it to your verdicts.

*Richard II's* value as first term in an epic-historical series is seriously flawed by its peculiar dependence on *Woodstock:*[8] peculiar since Shakespeare not only took items from it, but also *left behind* in it explanations badly needed in his play, items taken for granted, or as read, which produce puzzles that cannot be cleared up without reference to the earlier play. To some extent, then, *Richard II* as a play does not contain within itself the reason why it is thus and not otherwise. If so, the alleged epic scheme is faulty, since the "beginning" is not a beginning.

*Richard II* is about the fall and deposition of a King. The fall results from two events: *(a)* the quarrel of Bolingbroke and Mowbray, which Shakespeare invites us to focus down to the pin-point *hamartia* of throwing down the warder in the lists (see Mowbray's son in *2 Henry IV,* IV, i, 25–9); and *(b)* the falling-away of York, and all England, on Bolingbroke's landing. This second event has to do with Richard's failings as monarch: with "the state of England," which some critics make a main theme, although (Gaunt's reproaches apart) there is very little about it in the text. Ross (at II, i, 246) says, "The commons hath he pill'd with grievous taxes"; but that, as it happens, is a direct echo from *Woodstock* (I, iii, 112),[9] where "Plain Thomas," being mocked about his homespun frieze, says:

---

[8] Egerton MS. 1944, ed. Frijlinck, M.S.R., 1929; A. P. Rossiter, *Woodstock: A Moral History,* Chatto & Windus, 1946.

[9] References are to Rossiter's edition.

"did some here wear that fashion,/They would not tax and pill the commons so." In short, the connection between favourites and extravagance, extravagance and exaction, exactions and Richard's loss of power, is crystal-clear in *Woodstock* and nowhere else. In *Richard II* Willoughby takes up Ross with a mention of "daily new exactions," "As blanks, benevolences, and I wot not what"; and we wot not what neither. *Editors* tell us; but the fact is, there is precious little in Holinshed about "blanks"; nothing about "benevolences" (devised by Edward IV!); and one sentence about a *rumour* "that the King had set to farme the realme of England unto sir Wm. Scroope earle of Wiltshire...to Sir Jno. Bushie, sir Jno. Bagot, and sir Hy. Greene knights" (iii, 496, col. i, *ad fin.*). If we look at *Richard II*, taking it as it comes (as an audience *must*), we find: (1) *Before* Gaunt's accusations, only one inexplicit line by Richard, "We are enforc'd to farm our royal realm" (I, iv, 45); a bit more on blank charters following it, but no connecting of either with the evil influence of favourites. (2) It is only 190 lines *after* Gaunt's "Bound in with...inky blots and rotten parchment bonds," that Ross growls, "The Earl of Wiltshire hath the realm in farm" (II, i, 256). (3) *Between* these references lie Gaunt's two nearly-unintelligible charges: "rotten parchment bonds" and "Thy state of law is bondslave to the law" (II, i, 64 and 114). The Arden edition notes show these *are* obscurities: Both notes are nonsense.

Now these things are perfectly clear and straightforward to anyone who reads *Woodstock,* Acts II, III and IV of which are concerned with the rise to power of the favourites, headed by the villainous Lord Chief Justice Tresilian; their financial iniquities when *in* power (III and IV); and what "blanks" meant to the Commons (IV, iii). I can make but one point: The author of *Woodstock* scrambles and hashes history to make Richard's extortions a matter of legal iniquity: slavery to bonds, regal servitude to the law of contract.[10] And he therefore *stages* Richard presented with a legal instrument (a bond or lease), giving the favourites full command of the Exchequer and all the royal estates etc. in exchange for a monthly stipend of £7,000. That is what Gaunt is alluding to; and the whole difficulty of the financial wickedness of both Richard and the favourites in *Richard II* is simply that Shakespeare *alludes* and never explains. Nor is that all. Gaunt's accusations are not only explained by *Woodstock:* His terms of reproach derive from that text. England is

now leas'd out...
Like to a tenement or pelting farm;

10 He shifts back the fiscal tyranny from 1498 to a mythical date before 1488 (when Tresilian was hanged). Why does he do this? Because he was a Common-Law man, writing a moral history against the King's-Law men (i.e. Bacon as *versus* Coke). Hence the contradiction between his play and Shakespeare's on kingly right, as stated by Gaunt in *Richard II,* I, ii.

and later:

> Landlord of England art thou now, not King.
> Thy state of law is bondslave to the law....
> (II, i, 59–60; 113–14)

In *Woodstock,* IV, i, where Richard is presented with the bond, later read by Tresilian in full, and before the flattering Greene twists him round to it, Richard has a (cancelled) speech of apprehension or self-reproach: "We shall be censured strangely..." (when people think of the Black Prince)

> ...And we his son, to ease our wanton youth
> Become a landlord to this warlike realm,
> Rent out our kingdom like a pelting farm,
> That erst was held, as fair as Babylon,
> The maiden conqueress to all the world (IV, i, 146)

The term "landlord" is applied to Richard four times in this play: *inter alia* by the Ghost of Edward III:

> Richard of Bordeaux, my accursed grandchild...
> Becomes a landlord to my kingly titles,
> Rents out my crown's revenues... (V, i, 86 f.);

and by Gaunt himself:

> England now laments...
> Her royalties are lost: her state made base;
> And thou no king, but landlord now become
> To this great state that terrored christendom (V, iii, 104 f.)

The emphasis of iteration and the word "least" (not in Holinshed) show how Shakespeare's Gaunt has, so to speak, his past political experience in mind—in a play much rather than a Chronicle. This is not simply a source-hunter's game: It affects the whole moral complexion of Richard in Acts I and II, and alters both the colour of the theme and Shakespeare's reading of history.

It also bears on what we make of the *personæ,* as "characters" or as "symbols": especially the favourites, but, by repercussion, Gaunt too. In *Richard II* the blank-charter iniquity is less skimped; but only in *Woodstock* does the wickedness of income-tax returns signed "blank" (leaving the collector to invent the income) receive the emphasis we can call "normal." Nor, in Richard, is the dressy extravagance of favourites and Court made a clear cause. Shakespeare's Bushy, Greene and Bagot are nearly "blank-charters" themselves: once again because they are taken as *seen* (in their bad habits as they lived—on the stage); and "recognised" as shadows of vanity, flattery and contempt of good counsel, opposed symbolically and morally to what Gaunt stands for (which is identical with what he and York and Thomas of Woodstock stood for in *Woodstock:* in flat defiance of Chronicle and truth). Shakespeare's play leaves us wondering what vices they had; for apart from Bolingbroke's accusations of homosexuality (refuted by the Queen's behaviour throughout), they do not get beyond being a *1066 and All That* "bad thing."

Their real evil, which Shakespeare presents only by allusion, is that they *were* the political and moral opposites to Richard's "good old uncles," all of whom, in both plays, are economy, retrenchment, conservatism, public service and plain-Englishry. A phrase here points incontrovertibly to *Woodstock*. Gaunt's "My brother Gloucester, plain well-meaning soul" (II, i, 128), refers solely to the other play. "Plain homespun Thomas," who wears frieze at Court and is comically mistaken by a groom for an overdressed popinjay (III, ii), is, historically, a male Mrs. Harris. In Chronicle there is no such person: He is purely a *dramatis persona,* partly modelled on the good Duke Humphrey of *2 Henry VI* and with comparable moral functions. Against Dover Wilson's attempt to extract a "good" Gaunt from Froissart, I find that Shakespeare's Gaunt is the same "form" (or "shadow" in an allegory of State) as Thomas. By this I do not mean that either lacks "character": only that moral function, not history, determines their forms.

The most unquestionably historical thing that Woodstock does is to get murdered; and here the events of *Woodstock,* assumed to be known, have their most important bearing on the moral structure of Shakespeare's play: on the character of Richard, the mechanism of his fall, and the essential rights and wrongs behind the quarrel. No one can read *Richard II* and not encounter the problem, "Who killed Woodstock?" Bolingbroke accuses Mowbray of it; Gaunt tells the Duchess of Gloucester that Richard was responsible; Bagot and Fitzwater say it was Aumerle: they imply, moreover, that the murder took place *after* Bolingbroke was banished, and add that Mowbray said so (IV, i, 80). To say they are all liars is no more than they all say to one another. The whole thing makes sense, and makes the plot of Acts I and II far more coherent, as soon as we know that Woodstock was (1) kidnapped in a masque, with Richard and his favourites present; (2) conveyed to Calais, the Governor of which is called Lapoole in the play, but *was* Thomas Mowbray; and (3) there put to death (in a stirring scene) not by the Governor, but rather against his will, and by two experts in tidy murder sent from England.

Thus in the quarrel, Mowbray knows that Richard knows the truth, and that Bolingbroke knows most of it. Hence Richard's desire to quiet the pair, and his saying *he* will calm Norfolk, while Gaunt calms Bolingbroke. Hence his "How high a pitch his resolution soars!" (I, i, 109), when Bolingbroke has said that Gloucester's blood cries "to me for justice and rough chastisement." Hence, too, the riddling lines where Mowbray says:

> ...For Gloucester's death—
> I slew him not, but to my own disgrace
> Neglected my sworn duty in that case. (I, i, 132–4)

Reference to *Woodstock* suggests at once that the allusion is to Act V, i, where Woodstock appeals to Lapoole "by virtue of nobility" and "on that allegiance/Thou ow'st the offspring of King Edward's house" (V, i, 145 f.), when he fears murder. The lines in Shakespeare mean, then, that Mowbray admits he was Governor (which is known to everyone), and that he failed in his sworn duty to protect the blood royal (which again is obvious). But simultaneously he reminds Richard of *why* he failed (Richard threatened his life if Woodstock was not killed), while giving nothing away. For "I slew him not" is perfectly true of Lapoole himself: Woodstock was killed by agents, and all Lapoole-Mowbray did was not to prevent them.[11]

This criminal collusion with Mowbray *could* supply the motive for the stopping of the single-combat at Coventry. The principle of trial-by-arms is that it gives "the judgement of God"; and we may plausibly make the induction that Richard is afraid that God will give the right verdict. But it is only a reasonable *induction,* for Shakespeare gives no hint of Richard's motives. Character-critics are content to see here only an exhibition of Richard's exhibitionism: his self-regarding theatricality in the kingly role—even, perhaps, the actor-manager's vanity, in dramatically focusing all eyes on himself and dragging them away from the combatants (like a film-star at a prize-fight). That is there, no doubt: the Deposition-scene supports it, with Richard in a complex pageant of vanity, as the Middle Ages regarded it: stripping himself of kingly vanities, the pomps and glories of temporal rule; gazing in the glass of vanity; and yet, vanity of vanities, still making himself the focus of a dramatic contemplation of the essential human vanity, persistent though the robe is stripped, the mirror shivered.

But this act of throwing down the warder is of fatal consequence: fatal and fateful. From that one act a strict logic of events throws down Plantagenet and, inside ninety years, throws up Tudor. The logic of the eight-play series *and* the exact apprehension of the "tragedy" demand that

---

[11] Before dismissing *Woodstock,* let me remark that several of Dover Wilson's notes on *Richard II* (*New Cambridge* edn.) are unreliable, mainly because of his predisposition to lay a non-Shakespearean "old play" behind Shakespeare's, written by a wide-reading historian who potted many recondite chronicles. But the puzzle he makes of Bagot (who loses his head *en route* for Ireland and then apparently comes back to life again) vanishes if *Woodstock* is consulted; York's reference to "nor my own disgrace" (II, i, 168) is not a loose end, but alludes to the same Duke's "Disgraced our names and thrust us from his court" (*Woodstock,* III, ii, 4); and his attempt to make the phrase "upon pain of life" (I, iii, 140 and 153) a link with Froissart ("I have not found the phrase in any of the sources except Froissart...") fails completely, as it is used in *Woodstock,* IV, iii, 171.

we should know if it was *guilt* (and guilt of royal blood) which started this momentous sequence. If not, where is the beginning of the epic-drama? Further back. Then it has no unity. And in this case we cannot delve into *Woodstock* for the answer and come out certain.

We must be satisfied with a fair degree of probability and the absence of final certainty. The explanation of the King's desertion by England is writ large in *Woodstock*: favourites, vanities, extravagances, taxation, extortion, antipathy to sound counsel: all these are kingly vices. The explanation of the quarrel is there too: briefly, "Woodstock's blood," the wanton murder of a royal prince, epitome of the right-mindedness and political and social responsibility which are expressed in Gaunt. Integrate the causes of Richard's fall, and his confused actions throughout Acts I and II derive from a guilt, or guilts, out of which there is no clear path. Shakespeare knows this—indeed too well: He slips into the lecturer's commonest fault, of assuming that everybody must know what, as it happens, many do *not*. But this applies mainly to the first two acts alone. It explains Richard as he there appears, and explains too why a different Richard arrives from Ireland in Act III. It also suggests why Bolingbroke's intentions about the crown are left rather obscure. I believe that the *historic* fact is that there was a well-contrived conspiracy, leading to a well-timed landing. But Shakespeare took Halle's hint that Bolingbroke had no glimmer of what fate had in store for him: that chance would have him King (as we should say), and so chance crowned him. It is, after all, what he tells Warwick before his death:

> ...God knows, I had no such intent,
> But that necessity so bow'd the state
> That I and greatness were compell'd to kiss.
> (*2 Henry IV*, III, i, 72–4)

If, though, we accept the many hints in *Richard II* that Richard was a guilty *King*—and it is the guilt of the King, much rather than the innate wickedness of the man, that *Woodstock* emphasizes—then Bolingbroke's walk-in to kingship is itself one more instance of that process of retributive reaction which is the really *tragic* element in the History plays (the judgement of God in the process of history, as I suppose Professor Butterfield would call it). This retributive reaction, as a divinity that shapes the ends of England, is a principle which makes sense and logic of Bolingbroke's incredibly easy usurpation. Richard is *wrong,* but Bolingbroke's coronation is *not right*; and Richard's murder converts it to the blackest wrong. This greatly reduces the possibility of regarding Richard as a "royal martyr" or "sacrificial-king." It should also prevent our making Shakespeare a kind of sentimental conservative, looking nostalgically back, like Walter Scott, to the "great age" of Chivalry and showing us "the waning of the Middle Ages."

It implies a conception, or apprehension, of *history*. If the ills of England do not begin with Richard's deposition, then there is a dreary endlessness in this long sample of human affairs, sometimes cyclical, but always a conspectus of half-blinded actions and unpremeditated reactions, apparently with neither end nor beginning. Thus Shakespeare *"ends"* with the triumph of Henry V, pointing straight to Henry VI and all *that*: "Another Troy will rise and rot, another lineage feed the crow." The effect is to present the "historical process" as *obscure tragedy,* in which men are compelled, constrained, baffled and bent by circumstances in which their actions do *not* express their characters. Even in *Richard II* there are many light touches of irony, mainly the irony of frustration: for what makes such tragedy "obscure" is a kind of *stupidity* in events (in men and things), something far more confused and uncertain than Fate or Destiny. Hence the weariness of both Richard ("Learn, good soul,/To think our former state a happy dream": V, i, 17 f.) and King Henry (his invocation of sleep: *2 Henry IV,* III, i). The times are always out of joint: and the weak men, strong men, good men and bad men who try to re-articulate them, are *all* fumblers, or so compromised that their very skill is vain. As Pater said "No! Shakespeare's kings are not, nor are meant to be, great men."

But if we turn to Hamlet, is not that, too, in a different sense, an "obscure tragedy"? Obscure, in the sense that *Othello* is not, nor *Coriolanus,* nor *Antony and Cleopatra.* And though "the mystery of things" is heavy enough within *Macbeth* and *Lear,* they bear the mind beyond that iron curtain which shuts about the "History" world. Hamlet stands between: and its two worlds of action and sensibility have their somewhat shadowy counterparts in *Richard II.* It is not a dream of "sensibility" in any way like Hamlet's: rather, of sentiments, of the sentimentalist, as defined in Meredith's aphorism, quoted by Stephen Dedalus to Malachi Mulligan: "The sentimentalist is he who would enjoy without incurring the immense debtorship for a thing done."

The central experience in *Richard II* is its *middle,* the substance of Acts III and IV. The ceremonial or ritual scenes and styles do matter: Although only six scenes out of nineteen can be called "ritualistic" or formalized. They matter because of what they *contrast* with; for in that contrast there is a tonal and visual rendering of the contrast of Richard and his group and Bolingbroke and his, but more as *Weltanschauungen* or aspects of human experience than as just "characters."

However and whenever *Richard II* is played, the pageant-element is important (as much for 1955 as for 1595). But this element is double, not single. After the lists, etc., a new tone begins to emerge at the end of II, i, in the huddle of sullen earls plotting together after the fops have gone. Northumberland emerges there; and a grim meaning is given him at once in:

> Not so; even through the hollow eyes of death
> I spy life peering... (II, i, 270)

That is more than "character." When Bolingbroke lands, Northumberland is there beside him; and in III, i, and III, iii, I am sure that the *visual* contrast between these armed campaigners and the toy warfare of the lists, the brilliant and vapid refinement of the Court, are part of the play as images. Elizabethan eyes saw iron as we see khaki battle-dress and camouflage. And, significantly, Richard's words in banishing Bolingbroke foreshadow this very change: he would *avoid* the

> ...harsh-resounding trumpets' dreadful bray,
> And grating shock of wrathful iron arms.... (I, iii, 135–6)

But the iron comes; and with it a touch of iron in the verse: as witness Bolingbroke's opening lines in the scenes before and after Richard's speech on landing in Wales, "Dear earth, I do salute thee with my hand...." The answer to that is the efficient staff-officer's: "So that by this intelligence we learn/The Welshmen are dispers'd." (II, iii, 1). It is more than character-contrast: the verse, backed by the hardening of the human exteriors, the steel-framed faces, jars two worlds together. The same jar is in the Deposition-scene. It gives the play its meaning and experience, as a kind of tragic drama: the obscure tragedy, unclear, interesting, rather disheartening, of "Shakespearian history."

The nature of the jar—the nature of those two worlds—makes Richard less than the fully tragic hero. One is the half-fantasy world of the Court, where Richard's half-dream kingship reigns, with angels at his beck and serpents for his foes; the other is that other dream, of action, will and curt-worded decision, in which he is nothing, or a passive sufferer, a king of woes (or merely a king of words). In the mirror-episode the two dreams doubly confront each other. This it is that makes the Arden editor, following Pater, tell us Richard's nature is "that of the poet who has unfortunately had kingship thrust upon him." One need not reply, "If so, surely a very *bad* poet"; for the answer is in Dowden, or in what Dowden quotes from Kreyssig: "...he affords us the shocking spectacle of an absolute bankruptcy, mental and spiritual no less than in the world of outward affairs, caused by one condition only: that nature has given him the character of a Dilettante, and called him to a position which, more than any other, demands the Artist."[12]

---

12 Kreyssig, *Vorlesungen über Shakespeare* (ed. 1874), i. p. 189, quoted (in original) by Dowden, *Shakespere: His Mind and Art* (ed. 1892), p. 195.

# 11

# The Birth and Death of Falstaff Reconsidered

*Philip Williams*

In "Falstaff No Martyr," a paper read at a recent meeting of the South Atlantic Modern Language Association, Prof. Allan Gilbert said:

> Perhaps the most striking lack of the critics for many years and to no small extent at present is failure to consider the question: What are the proper limits of literary interpretation? Art is universal, we are told. But that hardly means that anything can be brought into the exposition of a speech or character. The middle ages...had a formula for exegesis.... Ridiculous enough, in our eyes, are some of their interpretations. But we may admire their clarity. A medieval preacher must have realized when he went over from the literal Samson to the allegorical Christ. But for a modern going from Falstaff, a fat man trying to run, to Falstaff the spirit of humanity, there is no post to mark the boundary. Do we have deduction straight from the play, or do we have the critic's fancy? Or, the boundaries of interpretation can be differently considered. Academics as we are here, we lay some importance on detailed study, even of the single word. How far can we go in allowing critics the very utmost from every word, from insisting on its absolute connection with every other word in the play? Or if they

*Reprinted from* Shakespeare Quarterly, *VIII (1957), 359–365 by permission of The Shakespeare Association of America, Inc.*

take the play just as something to be put on the stage, played so rapidly that a hearer cannot stop to reflect but must rely on a hurried impression, a total rather than a detailed effect, how far can we trust such an impression as adequate?

These are difficult questions, and I profess no answers. But a recent book on Shakespeare by the distinguished Lecturer in English at Christ Church, Oxford, and the review of that book by an even more distinguished American scholar afford a convenient case on which to speculate. I refer to Mr. J. I. M. Stewart's *Character and Motive in Shakespeare,* and "A Freudian Detective's Shakespeare," the long review of it by Prof. E. E. Stoll. The subject for consideration here can conveniently be limited to Stewart's final chapter, "The Birth and Death of Falstaff."

In this chapter, Stewart first discusses the inadequacies of the familiar critical approaches, and then, by drawing freely on the formulations of psychology and anthropology, offers what seems to him a more satisfactory interpretation. The objections to his predecessors are tightly argued and cogently expressed; but the book is a thin one, and there is room for little documentation of the author's own critical insights. Having canvassed the interpretations of Falstaff from Morgann to Dover Wilson, Mr. Stewart presents his own contribution:

> I suggest that Hal, by a displacement common enough in the evolution of ritual, kills Falstaff instead of killing the king, his father. In a sense Falstaff *is* his father; certainly a father-substitute in the psychologist's word; and this makes the theory of a vicarious sacrifice the more colourable.

For Prof. Stoll, this is arrant nonsense. He writes:

> And Falstaff. Whether in the hands of [Mr. Stewart] he or Leontes is the more astounding the reader shall now judge for himself. After repeating many of the vagaries of Maurice Morgann and his followers on the subject, Mr. Stewart ends up by making him symbolical, the victim of a fertility ritual, as in *The Golden Bough.* (After Freud Frazer, but Sir James, I trust, would of this have none; and again we can determine what Shakespeare's conception was *not.*) There is something "atavic" about the final rejection of him on the stage (to many of us now unacceptable) as there is, the critic thinks, also about the blinding of Gloucester, which reminds him (as possibly nobody else in the world) of Uranus castrated by his son Cronus (so long before Oedipus!) with the scythe. Similarly, the rejection is thought to be like the primeval religious rite of killing the king, and thus is made more acceptable. . . . But why, even if Shakespeare and the audience thus "instinctively" anticipated Freud and Frazer, Hal, the hero of Agincourt-to-be, should engage in a "vicarious sacrifice" of his real father, whose death he has mourned, does not satisfactorily appear. Nor does any reason why that should have reconciled the Elizabethan (however it may be with us) to the comic fat man's ignominious, though not unmerited end.

> And All this at Oxford, the Oxford of Arnold, Raleigh, the late illustrious Bradley, Ker, and Mackail!

It must be emphasized that Mr. Stewart does not claim uniqueness for his interpretation. "I hope it will be clear," he writes, "that what I am... concerned with is the *multiple* significance of the Falstaff story. To assert that Falstaff is the sacrificial object in a fertility ritual is not in the least to deny that he is (a good deal less remotely indeed) the Riot of a Morality (as Dover Wilson would have it)." Nor does Mr. Stewart deny that Falstaff "is" Prof. Stoll's braggart soldier, or Prof. Draper's down-and-out military man. His primary concern is why we, in the theatre if not in the study, accept the rejection and death as inevitable and right.

If we turn to the plays themselves, do we find that what Shakespeare wrote can possibly permit Mr. Stewart's startling interpretation, which proposes that instead of killing his real father, Hal kills Falstaff, a father-substitute; and that this killing is necessary before a diseased land can regain its health under a virile young king? Is this "deduction straight from the play," or is it "the critic's fancy"?

The antagonism between Prince Hal and his king-father is an important, and obvious, theme in these plays, from the forward-looking scene near the end of *Richard II* in which King Henry asks for news about his "unthrifty" son and adds, "If any plague hang over us 'tis he," to the death-bed scene near the end of *Henry IV, Part Two*, in which the king sums up the antagonism between father and son with the charge, "Thy life did manifest thou lovedst me not." Embedded in this antagonism are latent parricidal impulses, and King Henry IV is haunted by the vision of being slain by the son he has publicly rejected and whom he at times hates. For him, Hal is his "nearest and dearest enemy." When, at the battle of Shrewsbury, Hal rescues the king from Douglas, Henry is almost surprised:

> Thou hast redeem'd thy lost opinion,
> And show'd thou makest some tender of my life.

Hal's reply is curious, suggesting as it does that thoughts of his father's death had indeed not been absent from his mind:

> O God, they did me too much injury
> That ever said I hearkened for your death.
> If it were so, I might have let alone
> The insulting hand of Douglas over you
> Which would have been as speedy in your end
> As all the poisonous potions in the world,
> And saved the treacherous labour of your son.

When on his death-bed, Henry awakes to find the crown gone, taken by his son, the theme of parricide receives long and detailed statement:

This part of his conjoins with my disease
And helps to end me. See, sons, what things you are!
How quickly nature falls into revolt
When gold becomes her object!
For this the foolish over-careful fathers
Have broke their sleep with thoughts, their brains with care,
Their bones with industry;
For this they have engrossed and piled up
The cankered heaps of strange-achieved gold;
For this they have been thoughtful to invest
Their sons with arts and martial exercises:
When like the bee, culling from every flower
The virtuous sweets,
Our things packed with wax, our mouths with honey,
We bring it to the hive, and, like the bees,
Are murdered for our pains.

Hal then reenters, saying that he never thought to hear the king speak again. "Thy wish was father, Harry, to that thought," says the king, who then continues the parricide theme:

Thou hid'st a thousand daggers in thy thoughts
Which thou hast whetted on thy stony heart
To stab at half an hour of my life.

In Hal's reply to these charges, he shifts the parricidal impulse from himself to the crown: It is not I but the crown who kills my father:

I spake unto this crown as having sense,
And thus unbraided it: 'The care on thee depending
Hath fed upon the body of my father. . . .
[And] eat thy bearer up.' Thus most royal liege
Accusing it, I put it on my head,
To try with it, as with an enemy
That had before my face murdered my father.

In the corresponding scene in *The Famous Victories of Henry V,* based on hints found in the chronicles, Hal appears before the sick king with a drawn dagger. Shakespeare subtilizes his crude source, putting the daggers in Hal's mind rather than in his hand, but the overtones in both scenes are the same: parricide.

As a result of this antagonism between father and son, it is to be expected, the psychologist would say, that the son seeks a father-substitute. Given the character of the real father—sin-ridden, punctilious, lean, and cold—he would go further and predict what the father image would be: It would be, of course, a Falstaff, the opposite of the real father in all those qualities that the prince resents, and yet like enough the real father to make the identification possible. Falstaff, without a son of his own, has found that son in Hal; and Hal, rejecting and rejected by his real father, has found

Falstaff. It is right, the psychologist would add, that the ambivalent feeling of love-hate toward the real father be transferred to the father image, and this psychological insight may, in part at least, explain Hal's paradoxical attitude toward Falstaff.

Falstaff's role as father to Hal is unobtrusively developed throughout the plays, but in certain scenes the father-son relationship receives explicit statement. Falstaff's possessive paternalism is fully revealed in the rejection scene. "God save thy Grace, King Hal, my royal Hal! / God save thee, my sweet boy!" are the words with which the old knight greets the newly crowned king. This overt statement has been carefully prepared for.

Perhaps most important because of its initial position is the great tavern scene in *Part One* where, in the play impromptu, Falstaff becomes Hal's father. Hal commands him to "stand for my father," and the father ruffian complies willingly. Is it romanticising this scene to sense with what satisfaction Sir John says, "That thou art my son" (and so on)? I think not. Then comes the ominous word "depose." Hal becomes king, replacing Falstaff on the joint-stool throne. Comic, yes; but we have here acted out the major theme of the *Henry IV* plays. "When thou art king," introduced by Falstaff in his second speech in *Part One,* and echoed again and again by King Henry, runs like a refrain through the plays. The image of Falstaff as king-father being deposed by his prince-son is printed indelibly on our minds, and we are prepared for the rejection scene where the symbolic act of the play impromptu is literally enacted. In making the play impromptu deal with the father-son relationship, Shakespeare has again significantly deviated from his source, for in *The Famous Victories* the subject is Hal's encounter with the Chief Justice.

To emphasize the dual father roles of Falstaff and Henry IV, Shakespeare makes them parallel characters. Both Falstaff and Henry are mistaken for dead by Hal, who then reveals a curious mixture of grief and satisfaction over the supposedly dead bodies. Hal "robs" both Falstaff and Henry while they sleep: Falstaff of a tavern reckoning, Henry IV of the crown. The deaths of both Falstaff and Henry are surrounded by the aura of folklore and superstition: Falstaff passing to Arthur's bosom "just between twelve and one, even at the turning of the tide"; Henry IV dying in the Jerusalem Chamber after the river had "thrice flowed, no ebb between." In *Part Two,* the king's apostrophe to sleep is structurally balanced by Falstaff's apostrophe to sack. The cumulative effect of these and other parallels is to define the equivalency of their twin roles of father to the young prince.

But the most striking parallel between Falstaff and King Henry leads to the second part of Stewart's thesis. Much has been written about what happens to Falstaff in *Part Two*. It has been suggested that he is degraded, that his wit fails, that Shakespeare grows tired of him, that he becomes, somehow, an unsympathetic character. But the truth is, I think, that like Henry IV he grows old. In *Part One,* although his age and white hairs are not neglected, it is Falstaff's size that receives the greatest emphasis. In *Part Two,* although his girth has not decreased (in spite of Falstaff's claim to the contrary), the emphasis shifts to his age and infirmities. And Falstaff's growing old, his physical decay, parallels what happens to King Henry IV, who, in *Part Two,* also grows suddenly old and sick. In most of the historical scenes, and in many of the comic scenes, the infirmities of the king are stressed. The garden imagery of *Richard II* has been superseded by the imagery of disease, and Richard's prediction (that Henry quotes)

> The time will come that foul sin, gathering head,
> Shall break into corruption

becomes literally true. Under the guilt-ridden, infirm, old king, England itself has become diseased.

> The body of our kingdom,
> How foul it is, what rank diseases grow
> And with what danger, near the heart of it,

says the king, who is acutely aware that his own infirmities are reflected in the land he rules. Nor is he alone in making this primitive connection.

Do we not find here, surprising as it may at first appear, a classic example of a situation that anthropologists—and poets—have so thoroughly investigated—the wasteland? Under the rule of an infirm and guilty king, England has become diseased, and before regeneration can come—as it so obviously does under King Henry V—sacrificial rites must be performed. The penitential pilgrimage to the Holy Land, by which Henry hoped to expiate his guilt in Richard's murder, was never undertaken. On his death-bed, Henry is fully aware that his death is necessary to remove that stain from the succession. "And now my death," he says to Hal, "changes the mode." Hal too senses that the death of the king-father expiates past sins, but when he says

> My father has gone wild into his grave,
> For in his tomb lie my affections [that is, my sins]

he is speaking only half the truth. Into Henry's grave went the guilt of Richard's murder, but another grave, a more momentous sacrifice, is needed to bring regeneration to a wasted land.

In more ways than one, Falstaff is the only sufficient object for the sacrifice. Not only his person (and all that person symbolizes) but also his relationship to Hal marks him as the inevitable choice.

Dover Wilson long ago detected the sacrificial and symbolic quality in Falstaff. Commenting on the epithet "Martlemas" that Poins once employs, Wilson explains:

> Martlemas, or the feast of St. Martin, on 11 November, was in those days of scarce fodder the season at which most of the beasts had to be killed off and salted for the winter, and therefore the season for great banquets of fresh meat. Thus it had been for centuries, long before the coming of Christianity. In calling him a "Martlemas" Poins is at once likening Falstaff's enormous proportions to the prodigality of fresh-killed meat which the feast brought, and acclaiming his identity with Riot and Festivity in general.

To this, Mr. Stewart would add:

> But such festivals commemorate more than the need to reduce stock against a winter season. They commemorate a whole mythology of the cycle of the year, and of the sacrifices offered to secure a new fertility on the earth.... Perhaps we glimpse here a further reason why the rejection of Falstaff is inevitable—not merely traditionally and moralistically inevitable but symbolically inevitable as well. And this may be why, when in the theater, we do not really rebel against the rejection; why we find a fitness too in its being sudden and catastrophic.... For the killing carries something of the ritual suggestion, the obscure *pathos,* of death in tragedy.... And Falstaff is in the end the dethroned and sacrificed king, the scapegoat as well as the sweet beef. For Falstaff...so fit a sacrifice...to lard the lean, the barren earth, is of that primitive and magical world upon which all art, even with a profound unconsciousness, draws.

If Falstaff is ritually slain by Hal, if his death is necessary for the regeneration of a diseased land, we should expect to find further corroboration in the structure and imagery of the plays. One example, from each category will have here to suffice. It is significant, in terms of the structure of *Henry V,* that Hal does not "assume the port of Mars," does not become the hero-king, until *after* the death of Falstaff. He is uncomfortable in his new role of king in the last scenes of *Henry IV, Part Two,* and in the early scenes of *Henry V* there is much talk of his miraculous transformation, but it is only talk. Then, in Act II, scene iii, comes Falstaff's death, and Henry V's next words are:

> Once more unto the breach, dear friends, once more;
> Or close the wall up with our English dead!
> ...On, on, you noblest English
> Whose blood is fet from fathers of war proof!
> Fathers that, like so many Alexanders,
> Have in these parts from morn to even fought,
> And sheathed their swords for lack of argument.

For the first time, Henry V becomes in word and deed the national hero, the mirror of all Christian kings.

With a single image drawn from the rich storehouse of classic myth, Shakespeare sometimes found that he could present the essence of his play, a statement of its theme in miniature. In the first play of this tetralogy,

*Richard II,* he accomplished this, for the whole play is contained in Richard's lines,

> Down, down I come like glistering Phaeton,
> Wanting the manage of unruly steeds.

And he may, I think, have accomplished the same thing in the rejection scene with Falstaff's climactic line, "My King, my Jove, I speak to thee my heart!" For Hal is Falstaff's Jove, the son who deposes his king-father, old Saturn. It is only at this appropriate moment that Falstaff calls Hal Jove. He has never done so before, but Hal himself has made the identification. "It was Jove's case," he says as he dons the leather jerkin disguise to spy on Falstaff and Doll—Saturn and Venus as he calls them.

And for a final bit of evidence, not from the plays and yet not without significance: It is reassuring to note how often the critics have slipped unconsciously into the metaphor of making Falstaff a king and his rejection a dethronement or sacrifice. A. C. Bradley, who wrote, "[Shakespeare] created so extraordinary a being, and fixed him so firmly on his intellectual throne, that when he sought to dethrone him he could not," is only one of many whose intuitive understanding of the situation is revealed in the metaphors they chose to describe it. Even Stoll himself has written: "The king casts [Falstaff] off, but morally, officially, it is to his credit. The poet's hand here is a bit heavy, but he would simply convey to the audience that as King of England, Henry has broken with the past." Is it Shakespeare's hand that is heavy, or the hand of Hal as he runs bad humors on the knight and kills his heart?

In the final analysis, Stoll's own approach to Falstaff and Stewart's are curiously similar: both attempt to explain Falstaff by discovering his ancestors. Stoll found them in the *milites gloriosi* of Latin comedy; Stewart finds them in those ritually slain kings whose diverse histories and lingering traditions are so copiously recorded in *The Golden Bough.* Fortunately, literary paternity, unlike biological, does not preclude the possibility of more than one father, and Falstaff's family tree has many branches. If to those branches already traced by Stoll and the other literary genealogists, Stewart would add yet another, must we reject it because, for Stoll at least, it means an "instinctive anticipation" of Freud and Frazer?

I would suggest that Sigmund Freud did not endow only twentieth-century man with a subconscious mind. Nor did Sir James Frazer trace the survivals—in England long after Shakespeare's day—of the magical connection between old kings and the lands they ruled, of rites and rituals by which fertility was assured, merely to plague the historical critics of Shakespeare. It is not, however, Freudian psychology (so objectionable to Stoll) but Carl Jung's concept of the collective unconscious of the race which offers a possible further explanation of why, as Stewart claims, the rejection and death of

Falstaff are felt to be inevitable and just. Archetypal images of king-fathers and sacrificial rites are our inescapable heritage no less than they were Shakespeare's. We should be neither surprised nor alarmed that Shakespeare, in his greatest moments, penetrates this mysterious, rich, and largely unexplored region of the human psyche.

# 12

# The Renewal of the King's Symbolic Role: From *Richard II* to *Henry V*

*Joan Webber*

A central aspect of the Renaissance preoccupation with rhetoric is the recognition that traditional forms of language can become completely severed from reality. Reactions against stylized speech are in part a questioning of the orderly analogical and hierarchical world-view which such speech had upheld in literature, in the court, and in the pulpit. Conservatives like Ascham, believing wholeheartedly in the power of words, thought that rhetorical decorum was essential to the preservation of all values.[1] Some Puritan extremists, on the other hand, actively campaigning for a different kind of society, rejected ceremony and rhetoric altogether, and insisted upon spontaneous expression.[2] There were other, more moderate men who thought it possible to redirect the imaginative power of the old rhetoric and to reshape the old concepts without destroying them: the revision and renewal of the king's symbolic role, suggested by Shakespeare, is an effort to solve a political problem through creative use of language.



---

[1] Roger Ascham, *English Works*, ed. William Aldis Wright (Cambridge, 1904), pp. 265–266.

[2] See, for example, the summary of this trend, in John Donne, *The Sermons of John Donne*, ed. George R. Potter and Evelyn Simpson (Berkeley, 1953–1962), III, 368.

The history-play sequence that includes *Richard II,* the two parts of *Henry IV,* and *Henry V*, is, among other things, an analysis of the nature of kingship and royal rhetoric which directly concerns the relationship between language and reality. Richard's problem is twofold: as a fourteenth-century king, he has an attitude and a rhetoric that ignore his own human weakness; as he symbolizes a Renaissance king, he is attempting to sustain an order whose validity is coming into question. He has Ascham's faith in the saving power of language, but he lacks Ascham's awareness that form and content must be one, and by setting the two against one another, he constantly paralyzes action in his vicinity. His balanced clauses make tableaux out of life. Throwing his warder down, greeting the earth, arming his name, telling sad stories of the deaths of kings, he forces those around him simply to listen until he has played out his scene. But when he has finished, life goes on without him.

Bolingbroke, distrusting the rhetoric appropriate to the design he has destroyed, has no substitute for it except action, and no means to identify himself with his office or with other men. His anxiety to prove his charges against Mowbray with his body, his taciturn progress toward kingship, and his refusal to recognize the inspiring and unifying value of ceremonial display show him to be not unlike those Puritans who, in rejecting all the old symbols, with their pomp and rhetoric, rejected and condemned what we would call the imagination. Prior to the third act of *2 Henry IV,* he is out-talked, up-staged, and left off stage for whole acts at a time, and, save for several significant exceptions,[3] his rhetoric is alternately blunt and pedestrian, and hackneyed. We rarely see or hear majesty in him, as is half-mockingly made clear in the battle scene at the end of *1 Henry IV,* where the opposition cannot tell the king from his subjects. Lacking a leader who can control their sense of reality through his own control of language and ceremony the people of Henry's kingdom turn to undisciplined plots and schemes and day-dreams.

Having had before him in his boyhood the well-languaged Richard and the often unlanguaged Henry IV as two examples of imperfect kings, Harry Monmouth sets out to discover for himself how to be. A main theme of the two *Henry IV* plays is the education of a prince in rhetoric, and the central annunciation of this theme is the Earl of Warwick's defense of Hal's conduct:

> My gracious lord, you look beyond him quite.
> The Prince but studies his companions

---

[3] He is eloquent at the time of his exile, and again in a long speech to his son in *1 H. IV,* III, ii. The first passage is a rejection of the imagination: "O, who can hold a fire in his hand/ By thinking on the frosty Caucasus/ Or cloy the hungry edge of appetite/ By bare imagination of a feast?" (*R. II,* II, iii, 294–297). To him, imagination is not a practical thing.

Like a strange tongue, wherein, to gain the language,
'Tis needful that the most immodest word
Be look'd upon and learnt; which once attain'd
Your Highness knows, comes to no further use
But to be known and hated. So, like gross terms,
The Prince will, in the perfectness of time,
Cast off his followers; and their memory
Shall as a pattern or a measure live
By which his Grace must mete the lives of others,
Turning past evils to advantages. (*2 H. IV,* IV, iv, 67–77).

Warwick's use of the word "language" is not just a simile; Hal is quite literally studying strange tongues. Shakespearean characters, of course, are almost always identifiable by their speech patterns; but the variety in *Henry IV* is particularly rich. Henry IV's stilted and uncomfortable formality, Pistol's hackneyed borrowings from the old bombastic stage, Dame Quickly's disconnected malapropisms, Glendower's bardic eloquence, the carriers' doubly lewd chatter, Hotspur's headlong incoherence, Falstaff's Puritan aphorisms and his ready wit are all significant parts of Hal's milieu.

More significantly, these characters are frequently deluded by their own words or those of others. Dame Quickly believes Sir John's promises to marry her and make her a lady, and discounts his actions. Falstaff is so deep in the dream of a merry kingdom concocted out of his wit and Hal's that he cannot live beyond it. Glendower cannot brook the disruption of his attempt to spell-bind, to bear out in eloquence the significance of the portents attending his birth. Hotspur, like Richard, is kindled by a word to torrential descriptions of imagined glory: as Worcester says of him, "He apprehends a world of figures here,/ But not the form of what he should attend." (*1 H. IV*, I, iii, 209–210) Many-tongued Rumor broods over the opening of *2 Henry IV*, where the rebel armies too late begin to discuss the dangers of division between spirit and action (*2 H. IV*, I, i, 190–209), imagination and reality. (I, iii, 18–62) Even Henry IV is pathetically pleased to know that he dies in the Jerusalem chamber—that a *word* can validate his pledge of pilgrimage, and the prophecy that he will die in Jerusalem.

When the faculty of the imagination is considered in the Renaissance as anything more than a storehouse for sense impressions, it is often thought of as the Biblical "vain imagination" or fancy, a disruptive and disunifying activity which, when manifested in language, causes men to be misled by pleasing suggestions or emotive phrases that have no basis in reality.[4] It is

---

4 For the traditions, see Murray Wright Bundy, "The Theory of Imagination in Classical and Medieval Thought," *University of Illinois Studies in Language and Literature,* XII (1927), 183–472. These traditions are still active in the Renaissance. See Ruth Wallerstein, "Donnc and the Imagination," in *Studies in Donne,* ed. Barbara Davis (Ph.D. dissertation, Wisconsin, 1961).

this kind of process which operates in *Henry IV,* and is called by Lord Bardolph the "imagination proper to madmen." (*2 H. IV,* I, iii, 31–32) Truth needs a touchstone. State and Church had provided such touchstones in kings and bishops, God's earthly images. But these people have seen one true king proven false and thrust aside, and they know that Henry's right to the throne is dubious. In a sense a counterfeit himself, Henry IV is counterfeited by others on the battlefield; and counterfeiters of another kind rise up against him. The Archbishop of York was in the people's eyes "the imagin'd voice of God himself; / The very opener and intelligencer/ Between the grace, the sanctities of heaven/ And our dull workings." (*2 H. IV,* IV, ii, 16–22). In fact, says Prince John, the Archbishop's religious zeal is counterfeit.

Although an honest man, Henry IV is unable to unify and inspire his people because his own position is uncertain and because he does not know how to direct and control their imaginations. While Falstaff is never taken seriously, he does symbolize the disorder that fills an emotional and spiritual vacuum. He is a real threat because he wilfully confuses fiction with reality when, for example, he claims that he is the slayer of Hotspur, or that Poins means to make the Prince his brother-in-law. On the battlefield, when he casuistically concludes that "to counterfeit dying when a man thereby liveth, is to be no counterfeit, but the true and perfect image of life indeed" (*1 H. IV,* V, iv, 118–120) he is in effect proving that truth is falsehood. His road leads to spiritual anarchy, and the whole kingdom is going down that road.

Reason alone could not prevent such disintegration of meaning. So long as the medieval hierarchy continued to make sense, and so long as the king was believably God's anointed representative, the concept of kingship which Richard II attempts to realize was an imaginative as well as a rational one. When reason and imagination separate, as they do in *Richard II,* the bluff has to be called; the allegorical trappings have to be set aside in order that the real world may be recognized. Yet Henry IV is never able to make the real world clear and desirable, and in consequence his subjects fall prey to Richard's malady. Their plots and daydreams are not an attempt to recover the old hierarchy; but they are an attempt to recover the imaginative and unifying purpose which that hierarchy at its best had sustained. They are futile attempts because the people do not know what truth is or where to find it; and they come dangerously close to Falstaff's rejection of reason in his pursuit of pleasant and acceptable fancy.

The heir to the throne, in such times as these, might profitably employ his time by reading Quintilian, who, defining imagination in the usual negative way, suggests that fire can be fought with fire:

> When the mind is unoccupied or is absorbed by fantastic hopes or daydreams, we are haunted by these visions of which I am speaking to such an

> extent that we imagine that we are travelling abroad, crossing the sea, fighting, addressing the people, or enjoying the use of wealth which we do not actually possess, and seem to ourselves not to be dreaming but acting. Surely then it may be possible to turn this form of hallucination to some profit.[5]

The orator, presenting vivid images to his listeners, can come to control their minds. Medieval and Renaissance preachers, even while attacking imagination, work according to the same principles, using it in the service of reason, to restore the whole mind and heart of man to order and meaning.

The task that confronts Prince Hal is formidable. He has to propose a world-view more meaningful than Richard's, in a language more inspiring than Henry's, in order to lead his people out of confusion. He goes about his business at first simply by entering into the confusion, exploring the rhetorical worlds of his kingdom through a conscious trying-out of different roles, different kinds of speech. His awareness of what he is doing is important, for it immediately distinguishes him from all the other characters (with the partial exception of Falstaff), who are blindly seeking through rhetoric to make a world more to their liking. Throughout the two *Henry IV* plays, he devises and acts out one playlet after another. The echo scene, contrived by the Prince and Poins, with Francis as butt, springs from Hal's astonishment at the drawer's miniscule vocabulary, the extraordinary limitations of his ability to respond to the world. This episode is followed by another contrived scene, in which Falstaff as butt is undone by his own copiousness. Between the two, as a kind of interlude, he and Hal take turns playing the King and the Prince. Both imitations of Henry IV are euphuistic and noticeably wooden. The players are of course more concerned to laugh at each other here than to reproduce Henry's accents, but their mimicry is also a sidelong glance at the inadequacy of Henry's formal rhetoric. Hal is clearly aware that a king who, when he must be ceremonious, relies on outworn meaningless language, can be no more than the subject of buffoonery.[6]

Hal is the only character in *Henry IV* who speaks well both in prose and in verse; it is difficult, in fact, to tell what his true accent is, because throughout the play he is a verbal chameleon, adapting himself to the conventions of those with whom he associates. By mingling with the people, he learns their nature, and earns their respect on their own terms:

> They take it already upon their salvation that, though I be but Prince of Wales, yet I am the king of courtesy; and tell me flatly I am no proud Jack like Falstaff, but a Corinthian, a lad of mettle, a good boy (by the Lord,

---

[5] Quintilian, *Institutio Oratoria,* trans. H. E. Butler (London, 1921–1922), II, 433–435.

[6] As one example of Henry's style, a speech which completely alienates Hotspur includes lines 85–89 (*1 H. IV,* I, iii). Hotspur later quotes these lines in bitterness; and their rhetorical staleness is made apparent still later by Pistol in lines 177–182 (*2 H. IV,* II, iv).

> so they call me!), and when I am King of England I shall command all the good lads in Eastcheap. They call drinking deep, dying scarlet; and when you breathe in your watering, they cry "hem!" and bid you play it off. To conclude, I am so good a proficient in one quarter of an hour that I can drink with any tinker in his own language during my life. I tell thee, Ned, thou hast lost much honour that thou wert not with me in this action.
> (*1 H. IV,* II, iv, 9–24)

While Hal has as yet no stable language of his own, and has deliberately avoided a ceremonial role as prince, it is clear that he is practicing to be the kind of central and inspiring figure that his people require. When he is king, he will "command all the good lads in Eastcheap" because he has come to them in their language. His participation in their hitherto meaningless talk gives their talk and their lives a purpose that he can use.

The "I know you all" speech in *1 Henry IV* has been taken as a way of formally reassuring the reader that Hal will become a good king when the time is ripe. But a careful analysis of his behavior makes such reassurance almost unnecessary, for his activities are not play but play-acting; they teach him more about his subjects, and they teach him how to use rhetoric as an effective means of communication and leadership. He learns what Bolingbroke never understood, that bluntness is seldom convincing, that in order to persuade people, especially these people, who are suffering the effects of division between language and truth, imaginative and symbolic speech is required. The play-acting of *2 Henry IV* becomes increasingly serious from the time when Hal, masking his grief for his father, plays a drawer and unmasks Falstaff, to the final "scene" when Hal, thinking his father dead, takes the crown and plays king—and immediately afterward protests the purity of his intentions so well that Henry IV's doubts about his son are put to rest. In the king's mind, Hal's actual words would have been taken as treason; therefore, the Prince re-enacts the play in a way which he knows will appeal to his father. The same thing—though with intentionally opposite effect—happens with Falstaff. Falstaff ought to know his standing with Hal, for at the end of *1 Henry IV*, he hears the Prince say, thinking him dead on the battlefield, "O, I should have a heavy miss of thee/If I were much in love with vanity!" (V, iv, 105–106) But like most of the characters, Falstaff is not perceptive. Because Sir John cannot understand reality directly, Hal is forced into a symbolic rejection when he says, "I know thee not, old man."

While Quintilian's advice to the orator to "turn this form of hallucination to some profit" does foreshadow the Renaissance identification of the imagination with fancy and does in part describe Hal's cunning use of this tool, it is also true that Renaissance writers in practice understood the value of imagination very well. In criticism, even in the Middle Ages, the modern view is almost enunciated.[7] Certainly, at the end of *2 Henry IV*, the rejection of Falstaff is a rejection of vanity and of vain fancy.[8] In stating his case for order and authority, the Chief Justice explicitly appeals to Hal's imagination, and speaks of the king's "most royal image" as well as of the "image of his power" that is vested in law. The function of such images in binding together a kingdom is activated in the co-operating imaginations of the people. In *Henry V*, Rumor no longer acts as Chorus. The Chorus here invites the audience to participate in a dramatic production through use of their "imaginary forces"; Henry V is to elicit the same assistance from his subjects.

Vain fancy is permitted no freedom now. Having heard his people talking among themselves outside the court, both with and without knowledge of his presence, and having studied the relationship (or lack of it) between their words and their actions, he is not misled by flattery, by smooth speech, or by incompetent speech. He is able to dispose of rebellion before it comes to action (as Richard II and Henry IV could not), distinguishing, when the time comes, between the "smooth and even" bearing of Cambridge, Scroop, and Grey, and the "care and valour" of Fluellen, "though it appear a little out of fashion."

Whatever unifies the people must have worth and imaginative power; Henry V takes care that his war with France can be justified: There are grounds for the patriotic zeal that he means to create, just as there is a basis, in the skill of the players, for the imaginative response of the audience. (The analogy is not trivial, since Shakespeare intended to inspire Elizabethan patriotism.) Here, then, Henry gives his people a common aim, toward which they can direct all the energy that in the previous plays is so often set against the kingdom, or against reality, in illusions protected by rhetoric. He uses all the rhetorical and psychological knowledge picked up in play-acting to mould a nation together in loyalty and brotherhood. It is no accident that all the accents of England are represented on the battlefield. This is the final metamorphosis of the theme of language that begins in royal isolation, in the paralysis of action in *Richard II*, that is enlarged to a plenitude of almost random play-acting in *Henry IV*, and is now charged with coherent meaning and power, as rhetoric, royalty, and England are made one.

*Henry V* has always been known as a chauvinistic play. But this

---

[7] See Bundy, *op. cit.* Imagination comes closest to its modern meaning in such writers as Richard of St. Victor and Bernard of Clairvaux. For Renaissance usage, see Wallerstein, *op. cit.*

[8] It is significant that Henry here speaks to Falstaff in verse for the first time. Before this, there have been only one or two careless lines, and the couplets spoken in the presence of what Hal took to be the corpse of Falstaff at Shrewsbury.

particular kind of chauvinism is part of a very contemporary phenomenon. With the imminent collapse of the old institutions, people, even when they did not consciously foresee such destruction, were beginning to look for new absolutes. One (which in modified form was to become the indispensable absolute of the eighteenth century) was the belief that all men are alike, that in speaking for oneself, one speaks for all. Thus, for example, in the emerging genre of the essay, the first person is often used in a corporate sense. When Montaigne says "I," he means "we." And if the king is no longer so secure in the hierarchy of being—if Henry V prays to God rather than, like Richard, speaking for God—then he can achieve another kind of importance by speaking for all his people. He becomes the spirit of England.

There is no doubt where the leadership lies on the battlefields of France. Yet Henry's battle speeches show, not a desire for personal glory, but a wish to elevate his soldiers to share with him, to be brothers with him in action, and by this action to create a larger symbol of courage and greatness, for posterity. When he says, "But if it be a sin to covet honour, / I am the most offending soul alive," (IV, iii, 28–29), he speaks as he wants all who are with him to think; he speaks for their honor and for that of England. Working upon their imaginary forces, he gives them a reality impressive enough to capture their loyalty.

So far as the people are concerned, then, the king's symbolic role is successfully renewed. So far as the king himself is concerned, there are still problems, chief of which is the relationship between his public and his private self. Richard II became aware of his humanity too late; Henry IV was always too human and too vulnerable. Henry V would be both man and king. But if the king spends his youth acting out parts, if as king he consciously makes himself a symbol and turns hallucinations to some profit, to what extent can he remain a real and likeable person? I think now of his behavior toward Falstaff; his Machiavellian treatment of his subjects, his kingdom, and his foreign affairs; and of the faintly mechanical and very showy character of some of his speeches. All these things are justifiable and even necessary. They are the acts of a wise king. But while Henry's accession to the throne is supposed to have revealed his true nature, it does not actually do so. Despite his moving soliloquy before the battle of Agincourt, when, like his father, he speaks of the heavy price of ceremony, he is no clearer as an individual in this play than he was in *Henry IV*.

The courtship scene in the final act of *Henry V* typifies this problem. At first glance, it would seem that the calculating king is for once altogether human. The man who learned and united all the tongues of England must court a woman who speaks one language that he does not understand, and in accomplishing his task he makes one blunder after another. He speaks to her in prose. He claims Hotspur's dislike of poetry, "for these fellows of infinite tongue that can rhyme themselves into ladies' favours, they do always reason themselves out again." He lapses into the idiom that he and Falstaff used to parody the speech of kings. "A good leg will fall, a straight back will stoop, a black beard will turn white, a curl'd pate will grow bald, a fair face will wither, a full eye will wax hollow; but a good heart, Kate, is the sun and the moon." He even comes close to carrier-language: "If ever thou beest mine, Kate—as I have a saving faith within me tells me thou shalt—I get thee with scambling, and thou must therefore needs prove a good soldier breeder."

The frothy humor delights and surprises us, and perhaps keeps us from remembering that Henry wants to marry Katherine because it is expedient for him to do so. It is possible that he chooses the fumbling-suitor role deliberately. At any rate, some of the attitudes and poses that he strikes here are quite out of keeping with his character as we know it. And whether or not this is a deliberate role, it is certainly a symbolic one. The scene is a marriage of France with England, a uniting of the French people with the English. Henry acts as representative of his people, contrasting the straightforward bluntness of the one country with the suavity of the other, and showing off to France all the different aspects of the English character. He himself is neither plain soldier, nor loutish farmer, nor hater of poetry, nor euphuistic rhetorician, but he has subjects who farm and fight, speak plain and stilted English. Even the stress on his appearance, which has never been joked about before, despite abundant opportunity, reflects a rugged and warlike people, a land with a forbidding climate. Having made himself the Star of England and the center of his people's dreams, he cannot be simply a man. And it is because he loses individuality in being overtaken by his own symbol, because now England seems to speak through him whether or not he wills it to do so, that we forgive him his machinations. He is himself possessed by the diverse mortal strength that he nourished, unified, and controlled.

# COMEDIES

# 13

# *Love's Labour's Lost*

*Anne Barton**

In a sense the play has ended; an epilogue has been spoken by Berowne and that haunting and beautiful kingdom created by the marriage of reality with illusion destroyed, seemingly beyond recall. In the person of Marcade, the world outside the circuit of the park has at last broken through the gates, involving the people of the play in its sorrows and grim actualities, the plague-houses and desolate retreats, the mourning cities and courts of that vaster country overshadowing the tents and the fantastic towers of Navarre. Yet before the final dissolution of that minute and once isolated kingdom of the play, when some of the characters seem already to have disappeared and the others are preparing sadly to journey into the realms beyond the walls of the royal close, there is granted suddenly a little moment of grace. In the waning afternoon, all the people of the play return to the stage and stand quietly together to hear the song which "the two learned men have compiled in praise of the Owl and the Cuckoo," a song into which the whole of that now-vanished world of *Love's Labour's Lost*

*Reprinted from* Shakespeare Quarterly, *IV (1963), 411–426 by permission of the author and of The Shakespeare Association of America, Inc.*

* Dr. Anne (Righter) Barton, (née Roesen).

seems to have passed, its brilliance, its strange mingling of the artificial and the real, its loveliness and laughter gathered together for the last time to speak to us in the form of a single strain of music.

> When daisies pied and violets blue
> And lady-smocks all silver-white
> And cuckoo-buds of yellow hue
> Do paint the meadows with delight....

It is the landscape of the royal park that lies outstretched before us, a little world of thickets and smooth lawns, meadows and wooded hills. In the foreground, their appearance and speech as decorative and charming as the setting in which they have met to solemnize their vows of asceticism and study, stand four young men, Berowne, Dumain, Longaville, and that ruler of Navarre whose slender kingdom of foresters and dairy-maids, courtiers, pendants, and fools seems bounded by the park and its single, rustic village. Mannered and artificial, reflecting an Elizabethan delight in patterned and intricate language, Navarre's lines at the beginning of the play are nevertheless curiously urgent and intense.

> Let fame, that all hunt after in their lives,
> Live regist'red upon our brazen tombs,
> And then grace us in the disgrace of death;
> When, spite of cormorant devouring Time,
> Th' endeavour of this present breath may buy
> That honour which shall bate his scythe's keen edge,
> And make us heirs of all eternity.

With the King's first words, an expression of that peculiarly Renaissance relationship of the idea of Fame with that of Time and Death, a shadow darkens for a moment the delicate dream landscape of the park. Touched by this shadow, affected by its reality, the four central characters of *Love's Labour's Lost* enter the world of the play.

Fantastic and contrived as they are, those absurd vows to which the four friends commit themselves in the initial scene spring from a recognition of the tragic brevity and impermanence of life that is peculiarly Renaissance. For the people of the sixteenth century, the world was no longer the mere shadow of a greater Reality, the imperfect image of that City of God whose towers and golden spires had dominated the universe of the Middle Ages. While the thought of Death was acquiring a new poignancy in its contrast with man's increasing sense of the value and loveliness of life in this world, Immortality tended to become, for Renaissance minds, a vague and even a somewhat dubious gift unless it could be connected in some way with the earth itself, and the affairs of human life there. Thus there arose among the humanist writers of Italy that intense and sometimes anguished longing, voiced by Navarre at the beginning of *Love's Labour's Lost,* to attain "an immortality of glory, survival in the minds of men by the record of great deeds or of intellectual excellence. . . ."[1] At the very heart of the plan for an Academe lies the reality of Death, the Renaissance desire to inherit, through remarkable devotion to learning, an eternity of Fame, and thus to insure some continuity of personal existence, however slight, against the ravages of "cormorant devouring Time."

It is obviouss, however, from the very beginning of the play, that the Academe and the idea of immortality which it embodies must fail. Less remote and docile than Dumain and Longaville, existing upon a deeper level of reality within the play, the brilliant and sensitive Berowne, a Chorus character throughout, first realizes how unnatural the vows are, how seriously they trespass, despite their three-year limit, against the normal laws of life and reality. The paradox of the Academe and the reason why its failure is not only understandable but absolutely necessary lie in the fact that this elaborate scheme which intends to enhance life and extend it through Fame even beyond the boundaries of the grave would in reality, if successfully carried out, result in the limitation of life and, ultimately, in its complete denial. In their very attempt to retain hold upon life, the King and his companions, as Berowne alone understands, are cutting themselves off from it, from love, and the beauty of women, from all those simple sensuous pleasures of the world which have prompted the establishment of the Academe in the first place by making the "too much loved earth more lovely,"[2] and the thought of its loss in Death so unbearably grim.

Long before the appearance of those two delightful but sobering characters, Holofernes and Nathaniel, Berowne has seen the barrenness of learning that is divorced from life, the tragedy of those industrious men of science who find a name for every star in the western skies and yet "have no more profit of their shining nights/Than those that walk and wot not what they are." Even in the first scene of the play, before his love for Rosaline has made his perception deeper and more sensitive, Berowne realizes in some sense that the only way to deal with the bleak reality of Death and Time is to accept it, to experience as much of life's sensory loveliness as possible while the opportunity is still given. Implicit in his earliest lines is the knowledge, related somehow to the first group of the "Sonnets," that "we cannot cross the cause why we were born," and although he agrees at last to take the oath, it is through him that we first sense the conviction expressed by the play as a whole that this idea of intellectual glory is an essentially sterile one, that the price exacted is too great to pay for a fame and a memory on earth that will soon be lost in the unimagined reaches of Time.

---

1 Nesca Robb, *Neoplatonism of the Italian Renaissance* (London, 1935), p. 45.

2 Sir Philip Sidney, *The Defence of Poesie,* in *The Complete Works of Sir Philip Sidney,* ed. *Feuillerat* (Cambridge, 1923), III, 8.

It was one of Walter Pater's most famous dictums that "All art constantly aspires towards the condition of music,"[3] and in his beautiful essay on "Shakespeare's English Kings" he asserted more particularly that "into the unity of a choric song the perfect drama ever tends to return, its intellectual scope deepened, complicated, enlarged, but still with an unmistakable singleness, or identity, in its impression on the mind."[4] Such a unity is evident throughout *Love's Labour's Lost,* and, indeed, the quality of the whole is very much that of a musical composition, an inexorable movement forward, the appearance and reappearance in the fabric of the play of certain important themes, forcing the harmony into a series of coherent resolutions consistent with each other and with the drama as a whole. Berowne has scarcely finished speaking before his assertion that "every man with his affects is born,/Not by might mast'red, but by special grace" is echoed in the structure of the comedy itself, with the entrance of Constable Dull and the reluctant Costard, the first to disobey the edicts of the new Academe.

The little episode which follows is not only significant of the trend of future action but, in itself, one of the most delightful moments of the play. As the King reads Armado's incredible accusation and Costard tries feebly to avert impending doom by making Navarre laugh, it becomes obvious for the first time how much enchantment the play holds for the ear, how subtly it combines highly individual idioms of speech into a single conversation. *Love's Labour's Lost* is a play of many voices, and much of its beauty grows from the sheer music of their rise and fall, the exploitation of their differences of quality and tone, accent and complication. Here in the first scene, the frank simplicity of Dull, the awed monosyllables of Costard, are placed by Shakespeare in a deliberate musical relationship with the studied sentences of Longaville, the fantastic style of Armado, and the more attractive elegance of Berowne, and the whole episode is given the quality of a polyphonic composition half artificial and half real.

Beyond its humor and fascination of language, the Costard scene has, of course, a more serious purpose in the play, a purpose virtually identical with that fulfilled by a scene in *Measure for Measure.* In the later comedy, Angelo appears in the opening scene of the second act in a role analogous to Navarre's in *Love's Labour's Lost,* and the old counsellor Escalus in one similar to Berowne's. The scheme of justice which Angelo would enforce in Vienna is as ridiculously inflexible, as ignorant of the nature of human beings as Navarre's Academe, and it is protested by Escalus. Not, however, until the sudden entrance of Constable Elbow, an Austrian cousin of Dull's, and Pompey, who can in some measure be compared to Costard, does it become

---

3 Walter Pater, "The School of Giorgione," in *The Renaissance* (New York, n.d.), p. 111.

4 Pater, "Shakespeare's English Kings," in *Appreciations* (London, 1901), pp. 203–204.

completely obvious how impractical the system is, how helpless its high-minded idealism when forced to deal with real individuals, their private standards of morality and unpredictable human weaknesses. The fate of Angelo's justice is settled even before he himself has sinned against it, in the process of that riotous contention between Elbow, Froth, and Pompey, and in the same way, Navarre's Academe has failed before he and his friends are actually forsworn, from the moment that the real and intensely individual figures of Costard and Dull appear in their respective roles as transgressor and upholder. Among the lower social levels of the park, life itself destroys the King's scheme almost in the moment of its foundation.

Walter Pater found *Love's Labour's Lost* particularly charming in its changing "series of pictorial groups, in which the same figures reappear, in different combinations but on the same background,"[5] a composition, for him, like that of some ancient tapestry, studied, and not a little fantastic. The grouping of the characters into scenes would appear, however, to have been dictated by a purpose far more serious than the mere creation of such patterns; it is one of the ways in which Shakespeare maintains the balance of the play world between the artificial and the real, and indicates the final outcome of the comedy.

There are, of course, huge differences in the reality of the people who walk and speak together within the limits of the royal park. From the artificial and virtually indistinguishable figures of Dumain and Longaville, never really more than fashionable voices, the scale of reality rises gradually towards Berowne, in whom the marriage of a certain remote and fantastic quality with the delightful realism which first recognized the flaws in the Academe reflects the comedy as a whole, and reaches its apogee in the utter substantiality and prosaic charm of Constable Dull, who could never in any sense be accused of retreating into unreality, or affecting an elegant pose. Again and again, characters from different levels along this scale are grouped into scenes in a manner that helps to maintain the delicate balance of the play world; thus, in the first scene, with the incredible idea of the Academe and the sophisticated dialogue of Berowne and Longaville, Costard and the bewildered Dull are employed in much the same way that the mocking voice of the cuckoo is in the glowing spring landscape of the closing song, to keep the play in touch with a more familiar and real world, as well as to indicate the ultimate victory of reality over artifice and illusion.

As the first act ends, this theme is repeated again, and the inevitability of future events made even more clear with the abandonment of the edicts of the Academe by the very individual who was responsible for the deliverance of Costard into the righteous hands of Dull, the intense and serious Armado. The grave figure of the Spanish traveller is one of the most interesting and in

---

[5] Pater, *"Love's Labour's Lost,"* in *Appreciations,* p. 163.

a sense enigmatic to appear in *Love's Labour's Lost,* and his sudden love for Jaquenetta certainly the strangest of the five romances which develop within the park. Like Berowne, Armado is a very real person who is playing a part, but in his case it is far more difficult to separate the actor from the man underneath, and the pose itself is more complex than the fashionable role of Berowne. Even in his soliloquies, Armado seems to be acting to some invisible audience, and it is only in one moment at the end of the play that we are granted a glimpse of the man without the mask.

Romantic and proud, intensely imaginative, he has retreated into illusion much further than has Berowne, creating a world of his own within the world of the park, a world peopled with the heroes of the past, Samson and Hercules, Hector and the knights of Spain. Somehow, it is among these long-dead heroes that Armado really exists, rather than among the people of the play itself, and his bizarre language, so strange and artificial when placed beside the homely speech of Costard, was created for that remote, imaginative environment and possesses there a peculiar beauty and aptness of its own. A character with some of the isolation of Jaques, always separated from the gibes and chatter of Moth, he falls in love with Jaquenetta without accepting her as the real country-wench she is, but creates a little drama about the object of his passion in which his is the central role, and Jaquenetta appears in any likeness that he pleases, Delilah or Deianira. The illusion in which the real character of Armado lives has its own beauty and charm, but as the play progresses it becomes evident that this illusion is not strong enough to withstand the pressure of reality and must in the end be destroyed.

With the coming into the King's park of the Princess of France and her companions a new stage in the development of *Love's Labour's Lost* has been reached, and a theme we have not heard before begins slowly to rise in the musical structure of the play. Before the arrival of the ladies, it has been made clear that the Academe must fail, and it is no surprise when in the opening scene of the second act we find each of the four friends stealing back alone after the initial meeting to learn the name of his love from the obliging Boyet. As life itself breaks swiftly through the artificial scholarship of the court, the vitality of the play rises to an amazing height; the Academe is kept constantly before us, the reasons for its failure elaborated and made more plain, but at the same time, while the world of the royal park becomes more and more delightful, while masque and pageantry, sensuous beauty and laughter flower within the walls, it becomes slowly obvious that more than the Academe will be destroyed by the entrance of the ladies. Not only its scholarship, but the entire world of the play, the balance of artifice and reality of which it was formed, must also be demolished by forces from without the walls.

The Princess and her little retinue represent the first penetration of the park by the normal world beyond, a world composed of different and colder elements than the fairy-tale environment within. Through them, in some sense, the voice of Reality speaks, and although they seem to fit perfectly into the landscape of the park, indulge in highly formal, elaborate skirmishes of wit with each other and with the men, they are somehow detached from this world of illusion and artificiality in a way that none of its original inhabitants are. The contrived and fashionable poses which they adopt are in a sense less serious, more playful than those of the other characters, and they are conscious all the time, as even Berowne is not, that these attitudes are merely poses, and that Reality is something quite different. With them into the park they bring past time and a disturbing reminder of the world outside, and from them come the first objective criticisms which pass beyond the scheme of the Academe to attack the men who have formed it. Maria, remembering Longaville as she saw him once before in Normandy, criticizes in her first speech the unreality with which the four friends have surrounded themselves, and points out for the first time in the play the danger of attitudes which develop without regard for the feelings of others, of wit that exercises itself thoughtlessly upon all.

In the wit of the ladies themselves, it is a certain edge of reality, an uncompromising logic, which cuts through the pleasant webs of artifice, the courtly jests and elaborations in the humor of the men, and emerges victorious with an unfailing regularity. Unlike the women, the King and his companions play, not with facts themselves, but with words, with nice phrases and antithetical statements, and when their embroidered language itself has been attacked, their courteous offers disdained as mere euphemisms, they can only retire discomfited. Even Berowne is utterly defeated when he approaches Rosaline with his graceful conceits.

> *Ber.* Lady, I will commend you to mine own heart.
> *Ros.* Pray you, do my commendations;
>   I would be glad to see it.
> *Ber.* I would you heard it groan.
> *Ros.* Is the fool sick?
> *Ber.* Sick at the heart.
> *Ros.* Alack, let it blood.
> *Ber.* Would that do it good?
> *Ros.* My physic says "ay."

Witty as Berowne, as agile of mind, Rosaline attacks his conventional protestations with a wit based on realism, a ridicule spring from a consciousness of the absurdity of artifice. That Berowne could be expressing a real passion in these artificial terms never enters her mind; he is merely mocking her, and she defends herself in the most effective way she can.

Berowne is, however, like the King, Dumain, and Longaville, suddenly and genuinely in love. The Academe has been thoroughly demolished and now, in the fourth act, Shakespeare introduces, in the characters of Holofernes and Nathaniel, reminders of what such a scheme might have led to, examples of the sterility of learning that is unrelated to life. As usual, Dull, surely the most delightful of that illustrious Shakespearian series of dim-witted but officious representatives of constabulary law, appears with them as the realistic element in the scene, the voice of the cuckoo which mocks, unconsciously, the intricate speech of the two pedants. Bewildered as usual, Dull shows here a quality of stubbornness we had not quite expected in him, maintaining stolidly against the fantastic perorations of Holofernes and Nathaniel that the deer killed by the Princess was "not a haud credo; 'twas a pricket." It is one of the most charming of his infrequent appearances, matched only by that little scene later in the play in which, utterly stupefied by the conversation which he has endured from Holofernes and Nathaniel at dinner, he sits mute and quiescent through all the arrangements for the pageant of the Nine Worthies, only at the very last, when roused by another character, entering the dialogue at all to offer us a personal performance upon the tabor, a talent as engaging and unexpected in Dull as song is in the Justice Silence of *2 Henry IV*.

Unlike Dull, the schoolmaster and the curate are in some sense mere types, elements of a satire, but Shakespeare is after all not writing a treatise, and even though their absurdity is emphasized, the two have a certain charm of their own, and their interminable quibblings a faint and grotesque beauty. On a lower, less refined level, they reflect the love of words themselves that is visible throughout the play, reveling, not like Armado in the romance and wonder of the past, but in Latin verbs and bits of forgotten erudition, spare and abstract. As Moth says, "They have been at a great feast of languages and stol'n the scraps," and in their conversation the wisdom of ages past appears in a strangely mutilated form, the life drained from it, curiously haphazard and remote.

When in the third scene of Act Four, Berowne appears alone on the stage, we move from the two pedants to a higher level of reality, but one in which artifice is still present. Berowne's love for Rosaline is becoming increasingly intense, and although he seems at first only to be adopting another pose, that of melancholy lover, he is slowly becoming, as the play progresses, a more convincing and attractive figure, and his love more real.

> By heaven, I do love; and it hath taught me to rhyme and to be melancholy; and here is part of my rhyme, and here my melancholy. Well, she hath one of my sonnets already; the clown bore it, the fool sent it, and the lady hath it; sweet clown, sweeter fool, sweetest lady.

Often, beneath ornament and convention the Elizabethans disguised genuine emotion. Berowne's love for Rosaline is as sincere as Philip Sidney's for Stella, his longing as real as that of the unknown Elizabethan lover in Nicholas Hillyarde's strangest and most haunting miniature who stands in the attitude of a familiar poetic conceit, gaunt and disheveled, against a background of flames.

The episode which follows Berowne's introductory soliloquy is, of course, one of the finest in the entire play. It is the first of three scenes in *Love's Labour's Lost* which possess the quality of a play within the play, formal in construction, somehow contrived, always beautifully handled. Here, above the whole scene, Berowne acts as spectator and as Chorus, establishing the play atmosphere in his various asides, crying out upon the entrance of Longaville, "Why, he comes in like a perjure, wearing papers," or in a more general affirmation,

> "All hid, all hid"—an old infant play,
> Like a demigod here sit I in the sky,
> And wretched fools' secrets heedfully o'er-eye.

Throughout *Love's Labour's Lost,* the play is a symbol of illusion, of unreality, as it is in *A Midsummer Night's Dream,* and here it is employed to render the artificiality, the convenient but obvious device of having each of the four lovers appear alone upon the stage, read aloud the poem addressed to his lady, and step aside for the advance of the next one, not only acceptable, but completely delightful. In this play environment, a level of unreality beyond that of the comedy as a whole, the multiple discoveries are perfectly convincing, and the songs and sonnets read by the lovers the charming testimonies of a passion that is not to be questioned.

Through the comments of the spectator, Berowne, the scene is still, however, kept in touch with reality. From his wonderful, rocketing line upon the entrance of the King, "Shot, by heaven!" to the moment when he steps from his concealment in all the splendor of outraged virtue, Berowne's role is again analogous to that of the cuckoo in the closing song, mocking the lovers "enamelling with pied flowers their thoughts of gold,"[6] maintaining the balance of the play. When he actually appears among his shamefaced friends to chide them for this "scene of fool'ry," the play within the play ends, as the spectator becomes actor, and we return, with his beautifully sanctimonious sermon, to the more usual level of reality.

The sheer delight of the scene rises now towards its peak as, only a few lines after the close of the play scene, another and even more effective climax is built up. Costard appears with Berowne's own sonnet written to Rosaline, and suddenly the play rises into magnificence. "Guilty, my lord, guilty. I confess, I confess." Berowne has become more real and brilliant than ever before, and at the same time, his speech attains a power and a radiance new in the comedy, an utterance still fastidious, still choice, but less self-conscious, as he sums up for Navarre, Dumain, and Longaville all that Shakespeare has

---

[6] Sidney, "Astrophel and Stella, Sonnet III," in *Silver Poets of the Sixteenth Century,* ed. Bullett (London, 1947), p. 173.

been saying long before, in the Costard scene, in the fall from grace of Don Armado.

> Sweet lords, sweet lovers, O let us embrace!
> As true we are as flesh and blood can be.
> The sea will ebb and flow, heaven show his face;
> Young blood doth not obey an old decree.
> We cannot cross the cause why we were born,
> Therefore of all hands must be we forsworn.

Following these lines, there is a deliberate slacking of intensity, and the scene descends for a moment into a completely artificial duel of wits among the King, Berowne, and Longaville, on a somewhat hackneyed conceit. Berowne's toying with the various meanings of dark and light is as artificial and contrived as anything we have heard from him earlier in the play, but from these lines the scene suddenly rises to its final climax in that speech justifying the breaking of the vows, which is without doubt the most beautiful in the entire play. "Have at you then, affection's men-at-arms." Finally and completely, the Academe has crumbled, and it is Berowne, as is perfectly proper, who sums up all that the play has been saying up to this point in his exquisite peroration upon earthly love.

"Other slow arts entirely keep the brain,/And therefore, finding barren practisers,/Scarce show a harvest of their heavy toil." Holofernes and Nathaniel are indirectly brought before us, the symbols of learning divorced from life, and having thus disposed of scholarship, Berowne passes on to speak of Love itself, and the task of justifying his own perjury and that of his three friends. Gradually, his speech rises to a lyrical height unequalled in the rest of the play, his customary eloquence and delicacy of language transfigured and made splendid, the sincerity perfectly blended with the surviving mannerism. "And when Love speaks, the voice of all the gods/Make heaven drowsy with the harmony." With these two lines, the final climax of the scene has been reached, lines of an almost incredible beauty, sensuous and languid, their exact meaning a little puzzling perhaps, but communicating all that is necessary, in a realm beyond precise explanation.

After these lines, the speech loses something of its beauty, but its intensity remains and fires the King, Dumain, and Longaville. The action flares up suddenly in great, vibrant lines; "Shall we resolve to woo these girls of France?" "Saint Cupid, then! and, soldiers, to the field," and in a whirlwind of vitality and excitement the scene moves towards its close. "For revels, dances, masks, and merry hours,/Forerun fair Love, strewing her way with flowers." Yet, as is customary with Shakespeare, the scene ends quietly, with two thoughtful, foreboding lines which are prophetic of what is to come in the next act. As though he turned back for a second, musingly, in the act of going off with the others, Berowne, as Chorus, remarks more to himself and that deserted little glade which was the scene of the play within the play than to his retreating friends, "Light wenches may prove plagues to men forsworn; /If so, our copper buys no better treasure," lines which despite their apparent gaiety are curiously disturbing.

With the beginning of that long, last act, a turning point in the action of the play has been reached. The Academe defeated by life itself on all levels of the park, one might expect that *Love's Labour's Lost* would move now, as *Much Ado About Nothing* does in its final act, into an untroubled close, a romantic ending like that of the Beatrice-Benedick plot. As we have in some sense been told by the title, and by the comments of the ladies, such an ending is, in this case, impossible. From the Academe theme the play turns now to the destruction of the half-real world within the royal park, a destruction which, in the actual moment in which it is accomplished, is unexpected and shocking, and yet has been prepared for and justified by previous events within the comedy. As we enter the Fifth Act, shadows begin to fall across the play world. Life within the park, its brilliance and laughter, mounts higher and higher, yet it is the winter stanzas of the closing song that this act suggests, and a new darkness, a strange intensity forces the harmony of the play into unforeseen resolutions. Vanished now are the untroubled meadows of spring, and the landscape acquires a realism that is somehow a little harsh.

> When icicles hang by the wall,
> And Dick the shepherd blows his nail,
> And Tom bears logs into the hall,
> And milk comes frozen home in pail,
> When blood is nipp'd and ways be foul. . . .

With Act Five, the thought of Death enters the park. The play opened, of course, under the shadow of death, the great motivation of the Academe, but after that opening speech of Navarre's, it vanished altogether, never appearing again even in the imagery of the play until the entrance of the ladies. Significantly, it is they, the intruders from the outside world of reality, who first, in Act Three, bring death into the park itself. In this act, the Princess kills a deer, but in the lines in which the hunt is spoken of, those of Holofernes and the Princess herself, the animal's death is carefully robbed of any disturbing reality. After Holofernes has told us how "The preyful Princess pierc'd and pricked/A pretty, pleasing pricket," the fate of the deer is as unreal as the wooded landscape over which it ran. It might just as well have sprung to its feet and gamboled off when the forester's back was turned.

Not until Act Five does the death image become real and disturbing, and even here, until the final entrance of Marcade, it is allowed to appear only in the imagery, or else in the recollection by some character of a time and a place beyond the scope of the play itself, the country of France where

Katherine's sister died of her melancholy and longing, or that forgotten antiquity in which the bones of Hector were laid to rest. Appearing thus softened, kept in the background of the comedy, it is nevertheless a curiously troubling image, and as it rises slowly through the fabric of the play, the key of the entire final movement is altered. In the mask scene, Berowne, half-serious about his love and that of the King, Dumain, and Longaville, cries to the ladies,

> Write "Lord have mercy on us" on those three;
> They are infected; in their hearts it lies;
> They have the plague, and caught it of your eyes.
> These lords are visited; you are not free,
> For the Lord's tokens on you I do see.

and while the image is playfully treated still, it is surely a curious and grotesque figure, this marriage of love, the symbol throughout the comedy of life itself, with death. One cannot imagine such an image appearing earlier in the play, before the outside world, the echoes of its great plague bells sounding through desolate streets, the lugubrious cries of the watchmen marking the doors of the infected houses, began to filter obscurely through the little kingdom of the park.

It is the tremendous reality of death which will destroy the illusory world of Navarre as thoroughly as the gentler forces of life destroyed the Academe and the artificial scheme it represented, earlier in the play. At the very beginning of the Fifth Act, it is made apparent why this must happen, why it is completely necessary for the world of the comedy, despite its beauty and grace, to be demolished. The Princess and her gentlemen have been discussing the favors and the promises showered upon them by the King and his courtiers, laughing and mocking one another gently. Suddenly, the atmosphere of the entire scene is altered with a single, curious comment, a kind of overheard aside, made by Katherine, upon the real nature of Love. Rosaline turns to her, and as she remembers past time and a tragedy for which the god of Love was responsible then, the scene suddenly becomes filled with the presence of death.

> *Ros.* You'll ne'er be friends with him: 'a kill'd your sister.
> *Kath.* He made her melancholy, sad, and heavy;
> And so she died. Had she been light, like you,
> Of such a merry, nimble, stirring spirit,
> She might have been a grandam ere she died.
> And so may you; for a light heart lives long.

Against such a memory of the reality of love, the Princess sand her three companions place the fantastic protestations of Navarre, Berowne, Dumain, and Longaville. As we have seen, their love is genuine; it has made the character of Berowne immeasurably more attractive, caused him no little anguish of spirit, created that great speech of his at the end of Act Four. Beneath the delicate language, the elegance and the gaiety, lies a real passion, but the women from the world outside, where love has been coupled for them with death and reality, see only artifice and pose. The artificiality which has become natural to the four friends and the environment in which they live holds them from the accomplishment of their desire, for the ladies, hearing from Boyet of the masque in which their lovers intend to declare themselves, are unable to perceive in the scheme anything but attempted mockery and, in defending themselves, frustrate the serious purpose of the entertainment.

> They do it but in mocking merriment,
> And mock for mock is only my intent. . . .
> There's no such sport as sport by sport o'erthrown,
> To make theirs ours, and ours none but our own;
> So shall we stay, mocking intended game,
> And they well mock'd depart away with shame.

This masque scene is, of course, the second of the plays within the play, less delightful than the one before it, but immensely significant, the part of audience and commentator played in this instance by Boyet. As usual, the men are completely defeated by the ladies, the delicate fabric of their wit and artifice destroyed by the realistic humour of their opponents. Berowne, approaching the supposed Rosaline with a courteous request, "White-handed mistress, one sweet word with thee," is mercilessly rebuffed by the Princess—"Honey, and milk, and sugar; there is three"—and the charming illusion of the masque itself ruined by the satiric comments of Boyet who, unlike Berowne in the earlier play scene, actually insinuates himself into the unreal world of the entertainment, and totally upsets it.

Even when the exposure is complete and the men have asked pardon from their loves, the women think only that they have defeated a mocking jest directed against them, not that they have prevented their lovers from expressing a genuine passion. For the first time, Berowne reaches utter simplicity and humbleness in his love; his declaration to Rosaline at the end of the masque scene is touching and deeply sincere, but for her, this passion is still unbelievable, a momentary affectation, and she continues to mock her lover and the sentiments he expresses.

> *Ber.* I am a fool, and full of poverty.
> *Ros.* But that you take what doth to you belong,
>   It were a fault to snatch words from my tongue.
> *Ber.* O, I am yours, and all that I possess.
> *Ros.* All the fool mine?

More sensitive, gifted with a deeper perception of reality than his companions, Berowne seems to guess what is wrong, and he forswears "Taffeta phrases, silken terms precise,/Three pil'd hyperboles, spruce affectation,/Figures pedantical. . .," at least to Rosaline, but the rejection itself is somewhat artificial, and he remains afterwards with more than "a trick of the old rage."

The masque has failed, and Berowne's more direct attempt to announce to the ladies the purpose behind the performance and detect in them as answering passion has been turned away by the unbelieving Princess. At this point, Costard enters to announce that Holofernes and Nathaniel, Moth and Armado are at hand to present the pageant of the Nine Worthies, and the third and last of the plays within the play begins. As we enter this play scene, the vitality and force of the comedy reaches its apogee, but in its laughter there rings now a discordant note that we have not heard before. The actors themselves are, after all, no less sincere than Bottom and his troupe in *A Midsummer Night's Dream,* and they are a great deal more sensitive and easy to hurt. They are real people whose intentions are of the very best, their loyalty to their King unquestioned, and although their performance is unintentionally humorous, one would expect the audience to behave with something of the sympathy and forbearance exhibited by Duke Theseus and the Athenians.

The only civil members of the audience in *Love's Labour's Lost,* however, are the ladies. The Princess cannot resist one sarcasm upon the entrance of Armado, but it is addressed quietly to Berowne, before the play itself begins, while Armado is engrossed with the King and obviously does not hear. Thereafter, every one of her comments to the players is one of interest or pity: "Great thanks, great Pompey," "Alas, poor Maccabaeus, how hath he been baited," "Speak, brave Hector; we are much delighted." The players have only the Princess to appeal to in the storm of hilarity which assails them, and it is only she, realistic as she is, who understands that a play is an illusion, that it is to be taken as such and respected in some sense for itself, regardless of its quality. Like Theseus in *A Midsummer Night's Dream,* she realizes somehow that "the best in this kind are but shadows; and the worst are no worse, if imagination amend them,"[7] and when she addresses the players she is wise and sensitive enough to do so not by their own names, which she has read on the playbill, but by the names of those whom they portray, thus helping them to sustain that illusion which is the very heart of a play.

In contrast to that of the Princess, the behaviour of the men is incredibly unattractive, particularly that of Berowne. It is difficult to believe that this is the same man who spoke so eloquently a short time ago about the soft and sensible feelings of love, and promised Rosaline to mend his ways. Costard manages to finish his part before the deluge, and Nathaniel, although unkindly treated, is not personally humiliated. Only with the appearance of

---

[7] *A Midsummer Night's Dream,* V, i.

Holofernes as Judas Maccabaeus and Armado as Hector is the full force of the ridicule released, and it is precisely with these two characters that the infliction of abuse must be most painful. Costard, after all, is a mere fool; he takes part in the baiting of the others with no compunction at all, and Nathaniel throughout the comedy has been little more than a foil for Holofernes, but the village pedagogue is a more sensitive soul, and not at all unsympathetic.

Holofernes has his own reality, his own sense of the apt and the beautiful which, though perverse, is meaningful enough for him, and it is exceedingly painful to see him stand here on the smooth grass of the lawn, his whole subjective world under merciless attack, a storm of personal epithets exploding about him.

> *Dum.* The head of a bodkin.
> *Ber.* A death's face in a ring.
> *Long.* The face of an old Roman coin, scarce seen.
> *Boyet.* The pommel of Caesar's falchion.
> *Dum.* The carv'd bone face on a flask.
> *Ber.* Saint George's half-cheek in a brooch.

The laughter is unattractive, wild, and somehow discordant, made curiously harsh by the introduction of Berowne's "death's face," and it has little resemblance to the laughter which we have heard in the play before this, delicate, sophisticated, sometimes hearty, but never really unkind. When Holofernes cries at the last, "This is not generous, not gentle, not humble," he becomes a figure of real dignity and stature, restrained and courteous in the face of the most appalling incivility.

Meanwhile, around the pedagogue and his little audience the afternoon has been waning slowly into evening, long shadows falling horizontally across the lawn, and Boyet calls after the retreating Holofernes in a strangely haunting line, "A light for Monsieur Judas. It grows dark, he may stumble." A kind of wildness grips all the men, and though Dumain says in a weird and prophetic line, "Though my mocks come home by me, I will now be merry," Armado faces a jeering throng even before he has begun to speak. Of all the players, Armado is the one for whom we have perhaps the most sympathy. He is a member of the court itself, has had some reason to pride himself upon the King's favor, and has been good enough to arrange the pageant in the first place. The people represented in it are those who inhabit that strange world of his fancy, and one knows that his anguish is not alone for his personal humiliation, but for that of the long-dead hero he portrays, when he cries, "The sweet war-man is dead and rotten; sweet chucks, beat not the bones of the buried; when he breathed, he was a man." A little grotesque, as Armado's sentences always are, the line is nevertheless infinitely moving in its summoning up of great spaces of time, its ironic relation to the idea of immortality through fame expressed in the opening speech of the comedy. Not since the reference to Katherine's sister have we had such a powerful and disturbing image of death brought before us, death real and inescapable although still related to a world and a time beyond the play itself.

In the remaining moments of the play scene, the hilarity rises to its climax, a climax becoming increasingly harsh. During the altercation between Costard and Armado which results from Berowne's ingenious but unattractive trick, images of death begin to hammer through the fabric of the play. The painfulness of the realism grows as Armado, poor, but immensely proud, is finally shamed and humbled before all the other characters. For the first time in the play, the mask falls from Armado's face, and the man beneath it is revealed, his romanticism, his touching personal pride, the agony for him of the confession that in his poverty he wears no shirt beneath his doublet. Still acting, he tries feebly to pass off this lack as some mysterious and romantic penance, but the other characters know the truth; Armado knows they do, and the knowledge is intensely humilitating. The illusion of the role he has played throughout *Love's Labour's Lost* is destroyed for others as well as for himself, and he stands miserably among the jeers of Dumain and Boyet while complete reality breaks over him, and the little personal world which he has built up around himself so carefully shatters at his feet.

The other peole in the play are so concerned with Armado's predicament that no one notices that someone, in a sense Something has joined them. His entrance unremarked by any of the other characters, materializing silently from those shadows which now lie deep along the landscape of the royal park, the Messenger has entered the play world.

> *Mar.* I am sorry, madam, for the news I bring
> Is heavy in my tongue. The King your father—
> *Prin.* Dead, for my life!
> *Mar.* Even so; my tale is told.

There is perhaps nothing like this moment in the whole range of Elizabethan drama. In the space of four lines the entire world of the play, its delicate balance of reality and illusion, all the hilarity and overwhelming life of its last scene has been swept away and destroyed, as Death itself actually enters the park, for the first time, in the person of Marcade. Only in one Elizabethan madrigal, Orlando Gibbons' magnificent "What Is Our Life?" is there a change of harmony and mood almost as swift and great as this one, and it occurs under precisely the same circumstances, the sudden appearance among the images of life in Raleigh's lyric of "the graves that hide us from the searching sun"[8] the memory of the inescapable and tremendous reality of Death.[9]

---

8 Sir Walter Raleigh, "What Is Our Life?", *Silver Poets of the Sixteenth Century*, p. 296.

9 Wilfrid Mellers, in a series of lectures given on "Elizabethan and Jacobean Music," Stratford-upon-Avon, July, 1952.

Clumsy, as one always is in the presence of sudden grief, the King can think of nothing to say but to ask the Princess "How fares your Majesty?" a question to which she, from the depths of her sorrow and bewilderment, gives no reply, but prepares with the dignity characteristic of her to leave for France. Now, the men come forward uncertainly, and first the King and then Berowne, clinging still to a world no longer existing, attempt to express their love in terms which had been appropriate to that world, terms at first still incomprehensible to the women and then, at last, understood, but not altogether trusted.

As vows had begun the play, so vows end it. The King is assigned as his symbol of reality a "forlorn and naked hermitage" without the walls of the royal park, in the real world itself, in which he must try for a twelvemonth if this love conceived in the sunlit landscape of Navarre can persist in the colder light of actuality. For Dumain and Longaville, those shadowy figures, penances more vague but of a similar duration are assigned, and then at last, Berowne, shaken and moved to the depths of his being, inquires from Rosaline, who has been standing a little apart from the others, lost in thought,

> Studies my lady? Mistress, look on me;
> Behold the window of my heart, mine eye,
> What humble suit attends thy answer there.
> Impose some service on me for thy love.

Slowly, speaking with great care, Rosaline answers, and in the strangest and most grotesque of the penances, Berowne is condemned to haunt the hospitals and plague-houses of the world outside the park, to exercise his wit upon the "speechless sick," and try the power of his past role, the old artificiality that had no concern for the feelings of others, that humiliated Armado in the play scene, the careless mocks of the old world, upon the reality of the ailing and the dying. "A jest's prosperity lies in the ear/Of him that hears it, never in the tongue/Of him that makes it." It was this reality of actual living that Berowne was unconscious of when he led the unthinking merriment of the play scene just past. Yet, at the end of the year, love's labors will be won for Berowne, and he will receive Rosaline's love, not in the half real world of the park, but in the actuality outside its walls. Thus the play which began with a paradox, that of the Academe, closes with one as well. Only through the acceptance of the reality of Death are life and love in their fullest sense made possible for the people of the play.

The world of the play past has now become vague and unreal, and it is not distressing that Berowne, in a little speech that is really a kind of epilogue, should refer to all the action before the entrance of Marcade, the people who took part in that action and the kingdom they inhabited and in a sense created, as having been only the elements of a play. It is a play outside which the characters now stand, bewildered, a little lost in the sudden glare of actuality, looking back upon that world of mingled artifice and reality a trifle wistfully before they separate in the vaster realm beyond the royal park. Through *Love's Labour's Lost,* the play has been a symbol of illusion, of delightful unreality, the masque of the Muscovites, or the pageant of the Nine Worthies, and now it becomes apparent that there was a further level of illusion above that of the plays within the play. The world of that illusion has enchanted us; it has been possessed of a haunting beauty, the clear loveliness of those landscapes in the closing song, but Shakespeare insists that it cannot take the place of reality itself, and should not be made to. Always, beyond the charming, frost-etched countryside of the pastoral winter, like the background of some Flemish Book of Hours, lies the reality of the greasy kitchen-maid and her pot, a reality which must sooner or later break through and destroy the charm of the artificial and the illusory.

For us, however, knowing how Shakespeare's later work developed, and how the play image itself took on another meaning for him, there is a strange poignancy in this closing moment, with its confident assertion of the concrete reality of the world into which the characters are about to journey, the necessity for them to adjust themselves to that reality. Later, in *As You Like It* and *Hamlet* Shakespeare would begin to think of the play as the symbol, not of illusion, but of the world itself and its actuality, in *Macbeth* and *King Lear* as the symbol of the futility and tragic nature of that actuality, "that great stage of fools."[10] Yet he must always have kept in mind the image as it had appeared years before in the early comedy of *Love's Labour's Lost,* for returning to it at the very last, he joined that earlier idea of the play as illusion with its later meaning as a symbol of the real world, and so created the final play image of *The Tempest* in which illusion and reality have become one and the same, and there is no longer any distinction possible between them. The world itself into which Berowne and his companions travel to seek out reality will become for Shakespeare at the last merely another stage, a play briefly enacted,

> And, like the baseless fabric of this vision,
> The cloud-capp'd towers, the gorgeous palaces,
> The solemn temples, the great globe itself,
> Yea, all which it inherit, shall dissolve,
> And, like this insubstantial pageant faded,
> Leave not a rack behind. We are such stuff
> As dreams are made on; and our little life
> Is rounded with a sleep.[11]

---

10 *King Lear,* IV, vi.
11 *The Tempest,* IV, i.

# 14

# Structure in *A Midsummer Night's Dream*

*David Young*

## *"The Iron Tongue of Midnight Hath Told Twelve"*

The structure of *A Midsummer Night's Dream* involves, among other things, its time scheme, long considered a problem. The difficulties are well known; temporal references in the play are, like the references to the moon, inconsistent. Theseus and Hippolyta, at the beginning of the play, expect to wait four days until their marriage ceremony; count as they will, however, commentators are able to account for only three. There are various ways in which this discrepancy may be explained. It can be argued that Theseus and Hippolyta succumb to their impatience and move things up one day, or that everyone is anxious to seal the bonds between the quartet of lovers while they are harmoniously arranged. It is also quite possible that the occasion of the original performance was, in fact, four days before the wedding of the couple honored by the play and that Shakespeare never bothered to readjust this actual reference to the details of the plot. The discrepancies in the time scheme have also been used to support theories of revision. But the most sensible reaction is that of Kittredge:

> The time scheme of the drama has worried the critics a good deal and has helped them in spinning tenuous theories of revision. We need only observe that the four days and four nights contemplated by Hippolyta in I, i, 7–11, are not fully spanned. . . . No audience would note the discrepancy, for the night in the enchanted forest is long enough to bewilder the imagination.[1]

Hippolyta supports this when she says:

> Four days will quickly steep themselves in night;
> Four nights will quickly dream away the time. (I, i, 7–8)

The time in this play is indeed "dreamed away," so that undue concern about its exact chronology is a little like the mechanicals' anxious consultation of the almanac.

The temporal patterning of the play is more profitably examined in terms of its effect on the audience. What they witness is a movement from daytime in the city to nighttime in the woods, which then swings back to day again. All of this is controlled by the dramatist in a way that leaves no confusion about thc time of day or night at any given moment in the play.[2] We are carefully prepared for the nocturnal scenes first by the planning of the lovers, then by the rehearsal arrangements of the clowns. In the first night-scene at the opening of the second act, we are brought gradually to an awareness of night which is very like the gathering of dusk on a summer evening. There are oblique references in the opening lines to the moon, night, and starlight; these are balanced by visual images that do not suggest darkness. Puck next describes himself as a "wanderer of the night" and sketches two indoor nocturnal scenes. With Oberon's entrance and opening line—"Ill met by moonlight, proud Titania"—we have come to full night, but it is and will remain, for the most part, the peculiarly "glimmering" night which Oberon mentions a few lines later.

Similarly, we begin to anticipate the arrival of daylight long before it comes. "Cock crow" has been mentioned before the end of the second act. The end of the third act brings Puck's "this must be done with haste" speech and Oberon's reply, which fully prepares us for dawn. We have one more scene, however, before daybreak, that between Bottom and Titania. Then, with all the necessary magic performed, the fairies "hear the morning lark" and leave the stage; a horn blows, and Theseus and Hippolyta enter, bringing with them full daylight. This day-night-day pattern is all the audience knows and all it needs to know.

---

[1] Kittredge Edition, p. ix.

[2] Cf. the discussion of scene-setting techniques in this play in Arthur Colby Sprague, *Shakespeare and His Audience: A Study in the Technique of Exposition* (Cambridge, Mass., 1935), pp. 56 f.

Almost all, one should say, for the play takes one more turn back to darkness again, and the pattern becomes day-night-day-night. We are vaguely aware of this throughout the fifth act because Theseus has mentioned the need to while away the space between "after-supper and bedtime," a matter of some three hours. The "tedious brief" scene of Pyramus and Thisby, as if to make its oxymoron come true, takes up this time, for as it ends Theseus announces that it is past midnight. This is an excellent example of Shakespeare's illusory use of time for dramatic effect. It may not be credible to the scrupulous commentator that "Pyramus and Thisby" could occupy three hours, but it is perfectly credible to the audience, even though Theseus' announcement comes as something of a jolt. The jolt has a dramatic function, for the audience has nearly forgotton the fairies and their world. The lovers may think that they are out of the woods and free for good of their midsummer madness, but the audience is to be reminded that error, illusion, and mystery still exist. Theseus unwittingly aids this final twist by announcing that it is "almost fairy time." Then, as the mortals leave the stage, Puck replaces them with his superb nocturnal litany and all the fairies troop in to bless the marriages. By coming round to "fairy time" again, the play asserts the validity and constancy of both its worlds, day and night, reason and imagination. By returning from night to day it completes a circle; by reintroducing night it performs a figure eight.

Perhaps the most noticeable fact about time in *A Midsummer Night's Dream* is its minimization. In other Shakespearean plays it has a significant role in the workings of the plot. It untangles the knots of *Twelfth Night,* defeats the lovers in *Romeo and Juliet,* and appears before the curtain to divide *The Winter's Tale* in half. In *A Midsummer Night's Dream,* however, it neither starts nor finishes the action. The events in the woods are a suspension of reality, and their resolution, like their initiation, is extra-temporal. We know that one night has been passed in the woods. But what matters about Bottom's dream (as well as Titania's and the four lovers') is not when it happened or how long it lasted, but that its victim was somehow "translated," was absent from his usual self, another person in another place. In his own thick-witted way, Bottom touches on this when he says that his dream "hath no bottom." He is speaking of it in spatial terms, and such terms seem to be appropriate. Because of the minimization of time in *A Midsummer Night's Dream,* most discussions of its structure tend to emphasize spatial aspects—positioning of character groups, levels of awareness, spheres of action. It is these aspects of the play that we turn to next.

### *"By Some Illusion See Thou Bring Her Here"*

There are two worlds in *A Midsummer Night's Dream*—the kingdom of Theseus and the kingdom of Oberon, the one an orderly society, the other a confusing wilderness. The action of the play moves between the two, as two groups of characters from the real and reasonable world find themselves temporarily lost in the imaginary and irrational world. This pattern of action corresponds closely both to the religious morality and the romance, where the respective heroes often move on a narrative line that can be schematized as follows:[3]

*Morality:*

fall from grace / temporary prosperity of evil / divine reconciliation

*Romance:*

separation / wandering / reunion

As the secular drama came to supersede the religious, it branched out, and one of the variations, based on the pastoral ideal, presented the movement through bad fortune to good fortune in spheres of action already familiar from the romance:

*Pastoral Romance:*

society / wilderness / an improved society

The purest examples of this pattern in Shakespeare are *As You Like It* and the late romances, *Cymbeline, The Winter's Tale,* and *The Tempest,* but it may be found at work in plays as diverse as *Two Gentlemen* and *King Lear.* In *A Midsummer Night's Dream* it is present at its most comic pitch: the danger which initially sends the central characters into the wilderness is less severe than in, say, *As You Like It,* and the corresponding need for some sort of social reform is slight. The wilderness, as a result, comes to play a more dominant role. In the pastoral romances, it is usually a pseudo-ideal and a temporary haven. In *A Midsummer Night's Dream,* as personified in the fairies, it governs most of the action and controls most of the characters, recalling the more powerful forces of disruption at work in the mid-section of both morality and romance.

It will be noted that the spheres of action in these traditional narrative patterns do not alter significantly. It is the characters and, by imaginative extension, ourselves who alter as we move through the worlds in question, discovering their interaction. In *A Midsummer Night's Dream,* this process of discovery reveals that the opposing worlds seem to form concentric circles. At first, following the characters from Athens to the woods, we may feel that the two areas are simply adjacent, but as Theseus and daylight reenter

[3] I owe this schematization to a suggestion in David M. Bevington, *From Mankind to Marlowe* (Cambridge, Mass., 1962), p. 190.

the play, we realize that it is possible to enter the woods and reemerge on the other side into human society. Thus, Theseus and his world seem to envelop the world of the woods. But Oberon and Titania, as we learn early in the play and are reminded directly at the end, are not the subjects of Theseus. Their awareness exceeds his, and their world is larger, enveloping his; he is their unconscious subject. Thus we discover another and larger circle, enclosing the first two. Then comes Puck's epilogue, which reminds us that everything we have been watching is a play, an event in a theater with ourselves as audience. Here is a still larger circle, enveloping all the others. The process stops there, but the discovery of ever more comprehensive circles inevitably suggests that there is another one still to be discovered. This is not merely a trick or a display of artistic ingenuity; treating us as it does to an expansion of consciousness and a series of epistemological discoveries, it suggests that our knowledge of the world is less reliable than it seems.

Thus it is that the concentric circles described above can also be used to depict the spectrum of awareness formed by the characters in the play. These are more usually depicted as levels on a kind of rising ladder of intelligence and consciousness,[4] but the very action by which we learn of the differences, that of one character standing aside to watch characters who are less aware of a given situation, suggests the enclosing image of a circle or sphere. In the inmost circle are the mechanicals, and at their center stands Bottom, supremely ignorant of all that is happening. All of the humor derived from Bottom depends on his absolute lack of awareness joined to the absolute confidence with which he moves through the play. If this makes him amusing, it also makes him sympathetic, as if we unconsciously recognized his kinship not only with the other characters but with ourselves. The difference, after all, is one of degree.

In the next circle belong the lovers; they are not much better off than the clowns, but the fact that they are largely victims of enchantment rather than native stupidity gives them claim to a fuller awareness, since Bottom's enchantment never alters his behavior or his nature. The circle beyond belongs to Theseus and Hippolyta, who oversee the action from a distance and are not victimized by the fairies. Hippolyta deserves the further station, on the basis of her conversation with Theseus at the beginning of the fifth act. The fairies occupy the next circle, Titania first, because she is tricked by her husband, then Oberon and Puck. Even these two, however, are not at all times fully aware of the course of events, and we, the audience, watch them as they watch the others. The furthest circle, then, belongs to us. Or

---

[4] This is the way they are described in an excellent analysis by Bertrand Evans in his *Shakespeare's Comedies* (Oxford, 1960), pp. 33–46.

is it the furthest? Does not the playwright belong still further out, overseeing not only the events of the play but our reaction to them, enchanting us as Puck enchants the lovers?

The four groups into which the characters of *A Midsummer Night's Dream* fall present us with another spatial aspect of construction. The effect is like that of a fugue, in which we are simultaneously aware of several lines of movement and thus of position and interaction. Each of the four groups in the play has its own set of experiences. Since we know that these are occurring simultaneously, we are conscious of the location of each group and the ways in which the various actions impinge upon one another. This consciousness is essentially spatial; it requires harmonious resolution just as does the temporal action. If for no other reason, the fairies' entrance in the fifth act would be necessary as the final step in the series of group positionings. The other three groups have gathered there; the arrival of the fairies completes the choreography.

A large part of our interest in the comedy is directed to the way in which the four groups are handled. Their introduction, for example, is formal and at the same time intriguing enough to capture our interest as we gradually realize how the strands of action are to be divided. We meet each group in turn with whatever is necessary in the way of individual and group characterization as well as the details of exposition required to start each action. Theseus and Hippolyta begin the parade with their mood of revelry and a few key details about their wedding. Egeus bustles in, changing the tone and introducing the lovers' plot, with three of the four lovers present. The stage is then cleared for some conventional love dialogue, the plans which will initiate the action in the woods, and the introduction of the fourth lover. In the next scene, we meet the mechanicals and are treated to a full characterization of Bottom. The exposition prepares us for complications in the woods, but it also looks forward, as did that of Theseus, to the final events of the play. For the masque-like introduction of the fairy group, we shift to the second sphere of action. As the last details necessary to the exposition fall into place, Demetrius and Helena enter and the interwoven adventures of three of the groups begin, with Theseus and Hippolyta held in the background for the duration of the night.

It is clear by the time these four groups of characters have been introduced that we are witnessing an art that divides our attention among a number of subjects. The four groups are not unrelated. By the end of the exposition, all have been shown to have the royal wedding as a point of contact: it is the deadline set for Hermia by Theseus, the occasion for the clowns' performance, and the reason for the presence of the fairies. Other linkings and encounters will follow. Nonetheless, each group has a set of common characteristics and each will undergo a particular set of experiences.

The division of interest through multiplication of plots and characters is typical of Elizabethan drama, which has often been called an art of multiplicity.[5] As Madelaine Doran has shown, it originated in medieval practices of narration and staging and continued to be valued in the Renaissance even by those critics who were theoretically committed to the unities.[6] Those dramatists who practiced it risked chaos, since the traditional means of dramatic unification were not open to them. *A Midsummer Night's Dream* risks more than most. Not only does it avoid a single action, it has no central character to whom the various events are unmistakably related. Furthermore, it cannot even be said to have a single theme; its dispersal of interest among various groups and settings is a dispersal, in part, of subject matter as well. Yet Shakespeare achieves unity, partly through careful control of tone and setting and partly through his handling of the groups, a spatial organization which is almost geometrical in its order and which involves relationships within each group as well as among the four.

Our sense of the lovers' permutations, for example, is distinctly spatial; almost any discussion of them is apt to resort to diagrammatic figures.[7] We begin the play with a triangle, Lysander-Hermia-Demetrius, but we soon realize, as Helena's presence and importance is established, that it is in fact a quadrangle, with Helena the neglected corner. In the second act, Lysander's allegiance is suddenly switched, so that we have "cross-wooing," each man pursuing the wrong woman. We also have, as Baldwin points out,[8] a circle, since each of the four parties is pursuing another: Hermia is looking for Lysander; he is wooing Helena; she continues to love Demetrius; and he is still enamored of Hermia. This is the quadrangle at its most disrupted state, and two steps are necessary to repair it. The first of these comes in the third act, when Demetrius is restored to Helena. This reverses the original triangle, and Hermia becomes the neglected party. The fourth act finds the quadrangle in its proper state, each man attached to the right woman, restoring a situation which predates the beginning of the play.

These permutations are further complicated by the question of friendship. Each member of the quadrangle has, potentially, one love and two friends therein, but the shifting of love relationships disrupts the friendships as well. Lysander and Hermia are at the outset alienated from Demetrius

---

[5] Madelaine Doran, *Endeavors of Art* (Madison, Wis., 1954), quotes from Heinrich Wölfflin, *Principles of Art History* (London, 1932), p. 166, and discusses the concept in her first chapter. G. K. Hunter also uses it in his *Lyly,* p. 137 and n. He says the term is used by Rossiter in *English Drama From Early Times to the Elizabethans.* I have not found it there, but Rossiter discusses the concept on pp. 72 f. and in his Epilogue.

[6] See Doran, pp. 258–94.

[7] The most extensive analysis of this kind is by Baldwin, *Literary Genetics,* pp. 476 f.

[8] *Ibid.*

but friends of Helena, so much so that they tell her their secret. When Lysander falls in love with Helena, their friendship is of course destroyed; she thinks he is making fun of her. The next alteration, Demetrius' restoration to Helena, destroys the Hermia-Helena friendship: Hermia thinks Helena is somehow responsible; Helena thinks everyone is mocking her. Thus, the restoration of the proper love relationships also restores the friendships of all four; even Lysander and Demetrius, who were ready to fight to the death, are friends again at the end of the play.

The lovers' quadrangle is set within another calmer quadrangle involving the royal couples. We learn of its existence when Oberon and Titania meet. She immediately charges him with love of Hippolyta, "Your buskin'd mistress and your warrior love," and he counters:

> How canst thou thus, for shame, Titania,
> Glance at my credit with Hippolyta,
> Knowing I know thy love to Theseus? (II, i, 74–76)

There are cross-purposes, it appears, within this group as well. They do not, however, lead to the complications that beset the lovers. Theseus and Hippolyta are unaware of the fairies' marital difficulties. Moreover, the true occasion of the quarrel is the changeling boy, so that Oberon's practicing on Titania is all that is needed to restore the quadrangle to harmony and enable the fairies to join forces for the ritual blessing at the end.

Oberon solves his problems with Titania by finding her an absurd lover, thus creating a sort of mock triangle with Bottom as the oblivious third party. But Bottom is also a lover in his role of Pyramus and is part of another absurd triangle in which he plays not the intruding beast, lion or ass, but the rightful mate.

These geometrical figures are of course illusory, but by use of the analogy to which they point, we see more clearly the constant interaction among the four character groups, the collisions and entanglements which make their separate adventures interdependent. The lovers begin and end the play with an attachment to the court of Theseus and the revels surrounding his wedding. In between, they are the victims of their journey to the woods and consequent involvement with the fairies. The fairies, who have arrived to bless the royal wedding, are finally able to arrange two more and to solve their own difficulties through an involvement with the mechanicals. The mechanicals, intent on entertaining Theseus, unwittingly entertain Oberon and Puck as well. Their involvement with the lovers is more subtle. It is true that their entertainment finally has the four lovers as audience, but Bottom's adventures, as well as the play he stars in, provide a good deal of indirect comment on the lovers, most of it in the form of parody. This kind of relationship belongs to Shakespeare's practice of "mirroring," a spatial technique which deserves a section of its own.

*The Wat'ry Glass*

Shakespeare's device of using scenes, characters, and speeches to point up thematic relationships by means of reflection has only recently begun to receive critical attention.[9] The term "mirroring" is a useful one, recalling as it does Hamlet's remarks about art. To say that art mirrors nature is to suggest more than mere imitation; the process of reflection sends the image back to its origin and, presumably, stimulates thought. Ulysses and Achilles discuss the same notion in *Troilus and Cressida,* using Plato as a springboard. Before Ulysses turns the idea to Achilles' waning reputation, Achilles himself gives it a general application:

> For speculation turns not to itself,
> Till it hath travell'd and is mirror'd there
> Where it may see itself. This is not strange at all.
> (III, iii, 109–11)

Mirroring, then, while it may heighten mood and unify action, can also breed speculation. There is a good deal of evidence to indicate that Shakespeare used it specifically for "the parallel advancement of plot and idea."[10]

This function betrays the origins of mirroring; there had been dramatic devices with the same function and with reasonably similar techniques for some time. The parallel and simultaneous actions of medieval drama sometimes employed reflecting scenes and characters.[11] Medieval drama moves between the realistic and the allegorical so easily and frequently that we are not perhaps inclined to see sequential scenes as mirrors; it would be difficult at times to say which is primary and which reflective. Nonetheless, the fact that these dramas present scenes and characters that are different in kind and thematically alike relates them to the more sophisticated practices which were to follow. After all, *Gorboduc,* which uses allegorical dumb shows to reflect moral and philosophical content, is not very different and not much more sophisticated. Shakespeare's own eventual finesse with the technique in plays like *Lear* and *Hamlet* was the outgrowth of such painful and emblematic beginnings as the fly-killing scene in *Titus* and the dunghill and father-son scenes in the *Henry VI* cycle.

Mirroring in the comedies, less noticed than in the tragedies and histories, has a life and validity of its own. While Shakespeare uses it for the same purposes as in more serious plays, he also employs it concomitantly

---

9 Hereward T. Price, "Mirror-Scenes in Shakespeare," in *J. Q. Adams Memorial Studies* (Washington, D.C., 1948), pp. 101–13; Reuben A. Brower, *The Fields of Light* (New York, 1951), pp. 95–122; Maynard Mack, "The Jacobean Shakespeare: Some Observations on the Construction of the Tragedies," in *Jacobean Theatre,* Stratford-upon-Avon Studies 1 (New York, 1960), pp. 11–41.

10 Price, p. 103.

11 See, for instance, the Digby *Mary Magdalene* (in J. Q. Adams, *Chief Pre-Shakespearean Dramas,* pp. 225–42) in which realistic scenes are followed by scenes on separate allegorical stages which mirror the moral crises in the main action.

for comic effect. Perhaps its use as a comic device has distracted attention from its other functions, but mimicry, parody, and exaggeration can mean as much as more serious forms of imitation. The image returned by a fun-house mirror may provoke thought as well as laughter.

We have already noticed the paired characters in *A Midsummer Night's Dream* and noted how they lend symmetry to the plot. Shakespeare also takes advantage of them to set up reflections which underline key dramatic ideas. Thus, the near-identity of the lovers is used to stress the inadequacy of that kind of love which yields itself to irrationality and the consequent heavy demands upon both personality and intelligence. Demetrius and Lysander address the women they woo in the same conventional vocabulary of exaggerated praise, each mirroring the other's inadequacy. The women expose one another in similar fashion. Hermia has no sooner sworn her love by Cupid's bow and arrow and by "all the vows that ever men have broke" than Helena is on stage for her soliloquy, talking of winged Cupid and Demetrius' broken oaths in the same way. Thus, the two women who think themselves so different—one lucky in love, the other rejected—are shown to have an identity which, incidentally, foreshadows the events to come. Later on, in the woods, Helena herself employs the image of a mirror. Speaking of her earlier desire to be like Hermia, she accounts herself a failure:

> What wicked and dissembling glass of mine,
> Made me compare with Hermia's sphery eyne?
>
> (II, ii, 98–99)

It is at precisely this moment that Lysander wakes up and falls in love with her. "Transparent Helena," he shouts, not seeing in her the image of his folly. He too goes on to insist that she and Hermia are completely different. Throughout the night, the four lovers will peer at each other and always fail to see what the playwright makes so clear to us, their likenesses.

Much the same thing can be said about the royal pairs. It is appropriate that Theseus, as representative of daylight and right reason, should have subdued his bride-to-be to the rule of his masculine will. That is the natural order of things.[12] It is equally appropriate that Oberon, as king of darkness and fantasy, should have lost control of his wife, and that the corresponding natural disorder described by Titania should ensue. All the details in these dual situations have the same function. Both royal pairs love panoramas, but the landscapes they see are appropriately different. The means that each king employs to establish rule in his kingdom are significantly opposed. Even the Masters of the Revels of each monarchy, Philostrate and Puck, serve to strengthen the sense of contrast within likeness.

---

12 This point is extensively discussed in Olson, "*A Midsummer Night's Dream* and the Meaning of Court Marriage," pp. 101 ff. He cites the Theseus of *The Two Noble Kinsmen* as a more explicit example.

What we have here differs from the mirroring found in the tragedies. There, the tragic hero occupies the center of attention, while surrounding characters reflect him, as Horatio, Laertes, and Fortinbras mirror Hamlet, or while alternate scenes reflect his dilemma, as do the Gloucester scenes in *Lear*. In these plays, mirroring works mostly one way. Even the standard mirror device found in earlier comedies, the servant subplot, has this characteristic. Since *A Midsummer Night's Dream* cannot be said to have a central character, however, or even a central group of characters, any mirroring that takes place is necessarily reflexive or retroactive, throwing as much meaning on one scene, group, or character as on another. This is another illustration of the way in which diffusion marks this play, as well, I believe, as other Shakespearean comedies, where mirroring has the same two-way effect. If we could accept this, we would stop speaking of plot and subplot in Shakespearean comedy and recognize the uniqueness of its form. Nor need we be afraid of admitting to disunity. The continually rebounding reflections constantly strengthen identity, suggesting that everything we see is an aspect of the same situation and bringing to the play a startlingly organic unity. Again I think it accurate to stress the germinal role of *A Midsummer Night's Dream* in the development of this technique; while there are hints of it in *Love's Labour's Lost*, it was not until *A Midsummer Night's Dream* that Shakespeare found the means to use it fully.

If any group of characters in the play may be said to exist primarily for purposes of reflection, it is the mechanicals. This does not subordinate them in importance; they could easily claim supreme position as the busiest glasses in this comedy of reflection. What is more, they bring to the climax of the play its biggest and funniest mirror. Their reflective function is worth examining in some detail.

The mechanicals' first scene gives us hints of the echo and parody we are to have from them through the rest of the play. Their concern for an orderly handling of their task catches the theme Theseus has just sounded and will continue to sound throughout the play. Their respect for hierarchy recalls the issue raised by the entrance of Egeus and the lovers,[13] and their plans for rehearsal echo the plans of Demetrius and Hermia. Their confused use of language (e.g. "I will aggravate my voice") presents an aspect of the confusion that will later reign in the woods, and the paradoxes they blunder into, "lamentable comedy," "monstrous little voice," hint at the doubts about familiar categories—dreaming and waking, reason and imagination—with which the play will eventually leave us. The interlude about true love they plan to perform promises to mock the lovers we have just seen. Finally, Bottom's enthusiastic confidence that he can perform any role—tyrant, lover,

---

[13] "These common life characters...furnish a rule of ignorant common sense against which the vagaries of their superiors may be measured. So the first act closes by showing the persistence of order in the lower segment of society" (*Ibid.*, p. 106).

maiden, or lion—amusingly introduces us to the theme of metamorphosis, the activity which will dominate all experience in the woods.

All of these echoes, or pre-echoes, it should be added, are those that remain within the context of the play's events. Others, directed at the knowing audience, have already begun to parody such "outside" targets as bad plays, whining poetry, and court fashion. These mirrorings prepare the audience for the subtler parodies involved in the lovers' plot and dialogue, bring it into a closer relationship with the play, and open the way for some of the insights into the nature of dramatic illusion which the play ultimately provides.

Once in the woods, the clowns keep up a continuous comic counterpoint to the adventures of the lovers. When Hermia rushes off in search of errant Lysander ("Either death or you I'll find immediately"), the case of "Pyramus and Thisby" troops on ("Are we all met?") to rehearse another story of desperate love. By virtue of its versification, their language is more mechanical than what we have just heard from Lysander and will soon hear from Demetrius, but the vocabulary and tone are similar. Like Lysander and Demetrius, Bottom, playing the role of a faithful lover, finds himself the victim of a sudden transformation. The other clowns flee, but Bottom as Ass stays on to become the paramour of the fairy queen. Their beauty and beast tableaux alternate with the comings and goings of the lovers, each reflecting the absurdity of the other.

Verbal echoes strengthen the mirror relationships. Lysander swears to Helena that reason brings him to her:

> The will of man is by his reason sway'd;
> And reason says you are the worthier maid.
> Things growing are not ripe until their season;
> So I, being young, till now not ripe to reason;
> And touching now the point of human skill,
> Reason becomes the marshal to my will
> And leads me to your eyes. (II, ii, 115–21)

Bottom echoes him more sensibly when Titania first admits that she has fallen in love at first sight:

> Methinks, mistress, you should have little reason for that. And yet, to say the truth, reason and love keep little company together now-a-days. The more the pity that some honest neighbours will not make them friends.
> (III, i, 145–50)

Demetrius, once in the woods, thinks his problem is to find Hermia:

> Thou told'st me they were stol'n unto this wood;
> And here am I, and wood within this wood
> Because I cannot greet my Hermia. (II, i, 191–93)

The problem, as Bottom suggests, is much simpler than that:

> if I had wit enough to get out of this wood, I have enough to serve mine own turn. (III, i, 153–54)

Stupid as he may be, Bottom is not the victim of love's madness and so, throughout the night of errors, conducts himself with greater dignity and common sense. The distortive mirror can also serve as a corrective.

As object of Titania's affection, Bottom mirrors not only the Athenians, but the fairy queen's earlier loves as well. He is a kind of mock-Oberon, a role he tries valiantly to play, sending the fairies off on appropriate errands just as Oberon has sent Puck for the little Western flower, but of course his asshood keeps betraying him into unkingly needs:

> Methinks I have a great desire to a bottle of hay.
> Good hay, sweet hay, hath no fellow. (IV, i, 35–36)

Titania has also been, and will again be, in love with Theseus, and she has led him, as she leads Bottom, through "the glimmering night." Theseus has put such experiences behind him. He would probably agree with Quince that "A paramour is (God bless us!) a thing of naught" (IV, ii, 13–14). But Bottom's adventures offer a farcical reminder of events in Theseus' past. Thus, a clown's dream becomes one of the key mirrors in the play, reflecting almost all of the male characters in one way or another. Bottom is not the successful actor he had hoped to be, but he gets his chance to play a number of roles—not just lover and tyrant, but several kinds of lover and one or two kinds of tyrant; not lion, but a beast at least as interesting if not nearly as frightening.

"Pyramus and Thisby" is the climax of the mechanicals' reflective career. If it does not succeed in holding the mirror up to nature, it holds it up to almost everything else. "The best in this kind are but shadows," says Theseus. Shadows of what? Of the events and characters of *A Midsummer Night's Dream,* but the audience of "Pyramus and Thisby" may be partially pardoned for not recognizing their own images. The lovers, back from the woods and safely married, need not compare their experiences with those of Pyramus and Thisby in a less accommodating wood. Nor can they be expected so soon to recognize in the poetry of the play the inadequate language of their own vocabulary of love. Theseus and Hippolyta, too, have put their pasts behind them; nothing about this play is able to provoke their memories. The mechanicals, as with the other effects of the drama, fail in this function too; "speculation turns not to itself."

Not, that is, among the characters of the play. But we are also the audience of "Pyramus and Thisby" and have many comparisons to make. The resemblance between the "fond pageant" in the woods and the "tragical mirth" in the palace does not escape us, nor do the references to at least some of the other plays and the various dramatic and poetic conventions which the playwright finds hard to admire. Beyond these reflections we begin to discern an even larger one. Perhaps it is begun by Theseus' remarks about the poet, but it is the kind of insight that ought to be provoked by any play within a play, a mirror for the audience—drama relationship if ever there was one. Shakespeare exploits it thoroughly. Within a play about love written for a wedding, he puts a play about love written for a wedding. If "Pyramus and Thisby" is inept, it is also well-meaning and deserving of charity; so is *A Midsummer Night's Dream.* If Bottom and his fellows can expect sixpence a day for life as their reward, so perhaps does Shakespeare's company deserve generous remuneration. But there are contrasts too. Where the mechanicals fail at dramatic illusion, unity, and appropriateness, *A Midsummer Night's Dream* succeeds. The playwright manages to exploit the contrast as a kind of mild reminder that he knows his business; he can even afford to parody himself (assuming that this play follows *Romeo and Juliet*). This is perhaps what gave Max Beerbohm the impression that in this play, "we have the Master, confident in his art, at ease with it as a man in his dressing-gown, kicking up a loose slipper and catching it on his toe."[14]

The discerning audience will finally find in the mirror of the mechanicals' performance one more image—its own. They are bound to notice that "Pyramus and Thisby" does not have a very perceptive audience. Not that it deserves one, but as *A Midsummer Night's Dream* is superior to "Pyramus and Thisby," so, the playwright seems to hope, will its audience be superior. Elizabethan audiences, we know, were not always as attentive or polite as the actors and playwrights might wish. Perhaps they were being asked in this comedy, as well as in *Love's Labour's Lost,* to recognize their image and reform it altogether. Certainly they are given a chance to behave more astutely than the audience of "Pyramus and Thisby," to see to it that they are not quite as condescending as Theseus, as inconsistent as Hippolyta, as oblivious, when faced with their own images, as the lovers. The playwright, by placing them higher than any of the characters in the play, gives them every opportunity. If they should fail, they have only themselves to blame. There is just a hint of mockery in Puck's epilogue:

> If we shadows have offended,
> Thinke but this, and all is mended—
> That you have but slumb'red here
> While these visions did appear.
> And this weak and idle theme,
> No more yielding but a dream. (V, i, 430–35)

Anyone who is willing to admit that he has slept through this performance cannot claim to be very alert. In fact, he must inevitably be compared to

---

[14] Quoted in the New Cambridge Edition, p. xix.

those characters in the play who are willing to think that they have "dreamed" it, dismissing events which exposed them significantly. Shakespeare gives us our choice. We may remain within the outer circles of consciousness with Oberon, Puck, and himself, or we may doze off and fall inward toward the condition of Bottom and the lovers. In the mirror of *A Midsummer Night's Dream,* the spectator may find, even if he does not recognize, his very form and pressure.

# 15

# *The Merchant of Venice:* The Gentle Bond

*Sigurd Burckhardt*

## I

The danger of literary source-hunting is that it abets our natural tendency to discount things we believe we have accounted for. The source, once found, relieves us of the effort to see what a thing *is*; we are satisfied with having discovered how it got there. Shakespeare's plots—especially his comedy plots—have generally been at a discount; we have been content to say that the poet took his stories pretty much as he found them and then, as the phrase goes, "breathed life" into them, enriched them with his subtle characterizations and splendid poetry. That the dramatist must make his plot into the prime metaphor of his meaning—this classical demand Shakespeare was magnanimously excused from, the more readily because by the same token we were excused from the labor of discovering the meaning of complex and "improbable" plots.

*Reprinted from* ELH, A Journal of English Literary History, *XXIX, No. 3, September 1962, 239–262, by permission of The Johns Hopkins Press. This paper was read in April 1962 as the annual Tudor and Stuart Lecture at The Johns Hopkins University. It appears in a somewhat different form in Sigurd Burckhardt,* Shakespearean Meanings *(Princeton: Princeton University Press, 1968).*

But with the plot thus out of the way, other problems often arose. *The Merchant of Venice* is a case in point. Audiences persist in feeling distressed by Shylock's final treatment, and no amount of historical explanation helps them over their unease. It is little use telling them that their attitude toward the Jew is anachronistic, distorted by modern, un-Elizabethan opinions about racial equality and religious tolerance. They know better; they know that, in the play itself, they have been made to take Shylock's part so strongly that his end seems cruel. Nor does it do them much good to be told that Shakespeare, being Shakespeare, "could not help" humanizing the stereotype villain he found in his sources; Richard III and Iago are also given depth and stature, but we don't feel sorry for them. If we regard *The Merchant* as a play of character rather haphazardly flung over a prefabricated plot, we cannot join, as unreservedly as we are meant to, in the joyful harmonies of the last act; Shylock spooks in the background, an unappeased ghost.

The source of our unease is simple enough: Shylock gets more than his share of good lines. This is nowhere more evident than in the court-room scene, where he and Antonio, villain and hero, are pitted against each other in a rhetorical climax. Shylock is powerful in his vindictiveness:

> You'll ask me why I rather choose to have
> A weight of carrion flesh than to receive
> Three thousand ducats. I'll never answer that;
> But say it is my humour. Is it answer'd?
> What if my house be troubled with a rat
> And I be pleas'd to give ten thousand ducats
> To have it ban'd? What, are you answer'd yet?
> Some men there are love not a gaping pig;
> Some, that are mad if they behold a cat;
> And others, when the bagpipe sings i' th' nose,
> Cannot contain their urine: for affection,
> Master of passion, sways it to the mood
> Of what it likes or loathes. Now, for your answer:
> As there is no firm reason to be render'd
> Why he cannot abide a gaping pig;
> Why he, a harmless necessary cat;
> Why he, a swollen bagpipe; but of force
> Must yield to such inevitable shame
> As to offend, himself being offended;
> So can I give no reason, nor I will not,
> More than a lodg'd hate and a certain loathing
> I bear Antonio, that I follow thus
> A losing suit against him. Are you answer'd?

Antonio is grandiloquent:

> I pray you, think, you question with the Jew.
> You may as well go stand upon the beach

And bid the main flood bate his usual height;
You may as well use question with the wolf
Why he hath made the ewe bleat for the lamb;
You may as well forbid the mountain pines
To wag their high tops and to make no noise
When they are fretten with the gusts of heaven;
You may as well do anything most hard,
As seek to soften that—than which what's harder?—
His Jewish heart.

Both men use the triple simile in parallel structure, but the similarity serves only to bring out the difference. The toughness of Shylock's argument is embodied in the toughness of his lines, his passion in their speed and directness; this is a man who *speaks.* We might simply say that Shakespeare here is writing close to his dramatic best; but if by this time he was able to give his devils their due, why does he leave his hero shamed? Antonio's lines are flaccidly oratorical; his similes move with a symmetry so slow and pedantic that our expectations continually outrun them. He strains so hard for the grand that when he has to bring his mountainous tropes around to the point of bearing, they bring forth only a pathetic anti-climax: "You may as well do anything most hard." True, the burden of his speech is resignation; but it is feeble rather than noble, a collapse from overstatement into helplessness.

The historical critic may protest at this point that such a judgment reflects a modern bias against rhetoric, a twentieth-century preference for the understated and purely dramatic. But the qualities which make us rank Shylock's lines over Antonio's have long been accepted among the criteria by which we seek to establish the sequence of Shakespeare's plays, on the assumption that where we find them we have evidence of greater maturity and mastery. Nor is this only an assumption. In *The Merchant* itself there is a crucial occasion where these qualities are preferred and where, had the choice been different, the consequence would have been disaster for Antonio. The occasion is Bassanio's choice of the right casket; he rejects the golden one, because it is "mere ornament," and prefers lead:

thou meagre lead,
Which rather threat'nest than dost promise aught,
Thy plainness moves me more than eloquence.[1]

---

[1] My interpretation here rests on an emendation; F and Qq read "paleness," not "plainness." But the emendation has the support of most editors since Warburton—and of sound sense. Bassanio means to contrast the three metals; and though both silver —"thou pale and common drudge"—and lead are pale, it is contrary to his purpose, and to the logical structure of his speech, to fix on the one quality in which lead is *like* silver. The line as F has it would have to be read with a strong emphasis on "Thy"; but even then there is no reason why the paleness of lead should move Bassanio, when that of silver left him unmoved. Moreover, and most decisively, the word is clearly antithetical to "eloquence"; and while "plainness" yields a natural antithesis, "paleness" does not.

At a decisive moment, Bassanio's critical judgment is the same as ours; so that, when we find ourselves more moved by Shylock's plainness than by Antonio's eloquence, we have the best possible reason for feeling sure that Shakespeare intended us to be.

For Bassanio's judgment is "critical" in more senses than one: the play's happy outcome hangs on his taste. Had he judged wrongly, Portia could not have appeared in court to render her second and saving judgment. In the casket scene, the action turns on the *styles* of metals, conceived as modes of speech; the causalities of the play assume a significance which is, initially at least, only obscured by our being told that Shakespeare's plot is to be found in *Il Pecorone* and the *Gesta Romanorum*. Why does Portia come to Venice? Because Bassanio chooses plainness over eloquence. And how is Bassanio put into the position to make that choice? By Antonio's having bound himself to Shylock. That is how the causal chain of the story runs; it does not run from Fiorentino to Shakespeare.

And as in any good play, so here the causality reveals the meaning of the whole. It shows that the plot is *circular*: bound in such a way that the instrument of destruction, the bond, turns out to be the source of deliverance. Portia, won through the bond, wins Antonio's release from it; what is more, she wins it, not by breaking the bond, but by submitting to its rigor more rigorously than even the Jew had thought to do. So seen, one of Shakespeare's apparently most fanciful plots proves to be one of the most exactingly structured; it is what it should be: the play's controlling metaphor. As the subsidiary metaphors of the bond and the ring indicate, *The Merchant* is a play about circularity and circulation; it asks how the vicious circle of the bond's law can be transformed into the ring of love. And it answers: through a literal and unreserved submission to the bond as absolutely binding. It is as though Shakespeare, finding himself bound to a story already drawn up for him in his source, had taken it as the test of his creative freedom and had discovered that this freedom lay, not in a feeble, Antonio-like resignation, which consoles itself with the consciousness of its inner superiority to the vulgar exigencies of reality, but in a Portia-like acceptance and penetration of these exigencies to the point where they must yield their liberating truth. The play's ultimate circularity may well be that it tells the story of its own composition, of its being created, wholly given and intractably positive though it seems, by the poet's discovery of what it is.

## II

The world of *The Merchant* consists of two separate and mostly discontiguous realms: Venice and Belmont, the realm of law and the realm of love, the public sphere and the private. Venice is a community firmly established and concerned above all else with preserving its stability; it is a closed world, inherently conservative, because it knows that it stands and falls with the sacredness of contracts. Belmont, on the other hand, is open and potential; in it a union—that of lovers—is to be founded rather than defended. The happy ending arises from the interaction of the two realms: the bond makes possible the transfer of the action to Belmont, which then *re*-acts upon Venice. The public order is saved from the deadly logic of its own constitution by having been transposed, temporarily, to the private sphere.

But it is not a matter merely of transposition. Each realm has, as it were, its own language, so that the process is better described as a re-translation. Antonio's bonding is a necessary condition for Bassanio's winning Portia, but it is not a sufficient cause; the riddle of the caskets must be correctly *interpreted*. And in exactly the same way the winning of Portia is a necessary condition but not a sufficient cause for the redemption of the bond; it likewise cannot be bought but must be correctly interpreted. The language of love and liberality does not simply supersede that of "use" (=usuary) and law; it must first be translated from it and then back into it. Love must learn to speak the public language, grasp its peculiar grammar; Shylock, to be defeated, must be spoken to in his own terms. That he compels this retranslation is his triumph, Pyrrhic though it turns out to be.

The Jew draws his eloquence and dignity from raising to the level of principle something which by its very nature seems to deny principle: *use*. Antonio's most serious mistake—or rather failure of imagination—is that he cannot conceive of this possibility. He takes a fearful risk for Bassanio, but he cannot claim full credit for it, because he does not know what he is risking. Not only is he confident that his ships will come home a month before the day; he is taken in by Shylock's harmless interpretation of the "merry jest," the pound-of-flesh clause:

To buy his favour, I extend this friendship.

He is sure that the Jew wants to *buy* something, to make some kind of profit, and pleasantly surprised that the profit is to be of so "gentle" (=gentile) a kind; he cannot conceive that a greedy usurer would risk three thousand ducats for a profitless piece of carrion flesh. His too fastidious generosity prevents him from reckoning with the generosity of hatred:

...his flesh—what's that good for?
To bait fish withal!

So he blindly challenges the usurer—the very man he is about to use—to do his worst:

I am as like to call thee so again,
To spit on thee again, to spurn thee too.

> If thou wilt lend this money, lend it not
> As to thy friends; for when did friendship take
> A breed of barren metal of his friend?
> But lend it rather to thine enemy,
> Who, if he break, thou mayest with better face
> Exact the penalty.

(Little wonder that his later words about Shylock's hardness come off so feebly.) The worst he expects is the exacting of "barren metal"; that it will turn out to be a pound of his own flesh does not enter his haughtily gentle mind.

But the play, thanks largely to Shylock's imagination, insistently makes the point that metal is not barren; it does breed, is pregnant with consequences and capable of transformation into life and even love. Metal it is which brings Bassanio as a suitor to Belmont, metal which holds Portia's picture and with it herself. When Shylock runs through Venice crying: "My ducats and my daughter," we are as shallow as Venetian dandies and street urchins if we simply echo him with ridicule. Jessica and Lorenzo turn fugitive thieves for the sake of these ducats; it is only at the very end, and by the grace of Portia, that they are given an honest competence:

> Fair ladies, you drop manna in the way
> Of starved people.

In this merchant's world money is a great good, is life itself. When Antonio, again through Portia, learns that three of his argosies are "richly" come to harbor, he is not scornful of mere pelf but says:

> Sweet lady, you have given me life and living.

(Which makes him Shylock's faithful echo: "You take my life,/ If you do take the means whereby I live.") Bassanio, with Shylock's ducats, ventures to Belmont to win "a lady richly left" and so to rid himself of this debts; it is a good deal worse than irrelevant to blame him (as some gentlemen critics, of independent income no doubt, have done) for being a fortune hunter. One, perhaps *the* lesson Antonio is made to learn is a lesson in metal-breeding.

Shylock is imaginative not only about money and flesh but about speech. We are, I am convinced, meant to understand that he draws his bloody inspiration directly from Antonio. In the lines just before the stating of the clause, we are shown how intimately and subtly the Jew responds to words, how they trigger his imagination, which thus proves more charged and sure than Antonio's. (That is why he has the better lines.) When Antonio proudly says: "I do never *use* it," Shylock begins his story of Jacob's *ewes*; shortly thereafter, when his calculations—"Let me see, the *rate*. . ."—are brusquely interrupted by Antonio's impatient: "Well, Shylock, shall we be beholding to you?," he picks up the thread again but with a new twist:

> Signior Antonio, many a time and oft
> In the Rialto you have *rated* me.

This is how he is brought to the idea of making his metal breed flesh. Unlike Antonio, he does not speak in set pieces leading to sententious commonplaces, "as who should say: 'I am Sir Oracle,/And when I ope my lips, let no dog bark.' " *His* speech is for *use,* as it is of ewes; that is the secret of its effectiveness. Out of context his lines are not as quotable as many of Antonio's; but then we have reason to be suspicious of Shakespeare's quotable lines; Polonius is probably the most quoted of his characters. Shylock and Antonio provide the first major instance of Shakespeare's exploration of the conflict between noble-minded orators and less scrupulous but more effective speakers: between Brutus and Antony, Othello and Iago. The words of genuine speakers are so fully part of the dramatic situation, so organically flesh of the play's verbal body, that they resist excision. They grow, as truly dramatic speech must, from their circumstances and in turn change them; since the literal meaning of "drama" is "action," they are what they ought to be: language in action. It is because Shylock speaks this language that he is able to transform barren metal into living substance; the very mode of his speaking here becomes the mode of his doing.

## III

In Belmont the Jew's money promises to breed in a more literal sense: it helps to unite lovers. The equation money = offspring is pointed up by Gratiano, in a line which echoes Shylock's "My ducats and my daughter":

> We'll play them the first boy for a thousand ducats.

More precisely, the money makes the union possible; the consummation turns out to be rather more complicated.

I have stressed the differences between Belmont and Venice, but in one respect they are alike: both are governed by rigorously positive laws, which threaten to frustrate the very purposes they are meant to serve, but which must nevertheless be obeyed. In fact, the rule which governs Belmont —the covenant of the caskets—seems even more wilfully positive than that of Venice. More rigidly even than the law of the bond, it puts obedience above meaning, the letter above the spirit.

The harshly positive character of Venetian law is evident enough. When Bassanio pleads a kind of natural law, man's intuitive sense of justice, he is sternly corrected by Portia:

*Bass.* If this will not suffice, it must appear
That malice bears down truth. And I beseech you,
Wrest once the law to your authority;
To do a great right, do a little wrong,
And curb this cruel devil of his will.
*Por.* It must not be; there is no power in Venice
Can alter a decree established.
'Twill be recorded as a precedent,
And many an error by the same example
Will rush into the state. It cannot be.

But Portia here can still appeal to reason, can show that the law which is at the mercy of man's "sense of justice" fails of its purpose, even though, taken as positively binding, it may also frustrate that purpose. Nerissa, defending the wisdom of the casket test against Portia's rebellious complaints, has no argument to fall back on except authority and faith:

*Por.* I may neither choose who I would nor refuse who I dislike; so is the will of a living daughter curb'd by the will of a dead father. Is it not hard, Nerissa, that I cannot choose one nor refuse none?
*Ner.* Your father was ever virtuous, and holy men at their death have good inspirations.

The wisdom of the father's will can be proved only in the event.

The law of Belmont, then, demands submission quite as much as that of Venice; it too disallows mere feeling. But it differs in one decisive point: it permits, in fact (as the result shows) requires interpretation by *substance* rather than by letter. Aragon and Morocco fail because they try to interpret the lines inscribed on the caskets rather than the substance; they calculate which of the inscriptions correctly states the relation between their own worth, Portia's worth and the risk of choosing wrongly. For them the caskets are mere clues; what they are really concerned with is themselves and the object of their suit. It is this intrusion of their selves and their purposes that misleads them: they are enmeshed in their reckonings. The noteworthy thing about Bassanio is that he disregards the inscriptions; he lets the metals themselves speak to him (quite literally: he apostrophizes them as speakers). Once before the caskets, he seems almost to forget Portia, himself and his purpose. He does not look for signs, pointers along the way to his goal; he stops—and listens to the things themselves. And so he wins.

This being the quality of his choice, I am both intrigued by and suspicious of the ingenious theory that Portia surreptitiously gives Bassanio a clue through the "-ed" endings (rhyming with "lead") in the song: "Tell me where is fancy bred." If we think of the rhyme as having this effect on Bassanio, the theory is consistent with the tenor of his response to the caskets; the phonetic substance of the words would be what he unconsciously responds to. But if we think of the rhyme as a clue in the ordinary sense, intentionally placed and consciously interpreted, it would be out of tune with the quality of his chance, which lies in the rejection of even such clues as are legitimately provided. As often in Shakespeare, music liberates from the slavery of intention; it suspends, in a momentary harmony, the endless chase of means and meanings. Portia is eminently useful, and she is sought after, at least in part, because she can be of use; but that is not how she is won. At the moment of choice purpose is in abeyance, and the things themselves are given voice.

Yet this release into pure fancy is in its nature momentary; in human existence—and so in drama—purpose and use cannot long be set aside. "Fancy" is bred neither in the head nor in the heart, neither by will nor by thought; it is the child of pure vision. But being that, it lives only in the moment; its cradle is its grave. When the predestined pair is happily united and everything seems to have dissolved into pure concord, we are promptly reminded that there is an accounting still due back in prosaic Venice. Belmont is bound to Venice as surely as Antonio is to Shylock. If the bond were not acknowledged, the bliss of the lovers would remain private, encapsuled in the barren half-fulfilment of fancy and sheer, useless poetry, while in the public world of prose and use time and the law would run their deadly course. The parthenogenesis of fancy has no lasting issue; the union of Portia and Bassanio must remain unconsummated until after the retranslation to Venice:

> First go with me to church and call me wife,
> And then away to Venice to your friend;
> For never shall you lie by Portia's side
> With an unquiet soul.

## IV

At this point I had better deal with a question which may have troubled the reader for some time. I suggested that for Shakespeare the play he had been commissioned to do, or rather to rework (with a three-month deadline?) from a story already fixed, became the metaphor of the bondage he found himself in, and that the way to freedom he discovered was Portia's way of a radical and literal acceptance. Obviously this theory, if it is to be more than idle speculation, implies that Shakespeare did follow his source religiously; the question is: is this in fact true?

It would mean, for one thing, that Shakespeare did not, as used to be thought, graft the casket story from the *Gesta* onto the Fiorentino tale, but that this graft had already been made by the author of his immediate source. The evidence for such a source seems to me as conclusive as we can expect under the circumstances. In *The School of Abuse* Gosson mentions a play, no longer extant, which bore the title *The Jew* and showed "the greediness of worldly choosers and the bloody minds of usurers." The description fits the two main actions of Shakespeare's play so closely that we can hardly avoid regarding *The Jew* as his source; and so it has been regarded by most recent editors.

But the fact is that, as far as we can tell, Shakespeare did depart from his source in at least two important instances. The first of these is the inscription on the leaden casket. Gosson's phrase—"the greediness of *worldly* choosers"—shows that *The Jew* must still have had the *Gesta* inscription: "Whoso chooseth me shall find that God hath disposed to him." Shakespeare, while taking over the other two inscriptions as he found them, changed the leaden one to read: "Whoso chooseth me must give and hazard all he hath." If the very point of the play for him was that he felt bound to it and by it as it was, how did he come to take a liberty here?

His second assertion of independence is more substantial, although, as I shall try to show, less substantive; it is the Jessica-Lorenzo plot. It contains some echoes of Marlowe's *Jew of Malta,* but as a whole it appears to have been freely added by Shakespeare; no analogue to it has been found in any of his possible sources. Again: if he felt bound, whence this sudden flight of invention?

Before I take up these questions singly, I must note that they have one element in common: there seems to be no necessity for the departures. Bassanio, in choosing the leaden casket, gets no guidance from the inscription; insofar as his reference to threats and promises is an implicit allusion to the inscription, it is of a kind rather to frighten him off than to attract him. With the Jessica plot the puzzle is even greater; for not only does it not serve any useful purpose, it seems a perversely extraneous element in a story which was, to put it mildly, complicated enough without it. Yet I am persuaded that my general interpretation is confirmed—I would almost say verified—by these two elements.

To begin with the simpler one. In the Jessica plot Shakespeare breaks free of the bondage to his source and elopes into the untrammeled freedom of invention. Pure, spontaneous feeling governs the conduct of these lovers; they brush aside, without much compunction, the impediments to their union and celebrate careless honeymoons in Genoa, Belmont or wherever their fancy and Shylock's ducats take them. The one theme that accompanies them quite faithfully, however, is the difference of their religions; we are never allowed to forget that Jessica was a Jewess and Lorenzo is a Christian.

One of the important stipulations in the judgment on Shylock is that he become a Christian; and the compulsion leaves a bitter taste in our mouths. Again, *pace* the historians, who assure us that Shakespeare's audience understood the shot-gun, or rather halter, conversion as an undeserved mercy, since it was Shylock's sole chance of salvation. I don't know whether so totally mechanical a view of an adult's conversion and baptism was then seriously held. However that may be, Shakespeare takes particular pains to impress on us the violence and merciless secularity of this act of "grace." Gratiano has the last word on it and places it in the proper metaphorical context:

> In christening shalt thou have two godfathers:
> Had I been judge, thou shouldst have had ten more,
> To bring thee to the gallows, not the font.

We might think that the union of Jessica and Lorenzo would have offered a more harmonious means of conversion; the subplot, if it is designed for anything, seems designed to that very end. There could—I am tempted to say "should"—have been a final scene following the judgment, a scene with the satisfying, conciliatory finality and completeness we expect in comedies. As thus: Jessica and Lorenzo enter (perhaps from Genoa, bearing good tidings about Antonio's argosies); Shylock, already crushed, is urged by all to forgive his daughter and accept Lorenzo as his son-in-law; he still resists, claiming his religion; but finally Jessica's prayers prevail: he embraces Christianity and his new-found children. Antonio magnanimously renounces his claim to half of Shylock's property in favor of the lovers; Portia and Nerissa reveal themselves and are claimed by Bassanio and Gratiano; Antonio is asked to be honored guest at the triple wedding and godfather to Shylock. Curtain. I'll be so bold as to say that some such conclusion would have been a "natural": all the main characters on stage and in harmony, no need to return to Belmont and the business of the rings, no unresolved residue. As it is, Shylock exits unreconciled, while Jessica and Lorenzo moon in Belmont to no intelligible purpose, as they were brought there for no intelligible reason. I find it hard to imagine that Shakespeare, when he thought up the Jessica action, was not thinking of a conclusion somewhat along these lines, and that he was not fully aware of the complications and difficulties he needlessly created for himself by rejecting it. Why, then, did he?

The answer I am bound to by my interpretation—that it was not "so nominated in the bond," the source—only make matters worse. Neither was the Jessica story in his source; if he felt free to invent that, why couldn't he take another liberty and tie it into the main action, as he might so easily and satisfyingly have done? As it stands, the play would have more unity and coherence if the subplot were simply left out; if Shakespeare felt the need to add to it, why did he not at least add something that would help round matters out? Worse: why did he perversely refuse to make the addition serve the one end it seems so manifestly intended for?

Of course, a purpose for it *has* been discovered. As Quiller-Couch puts it: "But here Shakespeare comes in. His audience, conventionally minded, may accept the proffer of the bond as a jesting bargain made with bloodthirsty intent, to be bloodthirstily enacted; but a gentle Shakespeare cannot. There must be more incentive to hate, to lust for a literally bloody vengeance, than any past insult, however conventional, put upon him on the Rialto by Antonio, mildest of men, can dramatically supply." (Cambridge edition, 1926, p. xix). This, chastened into a prose somewhat more in keeping with the admirable precepts of the essay "On Jargon," would pretty well represent the critical consensus on the function of the Jessica plot. But it is not only implausible; it is demonstrably false. "Gentle Shakespeare"—the creator of Richard III and company—cannot create a vengeful Shylock? "Antonio, mildest of men"—who spits on Shylock, calls him a cur, and promises to do so again even as he is asking him for a loan—did not give Shylock ample cause for bloody hatred? But we need not even speculate about sufficiency or insufficiency of motive; the text is perfectly explicit and unambiguously refutes the theory that Shylock needed the elopement of his daughter to confirm him in the resolution to enforce the bond. In Belmont Jessica reports:

> When I was with him [i.e., *before her elopement*], I have heard him swear...
> That he would rather have Antonio's flesh
> Than twenty times the value of the sum
> That he did owe him.[2]

It is as though Shakespeare, suspecting that the subplot might be misinterpreted, had taken particular pains to prevent the misreading. But to no avail; the motive-mongers got the better of him. Here, as so often, the "psychological" explanation fails miserably—not because it is psychological, but because it is *ad hoc,* got up to explain away one difficulty and in doing so engendering a litter of others.

As almost always when Shakespeare puzzles us, the question to ask is not: why? but: what? If once we see the thing as it *is,* the question of its

---

[2] The most recent attempt to account for the Jessica action in this way (by John H. Smith, *JEGP* LX, [Jan. 1961], p. 19) has at least the virtue of dealing with these lines as a trouble spot. But the inevitable response is to explain them away; Jessica's statement, we are told, is neither true nor untrue; it is, rather, a Shakespearean stratagem to prepare us for Shylock's transformation into a blood-thirsty villain. Since Shakespeare, had he meant to prepare us for this, could have found any number of other ways of doing so, it remains unintelligible why he should have chosen the one way which was bound to confuse us about his real intentions.

purpose will commonly answer itself. As lovers, Jessica and Lorenzo stand in the sharpest imaginable contrast to Portia and Bassanio. Their love is lawless, financed by theft and engineered through a gross breach of trust. It is subjected to no test: "Here, catch this casket, it is worth the pains," Jessica says to Lorenzo to underscore the difference. The ring which ought to seal their love is traded for a monkey. They are spendthrift rather than liberal, thoughtless squanderers of stolen substance; they are aimless, drifting by chance from Venice to Genoa to Belmont. They are attended by a low-grade clown, who fathers illegitimate children (Launcelot), while Bassanio and Portia are served by a true jester, who marries in due form (Gratiano). Wherever we look, the Jessica-Lorenzo affair appears as an inversion of true, bonded love.

More: the spontaneous love-match remains fruitless and useless: it redeems no one but is itself in urgent need of redemption. There is one qualification to be made here; Jessica does have a function, which is repeatedly insisted on: she is to be the torch-bearer in the impromptu masque. But the light she casts is ambiguous and flickering as that of a torch; it illumines only her own shame:

> *Lor.* Descend, for you must be my torchbearer.
> *Jes.* What, must I hold a candle to my shames?
> They in themselves, good sooth, are too too light.
> Why, 'tis an office of discovery, love;
> And I should be obscur'd.

Also, the dramatic enterprise she is meant to serve in is

> vile. unless it may be quaintly order'd,
> And better, in my [Solanio's] mind, not undertook.

But in any case nothing comes of it:

> *Ant.* Fie, fie, Gratiano! where are all the rest?
> 'Tis nine o'clock; our friends all stay for you.
> No masque tonight; the wind is come about,
> Bassanio presently will go aboard.

The play of bonded and tested love, which was in danger of being delayed by these improvising masquers, is under way once more. A "strumpet wind" propels loves like Jessica's and Lorenzo's:

> How like a younker and a prodigal
> The scarfed bark puts from her native bay,
> Hugg'd and embraced by the strumpet wind!

How like a prodigal doth she return,
With over-weather'd ribs and ragged sails,
Lean, rent and beggar'd by the strumpet wind!

But now the wind has changed; blowing sternly and steadily, it drives the main action on its set and narrowly plotted course.

What, then, does this torch-lit subplot accomplish; why, it is now safe to ask, is it there at all? It is there to discover its own shame and uselessness and so, by contrast, to make clearer and firmer the outlines of bonded love. It is the abortive "masque," first planned by Shakespeare (I surmise) as an escape from the harsh letter of his bond, a means of rendering his intractable material more manageable. But when he discovered the much more hazardous and satisfying solution of unreserved submission, he turned the subplot to a new purpose, made it into something that should be "obscur'd" the *oscuro* in the chiaroscuro of the whole.

If this judgment of Jessica and Lorenzo seems too narrowly puritanical—and at odds, moreover, with their gorgeous lines about night and music at the opening of the last act—two things are to be remembered. *The Merchant* is a play of *use;* this word, among others, is rescued alike from Shylock's malice and Antonio's contempt. The people who ultimately count—Antonio, Bassanio, Portia and, in a negative way, Shylock—have all been useful, have freed and united not only each other but also the state. And they have done so—to repeat—by accepting the given, the letter of the law, as binding; something to be fulfilled, not evaded. The play's ethos, the standards by which we must judge, are defined by its causality: and the causality is wholly unambiguous. Here, as in the sphere of speech, it is action that counts, not sentiment, effect, not attitude; here too Shakespeare teaches us—and perhaps himself—the true meaning of "drama." Mere lyrical splendor is, in the world the play defines, a kind of sentimentality, a parasitical self-indulgence, possible only because, and insofar as, others bear the brunt of the law.

Which brings us to the concrete setting of the lyrical interlude. It opens with the oddly ambiguous hymn to night; what we are given is the genealogy of fly-by-night love: betrayal (Troilus and Cressida), disaster (Pyramus and Thisbe), desertion (Dido and Aeneas), sorcery (Medea) and theft (Jessica). Only with the arrival of good news from Venice does the tune change to the beautiful praise of music. And even then the music Lorenzo commands is not his but Portia's ("It is your music, madam, of the house"). She who pays the piper calls off the tune; to Lorenzo's borrowed authority ("Come, ho! and wake Diana with a hymn") there answers the real authority of the owner:

Peace, ho! the Moon sleeps with Endymion
And would not be awake'd. [*music ceases*]

Portia is known "as the blind man knows the cuckoo,/By the bad voice." Compared to the heavenly harmonies Lorenzo has summoned the voice *is* bad for it is the voice of daylight, of action. The scapegrace lovers have an unearned, nocturnal grace which transcends all that is earned and useful; if we are not moved by their concord of sweet sound, we are not to be trusted. But neither, clearly, were Jessica and Lorenzo to be trusted. Our surety lies in the sterner sound of redeemed prose which is won by the hazard of making the ethereal music of love answer to the letter of the law.

## V

If the Jessica story is thus a kind of inverse demonstration of the play's point, the changed inscription goes directly to the core of Shakespeare's meaning.

In writing *The Merchant* Shakespeare learned, by my interpretation, that his work as a commissioned playwright need not be servile, money-grubbing prostitution of his talent, that he need not make himself a motley to the view, gore his own thoughts and sell cheap what was most dear. There was dignity in his trade, truth and worth in the two hours' traffic of the stage. Antonio's sadness at the outset is, by his own description, that of a man who has to play a "part" arbitrarily assigned him; his restitution to happiness begins when he—though not fully aware of what he is doing—pledges his life to a binding contract and a literal "deadline." With this pledge things start to happen; "circulation" sets in. Trading with his talent is not in itself contemptible, an exploitation of something that should be employed only freely, for "gentle," liberal ends. It is, or can be, the beginning of action.

But this discovery entailed another—and a formidable risk. It meant that Shylock, the prophet of use and the bond, had to be built up—that his language had to be given the force and dignity which would sustain the claim Shakespeare was entering for profit-poetry. (Marlowe's Barabas was of no help to him; Barabas was a merchant-prince, with a language much more like Antonio's than like the lowly usurer's:

> What more may Heaven do for earthly men
> Than thus to pour out plenty in their laps,
> Ripping the bowels of the Earth for them,
> Making the Sea their servant, and the winds
> To drive their substance with successful blasts?

That is Antonio's grandiloquence, as Antonio's humbling is the humbling of Marlowe's "mighty line.") Characters who spoke in Shylock's idiom and cadence had been comic figures, meant to earn goodnatured smiles if they were good and to be despised if they were malicious. For the language they spoke was that in "common use," employed by common men for the mean and illiberal ends they are compelled to pursue. It was not gentle, noble—the idiom designed to give the poet's patrons and protectors a properly idealized image of themselves. The language of the stage—at least of characters deserving serious regard—was one of representation rather than action, or if action, then of "actions of state." Or it was a language of feelings—the "gentle" feelings allowed for within the conventions of courtly love. It moved in set pieces—lofty commentaries on an action that moved independently. If the action ended tragically, it was because the protagonists were star-crossed, or because the wheel of Fortune turned, or because they were guilty of *superbia* or some similar grand and splendid sins and crimes. If it ended happily, it did so because the proper feelings, dressed in the properly gentle language, had won out over loud-mouthed braggarts, mealy-mouthed parasites, foul-mouthed usurers and other ill-spoken folk. In either case the dramatic question was begged; the convention predetermined the issue and the judgment of the audience. Gentle was as gentle did; gentle talked as gentle did; ergo: gentle was as gentle talked—the syllogism of aristocratic sentimentality.

Had Shakespeare written three hundred years later, he might have had to fight free of a different kind of sentimentality—that of the naturalists. As it was—and because he was Shakespeare—he confronted the word "gentle" in all its tricky ambiguity: as meaning something purely external (well-born; Christian) as well as kind, generous, loving. He did not think that churlishness proved a man honest and uncorrupted; nor was he satisfied with making the tritely pious point that, alas! not every gentleman is a gentle man. His problem was a different one: to vindicate gentleness under conditions—social and (it is the same thing) linguistic conditions—which did not beg the question but put it.

Shylock puts the question. In his mouth the common language assumes a force which puts all genteel speech to shame and reduces gentle speech to impotence. It mocks, and makes a mockery of, all sentimental claims to a "higher truth," clothed in elevated and elevating rhetoric, which cannot produce its credentials in the only court there is: the state's. Shylock's language is positivism triumphant, scornful of gentle pretensions, forcing the gentles to confess that, when all the ornament is stripped away, they too have been relying on the positive laws of the social order. If Shylock were silenced by force or fiat—even by divine intervention—his triumph would only be more complete; for he would then have compelled the gentiles, or their god, openly to profess his own faith: positivism. An overruled Shylock would be what (I think it safe to guess) his predecessor of *The Jew* could never have been: a tragic hero.

The question the Jew puts is not confined to the class meaning of "gentle"; it probes with equal rigor the religious meaning. We have good reason to suppose that the language of Shakespeare's source begged the question of gentility; we *know* that it begged the question of Christianity. That is the point of the changed inscription. Simply by making the clearly labelled Christian choice, by proving himself a devout rather than a worldly chooser, the gentile of the earlier play gained the truth by which the Jew was vanquished. The test did not involve a risk but asked for a correct response; so that *The Jew* as a whole was not a drama, an action (with the absolute risk all true action involves), but a teaching machine, which in the end rewarded and reinforced the right answer with redemption, bliss and victory over the evil one. The Christian proved his superiority over the Jew merely by showing that he *was* a Christian and had learned his catechism—a religious tautology exactly analogous to the social one. To sum up: Shakespeare sees that the word "gentle" evades the social and religious issue by institutionalizing it. Through the power he gives to Shylock's dramatically ungentle speech and through the elimination of the religious solution, he submits to the hazard of a genuine test—not a schoolmaster's but a chemist's. His play is, so to speak, the *aqua regia* into which the world "gentle" is dropped to see if it is more than fool's gold.

It may be objected here that changing the inscription was, after all, no real risk. The plot was laid out for the poet and was sure to lead to a happy ending; not even the device by which that ending was achieved—Portia's judgment—had to be invented. But beyond the risk involved in changing the moral and dramatic balance between the usurious Jew and the noble Christian, Shakespeare had to confront, in simple fidelity to his source, the hazard that was its very meaning. He did not alter the story but restored it to itself by freeing it from a pious falsification. For its meaning was that it sprang from a series of ventures, of hazards; it was propelled by the risks Antonio, Bassanio, Portia and, up to a point, Shylock were willing to take. Its ethic was that of venture capitalism raised to the moral level; so that to make it pivot, at the decisive juncture, on an option to invest in God's own, gilt-edged securities was to deprive it of its truth. Shakespeare's change here, though of a kind opposite to that of the Jessica plot, is directed toward the same end: while through the "free lovers" he accented the outlines of the composition by adding shadows, in the test scene he removed a layer of pious overpainting. The picture as he leaves it is not changed but more itself than when he took it in hand; he is a restorer, not an adapter.

## VI

To return to the plot. Belmont, left to itself, would end in sterile self-absorption; Venice, left to itself, would end in silence. There is an odd logic working in Shylock's bond: with its seal and letter it gradually deadens even the Jew's powerful speech. Increasingly his lines become monotonous and monomaniacal; where we heard him, earlier, responding acutely and flexibly to Antonio's hard scantness, he now grows deaf:

> *Ant.* I pray thee, hear me speak.
> *Shy.* I'll have my bond; I will not hear thee speak.
> I'll have my bond; and therefore speak no more...
> I'll have no speaking; I will have my bond.

The theme is continued in the trial scene;

> I'll never answer that...
> I am not bound to please thee with my answers...
> Till thou canst rail the seal off my bond,
> Thou but offend'st thy lungs to speak so loud.

And finally:

> There is no power in the tongue of man
> To alter me. I stay here on my bond.

Thus "bond," in Shylock's mouth, comes to mean the opposite of speech and hearing; and since the state must sustain him, we come to the point where the community, to preserve itself, must prohibit communion. He who stands on the bond is no longer answerable and need no longer listen; the instrument of exchange threatens to render the body politic tongue-tied. A gap opens between the private and utterly ineffectual speech of men as men and the deadening, unalterable letter of the law. Portia's oft-quoted lines about the quality of mercy are remarkable not so much for their eloquence as for their impotence; they are of no use, fall on deaf ears, *do* nothing and so remain, in the literal sense, un-dramatic.

But at this point there is a reversal. Very much as Shylock learned, from Antonio's hardness, how to transform metal into flesh, so Portia now learns from Shylock himself the art of winning life from the deadly letter. So far she has given no hint that she has come with the solution ready: her last plea, interrupting as it does her already begun judgment, has the desperate urgency of a final, hopeless effort. When she asks Shylock to provide a surgeon to staunch the blood, does she know yet that it is on this point she will presently hang him? Or is it not rather Shylock himself who leads her to the saving inspiration?

> *Shy.* Is it so nominated in the bond?
> *Por.* It is not so express'd; but what of that?
> 'Twere good you do so much for charity.
> *Shy.* I cannot find it; 'tis not in the bond.

We cannot read Portia's mind and purposes, but this much is clear: here the crucial word is forced from her which then recurs in:

> This bond doth give thee here no jot of blood;
> The words *expressly* are "a pound of flesh."

The same process is at work as that which led to the framing of the bond; language, and with it Antonio and the state, have been revived and freed to act.

If we read Portia's judgment as a legal trick and Shylock's defeat as a foregone conclusion, the Jew's final humiliation must appear distressingly cruel. But there is good reason for reading the scene differently. Portia's ruling is one more hazard, and Skylock's moral collapse does not demolish the bond and all it stands for, but rather proves him unequal to the faith he has professed. Even after the judgment the issue is in doubt; it is still in Shyock's power to turn the play into a tragedy, to enforce the letter of the bond and to take the consequences. But at this point and before this choice he breaks, turns apostate to the faith he has so triumphantly forced upon his enemies. Having made the gentiles bow before the letter of the law, he is now asked to become, literally, a blood witness. But he reneges and surrenders the bond's power, and like a renegade he is flogged into gentleness.

That it is the apostate rather than the bond that is brought into contempt is made clear in the last act: the ring episode. We the spectators can view it as a mere frolic, because we know of Portia's double identity and so understand her threatening equivocations as being, in truth, binding pledges of fidelity. But Bassanio does not know and understand; to him the ring seems to continue the vicious circle of the bond. The cost of redeeming the public bond has been the forfeiture of the private one, the pledge of love; he now stands before Portia as Antonio stood before Shylock. His explanations, his appeals to circumstances and motives are in vain; she insists on the letter of the pledge and claims the forfeit. What redeems the bond of true love is not good intentions but the fact that Portia speaks with a double voice, functions both in Venice and in Belmont, is both man and woman ("the master-mistress of my passion," we may call her with Sonnet XX).

The ring is the bond transformed, the gentle bond. Since "bond" has dinned its leaden echo into our ears for the better part of four acts, "ring" is now made to ring out with almost comic but still ominous iteration:

> *Bass.* If you did know to whom I gave the ring,
> If you did know for whom I gave the ring,
> And would conceive for what I gave the ring,

And how unwillingly I left the ring,
When nought would be accepted but the ring,
You would abate the strength of your displeasure.
*Por.* If you had known the virtue of the ring,
Or half her worthiness that gave the ring,
Or your own honor to contain the ring,
You would not then have parted with the ring.

Like the bond, the ring is of a piece with flesh, so that we can hardly tell whether it has made flesh into metal or has itself become flesh:

A thing stuck on with oaths upon your finger,
And riveted with faith unto your flesh.

Flesh, therefore, may have to be cut for it:

Why, I were best to cut my left hand off.
And swear I lost the ring defending it.

And in the end Antonio must once again bind himself:

*Ant.* I once did lend my body for his wealth,
Which, but for him that had your husband's ring,
Had quite miscarried. I dare be bound again,
My soul upon the forfeit, that your lord
Will never more break faith advisedly.
*Por.* Then you shall be his surety.

Only with this renewal of the bond is the secret discovered, the true meaning of the equivocations revealed. Shylock has been defeated and dismissed, but the words which he almost succeeded in making synonymous with himself are not. They enter into the gentle contract of love, are requisite to the consummation; union, truth and faith are impossible without them.

So the action ends; or rather, the circle closes. The play comes round with Shakespeare's happy discovery that poetry is an equivocal language, public as well as private, common as well as gentle, useful as well as beautiful. The poet draws upon the social order's legal currency and so is bound and fully accountable. But by binding himself with Antonio instead of stealing with Lorenzo, he frees energies which will save the order from becoming deadlocked in a vicious circle of self-definition; by hazarding all he has on the chance of making personal unions possible, he frees himself from the twin futilities of uselessness and parasitical exploitation of the public currency. For himself and for Venice he gains Portia—the indefinable being who speaks most truly when she sounds most faithless, who frees us through an absolute literalness, who learns the grim prose of law in order to restore it to its true function. The gain will serve him for the time of the great romantic comedies; when, with *Julius Caesar* and *Hamlet,* he confronts the fact that the social order has neither the stability nor the good will he supposed, a new and much grimmer search will begin. The gentle bond will hold until Brutus speaks the tragic epilogue to *The Merchant of Venice:* "Portia is dead."

# 16

# The Alliance of Seriousness and Levity in *As You Like It*

*C. L. Barber*

*In a true piece of Wit all things must be*
*Yet all things there agree.*
—Cowley, quoted by T. S. Eliot in "Andrew Marvell"

*Then is there mirth in heaven*
*When earthly things made even*
*Atone together.*
—*As You Like It*

Shakepeare's next venture in comedy after *The Merchant of Venice* was probably in the Henry IV plays, which were probably written in 1597–98. Thus the Falstaff comedy comes right in the middle of the period, from about 1594 to 1600 or 1601, when Shakespeare produced festive comedy. *Much Ado About Nothing, As You Like It*, and *Twelfth*

*C.L. Barber,* Shakespeare's Festive Comedy *(Princeton, N.J.: © 1959 by Princeton University Press) pp. 222–239. Reprinted by permission of Princeton University Press.*

*Night* were written at the close of the period, *Twelfth Night* perhaps after *Hamlet. The Merry Wives of Windsor,* where Shakespeare's creative powers were less fully engaged, was produced sometime between 1598 and 1602, and it is not impossible the *All's Well That Ends Well* and even perhaps *Measure for Measure* were produced around the turn of the century, despite that difference in tone that has led to their being grouped with *Hamlet* and *Troilus and Cressida.*[1] I shall deal only with *As You Like It* and *Twelfth Night*; they are the two last festive plays, masterpieces that include and extend almost all the resources of the form whose development we have been following. What I would have to say about *Much Ado About Nothing* can largely be inferred from the discussion of the other festive plays. To consider the various other sorts of comedy which Shakespeare produced around the inception of the period when his main concern became tragedy would require another, different frame of reference.

*As You Like It* is very similar in the way it moves to *A Midsummer Night's Dream* and *Love's Labour's Lost,* despite the fact that its plot is taken over almost entirely from Lodge's *Rosalynde.* As I have suggested in the introductory chapter, the reality we feel about the experience of love in the play, reality which is not in the pleasant little prose romance, comes from presenting what was sentimental extremity as impulsive extravagance and so leaving judgment free to mock what the heart embraces. The Forest of Arden, like the Wood outside Athens, is a region defined by an attitude of liberty from ordinary limitations, a festive place where the folly of romance can have its day. The first half of *As You Like It,* beginning with tyrant brother and tyrant Duke and moving out into the forest, is chiefly concerned with establishing this sense of freedom; the traditional contrast of court and country is developed in a way that is shaped by the contrast between everyday and holiday, as that antithesis has become part of Shakespeare's art and sensibility. Once we are securely in the golden world where the good Duke and "a many merry men. . . fleet the time carelessly," the pastoral motif as such drops into the background; Rosalind finds Orlando's verses in the second scene of Act III, and the rest of the play deals with love. This second movement is like a musical theme with imitative variations, developing much more tightly the sort of construction which played off Costard's and Armado's amorous affairs against those of the nobles in Navarre, and which set Bottom's imagination in juxtaposition with other shaping fantasies. The love affairs of Silvius and Phebe, Touchstone and Audrey, Orlando and Rosalind succeed one another in the easy-going sequence of scenes, while the dramatist deftly plays each off against the others.

---

[1] For the chronology, see E. K. Chambers, *William Shakespeare* (Oxford, 1930) 1, 248–249 and 270–271.

## The Liberty of Arden

The thing that asks for explanation about the Forest of Arden is how this version of pastoral can feel so free when the Duke and his company are so high-minded. Partly the feeling of freedom comes from release from the tension established in the first act at the jealous court:

> Now go we in content
> To liberty, and not to banishment. (I, iii, 139–140)

Several brief court scenes serve to keep this contrast alive. So does Orlando's entrance, sword in hand, to interrupt the Duke's gracious banquet by his threatening demand for food. Such behavior on his part is quite out of character (in Lodge he is most courteous); but his brandishing entrance gives Shakespeare occasion to resolve the attitude of struggle once again, this time by a lyric invocation of "what 'tis to pity and be pitied" (II, vii, 117).

But the liberty we enjoy in Arden, though it includes relief from anxiety in brotherliness confirmed "at good men's feasts," is somehow easier than brotherliness usually is. The easiness comes from a witty redefinition of the human situation which makes conflict seem for the moment superfluous. Early in the play, when Celia and Rosalind are talking of ways of being merry by devising sports, Celia's proposal is "Let us sit and mock the good housewife Fortune from her wheel" (I, ii, 34–35). The two go on with a "chase" of wit that goes "from Fortune's office to Nature's" (I, ii, 43), whirling the two goddesses through many variations; distinctions between them were running in Shakespeare's mind. In Act II, the witty poetry which establishes the greenwood mood of freedom repeatedly mocks Fortune from her wheel by an act of mind which goes from Fortune to Nature:

> A fool, a fool! I met a fool i' th' forest, . . .
> Who laid him down and bask'd him in the sun
> And rail'd on Lady Fortune in good terms, . . .
> "Good morrow, fool," quoth I. "No, sir," quoth he,
> "Call me not fool till heaven hath sent me fortune."
> And then he drew a dial from his poke,
> And looking on it with lack-lustre eye,
> Says very wisely, 'It is ten o'clock.
> Thus we may see,' quoth he, 'how the world wags.
> 'Tis but an hour ago since it was nine,
> And after one more hour 'twill be eleven;
> And so, from hour to hour, we ripe and ripe,
> And then, from hour to hour, we rot and rot;
> And thereby hangs a tale.' (II, vii, 12–28)

Why does Jaques, in his stylish way, say that his lungs "began to crow like chanticleer" to hear the fool "thus moral on the time," when the moral concludes in "rot and rot"? Why do we, who are not "melancholy," feel such large and free delight? Because the fool "finds," with wonderfully bland wit, that nothing whatever happens under aegis of Fortune. ("Fortune reigns in gifts of the world" said Rosalind at I, ii, 44.) The almost tautological inevitability of nine, ten, eleven, says that all we do is ripe and ripe and rot and rot. And so there is no reason not to bask in the sun and "lose and neglect the creeping hours of time" (II, vii, 112). As I observed in the introductory chapter, Touchstone's "deep contemplative" moral makes the same statement as the spring song towards the close of the play: "How that a life was but a flower." When they draw the moral, the lover and his lass are only thinking of the "spring time" as they take "the present time" when "love is crowned with the prime." (The refrain mocks them a little for their obliviousness, by its tinkling "the only pretty ring time.") But Touchstone's festive gesture is *not* oblivious.

The extraordinary thing about the poised liberty of the second act is that the reduction of life to the natural and seasonal and physical works all the more convincingly as a festive release by including a recognition that the physical can be unpleasant. The good Duke, in his opening speech, can "translate the stubbornness of fortune" into a benefit: he does it by the witty shift which makes the "icy fang/And churlish chiding of the winter wind" into "counsellors/That feelingly persuade me what I am" (II, i, 6–11). The two songs make the same gesture of welcoming physical pain in place of moral pain:

> Come hither, come hither, come hither!
> Here shall he see
> No enemy
> But winter and rough weather. (II, v, 5–8)

They are patterned on holiday drinking songs, as we have seen already in considering the Christmas refrain, "Heigh-ho, sing heigh-ho, unto the green holly,"[2] and they convey the free solidarity of a group who, since they relax in physical pleasures together, need not fear the fact that "Most friendship is feigning, most loving mere folly."

Jaques' speech on the seven ages of man, which comes at the end of Act II, just before "Blow, Blow, thou winter wind," is another version of the liberating talk about time; it expands Touchstone's "And thereby hangs a tale." The simplification, "All the world's a stage," has such imaginative reach that we are as much astonished as amused, as with Touchstone's sum-

[2] See above pp. 113–116.

mary ripe and rot. But simplification it is, nevertheless; quotations (and recitations) often represent it as though it were dramatist Shakespeare's "philosophy," his last word, or one of them, about what life really comes to. To take it this way is sentimental, puts a part in place of the whole. For it only is *one* aspect of the truth that the roles we play in life are settled by the cycle of growth and decline. To face this part of the truth, to insist on it, brings the kind of relief that goes with accepting folly—indeed this speech is praise of folly, superbly generalized, praise of the folly of living in time (or is it festive abuse? the poise is such that relish and mockery are indistinguishable). Sentimental readings ignore the wit that keeps reducing social roles to caricatures and suggesting that meanings really are only physical relations beyond the control of mind or spirit:

> Then a soldier, . . .
> Seeking the bubble reputation
> Even in the cannon's mouth. And then the justice,
> In fair round belly with good capon lin'd. . .
> (III, vii, 149–154)

Looking back at time and society in this way, we have a detachment and sense of mastery similar to that established by Titania and Oberon's outside view of "the human mortals" and their weather.

## Counterstatements

That Touchstone and Jaques should at moments turn and mock pastoral contentment is consistent with the way it is presented; their mockery makes explicit the partiality, the displacement of normal emphasis, which is implicit in the witty advocacy of it.

> If it do come to pass
> That any man turn ass,
> Leaving his wealth and ease
> A stubborn will to please. . . (II, v, 52–55)

The folly of going to Arden has something about it of Christian humility, brotherliness and unworldliness ("Consider the lilies of the field. . ."), but one can also turn it upside down by "a Greek invocation to call fools into a circle" and find it stubbornness. Touchstone brings out another kind of latent irony about pastoral joys when he plays the role of a discontented exile from the court:

*Corin.* And how like you this shepherd's life, Master Touchstone?

*Touchstone.* Truly, shepherd, in respect of itself, it is a good life; but in respect that it is a shepherd's life, it is naught. In respect that it is solitary,

> I like it very well; but in respect that it is private, it is a very vile life. Now in respect it is in the fields, it pleaseth me well; but in respect it is not in the court, it is tedious. As it is a spare life, look you, it fits my humour well; but as there is no more plenty in it, is goes much against my stomach. (III, ii, 12–22)

Under the apparent nonsense of his self-contradictions, Touchstone mocks the contradictory nature of the desires ideally resolved by pastoral life, to be at once at court and in the fields, to enjoy both the fat advantages of rank and the spare advantages of the mean and sure estate. The humor goes to the heart of the pastoral convention and shows how very clearly Shakespeare understood it.

The fact that he created both Jaques and Touchstone out of whole cloth, adding them to the story as it appears in Lodge's *Rosalynde,* is an index to what he did in dramatizing the prose romance. Lodge, though he has a light touch, treats the idyllic material at face value. He never makes fun of its assumptions, but stays safely within the convention, because he has no securely grounded attitude toward it, not being sure of its relation to reality. Shakespeare scarcely changes the story at all, but where in Lodge it is presented in the flat, he brings alive the dimension of its relation to life as a whole. The control of this dimension makes his version solid as well as delicate.

Although both Jaques and Touchstone are connected with the action well enough at the level of plot, their real position is generally mediate between the audience and something in the play, the same position Nashe assigns to the court fool, Will Summers, in *Summer's Last Will and Testament.*[3] Once Jaques stands almost outside the play, when he responds to Orlando's romantic greeting: "Good day and happiness, dear Rosalind!" with "Nay then, God b'wi'you, and you talk in blank verse!" (IV, i, 31). Jaques' factitious melancholy, which critics have made too much of as a "psychology," serves primarily to set him at odds both with society and with Arden and so motivate contemplative mockery. Touchstone is put outside by his special status as a fool. As a fool, incapable, at least for professional purposes, of doing anything right, he is beyond the pale of normal achievements. In anything he tries to do he is comically disabled, as for example, in falling in love. All he achieves is a burlesque of love. So he has none of the illusions of those who try to be ideal, and is in a position to make a business of being dryly objective. "Call me not fool till heaven hath sent me fortune." Heaven sends him Audrey instead, "an ill-favour'd thing, sir, but mine own" (V, iv, 60)—not a mistress to generate illusions. In *As You Like It* the court fool for the first time takes over the work of comic commentary and burlesque from the clown of the earlier plays; in

---

[3] See above, Ch. 4, pp. 61–67.

Jaques' praise of Touchstone and the corrective virtues of fooling, Shakespeare can be heard crowing with delight at his discovery. The figure of the jester, with his recognized social role and rich traditional meaning, enabled the dramatist to embody in a character and his relations with other characters the comedy's purpose of maintaining objectivity.

The satirist presents life as it is and ridicules it because it is not ideal, as we would like it to be and as it should be. Shakespeare goes the other way about: he represents or evokes ideal life, and then makes fun of it because it does not square with life as it ordinarily is. If we look for social satire in *As You Like It,* all we find are a few set pieces about such stock figures as the traveller and the duelist. And these figures seem to be described rather to enjoy their extravagance than to rebuke their folly. Jaques, in response to a topical interest at the time when the play appeared, talks a good deal about satire, and proposes to "cleanse the foul body of th' infected world" (II, vii, 60) with the fool's medicine of ridicule. But neither Jaques, the amateur fool, nor Touchstone, the professional, ever really gets around to doing the satirist's work of ridiculing life as it is, "deeds, and language, such as men do use."[4] After all, they are in Arden, not in Jonson's London: the infected body of the world is far away, out of range. What they make fun of instead is what they can find in Arden—pastoral innocence and romantic love, life as it might be, lived "in a holiday humour." Similar comic presentation of what is not ideal in man is characteristic of medieval fool humor, where the humorist, by his gift of long ears to the long-robed dignitaries, makes the point that, despite their pageant perfection, they are human too, that *stultorum numerus infinitus est.* Such humor is very different from modern satire, for its basic affirmation is not man's possible perfection but his certain imperfection. It was a function of the pervasively formal and ideal cast of medieval culture, where what should be was more present to the mind than what is: the humorists' natural recourse was to burlesque the pageant of perfection, presenting it as a procession of fools, in crowns, mitres, caps, and gowns. Shakespeare's point of view was not medieval. But his clown and fool comedy is a response, a counter-movement, to artistic idealization, as medieval burlesque was a response to the ingrained idealism of the culture.

## "All Nature in Love Mortal in Folly"

I have quoted already in the Introduction a riddling comment of Touchstone which moves from acknowledging mortality to accepting the folly of love:

---

[4] Ben Jonson, *Every Man in his Humour, Prologue,* l. 21.

> We that are true lovers run into strange capers; but as all is mortal in nature, so is all nature in love mortal in folly. (II, iv, 53–56)

The lovers who in the second half of the play present "nature in love" each exhibit a kind of folly. In each there is a different version of the incongruity between reality and the illusions (in poetry, the hyperboles) which love generates and by which it is expressed. The comic variations are centered around the seriously-felt love of Rosalind and Orlando. The final effect is to enhance the reality of this love by making it independent of illusions, whose incongruity with life is recognized and laughed off. We can see this at closer range by examining each affair in turn.

All-suffering Silvius and his tyrannical little Phebe are a bit of Lodge's version taken over, outwardly intact, and set in a wholly new perspective. A "courting eglogue" between them, in the mode of Lodge, is exhibited almost as a formal spectacle, with Corin for presenter and Rosalind and Celia for audience. It is announced as

> a pageant truly play'd
> Between the pale complexion of true love
> And the red glow of scorn and proud disdain. (III, iv, 55–57)

What we then watch is played "truly"—according to the best current convention: Silvius, employing a familiar gambit, asks for pity; Phebe refuses to believe in love's invisible wound, with exactly the literal-mindedness about hyperbole which the sonneteers imputed to their mistresses. In Lodge's version, the unqualified Petrarchan sentiments of the pair are presented as valid and admirable. Shakespeare lets us feel the charm of the form; but then he has Rosalind break up their pretty pageant. She reminds them that they are nature's creatures and that love's purposes are contradicted by too absolute a cultivation of romantic liking or loathing: "I must tell you friendly in your ear,/Sell when you can! you are not for all markets" (III, v, 59–60). Her exaggerated downrightness humorously underscores the exaggerations of conventional sentiment. And Shakespeare's treatment breaks down Phebe's stereotyped attitudes to a human reality: he lightly suggests an adolescent perversity underlying her resistance to love. The imagery she uses in disputing with Silvius is masterfully squeamish, at once preoccupied with touch and shrinking from it:

> 'Tis pretty, sure, and very probable
> That eyes, which are the frail'st and softest things,
> Who shut their coward gates on atomies,
> Should be call'd tyrants, butchers, murtherers!
> ...lean but upon a rush,
> The cicatrice and capable impressure
> Thy palm some moment keeps; but now mine eyes,
> Which I have darted at thee, hurt thee not,... (III, v, 11–25)

Rosalind, before whom this resistance melts, appears in her boy's disguise "like a ripe sister," and the qualities Phebe picks out to praise are feminine. She has, in effect, a girlish crush on the femininity which shows through Rosalind's disguise; the aberrant affection is happily got over when Rosalind reveals her identity and makes it manifest that Phebe has been loving a woman. "Nature to her bias drew in that" is the comment in *Twelfth Night* when Olivia is fortunately extricated from a similar mistaken affection.

Touchstone's affair with Audrey complements the spectacle of exaggerated sentiment by showing love reduced to its lowest common denominator, without any sentiment at all. The fool is detached, objective and resigned when the true-blue lover should be

> All made of passion, and all made of wishes,
> All adoration, duty, and observance. (V, ii, 101–102)

He explains to Jacques his reluctant reasons for getting married:

> *Jaques.* Will you be married, motley?
> *Touchstone.* As the ox hath his bow, sir, the horse his curb, and the falcon her bells, so man hath his desires; and as pigeons bill, so wedlock would be nibbling. (III, iii, 79–83)

This reverses the relation between desire and its object, as experienced by the other lovers. They are first overwhelmed by the beauty of their mistresses, then impelled by that beauty to desire them. With Touchstone, matters go the other way about: he discovers that man has his troublesome desires, as the horse his curb; then he decides to cope with the situation by marrying Audrey:

> Come, sweet Audrey.
> We must be married, or we must live in bawdry.
> (III, iii, 98–99)

Like all the motives which Touchstone acknowledges, this priority of desire to attraction is degrading and humiliating. One of the hall-marks of chivalric and Petrarchan idealism is, of course, the high valuation of the lover's mistress, the assumption that his desire springs entirely from her beauty. This attitude of the poets has contributed to that progressively-increasing respect for women so fruitful in modern culture. But to assume that only one girl will do is, after all, an extreme, an ideal attitude: the other half of the truth, which lies in wait to mock sublimity, is instinct—the need of a woman, even if she be an Audrey, because "as pigeons bill, so wedlock would be nibbling." As Touchstone put it on another occasion:

> If the cat will after kind,
> So be sure will Rosalinde. (III, ii, 109–110)

The result of including in Touchstone a representative of what in love is unromantic is not, however, to undercut the play's romance: on the contrary, the fool's cynicism, or one-sided realism, forestalls the cynicism with which the audience might greet a play where his sort of realism had been ignored. We have a sympathy for his downright point of view, not only in connection with love but also in his acknowledgment of the vain and self-gratifying desires excluded by pastoral humility; he embodies the part of ourselves which resists the play's reigning idealism. But he does not do so in fashion to set himself up in opposition to the play. Romantic commentators construed him as "Hamlet in motely," a devastating critic. They forgot, characteristically, that he is ridiculous: he makes his attitudes preposterous when he values rank and comfort above humility, or follows biology rather than beauty. In laughing at him, we reject the tendency in ourselves which he for the moment represents. The net effect of the fool's part is thus to consolidate the hold of the serious themes by exorcising opposition. The final Shakespearean touch is to make the fool aware that in humiliating himself he is performing a public service. He goes through his part with an irony founded on the fact (and it is a fact) that he is only making manifest the folly which others, including the audience, hide from themselves.

Romantic participation in love and humorous detachment from its follies, the two polar attitudes which are balanced against each other in the action as a whole, meet and are reconciled in Rosalind's personality. Because she remains always aware of love's illusions while she herself is swept along by its deepest currents, she possesses as an attribute of character the power of combining wholehearted feeling and undistorted judgment which gives the play its value. She plays the mocking reveller's role which Berowne played in *Love's Labour's Lost,* with the advantage of disguise. Shakespeare exploits her disguise to permit her to furnish the humorous commentary on her own ardent love affair, thus keeping comic and serious actions going at the same time. In her pretended role of saucy shephered youth, she can mock at romance and burlesque its gestures while playing the game of putting Orlando through his paces as suitor, to "cure" him of love. But for the audience, her disguise is transparent, and through it they see the very ardor which she mocks. When, for example, she stages a gayly overdone take-off of the conventional impatience of the lover, her own real impatience comes through the burlesque; yet the fact that she makes fun of exaggerations of the feeling conveys an awareness that it has limits, that there is a difference between romantic hyperbole and human nature:

*Orlando.* For these two hours, Rosalind, I will leave thee.
*Rosalind.* Alas, dear love, I cannot lack thee two hours!
*Orlando.* I must attend the Duke at dinner. By two o'clock I will be with thee again.

> *Rosalind.* Ay, go your ways, go your ways! I knew what you would prove. My friends told me as much, and I thought no less. That flattering tongue of yours won me. 'Tis but one cast away, and so, come death! Two o'clock is your hour? (IV, i, 181–190)

One effect of this indirect, humorous method of conveying feeling is that Rosalind is not committed to the conventional language and attitudes of love, loaded as these inevitably are with sentimentality. Silvius and Phebe are her foils in this: they take their conventional language and their conventional feelings prefectly seriously, with nothing in reserve. As a result they seem naïve and rather trivial. They are no more than what they say, until Rosalind comes forward to realize their personalities for the audience by suggesting what they humanly are beneath what they romantically think themselves. By contrast, the heroine in expressing her own love conveys by her humorous tone a valuation of her sentiments, and so realizes her own personality for herself, without being indebted to another for the favor. She uses the convention where Phebe, being unaware of its exaggerations, abuses it, and Silvius, equally naïve about hyperbole, lets it abuse him. This control of tone is one of the great contributions of Shakespeare's comedy to his dramatic art as a whole. The discipline of comedy in controlling the humorous potentialities of a remark enables the dramatist to express the relation of a speaker to his lines, including the relation of naïveté. The focus of attention is not on the outward action of saying something but on the shifting, uncrystallized life which motivates what is said.

The particular feeling of headlong delight in Rosalind's encounters with Orlando goes with the prose of these scenes, a medium which can put imaginative effects of a very high order to the service of humor and wit. The comic prose of this period is first developed to its full range in Falstaff's part, and steals the show for Benedict and Beatrice in *Much Ado About Nothing*. It combines the extravagant linguistic reach of the early clowns' prose with the sophisticated wit which in the earlier plays was usually cast, less flexibly, in verse. Highly patterned, it is built up of balanced and serial clauses, with everything linked together by alliteration and kicked along by puns. Yet it avoids a stilted, Euphuistic effect because regular patterns are set going only to be broken to underscore humor by asymmetry. The speaker can rock back and forth on antitheses, or climb "a pair of stairs" (V, ii, 42) to a climax, then slow down meaningly, or stop dead, and so punctuate a pithy reduction, bizarre exaggeration or broad allusion. T. S. Eliot has observed that we often forget that it was Shakespeare who wrote the greatest prose in the language. Some of it is in *As You Like It*. His control permits him to convey the constant shifting of attitude and point of view which expresses Rosalind's excitement and her poise. Such writing, like the brushwork and line of great painters, is in one sense everything. But the whole design supports each stroke, as each stroke supports the whole design.

The expression of Rosalind's attitude towards being in love, in the great scene of disguised wooing, fulfills the whole movement of the play. The climax comes when Rosalind is able, in the midst of her golden moment, to look beyond it and mock its illusions, including the master illusion that love is an ultimate and final experience, a matter of life and death. Ideally, love should be final, and Orlando is romantically convinced that his is so, that he would die if Rosalind refused him. But Rosalind humorously corrects him, from behind her page's disguise:

> ...Am I not your Rosalind?
>
> *Orlando.* I take some joy to say you are, because I would be talking of her.
>
> *Rosalind.* Well, in her person, I say I will not have you.
>
> *Orland.* Then, in mine own person, I die.
>
> *Rosalind.* No, faith, die by attorney. The poor world is almost six thousand years old, and in all this time there was not any man died in his own person, videlicet, in a love cause. Troilus had his brains dash'd out with a Grecian club; yet he did what he could to die before, and he is one of the patterns of love. Leander, he would have liv'd many a fair year though Hero had turn'd nun, if it had not been for a hot midsummer night; for (good youth) he went but forth to wash him in the Hellespont, and being taken with the cramp, was drown'd; and the foolish chroniclers of that age found it was 'Hero of Sestos.' But these are all lies. Men have died from time to time, and worms have eaten them, but not for love.
>
> *Orlando.* I would not have my right Rosalind of this mind, for I protest her frown might kill me.
>
> *Rosalind.* By this hand, it will not kill a fly! (IV, i, 90–108)

A note almost of sadness comes through Rosalind's mockery towards the end. It is not sorrow that men die from time to time, but that they do not die for love, that love is not so final as romance would have it. For a moment we experience as pathos the tension between feeling and judgment which is behind all the laughter. The same pathos of objectivity is expressed by Chaucer in the sad smile of Pandarus as he contemplates the illusions of Troilus' love. But in *As You Like It* the mood is dominant only in the moment when the last resistance of feeling to judgment is being surmounted: the illusions thrown up by feeling are mastered by laughter and so love is reconciled with judgment. This resolution is complete by the close of the wooing scene. As Rosalind rides the crest of a wave of happy fulfillment (for Orlando's behavior to the pretended Rosalind has made it perfectly plain that he loves the real one) we find her describing with delight, almost in triumph, not the virtues of marriage, but its fallibility:

> Say 'a day' without the 'ever.' No, no, Orlando! Men are April when they woo, December when they wed. Maids are May when they are maids, but the sky changes when they are wives. (IV, i, 146–150)

Ordinarily, these would be strange sentiments to proclaim with joy at such a time. But as Rosalind says them, they clinch the achievement of the humor's purpose. (The wry, retarding change from the expected cadence at "but the sky changes" is one of those brush strokes that fulfill the large design.) Love has been made independent of illusions without becoming any the less intense; it is therefore inoculated against life's unromantic contradictions. To emphasize by humor the limitations of the experience has become a way of asserting its reality. The scenes which follow move rapidly and deftly to complete the consummation of the love affairs on the level of plot. The treatment becomes more and more frankly artificial, to end with a masque. But the lack of realism in presentation does not matter, because a much more important realism in our attitude towards the substance of romance has been achieved already by the action of the comedy.

In writing of Marvell and the metaphysical poets, T. S. Eliot spoke of an "alliance of levity and seriousness (by which the seriousness is "intensified)." What he has said about the contribution of wit to this poetry is strikingly applicable to the function of Shakespeare's comedy in *As You Like It:* that wit conveys "a recognition, implicit in the expression of every experience, of other kinds of experience which are possible."[5] The likeness does not consist simply in the fact that the wit of certain of Shakespeare's characters at times is like the wit of the metaphysicals. The crucial similarity is in the way the humor functions in the play as a whole to implement a wider awareness, maintaining proportion where less disciplined and coherent art falsifies by presenting a part as though it were the whole. The dramatic form is very different from the lyric: Shakespeare does not have or need the sustained, inclusive poise of metaphysical poetry when, at its rare best, it fulfills Cowley's ideal:

> In a true piece of Wit all things must be
> Yet all things there agree.

The dramatist tends to show us one thing at a time, and to realize that one thing, in its moment, to the full; his characters go to extremes, comical as well as serious; and no character, not even a Rosalind, is in a position to see all around the play and so be completely poised, for if this were so the play would cease to be dramatic. Shakespeare, moreover, has an Elizabethan delight in extremes for their own sake, beyond the requirements of his form and sometimes damaging to it, an expansiveness which was subordinated later by the seventeenth century's conscious need for coherence. But his extremes, where his art is at its best, are balanced in the whole work. He uses his broad-stroked, wide-swung comedy for the same end that the seventeenth-century poets achieved by their wire-drawn wit. In Silvius and Phebe he exhibits the ridiculous (and perverse) possibilities of that exaggerated romanticism which the metaphysicals so often mocked in their

[5] *Selected Essays, 1917–1932* (New York, 1932), pp. 255 and 262.

serious love poems. In Touchstone he includes a representative of just those aspects of love which are not romantic, hypostatizing as a character what in direct lyric expression would be an irony:

> Love's not so pure and abstract as they use
> To say who have no mistress but their muse.

By Rosalind's mockery a sense of love's limitations is kept alive at the very moments when we most feel its power:

> But at my back I always hear
> Time's winged chariot hurrying near.

The fundamental common characteristic is that the humor is not directed at "some outside sentimentality or stupidity," but is an agency for achieving proportion of judgment and feeling about a seriously felt experience.

*As You Like It* seems to me the most perfect expression Shakespeare or anyone else achieved of a poise which was possible because a traditional way of living connected different kinds of experience to each other. The play articulates fully the feeling for the rhythms of life which we have seen supporting Nashe's strong but imperfect art in his seasonal pageant. Talboys Dimoke and his friends had a similar sense of times and places when they let holiday lead them to making merry with the Earl of Lincoln; by contrast, the Puritan and/or time-serving partisans of Lincoln could not or would not recognize that holiday gave a license and also set a limit. An inclusive poise such as Shakespeare exhibits in Rosalind was not, doubtless, easy to achieve in any age; no culture was ever so "organic" that it would do men's living for them. What Yeats called Unity of Being became more and more difficult as the Renaissance progressed; indeed, the increasing difficulty of poise must have been a cause of the period's increasing power to express conflict and order it in art. We have seen this from our special standpoint in the fact that the everyday-holiday antithesis was most fully expressed in art when the keeping of holidays was declining.

The humorous recognition, in *As You Like It* and other products of this tradition, of the limits of nature's moment, reflects not only the growing consciousness necessary to enjoy holiday attitudes with poise, but also the fact that in English Christian culture saturnalia was never fully enfranchised. Saturnalian customs existed along with the courtly tradition of romantic love and an ambient disillusion about nature stemming from Christianity. In dramatizing love's intensity as the release of a festive moment, Shakespeare keeps that part of the romantic tradition which makes love an experience of the whole personality, even though he ridicules the wishful absolutes of doctrinaire romantic love. He does not found his comedy on the sort of saturnalian simplification which equates love with sensual gratification. He includes spokesmen for this sort of release in reduction; but they are never given an unqualified predominance, though they contribute to the atmosphere of liberty within which the aristocratic lovers find love. It is the latter who hold the balance near the center. And what gives the predominance to figures like Berowne, Benedict and Beatrice, or Rosalind, is that they enter nature's whirl consciously, with humor that recognizes it as only part of life and places their own extravagance by moving back and forth between holiday and everyday perspectives. Aristophanes provides a revealing contrast here. His comedies present experience entirely polarized by saturnalia; there is little *within* the play to qualify that perspective. Instead, an irony attaches to the whole performance which went with the accepted place of comedy in the Dionysia. Because no such clear-cut role for saturnalia or saturnalian comedy existed within Shakespeare's culture, the play itself had to place that pole of life in relation to life as a whole. Shakespeare had the art to make this necessity into an opportunity for a fuller expression, a more inclusive consciousness.

# 17

# *Much Ado About Nothing*[1]

*Barbara Everett*

*Much Ado About Nothing* is not, I think, among Shakespeare's most popular comedies. It lacks many of those perpetuating devices that we look for to give us a sense of timeless pleasure, of a "holiday" that is at once a sportive release and also, through lyricism, gives the faintest air of holiday blessedness and calm. It contains no sunlit or moonlit wood where every Jack finds his Jill. No heroine leaps happily into hose to find the sexless and timeless liberty of intellectual sport. There is no "play within a play" to strengthen the artifices that surround it with the solidity of comparative reality, and so to give their happy ending the stamp of truth. If "we did keep time, sir, in our snatches," it is not a snatch of perpetuity that is given in the songs of the play—no *Journeys end in lovers meeting,* nor *It was a lover and his lass,* nor *When daisies pied and violets blue*—but an omen of change: *Men were deceivers ever.* The play appears

*Reprinted from* Critical Quarterly, *III (1961), 319–335 by permission of the author and publisher.*

1 Read (with some minor alterations) to the Summer School on Shakespeare held in Stratford-on-Avon, September 1961, and printed here by permission of the Governors of the Royal Shakespeare Memorial Theatre.

to present, by contrast, a world rather for "working-days" than for "Sundays"; a world that is as formal, and potentially as harsh, as the comic world that probably preceded it, that of *The Merchant of Venice*. But the moneyed, legalistic, and formal world of Venice resolves at last into moonlit Belmont, from which one can see

> the floor of Heaven
> Thick inlaid with patines of bright gold.

The equally and beautifully formal Portia, in whom "The will of a living daughter is curbed by the will of a dead father" ceases to be a "Daniel come to judgment" and becomes a Diana in love, her homecoming heralded by Lorenzo and Jessica with lyrical myths and fables, and herself drawn into a dream from which she "would not be awaked."

*Much Ado About Nothing* is a play cut off from such pleasant natural resources. It is essentially "inland bred," and relies only on the natural forms of a great house where

> Ceremony's a name for the rich horn,
> And custom for the spreading laurel tree.

"Nature lovers" are offered only the flowers of rhetoric, the pleached arbour of wit, and the "dancing star" of human individuality. Not only the courteous, but the customary, matters in this play, not only the urbane, but the mundane: in fact, it is the unusual fusing of these into one world that is one of the individual characteristics of the play. The chief fact that makes this play unusual and individual (though there are other characteristics, which I shall discuss later, that develop straight out of earlier comedies) is the manner in which "time and place" do *not* "cease to matter," but matter very greatly.

It is not merely that the props of an urban or domestic existence—the window, the arras of a musty room, the church, the tomb, the wedding dress, the night-watchmen's staves, even the barber's shop—*are* important "props" in the world of this play. Nor is it merely that "time and place" have a crucial importance in the action:

> What man was he talked with you yesternight
> Out at your window betwixt twelve and one?
> Now if you are a maid, answer to this.

It is rather that the play concerns itself with what can only be called the most mundane or "local" fact in that world of love, in all its forms, that the comedies create: that is, that men and women have a notably different character, different mode of thinking, different system of loyalties, and, particularly, different social place and function. Not only this; but this is the first play, I think, in which the clash of these two worlds is treated with a degree of seriousness, and in which the woman's world dominates.

This is a rash generalisation and objections spring to mind. *All's Well That Ends Well* seems to indicate just such a victory. But not only does the style of parts of it, at least, suggest a date some time after *Much Ado About Nothing*; but also the character of Helen so dominates the play that no *meeting* of the two worlds can be said to be present: the play presents rather a deliberate reversal of a familiar situation, such as that presented by *Venus and Adonis,* or by another Helena's unhappy and outraged lines of midsummer madness:

> the story shall be chang'd;
> Apollo flies, and Daphne holds the chase;
> The dove pursues the griffin; the mild hind
> Makes speed to catch the tiger...

Similarly, the ladies in *Love's Labour's Lost* seem to hold the field at the end of the play when they turn the expected ending by proposing a trial of their perhaps rather complacent lovers. But this is a conclusion in which nothing is concluded—a Pyrrhic victory at best:

> Our wooing doth not end like an old play:
> Jack hath not Jill. These ladies' courtesy
> Might well have made our sport a comedy...

I am thinking rather of the way in which *Much Ado About Nothing* for the first time takes up and resolves matters which are either barely touched on or left unconcluded in earlier plays. The ladies' awareness in *Love's Labour's Lost*—that

> We are wise girls to mock our lovers so...
> You'll ne'er be friends with him; 'a killed your sister...
> He made her melancholy, sad and heavy,
> And so she died. Had she been light, like you,
> Of such a merry, nimble, stirring spirit,
> She might 'a been a grandam ere she died...

is present in all the earlier comedies, but the ladies, if the play is to end rightly, never are "light." One remembers the mourning Adriana, even in so light and cheerful a piece as the *Comedy of Errors:*

> Since that my beauty cannot please his eye
> I'll weep what's left away, and weeping die...

who stands by with Luciana while the men's doubleness is sorted out:

> Alas, poor women! Make us but believe,
> Being compact of credit, that you love us...
> We in your motion turn, and you may move us...

Or that "shallow story of deep love," the *Two Gentlemen of Verona,* in which the women's sympathetic solidarity—"I cannot choose But pity her"—is finally and necessarily subordinate to the men's chivalric friendship: "All that is mine in Silva I give thee." It is hardly necessary to mention the triumphant conclusion of *The Taming of the Shrew*; where the battered and hungry vixen Katherina steps forward at last as the most docile and dulcet of wives:

> Thy husband is thy lord, thy life, thy keeper,
> Thy head, thy sovereign; one that cares for thee...

Such suggestions are much more beautifully and subtly expanded in *A Midsummer Night's Dream.* They touch even the heroic lovers' plot, where Theseus kindly educates Hippolyta in dramatic criticism; but they are plainest in the two plots of the young lovers, and of Oberon and Titania. The doped and changeable Demetrius and Lysander at last manage, under Oberon's charge, to sort out their amorous inclinations; while Hermia and Helena stand by innocently throwing overboard a childhood loyalty which takes on an ornamental, emblematic, and Paradisaical peacefulness in contrast to their new world, which both at different times find "hellish":

> We, Hermia, like two artificial gods,
> Have with our needles created both one flower,
> Both on one sampler, sitting on one cushion,
> Both warbling of one song, both in one key...
> And will you rent our ancient love asunder,
> To join with men in scorning your poor friend?

The world of feminine loyalty that Titania clings to is even more interesting, in the rich and strange sensuousness with which it is presented. She keeps the Indian child out of loyalty to the physical world of "spiced Indian air, by night," "on Neptune's golden sands,"

> When we have laugh'd to see the sails conceive
> And grow big-bellied with the wanton wind...
> But she, being mortal, of that boy did die;
> And for her sake do I rear up her boy;
> And for her sake I will not part with him.

But she does, of course; Oberon's revenge is to give her loyalty to this mortal physical world full play. Dazed by her unseemly passion for an ass-headed Bottom, she at last hands over the child without a murmur, and is glad to get back her "fairy kingdom" of detached and aerial magic, in which she is always subordinate to an Oberon who has no such weaknesses, because no such loyalties.

Since *The Merchant of Venice* is the first play in which there appears a comic heroine who is also a great lady, one watches with interest to see what part the dominating Portia will play, how she will handle her subjection to the "will of a dead father," and whether she will prove to "fit her fancies to her fathers will" better than does Hermia. She and Bassanio equally "give and hazard all they have"; but it is, at least nominally, a man's world that they give themselves up to:

> her gentle spirit
> Commits itself to yours to be directed,
> As from her lord, her governor, her king.
> Myself and what is mine to you and yours
> Is now directed.

Portia is the salvation of the play; her wealth, her wits, and her pleading of a feminine quality of mercy—deeply Christian in its language and connotation, but allied too to that quality of compassion that is reserved for the women in the comedies—defeat the harshly logical and loveless intellectualism of Shylock. But they do so in masculine disguise, in a masculine court of law, and at the service of a chivalric friendship between men whose values Portia and Nerissa accept gaily, but seriously, at the end of the play. They lose, as women, the rings they have gained as men; the loyal and unhappily solitary friend Antonio is the peacemaker, being "bound again, His soul upon the forfeit" for the marriage, and is still in some sense master of the play.

It is here that the world of *Much Ado About Nothing* begins. There is no symbolic Antonio to keep the balance; the situation works itself out on its own resources. It does this by the characteristic of the play which has been sometimes regarded as a most happy accident of careless genius—the displacement of Claudio and Hero by Benedick and Beatrice as the play's dominating figures, in the course of what is "logical and necessary" in its action. This is brought about by allowing, more distinctively and fully than in any earlier comedy, a dance and battle—(a "merry war" in which not every "achiever brings home full numbers") of two worlds, which it is a gross, but serviceable, generalisation to call the "masculine" and the "feminine" worlds. And this in itself is achieved by the creation of a peculiarly social and domestic context—rarified, formal, and elegant, but still suggesting a social reality that makes the character of the sexes distinct. The sense of place, in its importance to the play, I have mentioned earlier; the sense of time has also an unusual function. One need only reflect on the obvious difference of age between Claudio and Hero, and Benedick and Beatrice—who play lightly with the idea of an obstinate, and therefore time-tried, celibacy; and ask oneself in what earlier comedy there is any differentiation other than that of Youth and Age. One can contrast, also, the references to past and future time that occur in earlier comedies with those in *Much Ado About Nothing*. " 'A killed your sister," in *Love's Labour's Lost*, or Helena's memory of "schooldays' friendship, childhood innocence," or Titania's memories of the sport on the Indian shore—all quoted above—have all, to varying degrees, an exquisite stylisation, an emblematic quality, that prevents their giving another temporal dimension to the play; they are an inset, not a perspective; an intensification of or contrast with the present, not an evocation of the past. But the casual, continual and colloquial harking-back in *Much Ado About Nothing* has a quite different effect.

> O, he's returned, and as pleasant as ever he was...
>
> He set up his bills here in Messina, and challenged Cupid at the flight; and my uncle's fool, reading the challenge, subscrib'd for Cupid, and challenged him at the birdbolt...
>
> They never meet but there's a skirmish of wit between them...
>
> In our last conflict four of his five wits went halting off...
>
> Indeed, my lord, he lent it me awhile; and I gave him use for it, a double heart for his single one...
>
> I have heard my daughter say she hath often dreamt of unhappiness, and waked herself with laughing...

One can, if one likes, play the same game with references to the future, contrasting *Love's Labour's Lost*'s

> You shall this twelvemonth term from day to day
> Visit the speechless sick, and still converse
> With groaning wretches...

with *Much Ado About Nothing*'s

> O Lord, my lord, if they were but a week married, they would talk themselves mad...
>
> I will live in thy heart, die in thy lap, and be buried in thy eyes; and, moreover, I will go with thee to thy uncle's...

This easy, humorous, and conversational manner, that refers to a past and future governed by customary event and behaviour, and that carries a sense of habitual reality in a familiar social group, gives the play the quality that it would be certainly unwise to call "realism"; it is an atmosphere easier to feel than to define. It is one of ennobled domesticity, aware of, touched by, and reflecting events in the outside world, but finally providing its own rules and customs: it is, in fact, a world largely feminine in character.

Into this world, at the beginning of the play, come the warriors, covered with masculine honours, cheerful with victory, and heralded importantly by a messsenger. They even bring their own style of figured public rhetoric with them:

> He hath borne himself beyond the promise of his age, doing in the figure of a lamb the feats of a lion...
> The fashion of the world is to avoid cost, and you encounter it...
> I had rather be a canker in a hedge than a rose in his grace; and it better fits my blood to be disdained of all than to fashion a carriage to rob love from any...

The "most exquisite Claudio," the "proper squire," is the flower of such a world; the plot that concerns him, and that seems at first to dominate the play, can be seen as the survival of all that is most formal, and least flexible, in the earlier comedies: a masculine game of romantic love with a firm—and sensible—business basis, the whole governed by an admirable sense of priorities in duty:

> I look'd upon her with a soldier's eye...
> But now I am return'd, and that war-thoughts
> Have left their places vacant, in their rooms
> Come thronging soft and delicate desires,
> All prompting me how fair young Hero is,
> Saying I lik'd her ere I went to wars...

If modern sentimentalism makes one dislike the foundation to Claudio's case—female good looks plus paternal income—it is as well to remember that it is an attitude embedded in all the comedies to date, whenever they touch on realism, and shared not only by Bassanio but—even though half-mockingly—by Benedick: "Rich she shall be, that's certain...fair, or I'll never look on her."

The beginning of the play, then, presents, in a social context, a company of young bloods, headed by the noble Don Pedro, who all hold together with a cheerful masculine solidarity. The "sworn brothers" are companions-in-arms, and if one deserts, there is cause for lamentation: "I have known when he would have walked ten mile afoot to see a good armour, and now will he lie ten nights awake carving the fashion of a new doublet." If Claudio dramatically distrusts Don Pedro at first—

> Let every eye negotiate for itself,
> And trust no agent; for beauty is a witch
> Against whose charms faith melteth into blood...

then the discovery of his mistake only strengthens his later trust in, and solidarity with, Don Pedro; and this trust is implicit even in the terms of his first doubt, which still postulates a male world of "negotiation" and "agents," against the hypnotic and possibly devilish enemy, Woman. Claudio's world, and Claudio's plot, are never "reformed"—in a dramatic, or moral sense—because they neither can nor need be changed; the simple course of loving, mistaking, and winning again, written from a specifically masculine point of view (again using the word masculine in its idiosyncratic sense here) that is half romance and half business, is a necessary backbone to the play, and holds the comedy together:

> Look, what will serve is fit: 'tis once, thou lovest;
> And I will fit thee with remedy.

And though Hero is in the course of it "killed, in some senses," as Dogberry might have said, she also gets her place in the world, and all is well. A comedy of romance needs something stable, limited, and circular, in which ends match beginnings, and in Claudio it gets this:

> Sweet Hero, now thy image does appear
> In the rare semblance that I loved it first...
> Another Hero!
> Nothing certainer...

But, if this world is not "reformed," it is to a large extent displaced; and the moment of that displacement is not hard to find:

> *Don Pedro.* Myself, my brother, and this grieved Count
> Did see her, hear her, at that hour last night
> Talk with a ruffian at her chamber window...
> *Exeunt Don Pedro, Don John, and Claudio.*
> *Benedick.* How doth the lady?

Left on stage we have a fainting and dishonoured girl; her wholly doubting and wretched old father, held to her only by paternal obligation; a wise and detached old Friar; and the dishonoured girl's cousin, in a rage of loyal devotion that is familial, sexual, and instinctual. One cannot help asking what the young, witty and independent soldier Benedick is doing in that gallery. He has broken the rules of the game, and entered upon a desertion far more serious than Claudio's ever appeared: he is crossing the boundaries of a world of masculine domination. How serious the desertion is, is indicated by his comic—but only partly comic—exchange with Beatrice, at the centre of their professions of love, that follow immediately on the church scene:

> *Ben.* Come, bid me do anything for thee.
> *Beat.* Kill Claudio.
> *Ben.* Ha! Not for the wide world.
> *Beat.* You kill me to deny it. Farewell.

"Kill Claudio" has become such a famous line that perhaps something of its importance, underlying its comic gesture of an unfeasible rage, has been lost. A pacific, sensible and level-headed bachelor is being forced toward a decision of alarming significance; and he accepts it. Beatrice's taunt "You dare easier be friends with me than fight with mine enemy" colours the whole of the end of the play, and produces the peculiar dramatic and psychological complexity of the scene of the challenge. In it, three characters, once a joint group of young men exchanging cheerful and witty backchat, begin to speak and think in two different worlds. Don Pedro's and Claudio's return to the old game between themselves—perfectly in place an hour earlier—becomes curiously embarrassing by the degree to which it can take no account of the dramatic change in Beatrice and Benedick's status, their siding with what the audience knows to be truth, or rather, a truer game than Don Pedro's and Claudio's:

> *Don Pedro.* But when shall we set the savage bull's horns on the sensible Benedick's head?
> *Claudio.* Yea, and text underneath, there dwells Benedick the married man?
> *Benedick.* Fare you well, boy: you know my mind. I will leave you now to your gossip-like humour; you break jests as braggarts do their blades, which God be thanked, hurt not. My lord, for your many courtesies I thank you. I must discontinue your company. Your brother the bastard is fled from Messina. You have among you killed a sweet and innocent lady. For my Lord Lackbeard there, he and I shall meet; and till then, peace be with him. (*Exit*).
> *Don Pedro.* He is in earnest. . . . What a pretty thing man is when he goes in his doublet and hose and leaves off his wit!

It is not sufficient to say simply that this effect is gained by some "change" in Benedick's—the witty Benedick's—character. It is rather that our own attitude has changed in the course of the play, so that something developing under the agency of the "important" characters has relieved them of their importance. Certain qualities, certain attitudes that have been found, in the earlier comedies, mainly confined to the women's and fools' parts, have here come into their own.

The plays have such artistic continuity that it is almost impossibly difficult to distinguish certain attitudes and feelings, and call *this* a specifically "feminine" attitude, or *that,* one belonging to a "fool" or "clown"; and the more mature the play, the more danger of falsifying there is. Perhaps it is merely possible to indicate certain speeches of Beatrice which do cohere into an attitude that utilises a "fool's" uncommitted wit and detached play of mind, together with a clown's grasp of earthy reality, yet committed in such a new way that they are given the effect of a female veracity against a masculine romanticism or formality.

> Yes, faith; it is my cousin's duty to make curtsy, and say 'Father, as it please you.' But yet for all that, cousin, let him be a handsome fellow, or else make another curtsy and say, 'Father, as it please me.'

The whole game of romantic passion was never glossed more conclusively than by her foreboding "I can see a church by daylight"; nor the silliness of romantic jealousy than by her sturdy description of Claudio as "civil as an orange, and something of that jealous complexion"; nor the game of formal, courteous and meaningless proposals—(Don Pedro's "Will you have me, lady?") than by her: "No, my lord, unless I might have another for working-days: your Grace is too costly to wear every day." (Certainly, Don Pedro does prove to be a costly guest, since he all but causes the death of his host's daughter.) The beautiful and formal scene that the men have arranged for the uniting of Claudio and Hero—"his Grace hath made the match, and all Grace say amen to it!" begins to be disarranged by Beatrice's detached sense ("Speak, Count, 'tis your cue") and she hastily has to give her "merry heart" the fool's harmless part in the play: "I thank it, poor fool, it keeps on the windy side of care." But the rising flight of her impertinence, which provokes Leonato to bustle her off the scene ("Niece, will you look to those things I told you of?") is not unacquainted with "care." Don Pedro's kindly and polite

> out of question, you were born in a merry hour

is met by her

> No, sure, my lord, my mother cried; but then there was a star danced, and under that was I born.

However light the reference, one goes back to the lamenting Adriana, out of place in a play of brisk farce; or the surprising seriousness of the reference in *Love's Labour's Lost* to Katharine's sister—

> He made her melancholy, sad and heavy,
> And so she died...

or the equally surprising seriousness of Titania's loyalty:

> But she, being mortal, of that boy did die...
> And for her sake I will not part with him...

The liaison of Claudio and Hero draws the "fools" Benedick and Beatrice into the play; and it is Beatrice who first here begins to show in her apparently detached wit, only partially revealed in her sparring with Benedick, the depth that the occasion demands. Marriage is seen here not as a witty dance of "wooing, wedding and repenting," but as the joining of Beatrice's "cousins," and her remarks have greater and more dangerous point. It is not surprising that on her exit Don Pedro sets afoot his second piece of matchmaking, since Beatrice patently needs a master. "We are the only love-gods."

It is only at the crisis of the play, in the church scene, that this dogged, loyal, and irrational femininity that characterises Beatrice comes into its own. The still hesitating and just Benedick is swept into her degree of belief simply by her obstinate passion of loyalty:

> Is 'a not approved in the height a villain that hath slandered, scorned, dishonoured my kinswoman? O that I were a man! What! bear her in hand until they come to take hands, and then with public accusation, uncovered slander, unmitigated rancour—O God that I were a man! I would eat his heart in the market-place.

Certainly her storms are comic; nevertheless our own sense at the end of the play of the limitations of the romantic background, and critics' unanimous conviction that Benedick and Beatrice "take over the play," is largely summed up by her own "Talk with a man out at a window! A proper saying!" and the comparative shallowness of the romanticism of the main plot very neatly and adequately summed up in her voluble harangue:

> Princes and Counties! Surely, a princely testimony, a goodly count, Count Comfect; a sweet gallant, surely! O that I were a man for his sake! or that I had any friend would be a man for my sake! But manhood is melted into curtsies, valour into compliment, and men are only turned into tongue, and trim ones too. He is now as valiant as Hercules that only tells a lie and swears it. I cannot be a man with wishing, therefore I will die a woman with grieving.

This is simultaneously a remarkable picture of a woman in a state of outraged temper, and an excellent piece of dramatic criticism. For Benedick, this is "Enough. I am engaged." The fools of the play have become the heroes.

To use the word "fools" is perhaps incautious: since, for one thing, Benedick's and Beatrice's speeches are characterised by a degree of sophistication and self command; and for another, the play itself has an excellent collection of clowns who do, noticeably, help to bring about the dénouement and save the day. But if one is attempting to explain the feeling of maturity and development that Beatrice and Benedick bring into the play, then it becomes apparent that a part of their strength comes from Shakespeare's drawing on resources of feeling expressed, in earlier comedies, as much by witty jesters and innocent clowns as by the kind of sophisticated commentators that one finds in Berowne and Rosaline. The sense of wisdom that they give is best glossed, perhaps, by Blake's "If the fool would persist in his folly, he would become wise."

Folly is an almost impossibly difficult thing to define. Perhaps one can say at least that the chief source of humour in Shakespeare's early comedies comes from a dichotomy between aspiration and actuality; the chief source of satisfaction, from the final resolution of these two things. If one looks at *Love's Labour's Lost* for instance, one sees a comic pattern repeated throughout. The young men first aspire toward a noble, beautiful, and impossible sublimity of monastic ascetism—

> brave conquerors, for so you are
> That war against your own affections
> And the huge army of the world's desires...

and then of course fall in love with the first females at the gate. Then again they aspire lyrically towards the heights of love—

> For valour, is not love a Hercules,
> Still climbing trees in the Hesperides?

and from this height it takes the clowns (who prove that Hercules is, after all, a mere Moth) and the women to bring them down, offering a second and harsher ascetism, in "some forlorn and naked hermitage"; or a second sphere for wit:

> To move wild laughter in the throat of death?
> It cannot be; it is impossible;
> Mirth cannot move a soul in agony.

If the hermitage and the hospital are not "actuality," they are nearer to being a figure for it, in the exquisite and formalised world of the play, than are the secluded and noble park-lands. The clowns and fools of the play suffer a similar fall, in aspiring toward similar nobilities of love and learning; and the actuality of the play that they perform proves the degree of their folly. Armado, who sees himself as Hector, must play the "Honest Troyan" by Jaquenetta; Costard's Pompey the Great finds himself merely the Big. But the fairly simple satire is transformed, in the games that both "high" and "low-life" characters play, in what is to prove the highly individual Shakespearian manner. Folly begins to transmute itself; out of this very discovery of the ridiculousness of aspiration, something not in itself ridiculous grows, generating a second movement upward:

> Let us once lose our oaths to find ourselves;
> Or else we lose ourselves to keep our oaths.
> It is religion to be thus forsworn;
> For charity itself fulfils the law,
> And who can sever love from charity?

This statement of what might be *gained* from folly is more clearly indicated and illustrated by some of the most surprising lines in the play. Armado, who is throughout genuinely ridiculous, is never more so than when enacting Hector. Yet he turns the laughter of the audience by his famous "The sweet war-man is dead and rotton; sweet chucks, beat not the bones of the buried; when he breathed, he was a man..." This is akin to Holofernes' suddenly serious rebuke to the mockery of the young lovers: "This is not generous, not gentle, not humble." For once more affecting than affected, Armado's plea for the dignity of the dead becomes a plea for the dignity of the fool; mortality, after all, makes equal fools of all men. "Get you to my lady's chamber, and tell her, let her paint an inch thick, to this favour she must come; make her laugh at that." Or—to gloss Armado from a later comedy—"as all is mortal in nature, so is all nature in love mortal in folly."

This suggestion, brilliantly scattered throughout *Love's Labour's Lost*—that dignity comes through an acceptance of folly; and that through this self-acceptance, and even better, self-knowledge, a man is twice a fool and yet "not altogether fool, my lord"—is present in *The Two Gentlemen of Verona* in a more solid and simple form. The noble chivalric love of the main characters transforms itself before our eyes into Launce and his dog. The dog is a bleak and simple positive in the play at the opposite end to Silvia's simple god-head; he is, so to speak, the god of love spelt backwards. "Ask my dog. If he say ay, it will; if he say no, it will; if he shake his tail and say nothing, it will." Launce's dog is infallible. To substitute a dog for a cold Petrarchan mistress is the simplest of comic tricks; but not so simple when done by genius.

> I think Crab my dog be the sourest-natured dog that lives: my mother weeping, my father wailing, my sister crying, our maid howling, our cat wringing her hands, and all our house in a great perplexity; yet did not this cruel-hearted cur shed one tear. He is a stone, a very pebble stone, and has no more pity in him than a dog.

All the possibilities of folly in idealistic love, and in the play, are "placed" by Launce's plaintive laments: "How many masters would do this for his servant? Nay, I'll be sworn, I have sat in the stocks for puddings he hath stolen, otherwise he had been executed..." And yet, as before, this is transformed satire. "I am but a fool, look you, and yet I have the wit to think my master is a kind of knave." In an idealistic world, earthy common-sense looks foolish enough; yet there is a savoir-faire, a calm satisfaction about Launce that makes us think again about folly. Launce gets what he wants: his dog.

Bottom is an expanded Launce; Launce with imagination, Launce sitting in the lap of the Gods. "Out of doubt he is transported." *A Midsummer Night's Dream* is so subtle and so integrated in its depiction of folly, that one hesitates to coarsen it by sketchy generalisation. The ridiculous and the beautiful grow so much closer together in this play that it is harmful to try to separate them: "Man is but an ass if he go about to expound this dream" is a good enough warning. But that one can quote this remark of

Bottom's indicates something of the growing complexity of the foolish nature. The young lovers, and the heroic couple, know the difference between dreaming and waking only by the common consent of their senses:

> The Duke was here...
> Why then we are awake...
> All their minds transfigured so together,
> More witnesseth than fancy's images,
> And grows to something of great constancy...

But to Bottom "a dream is a dream is a dream." He is both more rooted in a narrow, flat and earthly sense that makes nonsense of all dreams and games—of love or of magic or of dramatics—and more innocently capable of entering into them with easy belief, taking them for what they are.

> Let me play the lion too. I will roar that I will do any man's heart good to hear me; I will roar that I will make the Duke say, "Let him roar again, let him roar again...
> Tell them that I Pyramus am not Pyramus but Bottom the weaver. This will put them out of fear...

Books could be written—and probably have been—on the nature of dramatic illusion in *A Midsummer Night's Dream;* but one remark of Bottom's neatly clarifies the nature of dramatic belief, at least as far as the actor is concerned: "What beard were I best to play it in?" There may be little apparent similarity between a Bottom and a Beatrice; but her gift, too, is to "Find out Moonshine," and she, like Bottom, refuses to fall back on the evidence of the eyes and ears of noblemen to find out whether a dream is true or not: she trusts herself.

The folly of the clowns and naturals in *A Midsummer Night's Dream* is interesting, then, in its fertility; it lacks any nobility, but it leaves room for development. In the folly of Bottom there are the vestiges of wisdom, which could become self-knowledge. Theseus, the noblest figure in the play, can only judge; he has too much dignity to "play." Demetrius and the other young lovers "play," and are made fools of; but they can only judge other men's games, not their own. Bottom and the others have folly bred in the bone—an innocent, ignorant, and self-loving conviction of their own adequacy in a magical or artistic world—but they are also given a tough common sense that makes them, like Launce, and like the naturals in *Love's Labour's Lost,* twice fools, and not fools. "Sixpence a day in Pyramus, or nothing..." or "...No, I assure you, the wall is down that parted their fathers," shows something of a capacity at once to "play," and to "judge" the play.

Falstaff takes us far closer to Benedick and Beatrice, though his is a different world from theirs. Like Bottom, and like Launce, Falstaff is imperturbably at home in physical things (as Costard says: "It is the simplicity of man to hearken after the flesh." "If sack and sugar be a fault, God help the wicked!") and Falstaff wanders in a world of heroic values, both mocking them and mocked by them. "Let us be Diana's foresters, gentlemen of the shade, minions of the moon; and let men say we be men of good government, being governed, as the sea is, by our noble and chaste mistress the moon, under whose countenance we steal." This is a revitalising of Berowne's plea:

> Sweet lords, sweet lovers, O let us embrace.
> As true we are as flesh and blood can be.
> The sea will ebb and flow, heaven show his face;
> Young blood doth not obey an old decree...

but it is backed by the irony of self-knowledge.

Falstaff, like all clowns, elbows aside the rules of the world he lives in: "This chair shall be my state, this dagger my sceptre, this cushion my crown...And here is my speech. Stand aside, nobility." But his presence is more disturbing than that of any of the earlier clowns, by the increased degree of consciousness, and of self-consciousness, that he is given. The physical challenge of the "tun of man" is enormous; much more so is the intellectual challenge of his awareness, both of what he is, *and* of the world which he mocks and parodies. To a far greater extent than Bottom, Falstaff is both actor *and* critic, playing out his game, and judging it. "Dost thou hear me, Hal?...Do so, for it is worth the listening to..." "Gallants, lads, boys, hearts of gold, all the titles of good fellowship come to you! What, shall we be merry? Shall we have a play extempore?" Hal only barely dominates him by two simple devices, which give him something of the superiority of the jester over the natural. He stands, like a dwarf on a giant's shoulders, on the grandeur of History, of historic, and not imaginative, fact; and he is given a statement of consciousness and self-consciousness, in the first movement of the play, that "trumps" even Falstaff's:

> I know you all, and will awhile uphold
> The unyok'd humour of your idleness...

Falstaff's magnificent usefulness only begins to wear out in Part II of *Henry IV*. The game of politics begins to turn into the game of life itself, since Hal must "play the king" in all seriousness; that Falstaff's superlative wits detach themselves from *that* game arouses a certain sense of the need for yet another development of clowning.

> *Doll*. Thou whoreson little tidy Bartholomew boar-pig, when wilt thou leave fighting a days and foining a nights, and begin to patch up thine old body for heaven?
>
> *Falstaff*. Peace, good Doll! Do not speak like a death's-head; do not bid me remember mine end.

There are games—the second part of *Henry IV* suggests—in which the comic poise, that is generated by a knowledge of human ridiculousness and limitation, must generate something else to defeat that limitation.

> *Ben.* ...If a man do not erect in this age his own tomb ere he dies, he shall live no longer in monument than the bell rings and the widow weeps.
> *Beat.* And how long is that, think you?
> *Ben.* Question: Why, an hour in clamour, and a quarter in rheum.

So, in this colloquy between Benedick and Beatrice, one returns to *Much Ado.* Benedick and Beatrice are a delightful lesson in how the fool can "Serve God, love me, and mend." This they do by "persisting in their folly," in order to "become wise."

Their attitude at the beginning of the play is the comic stance of self-consciousness. Both gain dignity by an intellectual independence—by "sitting in a corner and crying Heigh-ho!" while they watch "everyone going to the world." This intellectual independence is largely a full and mocking knowledge—especially, at first, on Beatrice's side—of the physical realities underlying romantic aspirations. "But, for the stuffing...well, we are all mortal." Over and over again, "my uncle's fool" takes the place of Cupid. "Lord! I could not endure a husband with a beard on his face: I had rather lie in the woollen..." Mars as well as Cupid falls: the heroic warrior, who has done good "service" is "a very valiant trencherman; he hath an excellent stomach...(and is) a good soldier—to a lady." Yet the very intellectual detachment that gives a jester his dignity is the power to see general truths; and what is true of "mortals" must therefore be true also of Benedick and Beatrice, who are intellectually and dramatically joined to the hero and heroine of the main plot, by being friend and cousin to them, and by understanding—therefore sharing—their folly. Benedick's *ubi sunts* for bachelors derive their humour from the steadily-increasing knowledge that he is, like Barkis, going out with the tide: "In faith, hath not the world one man but he will wear his cap with suspicion? Shall I never see a bachelor of three score again?...Like the old tale, my lord: It is not so, nor 'twas not so, but indeed, God forbid it should be so!" Like Falstaff, Benedick is comic by being both actor and critic, and knows which way "old tales" go; and though he may cast himself as bachelor, "he never could maintain his part but in the force of his will." Benedick and Beatrice are "fooled" and "framed" by the dramatist even before they are "fooled" by the trick played on them by Don Pedro and the others; their detached intelligence is, by definition, an understanding of the way their "foolish" desires will go. "Shall quips and sentences and the paper bullets of the brain awe a man from the career of his humour? No: the world must be peopled."

Thus, when Benedick and Beatrice do "run mad," they suffer—like Falstaff in love—a loss of dignity the more marked by contrast with their intellectual detachment earlier. Benedick searching for double meanings, and Beatrice nursing a sick heart, a cold in the head, and a bad temper, are as "placed" within the others' play as are the clowns in *Love's Labour's Lost* or *A Midsummer Night's Dream,* attendant on the critique of their superiors. It is, of course, the church scene, and all that follows, that changes this, and shows their double "folly" coming into its own. Beatrice is loyal to Hero simply by virtue of an acquaintance with common sense physical realities—"Talk with a man out at a window! A proper saying!"—and by a flood of intuitive, irrational, and "foolish" pity and love, that instinctively recognizes the good when it sees it—good in Benedick, or in Hero; and Benedick is drawn to her, here, through very similar feelings. "Lady Beatrice, have you wept all this while?" In the professions of love that follow Benedick's opening, there are touches of great humour; but the scene is a serious one, nevertheless. Both Benedick and Beatrice gain a new and much more complex equilibrium and dignity; both pledge themselves by their "soul" to Hero's cause, and hence to each other. To be intelligent is to be aware "that we are all mortal"; and to be mortal is to be a fool; and therefore intelligent men are most fools; but to be a fool, in a good cause, is to be wise. This is an old paradox that echoes through and through Shakespeare's comedies, and after.

Because Beatrice and Benedick are "too wise to woo peaceably," they continue to bicker comfortably through the rest of the play, as though enjoying the mutual death of their individuality:

> Two distincts, division none.

Like Theseus' hounds, the quarrels of all the players grow, finally, into:

> Such gallant chiding...
> So musical a discord...
> Matched in mouths like bells, each under each.

An unlyrical play grows into a new and interesting harmony, as all the forms of folly in the play find "measure in everything, and so dance out the answer":

> Come, come, we are friends. Let's have a dance ere we are married, that we may lighten our own hearts and our wives' heels.
> We'll have dancing afterwards.
> First, of my word; therefore play, music.

Though the play can be summed up by the image of the dance, it is also a battle, in which certain things are lost. Hero's "death" is an illusion, but other things do seem to die out of the comedies: part of an old romantic ideal, and a sense of easy loyalty between young men. Rosalind's "Men have died from time to time, and worms have eaten them, but not for love. . ." and Antonio's bitter, though mistaken, reflections on friendship, both represent a kind of feeling that can be seen to emerge with some clarity in *Much Ado*. Some more important things take the place of what is lost, all perhaps developing out of the sense of that loss; a wisdom, balance, and generosity of mind and feeling, largely expressed through the women's rôles.

This paper has itself probably been unwise, unbalanced and ungenerous in all that it has omitted. I have concentrated only on certain elements in *Much Ado About Nothing* that interest me, and may have distorted them in the process. My intention has not been to present Shakespeare as an earnest—though early—leader of the feminist movement, but only to suggest the development, through the comedies, of certain feelings and attitudes which are a constituent part of the plays as a whole, but which do tend to be most clearly expressed through the women in them. In Messina, Arden, and Illyria the expression of humane principle, of generous and constant feeling, comes principally from the women—whether we choose to see them as symbols merely of an area of the mind possessed by both sexes in common, or whether we see Shakespeare creating a world in which some kind of distinctively female rationale is able to have full play, and to dominate the action. When, in tragedy, the action moves on to the battlements of civilisation, and beyond, the difference of the sexes becomes of minor importance, and the rôle of the women diminishes; they become little more than functions of the hero's mind, barely aware of the area in which that mind operates. Ironically, the heroic qualities which make the woman's stature minor by comparison can be seen as developing through and out of qualities confined largely to the women in the "mature" comedies; the values that are proved by their success in the comedies come to stand the proof of failure in the tragedies. Something of the tragic heroes' passionate constancy and painful knowledge, and something of the sane and honourable happiness that is felt most sharply in the tragedies by its absence, is first developed in the secure limitations of the "mature" comedies, and is chiefly expressed through the talkative and intelligent women who guide events and guard principles. So *Much Ado About Nothing* can be seen to have a certain aptness of title. The small world that it presents with such gaiety, wit, and pleasurable expertise, is perhaps relatively a "nothing" in itself; but a certain amount of the interest and delight it produces comes from the awareness that much can be held in little, and that in "nothing" can "grow. . . something of great constancy."

# 18

# *Twelfth Night* and The Morality of Indulgence

*John Hollander*

To say that a play is "moral" would seem to imply that it represents an action which concretizes certain ethical elements of human experience. It need not actually moralize at any point, nor need any of the characters in it state univocally a dogma, precept, or value that would coincide completely with the play's own moral intention. It was just this univocal didacticism, however, which characterized what was becoming in 1600 a prevailing comic tradition. The moral intent of the Jonsonian "comedy of humours" was direct and didactic; its purpose was to show

> the times deformitie
> Anatomiz'd in euery nerue and sinnew
> With constant courage, and contempt of feare.[1]

For moral purposes, a humour is an identifying emblem of a man's moral nature, graven ineradicably onto his physiological one. In the world of a

*Reprinted from* The Sewanee Review, *LXVIII, No. 2 by permission of the author and publisher.*

[1] Ben Jonson, *Every Man Out of His Humour* (1599), Induction, 11, 120–122.

play, a humour could be caricatured to such a degree that it would practically predestine a character's behavior. It was made to

> . . . so possesse a man, that it doth draw
> All his affects, his spirits and his powers,
> In their confluctions, all to runne one way,
> This may be truly said to be a Humour.

The emblematic character of the humour and the necessity for its use were affirmed even more directly by Sidney, whose dramatic theory Jonson seems to have greatly admired.

Now *Every Man In His Humour* was first acted in 1598, and it is known that Shakespeare appeared in it. He seems in *Twelfth Night* (for which I accept the traditional date of 1600–1601) to have attempted to write a kind of moral comedy diametrically opposed to that of Jonson, in which "the times deformitie" was not to be "anatomiz'd," but represented in the core of an action. For a static and deterministic Humour, Shakespeare substituted a kinetic, governing Appetite in the action, rather than in the bowels, of his major characters. In his plot and language, he insists continually on the fact and importance of the substitution. Characters in a comedy of humours tend to become caricatures, and caricatures tend to become beasts, inhuman personifications of moral distortions that are identified with physiological ones. I believe that it was Shakespeare's intention in *Twelfth Night* to obviate the necessity of this dehumanization by substituting what one might call a moral process for a moral system. While it is true that the play contains quite a bit of interesting discussion of humours as such, and that there is some correspondence between appetites and humours, it is equally true that the only person in the play who believes in the validity of humourous classifications, who, indeed, lives by them, is himself a moral invalid. I will have more to say about this later. At this point I merely wish to suggest that the primary effective difference between Shakespeare's and Jonson's techniques in making moral comedy is the difference between what is merely a display of anatomy, and a dramatization of a metaphor, the difference between a Pageant and an Action.

## II

The Action of *Twelfth Night* is indeed that of a Revels, a suspension of mundane affairs during a brief epoch in a temporary world of indulgence, a land full of food, drink, love, play, disguise and music. But parties end, and the reveller eventually becomes satiated and drops heavily into his worldly self again. The fact that plays were categorized as "revells" for institutional purposes may have appealed to Shakespeare; he seems at any rate to have analyzed the dramatic and moral nature of feasting, and to have made it the subject of his play. His analysis is schematized in Orsino's opening speech.

The essential action of a revels is: To so surfeit the Appetite upon excess that it "may sicken and so die." It is the Appetite, not the whole Self, however, which is surfeited: the Self will emerge at the conclusion of the action from where it has been hidden. The movement of the play is toward this emergence of humanity from behind a mask of comic type.

Act I, scene i, is very important as a statement of the nature of this movement. Orsino's opening line contains the play's three dominant images:

> If music be the food of love, play on.
> Give me excess of it, that, surfeiting,
> The appetite may sicken, and so die. (I, i, 1–3)

Love, eating, and music are the components of the revelry, then. And in order that there be no mistake about the meaning of the action, we get a miniature rehearsal of it following immediately:

> That strain again! It had a dying fall.
> Oh, it came o'er my ear like the sweet sound
> That breathes upon a bank of violets
> Stealing and giving odor! Enough, no more.
> 'Tis not so sweet now as it was before.
> O spirit of love, how quick and fresh art thou!
> That, notwithstanding thy capacity
> Receiveth as the sea, naught enters there,
> Of what validity and pitch soe'er,
> But falls into abatement and low price,
> Even in a minute! So full of shapes is fancy
> That it alone is high fantastical. (I, i, 4–15)

A bit of surfeiting is actually accomplished here; what we are getting is a proem to the whole play, and a brief treatment of love as an appetite. The substance of a feast will always fall into "abatement and low price" at the conclusion of the feasting, for no appetite remains to demand it. We also think of Viola in connection with the "violets Stealing and giving odor" for her actual position as go-between-turned-lover is one of both inadvertent thief and giver. The Duke's rhetoric is all-embracing, however, and he immediately comments significantly upon his own condition.

> Or, when mine eyes did see Olivia first,
> Methought she purged the air of pestilence!
> That instant was I turned into a hart,
> And my desires, like fell and cruel hounds,
> E'er since pursue me. (I, i, 19–23)

Like Actaeon, he is the hunter hunted; the active desirer pursued by his own desires. As embodying this overpowering appetite for romantic love, he serves as a host of the revels.[2]

The other host is Olivia, the subject of his desire. We see almost at once that her self-indulgence is almost too big to be encompassed by Orsino's. Valentine, reporting on the failure of his mission, describes her state as follows:

> So please my lord, I might not be admitted,
> But from her handmaid do return this answer:
> The element itself, till seven years' heat,
> Shall not behold her face at ample view;
> But, like a cloistress, she will veiled walk
> And water once a day her chamber round
> With eye-offending brine—all this to season
> A brother's dead love, which she would keep fresh
> And lasting in her sad remembrance. (I, i, 24–32)

"To season a brother's dead love": she is gorging herself on this fragrant herb, and though she has denied herself the world, she is no true anchorite, but, despite herself, a private glutton. The Duke looks forward to the end of her feast of grief,

> . . . when liver, brain, and heart,
> These sovereign thrones, are all supplied, and filled
> Her sweet perfections with one self king! (I, i, 37–39)

The trinitarian overtone is no blasphemy, but a statement of the play's teleology. When everyone is supplied with "one self king," the action will have been completed.

The first three scenes of the play stand together as a general prologue, in which the major characters are introduced and their active natures noted. Viola is juxtaposed to Olivia here; she is not one to drown her own life in a travesty of mourning. It is true that she is tempted to "serve that lady" (as indeed she does, in a different way). But her end in so doing would be the whole play's action in microcosm; the immersion in committed self-indulgence would result in the revelation of herself:

> And might not be delivered to the world
> Till I had made mine own occasion mellow,
> What my estate is. (I, ii, 42–44)

She will serve the Duke instead and use her persuasive talents to accomplish the ends to which his own self-celebrating rhetoric can provide no access. "I can sing," she says, "and speak to him in many sorts of music." Her

---

[2] See the extremely provocative commentary on the Duke's opening lines in Kenneth Burke, *The Philosophy of Literary Form* (Baton Rouge, 1941), pp. 344–349.

sense of his character has been verified; the Captain tells her that his name is as his nature. And "what is his name?" she asks. "Orsino," answers the Captain. Orsino—the bear, the ravenous and clumsy devourer. Her own name suggests active, affective music; and the mention of Arion, the Orpheus-like enchanter of waves and dolphins with his music, points up the connotation. Orsino's "music," on the other hand, is a static well of emotion in which he allows his own rhetoric to submerge: Viola's is more essentially instrumental, effective, and convincing.[3]

The third scene of Act I completes the prologue by further equating the moral and the physiological. Here we first encounter the world of what Malvolio calls "Sir Toby and the lighter people" (it is indeed true that there is none of Malvolio's element of "earth" in them). The continued joking about *dryness* that pervades the wit here in Olivia's house, both above and below stairs, is introduced here, in contrast to Olivia's floods of welling and self-indulgent tears. The idea behind the joking in this and the following scenes is that drinking and merriment will moisten and fulfill a dry nature. As Feste says later on, "Give the dry fool drink, then the fool is not dry." Toby's sanguine temperament and Aguecheek's somewhat phlegmatic one are here unveiled. They are never identified as such, however; and none of the wit that is turned on the associations of "humours," "elements" and "waters," though it runs throughout the play, ever refers to a motivating order in the universe, except insofar as Malvolio believes in it.

What is most important is that neither Feste, the feaster embodying not the spirit but the action of revelry, nor Malvolio, the ill-wisher (and the *bad appetite* as well), his polar opposite, appears in these introductory scenes. It is only upstairs in Olivia's house (I, v) that the action as such commences. The revel opens with Feste's exchange with Maria in which she attempts three times to insist on innocent interpretations of "well-hanged" and "points." But Feste is resolute in his ribaldry. Thus Olivia, momentarily voicing Malvolio's invariable position, calls Feste a "dry fool," and "dishonest"; Malvolio himself refers to him as a "barren rascal." From here on in it will be Feste who dances attendance on the revelry, singing, matching wit with Viola, and being paid by almost everyone for his presence. To a certain degree he remains outside the action, not participating in it because he represents its very nature; occasionally serving as a comic angel or messenger, he is nevertheless unmotivated by any appetite, and is never sated of his fooling. His insights into the action are continuous, and his every remark is telling, "*Cucullus non facit monachum*. That's as much as to say I wear not motley in my brain."[4] Indeed, he does not, but more important is

---

3 See my own "Musica Mundana and Twelfth Night" in *Sound and Poetry,* ed. Northrop Frye (New York, 1957), pp. 55–82, for an extended treatment of the use of "speculative" and "practical" music in the play.

4 Cf. *Measure for Measure,* V, i, 263, where Lucio refers in the identical words to the Duke disguised as Friar Lodowick.

the fact that his robe and beard are not to make him a *real* priest later on. And neither he as Sir Thopas, nor Olivia as a "cloistress," nor Malvolio in his black suit of travestied virtue, nor the transvestite Viola is what he appears to be. No one will be revealed in his true dress until he has doffed his mask of feasting. And although neither Feste nor Malvolio will change in this respect, it is for completely opposite reasons that they will not do so.

Every character in the play, however, is granted some degree of insight into the nature of the others. It is almost as if everyone were masked with the black side of his vizard turned inwards; he sees more clearly past the *persona* of another than he can past his own. Valentine, for the Duke, comments on Olivia, as we have seen before. Even Malvolio is granted such an insight. Olivia asks him "What manner of man" Caesario is; unwittingly, his carping, over self-conscious and intellectualized answer cuts straight to the heart of Viola's disguise: "Not yet old enough for a man, nor young enough for a boy, as a squash is before 'tis a peascod, or a codling when 'tis almost an apple. 'Tis with him in standing water, between boy and man. He is very well-favored and he speaks very shrewishly. One would think his mother's milk were scarce out of him" (I, v, 165–171).

The puns on "cod" and "codling" insist on being heard here, and as with the inadvertently delivered obscenity about Olivia's "great P's" and their source in the letter scene, Malvolio does not know what he is saying. The point is that Malvolio asserts, for an audience that knows the real facts, that Viola can scarcely be a male creature.

A more significant case of this hide-and-seek is Olivia's retort to Malvolio in the same scene: "O you are sick of self-love, Malvolio, and taste with a distempered appetite"; it provides the key to his physiological-moral nature. "Sick of self-love" means "sick with a moral infection called self-love," but it can also mean "already surfeited, or fed up with your own ego as an object of appetite." Malvolio's "distempered appetite" results from the fact that he alone is not possessed of a craving directed outward, towards some object on which it can surfeit and die; he alone cannot morally benefit from a period of self-indulgence. Actually this distemper manifests itself in terms of transitory desires on his part for status and for virtue, but these desires consume him in their fruitlessness; he is aware of the nature of neither of them. This is a brilliant analysis of the character of a melancholic, and Shakespeare's association of the melancholy, puritanic and status-seeking characters in Malvolio throws considerable light on all of them. The moral nature of the plot of *Twelfth Night* can be easily approached through the character of Malvolio, and this, I think, is what Lamb and his followers missed completely in their egalitarian sympathy for his being no "more than steward." For Malvolio's attachment to self-advancement is not being either aristocratically ridiculed or praised as an example of righteous bourgeois opposition to medieval hierarchies. In the context of the play's moral physiology, his disease is shown forth as a case of indigestion due to his self-love, the result of a perverted, rather than an excessive appetite.[5] In the world of feasting, the values of the commercial society outside the walls of the party go topsy-turvy: Feste is given money for making verbal fools of the donors thereof; everyone's desire is fulfilled in an unexpected way; and revellers are shown to rise through realms of unreality, disguise and luxurious self-deception. We are seduced, by the revelling, away from seeing the malice in the plot to undo Malvolio. But whatever malice there is remains peculiarly just. It is only Malvolio who bears any ill-will, and only he upon whom ill-will can appear to be directed. He makes for himself a hell of the worldly heaven of festivity, and when Toby and Maria put him into darkness, into a counterfeit-hell, they are merely representing in play a condition that he has already achieved.

The plot against Malvolio, then, is no more than an attempt to let him surfeit on himself, to present him with those self-centered, "time-pleasing" objects upon which his appetite is fixed. In essence, he is led to a feast in which his own vision of himself is spread before him, and commanded to eat it. The puritan concern with witchcraft and the satanic, and its associations of them with madness are carried to a logical extreme; and once Malvolio has been permitted to indulge in his self-interest by means of the letter episode, he is only treated as he would himself treat anyone whom he believed to be mad. His puritanism is mocked by allusions to his praying made by Toby and Maria; a priest (and a false, dissembling one at that, the answer to a puritan's prayer) is sent to him; and the implications of the darkness are eventually fulfilled as his prison becomes his hell.

It is interesting to notice how carefully Shakespeare analyzed another characteristic of the melancholic in his treatment of Malvolio. L. C. Knights has suggested[6] that the vogue of melancholy at the turn of the 17th century was occasioned to some degree by the actual presence in England of a large number of "*intellectuels en chômage*" (in Denis de Rougement's words), unemployed, university-trained men whose humanistic education had not fitted them for any suitable role in society. Malvolio is no patent and transparent university intellectual (like Holofernes, for example). He contrives, however, to over-rationalize his point (where the Duke will over-sentimentalize it) on almost every occasion. Even his first introduction of Viola, as has been seen before, is archly over-reasoned. His venture into exegesis of a text is almost telling.

It is not merely self-interest, I think, that colors the scrutiny of Maria's letter. His reading is indeed a close one: he observes that, after the first

---

[5] And Leslie Hotson has pointed out that his yellow stockings, as he later appears in them, are the true color of the Narcissus, as well as of the craven. See *The First Night of Twelfth Night* (London, 1954), p. 98f.

[6] *Drama and Society in the Age of Jonson* (Manchester, 1936), pp. 315–332.

snatch of doggerel, "The numbers altered." But Malvolio is incapable of playing the party-game and guessing the riddle. Of "M, O, A, I doth sway my life," he can only say "And yet, to crush this a little it would bow to me, for every one of these letters are in my name." He even avoids the reading that should, by all rights, appeal to him: Leslie Hotson has suggested that "M, O, A, I" probably stands for *Mare, Orbis, Aer* and *Ignis,* the four elements to which Malvolio so often refers. Malvolio himself fails as a critic, following a "cold scent" that, as Fabian indicates, is "as rank as a fox" for him in that it tantalizes his ambition.

But he continues to aspire to scholarship. In order to "let his tongue tang" with arguments of state, he intends to "read politic authors." His intrusion on the scene of Toby's and Andrew's merry-making involves a most significant remark: "Is there no respect of persons, time or place in you?" he asks. In other words, "Do you not observe even the dramatic unities in your revelling? Can you not apply even the values that govern things as frivolous as plays to your lives?" Coming from Malvolio, the ethical theorist, the remark feels very different from the remark made to Sir Toby by Maria, the practical moralist: "Aye, but you must confine yourself within the modest levels of order." Maria, presiding over the festivities, would keep things from getting out of hand. It is not only the spirit in which Malvolio's comment is uttered that accounts for this difference, however. I think that one of the implications is quite clearly the fact that Jonson's ordered, would-be-classic, but static and didactic comedy would disapprove of *Twelfth Night* as a moral play, and mistake its intention for a purely frivolous one.

The prank played on Malvolio is not merely an "interwoven" second story, but a fully-developed double-plot. Like the Belmont episodes in *The Merchant of Venice,* it is a condensed representation of the action of the entire play. In *Twelfth Night*, however, it operates in reverse, to show the other side of the coin, as it were. For Malvolio there can be no fulfillment in "one self king." His story effectively and ironically underlines the progress toward this fulfillment in everybody else, and helps to delineate the limitations of the moral domain of the whole play. In contrast to Feste, who appears in the action at times as an abstracted spirit of revelry, Malvolio is a model of the sinner.

The whole play abounds in such contrasts and parallels of character, and the players form and regroup continually with respect to these, much in the manner of changing of figurations in a suite of *branles*. Viola herself indulges in the festivities in a most delicate and (literally) charming way. She is almost too good a musician, too effective an Orpheus: "Heaven forbid my outside have not charmed her," she complains after her first encounter with Olivia. But as soon as she realizes that she is part of the game, she commits herself to it with redoubled force. If her "outside" is directed towards Olivia, her real identity and her own will are concentrated even more strongly on Orsino. In the most ironic of the love-scenes, she all but supplants Olivia in the Duke's affections. Orsino, glutting himself on his own version of romantic love, allows himself to make the most extravagant and self-deceptive statements about it:

> Come hither, boy. If ever thou shalt love,
> In the sweet pangs of it remember me;
> For such as I am all true lovers are,
> Unstaid and skittish in all motions else
> Save in the constant image of the creature
> That is beloved. (II, iv, 15–20)

This skittishness, beneath the mask of the ravenous and constant bear, is obvious to Feste, at least: "Now, the melancholy god protect thee, and the tailor make thy doublet of changeable taffeta, for thy mind is a very opal. I would have men of such constancy put to sea, that their business might be everything and their intent everywhere; for that's it that always makes a good voyage of nothing. (II, iv, 75–80)"

Orsino also gives us a curious version of the physiology of the passions on which the plot is based; it is only relatively accurate, of course, for he will be the last of the revellers to feel stuffed, to push away from him his heaping dish.

> There is no woman's sides
> Can bide the beating of so strong a passion
> As love doth give my heart, no woman's heart
> So big to hold so much. They lack retention.
> Alas, their love may be called appetite—
> No motion of the liver, but the palate—
> They suffer surfeit, cloyment and revolt.
> But mine is all as hungry as the sea
> And can digest as much. (II, iv, 96–104)

Viola has been giving him her "inside" throughout the scene, and were he not still ravenous for Olivia's love he could see her for what she is: a woman with a constancy in love (for himself and her brother) that he can only imagine himself to possess. She is indeed an Allegory of Patience on some baroque tomb at this point. She is ironically distinguished from Olivia in that her "smiling at grief" is a disguising "outside" for her real sorrow, whereas Olivia's is a real self-indulgent pleasure taken at a grief outworn. It is as if Olivia had misread Scripture and taken the letter of "Blessed are they that mourn" for the spirit of it. Her grief is purely ceremonial.

The "lighter people," too, are engaged in carrying out the action in their own way, and they have more business in the play than merely to make a gull of Malvolio. Toby's huge stomach for food and drink parallels the Duke's ravenous capacity for sentiment. The drinking scene is in one sense the heart of the play. It starts out by declaring itself in no uncertain terms. "Does not our life consist of the four elements?" catechizes Sir Toby. "Faith, so they say," replies Andrew, "but I think it rather consists of eating and drinking." No one but Feste, perhaps, really knows the extent to which this is true, for Andrew is actually saying "We are not merely comic types, mind you, being manipulated by a dramatist of the humours. The essence of our lives lies in a movement from hunger to satiety that we share with all of nature."

When Toby and Andrew cry out for a love song, Feste obliges them, not with the raucous and bawdy thing that one would expect, but instead, with a direct appeal to their actual hostess, Olivia. This is all the more remarkable in that it is made on behalf of everyone in the play. "O Mistress Mine" undercuts the Duke's overwhelming but ineffectual mouthings, Viola's effective but necessarily misdirected charming, and, of course, Aguecheek's absolute incompetence as a suitor. The argument is couched in purely naturalistic terms: "This feast will have to end, and so will all of our lives. You are not getting younger ('sweet and twenty' is the contemporaneous equivalent of 'sweet and thirty," at least). Give up this inconstant roaming; your little game had better end in your marriage, anyway." The true love "That can sing both high and low" is Viola-Sebastian, the master-mistress of Orsino's and Olivia's passion. (Sebastian has just been introduced in the previous scene, and there are overtones here of his being invoked as Olivia's husband.) Sebastian has, aside from a certain decorative but benign courtly manner, no real identity apart from Viola. He is the fulfillment of her longing (for she has thought him dead) and the transformations into reality of the part she is playing in the *ludus amoris*. The prognostication is borne out by Sebastian's own remark: "You are betrothed both to a man and maid." He is himself characterized by an elegance hardly virile; and, finally, we must keep in mind the fact that Viola was played by a boy actor to begin with, and that Shakespeare's audience seemed to be always ready for an intricate irony of this kind.

But if Viola and Sebastian are really the same, "One face, one voice, one habit, and two persons, A natural perspective that is and is not," there is an interesting parallel between Viola and Aguecheek as well. Both are suitors for Olivia's hand: Andrew, ineffectively, for himself; Viola for Orsino, and (effectively) for Sebastian. Their confrontation in the arranged duel is all the more ironic in that Andrew is an effective pawn in Toby's game (Toby is swindling him), whereas Viola is an ineffective one in the Duke's (she is swindling him of Olivia's love).

Feste's other songs differ radically from "O Mistress Mine." He sings for the Duke a kind of languorous ayre, similar to so many that one finds in the songbooks.[7] It is aimed at Orsino in the very extravagance of its complaint. It is his own song, really, if we imagine him suddenly dying of love, being just as ceremoniously elaborate in his funeral instructions as he has been in his suit of Olivia. And Feste's bit of handy-dandy to Malvolio in his prison is a rough-and-tumble sort of thing, intended to suggest in its measures a scrap from a Morality, plainly invoking Malvolio in darkness as a devil in hell. Feste shows himself throughout the play to be a master of every convention of fooling.

If Feste's purpose is to serve as a symbol of the revels, however, he must also take a clear and necessary part in the all-important conclusion. *Twelfth Night* itself, the feast of the Epiphany, celebrates the discovery of the "True King" in the manger by the Wise Men. "Those wits," says Feste in Act I, scene v "that think they have thee [wit] do very oft prove fools, and I that am sure I lack thee may pass for a wise man." And so it is that under his influence the true Caesario, the "one self king," is revealed.[8] The whole of Act V might be taken, in connection with "the plot" in a trivial sense, to be the other *epiphany,* the perception that follows the *anagnorisis* or discovery of classic dramaturgy. But we have been dealing with the Action of *Twelfth Night* as representing the killing off of excessive appetite through indulgence of it, leading to the rebirth of the unencumbered self. The long final scene, then, serves to show forth the Caesario-King, and to unmask, discover and reveal the fulfilled selves in the major characters.

The appearance of the priest (a real one, this time) serves more than the simple purpose of proving the existence of a marriage between Olivia and "Caesario." It is a simple but firm intrusion into the world of the play of a way of life that has remained outside of it so far. The straightforward solemnity of the priest's rhetoric is also something new; suggestions of its undivided purpose have appeared before only in Antonio's speeches. The priest declares that Olivia and her husband have been properly married:

> And all the ceremony of this compact
> Sealed in my function, by my testimony.
> Since when, my watch hath told me, toward my grave
> I have travelled but two hours. (V, i, 163–166)

It is possible that the original performances had actually taken about two hours to reach this point. At any rate, the sombre acknowledgment of the passage of time in a real world is there. Antonio has prepared the way earlier in the scene; his straightforward confusion is that of the unwitting

[7] The Rev. E. H. Fellowes, in *English Madrigal Verse* (Oxford, 1929), lists four different ayres with the conventional opening phrase, "Come away."

[8] For my interpretation of the last act I am indebted to Professor Roy W. Battenhouse's suggestions.

intruder in a masquerade who has been accused of mistaking the identities of two of the masquers.

That the surfeiting has gradually begun to occur, however, has become evident earlier. In the prison scene, Sir Toby has already begun to tire: "I would we were well rid of this knavery." He gives as his excuse for this the fact that he is already in enough trouble with Olivia, but such as this has not deterred him in the past. And, in the last scene, very drunk as he must be, he replies to Orsino's inquiry as to his condition that he hates the surgeon, "a drunken rogue." Self-knowledge has touched Sir Toby. He could not have said this earlier.

As the scene plays itself out, Malvolio alone is left unaccounted for. There is no accounting for him here, though; he remains a bad taste in the mouth. "Alas poor fool," says Olivia. "How have they baffled thee!" And thus, in Feste's words, "the whirligig of time brings in his revenges." Malvolio has become the fool, the "barren rascal." He leaves in a frenzy, to "be revenged," he shouts, "on the whole pack of you." He departs from the world of this play to resume a role in another, perhaps. His business has never been with the feasting to begin with, and now that it is over, and the revellers normalized he is revealed as the true madman. He is "The Madly-Used Malvolio" to the additional degree that his own uses have been madness.

For Orsino and Viola the end has also arrived. She will be "Orsino's mistress and his fancy's queen." He has been surfeited of his misdirected voracity; the rich golden shaft, in his own words, "hath killed the flock of all affections else" that live in him. "Liver, brain and heart" are indeed all supplied; for both Olivia and himself, there has been fulfillment in "one self king." And, lest there be no mistake, each is to be married to a Caesario or king. Again, "Liver, brain and heart" seems to encompass everybody: Toby and Maria are married, Aguecheek chastened, etc.

At the end of the scene, all exit. Only Feste, the pure fact of feasting, remains. His final song is a summation of the play in many ways at once. Its formal structure seems to be a kind of quick rehearsal of the Ages of Man. In youth, "A foolish thing was but a toy": the fool's bauble, emblematic of both his *membrum virile* and his trickery, is a trivial fancy. But in "man's estate," the bauble represents a threat of knavery and thievery to respectable society, who shuts its owner out of doors. The "swaggering" and incessant drunkenness of the following strophes bring Man into prime and dotage, respectively. Lechery, trickery, dissembling and drunkenness, inevitable and desperate in mundane existence, however, are just those activities which, mingled together in a world of feasting, serve to purge Man of the desire for them. The wind and the rain accompany him throughout his life, keeping him indoors with "dreams and imaginations" as a boy, pounding and drenching him unmercifully, when he is locked out of doors, remaining eternal and inevitable throughout his pride in desiring to perpetuate himself. The wind and the rain are the most desperate of elements, that pound the walls and batter the roof of the warm house that shuts them out, while, inside it, the revels are in progress. Only after the party is ended can Man face them without desperation.

It is the metaphor of the rain that lasts longest, though, and it recapitulates the images of water, elements and humours that have pervaded the entire play. Feste himself, who tires of nothing, addresses Viola: "Who you are and what you would are out of my welkin—I might say 'element' but the word is overworn." He adroitly comments on Malvolio's line "Go to; I am not of your element" by substituting a Saxon word for a Latin one. The additional association of the four elements with the humours cannot be overlooked. It is only Malvolio, of course, who uses the word "humour" with any seriousness: "And then to have the humour of State," he muses, as he imagines himself "Count Malvolio." Humours are also waters, however. And *waters,* or fluids of all kinds, are continually being forced on our attention. Wine, tears, seawater, even urine, are in evidence from the first scene on, and they are always being metaphorically identified with one another. They are all fluids, bathing the world of the play in possibilities for change as the humours do the body. Feste's answer to Maria in the prison scene has puzzled many editors; if we realize, however, that Feste is probably hysterically laughing at what he has just been up to, "Nay, I'm for all waters" may have the additional meaning that he is on the verge of losing control of himself. He is "for all waters" primarily in that he represents the fluidity of revelling celebration. And finally, when all is done, "The rain it raineth every day," and Feste reverts to gnomic utterance in a full and final seriousness. Water is rain that falls to us from Heaven. The world goes on. Our revels now are ended, but the actors solidify into humanity, in this case. "But that's all one, our play is done/And we'll strive to please you every day."

# 19

# *Troilus and Cressida:* The Uses of the Double Plot

*Norman Rabkin*

To many in each generation *Troilus and Cressida* must seem, as it did once to Tennyson, "perhaps Shakespeare's finest play."[1] On the stage it has had memorable if all too infrequent successes; in the study its muscular and iridescent intellectuality, its language and characterization have earned it the constant attention of Shakespeare's critics. Yet critics repeatedly imply their sense that *Troilus and Cressida* is a failure and find themselves obliged either to denounce it for its apparent idiosyncrasies or to explain them by seeing the play as a special phenomenon—an exercise for law students, a comical satire—not to be judged by the canons which we normally apply to Shakespeare. The range of statements that have been made about the play is as broad as can be imagined. Thus, for example, S. L. Bethell locates the problems of the piece in its "consciously philosophical" nature and Shakespeare's failure to merge the "story" and the "philosophy," so that "the story is an excuse for thought rather than the embodi-

*Reprinted from* Shakespeare Studies, *I (1965), 265–282 by permission of the author and publisher.*

[1] Jerome H. Buckley, *Tennyson: The Growth of a Poet* (Cambridge, Mass., 1960), p. 257.

ment of thought"[2]; while on the other hand Robert Kimbrough explains what he finds anomalous in the play by arguing that "the plot has no central drive, no consistent argument": Shakespeare has been too little willing to sacrifice the conventions which he has inherited from several traditions to achieve an intellectually coherent whole. "War and lechery generally confound all, but this overall theme has no general reverberation or universal ring as developed in this play. It opens in confusion and merely moves through more confusion to less confusion."[3] The play is damned on the one hand for the primacy of its theme, on the other for its themelessness.

For both of these critics the heart of the problem is the relation of "theme" or animating idea to action; and it should be noted that such critics as have achieved a measure of success with the play—Una Ellis-Fermor and L. C. Knights, for example—have done so precisely by confronting the question of the involvement of the theme in the play.[4] Not to recognize the extent to which an underlying idea relates the discrete elements of *Troilus and Cressida* to one another and explains Shakespeare's disposition of events is dangerously to misunderstand both the play's technique and its meaning. Ideas have a life in this play that they rarely have on the stage. What gives them that life is the way in which, built into a double-plot structure, they are made dramatic. *Troilus and Cressida* is perhaps the most brilliant of all instances of the double plot, that convention which gives a play the power to convey a complex theme implicitly through action and ironic language.[5] Through the use of the double plot, as in other ways through other conventions, Shakespeare and his contemporaries turned ideas into theater so that the two could scarcely be separated. Our understanding

---

[2] S. L. Bethell, *Shakespeare and Dramatic Tradition* (London, 1948), pp. 99–105. Professor Bethell's commitment to Eliot's dramatic practice leads him to regard what sounds like a vice in my paraphrase as a special virtue. The fact that he happens to be attracted to a drama that demands "dual consciousness" on the part of an audience attending to a story and a "philosophy" that work in opposite directions is not the issue with which I am concerned here though it is challenging. The point is rather that Professor Bethell sees a conflict between the play and its theme.

[3] Robert Kimbrough, "The *Troilus* Log," *SQ*, XV (1964), 205–206. Professor Kimbrough elaborates his argument in *Shakespeare's Troilus and Cressida and Its Setting* (Cambridge, Mass., 1964).

[4] Una Ellis-Fermor, " 'Discord in the Spheres': The Universe of *Troilus and Cressida*," *The Frontiers of Drama*, 3rd ed. (London, 1948); L. C. Knights, "The Theme of Appearance and Reality in *Troilus and Cressida*," *Some Shakespearean Themes* (London, 1959). A convenient summary of recent criticism of *Troilus and Cressida* can be found in Mary Ellen Rickey, " 'Twixt the Dangerous Shores: *Troilus and Cressida* Again," *SQ*, XV (1964), 3–13. Professor Rickey's own argument, that the unifying theme of the play is a corruption which consists in mistaking "prideful will and appetite" for honor and glory, will be seen to have its parallels to my own reading, though it stops short of seeing the uses to which this idea is put in the play, and the larger theme which it serves.

[5] I have attempted to formulate a statement about the nature and history of the convention in "The Double Plot: Notes on the History of a Convention," *Renaissance Drama*, I (1964), 55–69.

of the significance of the double plot has long since enriched our understanding of a number of Shakespeare's plays.[6] I should like to argue, by an analysis of the structure of *Troilus and Cressida,* that "the primary reason for [the play's] baffling, ambivalent final effect lies" not, as Professor Kimbrough claims, "with Shakespeare,"[7] but with our failure to recognize in Shakespeare's use of a dominant convention of his theater the key to the meaning of one of his greatest plays.

Despite the smoothness of the bond between them, *Troilus and Cressida* presents two distinct plots, as independent of one another as any in Shakespeare: the affair between Troilus and Cressida on the one hand, and the Greek ruse to bring Achilles back into the war and thus end it on the other. Each plot, or action, has its own beginning, middle, and end, and would in itself constitute a strong enough line for a play of its own; neither plot depends for its outcome on the course of the other. Even in such scenes as the Trojan council meeting, where Troilus irrelevantly speaks of the taking of a wife, or the exchange of the prisoners, which deeply concerns the progress of each action, the two plot lines remain separate. With its discrete plots which paradoxically seem to comprise a unified action, *Troilus and Cressida* resembles other plays in which Shakespeare modifies the convention of the double plot—*A Midsummer Night's Dream* and *King Lear,* for example, where we begin with a strong sense of separate plot lines only to learn that they are inextricably intertwined. Whether the illusion Shakespeare creates in a given play is that the actions are independent of one another or that they are, as in *Troilus and Cressida,* part of a complex and integrated whole, the result is always a structural sophistication so purely Shakespearean that perhaps we should not be suprised at the reluctance of centuries to recognize a shared convention in the double plots of Shakespeare and his contemporaries.

In *Troilus and Cressida* the double plot structure makes possible a thematic exposition, aesthetic rather than conceptual despite the philosophizing for which the play is so remarkable, that makes one realize most poignantly the inadequacy of rational analysis. Only by observing particulars in the order in which they appear, by considering each moment of the play in the contexts of both the whole play and the point at which it occurs, and by recognizing the effects achieved by the parallels between the autonomous plots can we stay clear of the traps into which the critic tempted

---

6 William Empson's "Double Plots" in *Some Versions of Pastoral,* first published in 1935, has been seminal, particularly with respect to *Troilus and Cressida* and *1 Henry IV,* though his discussions of those plays are more valuable for the avenues they open than for the conclusions they reach. Two recent studies which exemplify the kind of light double-plot analysis can shed on Shakespeare are Cecil C. Seronsy, " 'Supposes' as the Unifying Theme in *The Taming of the Shrew.*" *SQ,* XIV (1963), 15–30, and R. W. Dent, "Imagination in *A Midsummer Night's Dream,*" *SQ,* XV (1964), 115–130.

7 Kimbrough, "The *Troilus* Log," p. 205.

to make *a priori* statements may fall. My concern is thematic, to be sure. I am not, however, interested in formulating a "one- or two-word subject about which the [play] makes an ineffable statement," but rather with determining by an inductive reading of the whole play the principle which unifies and gives meaning to its discrete elements.[8] The analysis of a work whose genius is primarily structural must itself be structural.

Like a glittering and intricate spiderweb, the totality of the play seems implicated in its every node. Almost any point will do for a start. Let us take the end of the second scene, for example. Watching the heroes return from battle, Cressida and Pandarus have been fencing with each other, Pandarus maladroitly attempting to arouse his niece's interest in a young man toward whom she shows every evidence of indifference. As her uncle leaves, however, Cressida tells us that she actually prizes Troilus more than Pandarus can praise him:

> Yet hold I off. Women are angels, wooing:
> Things won are done; joy's soul lies in the doing.
> That she belov'd knows naught that knows not this:
> Men prize the thing ungain'd more than it is.[9] (I, ii, 312–315)

Conveyed in the first sententious speech of the play, Cressida's pessimism comes as a greater shock than the more conventional cynicism she has been demonstrating to her uncle, and is an important touch in a character study which will attempt to explain a notoriously inexplicable infidelity. But, like many such speeches in Shakespeare, Cressida's scene-ending soliloquy does not merely characterize: it raises a question. Is she right? Has a moment no value beyond its duration? Is expectation more satisfying than fulfillment? Is there no survival value in achievement?

As might be expected, Shakespeare is not overtly setting out the

---

[8] Sheldon Sacks, *Fiction and the Shape of Belief* (Berkeley and Los Angeles, 1964), p. 3. Professor Sacks' strictures against the casual use of the concept of "theme" are valuable (e.g., pp. 55–60). Like him, I find myself most concerned not with a writer's beliefs but with the "discernible and vital shape" such beliefs take in his works. Employing Professor Sacks' critical terminology, one might usefully study Shakespeare's plays in terms of their varying uses of the techniques of "represented action" and "apologue"; one of the things one might discover is that *Troilus and Cressida* disturbs its critics and inspires the kind of criticism it does because it is more like an "apologue" than most of Shakespeare's other plays. The debates, followed by episodes which seem to "prove" one or another position taken in them, are unusual in Shakespeare. And so is the fact that most readers, I suspect, though moved by the play's outcome, care less about the individual fates of the characters than they do about the thesis that has been made so painfully operative in the play's world by the end. Since my study is not taxonomic, however, I am not here concerned with proving that *Troilus and Cressida* is an "apologue."

[9] My text is George Lyman Kittredge, *The Complete Works of Shakespeare* (Boston, 1936).

thematic conclusion of the play, but he is preparing us for the exposition, sounding his theme in the minor so that we will think back, often and crucially, to Cressida's statement as new facets of the theme are revealed. Already we may be called back by the odd similarity of Cressida's self-justification to a remark that Troilus has just made, with savage irony, in the only other soliloquy so far in the play:

> Peace, you ungracious clamours! peace, rude sounds!
> Fools on both sides, Helen must needs be fair
> When with your blood you daily paint her thus! (I, i, 91–93)

Helen's value, that is, lies in the doing: if so many men fight for her, she must be worth fighting for. Like Cressida's soliloquy. Troilus' sardonic jibe merely foreshadows the arguments to come as to the subjectivity of value;[10] but like hers it has a dramatic significance that no one can miss who knows the old story, for, finding the fickle Helen "too starved a subject" for his sword, Troilus immediately and ironically turns to the praise of Cressida.

His theme adumbrated in the love plot, Shakespeare now begins to develop it in the war plot. Listening to the elaborate argumentation of the first Greek council scene (I, iii), the audience may be rather surprised to recognize in a discussion of matters that seem far removed from the love life of the Trojans a concern with the same questions that have already been raised within the walls of Ilium. Why have the gods prolonged the war for seven years? asks Agamemnon. The answer: because Jove wants to make trial of men. When fortune smiles all men seem alike in quality.

> But in the wind and tempest of her frown
> Distinction, with a broad and pow'rful fan,
> Puffing at all, winnows the light away,
> And what hath mass or matter, by itself
> Lies rich in virtue and unmingled. (I, iii, 26–30)

With comic alacrity the aged Nestor catches his commander's drift. Whatever it tells us about his intellectual independence, Nestor's repetition of the idea clarifies and reinforces it. He is neither the first nor the last Shakespearean character to make a statement which we must take more seriously than we do its speaker, and his performance here exemplifies Shakespeare's capacity simultaneously to strengthen dramatic illusion and to advance the theme. When the sea is smooth all boats seem equally competent, Nestor observes, but when it storms only the stoutest survive: "Even so/Doth valour's show and valour's worth divide/In storms of fortune" (I, iii, 45–47).

Again a metaphysical question underlies the speeches: what is the

10 The most lucid summary of the arguments over value in *Troilus and Cressida* is Miss Ellis-Fermor's. Her conclusion, that Shakespeare is attacking all value, is not mine.

value of a man? When can one be sure of that value? The answer suggested by Agamemnon and Nestor is that, as the medium in which fortune distributes adversity, time will ultimately distinguish true value. As the play develops, the idea of time as a process which defines and identifies value will grow increasingly complex and important as its role in both actions becomes clear; here it is being suggested for the first time, and as yet it may not seem particularly relevant.[11]

What follows immediately has all too often been taken as a formulation of the play's theme. Ulysses' great sermon on "the specialty of rule" delights the ear and lingers in the memory; it is a gorgeously imagined setting of an Elizabethan commonplace. Moreover, it is crucial in the play. Seldom if ever, however, does such a set piece explicitly enunciate the theme of a play by Shakespeare, and we should not simply assume that it does here. Brief reflection, in fact, should be sufficient for the realization that Ulysses' remarks do not hit dead center. What he does is to make us aware of the urgency of the Greeks' situation, of the dire condition of a society which has lost its old order, and of the dangers of surrendering reason to will, passion, and power. These concerns are indeed highly relevant to what goes wrong in both plots, and parallel in philosophical assumption to the debate about reason and passion; but they do not comprise the ultimate statement to be made about the universe of the play. When Ulysses so persuasively pictures the shaking of degree he is merely describing, not explaining; one might similarly account for juvenile delinquency by pointing out that many young people have lost their respect for established values. Ulysses' speech carries our attention from seven years of stalemate and the concern of the great generals to the delinquency of Achilles without allowing us to think of the latter as less important than the former, and this is a significant function: if the crucial understanding of Achilles' own attitude, at the center of the subplot, is reserved for a later point, its significance has at least been clearly signalled. But the comfortable ideas about order and disorder so often cited —most notably by Tillyard—as the chief importance of the speech do not really begin to answer the questions the play has been asking.

The idea which most looks forward to vigorous development in the play is that of time, whose winnowing function has been described by Agamemnon and Nestor. Already in this scene Ulysses, who is to make the play's most famous speech about time, speaks of it in an odd fashion as he proposes his trick to Nestor:

> I have a young conception in my brain;
> Be you my time to bring it to some shape. (I, iii, 312–313)

[11] L. C. Knights, p. 82, calls attention to the importance of time in the world of *Troilus and Cressida.*

Time is thus a midwife, attendant at an organic process. As he unfolds his plan. Ulysses continues to talk in the language of birth and growth:

> Blunt wedges rive hard knots. The seeded pride,
> That hath to this maturity blown up
> In rank Achilles must or now be cropp'd,
> Or, shedding, breed a nursery of like evil
> To overbulk us all. (I, iii, 316–320)

The imagery of the nursery takes us back to Agamemnon's account of the seven years' failure:

> Checks and disasters
> Grow in the veins of actions highest rear'd,
> As knots, by the conflux of meeting sap,
> Infects the sound pine, and diverts his grain,
> Tortive and errant from his course of growth. (I, iii, 5–9)

Ulysses' organic description of time finds its echo almost immediately in Nestor's response. Proposing an encounter between Hector and Achilles, the old man suggests that the success of the event

> Shall give a scantling
> Of good or bad unto the general;
> And in such indexes (although small pricks
> To their subsequent volumes) there is seen
> The baby figure of the giant mass
> Of things to come at large. (I, iii, 341–346)

Thus, by the end of the first council scene our attention has been drawn to a question of value and to a notion of time. How these matters are to be related to the play's theme is a larger question that in characteristically Shakespearean fashion withholds its question until later. But after the scurrilous interlude in which we first see Achilles, Ajax, and Thersites, the play takes up these matters again. Once again the scene is a council meeting, this time within Troy. And once again, as if to underline the symmetry between I, iii and II, ii, rational men make a mockery of reason: as Ulysses in the Greek camp both praised and exemplified the reason that stands in opposition to the universal wolf of appetite, yet found no better use for his reason than to trick Achilles, so Hector in Troy sees and rationally understands what action is necessary, yet impulsively acts against his own decision. Like the scene before Agamemnon's tent, the scene in Priam's palace concerns the war plot, but at a crucial moment in the argument Troilus reveals that his own attitude toward the return of Helen is based on his attitude toward Cressida; and at this moment the developing theme of the play begins to coalesce.

Like the Greeks, the Trojans are reassessing their situation; and like them they discover almost immediately that the attempt to justify what is happening to them leads to a discussion of value.

> *Hect.* Brother, she is not worth what she doth cost
> The holding.
> *Tro.* What's aught but as 'tis valu'd?

During the course of the argument, Troilus lets us understand what he meant, in the play's first soliloquy, by his jibe at Helen. To Hector, Helen's value is an objective quantity which, measured against the manhood lost in her defense, makes her surrender a moral necessity: "What merit's in that reason which denies/The yielding of her up?" Reason is the key word here, for objective evaluation is a rational process. And Troilus recognizes that reason is precisely the challenge he must answer:

> Nay, if we talk of reason,
> Let's shut our gates and sleep. Manhood and honour
> Should have hare hearts, would they but fat their thoughts
> With this cramm'd reason. Reason and respect
> Make livers pale and lustihood deject.

Distrustful of reason's ability to find excuses for selfish behavior—as indeed it does later when Hector backs out of his fight with Ajax on rational grounds—Troilus self-consciously espouses an irrational position:

> I take to-day a wife, and my election
> Is led on in the conduct of my will,
> My will enkindled by mine eyes and ears,
> Two traded pilots 'twixt the dangerous shores
> Of will and judgment. How may I avoid,
> Although my will distaste what it elected,
> The wife I chose? There can be no evasion
> To blench from this and to stand firm by honour.

Judgment may err in choice; will is changeable. All that is left is commitment, fidelity to the choices one has made regardless of the consequences; and committed behavior actually creates the worth of the object to which it is committed. From the sarcastic "O theft most base,/That we have stol'n what we do fear to keep" (II, ii, 93–94) it is a short distance to "But I would have the soil of her fair rape/Wip'd off in honourable keeping her" (II, ii,149–150). Helen has only such value as her defenders create—but that value is absolute.

Heroic, faithful, selfless, touching as Troilus' asseveration is, our accord with it is shortly to be subjected to considerable strain when we first meet Helen. From Euripides—perhaps even from Homer—to Giraudoux the story of Helen's rape has captivated the literary imagination because it so neatly puts the question: should the Trojan war, or any war, have been fought? This is the question that Shakespeare too is asking. Having set up Troilus' justification for the keeping of Helen, Shakespeare dramatically demolishes it within the same debate, even before Helen is introduced. "No marvel," Helenus remarks acidly to Troilus, "though you bite so sharp at reasons,/You are so empty of them" (II, ii, 34–35); and Hector makes a similar charge:

Or is your blood
So madly hot that no discourse of reason,
Nor fear of bad success in a bad cause,
Can qualify the same? (II, ii, 115–118)

Opposed to reason, after all, is will, almost synonymous in Shakespeare's English with blood. "The reasons you allege," Hector points out, "do more conduce/To the hot passion of distemp'red blood,/Than to make up a free determination/'Twixt right and wrong" (II, ii, 168–171). Hector objects that in rejecting reason in evaluation Troilus is committing himself to the dangers of subjectivity. "But value dwells not in particular *will,*" he argues, because the value of an object resides within the object:

'Tis mad idolatry
To make the service greater than the god;
And the will dotes that is attributive
To what infectiously itself affects,
Without some image of th' affected merit.

Will is the issue, then. Is Hector right in arguing that reason perceives value, or is Troilus in proposing that will projects value upon the object? Shakespeare insists that we be at least aware of the consequences of Troilus' belief, for the hero's most persuasive argument (II, ii, 61–96) is ended by the unanswerable screams of Cassandra:

Our firebrand brother Paris burns us all.
Cry Trojans, cry! a Helen and a woe!
Cry, cry! Troy burns, or else let Helen go.

The compressed argumentation of II, ii, then, has spelled out a dialectic that we have already seen developed in the first council scene; even more interestingly, it has translated that dialectic from its first adumbration in the initial soliloquies of the hero and heroine of the love plot to parallel arguments about will by Ulysses and Hector in the political world of the war plot. Most interesting of all, through a bold device Shakespeare calls attention to the symmetrically matched investigations of a single metaphysical question in the two plots. At the climax of Troilus' argument, the moment at which he must most convincingly advocate his proto-existentialist ethic, the willful hero makes an analogy between the two actions in which he is concerned:

> I take to-day a wife, and my election
> Is led on in the conduct of my will,
> My will enkindled by mine eyes and ears...

As a recent editor shrewdly notices, "the analogy between Troilus' choosing a wife and the rape of Helen as an act of revenge is, of course, a very false one."[12] But—as it will take the rest of the play to show—the analogy has a point. Immediately one sees the similarity between Helen and Cressida as foci of action who by one standard are worthless, and by another infinitely valuable.

In the main plot Cressida is going to remain the focus of the question of value. In the subplot, however, the same question is going to be asked most insistently not about Helen but about Achilles. Thus, avoiding the symmetry another dramatist might have attempted, Shakespeare creates the illusion of a universe that is not only coherent but also multitudinously rich. The kaleidoscopic fashion in which the dramatist begins to formulate the theme in his subplot in terms of one character only to complete it in terms of another is one of the marks of his genius in the play.

The next scene begins as another depressing interlude in which Achilles, Ajax, Thersites, and company revile each other—note how little of the Troilus and Cressida plot has been generated so far—but the scene grows more significant as Troilus' question, "What's aught but as 'tis valu'd?" becomes Achilles' question. The warrior has "much attribute," Agamemnon concedes to Patroclus; yet, because Achilles does not regard his own virtues virtuously, because he is "in self-assumption greater/Than in the note of judgment," because he overvalues himself, Achilles is losing the respect of his colleagues. There is a fatal disparity between the actual, inherent value of the hero, and the opinion of that value which Achilles holds. "Imagin'd worth," in Ulysses' words,

> Holds in his blood such swol'n and hot discourse
> That 'twixt his mental and his active parts
> Kingdom'd Achilles in commotion rages
> And batters down himself.

Like Hector talking of Troilus, Ulysses identifies overvaluation with blood, and the notion of will runs through his entire criticism of Achilles; even Hector's charge of idolatry ("'Tis mad idolatry/To make the service

---

[12] *Troilus and Cressida,* ed. Alice Walker, (Cambridge, 1957), p. 169.

greater than the god") finds an echo in Ulysses' "Shall he be worshipp'd/Of that we hold an idol more than he?" The question, what is Achilles? has not yet been formulated as it will be in coming scenes; but in the elaborately planned manner of *Troilus and Cressida* the materials have been gathered to make it possible.

In terms of both plot and theme, the exposition of the play is now over in both actions and the development section about to begin. Each plot has presented a woman who, because of the attitudes of those about her, raises the metaphysical question of value; and each has introduced as central male character a man whose patently exaggerated evaluation—of Cressida in Troilus' case, of himself in Achilles'—has been attacked as willful, a matter of blood by a character notably concerned with reason and its relation to social order. As the third act opens, Shakespeare leads us back to the love plot. He does so, however, in such a way as to keep alive in his audience's mind its similarity to the war plot, for the scurrilous episode between Helen and Pandarus plainly parallels the similar episode with which the preceding scene opened. Two passages (others might be cited) exemplify Shakespeare's technique:

II, iii

*Ther*. Agamemnon is a fool; Achilles is a fool; Thersites is a fool; and, as aforesaid, Patroclus is a fool.
*Achil*. Derive this, come.
*Ther*. Agamemnon is a fool to offer to command Achilles; Achilles is a fool to be commanded of Agamemnon; Thersites is a fool to serve such a fool; and Patroclus is a fool positive.
*Patr*. Why am I a fool?
*Ther*. Make that demand to the Creator. It suffices me thou art.

III, i

*Helen*. In love, i' faith, to the very tip of the nose!
*Par*. He eats nothing but doves, love, and that breeds hot blood, and hot blood begets hot thoughts, and hot thoughts beget hot deeds, and hot deeds is love.
*Pan*. Is this the generation of love —hot blood, hot thoughts, and hot deeds? Why they are vipers! Is love a generation of vipers?

The alacrity of such critics as Professor O. J. Campbell to agree with Thersites that in *Troilus and Cressida* "all the argument is a whore, and a cuckold" is easy enough to understand when in contiguous scenes, set in the play's two worlds, reason is so symmetrically travestied.[13] But it is important to observe that the milieux of Achilles and Ajax and of Pandarus and Helen are, though strikingly similar, only one level of a play in which moral seriousness is almost ubiquitous: even Cressida's betrayal, it is clear, has its philosophical basis.[14]

---

13 O. J. Campbell, *Comicall Satyre and Shakespeare's Troilus and Cressida* (San Marino, 1938).

14 See Empson (p. 39) on the function in *Troilus and Cressida* of "the comic character's low jokes" in establishing the play's unity.

As the scene in which Troilus and Cressida finally get together, III, ii stands at the center of the play. Not surprisingly, it picks up and develops the still emerging theme of the piece, once again simultaneously exposing a number of that theme's facets, but this time fully revealing it. In the first place, as everyone has noticed, the sensuality of Troilus' language gives away the quality of his love; more interestingly, it affirms the accuracy of Hector's unanswered charge that Troilus is moved by will, or blood, rather than by reason:

> I am giddy; expectation whirls me round.
> Th' imaginary relish is so sweet
> That it enchants my sense. What will it be
> When that the wat'ry palates taste indeed
> Love's thrice-repured nectar?

But this is not all. In his fear that expectation must exceed fulfillment—"This is the monstruosity in love, lady, that the will is infinite and the execution confin'd, that the desire is boundless and the act a slave to limit"—the lover shows himself in precise agreement with Cressida's initial reason for withholding herself from love: "Men prize the thing ungain'd more than it is."

Again: what is the relation between the thing and the value men place on it? Such repeated asking of the question—in relation to Achilles, his reputation, and his opinion of himself; to Helen, her intrinsic worthlessness, and the value that has already produced seven years of war; and now to the love of Troilus and Cressida—makes us recognize the justice of the epithet "problem play." As Troilus suggests a position new for him, the crucial scene hints at the play's answer to its basic question:

> Praise us as we are tasted; allow us as we prove. Our head shall go bare till merit crown it. No perfection in reversion shall have a praise in present. We will not name desert before his birth, and, being born, his addition shall be humble. (III, ii, 97–101)

With its suggestion that time will tell, Troilus' speech recalls the words of Agamemnon and Nestor at the Greek council meeting; moreover, it picks up the organic metaphors in which first Agamemnon, then Ulysses, and finally Nestor couched their discussion of time. In a climactic scene of the love plot Shakespeare is beginning to draw such images together in a significant pattern. Though its meaning does not yet become clear, the pattern emerges dramatically in the words of Troilus. We have heard once before, in Agamemnon's opening speech, of the winnowing function of time. Now, hopefully, Troilus inquires as to the probability of a fidelity in Cressida that might withstand the decay of the blood: he wishes that his

> integrity and truth to you
> Might be affronted with the match and weight
> Of such a *winnowed* purity in love!

How were I then uplifted! But, alas,
I am as true as truth's simplicity
And simpler than *the infancy of truth.*

The connection between Troilus and "unpractis'd infancy" (I, i, 12), the establishment of Troilus as one who "with great truth catch[es] mere simplicity" (IV, iv, 106), the notion of Troilus as innocent and faithful remain constants through the play. But of far greater significance is the picture of truth, like time, as an organic entity, something that has an infancy and a maturity. We shall hear more of it.

Immediately, however, follows one of the most striking dramatic moments in the play, and here it is that the argumentation of the play moves from dialogue into staged action as, through the use of a dramatic irony powerfully grounded in his audience's familiarity with the old story and the terms it has lent their language, Shakespeare allows a ritualistic tableau to act out for us what will happen when time, now in its infancy, shall grow old:

*Tro.* True swains in love shall in the world to come
Approve their truths by Troilus. When their rhymes,
Full of protest, of oath, and big compare,
Want similes, truth tir'd with iteration—
'As true as steel, as plantage to the moon,
As sun to day, as turtle to her mate,
As iron to adamant, as earth to th' centre'—
Yet, after all comparisons of truth,
As truth's authentic author to be cited,
'As true as Troilus' shall crown up the verse
And sanctify the numbers.
*Cres.* Prophet may you be!
If I be false, or swerve a hair from truth,
When time is old and hath forgot itself,
When water drops have worn the stones of Troy,
And blind oblivion swallow'd cities up,
And mighty states characterless are grated
To dusty nothing—yet let memory,
From false to false, among false maids in love,
Upbraid my falsehood! When th' have said, 'as false
As air, as water, wind, or sandy earth,
As fox to lamb, or wolf to heifer's calf,
Pard to the hind, or stepdame to her son'—
'Yea,' let them say, to stick the heart of falsehood,
'As false as Cressid.'

*Pan.* Go to, a bargain made! Seal it, seal it; I'll be the witness. Here I hold your hand; here my cousin's. If ever you prove false one to another, since I have taken such pain to bring you together, let all pitiful goers-between be called to the world's end after my name; call them all Pandars. Let all constant men be Troiluses, all false women Cressids, and all brokers-between Pandars! Say 'Amen.'

The debates in *Troilus and Cressida* may well be the most magnificent staged argumentation since Aeschylus. But the real measure of the play's greatness is to be taken at such moments as this, where an argument which originates as an abstraction from human experience is reëmbodied in such experience to give the illusion of life. Shakespeare is not telling us about time's function in determining value: he is showing us, and what he shows us is the theme of the play. The Troilus who has seen "the infancy of truth" will live to see his Cressida betray him before his eyes, and to exclaim "O withered truth" (V, ii, 46). And what will have happened in the time in which truth passes through its life-cycle will be the ironic fulfillment of each of the prophecies at the ritualistic ending of III, ii.

To suggest the nature and role of time in *Troilus and Cressida,* let me, recalling the notion of the spiderweb-like structure of the play, move forward for a moment to the beginning of IV, iii when Paris announces that the day of Cressida's removal to the Greek camp has arrived.

> It is great morning, and the hour prefix'd
> For her delivery to this valiant Greek
> Comes fast upon.

Steevens glossed "great morning" as "*Grand jour,* a Gallicism," and Delius noted in 1856 that the same phrase occurs in *Cymbeline,* IV, ii, 62.[15] No other explanation of the lines has ever been offered. Editors might well have referred us to another sense of "great" in *Pericles,* V, i, 107: "I am great with woe, and shall deliver weeping." In the passage in *Troilus and Cressida* as in the one in *Pericles,* "great" means "pregnant," indicating a condition that culminates in "delivery." The incessant personification of time in *Troilus and Cressida* is astonishing. Time is a monster, a witch, an arbitrator, a robber, a fashionable host; it is envious and calumniating, grows old and forgets itself, and walks hand in hand with Nestor. To recognize such a treatment of time, one need not agree with Professor G. Wilson Knight that time is the "arch-enemy," the issue on which the "love-interest turns";[16] but one must note the play's peculiar emphasis on the organic, almost personal nature of metaphysical process. The answer to Troilus' optimistic faith in the world's ability to meet his expectations of it is roundly answered by what the end of III, ii tells us: Cressida, like Troilus and Pandarus, is defined not by wishful thinking but by what each will become in time, and action which is not guided by that realization is going to come a cropper.[17]

---

[15] *Troilus and Cressida,* ed. H. N. Hillebrand, New Variorum ed. (Philadelphia, 1953), p. 212.

[16] *The Wheel of Fire* (New York, 1957), pp. 65, 68.

[17] The view of A. S. Knowland, in *"Troilus and Cressida," SQ,* X (1959), that time is identical in the play with mutability is an oversimplification, failing to note the organic metaphors constantly used to describe time's nature and action.

At the center of the play, then, the theme which has been taking shape from the beginning has become full and clear. As if by design, Shakespeare chooses this moment to stage the turning point in the action of the main plot, the making of the bargain which will send Cressida to the Greeks. The trade of prisoners naturally involves the war as well as the private affairs of Troilus and so we are back in the war subplot almost immediately. Again, if the play's structure is not a matter of conscious design, one must marvel at the intuitive genius which arranges that, immediately after the climactic exposition of the theme of the relation of time to value in the main plot, that theme should be dramatized with equal emphasis and clarity in the subplot. Thematically, III, ii and III, iii, one in the main, the other in the subplot, are the crucial scenes of the entire play.

Ulysses' trick has worked, and the neglected Achilles is driven to investigate the cause of the derision he sees aimed at him. Merit, he sees, has little to do with reputation:

> And not a man for being simply man
> Hath any honour, but honour for those honours
> That are without him, as place, riches, and favour,
> Prizes of accident as oft as merit.
> ...I do enjoy
> At ample point all that I did possess
> Save these men's looks, who do methinks find out
> Something not worth in me such rich beholding,
> As they have often given.

Claiming like Hamlet to paraphrase the book he is reading, Ulysses offers Achilles an explanation of his predicament that Cassius had once given to Brutus (in *Julius Caesar,* I, ii, 52ff.): man "Cannot make boast to have that which he hath,/Nor feels not what he owes, but by reflection." One perceives one's own value, that is, by seeing it reflected in the opinions of others. Pretending to find the position difficult to accept, Ulysses continues its exposition: if value is subject to the judgment of others, then "no man is the lord of any thing...Till he communicate his parts to others." Therefore, Achilles' qualities are forgotten while those of Ajax, "a very horse," receive universal admiration. "What things again most dear in the esteem,/And poor in worth!" Ulysses exclaims. Having noticed that his deeds do seem to have been forgotten, Achilles cannot deny what Ulysses has been saying, and he is ready to hear his shrewd opponent's explanation of the shortness of reputation:

> Time hath, my lord, a wallet at his back,
> Wherein he puts alms for oblivion,
> A great-siz'd monster of ingratitudes.
> Those scraps are good deeds past, which are devour'd
> As fast as they are made, forgot as soon

As done. Perseverance, dear my lord,
Keeps honour bright. To have done is to hang
Quite out of fashion, like a rusty mail
In monumental mock'ry.

How many moments of the play crystallize here: not only what Agamemnon and Nestor have already told us about time's determination of value, but also all that we have learned in the last scene; not only Achilles' discovery that what he has done will not retain its lustre but must be constantly renewed, but also Cressida's intuition of the ultimate reality of process ("Things won are done"):

Let not virtue seek
Remuneration for the thing it was! for beauty, wit,
High birth, vigour of bone, desert in service,
Love, friendship, charity, are subjects all
To envious and calumniating Time.

Ulysses' speech is profoundly pessimistic. For if the love plot has been telling us that value resides not in the valuer (Troilus, Achilles), but in the true nature of the object (Cressida, Achilles), the war plot makes explicit what the ritual at the end of III, ii dramatized: even the value in the object itself will be defined—and generally that definition is by a process of erosion—by time. By the kind of irony that the double plot in the hands of a master makes possible, the point is dramatically reinforced. As Achilles laments the course his career has taken in time, arrangements are in the making to take Cressida away from Troilus while simultaneously the lovers are enjoying what they take to be the sealing of their love's compact. When we next see Troilus he will be innocent of his impending loss, and the irony will recur. And when Troilus discovers the grim irony of his happiness, he will respond to it in a terse remark that Achilles might as well have made to Ulysses: "How my achievements mock me" (IV, ii, 71).[18]

His theme established, Shakespeare will vary it for the rest of the play in ways that it is not necessary, after so much analysis, to describe. A few points, however, in which the double-plot structure continues to make itself felt deserve brief notice. One is a new version of the question of merit, noteworthy because it applies—and is applied by the audience—even more vividly to a character in the main plot than to the subplot character it ostensibly describes. Paris asks Diomedes whether Menelaus or Paris himself "deserves fair Helen best." Diomedes, who as everyone in the audience knows is going to be Cressida's next lover—her Paris, as it were—answers as follows:

[18] It is significant that Ulysses has already complained that Achilles and Patroclus mock Greek "achievements" (I, iii, 81).

Both alike.
He merits well to have her that doth seek her,
Not making any scruple of her soilure,
With such a hell of pain and world of charge;
And you as well to keep her, that defend her,
Not palating the taste of her dishonour,
With such a costly loss of wealth and friends.
He like a puling cuckold would drink up
The lees and dregs of a flat tamed piece;
You, like a lecher, out of whorish loins
Are pleas'd to breed out your inheritors.
Both merits pois'd, each weighs nor less nor more;
But he as he, the heavier for a whore. (IV, i, 54–64)

The words precisely describe Cressida as the play's Thersites-voice might describe her in transit between Troilus and Diomedes. The predominant and unpleasant imagery of eating and drinking is only a version of Troilus' characteristic language in love.[19] The dregs to which Helen is reduced in masculine opinion hark back too neatly to be overlooked to an earlier prophecy:

*Tro.* What too curious dreg espies my sweet lady in the fountain of our love?
*Cres.* More dregs than water, if my fears have eyes. (III, ii, 73–75)

And, in the dazzling manner in which *Troilus and Cressida* works, giving the impression of a blinding flash, a single aesthetic moment, rather than of a discursive composition, Cressida's last note has already had its significant echo in Achilles' pain in the scene that follows it:

My mind is troubled like a fountain stirr'd,
And I myself see not the bottom of it. (III, iii, 308–309)

By its last acts the play vibrates at almost every point with this sort of cross-reference. Thus IV, v, a scene crucial to both plots, is larded with motifs and with variants of the theme. Let two excerpts speak for themselves. Agamemnon greets Hector:

Understand more clear,
What's past and what's to come is strew'd with husks
And formless ruin of oblivion;
But in this extant moment, faith and troth,
Strain'd purely from all hollow bias-drawing,
Bids thee with most divine integrity
From heart of very heart, great Hector, welcome.
(IV, v, 166–172)

---

[19] Though her interpretation of the phenomenon attempts, as often, to say more about Shakespeare than about what he is doing in a particular play, Miss Spurgeon astutely notices the "extraordinary number of food and cooking images in *Troilus*," *Shakespeare's Imagery and What It Tells Us* (Cambridge, 1935), Chart VI. Troilus' speech as he awaits Cressida *chez* Pandarus (III, ii, 20 ff.) is typical.

And Hector says a few moments later:

> The end crowns all,
> And that old common arbitrator, Time
> Will one day end it.

The last two acts consist primarily in the working out of the ironic prophecies in both plots. In the war plot the decision to keep Helen eventuates not in the glory that Troilus predicted, but in her continuing degradation (recall Diomedes' opinion) and in the utterly ignoble death of Hector himself, presaging the final catastrophe Cassandra has announced. Like a vengeful deity time has decided the debate in the Trojan camp. And in the love plot we have watched Cressida, in a ritualistic prefiguration of her future, passing lightly from the kisses of one Greek to the next. With Troilus we look on at her final act of betrayal; and we watch him arrive at a state, in which reason has become useless, that Ulysses has long since identified as the consequence of the behavior of Troilus' alter ego Achilles:

> O madness of discourse,
> That cause sets up with and against itself!
> Bi-fold authority, where reason can revolt
> Without perdition, and loss assume all reason
> Without revolt. This is, and is not, Cressid. (V, ii, 132–136)

As "the dragon wing of night o'erspreads the earth" (V, vii, 17)—again time is a personal force, the monster of ingratitudes, all too eager to gobble up human achievement—Achilles has ironically regained a reputation which his Myrmidons have stolen for him, and once again, even in the rush of the denouement, we are asked to contemplate the value of reputation. Troilus' last words reveal that he has learned at last the harsh reality that a man is what time proves he is, not what the optimist wishes him to be:

> Hence, broker, lackey; ignomy and shame
> Pursue thy life, and live aye with thy name.

Perhaps it is a signal of the difference between *Troilus and Cressida* and most of Shakespeare's plays that the idealistic hero, with whom for all our awareness of his error we have been led consistently to sympathize, should utter as a last speech words that so clearly reveal the diminution of his stature. Similar reduction affects us in the last appearance of other leading characters whose careers we have followed with concern: Cressida feebly chastizing herself for a disposition to follow Diomedes that she is scarcely capable of recognizing as contemptible, Achilles wretchedly crying the triumph won in fact by his roughneck vassals, Pandarus suddenly aged and bequeathing to the audience his venereal disease. Pandarus, whose coarse and heartless grumbling ends the play, is a paradigm of all the play's characters. In the magical conclusion of III, ii we have virtually seen etymology staged as Pandarus ironically prophesies the way in which he will become his name, and at the end we see the process complete. Regardless of their own intentions and the best potentialities within them, the major characters of the two plots have been transformed by a process over which none of them has control. That process is time, a time presented so consistently in organic terms that one comes finally to understand its inevitability: it grows according to its own will, not according to the desires of any individual.[20] And that process is the play's answer to the question of value: value exists not in the subjective will of the valuer or in the object he sees, but only in that object as time disposes of it. If this is not a satisfactory answer to a legitimate philosophical question, one must admit that very few readers have suspected that it was Shakespeare's intention in *Troilus and Cressida* to satisfy their skepticism or dispel their pessimism. But the play provides another kind of satisfaction which one seeks more legitimately perhaps in the theater, the aesthetic satisfaction of recognizing a structure brilliantly animated and made coherent by its complex relation to a thematic center.

If my account of *Troilus and Cressida* has been inordinately long, it has nevertheless only established the skeletal outline of the play's plan. That plan Shakespeare was shortly to modify in *King Lear,* which similarly but with even more mastery achieves a symphonic network of inner relationships that virtually defies expository analysis. In such plays the double plot has gone as far as it can go; it has become a form which, like all the great forms in the arts, is capable of saying what could not otherwise be said. I have found it almost impossible in discussing *Troilus and Cressida* not to speak at times in the language of the musicologist.[21] Though Pater's dictum that "all art constantly aspires towards the condition of music" has long since received the qualification it needs, it applies with singular aptness to Shakespeare's plays, and particularly to the double plot plays, where he makes the actions play one against the other so swiftly, so subtly, and so interdependently that they form an inseparable whole, a unity created by multiplicity. As the symphonist sets theme against theme, developing now one, now the other, intertwining and then separating them, and finally bringing his movement to a point of stasis at which the formal integrity of the whole releases a sense of completion, so, pre-eminently among the composers of double-plot plays, Shakespeare in such plays as *Troilus and Cressida* sets his plots one against the other, leading us to take pleasure from the insight afforded at each node at which they intersect, and to feel the whole only in the comprehension, conscious or unconscious, of the relation between parts.

---

[20] For a similar argument about the role of time as a figure for inevitable historical process in a play in which time is not presented organically, see Norman Rabkin, "Structure, Convention, and Meaning in *Julius Caesar,*" *JEGP,* LXIII (1964), 240–254.

[21] For a searching exploration of the appropriateness of such language to the criticism of Shakespeare, see John Palmer, *Political Characters of Shakespeare* (London, 1945), pp. 63–64.

# 20

# Shakespeare as Casuist: *Measure For Measure*

*Wylie Sypher*

Deny as we may that the dark comedies are autobiographical, our impression remains of Shakespeare going here and there in them to gore his own thoughts, to hold their equivocations in such precarious balance that they are always swinging from an allowed comic instability downward toward a moral twilight where the issues hang heavily and abstractly in doubt. *Troilus and Cressida, All's Well That Ends Well, Measure for Measure*—gradually the comedy narrows to legalistic maneuvers like the earlier tactic in *The Merchant of Venice.* But *The Merchant* at least offered Belmont, music, and the fabulous golden fleece for which Bassanio voyaged. The dramatic world of *Measure for Measure,* ruled—or not ruled—by the fantastical Duke who refuses to look too hard into dim corners, is the bleak territory of the Jacobean stage where brutality and lyric are in equipoise so venturesome that it can hardly be maintained. Vienna's darkest problems are darkly answered. In Vienna, where "there is scarce truth enough alive to make societies secure," there are laws for all faults,

> But faults so countenanc'd that the strong statutes
> Stand like the forfeits in a barber's shop,
> As much in mock as mark.

*Reprinted from* The Sewanee Review, *LVIII, (1950), No. 2 by permission of the author and publisher.*

The examination of these laws—a comic examination—is very theoretical and very intent, and does not end well. Because the Duke has not curbed Vienna's appetites during fourteen years, he undertakes a moral research: he deputes to the puritan Angelo the legal power to discipline lechery, then retires to watch Angelo's effort to violate Isabella, that hysterical virgin whose brother Claudio has got premature possession of Julietta's bed and thus is sentenced to die by Angelo's strict law. When his examination of the puritan hypocrisy is complete, the Duke reappears, reverses the law against Angelo himself, and re-establishes, with comic justice, his own genial exemption of sinners. In Vienna the quality of mercy is not strained. It drops freely upon the unholiest fellowships, which enjoy security enough to make them accurst.

With his customary acceptances G. Wilson Knight has written that the Duke, humanely tolerating the business of dark corners, represents a new Shakespearian ethic, a compassionate resignation to the illusions of life and death, a gospel dispensation, an almost mystic emancipation from sordid Vienna. This view seems charitable. The immediate comic implication, instead, is that under the good Duke there is no danger of Vienna's being unpeopled by continence. As for the moral research: the evasions of the law, the want of convincing measure for measure, the irresponsible graces of the Duke can easily be explained by the fashionable Jacobean stagecraft. Admittedly the Elizabethan and Jacobean characters are stereotyped, and the dramatic action is often so discontinuous that we cannot assign (to use Miss Bradbrook's term) any moral valency to the mercies of the Duke or even the substitution of Mariana for Isabella in the bed of Angelo. Doubtless we must allow the Jacobeans their theatrical license.

Nevertheless *Measure for Measure* is a notably dark comedy, a special revelation of a mentality of crisis, a Shakespearian center of indifference, perhaps, between the earlier comedies or tragedies and the final resolutions in *Antony and Cleopatra, Cymbeline,* and *The Tempest*. The very dramatic structure of *Measure for Measure* is an attempt to strike an equation between "mortality and mercy in Vienna." Or as Escalus asks, "Which is the wiser here, Justice or Iniquity?" Such a question, even when it is theatrically set, involves moral valencies. We do not raise the question: the comedy itself does. When Angelo suggests to Isabella the justice of saving her brother's life by her yielding to his lusts, his evil proposal is exploratory, tentative, hypothetical:

> . . . I subscribe not that, nor any other,
> But in the loss [loose?] of question.

Already Hamlet had held many questions in the loose, but these Danish speculations were temperamental—a reflex of the unhappy meditative nature of the Prince, not theoretic or abstract. In *Measure for Measure,* as in

*Troilus and Cressida,* questions are held with a kind of philosophic looseness, detached from the psychological texture of the drama, until the structure of the comedy becomes thematic.

The dramatic valency of the abstract issues is suggested by the very title *Measure for Measure,* but (if we presume that Shakespeare's intentions are disclosed in his metaphors) more directly by the image of counterfeiting and weighing that dominates the rhetoric. The central dramatic machine is the Duke's undertaking to see "the corrupt deputy scaled" (III, i). In assuming his office Angelo at once urges the Duke

> Let there be some more test made of my metal
> Before so noble and so great a figure
> Be stamp'd upon it. (I, i)

With this same image Claudio enters the close passage between mercy and mortality, complaining against Angelo

> Thus can the demigod authority
> Make us pay down for our offence by weight
> The words of heaven... (I, ii)

Isabella sustains the image, arguing that Angelo pardon Claudio because "We cannot weigh our brother with ourself" (II, ii). She will "bribe" Angelo "not with fond shekels of the tested gold" but with the chaste prayers of fasting maids (II, ii). In view of the major counterfeiting-weighing image Isabella's offer almost intimates that her extravagant virtue, her fasting prayers, her obsessional chastity are, as they prove to be, *not* "tested gold." Her very purity is a "bribe," an illegitimate tender, that may not abide the weighing. The ironic value of the counterfeiting image—particularly since Mariana is exchanged for the contracted Isabella in Angelo's bed—is doubled when Isabella pleads that she is woman and therefore frail:

> For we are soft as our complexions are,
> And credulous to false prints. (II, iv)

Her virginity—her "true" gold—is readily malleable to illegal uses. The ultimate Viennese irony, however, is Angelo's reply to Isabella, the neurotic virgin for whom the Duke manages to pass off the counterfeit Mariana in the dark: "Say what you can, my false o'erweighs your true" (II, iv). Angelo at least offers his fraud boldly. The Duke freely manipulates the same image: he is sure that Angelo only "hath made an assay of her virtue to practise his judgment" (III, i). His justice must be holy,

> More nor less to others paying
> Than by self-offences weighing. (III, ii)

And he will disguise Mariana to

> Pay with falsehood false exacting,
> And perform an old contracting. (III, ii)

It would appear that the only other play in which gold is so ulterior is *The Merchant;* there it carries a double valency: greed in Venice, romance in Belmont. In Vienna the recurrent weighing-counterfeiting figure, the attempt to strike measure for measure, suggests the balance of issues hanging in Shakespeare's mind.

The repulsive sexual imagery of the play has often been observed—Claudio's groping for trouts in a peculiar river, and Isabella's faith in authority that righteously "skins the vice o' th' top" (II, ii). When Angelo will persuade Isabella that her lying with him is "equal poise of sin and charity" (II, iv), the counterfeiting-weighing image becomes deeply involved with the sexual imagery. Angelo has just admitted "the strong and swelling evil of my conception." He cannot wink at Claudio's filthy vices on the ground that

> ...It were as good
> To pardon him that hath from nature stol'n
> A man already made, as to remit
> Their saucy sweetness that do coin Heaven's image
> In stamps that are forbid. (II, iv)

The nausea-sexual images have also been associated with the nausea-sexual images in *Hamlet.* This affiliation is closed by another image clustered in both plays with the counterfeiting-weighing-sexual-nausea images—the image of the looking-glass. A succession of three glass images occurs in the Isabella-Angelo scenes wherein Isabella comes to her recognition that the prenzie Angelo and all the law are "seeming, seeming." Angelo opens the glass-sexual image by referring Isabella to the law that

> ...like a prophet
> Looks in a glass that shows what future evils,
> Either new, or by remissness new-conceiv'd,

may be "hatch'd and born" (II, ii). Then Isabella confesses to him that women are credulous to false prints, and frail

> Ay, as the glasses where they view themselves;
> Which are as easy broke as they make forms. (II, iv)

These two images, occurring with the counterfeiting metaphors, culminate earlier in Isabella's cynical and convulsive reproach to Angelo:

...but man, proud man,
Dress'd in a little brief authority,
Most ignorant of what he's most assur'd,
His glassy essence, like an angry ape,
Plays such fantastic tricks before high heaven
As makes the angels weep; who, with our spleens,
Would all themselves laugh mortal. (II, ii)

The usual interpretation of man's glassy essence as his fragile soul doubtless conceals the same associations that cluster in Hamlet's frantic and disillusioned reproach to Gertrude: there is the same involvement—skinning vice o' th' top, counterfeiting, sexual nausea, the picture and the glass; *and* the brutality, disorder, and folly of the ape. Hamlet approaches his mother puritanically:

You go not till I set you up a glass
Where you may see the inmost part of you. (III, iv)

Then, after stabbing Polonius, he accuses Gertrude of the act that sets a blister on the fair forehead of innocent love:

Look here, upon this picture, and on this,
The counterfeit presentment of two brothers.

If Gertrude believes that his puritanical and hysteric disgust is madness, she

...will but skin and film the ulcerous place
Whilst rank corruption, mining all within,
Infects unseen.

The Queen must, tonight, refrain and lend an ease to abstinence by a counterfeit virtue, habit:

For use almost can change the stamp of nature.

As Hamlet approaches the ape-image he is afflicted by the same rhetorical fracture and abbreviation found in Isabella's glass-ape speech to Angelo; both Hamlet and Isabella are distraught by their discovery of "seeming, seeming," their new cynicism:

...'Twere good you let him know;
For who, that's but a queen, fair, sober, wise,
Would from a paddock, from a bat, a gib,
Such dear concernings hide? Who would do so?
No, in despite of sense and secrecy,
Unpeg the basket on the house's top,
Let the birds fly, and like the famous ape,

> To try conclusions, in the basket creep,
> And break your own neck down.

For Hamlet and Isabella, at their moment of most cynical insight, the symbol of human folly and irresponsibility is the ape, the gesturing, mimicking ape.

Yet the imagery in Hamlet is more internal; the Danish drama is played out far within the sensibility. The balance in Vienna between mercy and justice is thematic, a dramatic abstraction of the problem of equity to which Shakespeare gives an ambiguously hilarious answer. The situation of Angelo, not the character of Angelo, is the focus of the comedy. His corruption must be publicly scaled. The drama will be external. That is why Angelo, like Claudius, is mechanically aware of his situation, why his recognition of his sin is so clear but so unfelt, why his generalizations are so morally relevant but so psychologically irrelevant to the play. He views his guilt from a considerable distance—the distance of Claudius from his murder. Consequently he recognizes

> ...Most dangerous
> Is that temptation that doth goad us on
> To sin in loving virtue.

The conclusion is apt to Vienna, where all—Isabella and the Duke as well as Angelo—love virtue in excess. The Viennese moral crux is Angelo's baffled question upon his own hot response to the tantalizing virginity of Isabella: "The tempter or the tempted, who sins most?" The issue is before not only Angelo but Isabella, the Duke, Claudio, Mariana, and the audience. Shakespeare holds the reply in a comic shadow.

Isabella, pleading for the life of Claudio, finds herself "at war 'twixt will and will not."

> There is a vice that most I do abhor,
> And most desire should meet the blow of justice;
> For which I would not plead, but that I must.

No legal equation can compromise this war—neither the exactions by Angelo nor the exemptions by the Duke. Here, and in the courts of Venice, mercy and mortality are measured by the letter, are strained into a casuistry. G. Wilson Knight would say that the Duke suspends the precisions of the law in the name of an emancipating justice dimly comprehended but nevertheless accepted by an act of vision and faith:

> But, for those earthly faults, I quit them all;
> And pray thee take this mercy to provide
> For better times to come.

Yet impiety will continue to feast upon Vienna, and Escalus remains unanswered: "Which is the wiser here, Justice or Iniquity?" The Duke is sunny but ineffectual. His pardoning Barnardine, his benediction upon Claudio and Julietta, the quickening in Angelo's eye when he sees that he is safely matched with Mariana suggest that the laws still stand forfeit. The counterpoise of mercy and mortality remains precarious: the Duke is no Prospero. Neither is he the comic spirit, the lord of misrule, for he lacks the radiant assurance that men are legitimately and incorrigibly fools. His concern is not folly but sin; in Vienna he has "seen corruption boil and bubble 'till it o'er-run the stew." The paradox is that the Duke, attempting measure for measure, adopts a comic policy of misrule. His mercy is a sanction of license, a withdrawal of all law whatever except his own good will, a somewhat disastrous remission of order giving evil at once a clear field of operation in the person of Angelo. The question is not as Knight sees it, of enlarging a narrow law for one less parochial; it is simply the hypertrophy of mercy at the expense of justice.

The Duke's policy of misrule is a displacement of dramatic values. Ordinarily comedy strikes its equations—its measure for measure—under certain moral exemptions: according to the law of misrule, folly is legitimized. Or else the comic equation may be struck by a reversal, a contradiction: out of folly may come wisdom; out of disorder may come order. In Vienna the terms of these two separate comic equations have been displaced when the Duke's misrule—his tolerance of vice—becomes the principle of moral equity. No comic equilibrium follows, since the Duke has dislocated the comic exemptions into the alien territory of Vienna, where the need is for another, graver dispensation. Thus the play develops through a paradoxical derangement of order to a paradoxical re-establishment of order. In the moral twilight of Vienna the original indulgence of lechery is deranged by the puritanical "order" imposed by Angelo. This enforcing of the law is itself a "disorder" and gives occasion for the "comedy," the misrule, the dramatic disequilibrium. Then when the puritanical "disorder" is suspended at the return of the Duke (who is in this instance the comic lord of misrule) the mild and cynical Viennese "order" of sinning is re-instituted by the final remission of the laws against indulgence: the "comic" equation is balanced. The Duke, then, like almost everyone in the play, carries a double dramatic valency—comic irresponsibility and ethical responsibility (in this case opposed). Thus the measure of ducal justice swings in disequilibrium between comedy and the problem play. By his ambiguous policy the Duke represents both the principle of comic order( so far as he is merciful and winking) and the principle of comic disorder (so far as he withdraws his tolerance and permits Angelo to usurp the power of the law). By the same ambiguity Angelo becomes the principle of order (so far as he attacks the Viennese problem) and the principle of disorder (so far as he is the chaste villain who would hypocritically unpeople

Vienna with continence). By the same displacements Isabella is temptress (so far as she is prim) and victim (so far as Angelo is tempter). And Claudio, who has got Julietta with child, is at the same time guilty (before the necessary law) and innocent (under the injustice of the law). The comic equilibrium is always being upset by the moral displacements—or else the moral equilibrium by the comic displacements. There is no better evidence of the structural instability of this comedy, which so far as it is comic is immoral, and so far as it is moral (according to its own internal definitions) is not comic. This kind of fissure between "comedy" and "morality" does not open in the earlier and later plays. Here the issues are all held in the loose of question. The Duke occupies a position that is not tenable beyond the present Viennese occasion.

To think that he is the voice of a new gospel, a new ethics of mercy, a mystical insight is not merely to misread the play but to anticipate the authentic Shakespearian emancipation from the precisions of the law—a resolution between the letter and the spirit, the provincial and the universal, that came only in the final comedies or in *Antony and Cleopatra.* Prospero does not evade evil. The Duke does so shamelessly and benignly. His discourse on death, offered to the condemned Claudio, is no transcendental Prospero-view that we are such stuff as dreams, but rather the sort of platitude Friar Laurence had already addressed to the callow banished Romeo:

> Reason thus with life:
> If I do lose thee, I do lose a thing
> That none but fools would keep. A breath thou art,
> Service to all the skyey influences,
> That dost this habitation where thou keep'st
> Hourly afflict. Merely, thou art Death's fool...
> For thou dost fear the soft and tender fork
> Of a poor worm....

No one can question the theatrical economy and tact of such a speech, a view of death intended to console the wretched Claudio. But it is not more than theatrical tact; still less a triumphant mystic vision into our little lives and our eternal sleep. It is a rhetorical convenience, with a theatrical, not a religious, valency. To the Duke death and evil are illusory. Prospero never made this glib elocutionary mistake: Even in the seachanging island Antonio and Sebastian are unregenerate, and sin is so real and inexplicable that were he so minded Prospero could tell some tales; and the dark Caliban must at last be acknowledged his. In Vienna, on which impiety has feasted many a genial year, the Duke and Angelo and Claudio and Isabella and Barnardine and almost everyone *play* with evil—as of course in proper comedy they should. But suddenly the comedy is not properly thoughtless, and the delicate Viennese equipoise between the reckless will and the ridiculous will-not is violently shaken by Claudio's terrifying comment, as if from the blackness of the sepulcher, upon the Duke's easy rhetoric:

> Ay, but to die and go we know not where;
> To lie in cold obstruction and to rot;
> This sensible warm motion to become
> A kneaded clod, and the delighted spirit
> To bathe in fiery floods, or to reside
> In thrilling region of thick-ribb'd ice...
> ...'Tis too horrible!
> The weariest and most loathed worldly life
> That age, ache, penury, and imprisonment
> Can lay on nature is a paradise
> To what we fear of death.

Claudio's revelation—the archetypal discovery of the shade of Achilles wandering in the Cimmerian land, warning Odysseus over the empty ditch at the limits of the world—is not theatrical tact; it is heavily authentic with a desperation the Duke and the prurient Isabella cannot understand, for the Viennese mortality and mercy are too local, and the immediate comic task is only to evade or sophisticate the letter of the law and to keep it forfeit. Claudio's human terror has thrown the entire drama passionately beyond the loose of question into appalling certainties. No, *Measure for Measure* is not a new or a clear view of life. It may foretell a new view of life, an emancipation from provincial justice, but it is a center of indifference, a world of sullied motives and radiant good will, of romance and bestiality, of cleanliness and lechery, of responsibility and defection, of love and lust—and all counterpoised for the instant. In Vienna, as Angelo says, "we would, and we would not."

This brief counterpoise is really the structure of the play, which is built upon cynical repetitions. The Duke, after all, needs to face the problem he sought to elude. Angelo finds himself in Claudio's plight. Isabella, guarding her purity, necessarily passes upon her brother Claudio the same judgment as the hollow Angelo:

> O, fie, fie, fie!
> Thy sin's not accidental, but a trade.
> Mercy to thee would prove itself a bawd;
> 'Tis best that thou diest quickly.

Angelo already had said "It is the law, not I, condemn your brother." Viennese justice turns out to be only the original leniency that caused the withdrawal of the Duke. The opposed forces, the repetitions, are so strictly calculable that the very ironies of the action bear a tone of disillusion—the repressed hysteric Isabella appearing before the repressed compulsive Angelo with her explanation "I am come to know your pleasure," or the dissolute

Lucio urging Isabella's plea to Angelo with the advice "To him, I say! You are too cold." These ironies, in spite of their psychological color, are almost mechanical. The counterpositions are schematic, though the effects are indeterminate. Measure is not measure.

Such counterpositions and measures without determinate results, and irresolutely held, suggest a structure that might be called mannerist or baroque. According to one view baroque (or, more particularly, mannerism with its instabilities and disturbed accent) is a progressively arbitrary manipulation of the firm and harmonious symmetry of the Renaissance. This manipulation, a technical license, occurred with a loosening of forms, an experiment in equivalents, chiefly the daring opposition of one force unexpectedly against another, one surface against another, until movement and illusion were achieved. In architecture, for example, convex walls were swung against concave, one definite plane surface was counterpointed against another, or a succession of limited, rigid planes was arranged so that the composition appeared to "open" expansively. The mannerist or baroque painting or sculpture created its libertine movement by an illusion like that in *Measure for Measure*. The opposite forces or areas are calculable, but the effect and direction are inconclusive, spontaneous, incommensurate. A baroque tactic in painting was to establish very precise limiting planes or spaces arranged in a recessional sequence until an illusion of distance opened behind and within these circumscriptions—for instance, the views through solid Flemish rooms out into the sunlit confines of a walled and trimmed garden where the objects were diminished by forced perspective. The high Jesuitical ceilings were enclosed within painted cornices—a false architectural reference "above" which rose a succession of heavy foreshortened columns, architraves, and arches soaring "upward" into a false illimitable sky. This regress to the infinite—boundary vanishing behind boundary—is a deception essentially theatrical with a great energy that vibrates, by implication, far beyond the firmly denoted limits of the composition.

In Shakespeare's Viennese composition the arbitrary dispositions of the Duke appear to open spontaneously and generously beyond the provincial rigid statutes of the city toward a universal justice. The legal exactions are so manipulated, suspended, that the action appears to expand dynamically into a cosmic benevolence. In both instances the strategy is an implied negation of limits artificially and locally established for purely technical reasons. When these limits are negated, there appears a "release" or liberation. Since manneristic facility is always exploiting its own circumscriptions and definitions, both the definition and its negation are a theatrical figment, a contrivance, an effect. The structure is not only calculable but calculated with a very sophisticated, if not cynical, skill—although the total movement and direction may be incommensurate with an air of spontaneous triumph. The relation with casuistry is apparent: the Jesuitical tactic of seeming to regress to infinite mercy and justice through manipulating an arrangement of legalistic stipulations or "cases," each of local and special relevance. With this tactic penance becomes an illusion, a theatrical "performance"—perhaps like the conversion of the mechanical Angelo. The casuistic penance may be achieved in the act if not in the spirit. Or, as old Escalus (that accessory figure in the Viennese composition) keeps insisting, pardon may be the nurse of second woe.

In this sense *Measure for Measure* is casuistical because of its adjusting immediate legalism to ultimate indeterminations. The Viennese *do* play with evil. What looks like forgiveness is not; what looks like sin is not; what looks like lechery is not; what looks like brutality is not; what looks like chicanery is not; and so on—an infinite regression, an illusion of settlement and resolution and comedy. And all the while there are really lust and grossness, and, possibly, even love. All is in equipoise, yet all is in question and unsettlement. The temptation, as Angelo finds, is to sin in loving virtue. Vienna is a city of excesses; excess balanced by excess; inordinate license then inordinate penalty or inordinate pardon—an engaging perilous city without moderation, without measure. The corruption of Angelo and the benignity of the Duke prove to be as artifactual as the postures in mannerist sculpture. The structure is balanced, although the impression is not equilibrium but transcendence, mercy, and justice. The tension is drawn between the letter of the law and the whimsy of the Duke. Justice seems to be done, but we never know what Viennese justice is. The ducal will is not Prospero's or Sophocles' inexpressible recognition of the unwritten laws eternal in the heaven, imagined but not codified. The ducal mercy is not pulling down the stews; it is allowing Claudio to get premature possession of Julietta's bed. Against the winking Duke is the rigid Angelo, whose blood is snow-broth. The puritanism of Angelo is accepted, then negated; the laxity of the Duke is accepted, then negated. And the comedy apparently recedes apace into the intuitive unwritten law. Prospero's decisions are providential but not arbitrary. The Duke is, like the Jesuit, a humane casuist.

No other Shakespearian play holds brutality and lyric in such unresolved stress. The bawd Lucio, setting upon his errand of justice and mercy, approaches the nunnery to greet the bloodless Isabella "Hail, virgin—if you be." Coming from the grim midnight cells of Claudio and Barnardine, the Duke enters another world at the moated grange where Mariana is singing

> But my kisses bring again, bring again;
> Seals of love, but seal'd in vain, seal'd in vain.

At the instant when the Duke almost attains Prospero's transcendental vision after his nocturnal sordid intrigue in the prison, the dayspring comes clearly —like the pastoral cold dawns in Milton's youth. And in the dawn lies the bestial drunken Barnardine, too. So the Duke says "Look, the unfolding star calls up the shepherd. Put not yourself into amazement how these things should be. All difficulties are but easy when they are known. *Call your executioner, and off with Barnardine's head.*" The daystar, and the bloody, running headsman's block—without modulation; another counterposition with disturbing effect. Indeed there are few modulations in the play, where the psychological texture is managed only by oppositions. Isabella's obsession with her chastity ("More than our brother is our chastity") is inevitably the instrument by which she defiles the prurient Angelo, who moves to *his* temptation, also, by the way where prayers cross. His lust is inaccessible except to Isabella's obvious and tantalizing purity:

> ...Most dangerous
> Is that temptation that doth goad us on
> To sin in loving virtue. Never could the strumpet,
> With all her double vigour, art, and nature,
> Once stir my temper; but this virtuous maid
> Subdues me quite.

The fantastic tricks of Angelo and the Duke can be played only in a mannerist theater where reversals become easy. For Angelo, the devil is not the devil; in Vienna purity is the devil. Thus Angelo comes to his discovery that his blood is blood, not snow-broth, and that he was not begot between stock-fishes:

> Let's write good angel on the devil's horn;
> 'Tis not the devil's crest.

The ducal good humor is provocation to inverting an order that is itself an illusion. And the chastity of Isabella conceals the Oedipus-foulness: she fears that her brother's appetite has been inherited from her mother and says to Claudio,

> Heaven shield my mother play'd my father fair!
> For such a warped slip of wilderness
> Ne'er issu'd from his blood.

From his center of indifference Shakespeare has looked at Vienna askance and strangely. *Measure for Measure* is no translation from the written to the unwritten law, but a casuistry. The resolution of *All's Well That Ends Well,* too, is a mere legalism, a local adjustment; there are the same precise and calculated oppositions, setting an equation that promptly and spontaneously stabilizes itself within its narrow reckonings, yet leaves all in doubt. One cannot find in either play, however, the Jacobean confusions of Beaumont and Fletcher, who disguise their equations by a blurring of good and evil. That is a more dissolute casuistry. Shakespeare maintains his distinctions: the Duke is at Jesuitical pains to justify Mariana's lying with Angelo in the place of Isabella. The Viennese appetites are at least honest and sound in the sense that there is no overplus of glee in corrupting virgins. The flesh is simply wayward. There is no leering (as there is in *Troilus and Cressida*) at the pose of chastity; virginity is not itself an obscenity, as it often is in Beaumont and Fletcher. Shakespeare has, for this comic examination, simply held two local moralities, two definable virtues, in the loose of question: mortality and mercy—in Vienna.

The emancipation from this narrow overwrought dilemma will not come until *Cymbeline,* with the repentance of Posthumus, who after his suffering refuses to exact measure for measure, or to weigh the stamp between man and man. The counterfeiting image is resolved by the mercy of Posthumus in forgiving Imogen; and his forgiveness is the firstfruit of his humility, his profound new sense of guilt. For the repentant Posthumus justice is no longer written in the letter. It is ultralegal, and the counterfeit, he says, will do as well as the gold if it is offered contritely, as an oblation from the spirit to the spirit:

> 'Tween man and man they weigh not every stamp;
> Though light, take pieces for the figure's sake.

At last retribution is measured by the will, not by the scales.

Already, in *Measure for Measure,* Shakespeare may—unguardedly and dimly—have had the intimation of this larger justice. Throughout, Escalus, not the Duke, understands that the resolution must not be casuistical but ultra-legal. For Escalus the law is merely an instrument, not a definition of right and wrong. Mistrusting the legalism of both the Duke's evasions and Angelo's rigor, he insists that pardon is the nurse of second woe and yet that the law must

> ...be keen and rather cut a little
> Than fall, and bruise to death.

But in the unholy mirth of Vienna the voice of Escalus is so muffled that we never clearly hear how he meets the problem of mercy or mortality. There is deeper insight in Isabella's final plea to the Duke in behalf of Angelo, who is guilty before the law. Earlier, when Angelo had first been heated by Isabella's chastity, he had asked

> ...Is this her fault or mine?
> The tempter or the tempted, who sins most?

He had put the question as a casuistry. Isabella's appeal for his life is an answer beyond the measures of casuistry. It is a Posthumus-answer. As if by illumination the prim neurotic virgin wonderfully and suddenly repudiates the narrow Viennese definitions of virtue and vice and sees both herself and Angelo with the selfless resignation or perspective of the unwritten eternal laws of justice and mercy. She and Angelo, in their pallid filth, are alike guilty and innocent. They both share the human condition, and purity is indeed the devil in Vienna—it was her fate, she now sees, to corrupt the prenzie Angelo, and she must forgive him because she was the temptress:

> ...I partly think
> A due sincerity govern'd his deeds
> *Till he did look on me.* Since it is so,
> Let him not die.

This is neither evasion nor indifference, but regeneration. Not for Vienna, of course; but for Isabella, and conceivably for Shakespeare.

# 21

# *All's Well That Ends Well*

*R. G. Hunter*

In *All's Well That Ends Well,* the world of comedy is threatened not so much by strife as by mutability. Change, the second great enemy of love, beauty, and happiness, has brought the once charmed worlds of Rossillion and Paris to the point of final dissolution. Within the first fifteen lines of the play we learn that the fathers of this world are dead and that its king is near death, the victim of an incurable disease, against which he refuses to struggle. Constantly throughout the first part of the play, the old—the countess, Lafew, the king—remember and lament the past. They remember the nobility and honor of the dead Count Rossillion, the wisdom and skill of Helena's father, Gerard de Narbon, and their memories communicate the sense that irreplaceable virtues are in danger of passing from the world. The elegiac, autumnal tone of these opening scenes is close to that of the quatrains of Sonnet 73 with their images of bare boughs, twilight, and dying fire, and the effect of this beauty in *All's Well* is that described in the couplet of the sonnet: We love that best which we

*Reprinted from R. G. Hunter,* Shakespeare and the Comedy of Forgiveness *(New York: Columbia University Press, 1965) pp. 106–131 by permission of the author and publisher. Because of space, the editors have omitted some footnotes from the original article.*

must leave ere long. Like all autumnal beauty, it has a double force. It reminds us simultaneously that it will soon disappear, and that its decay will one day be our own.

*All's Well* presents us with a dying world, and if, as has been suggested, it is a problem play, its problem is a basic one—how do you rejuvenate a constantly dying race? The answer is one that we all know, and one that is suggested at the play's very opening when we discover, on-stage, not only an old man and an old lady, but a young man and a girl. Here, then, is our solution, and being members of the audience at a comedy, we recognize it. In romantic comedy, boy and girl mean love, love means marriage, marriage means sexual intercourse, means procreation, means the re-creation of an always dying world. And, of course, we are right. No sooner is the beautiful girl left alone than she confesses to us her passionate love for the handsome young man:

> My imagination
> Carries no fauour in't but *Bertrams.*
> I am vndone, there is no liuing, none,
> If *Bertram* be away. (I, i, 93–96)

If we are not surprised by this news, however, we are no more startled to learn that there are obstacles in the way of this love's fulfillment. In Act One, Scene One of a comedy, how could it be otherwise? Bertram and Helena are separated by more than Bertram's imminent departure:

> 'Twere all one,
> That I should loue a bright particuler starre,
> And think to wed it, he is so aboue me.
> In his bright radience and colaterall light,
> Must I be comforted, not in his sphere;
> Th'ambition in my loue thus plagues it selfe:
> The hind that would be mated by the Lion
> Must die for loue. (I, i, 96–103)

With remarkable economy, in little more than a hundred lines, Shakespeare has established his basic comic situation: a noble but dying world stands in need of the rejuvenating force of sexual love. That love is potentially present in Bertram and Helena, but, as always in romantic comedy, a barrier exists between boy and girl—in this case, the barrier of a great disparity in social position. As members of the audience, we appear to know where we are and we can settle ourselves to enjoy the destruction of the barrier and the vicarious pleasures that attend the fulfillment of love and the artistic creation of happiness. Though the heroine despairs of the possibility of achieving her desires, though she seems content, with Viola's mythical sister, to sit like patience on a monument, smiling at grief, we know better. Love, in romantic comedy, will find out the way.

It is at this moment in the play that Shakespeare, for the first time, does something slightly odd. It will not be the last time, for of all Shakespeare's comedies, this is certainly the oddest, the most uncomfortable, perhaps the least popular, and it is probable that in those elements that cause its oddity and discomfort, the clues to its special significance are to be found.

As amateurs of the various forms of literary romance, any audience, whether Elizabethan readers of chivalric or pastoral narrative, or moderns with an experience of Victorian fiction or Hollywood movies, would have, I should imagine, a not wholly formed but nonetheless definite expectation at this point in the play's action. We are expecting, surely, some sort of sign from the hero, some indication of the state of his emotions—the declaration of a passion that he, too, realizes to be hopeless, perhaps. Or even better, an expression of his determination to defy the prejudices of society, followed, of course, by the heroine's refusal to let him make the sacrifice. But instead of *"Enter Bertram,"* the stage direction at this point reads, *"Enter Parolles."* Instead of the *jeune premier* we are presented with the parasite, with one who is immediately identified for us as a liar, a fool, and a coward, and instead of a tender passage between hero and heroine, we are treated to some fifty lines of bawdy on the absurdity of remaining a virgin. It is not surprising that Shakespeare has been strongly reprehended for creating the scene. Quiller-Couch would like to cut it (and "the whole Parolles business") right out of the play, "like a wen." He finds it offensive and worse: "...such chat is more than offensive; it is pointless lacking a listener; and as we wish Helena to be, and as Boccaccio conceives Helena, she would have dismissed Parolles by a turn of the back. Shakespeare degrades her for us by allowing her to remain in the room with this impertinent."[1]

A shift in taste since Quiller-Couch's time has made it easier for the modern reader to enjoy Shakespeare's jokes about sex and tempts us to regard Edwardian attitudes toward them as quaint if not neurotic. We should not be too quick to dismiss Quiller-Couch's objections as absurd, however. They are absurd, but the absurdity they demonstrate is common to a great deal of the adverse criticism of *All's Well.* Again and again in the critical remarks on this comedy (and in one's own reactions to it) one notices the unconscious assumption that *All's Well* should really be another play altogether, and that Shakespeare wrote the one we have either by mistake or through a combination of perversity and incompetence. *We,* the argument appears to run, know perfectly well what should happen in the play, but Shakespeare seems to be unable to get it through his head what it is that we want him to do. *We* know what Helena is like but the author fails to provide us with a Helena who is "as we wish Helena to be." *All's Well* obstinately refuses to be as we like it.

---

[1] Quiller-Couch and Wilson (eds.), *All's Well That Ends Well,* introd. (by Quiller-Couch), pp. xxv.

Our expectations are consistently disappointed, our hopes are frustrated, and the romantic comedy that, after the first hundred lines, we had settled down comfortably to enjoy is again and again pulled out from under us in the most annoying and awkward way. So consistently does this occur that one must end, finally, by entertaining the suspicion that in writing *All's Well* Shakespeare had something other than our undisturbed comfort in mind, and by acknowledging the fact that an understanding of the play can be arrived at only through an attempt to deal with it on its own terms, as Shakespeare wrote it.

Parolles' bawdy is a case in point. His interchange with Helena is an odd and unexpected incident, but its reasons for being in the play are clear enough. Parolles tells some home truths, none of which Helena gives the slightest sign of ever having doubted. "Virginity," he tells her and us, is "too cold a companion." It is unnatural, self-consuming, suicidal, and, finally, unattractive:

> Losse of Virginitie is rationall encrease, and there
> was neuer Virgin got, till virginitie was first lost...
>
> . . . . . .
>
> your virginity, your old virginity, is like one
> of our French wither'd peares, it looks
> ill, it eates drily, marry 'tis a wither'd peare:
> it was formerly better, marry yet 'tis a
> wither'd peare. (I, i, 138–74)

Helena does more than tolerate this "offensive chat." She listens to it, and she clearly allows it to influence her state of mind. As G. K. Hunter points out, this dialogue

> is a free and frothy play upon the ideas which are fermenting...in Helena's (or rather Shakespeare's) mind, and the topic it turns upon—the use of virginity and the manner in which it can be laid out to best advantage—is obviously germane to the situation of a virgin yearning for honest marriage to a young nobleman.[2]

Its obvious effect upon Helena is to make her stop merely yearning and begin planning how she may lose her virginity, as she puts it, "to her own liking"—to Bertram and in marriage. She casts off the hopeless melancholy of her first soliloquy and substitutes for it the self-confidence of the second:

> Our remedies oft in our selues do lye,
> Which we ascribe to heauen: the fated skye
> Giues vs free scope, onely doth backward pull
> Our slow designes, when we our selues are dull. (I, i, 232–35)

---

[2] *All's Well That Ends Well,* introd., p. xlii.

This change from despair to determination is entirely in keeping with the comic spirit. Comedy, traditionally, is anything but dedicated to the preservation and exaltation of virginity, and Helena's desire to lose hers lawfully entirely befits a comic heroine. And yet her determination to marry Bertram unquestionably makes Helena something of an oddity among the usual heroines of romance. It is the function of the lady, ordinarily, to appear, at least, to be the pursued rather than the pursuer in a romantic narrative. According to Andrew Lang, "Every one would prefer the worm in the bud to feed on the damask cheek rather than to see 'Vénus toute entière à sa proie attachée,' as Helena attaches herself to Bertram."[3] Again, Shakespeare appears to have failed or refused to write this comedy as we would like it. An instructive example of how Lang's "every one" expects a heroine like Helena to behave can be found in Trollope's *Framley Parsonage*. There, too, the heroine, Lucy Robarts, is the daughter of a poor and recently deceased physician. There, too, the hero, Lord Lufton, is a great aristocrat of proud family. Lucy loves Lufton, but Lufton also loves Lucy, and far from pursuing him, Lucy refuses Lufton when he proposes and continues to refuse him until, in Volume III, his heretofore recalcitrant mother proposes for him.

In fact, *All's Well* is not a romantic comedy in the usual sense of the term. If we look to this play to gratify the expectations commonly raised by romantic comedy, we will be disappointed, and our frustration will make an understanding of the play impossible. It has been suggested that these frustrated expectations are a largely modern phenomenon and that the Elizabethan audience for whom the play was intended would have accepted it, with little discomfort, as a perhaps slightly odd but still quite satisfactory romantic drama. This is the argument of W. W. Lawrence in his excellent essay on the play, and by an intelligent examination of Shakespeare's source in Boccaccio and of analogous medieval stories, Professor Lawrence certainly manages to demonstrate the absurdity of objecting to Helena's "indelicacy" in pursuing Bertram, or to her use of the bed trick in catching him.[4] It is, however, in the play's departure from the traditional story that the argument from narrative and dramatic convention breaks down. Boccaccio's novella tells the story of a "clever wench" (to use Lawrence's term) who by curing the king gets herself married to a tough, unwilling aristocrat, who is nonetheless, "rather a good fellow." The new husband refuses to sleep with his lowborn wife and tells her that he will not do so until she has a child by him. His wife accepts the challenge and proves herself worthy of her husband by fulfilling the condition he has imposed upon her. When the clever wench reveals how clever she has been, the aristocrat accepts her as

3 "All's Well That Ends Well," *Harper's Magazine,* LXXXV (July, 1892), 216.
4 *Shakespeare's Problem Comedies.*

his wife. It is, as a matter of fact, a good story, and, straightforwardly dramatized, it could have made an amusing play. Shakespeare, however, did not choose to dramatize it straightforwardly. "The blackening of the character of Bertram is one of the most sweeping changes made by Shakespeare in the story as a whole."[5] Indeed by turning Bertram "into a thoroughly disagreeable, peevish and vicious person," Shakespeare has altered his story in a very basic way. Instead of a clever wench who must prove herself worthy of an aristocratic husband, we have an unworthy husband who must be made worthy of his wife. Shakespeare has chosen to transform his hero into an erring mortal in need of regeneration and forgiveness. Like the anonymous author of *Calisto and Melebea,* Shakespeare has changed his narrative source into a play of forgiveness, and it is as a comedy of forgiveness rather than as a purely romantic comedy that *All's Well* should be examined and judged. *All's Well* was never meant to please in the way that *As You Like It* or *Twelfth Night* please. Though the comedy of forgiveness is a subspecies of the genre romantic comedy, it is different enough in its conventions and in the expectations which it is designed to arouse and fulfill, to require that it be examined critically on the basis of criteria slightly but distinctly different from those by which we ordinarily judge purely romantic comedy. As a purely romantic comedy, *All's Well* is unquestionably a failure; as a comedy of forgiveness it may be only partially successful, but the successes it does achieve are frequently of a high order.

That we should mistake *All's Well* for a purely romantic comedy is not entirely our fault, for Shakespeare only gradually reveals to us that it is not. Indeed, one could say that for the first act and a half, the characters themselves are under the impression that they are appearing in an almost typical boy/girl romance. Helena and the countess, who learns of her love, believe that the barrier to love and happiness is the disparity in rank between Helena and Bertram. With her future mother-in-law's blessing, Helena sets about to destroy that barrier. In Elizabethan terms, Helena is the victim of Fortune, who has assigned her a worldly position which is inappropriate to her deserts. Helena's project in the first half of the play is to raise herself in Fortune to a position of equality with Bertram. Mark Van Doren has pointed out that one of Helena's favorite words is "nature,"[6] and well it might be, for if the goddess Fortuna has been niggardly in her gifts to Helena, the goddess Natura has been abundantly generous, and it is through the gifts of Nature that Helena means to overcome the opposition of Fortune. The king says of her:

> Shee is young, wise, faire,
> In these, to Nature shee's immediate heire:
> And these breed honour. . . . (II, iii, 140–42)

[5] *Ibid.,* p. 62.
[6] *Shakespeare,* p. 215.

Though she does not name them, Helena is clearly thinking of the power of her youth, intelligence, and beauty when she contemplates her chances of winning Bertram:

> The mightiest space in fortune, Nature brings
> To ioyne like, likes; and kisse like natiue things. (I, i, 238–39)

But, as Helena realizes, she must have a means by which to show her merit. That means is a symbolically powerful one—the king's disease.

Miss Jessie L. Weston[7] has made modern readers sufficiently conscious of the antiquity and symbolic force that is contained in the Arthurian motif of the dying king. Something of the same aura surrounds the king of France in *All's Well.* His figure is at the center of the play's sterile, dying world, and Helena's cure of him is an impressive and significant demonstration of her restorative power. That power is of two interrelated kinds. By restoring the king to his natural state of health, she is demonstrating again that she is the darling, the "immediate heir" of Nature. But the play strongly insists that she is more. Her cure of the king is "supernatural and causeless" (to quote Lafew). It is a direct result of the grace of God, whose instrument Helena is. "The greatest grace lending grace," (II, i, 164) she will cure the king, and she challenges him to try her ability with the words, "Of heaven, not me, make an experiment." (II, i, 157) This duality in Helena's nature is insisted on throughout the play. For Lavatch, the clown, she is at one moment "the sweete Margerom of the sallet, or rather the hearbe of grace," (IV, v, 16–17) but she has previously been Helen of Troy:

> Was this faire face the cause, quoth she,
> Why the Grecians sacked *Troy*... (I, iii, 58–59)

Helena is a beautiful and sexually attractive girl who is also a recipient of God's grace and a means by which it is transmitted to others. It is possible that her name has been chosen with both aspects of her nature in mind. She is, on the one hand, Helen, for whose beauty men launched ships and burned towers. On the other hand, she is Helena, who was the daughter of the notoriously merry old Coelus, Earl of Colchester, and one of the first and most famous of British saints. Her major accomplishments were to give birth to Constantine the Great and to discover the True Cross, by means of which she healed the sick and raised the dead. Though Protestant historians tended to take a jaundiced view of her story, she was by no means forgotten by Shakespeare's contemporaries. One of the London churches and the parish Shakespeare lived in during the 1590s were called after her and her name would presumably have had sacred connotations for the average Londoner.

It is impossible to say which of the two aspects of Helena—the sacred or the profane—is more important. Shakespeare keeps them constantly in

[7] *From Ritual to Romance.*

balance and to emphasize one at the expense of the other is to throw both character and play out of kilter. The scene in which Helena is introduced to the king is a good example of Shakespeare's strategy in preserving this balance. The scene ends with Helena at her most hieratic and sibylline, declaiming in highly formal rhymed verse her intention of serving as God's instrument in the cure of the king. But the episode begins with suggestions of a quite different kind. The job of convincing the king that he should give Helena an audience is assigned to old Lafew, and he goes about it bawdily—imitating the encomium of a pander, in order to amuse the king and arouse his interest:

I haue seen a medicine
That's able to breath life into a stone,
Quicken a rocke, and make you dance Canari
With sprightly fire and motion, whose simple touch
Is powerfull to arayse King *Pippen,* nay
To give great *Charlemaine* a pen in's hand
And write to her a loue-line. (II, i, 68–74)

Helena, Lafew is pretending to suggest, will put the debilitated king into a tumescent state,[8] and he makes his exit with the line:

I am *Cresseds* Vncle,
That dare leaue two together, far you well. (II, i, 97–98)

As with the earlier bawdy of Parolles, these speeches have functions beyond that of getting a laugh. They ensure that in our admiration for Helena's spirituality, we shall not forget her sexual attractiveness. And yet it seems possible that Shakespeare deliberately set Lafew's *double-entendres* within an action that would itself suggest spirituality for this scene is strongly reminiscent of another, previously dramatized by Shakespeare (or a collaborator), and familiar to his audience, in which the ruler of France is in grave danger and a simple country maiden is brought to him with assurances that she is the instrument of heaven sent to save the day. The resemblance to St. Joan may be fortuitous or unconscious, but even so, it can contribute to our idea of Helena.

That idea is complex, to say the least. Compounded of St. Helena and Helen of Troy, with hints of St. Joan and Cressida, Helena can fairly be called Shakespeare's most complicated comic heroine. Her complexity is the result of her function in *All's Well,* for the play demands a heroine who

[8] "Stone" (l.69) = testicle (cf. *Merry Wives,* I.iv.118); "arayse King Pippen" (l.72) "...a pen in's hand" (l.73); pen = the penis. (See Partridge, *Dictionary of Slang and Unconventional English,* p. 616.) For further bawdy in this scene see Halio, " 'Traitor' in *All's Well* and *Troilus and Cressida,*" *Modern Language Notes,* LXXII (June, 1957), 408–9.

combines, in their highest degrees, the attributes of sacred and profane love. On the human, secular level it is necessary that Helena regenerate a dying world in the ordinary human, secular way—sexually and procreatively. But on another level that regeneration must take place in ways other than the physical. The virtue as well as the bodily existence of a dying world must be re-created, and to achieve that, Helena's spiritual forces will be necessary.

The full extent of Helena's task is not apparent until she has cured the king. Before that, we had accepted her assumption that the barrier to the comic ending was, indeed, the disparity in rank between hero and heroine. Now we find out that we have been wrong. The barrier that stands between Helena and Bertram is Bertram. The scene in which we make this discovery is an equivalent to the church scene in *Much Ado*. But though Claudio's outburst there is more violent in language and emotion than Bertram's in the later play, the effect of both as violations of the comic spirit is the same, and, if anything, Bertram's interruption of festivity leaves us more frustrated and uncomfortable than Claudio's.

The festive quality of the scene within which Shakespeare has placed Bertram's rejection of Helena is interesting. There is a ceremoniousness about the business of Helena's choice of a partner that has caused it to be staged as a ballet and compared to a Levantine slave market. It is also reminiscent of another and very common ritual—a children's game, a choosing or kissing game, like "Post Office." Indeed, the whole incident resembles a children's party with the old folks, the king and Lafew, looking benignly on while the birthday girl selects her partner. And as frequently happens on such occasions there is one guest who spoils the fun by refusing to play if he has to be "it." The petulance of Bertram at this moment reveals suddenly that the object of Helena's pursuit is not a fairy-tale prince, a romantic hero, but a spoiled, immature, self-centered snob. Like Claudio, Bertram denies us our comic pleasures, but while Claudio acts as badly as Bertram, he at least acts upon the discreditable motives of a grown man—outraged honor, however misguided, and sexual revulsion, however irrational—and he is suffering while he acts. Bertram does not have even these excuses for his offense.

To be sure, Bertram's refusal to accept Helena as his wife is in part a matter of principle. He is a ward of the king, so that the king has the legal right, as his guardian as well as his lord, to marry him where he chooses. Bertram, however, has the legal right to refuse his guardian's choice of a partner if the proposed marriage entails what was called "disparagement"—marriage to a person of a lower social class. He attempts to exercise that right:

> A poore Physitians daughter my wife? Disdaine
> Rather corrupt me euer. (II, iii, 124–26)

The king then tries to persuade Bertram with the familiar Renaissance argument that true nobility is not the exclusive possession of the aristocracy. An aristocrat may be essentially ignoble while commoners frequently display noble qualities. These are commonplaces hallowed by repetition through the centuries, but the king does not stop with them. He proceeds to point out that he can endow the already naturally endowed Helena with the additional gifts of Fortune, thus making her the equal in every way of Count Rossillion:

> If thou canst like this creature, as a maide,
> I can create the rest: Vertue, and shee
> Is her owne dower: Honour and wealth, from mee.
>
> (II, iii, 153–55)

The king is not proposing to force Bertram to marry his inferior. Rather, he will raise Helena to Bertram's material and social level. In the reigns of Elizabeth and James I, it would have been unwise to deny the monarch's ability to do this, and Bertram does not attempt it. Instead, he rejects Helena as a woman: "I cannot loue her, nor will strive to doo't" (II, iii, 156).

Bertram, at this point, stops trying to justify himself, and the king, in turn, abandons all attempt to reason with him and produces the royal power. The result is impressive and gives one an inkling of why contemporary courtiers were shaken even by the distant memory of one of Elizabeth's losses of temper. Bertram capitulates completely and admits what he had never denied—that the king has it in his power to ennoble Helena. He does not, however, recant his refusal to love her and we must ask ourselves what, finally, inspires or accounts for that refusal.

The "children's party" quality of the scene of rejection underlines one of Bertram's most important characteristics—his extreme immaturity. Bertram is very young, chronologically nineteen, perhaps, and psychologically even younger. He is young, however, in an odd way. His reaction to the situation he finds himself in is not that of an ordinary late adolescent. It is understandable enough that he should oppose the king's insistence that he marry a woman of the king's choosing, but his behavior after he has been forced to capitulate is less comprehensible. One would expect him, after the marriage ceremony, to take stock of the situation. He would find himself married to a young, intelligent, and charming girl whose influence with the king was likely to procure him great worldly advantage. He would also discover that he had acquired a wife of great beauty and sexual attractiveness. Under the circumstances it seems likely that for the average nineteen-year-old—for the average man of any age, perhaps—having to "bed" Helena would be, not the final indignity, but the first consolation.

Bertram's refusal to consummate his marriage cannot, surely, be attributed simply to his refusal to recognize Helena's true nobility. It must also be the result of his failure to feel sexual desire for his young and attractive wife. As we have seen, Shakespeare has been at great pains to make it clear that Helena is, in fact, more than ordinarily desirable and that the reason for Bertram's refusal to "bed" her is clearly not to be discovered in Helena. Whatever its source, nothing could be more inimical to the spirit of romantic comedy than this refusal of sexual love. That the ostensible hero of a comedy should reject, for any reason, the pleasure, beauty and happiness of the act of love is shocking enough to the comic sensibilities. Claudio, Posthumus, and Leontes, however, are at least provided with a comprehensible reason: they have wrongly suspected the women they love of unchastity, and, as a result, their love has turned to hatred. Bertram's rejection of love, by comparison, is simply perverse, and in refusing to make love to Helena, he refuses not only his own pleasure, but the means which nature has provided for the defeat of mutability. By doing so, he sets himself against the emotional movement of the play he is appearing in, and leaves his audience baffled, frustrated, and annoyed.

But, of course, our frustration and annoyance are only beginning. Shakespeare will proceed to have Bertram behave more and more unpleasantly until the final moments of the play. It is only natural, perhaps, that, confronted by this series of unpleasant actions on the part of a "hero," we should search for an explanation of them, a tidy, logical "reason" for Bertram's bad behavior. Since, for example, it is clear that the reason for Bertram's refusal to "bed" Helena is not to be discovered in Helena, where, we ask ourselves, is it to be discovered? A common solution, and one that is to some extent justified by the play, is to find it in Parolles. It is tempting to try to ameliorate, somewhat, the play's central difficulty by shifting the blame for Bertram's ignobility onto a figure who can be seen as his bad angel, as a version of the old Vice, who tempts Bertram and leads him astray. If Parolles could be so seen, could be found to function in the play as a surrogate for the audience's dislike of his master, if we could legitimately allow Parolles to serve as a scapegoat for Bertram, as Don John serves for Claudio, and Iachimo serves for Posthumus, the difficulty of forgiving Bertram at the play's end would be considerably eased.

Evidence for so regarding Parolles can be found within the play. He is described precisely as the ignoble misleader of noble youth by several of the more clear-seeing figures in the comedy. The Old Countess characterizes him as:

> A verie tainted fellow, and full of wickednesse,
> My sonne corrupts a well deriued nature
> With his inducement. (III, ii, 90–92)

And when, toward the end of the play, Lafew has decided to marry his daughter to Bertram, he similarly excuses his future son-in-law:

> No, no, no your sonne was misled with a
> snipt taffata fellow there, whose villanous
> saffron wold haue made all the vnbak'd and
> dowy youth of a nation in his colour. (IV, v, 1–4)

These statements, of course, influence our view of the relationship between Parolles and Bertram. They do not, however, completely define that relationship for they do not accurately describe what has been presented to us by the action of the play. There are undoubtedly elements of the old Vice and the evil councilor in Parolles, but they are not of a kind or of an intensity to serve as full excuses for Bertram's actions. Parolles is unquestionably a low fellow and far from suitable company for the young, but we never see him actively misleading, tempting, or corrupting Bertram. It is Bertram who has the evil impulses and suggests the ignoble actions. Parolles need do no more than second the motion. He is a parasite, a yes-man, rather than a corrupter of youth. The scene in which Bertram decides to desert his wife and run away to Italy is an excellent example of the relashionship:

> *Ros.* Vndone, and forfeited to cares for euer.
> *Par.* What's the matter sweet-heart?
> *Ros.* Although before the solemne Priest I haue
> sworne, I will not bed her.
> *Par.* What? what sweet-heart?
> *Ros.* O my Parrolles, they have married me:
> Ile to the *Tuscan* warres, and neuer bed her.
> *Par. France* is a dog-hole, and it no more merits,
> The tread of a mans foot: too'th warres. (II, iii, 276–82)

Far from leading Bertram into temptation, Parolles is lamentably slow to discover exactly what he is expected to agree to. The most we can blame Parolles for is his failure to disapprove of Bertram's plans. He does perform a portion of the Vice's function in that he provides an atmosphere of complaisance to sin, but as an active tempter, he is highly ineffective. Even when he serves as a go-between for Bertram in the attempted seduction of Diana, we discover that, far from encouraging Diana to commit adultery, Parolles is double-crossing his master and trying to get the girl for himself.

That "the relationship of the two is not that of misleader and misled"[9] is clearest in the last act of the play. By the time of Bertram's return to France, the true character of Parolles has been made clear to him as a result of the plot concocted for that purpose by the two French lords. Bertram has dismissed Parolles from his favor, and if Parolles had been previously responsible for Bertram's ignoble actions, we would be justified in expecting Bertram to begin acting decently once he had been removed from the influence of his bad angel. Nothing of the sort happens. In the final scene of

---

[9] Rossiter, *Angel with Horns,* ed. Storey, p. 96.

the play, Bertram's behavior surpasses, in loutishness, everything he has achieved up to that point. His treatment of Diana makes it quite clear that nothing outside his own character is needed to inspire Bertram to dishonorable actions.

Parolles is a symptom rather than a cause of Bertram's disease—for Bertram's very nature is diseased. Just as the king's natural state of health is corrupted by his illness, so Bertram "corrupts a well-derived nature." To cure him Helena must, in a sense, repeat, on a spiritual and psychological plane, the miracle of the king's restoration to health, and Parolles serves as the fistula, the symptom by which Bertram's malady can be recognized. Bertram's admiration for this fool and coward is a logical complement to his detestation of Helena. A part of Bertram's corruption is the result of his inability to perceive the true nature of others. He can see neither Parolles nor Helena for what they truly are. This failure of perception is, itself, only an indication of another and, to the Elizabethan, far more dangerous failure—for Bertram is also unable to perceive and to differentiate between the nobility and ignobility within his own character. His admiration for Parolles provides an example of the first of these failures. Parolles' unmasking and subsequent forced assumption of his true role in the world of the play will, as we shall see, provide an action analogous to that in which Bertram is similarly dealt with. It is as symptom and as analogue, rather than as tempter, that Parolles functions most importantly in *All's Well.*

Bertram's refusal to go to bed with Helena cannot, then, be explained either as the result of Helena's lack of sexual desirability or of the malign influence of Parolles. Neither can we justifiably suspect that Bertram is unable to feel ordinary sexual desire. His determined pursuit of Diana is sufficient proof that he is capable of heterosexual lust. But it is perhaps time to call a halt to our search for motivations and to think, for a moment, of the significance of Bertram's recalcitrance in terms of the action of the play as a whole. That recalcitrance appears to be at the center of the play's meaning, but there is little reason to believe that Shakespeare therefore felt called upon to account for it either with strict psychological realism or by providing any of the tidy "motives" which some academic critics still naïvely regard as explanations for human action. Bertram's intransigence is Shakespeare's *donné*. He dramatizes it, considers it, comments on it, but he does not explain it. Some of its implications for the play as a whole are clear enough. Man sometimes inexplicably rebels against his own good—against both what is good for him and what is good within him. This is what Bertram does, not only in his treatment of Helena, but consistently throughout the play. To look for motives in the ordinary sense of the word will be to look in vain, for Bertram acts, not out of a rational desire for his own good, but from an inexplicable but by no means uncommon desire for self-damage. Or, to put it in Elizabethan terms:

Of ourselves and by ourselves, we are not able either to think a good thought, or work a good deed: so that we can find in ourselves no hope of salvation, but rather whatsoever maketh unto our destruction.[10]

The two French lords, Shakespeare's chorus to the third and fourth acts of *All's Well,* comment specifically upon Bertram as his own enemy, and extend their remarks to include us all:

*Cap. E.* Hee hath peruerted a young Gentlewoman heere in *Florence,* of a most chaste renown, & this night he fleshes his will in the spoyle of her honour: hee hath hath giuen her his monumentall Ring, and thinkes himself made in the unchaste composition.
*Cap. G.* Now God delay our rebellion as we are our selues, what things are we.
*Cap. E.* Meerely our owne traitours. And as in the common course of all treasons, we still see them reueale themselues, till they attaine to their abhorr'd ends: so he that in this action contriues against his owne Nobility in his proper streame, ore-flowes himselfe. (IV, iii, 13–24)

Shakespeare has been at some pains to show us, in the incident of Bertram's attempted seduction of Diana, a man not only contriving against his own nobility, but inspired to do so by an absurdly and ironically misguided sensuality. In order to "flesh his will," Bertram is ready to betray anything. He breaks, first, his marriage vows, then violates his personal honor with a string of lying promises to Diana, and finally, in agreeing to give Diana his "monumental ring," he symbolically betrays the honor of his family. Family honor, the motive upon which he has insisted in refusing to consummate his marriage with Helena, he is willing to pawn for a few moments of adulterous lust in the pitch dark with Diana. The dark contains, not Diana, but the detested Helena, and Bertram is unaware of the difference.

Helena's substitution of herself for Diana is immediately inspired by Bertram's taunting assertion that he will not sleep with his wife until he has had a child by her. By deceiving him, Helena saves her husband from the violation of his marriage vows and of his honor. In addition, Helena is able to trick Bertram into performing his necessary role in the physical regeneration of the dying world of Rossillion, for lust will serve as well as love for that, and Helena need only direct lust toward its morally and legally sanctioned object. The fact that she is able to do so without lust's being aware of what is happening inspires her to make a profound and disquieting comment upon the nature of male sexuality:

But O strange men,
That can such sweet vse make of what they hate,
When sawcie trusting of the cosin'd thoughts
Defiles the pitchy night, so lust doth play
With what it lothes, for that which is away. (IV, iv, 24–28)

---

[10] Griffiths, ed., *Certain Sermons or Homilies Appointed to Be Read In Churches In The Time of Queen Elizabeth of Famous Memory,* p. 19.

Although Helena's knowledge is the result of her deception of Bertram, it is clear that her comments are not meant to be limited to those (surely rare) unfortunates who are victims of the bed trick. The truth that lust is more a mental than a physical phenomenon has been fully revealed by Bertram's passionate response to the mistaken thought that the woman he detests is the woman he desires. But the application of the truth goes beyond Bertram, beyond the deceived to the self-deceived, for the cozened thoughts of the lustful are ordinarily self-cozened and we deceive ourselves into accepting the loathesome as a substitute for the desirable. Helena's statement suggests an even deeper insight into the duality of sexual desire, however, for men, she ambiguously tells us, make sweet use of *what* they hate. Sexual desire makes it possible for men to enjoy not only a partner they detest, but an act they detest. Lust, as opposed to love, contains a hatred for the sexual act itself.

Bertram's attempted seduction of Diana and his deception by the bed trick reveal the corruption of his nature and, by implication, the corruption of all male sexuality when it is dominated by lust. Bertram selects the corrupt and ignoble alternative when forced by his sexual desires to find an object for them. He rejects the sexuality which is sanctioned and, indeed, enjoined upon him by his marriage vows, because he prefers an adulterous liaison which he can obtain only by ignoble lying and bribery. He believes that he seduces Diana because of his overwhelming sensual desire for her, and yet he is able to satisfy that desire by a brief moment in the dark with another woman, with the very woman whom he professes to loathe so intensely that he will not have sexual relations with her. By this irrational rejection of his own good, Bertram is doing more than demonstrate the truth of the proposition that "Passion and reason self-division cause." Bertram is not self-divided; he is self-deceived and self-ignorant. He seems totally unaware of the ignobility of his own nature and, as a result, he is in a perilous state, indeed. Again the comments of the French lords are to the point:

> *Cap. G.* The webbe of our life, is of a mingled yarne, good and ill together: our vertues would bee proud, if our faults whipt them not, and our crimes would dispaire if they were not cherish'd by our vertues. (IV, iii, 77–80)

Bertram is ignorant of his faults and consequently ignorant of his virtues. Until she has brought her husband to a state of self-knowledge, Helena will not have completed her task of restoring the dying world of Rossillion. The honor of Bertram's father has not reappeared in the son, and so long as that is the case, the world of Rossillion is only superficially alive, for honor is the soul of that world, and

> this is honours scorne,
> Which challenges it selfe as honours borne,
> And is not like the sire. . . . (II, iii, 144–46)

Helena has cured the king and, by obtaining Bertram's ring and becoming pregnant by him, she has fulfilled the tasks which her husband imposed upon her. The dying world of the play's opening scene has been restored to health and fertility. It now remains for Helena to restore Bertram to that state of honor which, we are told, is naturally his. This she can do only by forcing self-knowledge upon him.

The method by which this end is achieved is both predicted and explained by the analogous action of Parolles' unmasking. The two French lords undertake this project specifically in the hope that it will force Bertram to confront the true nature, not so much of Parolles, as of himself:

> I would gladly haue him see his company
> anathomiz'd, that hee might take a measure
> of his owne iudgements, wherein so curiously
> he had set this counterfeit. (IV, iii, 37–40)

Their hopes, for the time being, prove fruitless, for Bertram's self-esteem needs harsher methods for its correction than the revelation of someone else's weakness. The plot of the drum does, however, provide Shakespeare with a method of demonstrating how a man may be forced to act in accordance with his own nature.

The basic difference between the unmasking of Parolles here and the unmasking of Bertram in the last act is that Parolles learns nothing about himself because he has never been the victim of any illusions about what he is. He, like everyone else in the play, except Bertram, is perfectly well aware that Parolles is a coward and a knave. In order to profit by Bertram's credulity, Parolles is willing to pretend to be what he is not, but he knows that he is playing a role and he curses himself when he begins playing it too realistically:

> What the diuell should moue mee to vndertake
> the recouerie of this drumme, being not ignorant of the
> impossibility, and knowing I had no such purpose? (IV, i, 34–36)

Again the comments of the French captains underline the point: "It it possible that he should know what hee is, and be that he is?" It is, indeed, possible, though unlike Parolles, most of us manage to prevent ourselves from knowing what we are. There is, however, nothing immoral about ignobility so long as one cannot be and does not pretend to be noble. Pretensions to nobility can be dangerous to society for they may lead to misplaced trust. In deflating Parolles' pretensions, the French lords are performing a public service, and the way in which they go about it has a strong resemblance to the way in which Helena goes about the cure of Bertram.

Like Bertram in his desire for Diana, Parolles, in his desire for life, is ready to promise anything, compromise anything, betray anyone. Like Bertram, the blindfolded Parolles is caught in the dark, and just as Bertram commits adultery with his wife, Parolles betrays his comrades to his comrades. When the blindfold is removed from his eyes, Parolles realizes that he has revealed his true nature beyond hope of concealment or excuse. His reaction is to accept that nature and decide to live by it:

> Rust sword, coole blushes, and *Parrolles* liue
> Safest in shame: being fool'd, by fool'rie thriue;
> There's place and meanes for euery man aliue.
> Ile after them. (IV, iii, 370–73)

By becoming a tame toady to Lord Lafew, he discovers the place in the world that is proper to him.

It is necessary to keep the unmasking of Parolles in mind when one approaches the last scene of the play—a highly uncomfortable piece of theater which has been generally held to result in the failure of the comedy as a whole. Parolles thinks he is safe in defaming his fellow soldiers—Captain Dumain, for example:

> I know him, a was a Botchers Prentize in *Paris,*
> from whence he was whipt for getting the Shrieues fool
> with childe, a dumbe innocent that could not
> say him nay. (IV, iii, 207–10)

By doing so, he hopes to save his life. Bertram thinks he is safe in defaming Diana:

> She's impudent my Lord,
> And was a common gamester to the Campe. (V, iii, 187–88)

By doing so, he hopes to save his reputation. When the truth dawns upon Parolles, he has no choice but to become himself and to turn to the charity of his fellow men in the hope that they will accept him as he is. The truth which dawns upon Bertram is more complex. He realizes, first that the girl whom he thinks he has seduced and whom he has had no compunction about slandering, is, in fact, innocent, and has revealed to the king, the countess, and the court of France that Bertram is a lying, promise-breaking seducer. Like Parolles when the blindfold is removed, Bertram must face the fact that the truth about him is irretrievably known, but we have also the sense that for the first time the truth about Bertram has been revealed to Bertram himself.

In Bertram's case, then, the blindfold is removed from the inner eye of conscience, and *humanum genus* is able, as a result, finally to see the evidence of his own corruption. That revelation is no more fortuitous than the unmasking of Parolles. The French lords have played a socially valuable practical joke which results in the return of Parolles to his appropriate station in the world. Like them, Helena has arranged a salutary discomfiture—that of her erring husband. In doing so, she has once again served as the instrument of God's grace. As Clifford Leech puts it, "Helena, in her curing of the King, is a dispenser of divine grace, and in her definitive subjection of Bertram she is setting his foot on the path of Christian virtue."[11] For Bertram, the descent of grace equals the access of self-knowledge, and because "the turning of the heart unto God is of God,"[12] the means by which that "turning" is achieved must be of God, too. Helena is the instrument which heaven has employed in working out its designs:

> Whatsoever God doeth, he bringeth it about by his instruments ordained thereto. He hath good angels, he hath evil angels; he hath good men, and he hath evil men; he hath hail and rain, he hath wind and thunder, he hath heat and cold; innumerable instruments hath he, and messengers...[13]

Helena is such an instrument and messenger.

The Old Countess, reflecting on her son's flight to Italy, asks:

> What Angell shall
> Blesse this vnworthy husband...? (III, iv, 26–27)

The answer, of course, is Helena, as the countess goes on to explain in the lines that follow:

> he cannot thriue,
> Vnlesse her prayers, whom heauen delights to heare
> And loues to grant, repreeue him from the wrath
> Of greatest Iustice. (III, iv, 27–30)

These lines describe Helena, but they do so in terms that inevitably suggest the Virgin Mary. The Arden editor believes that "a straightforward reference to the Virgin as intercessor is too Popish to be probable,"[14] but a more "Popish" activity than a barefoot pilgrimage to Santiago da Compostella is difficult to imagine, and yet Helena has just left on such an errand when these lines are spoken of her. Shakespeare evokes the Virgin here because Helena's function in the play is similar to that of the Mother of God in the "Popish" scheme of things. Both serve as means through which the grace of

---

11 "The Theme of Ambition in *All's Well That Ends Well,*" *ELH,* XXI (March, 1954), p. 20.

12 Griffiths, *Homilies,* p. 571.

13 *Ibid.,* p. 516.

14 Hunter, p. 82.

God can be communicated to man. Nor is this similarity surprising, for, considered historically, the charitable heroines of the comedy of forgiveness are literary descendants of the Virgin in the medieval narrative and dramatic "Miracles of Our Lady." Ordinarily their function is simply to be sinned against and to forgive, but unlike Hero, Imogen, and Hermione, Helena is called upon to serve as the active agent in the regeneration of the erring hero.

Two main objections, largely inspired by that regeneration, have been raised to the happy ending of *All's Well.* The first of these sees the forgiveness of Bertram as a violation of poetic justice. For Dr. Johnson, Bertram's felicity is not deserved. Bertram is merely "dismissed to happiness,"[15] after a series of sneaking profligacies, and Dr. Johnson cannot, therefore, reconcile his heart to him. Against this objection no defense is possible except a very basic one. Poetic justice is *not* served by the comedies of forgiveness. It is not meant to be served, because these comedies celebrate another virtue—charity. The second objection is more complicated in its implications. Critics of this play have felt (as far as I know, without exception) that the final scene of the play fails because Bertram's regeneration is unconvincing. There can be no doubt that, indeed, the scene does so fail for a modern audience. We do not believe in the regeneration. It is not communicated to us.

The reasons for that failure of communication need careful consideration, however. The general feeling seems to be that Shakespeare fell back on a rather shallow theatrical convention for the denouement of this play. According to Quiller-Couch, "*All's Well* has no atmosphere save that of the stage. . . . It is a thing 'of the boards' "[16] and such a "thing,'" we assume, does not deserve the name of great drama and is unworthy of a great dramatist. Robert Y. Turner, in a recent essay, has shown how common a theatrical event such arbitrary regenerations were in the drama of Shakespeare's time, but, as Turner points out, this use of a literary commonplace "will not justify Shakespeare's workmanship. It merely tells us that *All's Well* is a failure of one kind and not another."[17] And yet, theatrical conventions of this sort are not simply arbitrary or purely formal. They succeed because they refer to and draw upon the shared beliefs of an audience.

The final scene of *All's Well* draws upon and refers to a belief in the reality of the descent of grace upon a sinning human. The Elizabethan audience believed in such an occurrence not as a theological abstraction, but as an everyday psychological possibility. What happens to Bertram would, I think, have been clear to Shakespeare's contemporaries. The scales fall from

---

15 Johnson, III, 399.

16 Quiller-Couch and Wilson, *All's Well That Ends Well,* introd. (by Quiller-Couch) p. xxxiv.

17 "Dramatic Conventions in *All's Well That Ends Well,*" *PMLA,* LXXV (December, 1960), 502.

Bertram's eyes, he sees what he has done, and he is filled with shame and a sense of the necessity for pardon:

> We have a common experience of the same in them which, when they have committed any heinous offence or some filthy and abominable sin, if it once to light, or if they chance to have a through feeling of it, they be so ashamed, their own conscience putting before their eyes the filthiness of their act, that they dare look no man on the face, much less that they should be able to stand in the sight of God.[18]

Out of such an experience, a new man is born:

> After his repentance he was no more the man that he was before, but was clean changed and altered.[19]

A Renaissance audience would not, I think, have considered even Bertram incapable of that alteration.

By referring the characters and events of *All's Well* to the Christian concepts which help to explain them, I am not, I hope, maintaining that this comedy is a Christian allegory, a Christian parable, or a Christian homily. It is a secular comedy concerned with this world and with the relationships between men and women in this life. It was, however, written for a Christian audience and it draws naturally upon a Christian view of the world. It is, furthermore, cast in a traditionally Christian dramatic form—that of the play of forgiveness.

---

18 Griffiths, *Homilies,* p. 584.
19 *Ibid.,* p. 580.

# 22

# Recognition in *The Winter's Tale*

*Northrop Frye*

In structure *The Winter's Tale,* like *King Lear,* falls into two main parts separated by a storm. The fact that they are also separated by sixteen years is less important. The first part ends with the ill-fated Antigonus caught between a bear and a raging sea, echoing a passage in one of Lear's storm speeches. This first part is the "winter's tale" proper, for Mamillius is just about to whisper his tale into his mother's ear when the real winter strikes with the entrance of Leontes and his guards. Various bits of imagery, such as Polixenes' wish to get back to Bohemia for fear of "sneaping winds" blowing at home and Hermione's remark during her trial (reproduced from *Pandosto*) that the emperor of Russia was her father, are linked to a winter setting. The storm, like the storm in *King Lear,* is described in such a way as to suggest that a whole order of things is being dissolved in a dark chaos of destruction and devouring monsters, and the action of the first part ends in almost unrelieved gloom. The second part is a

*"Recognition in The Winter's Tale," by Northrop Frye, pp. 235–46 in* Essays on Shakespeare and Elizabethan Drama in Honor of Hardin Craig, *edited by Richard Hosley. Reprinted by permission of the publishers, University of Missouri Press, Columbia, Missouri.* 

tragi-comedy where, as in *Cymbeline* and *Measure for Measure,* there is frightening rather than actual hurting. Some of the frightening seems cruel and unnecessary, but the principle of "all's well that ends well" holds in comedy, however great nonsense it may be in life.

The two parts form a diptych of parallel and contrasting actions, one dealing with age, winter, and the jealousy of Leontes, the other with youth, summer, and the love of Florizel. The first part follows Greene's *Pandosto* closely; for the second part no major source has been identified. A number of symmetrical details, which are commonplaces of Shakespearian design, help to build up the contrast: for instance, the action of each part begins with an attempt to delay a return. The two parts are related in two ways, by sequence and by contrast. The cycle of nature, turning through the winter and summer of the year and through the age and youth of human generations, is at the center of the play's imagery. The opening scene sets the tone by speaking of Mamillius and of the desire of the older people in the country to live until he comes to reign. The next scene, where the action begins, refers to Leontes' own youth in a world of pastoral innocence and its present reflection in Mamillius. The same cycle is also symbolized, as in *Pericles,* by a mother-daughter relationship, and Perdita echoes Marina when she speaks of Hermione as having "ended when I but began." In the transition to the second part the clown watches the shipwreck and the devouring of Antigonus; the shepherd exhibits the birth tokens of Perdita and remarks, "Thou mettest with things dying, I with things new-born." Leontes, we are told, was to have returned Polixenes' visit "this coming summer," but instead of that sixteen years pass and we find ourselves in Bohemia with spring imagery bursting out of Autolycus's first song, "When daffodils begin to peer." If Leontes is an imaginary cuckold, Autolycus, the thieving harbinger of spring, is something of an imaginative cuckoo. Thence we go on to the sheep-shearing festival, where the imagery extends from early spring to winter evergreens, a vision of nature demonstrating its creative power throughout the entire year, which is perhaps what the dance of the twelve satyrs represents. The symbolic reason for the sixteen-year gap is clearly to have the cycle of the year reinforced by the slower cycle of human generations.

Dramatic contrast in Shakespeare normally includes a superficial resemblance in which one element is a parody of the other. Theseus remarks in *A Midsummer Night's Dream* that the lunatic, the lover, and the poet are of imagination all compact. Theseus, like Yeats, is a smiling public man past his first youth, but not, like Yeats, a poet and a critic. What critical ability there is in that family belongs entirely to Hippolyta, whose sharp comments are a most effective contrast to Theseus's amiable bumble. Hippolyta objects that the story of the lovers has a consistency to it that lunacy would lack, and everywhere in Shakespearian comedy the resemblance of love and lunacy is based on their opposition. Florizel's love for Perdita, which transcends his duty to his father and his social responsibilities as a prince, is a state of mind above reason. He is advised, he says, by his "fancy":

> If my reason
> Will thereto be obedient, I have reason;
> If not, my senses, better pleased with madness,
> Do bid it welcome.

Leontes' jealousy is a fantasy below reason, and hence a parody of Florizel's state. Camillo, who represents a kind of middle level in the play, is opposed to both, calling one diseased and the other desperate. Both states of mind collide with reality in the middle, and one is annihilated and the other redeemed, like the two aspects of law in Christianity. As the Gentleman says in reporting the finding of Perdita, "They looked as they had heard of a world ransomed, or one destroyed." When Leontes has returned to his proper state of mind, he echoes Florizel when he says of watching the statue,

> No settled senses of the world can match
> The pleasure of that madness.

The play ends in a double recognition scene: the first, which is reported only through the conversation of three Gentlemen, is the recognition of Perdita's parentage; the second is the final scene of the awakening of Hermione and the presenting of Perdita to her. The machinery of the former scene is the ordinary *cognitio* of New Comedy, where the heroine is proved by birth tokens to be respectable enough for the hero to marry her. In many comedies, though never in Shakespeare, such a *cognitio* is brought about through the ingenuity of a tricky servant. Autolycus has this role in *The Winter's Tale,* for though "'out of service" he still regards Florizel as his master, and he has also the rascality and the complacent soliloquies about his own cleverness that go with the role. He gains possession of the secret of Perdita's birth, but somehow or other the denouement takes place without him, and he remains superfluous to the plot, consoling himself with the reflection that doing so good a deed would be inconsistent with the rest of his character. In *The Winter's Tale* Shakespeare has combined the two traditions which descended from Menander, pastoral romance and New Comedy, and has consequently come very close to Menandrine formulas as we have them in such a play as *Epitripontes*. But the fact that this conventional recognition scene is only reported indicates that Shakespeare is less interested in it than in the statue scene, which is all his own.

In *Measure for Measure* and *The Tempest* the happy ending is brought about through the exertions of the central characters, whose successes are so remarkable that they seem to many critics to have something almost supernatural about them, as though they were the agents of a divine providence. The germ of truth in this conception is that in other comedies of the same general structure, where there is no such character, the corresponding dramatic role is filled by a supernatural being—Diana in *Pericles* and Jupiter in *Cymbeline. The Winter's Tale* belongs to the second group, for the return of Perdita proceeds from the invisible providence of Apollo.

In *Pericles* and *Cymbeline* there is, in addition to the recognition scene, a dream in which the controlling divinity appears with an announcement of what is to conclude the action. Such a scene forms an emblematic recognition scene, in which we are shown the power that brings about the comic resolution. In *The Tempest,* where the power is human, Prospero's magic presents three emblematic visions: a wedding masque of gods to Ferdinand, a disappearing banquet to the Court Party, and "trumpery" (IV, i, 186) to entice Stephano and Trinculo to steal. In *The Winter's Tale* Apollo does not enter the action, and the emblematic recognition scene is represented by the sheep-shearing festival. This is also on three levels. To Florizel it is a kind of betrothal masque and "a meeting of the petty gods"; to the Court Party, Polixenes and Camillo, it is an illusion which they snatch away; to Autolycus it is an opportunity to sell his "trumpery" (IV, iv, 608) and steal purses.

An emblematic recognition scene of this kind is the distinguishing feature of the four late romances. As a convention, it develops from pastoral romance and the narrative or mythological poem. The sheep-shearing festival resembles the big bravura scenes of singing-matches and the like in Sidney's *Arcadia,* and *The Rape of Lucrece* comes to an emblematic focus in the tapestry depicting the fall of Troy, where Lucrece identifies herself with Hecuba and Tarquin with Sinon, and determines that the second Troy will not collapse around a rape like the first one. In the earlier comedies the emblematic recognition scene is usually in the form of burlesque. Thus in *Love's Labour's Lost* the pageant of Worthies elaborates on Don Armado's appeal to the precedents of Solomon, Samson, and Hercules when he falls in love; but his appeal has also burlesqued the main theme of the play. The allegorical garden spisode in *Richard II* represents a similar device, but one rather different in its relation to the total dramatic structure.

In any case the controlling power in the dramatic action of *The Winter's Tale* is something identified both with the will of the gods, especially Apollo, and with the power of nature. We have to keep this association of nature and pagan gods in mind when we examine the imagery in the play that reminds us of religious, even explicitly Christian, conceptions. At the beginning Leontes' youth is referred to as a time of paradisal innocence; by the end of the scene he has tumbled into a completely illusory knowledge of good and evil. He says:

> How blest am I
> In my censure, in my true opinion!
> Alack, for lesser knowledge! How accurs'd
> In being so blest!

Or, as Ford says in *The Merry Wives,* "God be praised for my jealousy!" The irony of the scene in which Leontes is scolded by Paulina turns on the fact that Leontes tries to be a source of righteous wrath when he is actually an object of it. Hermione's trial is supposed to be an act of justice and the sword of justice is produced twice to have oaths sworn on it, but Leontes is under the wrath of Apollo and divine justice is his enemy. The opposite of wrath is grace, and Hermione is associated throughout the play with the word grace. During the uneasy and rather cloying friendliness at the beginning of the play Hermione pronounces the word "grace" conspicuously three times, after which the harsh dissonances of Leontes' jealousy begin. She also uses the word when she is ordered off to prison and in the only speech that she makes after Act III. But such grace is not Christian or theological grace, which is superior to the order of nature, but a secular analogy of Christian grace which is identical with nature—the grace that Spenser celebrates in the sixth book of *The Faerie Queene.*

In the romances, and in some of the earlier comedies, we have a sense of an irresistible power, whether of divine or human agency, making for a providential resolution. Whenever we have a strong sense of such a power, the human beings on whom it operates seem greatly diminished in size. This is a feature of the romances which often disappoints those who wish that Shakespeare had simply kept on writing tragedies. Because of the heavy emphasis on reconciliation in *Cymbeline,* the jealousy of Posthumus is not titanic, as the jealousy of Othello is titanic; it expresses only a childish petulance about women in general: "I'll write against them, Detest them, curse them." Similarly Leontes (as he himself points out) falls far short of being a somber demonic tyrant on the scale of Macbeth, and can only alternate between bluster and an uneasy sense of having done wrong:

> Away with that audacious lady! Antigonus,
> I charg'd thee that she should not come about me.
> I knew she would.

This scaling down of the human perspective is in conformity with a dramatic structure that seems closely analogous to such Christian conceptions as wrath and grace. But the only one of the four romances in which I suspect any explicit—which means allegorical—references to Christianity is *Cymbeline.* Cymbeline was king of Britain at the birth of Christ, and in such scenes as the Jailer's speculations about death and his wistful "I would we were all of one mind, and that mind good," there are hints that some far-reaching change in the human situation is taking place off-stage. The play ends on the word "peace" and with Cymbeline's promise to pay tribute to Rome, almost as though, as soon as the story ended, another one were to begin with Augustus Caesar's decree that all the world should be taxed.

No such explicit links are appropriate to *The Winter's Tale,* though it is true that the story does tell of a mysterious disappearing child born in the winter who has four father-figures assigned to her: a real one, a putative one who later becomes her father-in-law, a fictional one, Smalus of Libya in Florizel's tale, and a shepherd foster-father. This makes up a group of a shepherd and three kings, of whom one is African. The first part of *The Winter's Tale* is, like *Cymbeline,* full of the imagery of superstitious sacrifice. Leontes, unable to sleep, wonders if having Hermione burnt alive would not give him rest. Antigonus offers to spay his three daughters if Hermione is guilty, though he would prefer to castrate himself. Mamillius, whom Leontes thinks of as a part of himself, becomes the victim necessary to save Leontes, and the exposing of Perdita is attended by a sacrificial holocaust. Not only is Antigonus devoured by a bear, but the ship and its crew were "Wrecked the same instant of their master's death and in the view of the shepherd; so that all the instruments which aided to expose the child were even then lost when it was found." In contrast, the restoring of Perdita to her mother is an act of sacramental communion, but it is a secular communion, and the "instruments" aiding in it are the human arts. The main characters repair to Paulina's house intending to "sup" there, and are taken into her chapel and presented with what is alleged to be a work of painting and sculpture. Hermione, like Thaisa in *Pericles,* is brought to life by the playing of music, and references to the art of magic follow. Art, therefore, seems part of the regenerating power of the play, and the imagination of the poet is to be allied with that of the lover as against that of the lunatic.

Apart from the final scene, at least three kinds of art are mentioned in the play. First, there is the art of the gardener who, according to Polixenes' famous speech, may help or change nature by marrying a gentler scion to the wildest stock but can do so only through nature's power, so that "the art itself is nature." This is a sound humanist view: it is the view of Sidney, who contrasts the brazen world of nature with the golden world of art but also speaks of art as a second nature. Sidney's view does not necessitate, but it is consistent with, his ridiculing of plays that show a character as an infant in one act and grown up in the next, and that mingle kings and clowns in the same scene. It is also the view of Ben Jonson who, recognizing a very different conception of nature in Shakespeare's romances, remarked good-humoredly that he was "loth to make nature afraid in his plays, like those that beget tales, tempests, and suchlike drolleries." We note that Polixenes' speech entirely fails to convince Perdita, who merely repeats that she will have nothing to do with bastard flowers:

> No more than, were I painted, I would wish
> This youth should say 'twere well, and only therefore
> Desire to breed by me. . . .

—a remark which oddly anticipate the disappearance of the painted statue of Hermione into the real Hermione. It also, as has often been pointed out, fails to convince Polixenes himself, for a few moments later we find him in a paroxysm of fury at the thought of his own gentle scion marrying the wild stock of a shepherd's daughter. Whatever its merits, Polixenes' view of art hardly seems to describe the kind of art that the play itself manifests.

Secondly, there is the kind of art represented by Julio Romano, said to be the painter and sculptor of Hermione's statue, a mimetic realist who "would beguile Nature of her custom, so perfectly is he her ape." But it turns out that in fact no statue has been made of Hermione, and the entire reference to Romano seems pointless. We do not need his kind of art when we have the real Hermione, and here again, whatever Romano's merits, neither he nor the kind of realism he represents seems to be very central to the play itself. The literary equivalent of realism is plausibility, the supplying of adequate causation for events. There is little plausibility in *The Winter's Tale,* and a great deal of what is repeatedly called "wonder." Things are presented to us, not explained. The jealousy of Leontes explodes without warning: An actor may rationalize it in various ways; a careful reader of the text may suspect that the references to his youth have touched off some kind of suppressed guilt; but the essential fact is that the jealousy suddenly appears where it had not been before, like a second subject in a piece of music. "How should this grow?" Polixenes asks of Camillo, but Camillo evades the question. At the end of the play Hermione is first a statue, then a living woman. The explanations given do not satisfy even Leontes, much less us. He says:

> But how, is to be question'd; for I saw her,
> As I thought, dead, and have in vain said many
> A prayer upon her grave.

As often in Shakespeare, further explanations are promised to the characters, but are not given to the audience: Paulina merely says, "it appears she lives."

Thirdly, though one blushes to mention it, there is the crude popular art of the ballads of Autolycus, of which one describes "how a usurer's wife was brought to bed of twenty money-bags at a burden." "Is it true, think you?" asks Mopsa, unconsciously using one of the most frequently echoed words in the play. We notice that Shakespeare seems to be calling our attention to the incredibility of his story and to its ridiculous and outmoded devices when he makes both Paulina and the Gentlemen who report the recognition of Perdita speak of what is happening as "like an old tale." The magic words pronounced by Paulina that draw speech from Hermione are "Our Perdita is found," and Paulina has previously said that the finding of Perdita is "monstrous to our human reason." And when one of the Gentlemen says "Such a deal of wonder is broken out within this hour that ballad-makers cannot be able to express it," we begin to suspect that the kind of art manifested by the play itself is in some respects closer to these "trumpery" ballads than to the sophisticated idealism and realism of Polixenes and Romano.

My late and much beloved colleague Professor Harold S. Wilson has called attention to the similarity between Polixenes' speech and a passage in Puttenham's *Arte of English Poesie* (1589), which in discussing the relation of art and nature uses the analogy of the gardener and the example of the "gillyvor." Puttenham also goes on to say that there is another context where art is "only a bare imitator of nature's works, following and counterfeiting her actions and effects, as the Marmoset doth many countenances and gestures of man; of which sort are the arts of painting and carving." We are reminded of Romano, the painter and carver who is the perfect "ape" of nature. The poet, says Puttenham, is to use all types of art in their proper place, but for his greatest moments he will work "even as nature her self working by her own peculiar virtue and proper instinct and not by example or meditation or exercise as all other artificers do." We feel that Puttenham, writing before Shakespeare had got properly started and two centuries earlier than Coleridge, has nonetheless well characterized the peculiar quality of Shakespeare's art.

The fact that Leontes' state of mind is a parody of the imagination of lover and poet links *The Winter's Tale* with Shakespeare's "humor" comedies, which turn on the contrast between fantasy and reality. Katharina moves from shrew to obedient wife; Falstaff from the seducer to the gull of the merry wives; the King of Navarre and his followers from contemplative pedants seeking authority from books to helpless lovers performing the tasks imposed on them by their ladies. Similarly when Florizel says that his love for Perdita

> cannot fail but by
> The violation of my faith; and then
> Let nature crush the sides o' th' earth together
> And mar the seeds within!...

—he is supplying the genuine form of what Camillo describes in parallel cosmological terms:

> you may as well
> Forbid the sea for to obey the moon,
> As or by oath remove or counsel shake
> The fabric of his folly, whose foundation
> Is piled upon his faith.

Puttenham begins his treatise by comparing the poet, as a creator, to God, "who without any travail to his divine imagination made all the world of nought." Leontes' jealousy is a parody of a creation out of nothing, as the insistent repetition of the word "nothing" in the first act indicates, and as Leontes himself says in his mysterious mumbling half-soliloquy:

Affection, thy intention stabs the centre!
Thou dost make possible things not so held,
Communicat'st with dream—how can this be?
With what's unreal thou coactive art,
And fellow'st nothing.

A humor is restored to a normal outlook by being confronted, not directly with reality, but with a reflection of its own illusion, as Katharina is tamed by being shown the reflection of her own shrewishness in Petruchio. Similarly Leontes, in the final scene, is "mocked with art," the realistic illusion of Romano's statue which gradually reveals itself to be the real Hermione.

In the artificial society of the Sicilian court there are Mamillius, the hopeful prince who dies, and the infant Perdita who vanishes. In the rural society of Bohemia there are the shepherdess Perdita who is "Flora Peering in April's front," and Florizel who, as his name suggests, is her masculine counterpart, and the Prince Charming who later reminds Leontes strongly of Mamillius and becomes Leontes' promised heir. Perdita says that she would like to strew Florizel with flowers:

like a bank for love to lie and play on.
Not like a corse; or if, not to be buried,
But quick and in mine arms.

The antithesis between the two worlds is marked by Polixenes, who is handed "flowers of winter" and who proceeds to destroy the festival like a winter wind, repeating the *senex iratus* role of Leontes in the other kingdom. But though he can bully Perdita, he impresses her no more than Leontes had impressed Hermione. Perdita merely says:

I was not much afeard; for once or twice
I was about to speak and tell him plainly
The selfsame sun that shines upon his court
Hides not his visage from our cottage but
Looks on alike.

There is a faint New Testament echo here, but of course to Perdita the god of the sun would be Apollo, who does see to it that Polixenes is outwitted, though only by the fact that Perdita is really a princess. As always in Shakespeare, the structure of society is unchanged by the comic action. What happens in *The Winter's Tale* is the opposite of the art of the gardener as Polixenes describes it. A society which is artificial in a limited sense at the beginning of the play becomes at the end still artificial, but natural as well. Nature provides the means for the regeneration of artifice. But still it is true that "The art itself is nature," and one wonders why a speech ending with those words should be assigned to Polixenes, the opponent of the festival.

The context of Polixenes' theory is the Renaissance framework in which there are two levels of the order of nature. Art belongs to human nature, and human nature is, properly speaking, the state that man lived in in Eden, or the Golden Age, before his fall into a lower world of physical nature to which he is not adapted. Man attempts to regain his original state through law, virtue, education, and such rational and conscious aids as art. Here nature is a superior order. In poetry this upper level of nature, uncontaminated by the sin and death of the fall, is usually symbolized by the starry spheres, which are now all that is left of it. The starry spheres produce the music of the spheres, and the harmony of music usually represents this upper level of nature in human life.

Most Shakespearian comedy is organized within this framework, and when it is, its imagery takes on the form outlined by G. Wilson Knight in *The Shakespearean Tempest* (1932). The tempest symbolizes the destructive elements in the order of nature, and music the permanently constructive elements in it. Music in its turn is regularly associated with the starry spheres, of which the one closest to us, the moon, is the normal focus. The control of the tempest by the harmony of the spheres appears in the image of the moon pulling the tides, an image used once or twice in *The Winter's Tale.* The action of *The Merchant of Venice,* too, extends from the cosmological harmonies of the fifth act, where the moon sleeps with Endymion, to the tempest that wrecked Antonio's ships. In *Pericles,* which employs this imagery of harmony and tempest most exhaustively, Pericles is said to be a master of music, Cerimon revives Thaisa by music, Diana announces her appearance to Pericles by music, and the final recognition scene unites the music and tempest symbols, since it takes place in the temple of Diana during the festival of Neptune. Music also accompanies the revival of Hermione in the final scene of *The Winter's Tale.* All the attention is absorbed in Hermione as she begins to move while music plays; and we are reminded of Autolycus and of his role as a kind of rascally Orpheus at the sheep-shearing festival: "My clown. . .would not stir his pettitoes till he had both tune and words; which so drew the rest of the herd to me that all their other senses stuck in ears. . . . No hearing, no feeling, but my sir's song, and admiring the nothing of it." Here again Autolycus seems to be used to indicate that something is being subordinated in the play, though by no means eliminated.

In another solstitial play, *A Midsummer Night's Dream,* the cosmology is of this more conventional Renaissance kind. In the middle, between the world of chaos symbolized by tempest and the world of starry spheres symbolized by music, comes the cycle of nature, the world of Eros and Adonis, Puck and Pyramus, the love-god and the dying god. To this middle world the fairies belong, for the fairies are spirits of the four natural elements, and their dissension causes disorder in nature. Above, the cold fruitless moon of Diana, whose nun Hermia would have to be, hangs over the action. While a mermaid is calming the sea by her song and attracting the stars by the power of harmony, Cupid shoots an arrow at the moon and its vestal: it falls in a parabola on a flower and turns it "purple with love's wound." The story of Pyramus is not very coherently told in Peter Quince's play, but in Ovid there is a curious image about the blood spurting out of Pyramus in an arc like water out of a burst pipe and falling on the white mulberry and turning it purple. Here nature as a cycle of birth and death, symbolized by the purple flower, revolves underneath nature as a settled and predictable order or harmony, as it does also in a third solstitial play, *Twelfth Night,* which begins with an image comparing music to a wind blowing on a bank of violets.

But in *The Winter's Tale* nature is associated, not with the credible, but with the incredible: Nature as an order is subordinated to the nature that yearly confronts us with the impossible miracle of renewed life. In Ben Jonson's animadversions on Shakespeare's unnatural romances it is particularly the functional role of the dance, the "concupiscence of jigs," as he calls it, that he objects to. But it is the dance that most clearly expresses the pulsating energy of nature as it appears in *The Winter's Tale,* an energy which communicates itself to the dialogue. Such words as "push" and "wild" (meaning rash) are constantly echoed; the play ends with the words "Hastily lead away," and we are told that the repentant Leontes

> o'er and o'er divides him
> 'Twixt his unkindness and his kindness; th' one
> He chides to hell and bids the other grow
> Faster than thought of time.

Much is said about magic in the final scene, but there is no magician, no Prospero, only the sense of a participation in the redeeming and reviving power of a nature identified with art, grace, and love. Hence the final recognition is appropriately that of a frozen statue turning into a living presence, and the appropriate Chorus is Time, the destructive element which is also the only possible representative of the timeless.

# 23

# New Uses of Adversity: Tragic Experience in *The Tempest*

*Stephen Kitay Orgel*

*The Tempest,* Hemminge and Condell tell us, is a comedy. And yet, if it is read with more concern for Shakespeare's chronology than for his editors' notions of *genre*—read, that is, as a work that develops out of the great tragedies—it will be apparent how much the tragic view of life is present in the play. Even the earliest and lightest Shakespearean comedies—*The Two Gentlemen of Verona, The Comedy of Errors*—have their tragic elements, their potential disasters. This same quality becomes a very serious threat to the worlds of *The Merchant of Venice* and *Much Ado About Nothing,* and largely controls the tone of *Measure for Measure* and *All's Well that Ends Well,* plays which are, in form at least, still clearly comedies.

Similarly, behind the great tragedies lies not simply the progression of plays from *Titus Andronicus* through *Richard III* and *Richard II* to *Romeo and Juliet* and *Julius Caesar,* but also, and just as significantly, the whole range of Shakespearean comedy. The plays suffer greatly by being cut off from each other, placed in those neat piles of comedies, histories, tragedies that are the folio editors' contribution to our sense of Shakespeare. The rich world of *The Merchant of Venice,* which Shakespeare so often and so deliberately moves close to disaster; or the feasting and frustration of *Twelfth Night,* which concludes with a sense that the party is very much over and a song that is to reappear in *Lear,* turn easily enough into the worlds of *Measure for Measure* and *Troilus and Cressida*—worlds of greed, lust, disease. That the next step was, logically, into the great tragedies seems an obvious enough perception. Still, let us recall that the logical step after *Richard II* was into tragedy also; but it was a step Shakespeare evidently felt unprepared to take. In a perfectly literal way, then, comedy served Shakespeare as the training ground for tragedy. In the same way the late comedies, *Pericles, The Winter's Tale,* and *The Tempest,* are filled with a sense of life learned through the tragedies; however qualified the suffering, however happy the resolution, each of them deals richly and seriously with experience which is essentially tragic. It is from this aspect that I wish to consider *The Tempest.*

Simply on the level of action, *The Tempest* has a great deal to connect it with tragedy: the shipwreck, the uninhabited islands, the potential murders. Indeed, to most of the victims of the wreck, the play seems very much like a tragedy. Certainly for Alonso there is nothing till the very end to mitigate the strongest sense of loss and desolation the play presents. And yet the viewpoint of Prospero continuously qualifies that tragic sense, and reminds us that the drama cannot turn fully into tragedy. This sort of double viewpoint is nothing new in Shakespeare's comedy; Portia in *The Merchant of Venice* and the Duke in *Measure for Measure* provide something analogous; and, as with Prospero, in both cases it is their greater awareness, their heightened perceptiveness, which manages to subvert the tragedy. Portia is simply shrewder than anyone else; and the Duke has a better, fuller understanding of human nature, as well as something of the same control over the action that Prospero has. In both their plays the claims of reason and humanity are asserted over disorder, passion, violence—mercy over revenge, however justified; forgiveness and reconciliation over retribution, however merited. But there is a significant distinction to be drawn between these two examples and *The Tempest.* In *The Merchant of Venice* and *Measure for Measure* the tragedy is averted through intelligence and sympathy, perfectly ordinary qualities, perhaps somewhat heightened, which we may be expected to find in ourselves. But Prospero's claims are explicitly, unabashedly extraordinary; they are the claims of fantasy taken—as we cannot take it—literally. But the play does take it very literally; Prospero's power is the power of imagination, and it is something no other character possesses. The powerful imagination, a concept we tend to treat as an easy metaphor, is translated here into terms of action. We are continuously aware of the extent to which this world is controlled by Prospero and is even at times indistinguishable from him. The elements obey him; natural forces are an extension of his will, an external manifestation of his mind, and have, consequently, explicitly human qualities like pity and gratitude. The shipwreck, the attempted murders, the loss and desolation, are qualified here by the ubiquitous presence of the magician of the island, who has banished the wicked witch, who can command the winds and the sea, and who has as his servants the spirits of nature, all the creatures of the imagination. For Prospero, indeed, idea and action, metaphor and drama merge; the distinction between thinking a thing and doing it has essentially disappeared.

Obviously an actualized metaphor represents a different kind of action, a different notion of what it is to *act,* from the kind we ordinarily find presented in drama. But the magician and his metaphors are only a part of the play; and there is another part interwoven with it which we might call, for most of its length, at least, *The Tragedy of the Tempest.* We may tend to slight the seriousness of this aspect of the drama, overshadowed as it is by the omnipotent figure of Prospero. Nevertheless, the play opens with it: plunges us into the midst of an image of disordered nature, *the tempest,* which had served King Lear as an image for the chaos of his state and of his mind. And the opening scene on the ship, brief as it is, refers us back to *Lear* in a number of ways. The boatswain's charge to the courtiers that "you do assist the storm," his taunting "What cares these roarers for the name of King?" and "use your authority," should all remind us that Lear's tone to the elements, in a play precisely about royal authority, was one of command: "Blow, winds, and crack your cheeks!" Now, "the name of King" in its immediate context may also, if we are thinking about *Lear,* work in exactly the opposite direction; it may recall to us that throughout Lear's tempest, the king has nothing but "the name of King"; that once stripped of authority and sent into the storm, he becomes "unaccommodated man." This is a serious foreboding of what we may expect to happen to the king in *this* tempest—Alonso, wrecked on an island and threatened by both the violence of nature and the human passions of selfishness, greed and jealousy which are so evident among his followers on the ship.

Nevertheless, the boatswain's question, "What cares these roarers for the name of King?" is in the larger context ironic; for the storm *is* under the control of Prospero. As we pass from the chaos and helplessness of the ship to the authority which the winds actually obey, we are presented with a contrasting scene of order, compassion, and an almost intolerable innocence. Miranda's description of the storm we have just experienced shows us that nature, both human and elemental, has other aspects. The passage is worth pausing over because it announces a number of themes which are to be of importance throughout the play:

> If by your Art, my dearest father, you have
> Put the wild waters in this roar, allay them.
> The sky, it seems, would pour down stinking pitch,

> But that the sea, mounting to th'welkin's cheek,
> Dashes the fire out. O, I have suffered
> With those that I saw suffer! A brave vessel,
> (Who had, no doubt, some noble creature in her,)
> Dash'd all to pieces. O, the cry did knock
> Against my very heart! Poor souls, they perish'd!
> Had I been any god of power, I would
> Have sunk the sea within the earth, or ere
> It should the good ship so have swallow'd, and
> The fraughting souls within her.[1] (I, ii, 1–13)

The storm to Miranda presents an image of the whole universe in conflict, but her concern is not a metaphysical one. She fastens her attention on the destruction of the ship, as we have just done, and in contrast to the selfishness and insensitivity we have observed in the first scene, her sympathy and compassion are immediate and unqualified. "O, I have suffered/ With those that I saw suffer," she says, and that characteristic immediacy in her responses, that reciprocal suffering, is an analogue on the human level of the reciprocal violence she has perceived in the tempest. Similarly, her image of the wreck is at once translated into an image of her feelings about it: the "vessel... dash'd all to pieces" emits for her a cry which "did knock against my very heart." Miranda's suffering is apparent the first moment we see her; it is very real and quite uncomplicated, and it is only the first instance of many in a play which is full of suffering. Yet her compassion, real as it is, also has a certain element of shallowness, or at least of inexperience about it. She assumes "some noble creature" must be in the ship—whereas we, who have just come through the first scene, may tend to doubt it. In her innocence she idealizes whatever she experiences, and every statement she makes, all her observations and attitudes, are continually modified for us by the play's context. Here, the apparent futility of her last remark ("Had I been any god of power...") is qualified by the fact that Prospero *is* the "god of power" that his daughter wishes to be. As soon as we are on the island, the assertion of human control over the tempest, so ironic in the context of the first scene, is intended perfectly literally. But it is a special kind of power Miranda invokes from her father, and her word for it is *art*.

*Our* awareness of Prospero's power, however, is conveyed here not through his magical apparatus, the wand and the cloak he is to remove with the words "Lie there, my art," but simply through the tone of his reply:

> Be collected:
> No more amazement: tell your piteous heart
> There's no harm done.
> *Mir.* O, woe the day!
> *Pros.* No harm.
> (I, ii, 13–15)

[1] Quotations are from the Arden edition of *The Tempest,* ed. Frank Kermode, 6th ed. (Cambridge: Harvard University Press, 1958).

He speaks as one speaks to a child, simply, gently and firmly; more important, he speaks with a sureness and succinctness which, in tragedy, are possible only at the very end. His tone is that of a character with a full comprehension of the experience of the drama; and the sense it gives us is of a mind achieving full control of itself, so that when Prospero proceeds to explain the background of the play in the subsequent recitation of his sufferings, we feel that we can with understanding participate in the end of a long and complex action. We have been dramatically prepared, that is, for the recitation simply by Prospero's tone.

Prospero's magic power is directly related to his control over his past suffering, and we see him working out the last traces of bitterness and vindictiveness in the sharp expostulations that punctuate that speech to his daughter—"Dost thou attend me?" "I pray thee mark me." "Dost thou hear?" (These are not to be taken as evidence that Miranda's attention is wandering, though they are usually, ludicrously, treated as such in productions of the play; Miranda's reply to "Dost thou hear?"—"Your tale, sir, would cure deafness"—betrays humor as well as sympathy.) What we see as Prospero describes the loss of his dukedom is his retrospective suffering being played out before our eyes. But the controlling of the experience is evident too, as the tone of Prospero's monologue moves from violence against his enemies to a wry and familiar but most untypical playfulness with his daughter ("Well demanded, wench..."), and finally to the tone of "Now I arise" and "I am ready now"; to that tone of authority and sureness which we observed in his first lines and which are characteristic of him throughout the play.

Prospero's suffering, then, is essentially behind him. By contrast, the play presents a variety of characters in varying degrees of grief or passion. The first of these, and, after Miranda, probably the least complicated, is Ferdinand. We see him shipwrecked and desolate after the storm; but what we hear is Ariel singing:

> Come unto these yellow sands,
>   And then take hands:
> Courtsied when you have and kiss'd
>   The wild waves whist:
> Foot it featly here and there,
>   And sweet sprites bear
> The burthen. (I, ii, 377–383)

The usual editorial interpretation of "the wild waves whist" as an absolute construction is syntactically unnecessary and renders the song meaningless. The song is about relationships in nature between the spirits and the elements, about kissing the waves into silence, quieting the tempest with love. Ferdinand comments:

Where should this music be? i'th'air or th'earth?
It sounds no more: and, sure, it waits upon
Some god o'th'island. Sitting upon a bank,
Weeping again the King my father's wrack,
This music crept by me upon the waters,
Allaying both their fury and my passion
With its sweet air: thence I have follow'd it,
Or it hath drawn me rather. (I, ii, 390–397)

Ferdinand is overcome with grief, but the first thing we sense about him is a continual tone of wonder, like Miranda's, an almost passive receptiveness to experience of all kinds. His nature is very close to the elemental nature that surrounds him; the fury of the waves and his own passion are scarcely to be distinguished, and Ariel's music has the same effect on both. (Ferdinand shows himself, incidentally, more perceptive than most editors: "allaying... their fury" is simply a paraphrase of Ariel's "kiss'd/ The wild waves whist.") The "sweet air" is both the musical strain and the element, the atmosphere. The double sense of "air" is only one example of an ambiguity that functions throughout this play, where all the elements may serve as metaphors for something else. (So, for example, earlier in the scene [1.316] Prospero addresses Caliban as "earth.") Finally the whole experience becomes ambiguous to Ferdinand; he becomes uncertain whether he has been active or passive, whether he has followed the music or been drawn by it. But his sense of the experience is perfectly correct; he perceives that the music "waits upon/ Some god o' th' island," and he is fully aware of its effect.

We keep being reminded that there is something special about nature on the island. Ariel sings again:

Full fadom five thy father lies;
  Of his bones are coral made;
Those are pearls that were his eyes:
  Nothing of him that doth fade,
But doth suffer a sea-change
Into something rich and strange. (I, ii, 399–404)

Now that nature has been calmed, Ariel proceeds to deepen this mysterious experience. His song is about nature becoming art; and in it, disaster and death involve not decay and loss, but a transformation into something wonderful, something almost directly opposite to loss, tremendous richness. And the word for that transformation is *suffer*. We may recall Miranda's analogous use of "art" to describe a quality defined in the first scene as "command" and "authority." In Ariel's song we begin to be aware that the whole concept of *suffering* is now undergoing a sea-change. It is not being diminished at all, but we are seeing it from a different viewpoint, whereby the endurance of violence and destruction leaves us infinitely richer. That richness has been taken perfectly literally by the song; the drowned man has become a work of art, and the transformation has been effected by the art of the figure who has suffered most, and whose very name conveys the richness he embodies: Prospero.

Ferdinand, insofar as he can, understands all this perfectly: "The ditty does remember my drown'd father./ This is no mortal business, nor no sound/ That the earth owes" (I, ii, 408–410). He again paraphrases the song; the wonder is still there, but so is the awareness: to the limits of his information, he knows exactly what is going on. And his sense of things again is accurate. "This is no mortal business" means a number of things, but one thing it certainly means is "this is nothing to do with death." We are watching the beginning of a transformation of Ferdinand's grief into something else. It is precisely the awareness and receptivenss we have observed that make him the right man for Miranda; and especially, it is his sense of wonder that makes him immediately aware of the wonder that *is* Miranda, whose very name means "something to be wondered at."

Ferdinand's suffering is, as we have seen, relatively uncomplicated, though it is not so simple as Miranda's. Ferdinand is not merely experiencing sympathetic feelings; he has undergone a real and great loss. His father's case, however, is a different matter. Alonso suffers more deeply in the play than any other character, and though the play is certainly not primarily about Alonso, his experience has a dramatic significance which in the total picture is second only to Prospero's.

The first scene of Act II returns us to a good deal of the tone and personnel of the opening of the play. Squabbling, selfishness, and insensitivity provide the setting for Alonso's grief. For over a hundred lines he says nothing but "Prithee, peace," until at last, goaded by Antonio's and Sebastian's talk of his daughter's wedding (from which they were returning when the tempest occurred), he passionately replies:

> You cram these words into mine ears against
> The stomach of my sense. Would I had never
> Married my daughter there! for, coming thence,
> My son is lost and, in my rate, she too,
> Who is so far from Italy removed
> I ne'er again shall see her. O thou mine heir
> Of Naples and of Milan, what strange fish
> Hath made his meal on thee? (II, i, 102–109)

Even without recalling the sensitivity and perceptiveness that went with Ferdinand's simple grief, we must be aware that this is a rather crude way to talk about the death of a son. Admittedly Alonso is with a crude group, and the main intention of his words is simply to get Sebastian and Antonio to be quiet and leave him alone. Still, we are given an immediate contrast of tone in Francisco's reply:

> Sir, he may live:
> I saw him beat the surges under him,
> And ride upon their backs; he trod the water,
> Whose enmity he flung aside, and breasted
> The surge most swoln that met him; his bold head
> 'Bove the contentious waves he kept, and oared
> Himself with his good arms in lusty stroke
> To th' shore, that o'er his wave-worn basis bowed,
> As stooping to relieve him: I not doubt
> He came alive to land. (II, i, 109–118)

The tone is one of nobility and respect; Francisco speaks with the sort of heroic rhetoric we recall from *Julius Caesar* and *Antony and Cleopatra.* This is the way kings *should* talk. By contrast, our first sense of Alonso is of insensitivity, coarseness, and a general tastelessness in the quality of his suffering. We feel a good deal more kindly toward him by the end of the play, but aversion must necessarily be our first response, and is inevitably strengthened by what we already know about Alonso from Prospero's narrative.

The response, though, begins at once to be qualified. To Sebastian's incredibly tasteless accusation "The fault's your own" (l.131), Alonso replies sharply and immediately, "So is the dear'st o' th' loss," and we feel the rightness of the reply as well as its sincerity. Notice, too, how it picks up and transforms the metaphor Ariel had used singing to Ferdinand of Alonso's own death. That loss became a new richness; this is just the opposite, and "dearest" provides Shakespeare with another functional ambiguity. The sense of the line is of a richness lost with no metaphor to qualify the desolation.

Nevertheless, "The fault's your own" is of course precisely right; Alonso's suffering is involved with his guilt. This is what gives his tone a bitterness alien to his son's grieving. In a later scene, when Ariel confronts Alonso as he has confronted Ferdinand, the king's guilt is seen as a central issue in the drama, a motivation for the whole action:

> *Ariel.* You are three men of sin, whom Destiny—
> That hath to instrument this lower world
> And what is in't,—the never-surfeited sea
> Hath caus'd to belch up you. . . .
> I and my fellows
> Are ministers of Fate. . . .
> But remember—
> For that's my business to you,—that you three
> From Milan did supplant good Prospero:
> Expos'd unto the sea, which hath requit it,

Him and his innocent child: for which foul deed
The powers, delaying, not forgetting, have
Incens'd the seas and shores, yea, all the creatures,
Against your peace. Thee of thy son, Alonso,
They have bereft; and do pronounce by me
Ling'ring perdition—worse than any death
Can be at once—shall step by step attend
You and your ways; whose wraths to guard you from,—
Which here, in this most desolate isle, else falls
Upon your heads,—is nothing but heart-sorrow
And a clear life ensuing. (III, iii, 53–82)

Ariel declares himself an agent of *Fate,* and the first thing we should remark is that this is not true; it is only something like the truth, which has been related in a way that these three men of sin and rather limited sensibility can understand—and only Alonso understands it. (No such explanation, we recall, was necessary for Ferdinand.) From then on, the speech is not only complex and majestic verse but very straight talk indeed: Ariel has to remind Alonso of what he has done, and why he merits punishment. "Ling'ring perdition—worse than any death/ Can be at once" is to be his fate. The spirit explicitly points the way toward not redemption, not reconciliation, but simply toward some mitigation of the punishment and of the guilt. The way is precisely one it has never occurred to Alonso to take; it involves an awareness of his crime and a sense of his responsibility.

This speech has been tailored to fit the requirements of Alonso's sensibility; that is, it presents the truth, or a version of it, in the only terms he can understand. It works; and the way we know it works is that something new happens in the verse he speaks. "O, it is monstrous, monstrous!" he cries, as Ariel's words make him aware for the first time of his crime, or of the punishment, or simply of the fact that he lives, after all, in a world where something like retribution actually exists. His sense of horror and surprise rushes in on him all at once, bringing with it a revelation. All at once, Alonso speaks a different language; the crudeness of that earlier perception of Ferdinand's death is now replaced by a new tone and an altered sensibility:

O, it is monstrous, monstrous!
Methought the billows spoke, and told me of it;
The winds did sing it to me; and the thunder,
That deep and dreadful organ-pipe, pronounc'd
The name of Prosper: it did bass my trespass.
Therefor my son i' th' ooze is bedded; and
I'll seek him deeper than e'er plummet sounded,
And with him there lie mudded. (III, iii, 95–102)

The language of this is obviously, suddenly, rich and complex; Alonso suddenly perceives a whole new range of experience. He has, in fact, *suffered* that sea-change before our eyes. We may recall Ferdinand's pun on "sweet air," and see that for the first time Alonso is perceiving the elements in terms of music, and not of destruction. It is now possible for him to repent, to ask Prospero's pardon when the time comes, and ultimately to be reconciled with him and reunited with his son. The sense he has of all this, however, may still strike us as a little oversimplified: the cause-and-effect relationship he finds between his crime and this retribution does not actually exist, although it may be as close as he can come to a real understanding of the action. On the other hand, nobody in the play has a better sense of it except Prospero, and he, of course, is directly responsible for the action. Let us, then, look back now, and consider what it is that Prospero does in *The Tempest*.

I have remarked earlier that Prospero's kind of action is significantly different from that of the other characters in the play; that is, Prospero alone is not limited to ordinary dramatic action; his awareness, his intelligence, and particularly his imaginative power have all been translated into terms of physical action: his metaphors have been actualized, or taken literally. Therefore our sense of his "art," his magic power, is that it is really a kind of heightened awareness and intelligence. Certainly he is aware of everything that happens in the play; and since, as we have seen, all his action is mental action, for Prospero to be *aware* of something is to be in control of it.

The magic, then, is something like Bacon's idea of science; not spells and witchcraft, but a complete understanding of nature. We may recall, too, that for Bacon the purpose of scientific inquiry was precisely to be able to control nature as Prospero does. But *nature* has larger meanings in the play, as it has in *Lear*. It means weather—*The Tempest*—and by extension an unseen and constantly active universe which is personified in the spirits whom Prospero has at his command. This is "elemental nature," and the *elements* keep reappearing in the play's imagery—the elements of wind and rain, and the four basic elements that compose the world: earth, water, fire, and air. Significantly, too, the most volatile of these, Ariel, the spirit of air, is Prospero's servant. The magician has released Ariel from the tree where "the damn'd witch Sycorax. . .in her most unmitigable rage" had imprisoned him; nature suffered under the passionate, unnatural sorceress, and Prospero has relieved that suffering. An act of kindness has moved Ariel: Elemental nature, even the volatile air, can feel gratitude. In contrast, the play presents the other sort of nature—human nature—and we may remember, along with the most agonizing scenes from *Lear,* a song from comedy:

> Blow, blow thou winter wind,
> Thou art not so unkind
> As man's ingratitude.

Constantly throughout the play, elemental nature is invested with human qualities, while human nature is seen as base and vicious. The antithesis is made very clear when, right after we have witnessed the violence of the storm in the opening scene, Prospero describes how he and Miranda had been set adrift:

> there they hoist us,
> To cry to th' sea that roar'd to us; to sigh
> To th' winds, whose pity, sighing back again,
> Did us but loving wrong. (I, ii, 148–151)

We find here that same immediacy of reciprocal response between elemental nature and human feeling that we noticed the first time we saw Miranda. Her nature, in its innocence, is the closest in the play to the nature of the elements. She is perfectly safe on the island because—with one significant exception, which we shall consider presently—the elements are all she has to deal with. But Prospero is about to return to society, to a world of *human* nature, and Miranda's innocence, therefore, must yield to education. "I pray thee, mark me," says Prospero, "that a brother should/ Be so perfidious!" (ll. 67–68). She must be taught, like Hamlet, "that one may smile and smile and be a villain."

In the world of *The Tempest,* Miranda is one extreme of human nature. The opposite extreme is the figure Prospero calls "the beast Caliban." He is usually treated by commentators as a foil to Ariel—the airy spirit versus the earthy monster—but this seems to me only part of the truth. For one thing, it implies an evaluation of elemental nature—air is good, earth is bad—that is really only incidental in the play. Such value judgments are, on the whole, reserved for human nature, for characters with motives. Furthermore, to contrast Caliban with Ariel may lead us to ignore a contrast that the play clearly does set up between Caliban and Miranda. Both were raised on the island, both equally inexperienced, both the objects of Prospero's loving care; but Miranda's nature turns toward order, obedience, compassion, and reason; and Caliban's toward violence, destruction, the indulgence of appetites, sensual passion, and particularly lust. The situation is presented almost as a scientific experiment: If two children brought up under the same conditions behave differently, we may argue that they are different *by nature*. Miranda has been carefully educated; Caliban is incapable of learning. The two are contrasted throughout the play. For example, they have precisely the same response to the first strangers they have ever seen; both idealize them. Miranda says of Ferdinand, "I might call him/ A thing divine"; Caliban says of Stephano, "that's a brave god." And by the end of the play they have both learned a good deal about human nature. Caliban is quite disenchanted, Miranda is wide-eyed with wonder; but he has instinctively—that is, *naturally*—made the wrong choice, and she has made the right one.

Prospero is very hard on Caliban; perhaps, we may feel, too hard. Certainly in this case our sympathies are engaged in a most unexpected way. Prospero's attitude, and our response to it, play a large part in determining the total effect of the play, and it is worth pausing to consider them in general terms. We may begin by nothing that whatever harshness Prospero expresses the play justifies at once when Caliban, reminded that he had repaid all his master's kindness by trying to rape Miranda, is both unrepentent and retrospectively lecherous. Furthermore, Caliban is the only figure in this world for whom a direct relationship between crime and retribution (such as Ariel has described to Alonso) has always actually existed; to Caliban, that is, Ariel and the spirits of nature, creatures of Prospero's imagination, really are "ministers of Fate." Caliban suffers horribly at Prospero's hands, but unlike people a little higher on the scale of human nature, his suffering does not change him. He learns nothing from it—not even how to avoid it. Prospero finds him unregenerate and inhuman.

Nevertheless, the problem of our sympathy remains. To say this is not to be sentimental about Caliban; the point is that *our* sense of this figure is different from Prospero's—that is, this is the one place in the play where what Prospero says and what we perceive do not coincide. We shall consider why presently. Here it is sufficient to note that Prospero's description accounts only for the invective, the violence, the *bad nature* of Caliban; it accounts for remarks like, "You taught me language, and my profit on't/ Is, I know how to curse." We hear more than cursing in Caliban's language. If we stop to consider how we know what the island is like, where our sense of its lushness and particularity comes from, we shall realize that it comes almost entirely from Caliban—from verse like this:

> I prithee, let me bring thee where crabs grow;
> And I with my long nails will dig thee pig-nuts;
> Show thee a jay's nest, and instruct thee how
> To snare the nimble marmoset; I'll bring thee
> To clustering filberts, and sometimes I'll get thee
> Young scamels from the rock. (II, ii, 167–172)

It is the specificity that is important here; such catalogues of a full and wild nature communicate considerable vitality, and tell us something about the island that is not conveyed by Ariel's singing. Even Caliban's invective has an unexpected richness. We should look too at his description of how Prospero's spirits torture him:

> Sometime like apes, that mow and chatter at me,
> And after bite me; then like hedgehogs, which
> Lie tumbling in my barefoot way, and mount

Their pricks at my footfall; sometime am I
All wound with adders, who with cloven tongues
Do hiss me into madness. (II, ii, 9–14)

Here we perceive that he too is fully aware of a continuously active—for him, horribly active—universe. Nor is his awareness limited only to ugly things, and he produces one of the great set pieces of the play:

Be not afeard; the isle is full of noises,
Sounds and sweet airs, that give delight, and hurt not.
Sometimes a thousand twangling instruments
Will hum about mine ears; and sometime voices,
That, if I then had wak'd after long sleep,
Will make me sleep again: and then, in dreaming,
The clouds methought would open, and show riches
Ready to drop upon me; that, when I wak'd
I cried to dream again. (III, ii, 133–141)

Of course, the fact that this is addressed to Stephano (whose only response is, "I shall have my music for nothing") will keep us from too uncritical an admiration for Caliban's sensibility. It is also true that the wonderful quality of the island becomes here an image of frustration for Caliban—frustration both in the dream and out of it, because even if the riches did descend, what value would they have on the island? Nevertheless, the primary effect of the passage is of a marvelous and rich fantasy, a dream world which, at rare moments, may merge with the real world to give even the most unregenerate sufferer a respite.

Our sense of Caliban, then, is of violence, cunning, but also of something else we cannot dismiss as Prospero does: a sensuous and fantastic perception of certain kinds of experience. Caliban is the mind that cannot learn, that will not impose controls on its passion; he is the creature for whom *passio*—suffering—has no meaning. In a very different way from Prospero, he does not distinguish between the world of his fantasies and the real world, and in an important sense the island is as much the realm of Caliban's imagination as of Prospero's. But Caliban's creativity, from the lowest level of his lust to the highest of his fantasy, is chaotic and unreasoning, whereas Prospero's is controlled; his power is "art."

It is precisely what Caliban represents, passion unmitigated by any moral sense, will unmoved by any ties of love or faith, that has been the chief danger to Prospero's life. These are the qualities we observed on the ship in the opening scene of the play; and certainly both Prospero's account of his past, and the ease with which Caliban makes gods of Stephano and Trinculo, imply that there is a place for Calibans in the world of Milan and Naples. Prospero's twelve years of suffering have in part been educating him to an awareness of what that world is really like. But on the island, at least, for Prospero to be aware is to control; and his control of "nature" is a control not only of the elements but of his own base nature as well, of the Caliban in himself. What cannot, like Alonso, be educated, can at least, like Stephano and Trinculo, be kept in abeyance or foiled. So nothing Caliban represents is attractive to Prospero any more—not even the sensuous richness of the fantasy, because it is unreasoning and uncontrolled. And this must be a measure of how far Prospero is beyond us, too, with our sympathy for unregenerate nature. We too are being instructed.

Prospero leads the play, then, through suffering to reconciliation and a new life. He moves the action first toward the revelation which is Alonso's salvation, and second toward the wedding masque (IV, i), with its vision of an ordered nature and bountiful fruition. This is Prospero's creation, the most palpable example we are shown of his art.

The masque is first of all an interruption of the dramatic action, a point at which we lose our sense of the progress of time. It is important to remark this, because both the chronology of the action and the length of time it occupies are worked out with considerable care and ingenuity in the play. In fact this and *The Comedy of Errors* are the only Shakespeare plays in which the amount of time represented and the time actually consumed in performance substantially coincide. Therefore it is especially significant that the masque has a very different sort of time scheme from the play.

Time is an essential element of what we ordinarily mean by drama. People act on each other, things happen in time. In comedy, it is not only the medium but also the agent that solves all problems. In tragedy, time has a different aspect: for Hamlet, "the *time* is out of joint"—both the age and the sequence of events, but not the court or the world or particular people—and time begins to look more like an enemy, like that archetype Elizabethan villain Mutability, involving the action in change, decay, and death. The action of *The Tempest,* as we have seen, partakes of both these senses of time, the comic and the tragic. But the masque requires a pause in that action, and partakes, as we shall see, of neither.

The plot of *The Tempest,* then, loses nothing if the masque is omitted, as it usually is in modern productions. Indeed, Prospero himself contributes to our initial sense of its unimportance by referring to it as "some vanity of mine art." Nevertheless, this attitude has been thoroughly qualified for us by the masque itself when Ferdinand interrupts it to pronounce it "a most majestic vision, and/ Harmonious charmingly." Majesty, the qualities of the ruler generally, has been one of the chief concerns of the play; and harmony, or music, has provided much of its metaphor, its poetic structure. Ferdinand, then, perceives an integral connection between the vision and his experience (and ours) on the island. *We* may perceive that the connection is dramatically integral as well. At the beginning of Act IV, when Prospero releases Ferdinand and offers him Miranda's hand in marriage, a new formality and ceremoniousness of tone set the scene in which vows are to be pronounced and the lovers' plot resolved. "Here, afore Heaven," says Prospero, "I ratify this my rich gift," and thereby prepares us for the solemn celebration represented by the masque. But something remarkable happens to the dramatic verse as well:

> Then, as my gift, and thine own acquisition
> Worthily purchas'd, take my daughter: but
> If thou dost break her virgin-knot before
> All sanctimonious ceremonies may
> With full and holy rite be minister'd,
> No sweet aspersion shall the heavens let fall
> To make this contract grow; but barren hate,
> Sour-ey'd disdain, and discord shall bestrew
> The union of your bed with weeds so loathly
> That you shall hate it both: therefore take heed,
> As Hymen's lamps shall light you. (IV, i, 13–23)

As the play looks forward to "sanctimonious ceremonies"—as the action moves toward the masque—the verse begins to use personifications instead of metaphors. "Barren hate, sour-ey'd disdain and discord," and Hymen are figures out of an allegory, and a masque is precisely an allegory put onto a stage. The dialogue, the movement of the poetry, correspondingly becomes more formal. Ferdinand's elaborate reply might almost be a prescribed one, and Prospero with his "fairly spoke" gives the sense that his prospective son-in-law has indeed given the right answer.

The threatening figures Prospero has invoked in the passage just cited, hate, disdain, discord, have been sowing weeds on the marriage bed, which should be fruitful. In contrast, the masque itself opens with an invocation of Ceres, a grain goddess and the deity who presides over the harvest. We find, logically enough, images of growth and fruition in the masque. But the fertility implied here is of quite a different sort from what we have found on the island. Caliban is a hunter and fisherman; the islanders live on wild things. But the masque is about agriculture, and refers us to a highly civilized society—Ceres even remarks on "this short-grass'd green" (l.83): This action takes place on a well-kept lawn. The season adduced is "spongy April," the very beginning of the agricultural year. Crops have not quite begun to sprout yet, and similarly the nymphs are "cold" and "chaste," the bachelor with spring fever is "lass-lorn" (ll. 65–68). But as the masque continues, the season changes. After a scant fifty lines we find "Vines with clust'ring bunches growing; / Plants with goodly burthen bowing" (ll. 112–113). And shortly before Prospero stops the performance, Iris invokes the "sunburn'd sicklemen, of August weary" (l.134): it is now harvesttime. A whole season of growth, fruition, and harvest has been encompassed in about seventy-five lines.

It is clear enough what the masque is doing The play is at this point moving away from the island and back to civilization. The natural bounty of the island has up to this point been presented entirely in Caliban's terms. Now the masque gives us Prospero's terms; not "dams for fish," "clust'ring filberts and young scamels," whatever they are, but an ordered and orderly agriculture. This is a world with a different sense of time and another kind of nature. We ought also to be aware that something is missing from the natural world the masque depicts. There is, in this cycle of seasons, no winter. Indeed, Ceres is explicit about it: "Spring come to you at the farthest/ In the very end of harvest" (ll. 114–115)—after autumn, that is, spring will return at once. And something else is missing from this world. It is the whole sense of darkness, the undertone of tragedy that fills the play. We may remark how lightly the one tragic allusion is treated:

> *Ceres.* Tell me, heavenly bow,
> If Venus or her son, as thou dost know,
> Do now attend the queen? Since they did plot
> The means that dusky Dis my daughter got,
> Her and her blind boy's scandal'd company
> I have forsworn. (IV, i, 86–91)

Ceres, speaking of the rape of her daughter Proserpina, uses not a tone of tragic bereavement, but one of social outrage. This is all the more to the point since it is precisely that abduction which is directly responsible for the very fact that winter exists at all in nature.

There is, then, in this cycle of the seasons of birth, fruition, and harvest, no winter—no death. So, when Prospero interrupts, it is to stress that what is missing from the masque is nevertheless very real. The vision of permanence is in danger of blinding us to the necessities of the moment, for it is precisely death in the persons of Stephano, Trinculo, and Caliban that is threatening now. Throughout this short play, Prospero's special quality has been, above all, an awareness of *time,* of the right moment, the exact instant when action must be taken:

> By accident most strange, bountiful Fortune,
> (Now my dear lady) hath mine enemies
> Brought to this shore; and by my prescience
> I find my zenith doth depend upon
> A most auspicious star, whose influence
> If now I court not, but omit, my fortunes
> Will ever after droop; (I, ii, 178–184)

and the repeated *"now"* looms large throughout the drama. We have observed that the chronology of the action is worked out with remarkable precision, and the play makes a point of letting us know how close the correspondence is between the duration of the performance and the length of time it represents. Both Alonso and the boatswain remark in the last scene that the wreck occurred less than three hours before; and one sense we ought to have is of how quickly the whole action has happened—a sense that Prospero has indeed seized the decisive moment. His safety and the success of his designs depend on his awareness of time as dramatic, as a series of crises. But the masque is presenting a world which is an eternal and unchanging cycle, a world without drama, without crises, without immediacy, and in a very real sense there is in the action of the play—in the prosecution of Prospero's designs—no *time* for the masque.

So Prospero's "majestic vision" has a double aspect. It is finally the only place in the play where Caliban's sense of the richness of the island, which is necessarily our sense as well, is qualified; where we see, as we must see, that there is a better kind of natural bounty, an ordered nature in which man lives not as a predator but as a part. It shows us, in fact, Prospero's sense of nature, one ideal of the world of Prospero's imagination. But the masque-vision is also, paradoxically, a threat to that ideal, which depends so utterly on the magician's complete awareness of all parts of his world. We must, then, take Prospero's comment on his masque very seriously:

> Our revels now are ended. These our actors,
> As I foretold you, were all spirits, and
> Are melted into air, into thin air:
> And, like the baseless fabric of this vision,
> The cloud-capp'd towers, the gorgeous palaces,
> The solemn temples, the great globe itself,
> Yea, all which it inherit, shall dissolve
> And, like this insubstantial pageant faded,
> Leave not a rack behind. We are such stuff
> As dreams are made on; and our little life
> Is rounded with a sleep. (IV, i, 148–158)

"Our revels now are ended": *revels* is a technical theatrical term for a masque, and has its modern sense in addition. The serious business of the play, then, the tragic world of Alonso, the treachery of Sebastian and Antonio, the conspiracy of Stephano, Trinculo, and Caliban, all are now at hand. The speech follows that most crucial moment in the play when Prospero's awareness of a world of fancy has made him forgetful for the first time of the real world, has almost deprived him of his control over the action and thereby almost turned the drama to tragedy. The dangers of an uncontrolled imagination such as Caliban's are now brought dramatically and immediately home to us in the very person of Prospero. For the magician, returned to the hard facts of the play's continuing action, the world of imagination is rapidly vanishing. But the realities of Prospero's world are also the play's metaphors; the spirits have, literally, "melted into air," and they now provide a poetic analogue of the larger reality of life outside the drama:

...the great globe itself,
Yea, all which it inherit, shall dissolve
And, like this insubstantial pageant faded,
Leave not a rack behind.

This does more than move us beyond the world of the play. "Pageant" is another technical term, meaning both a stage and the setting on it, and "the great globe" was also, of course, literally the scene of the action. The theatrical terminology, the striking ambiguity, are ultimately to be taken up and justified in Prospero's epilogue, where his awareness extends not only beyond the fictive world but beyond the limits of his theater as well; where, acknowledging himself an actor on a stage, he takes on both the audience's understanding and the dramatist's control. Similar conclusions offered by Puck and Feste are in their plays perfectly conventional; but the epilogue to *The Tempest* has a power and point that derive from its organic relation to a movement within the drama; and it is the revels speech that makes this possible. The ability to think metaphorically, which only Prospero possesses, is in the revels speech directly related to the strongest and fullest sense of reality in the play. Nowhere else except in his epilogue is the extent of Prospero's awareness larger or clearer, and the world he summons up, the kinds of relationships he establishes, are ones of which Miranda and Ferdinand cannot even conceive. Ferdinand had thought the masque a happy ending to his adventures, but Prospero's play has only just reached its climax.

In a sense, it is the implications of the masque that have brought the play to this climax; and Prospero's interruption is full of a consciousness of the dangers not only of the conspiracy he has forgotten but also of the imaginative world that has tempted him to forget it. Ferdinand's comment during the masque had led him to plead, "Let me live here ever;/ So rare a wonder'd father and a wise/ Makes this place Paradise"; but Prospero at the end of the masque is implicitly criticizing both that "Paradise" and his son-in-law's callowness as he urges Ferdinand, "be cheerful, sir./ Our revels now are ended." The conclusion of the revels, the vision of the masque as an "insubstantial pageant," and all that that vision implies for Prospero, provide a vital transition in the play to the renunciation of extraordinary powers and the return to the ordinary world.

That the transition is a painful one for Prospero to make is apparent enough from its violence. Ferdinand remarks, "Your father's in some passion/ That works him strongly"; Miranda observes, "Never till this day/ Saw I him touch'd with anger, so distemper'd" (II, 143–145). Both perceive how uncharacteristic his behavior is, though Miranda might have recalled the several outbursts that punctuated her father's earlier tale of his sufferings. Prospero's momentary return to passion, striking in the first act and even more evident in the fourth, takes on still greater significance as the play moves to its conclusion, returning its figures to society, and linking the magician at last more with the world of humanity than with the elements.

The opening of the fifth act, then, finds Prospero asserting not his magical power over his victims, but his human sympathy with them, and renouncing not the world of Milan and Naples, but the island and his art. Ariel has been moved by the plight of the king and his followers; Prospero, who comprehends both Ariel and Alonso, both nature and man, comments:

> Hast thou, which are but air, a touch, a feeling
> Of their afflictions, and shall not myself,
> One of their kind, that relish all as sharply
> Passion as they, be kindlier mov'd than thou art?
> Though with their high wrongs I am struck to th' quick,
> Yet with my nobler reason 'gainst my fury
> Do I take part: the rarer action is
> In virtue than in vengeance: they being penitent,
> The sole drift of my purpose doth extend
> Not a frown further. (V, i, 21–30)

It is *natural* to forgive, to be guided by reason, but—and this is what is striking about the speech—both passion and the desire for revenge are here seen to be natural as well. Vengeance is properly the Lord's, and Prospero is coming to seem less and less like God. If repentance is demanded of Alonso, mercy is equally demanded of Prospero. Here we may recall Miranda's use of "art" and Ariel's of "suffer," and remark that Prospero's word for the alternative to "vengeance" is not mercy, but something much larger: "virtue." This is the quality which is to replace Prospero's magic, and by this point in the play it includes everything that magic had represented: for Prospero the restored Duke, power and justice. So this one action toward which the drama has been moving, Prospero's pardon of his enemies, is the culmination of his "art" and implies a whole way of life for the good ruler he will become.

This is followed by the great monologue "Ye elves of hills, brooks, standing lakes, and groves," in which Prospero anatomizes the world he has controlled and is leaving, the world of nature and its spirits, and even of the dead:

> graves at my command
> Have wak'd their sleepers, op'd, and let 'em forth
> By my so potent Art. But this rough magic
> I here abjure; (V, i, 48–51)

and in the space of a single line the renunciation takes place; we see the "potent Art" become "rough magic" before our eyes.

Where, then, at the end, are we left? The play ends happily, certainly; the potential violence, the incipient disaster have been averted. The tragedy, that is, *has* been qualified. But unlike *Measure for Measure* or *All's Well that*

*Ends Well,* it has been qualified in a way that does not diminish or dismiss any of the play's tragic implications. There is no sense at the end of *The Tempest* that everything is all right now. Alonso's repentance and the restoration of Prospero's dukedom solve two old problems; but they are by no means the only problems the play has presented. When Miranda sees all the shipwreck victims finally assembled, she marvels "how beauteous mankind is! O brave new world,/ That has such people in't!" But two of the people in it are Sebastian and Antonio; and Prospero's brief answer, "'Tis new to thee," implies that there are old problems Miranda cannot even conceive of, as well as a good deal of unfinished business. Prospero's "art" still enables him to promise "auspicious gales" for the voyage home—the voyage away from elemental nature and back to society, a world full of people. But we know what *human* nature can be like; and Prospero, leaving the island, is beyond magic and has only his virtue to protect him.

# TRAGEDIES

# 24

# *Romeo and Juliet*

*M. M. Mahood*

## 1

*Romeo and Juliet* is one of Shakespeare's most punning plays; even a really conservative count yields a hundred and seventy-five quibbles. Critics who find this levity unseemly excuse it by murmuring, with the Bad Quarto Capulet, that "youth's a jolly thing" even in a tragedy. Yet Shakespeare was over thirty, with a good deal of dramatic writing already to his credit, when *Romeo and Juliet* was first performed. He knew what he was about in his wordplay, which is as functional here as in any of his later tragedies. It holds together the play's imagery in a rich pattern and gives an outlet to the tumultuous feelings of the central characters. By its proleptic second and third meanings it serves to sharpen the play's dramatic irony. Above all, it clarifies the conflict of incompatible truths and helps to establish their final equipoise.

Shakespeare's sonnet-prologue offers us a tale of star-crossed lovers and

*Reprinted from M. M. Mahood,* Shakespeare's Wordplay *(London: Methuen & Company, Ltd., 1957), pp. 56–72 by permission of the publisher.*

'The *fearfull passage* of their *death-markt* loue'.[1] *Death-marked* can mean 'marked out for (or by) death; foredoomed'. If, however, we take *passage* in the sense of a voyage (and this sub-meaning prompts *trafficque* in the twelfth line) as well as a course of events, *death-marked* recalls the 'euer fixed marke' of Sonnet 116 and the sea-mark of Othello's utmost sail and suggests the meaning "With death as their objective." The two meanings of *fearful* increase the line's oscillation; the meaning "frightened" makes the lovers helpless, but they are not necessarily so if the word means 'fearsome' and so suggests that we, the audience, are awe-struck by their undertaking. These ambiguities pose the play's fundamental question at the outset: is its ending frustration or fulfilment? Does Death choose the lovers or do they elect to die? This question emerges from the language of the play itself and thus differs from the conventional, superimposed problem: is *Romeo and Juliet* a tragedy of Character or of Fate? which can be answered only by a neglect or distortion of the play as a dramatic experience. To blame or excuse the lovers' impetuosity and the connivance of others is to return to Arthur Broke's disapproval of unhonest desire, stolen contracts, drunken gossips and auricular confession. Recent critics have, I believe, come nearer to defining the play's experience when they have stressed the *Liebestod* of the ending and suggested that the love of Romeo and Juliet is the tragic passion that seeks its own destruction. Certainly nearly all the elements of the *amour-passion* myth as it has been defined by Denis de Rougemont[2] are present in the play. The love of Romeo and Juliet is immediate, violent and final. In the voyage imagery of the play[3] they abandon themselves to a rudderless course that must end in shipwreck:

> Thou desperate Pilot, now at once run on
> The dashing Rocks, thy seasick weary barke:
> Heeres to my Loue. (V, iii, 117–19)

The obstacle which is a feature of the *amour-passion* legend is partly external, the family feud; but it is partly a sword of the lovers' own tempering since, unlike earlier tellers of the story, Shakespeare leaves us with no explanation of why Romeo did not put Juliet on his horse and make for Mantua. A *leitmotiv* of the play is Death as Juliet's bridegroom; it first appears when Juliet sends to find Romeo's name: "if he be married, My graue is like to be my wedding bed." At the news of Romeo's banishment Juliet cries "And death not Romeo, take my maiden head," and she begs her mother, rather

---

[1] L.9. The prologue is not given in the Folio, but is found in the second, third and fourth Quartos. My quotations in this chapter are all from the Shakespeare Association facsimile of the Second Quarto.

[2] *L'Amour et l'Occident* (Paris 1939).

[3] See Kenneth Muir and Sean O'Loughlin, *The Voyage to Illyria* (1937), p. 72.

than compel her to marry Paris, to"make the Bridall bed / In that dim Monument where Tibalt lies." The theme grows too persistent to be mere dramatic irony:

> O sonne, the night before thy wedding day
> Hath death laine with thy wife, there she lies,
> Flower as she was, deflowred by him,
> Death is my sonne in law, death is my heire.
> My daughter he hath wedded. (IV, v, 35–9)

Romeo, gazing at the supposedly dead Juliet, could well believe

> that vnsubstantiall death is amorous,
> And that the leane abhorred monster keepes
> Thee here in darke to be his parramour. (V, iii, 103–5)

Most significant of all, there is Juliet's final cry:

> O *happy* dagger
> This is thy sheath, there rust and let me *dye*. (V, iii, 169–70)

where *happy* implies not only "fortunate to me in being ready to my hand" but also 'successful, fortunate in itself' and so suggests a further quibble on *die*. Death has long been Romeo's rival and enjoys Juliet at the last.

In all these aspects *Romeo and Juliet* appears the classic literary statement of the *Liebestod* myth in which (we are told) we seek the satisfaction of our forbidden desires; forbidden, according to Freud, because *amour-passion* is inimical to the Race, according to de Rougemont because it is contrary to the Faith. Shakespeare's story conflicts, however, with the traditional myth at several points. Tragic love is always adulterous. Romeo and Juliet marry, and Juliet's agony of mind at the prospect of being married to Paris is in part a concern for her marriage vow: "My husband is on earth, my faith in heauen." Again, Romeo faces capture and death, Juliet the horror of being entombed alive, not because they want to die but because they want to live together. These woes are to serve them for sweet discourses in their time to come. In contrast to this, the wish-fulfilment of the *Liebestod* is accomplished only by the story of a suicide pact. Drama has furnished many such plots since the middle of the last century. Deirdre and her lover deliberately return to Ireland and the wrath of Conchubar because it is "a better thing to be following on to a near death, than to be bending the head down, and dragging with the feet, and seeing one day a blight showing upon love where it is sweet and tender." What makes Synge's play a tragedy is that the blight does show before the lovers are killed. By itself, the suicide pact offers the audience wish-fulfilment and not *katharsis*. The good cry we enjoy over the worn reels of *Meyerling* bears only a remote relationship to the tragic experience of *Romeo and Juliet.*

The real objection to reading *Romeo and Juliet* as the *Liebestod* myth in dramatic form is that it is anachronistic to align the play with pure myths like that of Orpheus and Eurydice or with the modern restatement of such myths by Anouilh and Cocteau. Shakespeare's intention in writing the play was not that of the post-Freud playwright who finds in a high tale of love and death the objective correlative to his own emotions and those of his audience. We may guess that the story afforded Shakespeare an excited pleasure of recognition because it made explicit a psychological experience; but he did not, on the strength of that recognition, decide to write a play about the death wish. Like Girolamo de la Corte, whose *History of Venise* appeared about the time *Romeo and Juliet* was first acted, Shakespeare believed his lovers to be historical people. He read and retold their adventures with the detached judgment we accord history as well as with the implicated excitement we feel for myth. The story is both near and remote; it goes on all the time in ourselves, but its events belong also to distant Verona in the dog days when the mad blood is stirred to passion and violence. The resultant friction between history and myth, between the story and the fable, kindles the play into great drama. When we explore the language of *Romeo and Juliet* we find that both its wordplay and its imagery abound in those concepts of love as a war, a religion, a malady, which de Rougemont has suggested as the essence of *amour-passion.* If the play were pure myth, the fictionalising of a psychological event, all these elements would combine in a single statement of our desire for a tragic love. But because the play is also an exciting story about people whose objective existence we accept during the two hours' traffic of the stage, these images and quibbles are dramatically 'placed'; to ascertain Shakespeare's intentions in using them we need to see which characters are made to speak them and how they are distributed over the course of the action.

## 2

Act I begins with some heavy-witted punning from Sampson and Gregory—a kind of verbal tuning-up which quickens our ear for the great music to come. The jests soon broaden. This is one of Shakespeare's most bawdy plays, but the bawdy has always a dramatic function. Here its purpose is to make explicit, at the beginning of this love tragedy, one possible relationship between man and woman: a brutal male dominance expressed in sadistic quibbles. After the brawl has been quelled, the mood of the scene alters "like a change from wood wind, brass and tympani to an andante on the strings"[4] in Benvolio's tale of Romeo's melancholia; and Romeo himself appears and expresses, in the numbers that Petrarch flowed in, the contrary relationship of the sexes: man's courtly subjection to women's tyranny. Rosaline is a saint, and by his quibbles upon theological terms Romeo shows himself a devotee of the Religion of Love:

> She is too faire, too wise, wisely too faire,
> To merit blisse by making me *dispaire.* (227–8)

Love is a sickness as well as a cult, and Romeo twists Benvolio's request to tell in sadness (that is, seriously) whom he loves, to an expression of *amour-maladie:*

> A sicke man in *sadnesse* makes his will:
> A word ill vrgd to one that is so ill. (208–9)

It is characteristic of this love learnt by rote from the sonnet writers that Romeo should combine images and puns which suggest this slave-like devotion to his mistress with others that imply a masterful attack on her chastity.[5] Love is a man of war in such phrases as "th' incounter of assailing eies" which, added to the aggressive wordplay of Sampson and Gregory and to the paradox of 'ô brawling loue, ô louing hate', reinforce the theme of ambivalence, the *odi-et-amo* duality of passion.

All the Petrarchan and anti-Petrarchan conventions are thus presented to us in this first scene: love as malady, as worship, as war, as conquest. They are presented, however, with an exaggeration that suggests Romeo is already aware of his own absurdity and is "posing at posing." "Where shall we dine?" is a most unlover-like question which gives the show away; and Benvolio's use of "in sadnesse" implies that he knows Romeo's infatuation to be nine parts show. Romeo is in fact ready to be weaned from Rosaline, and the scene ends with a proleptic pun that threatens the overthrow of this textbook language of love. "Examine other bewties" Benvolio urges, but for Romeo, "Tis the way to call hers (exquisit) in question more." By *question* he means, with a play upon the etymology of *exquisite,* "consideration and conversation"; but we guess, if we do not know, that Rosaline's charms will be called into question in another sense when set beside the beauty of Juliet.

Love in Verona may be a cult, a quest or a madness. Marriage is a business arrangement. Old Capulet's insistence to Paris, in the next scene, that Juliet must make her own choice, is belied by later events. Juliet is an

[4] Harley Granville-Barker, *Prefaces to Shakespeare, Second Series* (1930), p. 6.

[5] See G. E. Matthews, "Sex and the Sonnet," *Essays in Criticism* II (1952), pp. 119–37.

heiress, and her father does not intend to enrich any but a husband of his own choosing:

> *Earth* hath swallowed all my hopes but she,
> Shees the hopefull Lady of my *earth.* (I, ii, 14–15)

This quibbling distinction between *earth* as the grave and *earth* as lands (as Steevens points out, *fille de terre* means an heiress) is confounded when Juliet's hopes of happiness end in the Capulets' tomb. We recall the dramatic irony of this pun when Old Capulet speaks his last, moving quibble:

> O brother Mountague, giue me thy hand,
> This is my daughters *ioynture,* for no more
> Can I demaund. (V, iii, 296–8)

The ball scene at Capulet's house is prologued by a revealing punning-match between Romeo and Mercutio. Romeo's lumbering puns are the word-play of courtly love: the other masquers have nimble soles, he has a soul of lead: he is too bound to earth to bound, too sore from Cupid's darts to soar in the dance. Mercutio's levity, on the other hand, is heightened by his bawdy quibbles. Mercutio appears in early versions of the tale as what is significantly known as a ladykiller, and his dramatic purpose at this moment of the play is to oppose a cynical and aggressive idea of sex to Romeo's love-idolatry and so sharpen the contrast already made in the opening scene. Yet just as Romeo's touch of self-parody then showed him to be ready for a more adult love, so Mercutio's Queen Mab speech implies that his cynicism does not express the whole of his temperament. The falsity of both cynicism and idolatry, already felt to be inadequate by those who hold these concepts, is to be exposed by the love between Romeo and Juliet. Like Chaucer two centuries previously, Shakespeare weighed the ideas of the masterful man and the tyrannical mistress and wisely concluded that "Love wol nat be constreyned by maistrie."

For the ball scene, Shakespeare deploys his resources of stagecraft and poetry in a passage of brilliant dramatic counterpoint. Our attention is divided, during the dance, between the reminiscences of the two old Capulets (sketches for Silence and Shallow) and the rapt figure of Romeo who is watching Juliet. Nothing is lost by this, since the talk of the two pantaloons is mere inanity. We are only aware that it has to do with the passage of years too uneventful to be numbered, so that twenty-five is confused with thirty; simultaneously we share with Romeo a timeless minute that cannot be reckoned by the clock. Yet the old men's presence is a threat as well as a dramatic contrast. They have masqued and loved in their day, but "'tis gone, 'tis gone, 'tis gone."

Romeo's first appraisal of Juliet's beauty is rich not only in its unforgettable images but also in the subtlety of its wordplay. Hers is a "Bewtie too rich for vse, for earth too deare." When we recall that *use* means "employment," "interest" and "wear and tear" that *earth* means both "mortal life" and "the grave," that *dear* can be either "cherished" or "costly" and that there is possibly a play upon *beauty* and *booty* (as there is in *Henry IV* part 1, I, ii, 28), the line's range of meanings becomes very wide indeed. Over and above the contrast between her family's valuation of her as sound stock in the marriage market and Romeo's estimate that she is beyond all price, the words contain a self-contradictory dramatic irony. Juliet's beauty is too rich for use in the sense that it will be laid in the tomb after a brief enjoyment; but for that very reason it will never be faded and worn. And if she is *not* too dear for earth since Romeo's love is powerless to keep her out of the tomb, it is true that she is too rare a creature for mortal life. Not all these meanings are consciously present to the audience, but beneath the conscious level they connect with later images and quibbles and are thus brought into play before the tragedy is over.

The counterpoint of the scene is sustained as Romeo moves towards his new love against the discordant hate and rage of her cousin. Tybalt rushes from the room, threatening to convert seeming sweet to bitter gall, at the moment Romeo touches Juliet's hand. The lovers meet and salute each other in a sonnet full of conceits and quibbles on the Religion of Love—"palme to palme is holy Palmers kis"; "grant thou least faith turne to dispaire"; "Saints do not moue"—for the place is public and they must disguise their feelings beneath a social persiflage. The real strength of those feelings erupts in Romeo's pun—"O *deare* account!"—and in Juliet's paradox—"My onely loue sprung from my onely hate"—when each learns the other's identity, and the elements of youth and experience, love and hate, which have been kept apart throughout the scene, are abruptly juxtaposed. Then the torches are extinguished and the scene ends with a phrase of exquisite irony, when the Nurse speaks to Juliet as to a tired child after a party: "Come lets away, the strangers all are gone." Romeo is no longer a stranger and Juliet no longer a child.

A quibbling sonnet on love between enemies and some of Mercutio's ribald jests separate this scene from that in Capulet's orchard.[6] It is as if we must be reminded of the social and sexual strife before we hear Romeo

---

6 Mercutio's "This field-bed is too cold for me to sleepe" seems to be an echo of the Nurse's words to the lovers in Broke's poem:

> Loe here a fielde, (she shewd a fieldbed ready dight)
> Where you may, if you list, in armes, revenge your selfe by fight.

As often with Shakespeare, a piece of rhetorical decoration in the source has become an integral part of the play's imagery, by prompting its quibbles on love as war.

and Juliet declare the perfect harmony of their feelings for each other. At first Romeo seems still to speak the language of idolatry, but the "winged messenger of heauen" belongs to a different order of imagination from the faded conceits of his devotion to Rosaline. The worn commonplaces of courtship are swept aside by Juliet's frankness. One of the few quibbles in the scene is on *frank* in the meanings of "generous" and "candid, open," and it introduces Juliet's boldest and most beautiful avowal of her feelings:

> *Rom.* O wilt thou leaue me so vnsatisfied?
> *Iul.* What satisfaction canst thou haue to night?
> *Rom.* Th'exchange of thy loues faithful vow for mine.
> *Iul.* I gaue thee mine before thou didst request it:
> And yet I would it were to giue againe.
> *Rom.* Woldst thou withdraw it, for what purpose loue?
> *Iul.* But to be franke and giue it thee againe,
> And yet I wish but for the thing I haue,
> My bountie is as boundlesse as the sea,
> My loue as deepe, the more I giue to thee
> The more I haue, for both are infinite. (II, ii, 125–35)

Thus the distribution of wordplay upon the concepts of love-war, love-idolatry, love-sickness, serves to show that the feelings of Romeo and Juliet for each other are something quite different from the *amour-passion* in which de Rougemont finds all these disorders. For Romeo doting upon Rosaline, love was a malady and a religion; for Mercutio it is sheer lunacy ('a great naturall that runs lolling vp and downe') or a brutal conquest with no quarter given. All these notions are incomplete and immature compared to the reality. When Romeo meets Mercutio the next morning a second quibbling-match ensues in which the bawdy expressive of love-war and love-madness is all Mercutio's. Romeo's puns, if silly, are gay and spontaneous in comparison with his laboured conceits on the previous evening. Then, as he explained to Benvolio, he was not himself, not Romeo. Now Mercutio cries: "now art thou sociable, now art thou Romeo." In fact Romeo and Juliet have experienced a self-discovery. Like Donne's happy lovers, they "possess one world, each hath one and is one"; a world poles apart from the Nirvana quested by romantic love. The play is a tragedy, not because the love of Romeo for Juliet is in its nature tragic, but because the ending achieves the equilibrium of great tragedy. The final victory of time and society over the lovers is counterpoised by the knowledge that it is, in a sense, *their* victory; a victory not only over time and society which would have made them old and worldly in the end (whereas their deaths heal the social wound), but over the most insidious enemy of love, the inner hostility that "builds a Hell in Heaven's despite" and which threatens in the broad jests of Mercutio. For we believe in the uniqueness of Romeo's and Juliet's experience at the same time as we know it to be, like other sublunary things, neither perfect nor permanent. If our distress and satisfaction are caught up in the fine balance of great tragedy at the end of the play, it is because, throughout, the wordplay and imagery, the conduct of the action and the grouping of characters contribute to that balance. The lovers' confidence is both heightened and menaced by a worldly wisdom, cynicism and resignation which, for the reason that candleholders see more of the game, we are not able to repudiate as easily as they can do.

## 3

The play's central paradox of love's strength and fragility is most clearly expressed in the short marriage scene (II, vi). On the one hand there is Romeo's triumphant boast:

> come what sorrow can,
> It cannot counteruaile the exchange of ioy
> That one short minute giues me in her sight:
> Do thou but close our hands with holy words,
> Then loue deuouring death do what he dare,
> It is inough I may but call her mine. (3–8)

On the other hand there are the forebodings of Friar Laurence:

> These violent delights haue violent endes,
> And in their triumph die like fier and powder:
> Which as they kisse *consume,* (9–11)

where *consume* means both "reach a consummation" (*N.E.D.* v.2) and burn away, be destroyed." These conflicting themes of satisfaction and frustration coalesce in the Friar's words on Juliet's entry:

> Here comes the Lady, Oh so *light* a foote
> Will *nere weare out* the euerlasting flint. (16–17)

An ambiguity of pronounciation between "near" and "ne'er" and another of meaning in *wear out*[7] enable us to distinguish four possible readings here before, with cormorant delight, we swallow the lot. Juliet's foot is so light that

(i) it will never wear away the everlasting flint;
(ii) it will never last it out;
(iii) it will nearly outlast it;
(iv) it will nearly wear it away.

---

7 As in the shoe polish advertisement: "They're well-worn but they've worn well." For discussion of the *Romeo and Juliet* passage see the correspondence in the *T.L.S.* for April 3, 17 and 24 and May 1, 1943.

The first of these is the obvious meaning, platitudinously suited to the speaker. The second anticipates our fear that the lovers are too beset with enemies on the hard road of life to be able to last the course, whereas the third contradicts this by saying that Juliet's love and beauty, because time will not have the chance to wear them away, will last in their fame nearly as long as the rocks of earth. And this contradiction is heightened by (iv) in which *light* has a suggestion of Juliet's luminous beauty,[8] and the flint is that of a flintlock; so that the line is connected with the sequence of paradoxical light images running through the play. Love is spoken of as a sudden spark or a flash of lightning. Juliet's forebodings in the balcony scene—

> I haue no ioy of this contract to night,
> It is too rash, too vnaduisd, too sudden,
> Too like the lightning which doth cease to bee,
> Ere one can say, it lightens (II, ii, 117–20)

—are deepened here by the Friar's talk of fire and powder and again in the next act by his reproaches to Romeo:

> Thy wit, that ornament, to shape and loue,
> Mishapen in the conduct of them both:
> Like powder in a skillesse souldiers flaske,
> Is set a fier by thine owne ignorance. (III, iii, 129–32)

In sum, love is as easily extinguishable as it appears to Lysander in *A Midsummer Night's Dream*:

> Briefe as the lightning in the collied night,
> That (in a spleene) vnfolds both heauen and earth;
> And ere a man hath power to say, behold,
> The iawes of darknesse do deuoure it vp:
> So quicke bright things come to confusion. (I, i, 145–9)

Yet Romeo, when he experiences "a *lightning* before death," uses the pun not only to imply that he has enjoyed a lightning brief happiness before being

> Dischargd of breath,
> As violently, as hastie powder fierd
> Doth hurry from the fatall Canons wombe, (V, i, 63–5)

but also to sustain the image of Juliet's luminous beauty which makes "This Vault a feasting presence full of light." For alongside the images of sparks, torches, lightning, are others which associate Romeo and Juliet with the unquenchable heavenly lights. Mercutio's "We waste our lights in vaine,

[8] There are previous puns on *light:*
Away from light steales home my heauie sonne (I, i, 142); Being but heauie I will beare the light (I, iv, 12); And not impute this yeelding to light loue, Which the darke night hath so discouered (II, ii, 105–6).

light lights by day" is ironically apposite to Romeo's love of Rosaline, who is a mere candle before the sun that breaks from Juliet's window. Two passages which have been slighted as conceits are an essential part of this theme:

> Two of the fairest starres in all the heauen,
> Hauing some busines do[9] entreate her eyes,
> To twinckle in their spheres till they returne.
> What if her eyes were there, they in her head,
> The brightnesse of her cheek wold shame those stars,
> As day-light doth a lampe, her eye in heauen,
> Would through the ayrie region streame so bright,
> That birds would sing, and thinke it were not night. (II, ii, 15–22)

> Giue me my Romeo, and when I shall die,
> Take him and cut him out in little starres,
> And he will make the face of heauen so fine,
> That all the world will be in loue with night,
> And pay no worship to the garish Sun. (III, ii, 21–5)

Romeo and Juliet stellify each other, the love which appears to be quenched as easily as a spark is extinguished is, in fact, made as permanent as the sun and stars when it is set out of the range of time.

The same paradox is sustained by the flower images which are closely associated with those of light. The "gather the rose" theme was of course inevitable in a love tragedy of the High Renaissance. Shakespeare's rose imagery, however, is more than rhetorical, and serves to stress the central themes of the play.[10] The rose was dramatically appropriate as a love symbol because it was so often a prey to the invisible worm: "Loathesome canker liues in sweetest bud." Romeo is devoured by his infatuation for Rosaline "as is the bud bit with an enuious worme" and the Friar, gathering herbs, moralises over the adulteration of the good in a life by its evil until "the Canker death eates vp that Plant." Romeo and Juliet are spared this. Death lies on Juliet just as its earlier semblance had done

> like an vntimely frost,
> Vpon the sweetest flower of all the field. (IV, v, 28–9)

This early frost forestalls the heat of the sun as well as the blight in the bud, since a further fitness of the image consists in the speed with which both roses and "fresh female buds"[11] bloom and wither in the south. Although Lady Capulet seems never to have been young she tells Juliet

---

[9] For the Second Quarto's *to*.

[10] As the author of *2 Henry VI,* Shakespeare must almost unconsciously have connected rose images with the rivalry of two great houses. For the light-flowers cluster see I, i, 139–45 and 156–8; I, ii, 24–30; II, ii, 117–22.

[11] I borrow the phrase from the Bad Quarto. The accepted texts have "fresh fennell buds."

> I was your mother, much vpon these years
> That you are now a maide, (I, iii, 72–3)

and the cruelty of Verona's summer is implicit in Old Capulet's words:

> Let two more Sommers wither in their pride,
> Ere we may thinke her ripe to be a bride. (I, ii, 10–11)

The marriage scene, after its strong statement of love as the victor-victim of time, closes with a quibbling passage already discussed[12] in which Romeo and Juliet defy time's most powerful allies. Romeo, in an image of music, challenges the notion that passion is discordant by nature, Juliet rejects the prudence of social considerations in her declaration of love's richness—"I cannot sum vp sum of halfe my wealth." This last image is a foretaste of *Antony and Cleopatra,* and it would be interesting to compare the success of love's three enemies in Shakespeare's three double-titled tragedies. In *Troilus and Cressida* they win hands down. Society, in the shape of the Trojan War, again compels secrecy and again separates the lovers; the inner corruption of love itself makes Cressida unfaithful; and the burden of the play is that "Loue, friendship, charity, are subiects all To enuious and calumniating time." By contrast, *Antony and Cleopatra* is a clear victory for the lovers. Society, seen as the pomp of Rome, is a world well lost; the dismal drunken party we witness on Pompey's barge contrasts poorly with the revels of Antony and Cleopatra—which are left to our imagination. The lovers are old and wise enough to be reconciled to the ambivalence of their feelings, which is implicit in the play's imagery. Finally, time cannot harm them when they have eternity in their lips and eyes; at the end of the play Cleopatra is again for Cydnus to meet Mark Antony.

In *Romeo and Juliet* love's enemies have a Pyrrhic victory which begins with the slaying of Mercutio at the beginning of Act III. Like many of Shakespeare's characters, Mercutio dies with a quibble that asserts his vitality in the teeth of death. He jests as long as he has breath; only if we ask for him *tomorrow* shall we find him a grave man. But it is grim joke, to accompany a dying curse. The Elizabethans, who believed in the power of curses, would have seen in the play's subsequent events the working-out of Mercutio's cynical knowledge that love is inseparably commingled with hate in human affairs. Romeo kills Tybalt, the cousin whose name he now tenders as dearly as his own. Juliet responds to the news with an outburst—"O serpent heart hid with a flowring face..." which, by recalling the loving hate of Romeo's infatuation with Rosaline, threatens the harmony and permanence of the love between Romeo and Juliet. She recovers her balance, but we have felt the tremor and know that even these lovers cannot sustain many such shocks.

---

12 See above, p. 13.

Some of the most notorious puns in Shakespeare occur in this scene between Juliet and her Nurse, when the Nurse's confusion misleads Juliet into thinking Romeo has killed himself:

> Hath Romeo slaine himselfe? say thou but *I*,
> And that bare vowell *I* shall poyson more
> Then the death darting[13] *eye* of Cockatrice,
> *I* am not *I*, if there be such an *I*.
> Or those *eyes* shut[13], that makes thee answere *I*:
> If he be slaine say *I*, or if not, no. (III, ii, 45–50)

Excuses might be made for this. It does achieve a remarkable sound-effect by setting Juliet's high-pitched keening of 'I' against the Nurse's moans of 'O Romeo, Romeo.' It also sustains the eye imagery of Juliet's great speech at the opening of this scene: the runaways' eyes, the blindness of love, Juliet hooded like a hawk, Romeo as the eye of heaven. But excuses are scarcely needed since this is one of Shakespeare's first attempts to reveal a profound disturbance of mind by the use of quibbles.[14] Romeo's puns in the next scene at Friar Laurence's cell are of the same kind: flies may kiss Juliet, but he must fly from her; the Friar, though a friend *professed,* will offer him no sudden mean of death, though ne'er so mean; he longs to know what his concealed lady says to their cancelled love. This is technically crude, and perhaps we do well to omit it in modern productions; but it represents a psychological discovery that Shakespeare was to put to masterly use in later plays. Against this feverish language of Romeo's, Shakespeare sets the Friar's sober knowledge that lovers have suffered and survived these calamities since the beginning of time. For the Friar, "the world is broad and wide," for Romeo, "there is no world without Verona wall." When the Friar tries to dispute with him of his "estate," the generalised, prayer-bookish word suggests that Romeo's distress is the common human lot, and we believe as much even while we join with Romeo in his protest: "Thou canst not speak of that thou dost not feele." Tragedy continually restates the paradox that "all cases are unique and very similar to others."

The lovers' parting at dawn sustains this contradiction. Lovers' hours may be full eternity, but the sun must still rise. Their happiness has placed them out of the reach of fate; but from now on, an accelerating series of misfortunes is to confound their triumph in disaster without making it any less of a triumph. With Lady Capulet's arrival to announce the match with Paris, love's enemies begin to close in. Juliet meets her mother with equivocations which suggest that Romeo's "snowie Doue" has grown wise as serpents since the story began, and which prepare us for her resolution in feigning death to remain loyal to Romeo:

---

13 For the Second Quarto's *arting* and *shot*.

14 He had already done so in *Two Gentlemen of Verona*, but the device is less startling in a comedy.

> Indeed I neuer shall be satisfied
> With Romeo, till I behold him. Dead
> Is my poore heart so for a kinsman vext.[15] (III, v, 94–6)

This is a triple ambiguity, with one meaning for Juliet, another for her mother and a third for us, the audience: Juliet will never in fact see Romeo again until she wakes and finds him dead beside her.

A pun which has escaped most editors is made by Paris at the beginning of Act IV. He tells the Friar he has talked little of love with Juliet because "Venus smiles not in a house of teares." Here *house of tears* means, beside the bereaved Capulet household an inauspicious section of the heavens—perhaps the eighth house or "house of death." Spenser's line "When oblique Saturne sate in the house of agonyes"[16] shows that the image was familiar to the Elizabethans, and here it adds its weight to the lovers' yoke of inauspicious stars. But this is one of very few quibbles in the last two acts. The wordplay which, in the first part of the play, served to point up the meaning of the action is no longer required. What quibbles there are in the final scenes have, however, extraordinary force. Those spoken by Romeo after he has drunk the poison reaffirm the paradox of the play's experience at its most dramatic moment:

> O *true* Appothecary:
> Thy drugs are *quicke*. Thus with a kisse I die. (V, iii, 119–20)

Like the Friar's herbs, the apothecary's poison both heals and destroys. He is *true* not only because he has spoken the truth to Romeo in describing the poison's potency, but because he has been true to his calling in finding the salve for Romeo's ills. His drugs are not only speedy, but also *quick* in the sense of "life-giving." Romeo and Juliet "cease to die, by dying."

It is the prerogative of poetry to give effect and value to incompatible meanings. In *Romeo and Juliet,* several poetic means contribute to this end: the paradox, the recurrent image, the juxtaposition of old and young in such a way that we are both absorbed by and aloof from the lovers' feelings, and the sparkling wordplay. By such means Shakespeare ensures that our final emotion is neither the satisfaction we should feel in the lovers' death if the play were a simple expression of the *Liebestod* theme, nor the dismay of seeing two lives thwarted and destroyed by vicious fates, but a tragic equilibrium which includes and transcends both these feelings.

---

[15] The Arden editor, following Theobald's reading, prints it thus:
> Indeed, I never shall be satisfied
> With Romeo, till I behold him—dead—
> Is my poor heart so for a kinsman vex'd.

[16] *The Faerie Queene,* II, ix, 52.

# 25

# "Or Else Were This a Savage Spectacle"

*Brents Stirling*

Modern readers are prone to find the tragedy of Brutus in his rigid devotion to justice and fair play. Many members of the Globe audience, however, believed that his virtues were complicated by self-deception and doubtful principle. In sixteenth-century views of history the conspiracy against Caesar often represented a flouting of unitary sovereignty, that prime point of Tudor policy, and exemplified the anarchy thought to accompany "democratic" or constitutional checks upon authority. Certain judgments of Elizabethan political writers who refer to Brutus are quite clear upon this point.[1] Although naturally aware of his disinterested

*From Unity in Shakespearian Tragedy: the Interplay of Theme and Character, 1956, pp. 40–54. Copyright 1956 by Columbia University Press. Reprinted by permission of the author and the publisher.*

[1] See the discussion in J. E. Phillips's *The State in Shakespeare's Greek and Roman Plays* (New York, 1940), pp. 172ff. Mr. Phillips quotes at length from such typical spokesmen as Sir Thomas Elyot and Thomas Craig. His analysis of *Julius Caesar* on the basis is also illuminating. See also the present author's *The Populace in Shakespeare* (New York, 1949), p. 147, for a condemnation by William Covell of Romans who aroused civil dissension by covering their purposes "with the fine terms of a common good, of the freedom of the people, of justice. . . ." The parallel with Brutus is a very close one, and Covell, moreover, explicitly avows a topical relation of such Roman history to the civil tensions of Elizabethan England.

honor and liberality, contemporary audiences could thus perceive in him a conflict between questionable goals and honorable action, a contradiction lying in his attempt to redeem morally confused ends by morally clarified means. The Elizabethan tragedy of Brutus, like that of Othello, is marked by an integrity of conduct which leads the protagonist into evil and reassures him in his error.

The distinction between modern and Elizabethan views of *Julius Caesar* is not the point of our inquiry, but it is a necessary beginning, for the older view of Brutus determines both the symbolic quality and the structure of the play. I hope to show that a sixteenth-century idea of Brutus is as thoroughly related to Shakespeare's art as it is to his meaning.

When a dramatist wishes to present an idea, his traditional method, of course, is to settle upon an episode in which the idea arises naturally but vividly from action and situation. Such an episode in *Julius Caesar* is the one in which Brutus resolves to exalt not only the mission but the tactics of conspiracy: having accepted republicanism as an honorable end, he sets out to dignify assassination, the means, by lifting it to a level of rite and ceremony.[2] In II, i, as Cassius urges the killing of Antony as a necessary accompaniment to the death of Caesar, Brutus declares that "such a course will seem too bloody. . . ,/ To cut the head off and then hack the limbs." With this thought a sense of purpose comes over him: "Let's be sacrificers, but not butchers, Caius." Here his conflict seems to be resolved, and for the first time he is more than a reluctant presence among the conspirators as he expands the theme which ends his hesitation and frees his moral imagination:

> We all stand up against the spirit of Caesar,
> And in the spirit of men there is no blood;
> Oh, that we then could come by Caesar's spirit,
> And not dismember Caesar! But, alas,
> Caesar must bleed for it! And, gentle friends,
> Let's kill him boldly, but not wrathfully;
> Let's carve him as a dish fit for the gods,
> Not hew him as a carcass fit for hounds.

This proposed conversion of bloodshed to ritual is the manner in which an abstract Brutus will be presented in terms of concrete art. From the suggestion of Plutarch that Brutus' first error lay in sparing Antony, Shakespeare moves to the image of Antony as a limb of Caesar, a limb not to be hacked because hacking is no part of ceremonial sacrifice. From Plutarch's description of Brutus as high-minded, gentle and disinterested, Shakespeare

---

[2] My article on the ritual theme in *Julius Caesar* (*PMLA,* LXVI, pp. 765ff.) appeared in 1951 as an early draft of this chapter. Some of my principal observations have been repeated by Ernest Schanzer in a recent essay ("The Tragedy of Shakespeare's Brutus," *ELH* [March, 1955], pp. 1ff.; see pp. 6–8).

proceeds to the Brutus of symbolic action. Gentleness and disinterestedness become embodied in the act of "unwrathful" blood sacrifice. High-mindedness becomes objectified in ceremonial observance.

A skeptical reader may ask why the episode just described is any more significant than a number of others such as Brutus' scene with Portia or his quarrel with Cassius. If more significant, it is so only because of its relation to a thematic design. I agree, moreover, that Shakespeare gains his effects by variety; as a recognition, in fact, of his complexity I hope to show that the structure of *Julius Caesar* is marked by reference both varied and apt to Brutus' sacrificial rite, and that this process includes expository preparation in earlier scenes, emphasis upon "mock-ceremony" in both earlier and later scenes, and repeated comment by Antony upon butchery under the guise of sacrifice—ironical comment which takes final form in the parley before Philippi.

Derived in large measure from Plutarch, but never mechanically or unselectively, the theme of incantation and ritual is thus prominent throughout *Julius Caesar,* and this is no less true at the beginning than during the crucial episodes of Acts II and III. In the opening scene of the play we are confronted with a Roman populace rebuked by Marullus for ceremonial idolatry of Caesar:

> And do you now put on your best attire?
> And do you now cull out a holiday?
> And do you now strew flowers in his way
> That comes in triumph over Pompey's blood?

For this transgression Marullus prescribes a counter-observance by the citizens in immediate expiation of their folly:

> Run to your houses, fall upon your knees,
> Pray to the gods to intermit this plague
> That needs must light on this ingratitude.

To which Flavius adds:

> Go, go, good countrymen, and for this fault,
> Assemble all the poor men of your sort;
> Draw them to Tiber banks, and weep your tears
> Into the channel, till the lowest stream
> Do kiss the most exalted shores of all.

And after committing the populace to these rites of atonement for their festal celebration of Caesar, the two tribunes themselves leave to remove the devotional symbols set up for his welcoming. "Go you. . . towards the Capitol;/ This way will I. Disrobe the images/ If you do find them decked with ceremonies./ . . . let no images/ Be hung with Caesar's trophies." It is the hope of Flavius that these disenchantments will make Caesar "fly an ordinary pitch,/ Who else would soar above the view of men."

Act I, scene ii is equally unusual in carrying the theme of ritual. It is apparent that Shakespeare had a wide choice of means for staging the entry of Caesar and his retinue; yet he selects an entry based upon Plutarch's description of the "feast Lupercalia" in which the rite of touching or striking barren women by runners of the course is made prominent. Caesar, moreover, after ordering Calpurnia to be so touched by Antony, commands: "Set on; and leave no ceremony out." It can be said, in fact, that the whole of this scene is written with ceremonial observance as a background. Its beginning, already described, is followed by a touch of solemnity in the soothsayer's words; next comes its main expository function, the sounding of Brutus by Cassius, and throughout this interchange come at intervals the shouts and flourishes of a symbolic spectacle. When the scene is again varied by a formal reentry and exit of Caesar's train, Casca remains behind to make a mockery of the rite which has loomed so large from off-stage. Significantly, in Casca's travesty of the ceremonial crown-offering and of the token offering by Caesar of his throat for cutting, Shakespeare has added a satirical note which does not appear in Plutarch.

The process, then, in each of the two opening episodes has been the bringing of serious ritual into great prominence, and of subjecting it to satirical treatment. In the first scene the tribunes denounce the punctilio planned for Caesar's entry, send the idolatrous crowd to rites of purification, and set off themselves to desecrate the devotional images. In the second scene a multiple emphasis of ceremony is capped by Casca's satire which twists the crown ritual into imbecile mummery. At this point, and in conformity with the mood set by Casca, occurs Cassius' mockery in soliloquy of Brutus:

> Well, Brutus, thou art noble; yet I see
> Thy honorable mettle may be wrought
> From that it is dispos'd; therefore it is meet
> That noble minds keep ever with their likes;
> For who is so firm that cannot be seduc'd?

The next scene (I, iii) is packed with omens and supernatural portents, a note which is carried directly into II, i where Brutus, on receiving the mysterious papers which have been left to prompt his action, remarks,

> The exhalations whizzing in the air
> Give so much light that I may read by them.

Appropriately, the letters read under this weird glow evoke his first real commitment to the "cause":

O Rome, I make thee promise
If the redress will follow, thou receivest
Thy full petition at the hand of Brutus!

Now appear his lines on the interim "between the acting of a dreadful thing/ And the first motion" in which "the state of man/Like to a little kingdom, suffers then/The nature of a insurrection." This conventional symbolizing of political convulsion by inward insurrection is followed by the soliloquy on conspiracy:

O, then by day
Where wilt thou a cavern dark enough
To mask thy monstrous visage? Seek none, Conspiracy!
Hide it in smiles and affability.

The conflict within Brutus thus becomes clear in this scene. First, the participant in revolution suffers revolution within himself; then the hater of conspiracy and lover of plain dealing must call upon Conspiracy to hide in smiling courtesy.

We have now reached the critical point (II, i, 154ff.) to which attention was first called, an outward presentation of Brutus' crisis through his acceptance of an assassin's role upon condition that the assassins become sacrificers. Already a theme well established in preceding scenes, the idea of ritual is again made prominent. As the soliloquy on conspiracy closes, the plotters gather, and the issue becomes the taking of an oath. Brutus rejects this as an idle ceremony unsuited to men joined in the honesty of a cause and turns now to the prospect of Caesar's death. This time, however, honorable men do need ceremony, ceremony which will purify the violent act of all taint of butchery and raise it to the level of sacrifice. But although Brutus has steadied himself with a formula his conflict is still unresolved, for as he sets his course he "unconsciously" reveals the evasion which Antony later will amplify: to transmute political killing into ritual is to cloak it with appearances. We began with Brutus' passage on carving Caesar as a dish for the gods; these are the lines which complete it:

And let our hearts, as subtle masters do,
Stir up their servants to an act of rage,
And after seem to chide 'em. This shall make
Our purpose necessary and not envious;
Which so appearing to the common eyes,
We shall be called purgers, not murderers.

The contradiction is interesting. In an anticlimax, Brutus has ended his great invocation to ritual with a note on practical politics: our hearts shall stir us and afterward seem to chide us; we shall thus "appear" to the citizenry as purgers, not murderers.

Shakespeare never presents Brutus as a demagogue, but there are ironical traces of the politician in him which suggest Covell's adverse picture of Roman liberators.[3] It is curious, in fact, that although Brutus is commonly thought to be unconcerned over public favor, he expresses clear concern for it in the passage just quoted and in III, i, 244–51, where he sanctions Antony's funeral speech only if Antony agrees to tell the crowd that he speaks by generous permission, and only if he agrees to utter no evil of the conspiracy. Nor is Brutus' speech in the Forum wholly the nonpolitical performance it is supposed to be; certainly Shakespeare's Roman citizens are the best judges of it, and they react tempestuously. Although compressed, it scarcely discloses aloofness or an avoidance of popular emotive themes.

Act II, scene ii now shifts to the house of Caesar, but the emphasis on ritual continues as before. With dramatic irony, in view of Brutus' recent lines on sacrificial murder, Caesar commands, "Go bid the priests do present sacrifice." Calpurnia who has "never stood on ceremonies" (omens) is now terrified by them. News comes that the augurers, plucking the entrails of an offering, have failed to find a heart. Calpurnia has dreamed that smiling Romans have laved their hands in blood running from Caesar's statue, and Decius Brutus gives this its favorable interpretation which sends Caesar to his death.

The vivid assassination scene carries out Brutus' ritual prescription in dramatic detail, for the killing is staged with a formalized approach, ending in kneeling, by one conspirator after another until the victim is surrounded. This is met by a series of retorts from Caesar ending in "Hence! Wilt thou lift up Olympus," and the "sacrifice" is climaxed with his "Et tu Brute!" The conspirators ceremonially bathe their hands in Caesar's blood, and Brutus pronounces upon "this our lofty scene" with the prophecy that it "shall be acted over/In states unborn and accents yet unknown!"

The mockery in counterritual now begins as a servant of Antony enters (III, i, 121) and confronts Brutus:

> Thus, Brutus, did my master bid me kneel,
> Thus did Mark Antony bid me fall down;
> And being prostrate, thus he bade me say:
> Brutus is noble, wise, valiant, and honest.

Here a threefold repetition, "kneel," "fall down," and "being prostrate," brings the ceremonial irony close to satire. Following this worship of the new idol by his messenger, Antony appears in person and with dramatic timing

---

[3] See the reference and quotation in note 1.

offers himself as a victim. In one speech he evokes both the holy scene which the conspirators so desired and the savagery which underlay it:

> Now, whilst your purpled hands do reek and smoke,
> Fulfill your pleasure. Live a thousand years,
> I shall not find myself so apt to die;
> No place will please me so, no mean of death,
> As here by Caesar, and by you cut off.

The murder scene is thus hallowed by Antony in a manner which quite reverses its sanctification by the conspirators. Brutus, forbearing, attempts to mollify Antony with his cherished theme of purgation:

> Our hearts you see not. They are pitiful,
> And pity to the general wrong of Rome—
> As fire drives out fire, so pity pity—
> Hath done this deed on Caesar.

Antony's response is again one of counterceremony, the shaking of hands in formal sequence which serves to make each conspirator stand alone and unprotected by the rite of blood which had united him with the others. The assassins had agreed as a token of solidarity that each of them should stab Caesar. Antony seems to allude to this:

> Let each man render me his bloody hand.
> First, Marcus Brutus, will I shake with you;
> Now, Caius Cassius, do I take your hand;
> Now, Decius Brutus, yours; now yours, Mettellus;
> Yours, Cinna; and, my valiant Casca, yours;
> Though last, not least in love, yours, good Trebonius.
> Gentlemen all,—alas what shall I say?

It is then that Antony, addressing the body of Caesar, suddenly delivers his first profanation of the ritual sacrifice:

> Here wast thou bay'd brave hart;
> Here didst thou fall; and here thy hunters stand,
> Sign'd in thy spoil, and crimson'd in thy lethe.

And lest the allusion escape, Shakespeare continues Antony's inversion of Brutus' ceremonial formula: the dish carved for the gods is doubly transformed into the carcass hewn for hounds with further hunting metaphors of Caesar as a hart in the forest and as "a deer strucken by many princes." Brutus agrees to give reasons why Caesar was dangerous, "or else were this a savage spectacle," and the stage is set for what may be called the play's chief counterritual. Only Brutus, who planned the rite of sacrifice, could with such apt irony arrange the "true rites" and "ceremonies" which are to doom the conspiracy.

> I will myself into the pulpit first
> And show the reason of our Caesar's death.
> What Antony shall speak, I will protest
> He speaks by leave and by permission,
> And that we are contented Caesar shall
> Have all true rites and lawful ceremonies.

But exactly after the manner of his speech announcing the ritual sacrifice (II, i) Brutus concludes again on a note of policy: "It shall advantage more than do us wrong."

Next follows Antony *solus* rendering his prophecy of "domestic fury and fierce civil strife" symbolized in Caesar's ghost which will

> Cry "Havoc," and let slip the dogs of war,
> That this foul deed shall smell above the earth.

The passage is similar in utterance, function, and dramatic placement to Carlisle's prophecy on the deposition of Richard II, and for that reason it is to be taken seriously as a choric interpretation of Caesar's death. Significantly, the beginning lines again deride Brutus' erstwhile phrase, "sacrificers but not butchers":

> O, pardon me, thou bleeding piece of earth,
> That I am meek and gentle with these butchers!

It is unnecessary to elaborate upon the Forum scene; Antony's oration follows the speech of Brutus with consequences familiar to all readers. But there is an element in Antony's turning of the tables which is just as remarkable as the well-known irony of his references to "honorable men." If we remember that Shakespeare has emphasized ritual at various planes of seriousness and of derision, the conclusion of Antony's speech to the populace will link itself with the previous theme. For here Antony reenacts the death of Caesar in a ritual of his own, one intended to show that the original "lofty scene" presented a base carnage. Holding Caesar's bloody mantle as a talisman, he reproduces *seriatim* the sacrificial strokes, but he does so in terms of the "rent" Casca made and the "cursed steel" that Brutus plucked away with the blood of Caesar following it. Again, each conspirator had struck individually at Caesar and had symbolically involved himself with the others; for the second time Antony reminds us of this ritual bond by recounting each stroke, and his recreation of the rite becomes a mockery of it. Brutus' transformation of blood into the heady wine of sacrifice is reversed both in substance and in ceremony.

For the "realists" among the conspirators what has occurred can be summed up in the bare action of the play: the killing of Caesar has been accomplished, but the fruits of it have been spoiled by Brutus' insistence that Antony live and that he speak at Caesar's funeral. "The which," as North's Plutarch has it, "marred all." With reference to Brutus, however, something much more significant has been enacted; the "insurrection," the contradiction, within him has taken outward form in his attempt to purify assassination through ceremony. This act, not to be found in Plutarch,[4] symbolizes the "Elizabethan" Brutus compelled by honor to join with conspirators but required by conscience to reject Conspiracy.

We have followed the ritual theme in *Julius Caesar* from early scenes to point of Antony's oration, at which it is completely defined. There remains, however, a terminal appearance of the theme in the first scene of Act V. The ultimate clash between the idealism of Brutus and Antony's contempt for it comes during the parley on the eve of Philippi, at which Antony again drives home the old issue of ceremonial imposture. Brutus has observed that his enemy wisely threats before he stings; the reply is Antony's last disposition of the sacrificial rite:

> Villains, you did not so when your vile daggers
> Hack'd one another in the sides of Caesar,
> You show'd your teeth like apes, and fawn'd like hounds,
> And bow'd like bondmen, kissing Caesar's feet;
> Whilst damned Casca, like a cur, behind
> Struck Caesar on the neck.

---

[4] A reference at this point to Plutarch will serve both to clarify my meaning and to allay some natural doubts concerning the dramatist's intention. While it is true that the ritual murder of Caesar is Shakespeare's own contribution, the expository preparation for it in Act I comes from an episode in Plutarch in which Antony concludes the Lupercalian rites by offering a laurel crown twice to Caesar, and in which the tribunes are described as desecrating ritual offerings (*Shakespeare's Plutarch,* I, 92–3; see also II, 19–20). Hence we have basic ritual materials for Shakespeare's first two scenes present in one convenient block of his source which also offered a convenient beginning for the play. Does this prevent us from attaching significance to the unusual presence of ritual elements in the exposition scenes? I believe it does not, for two reasons. First, the choice of source material by a dramatist is itself significant; Shakespeare could have started the play with other episodes in Plutarch or with scenes of his own invention. Secondly, it is immaterial whether he began *Julius Caesar* with this episode in his source and, because of its wealth of ritual detail, was led to the theme of ritualized assassination, or whether he began with the theme and chose source materials for exposition which agreed with it. In either case the same remarkable unity between earlier and later parts of the play would have been achieved, and it is this unity which is important. Guesses about its origin in the playwright's composition are profitless. We do know that Shakespeare's Brutus plans the killing of Caesar as ritual, while Plutarch presents it as the very opposite of this. Plutarch's description of the assassination emphasizes, in fact, its resemblance to the hunting down of an animal, the very effect Brutus seeks explicitly to avoid in the "carcass-hounds" figure, and the one which Antony magnifies in his counter-emphasis of imagery drawn from hunting. North notes it thus: "Caesar turned him nowhere but he was stricken at by some...and was hacked and mangled among them, as a wild beast taken of hunters." (*Shakespeare's Plutarch,* I, 101–2.)

Antony invokes the "hacking" which Brutus earlier foreswore, and he again inverts the cherished formula of sacrifice: once more the dish carved for gods becomes the carcass hewn for hounds. Over the body of Caesar he had previously employed the hunting-hound figure ("Here wast thou bay'd, brave hart."); the apes, the hounds, and the cur of these lines complete his vengeful irony of metaphor.

What, finally, is to be inferred from Antony's concluding passage on "the noblest Roman of them all"? Commonly found there is a broad vindication of Brutus which would deny an ironical interpretation. When Antony's elegiac speech is read plainly, however, its meaning is quite limited: it declares simply that Brutus was the only conspirator untouched by envy, and that, in intention, he acted "in a general honest thought/And common good to all." The Elizabethan view of Brutus as tragically misguided is thus consistent with Antony's pronouncement that he was the only disinterested member of the conspiracy. But Brutus is not to be summed up in an epitaph; as the impersonal member of a conspiracy motivated largely by personal ends, he sought in a complex way to resolve his contradiction by depersonalizing, ritualizing, the means.

Shakespeare's achievement, however, is not confined to the characterization of a major figure, for we have seen that the ceremonial motive extends beyond the personality of Brutus into the structure of the play. Exposition stressing the idea of ritual observance leads to the episode in which Brutus formulates the "sacrifice," and clear resolution of the idea follows in event and commentary. Structural craftsmanship thus supplements characterization and the two combine, as in *Richard II,* to state the political philosophy implicit in the play.

# 26

# Speak Hands for Me: Gesture as Language in *Julius Caesar*

*Robert Hapgood*

No less than Antonin Artaud or Gordon Craig, Shakespeare was a maker of total dramatic experiences. Despite the sparseness of his stage-directions, recent work has shown that we can make out enough of his use of non-verbal elements (props, gestures, stage-pictures) to appreciate his plays as pieces of "total theatre." As a further effort in this direction, I should like to look closely at the gestures in *Julius Caesar,* founding my analysis on gestures positively indicated in Shakespeare's text while drawing illustrations from performances I have seen or read about.

Stabbing; rising; falling; leading; following; gathering; dispersing; shaking hands, weeping, and other "shows of love"—these comprise the basic vocabulary of gesture and movement in *Julius Caesar.* They occur again and again, and in patterns, the dominant one being that of reversal.

This pattern is best seen in the acts of falling and rising. Caesar is at first on high. In Plutarch, he displays his power by sitting while others stand. In Shakespeare, the repeated references to him as one who would rise too high suggest that he should somehow be literally above the rest, and Cassius confirms that his underlings must bend their bodies if Caesar care-

*Reprinted from* Drama Survey, *V (1966), 162–170 by permission of the author and publisher.*

lessly but nod on them. Beyond that, Caesar might well hold himself with an imperiousness equal to his third-person "Caesars" (he uses the royal "we" just before his "coronation"). In the MGM motion picture, Louis Calhern as Caesar was simply taller than everyone else. That was too easy a solution, however; for it missed the artificiality in his ascendancy, a quality Shakespeare stresses by making Caesar's exaltation very self-conscious (just before his fall he compares himself to the Northern Star and Olympus) and very obviously belied by his falling-sickness. The effect was better conveyed by the downward camera-angle when Cassius beneath a towering statue of Caesar spoke of him as a Colossus.

Caesar's metaphorical "fall" from power is also visually realized and emphasized. Calling attention to the stage-picture, Antony laments after the assassination: "here didst thou fall; and here thy hunters stand"—an image which the elder Booth as Cassius pushed still further (Sprague reports), striding right across the body of dead Caesar as he made his exit. Caesar's former underlings not only "stand" but rise, reaching their zenith when Brutus ascends the pulpit for his oration. But when Antony then rises to speak, he reverses the fall of Caesar (the First Pleb cries "Take up the body") in such a way that those who made him fall, fall themselves. In defeat, Brutus finds the apt image:

> Our enemies have beat us to the pit:
> It is more worthy to leap in ourselves
> Than tarry till they push us.

Here, as often, the image called up in the dialogue clarifies and extends the stage-image we actually see when Brutus dies.

Always, Antony is the agent of such reversals. Yet they are not entirely his doing: the conspirators make themselves vulnerable by putting a twist on their acts that ultimately brings them full circle. This "boomerang" effect is also clear in the gestures of falling. The conspirators contrive to rise by throwing themselves down in false supplication before Caesar, thus surrounding him. Their falsity is emphasized by contrast with the parallel scenes immediately before, in which Portia and then Calpurnia kneel to their husbands in true prayer, and by the obvious exaggeration of their own abasement, which Caesar at the time and Antony later deride. There is a special aptness, hence, about the way Antony begins his counterplot. He sends a messenger carefully instructed in false falling:

> Thus, Brutus, did my master bid me kneel;
> Thus did Mark Antony bid me fall down;
> And being prostrate, thus he bade me say...

Note the calculated rather than spontaneous movement ("my master bid me") and the explicitly exaggerated abasement (the servant not only kneels but falls down prostrate before them): Thus boldly does Shakespeare underline the effect of a perverted gesture returning on its perverters.

In the same way, Antony turns the conspirators' false "shows of love" back upon the falsifiers. A dominant visual effect of the play is the growth and destruction of the conspiracy before our eyes. Like the ten little Indians, first there is one (Cassius), then two (as Casca commits himself with "Hold, my hand"), then three (as Cinna rushes in, clearly another "incorporate/To our attempts"); these three, with three more, then come to Brutus; and soon, except for the final addition of Ligarius, the faction is complete, as Brutus cries: "Give me your hands all over, one by one." Then they add Caesar, falsifying the "shows of love" by which they have truly bound themselves to one another, as they "like friends" escort Caesar to the Senate. Their falsity reaches its climax with Brutus' ruefully sly equivocation just before the assassination: "I kiss thy hand, but not in flattery, Caesar." It is fitting, then, that Antony should begin the undoing of their compact (given final affirmation when they bathe their hands in Caesar's blood) by shaking each man's "bloody hand" in false show of amity. Antony's success is immediate. After this scene, we will see no more of the group except for Cassius and Brutus, and they die separately.

All of the gestures which have been twisted from their normal significance in the course of the play return to norm at the end. The act of lying down is purged of policy: Varro, Claudius, Lucius, and finally Strato, sleep; Cassius, Titinius, and then Brutus at last "lie upon the ground," dead. Love is truly shown by numerous handshakes, although these are now mostly in farewell. Even the conspirators' false tasting of wine with Caesar comes right when Brutus and Cassius celebrate their reconciliation by sharing a bowl of wine.

The complete reversal pattern is apparent in the way the stabs by Caesar's assassins return to their own proper entrails. As always, it is Antony who turns the conspirators' blows back upon themselves. The moment of reversal comes in his funeral oration, as he recounts their strokes:

> Look, in this place ran Cassius' dagger through.
> See what a rent the envious Casca made:
> Through this the well-beloved Brutus stabb'd...

Through Antony's "counter-ritual," as Brents Stirling aptly calls it, the very stabbings that clinched the success of the conspiracy help to undo it.

Before the assassination, Casca—the first to strike—is the only Roman who draws a weapon. He enters I, iii, with his sword drawn, explaining "I ha' not since put up my sword—/Again the Capitol I met a lion/Who glared upon me, and went surly by." (A few speeches later, Cassius will confirm the foreshadowing by saying that Caesar "roars/As doth the lion in the Capitol.") The other positive instance comes in II, i, when he uses his sword as a pointer: "Here, as I point my sword, the sun arises." Since it here seems completely natural for him to make free with his sword, I suspect that he should draw it frequently. He might well use his sword to stress his wish that he had taken Caesar at his word when "he plucked me ope his doublet and offered [the crowd] his throat to cut," and might make further use of it, then, to emphasize "If Caesar had stabbed their mothers, they would have done no less."

Relevantly, Shakespeare adds a curious detail to Plutarch's account of the slave who "did cast a marvelous burning flame out of his hand." As Casca tells it, the slave "Held up his *left* hand which did flame and burn." So thoroughly has Shakespeare prepared for the moment when Casca is the first to rear his hand against Caesar, it seems likely that he wanted Casca to "rear his hand" at this point, too; and since Casca already had his sword in his right hand, only his left hand was free. Edmond O'Brien as Casca in the MGM motion picture gestured thus, with cocked left arm and clinched fist. Very effective, too, was the way he clutched his dagger at: "So can I./So can every bondsman in his own hand bear/The power to cancel his captivity." Cassius had just before been talking about suicide, but O'Brien's gesture was more suggestive of murder.

Until he stabs Caesar, Casca's use of his weapon is straightforward. The gesture of stabbing is not twisted from its normal significance until Brutus' attempt to construe an act of betrayal and assassination into a sacrifice. With all of the conspirators but Brutus, the distortion is obvious. As a matter of policy, they merely pretend to share the sacrificial version of the killing that is to Brutus a matter of principle. Hence they are vulnerable to Antony's exposé of their hackings.

Is Brutus also culpable? That is of course *the* question of the play. Certainly he is not culpable in the same way as the others, for there is no real doubt of his sincerity in wishing to "carve Caesar as a dish fit for the gods." Yet for all his high-mindedness (indeed, because of it), he as much as they is engaged in construing the act of stabbing into something it isn't—Shakespeare shows him in the very process of self-deceptively "fashioning it thus." There seems to be truth in Antony's parody:

> In your bad strokes, Brutus, you give good words;
> Witness the hole you made in Caesar's heart,
> Crying "Long live! Hail, Caesar!"

Still more tellingly, when Brutus requests Volumnius to hold his sword while he runs on it, Volumnius' reply bears a penetrating irony: "That's not an office for a friend, my lord."

Everything suggests that Brutus' blow, which certainly comes last, should be sharply distinct from those of the others. Doubtless, Mansfield's version went too far; as Sprague records it: "Tenderly, sorrowfully, sacrificially the patriot laid his blade on the bleeding throat of his friend, the point directed to his own heart." Yet somehow Brutus' well-meaning but misguided conception of himself as sacrificer not butcher needs to be recalled. That he is misguided will probably be clear enough from the bloodiness of the savage spectacle itself. If not, Caesar's translation of it from a political to a personal context should make it so. For Caesar plainly receives the unkindest cut of all differently from the blows of the others. He is one of many—with Portia, Antony, Cassius—who come to realize that the price of Brutus' love is submission to the sword, and who voluntarily pay it. As North's Plutarch describes it: "Caesar did still defend himself against the rest, running every way with his body, but when he saw Brutus with his sword drawn in his hand, then he pulled his gown over his head and made no resistance." "Et tu, Brute?—Then fall Caesar!" should be spoken *before* Brutus strikes.

Like the other gestures, that of stabbing does not come to rights again until the action moves to the battlefield, with its straightforward swordplay. It is there, too, that the reversal pattern comes full circle. This is worked out with remarkable nicety, Cassius' suicide differing in kind from Brutus' exactly as did their stabbings of Caesar. Cassius, who killed Caesar as an act of hate, receives his own death-blow in the same spirit: "Caesar, thou art revenged/Even with the sword that killed thee." Brutus, who thought of the slaying of Caesar as an act of sacrifice, sacrifices himself accordingly, fulfilling his earlier promise: "as I slew my best lover for the good of Rome, I have the same dagger for myself when it shall please my country to need my death." Where Cassius *is struck* by Pindarus, Brutus *runs on* his sword, held by Strato, and avows: "Caesar, now be still./I killed not thee with half so good a will."

Although Brutus participates in the general pattern of reversal, his characteristic pattern is one of emergence, in which a gesture is at first restrained and then progressively released. He is at first a model of stoic self-control. His calm is not, to be sure, that of true serenity. Certainly it is not the mild gentleness of James Mason in the movie. Instead it is the kind of tense, willed self-control of insurrection-within that Eric Porter portrayed in the BBC-TV version. "Self-subdued" is the way Macready put it. In this, he is like Caesar, whose first impulses—to heed the soothsayer, the priests, his wife, his own intuitive fears—could have saved his life had he not subjugated them to his thrust toward ascendancy. In direct contrast stand their wives, Calpurnia giving way altogether to her fears and even Portia, despite her "man's mind," failing to restrain her woman's heart. At an ultimate extreme is the impulsiveness of the Roman commoners, uncritically sympathetic and demonstrative toward whoever makes an appeal to them.

Amid the hurly-burly of Rome, Brutus is at first so calm as to seem inert. His immobility (he does not even go to watch the rites) contrasts with the "quick spirit" of Antony, the Lupercalian runner. Actors have made the most, too, of a contrast with Cassius. In his life of Booth, Winter comments on "Kemble's slow, stately, massive walk, in Brutus, as contrasted with Young's quick, nervous, restless pace, as Cassius"—a contrast which Winter found equally striking when Booth and Barrett played the roles. The movie exaggerated this contrast outlandishly, with John Gielgud's Cassius all forward-thrust (striding forcefully ahead during his soliloquy) while James Mason's Brutus was not merely immobile but in retreat, both Cassius and Portia physically pursuing him. Characteristically, this Brutus backed away to the statue of Pompey at Caesar's assassination, and in fact never did come fully into action. The most he did, in the quarrel scene, was stand his ground.

In this respect, the film's choreography directly contradicted Shakespeare's. For Shakespeare's Brutus soon goes into action, a process precisely marked in his assumption of leadership. In their first interview, Brutus feels that it is Cassius who would "lead" him into dangers. When Brutus first joins the conspiracy, his leadership takes the form not of positive action but of vetoing the proposals of the others—not to include Cicero ("he will never follow anything/That other men begin"), not to kill Antony. His assumption of positive, physical leadership is marked by the scene with sick Ligarius, who discards his sickness, asks Brutus to "bid me run," and declares: "I follow you/To do I know not what; but it sufficeth/That Brutus leads me on." Brutus responds: "Follow me then." After the assassination, Cassius declares: "Brutus shall lead, and we shall grace his heels"; Brutus directs Antony to "follow us" with Caesar's body; and he asks the people to "follow me and give me audience, friends." The throng that had followed Caesar at the heels does so.

Once Brutus is under way, there is no stopping him! Against Cassius' cautions, he insists on letting Antony speak at the funeral; he insists on engaging in the battle of Philippi. In the battle, perceiving but cold demeanor in Octavius' wing, Brutus decides that "Sudden push gives them the overthrow" and sends Messala with bills to his legions: "Ride, ride, Messala! Let them all come down." Bell's edition made the dramatic point explicit by substituting "Haste, haste." In the next scene, Titinius explains the disastrous results: "Brutus gave the word too early,/Who, having some advantage on Octavius/Took it too eagerly. His soldiers fell to spoil."

It is one of the central ironies of Brutus' tragedy that after a lifetime of self-restraint, he dies on the threshold of a new life of free and open expression. For in addition to his rush into battle, Brutus "lets himself go" enough to quarrel with Cassius and to brave Antony and Octavius. Only after such releases does true repose come, when Brutus sits and rests on a rock just before his death.

Ironically, Brutus' suppressed impulses to act are no sooner released than they in turn release disastrous counteractions. In life, Caesar, like Brutus, prided himself on being "unshaked of motion"; but when Brutus kills him, his spirit "ranges for revenge" and continues to "walk abroad" until Brutus runs on his sword. Only then can Caesar "be still." Similarly, as Brutus takes leadership away from Cassius and then Caesar, Antony—Caesar's best follower—takes leadership away from Brutus; at the funeral, the people say of Antony: "we'll follow him, we'll die with him." The counter-action does not, of course, go so far that Brutus and Cassius are themselves made to follow Antony; indeed, their suicides are in part prompted by their refusal "to be led in triumph/Through the streeets of Rome." But Brutus' man Strato, who held his sword, does end up following Octavius. Leadership having passed from Antony to Octavius (for a visual instance see V, i, 68), Messala suggests at the end: "Octavius, then take him to follow thee."

There is one gesture that combines the emergence and reversal patterns, that of weeping and mourning. Antony's mourning soliloquy to the "bleeding piece of earth" and his private tears over Caesar's corpse are genuine. In contrast, Brutus a little later talks about weeping for Caesar, but his tears are abstract and rhetorical, not real. Antony then turns this controlled "grief" back upon Brutus by recalling in his oration that when the poor have cried, Caesar hath wept; by shedding his own artful yet real tears; and by drawing gracious drops from the populace. Thus the "reversal" of the gesture is accomplished. Its emergence is confined to Brutus, who must suffer many losses before he can give normal expression of grief. Portia, driven distract by her own sorrows for him, dies unwept by him. Because of their falling-out, Cassius "could weep/My spirit from mine eyes," but not Brutus; even at Cassius' death, Brutus' promise of mourning is for the future:

> I owe moe tears
> To this dead man than you shall see me pay.
> I shall find time, Cassius; I shall find time.
> Come, therefore, and to Thasos send his body.
> His funerals shall not be in our camp,
> Lest it discomfort us.

The inadequacy of Brutus' response is pointed by contrast with Titinius' suicidal way of "mourning" for Cassius which has come just before. For whom does Brutus first weep? For himself!—and his lost cause. Just before his suicide, Clitus remarks: "now is that noble vessel full of grief,/That it runs over even at his eyes." After this final release, a return to norm is also emphasized. The eulogy which Antony delivers over Brutus is genuine, without the demagoguery of his oration over Caesar. The rites of mourning which Octavius promises Brutus are without the calculation that tainted Brutus' for Caesar.

What is the upshot of these patterns of gesture? They seem to me to imply a mordant critique of the Roman way of life. In Shakespeare's Rome (in this play as in his other Roman plays) spontaneous, direct expression of natural impulses is regarded as a weakness—a trait of women and the throng. Such impulses must be suppressed or elevated or in some other way given purposeful direction, whether that of principle or policy. In this way of life, control is all. That is why the dialogue of *Julius Caesar* is full of explicit appeals to codes of honor, family pride, and ultimate goals: The unregenerate life of impulse never ceases its claims and must constantly be ruled.

Yet try as these Romans will, they cannot finally construe the significance of their actions to suit themselves. Temporarily, yes. But the language of gestures is a hard one in which to tell a lie. It is continually revealing the human being beneath the toga. It is as if these gestures were governed by a self-regulating norm of human conduct which insists at last on having its way: However a gesture may be suppressed, it emerges; however a gesture may be distorted, it boomerangs on its distorters and returns to normal.

Antony is the agent of this human norm, beating the manipulators at their own game. He never himself distorts the significance of a gesture until it has already been distorted. The irony is that he himself becomes infected with the disease he helps to purge. His former spontaneity replaced by calculation, he coldbloodedly "pricks down" relatives for death (a visual echo of the stabbing?) and determines how to cut off some charge in Caesar's legacies. Hence, he like the other shrewd contrivers must make a final return to norm.

This norm is one of open, direct, spontaneous, true action and reaction. It is best seen in the latter part of the play when the action moves out of Rome to the battlefield. Brutus' impulses to act and to express friendship and grief are there released and the main thematic gestures are given undistorted expression. Its ascendancy promises stability at the close, but no more than that. For there is nothing secure or comforting about this norm; indeed there is something sardonic about its workings. Its unblinking assertion of the claims of humanity is conservative and limiting, reducing even the noblest aspirations of the mind to the ineluctabilities of the body and its actions. Moreover, adherence to it makes one vulnerable in a way that can be as disastrous as denying it. Where sheer calculation on Cassius' part might well have succeeded, it is his love for Brutus and his direct, spontaneous expression of it which lead him to progressively more disastrous concessions. Even more, what may be Brutus' most spontaneous act—his too early command to attack—proves to be his undoing.

The conflict of impulse and control in *Julius Caesar* is thus thoroughgoingly tragic. The life of impulse comes out as preferable, I believe. But its price is as high as that of control, and both cost too much.

# 27

# *Hamlet:* The Analogy of Action

*Francis Fergusson*

## Ritual and Improvisation: Hamlet's Play as the Center

Shakespeare's theater, because of its ancient roots and its central place in society, permitted the development of ritual drama—or at least a drama which had this dimension as well as others. In the structure of *Hamlet* the rituals, as distinguished from the plots, serve to present the main action at various points in its development. Shakespeare uses them in much the same way in which Henry James used his "social occasions" to present the main theme of *The Awkward Age*. The structure of *Hamlet* could be described in Henry James's words: "A circle consisting of a number of small rounds disposed at equal distance about a central object. The central object was my situation, my subject in itself, to which the thing would owe its title, and the small rounds represented so many distinct lamps, as I liked to call them, the function of each of which would be to light up with all due intensity one of its aspects. . . . I revelled in this notion of the Occasion as a thing by itself." That is the important point: the social rite cr occasion is taken as a thing by itself; it enables the author to assemble his *dramatis*

*Reprinted from Francis Fergusson,* The Idea of a Theater *(Princeton: Princeton University Press, 1949) pp. 120–141 by permission of the publisher.*

*personae* in a wider light than any of their individual intelligences could provide. If my analysis of *Hamlet* is correct, the rituals (though they have deeper meanings than James's social gatherings) are also "occasions" of this kind: lamps lighting the rottenness of Denmark (the basic situation of the play) and the many-sided action which results, at various points in its course, and in various aspects.

In the table showing the relation of the plot to the ritual scenes and the improvisations, the players' scene is at the center. It has a ritual aspect, it is Hamlet's most ambitious improvisation, and it is the climax and peripety of the whole complex plot-scheme. If one can understand this scene, one will be close to grasping Shakespeare's sense of the theater, and his direct, profoundly histrionic dramaturgy.

The prologue contains two rituals, the changing of the guard and Claudius' first court. The changing of the guard is conducted by the honest and simple-minded soldiers, in perfect good faith: the welfare of the state is conceived in the most obvious and acceptable terms, and with the solemnity and authority of the military function. The motives of the soldiers are not impugned; and the only ironic angle we get on this scene is due to the arrival of the Ghost, which clearly suggests that the military rite is not an appropriate means for dealing with the actual danger. Claudius' court, on the other hand, is conducted by the new King; and here we feel (both in the light of Hamlet's disabused view of Claudius, and in the light of the visit of the Ghost) that there is something false about Claudius' discharge of the royal function. Together the two scenes establish the fact of danger and the common concern with the threatened welfare of the state. But they throw ironic lights upon each other. The point of view of the regime is in conflict with that of the simple soldiers. Neither the soldiers nor the regime have the magic for dealing with the Ghost; and it appears that the rituals of the state in general are false or mistaken.

The many conflicts, which the prologue presents as it were in suspension, are further developed (though without coming to direct issue) during the rest of the first act, the second act, and the first scene of Act III. Then (bringing the climax, peripety, and recognition) comes Hamlet's improvised ritual, the players' scene. Hamlet, as the "chief reflector," the widest consciousness in literature, as Henry James called him, is aware of what the soldiers see, of what Claudius sees, and of what the Ghost sees, and he is torn by all the conflicts implicit in these partial values and myopic vested interests. His "ritual occasion" is thus an answer to both rituals in the prologue; and at the same time (because he has also seen what the Ghost sees) it is an answer to, and a substitute for, the inadequate or false ritual order of Denmark. It is itself a "ritual" in that it assembles the whole tribe for an act symbolic of their deepest welfare; it is false and ineffective, like the other public occasions, in that the Danes do not really understand or intend the enactment which they witness. It is, on the other hand, not a true ritual, but an improvisation—for here the role of Hamlet, as showman, as master of ceremonies, as clown, as night-club entertainer who lewdly jokes with the embarrassed patrons—Hamlet the ironist, in sharpest contact with the audience on-stage and the audience off-stage, yet a bit outside the literal belief in the story: it is here that this aspect of Hamlet's role is clearest. But notice that, if Hamlet is the joking clown, he is also like those improvising Old Testament prophets who, gathering a handful of dust or of little bones, or a damaged pot from the potter's wheel, present to a bland generation a sudden image of their state. It is in the players' scene that the peculiar theatricality of *Hamlet*—ritual as theater and theater as ritual; at once the lightest improvisation and the solemnest occasion—is most clearly visible.

What then is the image, the parable, the "fear in a handful of dust," which Hamlet thus places—with all the pomp of court and all the impudence of the night-club entertainer—in the very center of the public consciousness of Denmark?

The most detailed analysis I know of the players' scene is Mr. Dover Wilson's, in his excellent book, *What Happens in Hamlet.* The reader is referred to that study and to its companion-piece, Granville-Barker's book on *Hamlet,* for a discussion of the theatrical problems which the scene presents and for an understanding of the complexity of the scene as a whole, wherein the focus of the audience's attention is shifted from Hamlet (the "central reflector") to Horatio, to the Queen, to Ophelia, to the King—as though the play-within-a-play were being lighted from many angles by reflection from many mirrors. My purpose here is only to describe Hamlet's play itself, in order to show how it reveals the malady of the regime in all its ambiguity, mystery, and spreading ramifications. For this little play is indeed an all-purpose mousetrap—and it catches more than the conscience of the King.

First of all, the play presents the hidden crime (the murder of a king and the more or less incestuous theft of his queen and his throne) upon which, as in *Oedipus,* all the threads of the interwoven plots depend. It is the presentation of this literal fact which has the immediate effect upon the innocent bystanders of the court and upon the innocent groundlings in the audience, though in Hamlet's violent view none are innocent. Because the security of the regime and the purposes of its supporters depend either upon ignorance or concealment, the public representation of the crime is itself an act of aggression, Hamlet's attack, the turning point in the story. This attack reaches the guilty Claudius first, Gertrude second, Polonius third, then Laertes and Ophelia. And at length it clears the way for Fortinbras, the new faith and the new regime.

But though the fact of murder, incest, and usurpation is clearly presented, the time of the murder—is it still to come?—is vague; and the *dramatis personae* in the playlet are shifted about in such a way as to leave the identity of the criminal in question, and so to spread the guilt. The actual crime was that of Claudius; but in the play the guilty one is nephew to the King. This could mean (as Polonius and Gertrude seem to think) a direct threat by Hamlet to Claudius; it also means that Hamlet (who had admitted to himself a "weakness and melancholy" which makes him subject to devilish solicitations, and who had assured Ophelia, that "I am myself indifferent honest, yet I could accuse me of such things it were better my mother had not borne me") had granted Claudius, in advance, that he too is at least potentially guilty. Neither Hamlet nor Shakespeare seem to rule out a Freudian interpretation of the tangle; Hamlet comes close to representing himself as the diagrammatic son of the Oedipus complex, killing the father and possessing the mother. Yet his awareness of such motivations lifts the problems from the level of pathology to that of drama; he sees himself, Claudius, Denmark, the race itself, as subject to greeds and lusts which the hypocritical façade of the regime guiltily conceals.

Thus the literal meaning of the playlet is the fact of the crime; but the trope and the anagoge convey a picture of the human in general as weak, guilty, and foolish: the deepest and most sinister version of the malady of Claudius' regime in Denmark. This picture should emerge directly from the staging of the playlet before the corrupt and hypocritical court, under the inspired and triumphant irony of the regisseur-prince. The whining of pipes, the parade of mummers, the wooden gestures of the dumb-show, the tinkle of the rhymes, should have the magical solemnity of a play-party or children's singing-game ("London bridge is falling down"). Yet because of the crimes represented, this atmosphere is felt as unbearably weak and frivolous, a parody of all solemn rites. If this playlet invokes the magic potency of the theater ("the play's the thing") it does so with as much despairing irony as love. The staging is crude and childish: Hamlet's actors vainly take things into their own hands, and the court audience is as condescendingly unperceptive (until the scandal dawns on them) as any cynical crowd at a Broadway opening.

Hamlet's audience on-stage (and perhaps off-stage as well) misses the deeper meanings of his play. Yet he and his author have put it as simply as possible in the weary couplets of the Player-King. The Player-King seems to stand for Hamlet's father, and thus for the Ghost; and he speaks in fact with the clarity but helplessness (in this world) of the dead—addressing the frivolous Player-Queen without much hope of understanding. Since he is Hamlet's puppet, he speaks also for Hamlet, and since he is the King, he stands also for Claudius. Claudius, in the course of the play, will gradually acquire a helplessness like that of the Ghost; a faithlessness and an indecision like that of Hamlet. It is the function of the Player-King to state as directly as possible that gloomy and fatalistic sense of human action which is the subject of the play, and which all the various characters have by analogy.

The way to show this in detail would be to study the action of each character and to show what frivolity and gloomy faithlessness they have in common, but this would take too long. The point may be briefly illustrated by juxtaposing a few utterances of Hamlet and Claudius with analogous couplets of the Player King:

*Hamlet*. There's a divinity that shapes our ends,
Rough-hew them how we will.
Was't Hamlet wronged Laertes? Never Hamlet:
...Hamlet denies it.
Who does it then? His madness. (V, ii)

*Claudius*. My stronger guilt defeats my strong intent:
And, like a man to double business bound,
I stand in pause where I shall first begin,
And both neglect. (III, iii)
Not that I think you did not love your father,
But that I know love is begun by time,
And that I see, in passages of proof,
Time qualifies the spark and fire of it.
There lives within the very flame of love
A kind of wick or snuff that will abate it,
And nothing is at a like goodness still,
For goodness, growing to a plurisy,
Dies in his own too much. That we would do,
We should do when we would, for this "would" changes
And hath abatements and delays as many
As there are tongues, are hands, are accidents;
And then this "should" is like a spendthrift sigh,
That hurts by easing. (IV, vii)

*Player*. Our wills and fates do so contrary run
*King*. That our devices still are overthrown,
Our thoughts are ours, their ends none of our own.
What to ourselves in passion we propose,
The passion ending, doth the purpose lose.
Purpose is but the slave to memory
Of violent birth, but poor validity.

The speeches of Hamlet and Claudius which I have quoted come late in the play, when both of them gain a deathly insight into their destinies—the hidden and uncontrolled springs of their own and others' actions. Even Claudius sees so deeply at this moment that he gets the sense of human action which all the characters have by analogy. His speech to Laertes (Act IV, scene vii) is, moreover, both made more ironic and more general by being addressed to Laertes in order to deceive him into a course which is contrary to his deepest purposes and best interests. As for Hamlet, his sense of pathos, of the suffering of motivations beyond our understanding or control, does not save him from violent outbursts any more than that of Claudius does. Shakespeare usually grants his victims a moment of great clarity when it is too late—and then shows them returning, like automatons, to "ravin down their proper bane" and die.

But the chief point I wish to make here is that the Player King presents very pithily the basic vision of human action in the play, at a level so deep that it applies to all the characters: the guilty, the free, the principals, the bystanders, those in power and the dispossessed. This vision of course comes directly from the crime of Claudius and the other "accidental judgements, casual slaughters, purposes mistook" (as Horatio describes them when summing up for Fortinbras) upon which the complicated plot depends; yet this generalized vision is more terrible than any of the particular crimes, and much more important for understanding Hamlet's motivation. To this point I shall return later.

The immediate effect of Hamlet's play comes by way of the concrete scandal which brings the climax and peripety of the narratives. The presentation of the play is Hamlet's attack; it succeeds; it convicts Claudius' regime, and "the lives of many" that depend upon it, of impotence and corruption. After that revelation all is lost (just as Macbeth is lost after the banquet scene)—and the desperate devices of the King and Laertes, the brief folly of Polonius, and the unimpeded progress of Fortinbras, in the healthy rhythm of the march, are seen as clearly fated or doomed.

For this reason also the "rituals" which follow the players' scene have a different quality from those which precede it. Since the regime has lost its manna—been "shown up"—the rituals in Acts IV and V, marking the stages of the collective pathos and epiphany, are clearly presented as mad or evil. Ophelia's mad ritual presents the "sparagmos" or tearing asunder of the individual and society at once ("schism in the state and schism in the soul"); mingling marriage and funeral, lewdness and prettiness, love and destruction to the accompaniment of plotting and rebellion. Ophelia's funeral is a real death but a "maimèd rite"; the duel between Hamlet and Laertes is ostensibly a ritual and actually a murder. With the assembling of the court and the royal family for the duel, the picture of Claudius' regime (the collective revelation of his black masses) is complete.

In the succession of "ritual scenes" with its center and climax in Hamlet's little play, it is obvious that Hamlet himself plays a central role. In the two rituals of the prologue he is, like the audience, a mere puzzled and troubled bystander. After the hidden struggles of Acts I, II, and III, he presents, with his play, his own black mass, his own parody of a rite. He does not appear for the "tearing asunder" of Ophelia's madness, for this marks the pathos of the regime, and of the lives that depend directly on it; and his life (wherever it may be) has already withdrawn from all loyalty to Claudius' Denmark. But he returns to record Ophelia's truncated funeral in his cold, spent, but clear awareness; and to take his fated role in the duel at the end. I have endeavored to study the rituals as marking the progress of the "play as a whole"; but it is evident that in the play, and in the order of the rituals, Hamlet himself is both chief "agonist" and central "reflector." With this in mind it is possible to offer an interpretation of the role of Hamlet in relation to Shakespeare's idea of the theater, and the traditional social values which the play assumes.

## An Interpretation of the Role of Hamlet

> "For, by the image of my cause, I see
> The portraiture of his."

Oedipus, as I have pointed out, starts out as the hero, the triumphant human adequate to rule, and ends, like Tiresias, a scapegoat, a witness and a sufferer for the hidden truth of the human condition. The play starts with the conflict and contrast between Oedipus and Tiresias, shows the steps of Oedipus' dismemberment, and ends when he is blind and all-seeing and helpless, as Tiresias was in the beginning. Hamlet is apparently thought of as undergoing a similar transformation, from hero to scapegoat, from "the expectancy and rose of the fair state" to the distracted, suffering witness and victim of Act V. But this development is not neatly laid out for him according to a publicly understood series of struggles: He feels his way toward it, not with public sanction but against the faithless worldliness of the Danes. It is not until Act V that his martyr-like destiny "feels right" to him.

We see him in the first three acts of the play as a puzzled and, as it were, unconvinced hero and prince. He knows that "the times are out of joint" and that he is born to set them right; he knows that the Prince should be moved by honor and ambition: But he cannot reconcile this worldly code with his sense of evil in Denmark nor with the otherworldly solicitations of his Ghost-father. From Corneille to Dryden the ethical values of "honor" will be taken as sufficient basis for the drama of human life; but Hamlet's sense of his own and Denmark's condition contradicts this simplified philosophy. When he looks at Laertes, that "noble youth," he envies him—envies, at least, his simple and honorable motivations. When he looks at Fortinbras, he envies him the ability to risk his own and other lives for honor—"even for an eggshell." If he could accept this code, he would feel that the murder of Claudius would heal the schism in his own soul and in society; but just as his sense of evil preceded his knowledge of Claudius' literal guilt, so he cannot believe that the literal punishment of Claudius (an eye for an eye) will cure the damage he has done. And so his drama becomes far deeper than a simple revenge play.

If Hamlet is not content with the simple soldierly code of honor, it is because he sees too deeply and skeptically into that cosmic setting of human life which Shakespeare's theater symbolically represented. He sees beyond the tiny human involvements of the foreground to the social order indicated by the stage house façade and, above that, to the order in the stars implied by the canopy over his head. This is especially clear in his first scene with Rosencrantz and Guildenstern (Act II, scene ii). It is in this scene that he makes the great speech on Man which Tillyard quotes as an exposition of the traditional ordered universe. But the speech ends bitterly: "And yet, to me, what is this quintessence of dust?"

Though Hamlet accepts this order, he does not know where he belongs in it; he is not even sure which way is up. He would have felt the force of that remark of Heracleitus which Eliot uses as epigraph to *Burnt Norton:* "The way up and the way down are one and the same" His intellect plays over the world of the religious tradition with an all-dissolving irony like that of Montaigne in the *Apologie de Raimond Sebonde:* a truly double-edged irony, for he can neither do with nor do without the ancient moral and cosmic order.

That is why he has a despairing fellow-feeling for Rosencrantz and Guildenstern. He knows them for little trimmers, neither for God nor for the Devil, but "for themselves," like the dim figures in Dante's Limbo: "indifferent children of the earth," "Fortune's privates," as they call themselves. He is himself anything but indifferent, yet he does not at that moment know how to care, and so he feels himself, like them, lost between "greatness" and the chill of mere bodily "weight" and utter faithlessness at the bottom of the universe. Thus he is troubled with "bad dreams":

> *Guil.* Which dreams, indeed, are ambition, for the very substance of the ambitious is but the shadow of a dream.
> *Ham.* A dream itself is but a shadow.
> *Ros.* Truly, and I hold ambition of so airy and light a quality that it is but a shadow's shadow.
> *Ham.* Then are our beggars bodies, and our monarchs and outstretched heroes the beggars' shadows. Shall we to the court? for, by my fay, I cannot reason.

Hamlet draws the deduction which troubles *him,* but not Rosencrantz and Guildenstern: If ambition like Fortinbras' is illusory, what, in Denmark, is to show us the way, and prevent us from taking the "shadow as a solid thing"?

It would be an exaggeration to say that Hamlet envies these two as he envies Fortinbras and Laertes. But his fellow-feeling for them—call it sympathy, or a sense of the analogy between them, or seeing their cause as mirroring his—comes, like his envy, from the fact that he himself is lost. Until the success of his play, Hamlet feels his over-quick sympathy as a weakness and covers it up with murderous sarcasm. On his return from England, he has accepted it, and in Act V his abnormally quick sympathy has acquired some of the quiet of the vision integrated and lived-up-to, some of the breadth of charity.

What has intervened is chiefly the presentation of his play. When the players come and do a speech for Hamlet, he envies *them*; but at this time it turns out that he has found a real clue to his own action. He cannot act like a simple soldier, but he can employ the theater in an equally dangerous, and far more significant, project. He can use it as a trap for the conscience of the King, and at the same time as a test of his own and the Ghost's vision. Thus empirically, or improvisationally, feeling his way through the concrete elements of his situation, he finds his own proper line of action, and a use of the theater very much like that which two other autobiographical characters of Shakespeare make of it.

The two other characters who use the theater in this way are the Duke in *Measure for Measure* and Prospero in *The Tempest*. These two plays are, of course, very different from each other and from Hamlet. But the analogies between the three dispossessed rulers, and their attempts to purify the spiritual atmosphere of their societies by means of significant shows, are close enough to throw a good deal of light on the nature of the role of Hamlet.

The "Duke of dark corners" is dispossessed and anonymous much as Hamlet is, even though he himself had rejected the official role of ruler. His theatricality consists in casting Angelo and Claudio and Isabella for tragic roles, and then moving about behind the scenes like a nervous regisseur, to make sure that the moral of the drama is clear, and yet that the real tragedy does not go too far. The play he arranges is almost a practical joke; yet, like Hamlet's play, it both tests and reveals a wider and healthier vision of human society than Vienna publicly accepts. And by this means he proposes to substitute the rule of charity for Angelo's blind and univocal conception of Mosaic justice. *Measure for Measure* has been called a problem comedy, and it has, in fact, a discursive clarity, a kind of modern intellectuality, quite unlike *Hamlet*. But with this reservation, the Duke as regisseur-prince is very closely akin to Hamlet in that role.

*The Tempest* has neither the analytic naturalism of *Hamlet* nor the "thesis" quality of *Measure for Measure*. It partakes of the qualities of myth, of Medieval allegory, and of dream; as though Shakespeare's mind, at the end of his career, were in that state which Dante knew, in the early morning, at the threshold of the Mount of Purgatory:

> e che la mente nostra, peregrina / più dalla carne e men da' pensier presa, / alle sue vision quasi è divina. (Canto IX)
>
> *When our mind, wandering farther from the flesh and less caught by thought, is in its visions almost prophetic.*

The basic *donné* of the play is the magic of Prospero. And hence the shows with which he purges the worldly exiles from Milan can be close to the very idea of such shows. Mr. Colin Still (in *The Timeless Theme*) has traced in them many ancient ritual themes. It is in this play that Shakespeare comes to terms with his own imaginative power as a wielder of the theater—indicating its use in the service of truth, and its limitations as a means of salvation. For at the end, when Prospero has demonstrated both the magic power of the theater and its use, he buries his book and staff and prays for grace. He has a ripeness and a clarity and a power which Hamlet lacks, but for that very reason he helps one to see what Hamlet, with his play, was trying to do.

Hamlet, more than either the Duke or Prospero, is defenseless and uninstructed in the midst of life; and if he stumbles on the theater as a means of realizing his vision and his anonymous being, he does not clearly understand what he has accomplished. When the King rises after the play, Hamlet takes his success with almost childish pleasure: "Would not this, sir, and a forest of feathers, if the rest of my fortunes turn Turk with me, with two Provincial roses on my razed shoes, get me a fellowship in a cry of players, sir?" The delight is, of course, partly ironic; moreover he has still to confirm his success with his mother and the King. Even after those two interviews he is puzzled and tormented; he does not really feel that he has done his part, borne his witness, taken his stand, until he returns from England. By that time his testimony has had its effect: the regime is wounded beyond repair, and he himself is doomed.

In Act V, while he records in the graveyard the vision of death—literal death and the death of society, to the accompaniment of the clowns' heartless equivocations—and finally suffers the truncated funeral of Ophelia—he feels that his role, all but the very last episode, has been played. He is still uncertain what this will be, still feels that it must include the killing of Claudius: "Is't not perfect conscience to quit him with this arm?" His personal hatred for the King is sharp as ever; but he is content, now, to let the fated end come as it will. "It will be short: the interim is mine; and a man's life's no more than to say 'one'." He feels, I think, whether he or his author would put it so or not, that he is ready to take the consequences of his revelation, to suffer for that truth: "Thou wouldst not think how ill's all here about my heart; but it is no matter.... It is such a kind of gain-giving as would perhaps trouble a woman.... The readiness is all." One could say that he feels the poetic rightness of his own death. One could say, with Ernest Jones, that because of his Oedipus complex he had a death-wish all along. Or one could say that his death was the only adequate expiation for the evil of Denmark, according to the ancient emotional logic of the scapegoat; or one could say that only by accepting death to prove it could the truth of his vision be properly affirmed.

However one may interpret it, when his death comes it "feels right," the only possible end for the play. Horatio makes music for his going-off like that which accompanies Oedipus' death at Colonnus: "Good night, sweet prince, and flights of angels sing thee to thy rest." And Fortinbras treats him like one of those honor-seekers that had puzzled him all along, as though in his career the hero had somehow been subsumed in the martyr: "Let four captains bear Hamlet, like a soldier, to the stage." We are certainly intended to feel that Hamlet, however darkly and uncertainly he worked, had discerned the way to be obedient to his deepest values, and accomplished some sort of purgatorial progress for himself and Denmark.

I am aware that this interpretation of the role of Hamlet is open to the same sort of objections as all other interpretations; there is no substitute for the direct knowledge which a good performance of the play would give. But I think that Shakespeare, in writing the play, was counting on such a performance, and upon the willing make-believe of his audience and his performers. The elements of the Tudor monarchy, of the emblematic stage of the Globe, and of the traditional cosmos they stood for, were accepted for the purposes of the play as real; and within the concrete elements of this scene the role of Hamlet has its own logic.

## Analogous Action: An Interpretation of the Play

> "For goodness, growing to a plurisy,
> Dies in his own too much."

The remark of the King, which he uses as a warning to Laertes, and which I have used to describe Hamlet's over-quick and over-subtle sympathy, applies also to Shakespeare's principles of composition in the play as a whole. Shakespeare's sense of analogy is perhaps too productive, burgeoning too richly in all directions, as though the dramatic life he had got hold of gave him more instances than he needed. Yet it is my belief that the life itself, the germ, the "unity" is there, however overlaid with elaborations and confusingly illumined from many directions.

Miss Caroline Spurgeon discerned this underlying life, quite accurately, as a result of her studies of the metaphors in the play: "To Shakespeare's pictorial imagination," she writes, "the problem in *Hamlet* is not predominantly that of the will and reason, of a mind too philosophic or a nature temperamentally unfitted to act quickly: he sees it pictorially *not as the problem of an individual at all,* but as something greater and even more mysterious, as a *condition* for which the individual himself is apparently not responsible, any more than the sick man is to blame for the infection which strikes and devours him, but which, nevertheless, in its course and development, impartially and relentlessly annihilates him and others, innocent and guilty alike. That is the tragedy of *Hamlet,* and it is perhaps the chief tragic mystery of life."

Miss Spurgeon offers a kind of scientific proof of her view of the play by showing that the predominant metaphors are those of disease. An analysis of the play as the imitation of action gives the same result. The action of the play as a whole is "to identify and destroy the hidden imposthume which is endangering the life of Denmark." But because the source of infection is hidden, and there is no general agreement about its nature or location, the action of the play is predominantly in the passive mode—the suffering of forces not controlled or understood, rather than the consistent drive of an intelligible purpose. *Hamlet* is, like *The Cherry Orchard,* in its essential structure an "ensemble pathos," broken from time to time by the spasmodic moves of one or two of the characters.

This action is realized in many analogous ways in the contrasted characters. Claudius, who identifies the health of Denmark with the safety of his own corrupt regime, and therefore merely wishes to hold what he has, gradually comes to feel that the imposthume which poisons the communal life and his own is Hamlet: "for like the hectic in my blood he rages." Polonius, the chief figure in the comic sub-plot, also identifies the health of the body politic with the status quo; and for him the dis-ease is only the normal but troublesome fires of youth: Laertes' appetite for drabbing and gambling, Hamlet's infatuation for Ophelia—both to be cured by a judicious mixture of discipline and indulgence, which his age and experience can easily concoct.

Gertrude and Ophelia (like other women pictured by Shakespeare) define their actions and their beings only with reference to their men; and since they both have a stake in the regime, and at the same time in the rebellious Hamlet, they suffer the worst of the disease itself. In the economy of the play, they are symbols and measures of the health of the body politic —glamorous signs of what might have been, and torn and dishonored images of what is.

Hamlet himself, as we saw, comes the closest to seeing the whole range of the disease, as it spreads from the immediate guilt of Claudius to ruin all dependent lives. And we have seen that the adequate response to the rottenness of Denmark, as he sees it, is not a simple, purposive course of action, but a bearing-witness and a suffering-for-the-truth.

The characters have not only analogous objects of their actions, they all act in a similar way, indirectly. Polonius has his "windlasses" and his "assays of bias." Claudius acts only through intermediaries: Polonius, Rosencrantz and Guildenstern, Laertes. Ophelia acts as the puppet of her father, and Hamlet by means of his symbolic play. The Gravedigger speaks in equivocations, and Osric in such a "yesty collection" of ornamental clichés that he is barely comprehensible.

In defining the action of the play as a whole, the one underlying "essence" which the actions of the various characters "adumbrate" in their different ways, the character of Claudius is all important—not because he sees more, or realizes a deeper life, but because as head of the state he is, *de facto,* the one center of "weight" and of "greatness." As Tudor monarch, father, king, and high-priest—the massy wheel upon which the lives of the many depend—he makes, so to speak, the spiritual weather in Denmark. It is his particular kind of spiritual night—his motionless worldly presence, like a wall; his gratified lust ("fat weed on Lethe wharf," "things rank and gross in nature")—which defines the action in *Hamlet*. In such a nonconducting atmosphere, all purposes are short, hidden, and mistook, and they soon sink into frightened or oblivious stagnation. As long as he rules, "Denmark is a prison," "one of the worst" of the world's many confines, closed away from Dante's "dolce mondo."

From this point of view, Claudius' place in the economy of the play is like that of Macbeth in his play: Shakespeare thinks of the usurper in both cases as defining the "scene" and thereby the action of the play. Macbeth is in his moral being quite unlike Claudius; and he produces a different action and a different rhythm in the play as a whole. Macbeth is like a man running down-hill to escape himself: however fast he goes, "the pauser, reason," is still with him. In his depraved career he lays an irrational and obsessive basis for all human thought and intercourse; hence every action is paradoxical and unnatural. Even the peripety, when Macduff, Malcolm, and Ross are forced to take action against Macbeth, is realized as a tissue of denials and paradoxes. The final assault upon the castle is (in spite of its healthy marching rhythm) unreasonable and unnatural too. The wood moves, the leader is unborn of woman, and the soldiers are sustained by the super-rational, the miraculous blessings and graces that hang about King Edward's throne.

Mr. Kenneth Burke has pointed out that "action" may be defined in terms of "scene." This is one of the principles of composition in the *Divine Comedy*: human actions are presented in an orderly succession of scenes which concretely realize and define them. But Dante's tremendous subject was human life and action in general, while the subject of a Shakespearean tragedy is, more immediately, human action under a particular regime, or at a particular historic moment. His dramatis personae are seldom seeking salvation directly, but rather trying to realize a human life in a concrete society. That is why an analysis like Miss Spurgeon's is so suggestive, and takes one so far toward an understanding of the play as a whole—much further, for example, than the attempt to rationalize Hamlet's character, as though Shakespeare had been writing a drama of the individual will and reason only.

Yet there are dangers in an analysis based on metaphor. Such an analysis leaves *Hamlet* at the level of the romantic lyric, as though its "logic" were a logic of feeling only, and its principles of composition those of "association and contrast," as Mr. Burke calls them. Such an analysis works better for *Tristan* than for *Hamlet,* for it leaves out the substantial elements (the beings of the individual characters, the stable elements in the traditional cosmos) which underlie the associated or contrasted *qualities* of their lives, the "atmosphere" or feeling tone of the play. Miss Spurgeon's lyrical or subjective or qualitative analysis needs to be supported and extended by a more realist analysis, one based for instance on the four levels of Medieval symbolism.

According to this system, the analogous actions of the characters in their attempts to destroy the hidden disease of Denmark would constitute the "trope" or moral meaning of the play. The rottenness of the regime itself, from which they all suffer, could be called the "allegory," for it refers to a particular moment in history when a corrupt regime falsifies the life of the community. We have seen that in *Hamlet,* as in *Macbeth,* Shakespeare takes this historic moment as defining his subject. But Shakespeare is no Spenglerian determinist; in spite of his worldly focus, his preoccupation with social order, and his feeling for the "divine sanction" of kingship, he places Claudius' Denmark in a wider setting; and this "placing" of Claudius' regime is the anagoge, the meaning of the play in relation to ultimate values.

Miss Spurgeon records the fact that there is in *Hamlet* a series of images contrasting with those of disease and darkness; and, indeed, from the first we are made to feel that the condition of the Danes is not the human condition *überhaupt* but only a particular version of it. Ophelia's description of Hamlet, "What a noble mind is here o'erthrown," contrasts his present plight with what she feels to be his natural role: "the expectancy and rose of the fair state." Hamlet's description of his father, in his terrible interview with his mother, has a similar effect—to make us feel that a natural and divinely sanctioned order has been betrayed and lost. And in his famous speech on "man, the paragon of animals," though the context gives it depths of irony, Hamlet unrolls the traditional moral order as both good and true though he has somehow lost a vital relation to it. But it is chiefly in Act V that Claudius' regime is seen for what it is, brought to its temporal end, and placed in a wider and therefore truer scene.

Act V unrolls for us, first of all, a picture of Denmark after it has been torn asunder, its deathliness or its nonentity laid as it were flat and open to the eye of the audience and the eyes of Hamlet. The vision, as usual in Shakespeare, is firmly based upon the most concrete sensory impact (like the darkness of Act I, scene i) and proceeds then to elaborate ever wider and more complex perspectives. The basic sensual impression is the brutal digging up of skulls; then comes the solemn-joyful equivocating of the clowns—a denial of all meaning, the end result of Claudius' falsity. With this goes a series of hints of social disorder: the dead receive no respect; the professions, especially law, are laughably helpless; "the age is grown so picked that the toe of the peasant comes so near the heel of the courtier, he galls his kibe." As for the courtiers, we shall presently have Osric: "He did comply with his dug before he sucked it." Osric corresponds to Rosencrantz and Guildenstern, a more shameless hypocrite and time-server, much as the clowns correspond to Polonius in their complacent irrelevancy but speak in equivocations where Polonius, less deathly, merely rationalizes upon false premises.

From this opening impression of literal death and meaninglessness in many forms comes the funeral of Ophelia, the "maimèd rite." I have already pointed out its place in the succession of rituals. It is full of cross-references: to the funerals of Hamlet the first and Polonius; to Gertrude's corrupt marriage; to the marriage of Ophelia and Hamlet, which never occurred; and to Ophelia's mad mixture of funeral and marriage.

The second scene of Act V, with the duel between Hamlet and Laertes, shows the denouements of all the intrigues in the play: Polonius is avenged by Laertes; Laertes, like Hamlet, falls victim to Claudius' deceits; Gertrude follows Ophelia; Hamlet kills the King at last, and Fortinbras finally appears upon the Danish scene, the new faith and hope which Claudius no longer prevents. But these events, which literally end the narratives in the play, and bring Claudius' regime to its temporal end, tell us nothing new but the fact: that the sentence, which fate or providence pronounced long since, has now been executed. It is the pageantry, the ceremonial mummery, in short the ritual character of this last scene which makes us feel it as the final epiphany, the showing-forth of the true nature of Claudius' regime.

The staging of this scene is parallel to that of Claudius' first court (Act I, scene ii) and to that of the players' scene. It is the last time we see all the dramatis personae gathered to celebrate the social order upon which they all depend. But whereas we saw Claudius' first court as smooth, plausible, almost majestic, and ostensibly devoted to guarding the welfare of all the subjects, we see this last court, all in mourning, for the deathtrap it is. The vision of Claudius' Denmark which Hamlet's play presented as a parable, is now brilliantly and literally visible. As soon as we glimpse it with this literal clarity, it is gone like a bad dream, and we are returned, with the healthy rhythms of young Fortinbras, to the wider world of the order of nature, with the possibility at least of divine sanction.

Thus the "placing" of the play follows immediately upon the completion of its action. Fortinbras is the agent; and in the scheme of the whole the role of Fortinbras, though it is very economically developed, is of major importance.

I have already pointed out that Fortinbras' story is one of the variations on the son-father theme. When we first hear of Fortinbras he, like Hamlet (and later, Laertes), is trying to avenge a dead and dishonored father. Like Hamlet, he has an uncle who stands *in loco parentis.* Like Laertes, he is a simple and noble youth, expending his high spirits upon the worldly code of "honor," yet at the same time he is a "good child," obedient to age—so that when his uncle tells him to, he is quite willing to turn his martial ambitions from the Danes to the Poles. But unlike both Hamlet and Laertes he does not live under Claudius' shadow: His obedience is not (like Laertes' obedience to Claudius) misplaced—and his life works itself out (as we hear) in a region free of the Danish infection.

Thus the role of Fortinbras, in *Hamlet,* corresponds to those of Malcolm, Macduff, and King Edward in *Macbeth.* Like them, he is felt as a constant, though off-stage, threat to the corrupt regime. Like them, he does not appear in the flesh until after the peripety and, though we feel his approach, does not enter Denmark until Claudius is gone. Like Malcolm and Macduff, he has his own version of the main action of the play. He moves and fights in the dark as much as his contemporaries, Hamlet and Laertes; but his darkness is not the artificial shadow of Claudius but the natural darkness of inexperience. He confronts it with a kind of sanguine natural faith, "exposing all that's mortal and unsure even for an egg-shell"—as he could not (Laertes' example is there to prove it) in Denmark. That is why he cannot enter Denmark until the end. In the same way, in *Macbeth,* we are not ready for Macduff's and Malcolm's reception of Grace until Macbeth and his Queen have reached the nightmarish stalemate of the banquet scene. When the avengers appear before Macbeth's castle, they show him that there is another way to "outrun reason"; and when Fortinbras comes in at the end, he places the action we have seen in Denmark, both with reference to the wider world from which he comes, and with reference to his healthier version of "the fight in the dark," the "quest for the unseen danger." Fortinbras' darkness of natural faith is the last variation, this time in a major key, which Shakespeare plays upon his great theme.

This does not mean that Fortinbras, either in his character or in his vision, provides an answer to Hamlet's "problem"—nor does it mean that his example is intended to show that the experience of the play was simply illusory. This experience was "real," just as Dante's experience of Hell was real—though this is the region of low ceilings, and of those who have lost the good of the intellect. Hamlet sees a great deal that Fortinbras will never see; but Hamlet, who has his own limited being, is defined by it and by the spiritual realm in which he moves; and this is not all of life. Fortinbras does not destroy, he "places" the action of the play by suddenly revealing a new analogue of this action. The effect, once more, is not to provide us with an intellectual key, an explicit philosophy, but to release us from the contemplation of the limited mystery of Denmark by returning us to the wider mystery of life in the world at large.

Thus it seems to me that the elements of Shakespeare's composition (like those of Sophocles and Dante before him) are not qualities, like those of the romantics with their logic of feeling, not abstract concepts, like those of the dramatists of the Age of Reason, with their clear and distinct moral ideas, but beings, real people in a real world, related to each other in a vast and intricate web of analogies.

I know that analogy is a very difficult concept to use with accuracy. (I have endeavored to raise some of the questions connected with it elsewhere.) At this point I merely wish to point out that the anagoge, or ultimate meaning of the play, can only be sought through a study of the analogical relationships within the play and between the world of Denmark and the traditional cosmos. There are the analogous actions of all the characters, pointing to the action which is the underlying substance of the play. There are the analogous father-son relationships, and the analogous man-woman relationships. There are the analogous stories, or chains of events, the fated results of the characters' actions. And stretching beyond the play in all directions are the analogies between Denmark and England; Denmark and Rome under "the mightiest Julius"; Hamlet's stage and Shakespeare's stage; the theater and life. Because Shakespeare takes all these elements as "real," he can respect their essential mystery, not replacing them with abstractions, nor merely exploiting their qualities as mood-makers, nor confining us in an artificial world with no exit. He asks us to sense the unity of his play through the direct perception of these analogies; he does not ask us to replace our sense of a real and mysterious world with a consistent artifact, "the world of the play."

If Shakespeare's Hamlet is realist in the tradition represented by Sophocles and Dante, if he composes by analogy rather than by "qualitative progression" or "syllogistic progression," then the question of *Hamlet* as an artistic success appears in a different light. Because it is rooted in an ancient tradition, and in a theater central to its culture, it is not only a work of art, but a kind of more-than-individual natural growth, like the culture itself, and Shakespeare is not so much its inventor as its god-like recorder: "Cuando amor spira, vo significando." The question is not whether the subject Shakespeare intends is there, but whether it is there in too bewildering a richness and complexity. The besetting sin of the Renaissance, as Pico foresaw, was an overindulgence in the imagination as it discerns analogies of every kind. M. Gilson has explained how even Bonaventura could abuse his gift for analogizing, losing at times the distinction between real analogy and the superficial correspondences which his faith led him to see. And Mr. Scott Buchanan in *Poetry and Mathematics* asks the suggestive question, at what point in history, and by what process, was the clue to the vast system of Medieval analogies lost, the thread broken, and the way cleared for the centerless proliferations of modern culture?

Of this question too Shakespeare seems to have been prophetically aware. Like Hamlet, he felt, perhaps, too wide a sympathy, too precise a scruple. His endless sense of analogical relationships, though a good, *could* "grow to a plurisy." And *Hamlet* can be regarded as a dramatization of the process which led, in the Renaissance, to the modern world and its fragmentary theaters.

# 28

# Shakespeare's Theatrical Symbolism and Its Function in *Hamlet*

*Charles R. Forker*

## I

A rapid glance at any concordance will reveal that Shakespeare, both for words and metaphors, drew abundantly from the language of the theater. Terms like *argument, prologue, stage, pageant, scene, player, act, actor, show, audience, rant*—these and their cousins which evoke dramatic connotations occur again and again throughout his plays in instances which range from very literal or technical significations to highly figurative and symbolic ones. This constant recourse to dramatic vocabulary suggests an analogy in Shakespeare's mind between life and the theater—an analogy which he himself makes explicit and which even the name of his own theater, the Globe, reinforces. Examples are not far to seek. Everyone will recall the

*Reprinted from* Shakespeare Quarterly, *XIV (1963), 215–229 by permission of the author and of The Shakespeare Association of America, Inc.*

Since this essay was accepted for publication, two other studies have appeared that in part anticipate my own conclusions: G. C. Thayer, "*Hamlet:* Drama as Discovery and as Metaphor," *Studia Neophilologica, XXVIII,* 118–129; and Ann Righter, *Shakespeare and the Idea of the Play* (Cambridge, 1962). Miss Righter's valuable book treats the development of the actor-audience relationship from the beginnings of English drama and analyzes the significance of the play metaphor throughout Shakespeare's works.

famous references of Jaques ("All the world's a stage...")[1] and Macbeth ("Life's but...a poor player,/That struts and frets his hour upon the stage..."); and there are many others. Not infrequently the figure is associated with pain or death and the relation of man to the cosmos; hence, it becomes a natural focus for the idea of tragedy. The Duke in *As You Like It* speaks of the world as a "universal theatre" which "Presents more woeful pageants than the scene/Wherein we play..."; Lear with the penetration of madness bewails that "we are come/To this great stage of fools"; and Richard of Bordeaux, the actor-king, glances back over his life to find it as unreal and as temporary as a play—"a little scene,/To monarchize, be fear'd, and kill with looks".

That Shakespeare should have conceived of man as an actor, the world as a stage, and the universe as its backdrop is not extraordinary, for, apart from the fact that he himself played the triple role of actor, playwright, and part-owner of a theater, the metaphor was a Renaissance commonplace. The motto of the Globe, *"Totus mundus agit histrionem"*, is only the most succinct expression of an idea extended to greater length in Montaigne, in Erasmus' *Praise of Folly,* in Romei's *Courtier's Academie,* and in the works of Shakespeare's fellow dramatists, as, for instance, the Induction to Marston's *Antonio and Mellida.*[2]

The intention of this essay is to analyze some of the elaborate ramifications of the theater symbol as it functions throughout *Hamlet,* to suggest that by re-examining the play with emphasis on the theme of acting, we may reach certain new perceptions about its dramatic architecture and see some of its central issues (Hamlet's delay, for instance, his disillusionment and madness, his intrigue with Claudius, his relation to his mother, his knowledge of himself) in fresh perspective. Before, however, we consider the one play of Shakespeare that embodies his most personal statements on the drama, let us make some further generalizations about the complexity of aesthetic response which theatrical imagery entails and the relation of this complexity to the idea and nature of tragedy.

S. L. Bethell[3] points out that references to the theater in a public performance elicit a double or "multi-conscious" reaction from the audience. Suppose Humphrey Bogart (at the local cinema) corners his gangster with a loaded revolver and sneers that the bullets are real, not blanks "like in the movies." The chief effect of this remark is to establish verisimilitude. We are invited to compare what is happening on the screen with cruder versions of the same thing which we have seen before, and the implication is

---

1 My citations throughout are to *The Complete Works of Shakespeare,* ed. G. L. Kittredge (Boston, 1936).

2 The theatrical trope is ancient. E. R. Curtius in *European Literature and the Latin Middle Ages* (London, 1953), pp. 138–144, traces its permutations from Plato to Hofmannsthal.

3 *Shakespeare and the Popular Dramatic Tradition* (London, 1948), pp. 31–41.

that we know a hawk from a handsaw. But at the same time the remark distances the performance by reminding us that we are after all looking at a film and not at real life. The response is the same in Shakespeare, but its duality is more constant there, not only because the theatrical references are more frequent and the actors are people instead of pictures, but because the Elizabethans, lacking our naturalistic visual aids, had to rely much more than we are accustomed to do upon the symbolic suggestiveness of the spoken word. So, when Fabian comments in *Twelfth Night,* apropos of gulling Malvolio: "If this were play'd upon a stage now, I could condemn it as an improbable fiction," or when Cleopatra inveighs against her would-be captors with "...I shall see/Some squeaking Cleopatra boy my greatness/I' th' posture of a whore", the audience responds to the situation on a dual plane of reality. They are aware of play-world and real world at once. The opposition between appearance and reality, between fiction and truth, is maintained; yet the appearance seems more real and the fiction more true.

In *Hamlet* this duality functions almost constantly, not only because there is so much reference to playing and to related aspects of the fictional world, both literally and figuratively, but because the center of the play itself is largely concerned with the arrival of the players at Elsinore and the "mouse-trap" that constitutes the climax or turning point of the plot.[4] Since Hamlet as a dramatic character is manifestly interested in the aesthetics of drama and its analogy to his own emotional predicament ("What's Hecuba to him, or he to Hecuba...?" [II, ii, 585]), the conflicts generated are teasingly complex. The theatrical references urge us to a sympathetic union with the characters, their actions and their feelings, and at the same time give them the objective reality of artifice through aesthetic distance. The world of the play becomes at once both more and less real than the actual world, and we are required to be aware of this relationship inside as well as outside the play.

The idea of theater therefore embodies one of the mysterious paradoxes of tragedy, the impingement of appearance and reality upon each other. This is the very problem that obsesses Hamlet throughout the play and that eventually destroys both guilty and innocent alike. What is real seems false and what is false seems real. Spiritual growth, Shakespeare seems to say, is an extended lesson in separating out the components of the riddle and in

---

[4] Properly speaking, the device of play-within-play adds another plane of reality, making the response a triple or (if the anagogical level is included) a quadruple one. Looked at in this way, the gradations of actuality resemble a Platonic ladder, for the play-within-play is an image of an image of an image. Real actors pretend to be actors entertaining an actor-audience, who, in turn, entertain a real audience, who are metaphorically actors on the world's stage and hence "walking shadows" of an ultimate cosmic reality, of which they are but dimly aware. In reverse, the movement can be graphed as follows: ULTIMATE REALITY—ACTUAL WORLD—PLAY WORLD—PLAY-WITHIN-PLAY-WORLD.

learning to recognize and cope with one in the "role" or "disguise" of the other. Hence the theater to Hamlet, to Shakespeare, and to the audience becomes a symbol for making unseen realities seen, for exposing the secret places of the human heart and objectifying them in a way without which they would be unbearable to look upon. We see into ourselves, as it were, through a looking-glass. Thus the mirror image is connected in Hamlet's mind with acting and, by extension, with other forms of art which penetrate hypocrisy and pretense:

> ...the purpose of playing... is, to hold, as 'twere, the mirror up to nature; to show virtue her own feature, scorn her own image, and the very age and body of the time his form and pressure. (III, ii, 21–25)

Later in the closet scene Hamlet verbally acts out his mother's crimes before her and teaches her by means of "counterfeit presentment" the difference between Hyperion and a satyr: "You go not till I set you up a glass/Where you may see the inmost part of you" (III, iv, 19–20). In Ophelia's description of Hamlet as "The glass of fashion and the mould of form,/Th' observ'd of all observers" (III, i, 161–162), the mirror and actor images coalesce as a symbol of truth reflected.

The very court of Denmark is like a stage upon which all the major characters except Horatio take parts, play roles, and practice to deceive. The irony is that Hamlet himself must adopt a pose in order to expose it in others. *All* the world's a stage. But for him pretense may entail revelation; Claudius "acts" only to conceal. Since, for Hamlet, the end of playing is to show virtue her own feature and scorn her own image, he not only sees through false appearances ("Seems, madam? Nay, it is. I know not 'seems' " [I, ii, 76]) but also feigns in order to objectify his inner feelings; he both uses and recognizes "honest artifice." He welcomes the players enthusiastically and approves their art. One piece in their repertory, part of which he has memorized, he chiefly loves because there is "no matter in the phrase that might indict the author of affectation." It shows "an honest method, as wholesome as sweet" (II, ii, 461–463). His antic disposition, although a smoke screen to protect him from his enemies, is also a dramatic device which allows Hamlet to express to himself and to the audience the nagging pain and disgust which the world of seeming has thrust upon him. It is by acting himself that he penetrates the "acts" of Polonius, of Rosencrantz and Guildenstern, of Gertrude, and even of the innocent Ophelia, upon whom her father has forced a role of duplicity.

The true appearances of things are revealed by phenomena from outside the world of Elsinore, by the Ghost who brings a vision of reality from the dead and by the players who bring another vision of truth from art. Thus the action of the play inhabits three kingdoms, and Claudius, a false king, is hedged on both sides by images of truth—on one side by old Hamlet, the "royal Dane", and on the other by a player-king.[5] It is one of the significant ironies of the play that the player's acting prompts Hamlet to action, that the action he chooses is a theatrical one, and that Claudius, himself perhaps the arch actor, is made to look upon his own deepest secret through the agency of drama. Thus, at one pole of the tragic magnet, the theater is the symbol of inner truth. Just as the player's speech is true for Hamlet[6] and *The Murder of Gonzago* all too true for Claudius, so *Hamlet, Prince of Denmark* is truth for us. There is a sense in which the characters there are the abstract and brief chronicles of the time ("The players cannot keep counsel; they'll tell all" [III, ii, 151]), and we are guilty creatures sitting at a play.

But if the stage equals truth at its highest level, it also equals falsity at its lowest. Throughout Shakespeare's other plays but especially in *Hamlet* "playing" is the stock metaphor for pretense and hypocrisy. The tragedy as a whole is a tissue of intrigue and counter-intrigue, a scaffold for "unnatural acts" and "purposes mistook," all "put on by cunning and forc'd cause" (V, ii, 392–395). The idea of falsity is therefore closely allied to the mention of actors, particularly bad ones, and indeed most references to them throughout Shakespeare are pejorative.[7] Actors all too often out-Herod Herod, strut and fret upon the stage, or tear a passion to tatters. They are false, not because they imitate humanity, but because they imitate it so abominably. They pervert the dramatic function by concealing inner reality under a crude show of outward affectation.

When the analogy of acting (in this complex of associations) is applied to character, it of course implies moral weakness or corruption. It is this thrust of the metaphor which points to Claudius, Gertrude, Polonius, Laertes, and Osric as players on the world's stage, bad actors (with all the ambiguity the world contains) because they conceal the truth either from themselves or from their fellows or both. Ophelia and Reynaldo are players with a difference, for they do not act as free agents like the others, but have been cast in their roles by Fortune. Rosencrantz and Guildenstern occupy an ambiguous position between these extremes. Having no reason to suspect Claudius' secret crimes or, later on, his design upon Hamlet's life, they are obliged to carry out their sovereign's orders. Nevertheless, there is an unsavory side to their behavior which makes them more than simple dupes.

---

[5] I am indebted for some of the ideas in this essay to Mr. H. V. D. Dyson of Merton College, Oxford. See especially "The Emergence of Shakespeare's Tragedy", *Proceedings of the British Academy,* XXXVI (1950), 69–93.

[6] For a full explication of the player's speech and its symbolic relation to major themes in *Hamlet,* see Harry Levin, *Kenyon Review,* XII (1950), 273–296.

[7] Ulysses describing Achilles as an actor (*Troilus and Cressida,* I, iii, 151–158), Buckingham satirizing the "ham" (*Richard III,* III, v, 5–7), and Hamlet giving advice to the players (*Hamlet* III, ii, 2–3) are typical examples.

They are natural meddlers, and, as Hamlet says, "they did make love to this employment" (V, ii, 57). Hamlet himself is symbolically the most complex type of the actor and, therefore, a special case, for Shakespeare has gathered up into his character all the self-contradictions and subtle paradoxes which the symbol can express. Hamlet is caught in a maze of antinomies. He both chooses his "role" and has it forced upon him by fate. He must live in the divided worlds of good and evil, of fact and fiction, of actuality and feigning, of spectator and performer. His part requires of him both action and passivity, and he is constantly stepping out from behind his mask to serve as chorus to his own tragedy.

The figure of the actor in *Hamlet* may therefore be viewed as a symbolic focus for the idea of tragic conflict—man divided against himself, forced in his brief hour upon the stage to play conflicting roles and torn between the compulsion to act *(to do)* and the need to pretend and hence *not* to do. Man as actor must reconcile reason with passion, the beast with the angel, the will with the imagination, and his dignity with his wretchedness. And as tragedy, for the audience, represents the ordering of its own inner divisions, so "acting" for Hamlet is his way of objectifying the various modes of his own self-awareness. The theater audience can preserve a comforting detachment, for its involvement is purely imaginative. The spectators know that *Hamlet* is only a play. But Hamlet, the character, is not so sure, for the action in which he takes part is real from one point of view and unreal from another. Claudius' relation to theatrical performance is something else again, for he is tented to the quick by it. At one point, he cannot maintain any detachment at all. The extent to which acting is real or illusory depends largely upon the position of the observer, and we, like Hamlet himself, are permitted to shift position in our imaginations and to look upon the fiction from both sides of that hypothetical curtain which divides the stage from the pit. Claudius does not have that privilege.

It will surely be apparent by this time that the various facets of the theater-life equivalence (particularly when it is dramatized upon a stage) constantly threaten to blur into one another. The blurring results, in part, from the critic's method of abstracting meanings which Shakespeare embodies organically, and it should remind us that tragedy is a mystery to be shared rather than a problem to be solved.

To sum up, the symbol of the actor is important and implies (particularly in *Hamlet*) a good many meanings: metaphorically, he may stand for both true and false seeming and for doer and pretender; at times he may serve as audience to his own performance and to those of the other actors on the stage or as chorus to both. He may function both as the observer and the observed, playing in more than one sphere of reference at once. Lastly, he can symbolize tragedy itself—man as ephemeral, man as Fortune's fool, man as self-aware, and man divided against self. If we keep these generalizations in mind, it should be possible to trace the dramatic structure of Shakespeare's most popular play in terms of its theatrical symbolism and to see its progress (metaphorically as well as literally) as a series of "scenes" and "acts" in which the characters "play" to each other, combining and alternating between the roles of spectator and performer.

## II

The overriding symbol of Elsinore as a stage upon which the people do not always recognize each other in their shifting roles is immediately hinted in the nervous first lines (spoken upon a "platform") of the opening scene:

> *Ber.* Who's there?
> *Fran.* Nay, answer me. Stand and *unfold* yourself.

Marcellus and Horatio enter presently, and it soon becomes apparent that they are there to *watch* an appearance of some kind. This is, of course, the Ghost, which Horatio successively refers to throughout the course of the scene as "fantasy", "image", and "illusion". Already at the very outset, we are shown a scene within a scene. The Ghost is a kind of show, and the other characters on the stage are its audience. This relationship immediately raises the mysterious appearance-reality question in our minds, for we do not know as yet what to make of the apparition. Horatio, who serves throughout the play as a medial figure between stage world and real world, a kind of *raisonneur* whose reactions we watch as a guide to our own, fills in the political background for us, and the scene ends with the decision to acquaint Hamlet with the supernatural phenomenon just witnessed.

The next episode, played, we discover, in the king's *audience* chamber, gives us our first glimpse of the Danish court and its dominant figure. This, too, is a kind of performance, though it only emerges as such very gradually in the light of details which are added later. Claudius makes a formal speech from the throne, putting as fair a face as possible on his "o'er hasty marriage" and "our dear brother's death." In its extensive use of doublets the speech communicates a hint of duplicity. After the ambassadors are received and Laertes has been granted his suit, our attention turns to Hamlet, the solitary and silent auditor who refuses to be drawn into Denmark's "act", remaining on the periphery to comment bitterly on the difference between "seems" and "is." When his mother remarks about the "nighted colour" of his mourning costume, he replies in a metaphor from the stage:

> These indeed seem,
> For they are actions that a man might play;
> But I have that within which passeth show—
> These but the trappings and the suits of woe. (I, ii, 83–86)

Hamlet is not deceived by the "cheer and comfort" of the king's eye nor persuaded by the queen's plea that he "look like a friend on Denmark." In the soliloquy that follows he acts as chorus, emphasizing to the audience the discrepancy he feels between fictional reality or absent truth and actual, present hypocrisy. He compares himself to Hercules, Gertrude to Niobe, the dead king to Hyperion, and Claudius to a satyr. His speech ends with the realization that he too must play a role, and we understand that "acting" represents inner conflict: "But break my heart, for I must hold my tongue" (I, ii, 159). Now Horatio "delivers" the "marvel" of the apparition to Hamlet, which the prince receives excitedly in contrast to the words he has just heard from the king and queen. He will be a willing spectator to this appearance, and he enjoins Horatio to adopt his pose: "Give it an understanding but no tongue" (I, ii, 250). Thus Hamlet is already involved in a double role: he will be both "actor" and "audience" at once.

The theme of acting is now echoed in the underplot. Laertes, about to depart for France, adopts the role of worldly-wise big brother and warns Ophelia not to take the appearance of Hamlet's love for truth. Her best safety lies in fear (a euphemism for pretense), for "The chariest maid is prodigal enough/If she *unmask* her beauty to the moon" (I, iii, 36–37). Ophelia sees through his performance, however, and counters with her own distinction between the "ungracious" role of pastor and the "puff'd and reckless libertine" beneath it (I, iii, 47–49). Polonius now enters to give his son some fatherly advice in the same tone Laertes had used to his sister. The roles are reversed and actor-father now performs to auditor-son. His counsel is a lesson in cautious appearance: "Give thy thuoghts no tongue,/ Nor any unproportion'd thought his act" (I, iii, 59–60). His concluding words, "This above all—to thine own self be true" (I, iii, 78), ironically point up to the audience the contrast between "seems" and "is." After Laertes' departure, Polonius repeats his son's warning to Ophelia, and since Hamlet's vows are but "springes to catch woodcocks," he orders her to play a part unnatural to her and to refrain from conversation with the prince. Acting for Ophelia, as for Hamlet, symbolizes inner division. She, too, must hold her tongue.

In terms of the theatrical symbolism, the situation on stage at the Ghost's second appearance is the same as before, with the difference that Hamlet is now the principal spectator at a performance to which Horatio (in an earlier scene) had spoken the prologue. To the verbal part of the Ghost's revelation, he is the sole auditor. Although Hamlet is not quite certain intellectually of the Ghost's "honesty," the emotional effect both for him and for us is that of truth disclosed: "Pity me not, but lend thy serious hearing/To what I shall *unfold*" (I, v, 5–6). And now the prince learns the extent to which Claudius had been feigning in the court scene—that "the whole ear of Denmark" has been "Rankly abus'd" (I, v, 36–38). The Ghost also refers to Gertrude's hypocrisy, calling her "my most seeming-virtuous queen (I, v, 46). After the apocalyptic disclosure, Hamlet's answer to his father's words, "Remember me," is:

> Ay, thou poor ghost, while memory holds a seat
> In *this distracted globe.* (I, v, 96–97)

Thus Shakespeare, in a triple pun (one meaning of which is unfortunately lost in modern performance) gathers up several aspects of reality into a single phrase and allows the audience to respond multi-consciously. The "distracted globe" (literally "mind" or "head") represents Hamlet's inner world, his divided self, his microcosm, and by extension, it connects the real world, the macrocosm, with the theatrical world through the mention of the very theater in which the play was being performed. Hamlet's reaction to what the Ghost has told him underlines the crucial split between actor as true and false seeming. The Ghost himself plays the first role in this ambivalence and, by doing so, turns Hamlet's attention upon the false actor, the usurper who "may smile, and smile, and be a villain" (I, v, 108). Hamlet is caught between the two illusions, that which reveals and that which conceals the truth. In order to reconcile the two symbolic worlds, for they are "out of joint," he must act in the true world by "acting" in the false one. The "antic disposition," then, is truly to be a double role. To Hamlet himself and to the real audience it will mean one thing; to the court audience at Denmark, it will signify quite another.

The opening of Act II takes us back to the underplot with Polonius sending Reynaldo to spy on Laertes in Paris. His directions to the servant are truly a lesson in "seeming," and the speech may be regarded as a humorously ironic counterpart to Hamlet's later lesson to the players on how a "bait of falsehood" may take a "carp of truth" (II, i, 63). Ophelia enters to recount to her father (now in the role of audience) the scene of Hamlet's distracted appearance to her in the guise of a madman. This instance of Hamlet's behavior is a scene (like the queen's description of Ophelia's death) which the audience sees at one remove from actuality through the speech of an actor as narrator. But it is clear from Ophelia's words that Hamlet has already assumed his dual role, for the sincerity of true feeling shows through the guise of affected madness. The tone of the speech also indicates that Ophelia is moved, though she does not understand what lies behind the "antic disposition." The prying Polonius is fooled by his daughter's recital, and Hamlet's performance conceals from him what it reveals to us.

In the next scene we are introduced to Rosencrantz and Guildenstern attending upon the king and queen. The two carbon-copy courtiers are told of Hamlet's transformation, informed that neither the "exterior nor the inward man/Resembles that it was" (II, ii, 6–7), and assigned the job of spying on him, even as Reynaldo had been charged with a similar task in the preceding scene. Claudius, the actor who hides behind a mask of smiling, enlists two other actors who will attempt to "play upon" Hamlet; and we know that he too is wearing a mask. A chain of "playings" is thus set in motion in which the disguises on both sides will either succeed or fail depending on how much the opposing side knows.[8] The theater audience, of course, may enter into these "playings" more and more omnisciently as the plot unfolds.

After Voltimand and Cornelius report the news of Norway's alliance to Denmark and Polonius with more "art" than "matter" has mistakenly diagnosed the cause of Hamlet's madness to the royal pair, the theatrical parallel is again apparent in the decision to "find/Where truth is hid" (II, ii, 158) through what amounts to another little play-within-the-play. In this production Polonius and the king will play audience "behind an arras," and Ophelia will act the ingenue in order to trap Hamlet into a confession of his true feelings.

Now Hamlet enters playing his role of madness, and the king and queen withdraw to let Polonius "board him." "Actor" confronts "actor," and Shakespeare, for the first time, fully exploits the tragicomic possibilities of Hamlet's dual role—Hamlet playing to himself and the audience and Hamlet playing to Polonius. Throughout this episode and the next (which substitutes Rosencrantz and Guildenstern for Polonius in the symbolic pattern) the ironic disjunction between pretense and sincerity is stressed again and again as Hamlet penetrates the disguise of his opponent:

> *Pol.* Honest, my lord?
> *Ham.* Ay sir. To be honest, as this world goes, is to be one man pick'd out of ten thousand. (II, ii, 177–179)[9]

And Hamlet to the stage twins: "...there is a kind of confession in your looks, which your modesties have not craft enough to colour" (II, ii, 289–290).

A little later the players are announced to the prince. If man delights not him, they do, and it is at this point that Shakespeare begins to play explicitly upon the paradoxes of the theatrical process itself. Since the players' art for Hamlet symbolizes a kind of artifice which is at least potentially "good," being at once more true and more unreal than the "acting" of the court, the company serves as both contrast and parallel to the people who surround

---

8 Hamlet, of course, has the distinct advantage in this contest of acting. He knows, or rather, strongly suspects, Claudius' secret, but the king is kept guessing about Hamlet until the "mousetrap" and even then, he is not sure *how much* his nephew knows.

9 Even Polonius can see a ray of truth through Hamlet's disguise, though the disguise itself deceives him: "How pregnant sometimes his replies are! a happiness that often madness hits on, which reason and sanity could not so prosperously be delivered of" (II, ii, 211–213).

him. The actors have come to Elsinore by reason "of the late innovation" (the current popularity of the "little eyases"), and Hamlet can identify himself with them, because he too is suffering from a late innovation of a different sort.[10] Also the reference to the war of the theaters may remind the Globe audience that they are witnessing symbolically another kind of theatrical warfare on the stage of Denmark. At any rate, Hamlet likes honest actors because feigning is their job (as it is now his own) and has for its object, ideally at least, the revelation of truth, so that, from one point of view, a bond of sympathy exists between him and them. But their profession also suggests to him the symbolic link between acting and the hypocrisy of the real world which so disgusts him, and he comments bitterly on this idea by drawing a parallel between the fickleness of the public's response to good and bad acting and the fickleness of Danish subjects to a good and bad king (II, ii, 378–382). In both cases, fashionable appearance rather than true worth is the criterion of value. Polonius, of course, though he is indeed an actor in the world of hypocrisy and likes to account himself a critic of the drama, sees no such fine distinctions, as he proves a little later by his reaction to the player's speech. For him theatrical art is just make-believe.

The players enter, and Hamlet asks for a taste of their quality, specifying a particular speech which he loves from "Aeneas' tale to Dido." The significance of this speech and its content are, of course, integral to the theatrical symbolism of the play. Professor Levin has already given it such exhaustive analysis in the essay previously cited[11] that I should only be repeating him to discuss the matter at length. It is necessary to point out, nonetheless, that this episode constitutes another of our plays-within-the-play, with this difference—that the artifice here is quite literal as well as figurative in effect.[12] Hamlet begins to recite the speech, and the players and Polonius serve as audience. After thirteen lines, Hamlet breaks off, directing the first player to continue, so that the audience-actor relationship is reversed on the stage. The fact that Hamlet himself gives part of the speech indicates how closely he identifies himself and his own situation with its content; for the lines dramatize for him, both through contrast and parallelism, the very feelings about which he is otherwise constrained to be silent—grief for his murdered father, his mother's lack of grief, his uncle's cruelty, and the

---

[10] It is very possible that Shakespeare reinforced the connection at this point by another actual allusion to the Globe theater, the emblem of which is traditionally thought to have been a figure of Hercules carrying the world on his shoulders: "*Ham.* Do the boys carry it away? *Ros.* Ay, that they do, my lord—Hercules and his load too" (II, ii, 376–377). If so, the effect would be to enhance audience participation in the symbolism.

[11] See note 6 above.

[12] Kittredge notes in his edition that the exaggerated style of the speech itself is quite necessary to preserve the distinction between the two fictional levels of art and art-within-art.

pressing necessity for revenge. Not only does the speech make real to him "the very age and body of the time," revealing, as the Ghost had done, truth beneath the appearances of things; it also forces upon him the depressing realization that the player's speech was but a "dream of passion," a mere fiction, whereas his own motive for passion is horribly real. Art is seen, then, as having both more and less reality than life itself, and our relation to *Hamlet* is precisely analogous to Hamlet's relation to the player. Hence the speech provides Hamlet with a cue for action. Stepping once more out of his role as actor (by convention of the soliloquy), Hamlet clarifies the meaning of the player's speech to the audience and tells them that the play's the thing wherein a player-king will catch the conscience of a real king. But even as he moves towards action, he is encircled by more doubts:

> The spirit that I have seen
> May be a devil; and the devil hath power
> T' assume a pleasing shape. . . . (II, ii, 626–628)

The Ghost, too, may be a kind of "actor." We are caught up in paradox within paradox. As commentator, Hamlet stands upon a stage in London; as tragic protagonist, standing upon a stage in Denmark, he wrestles with three worlds of seeming, and looks backward to the Ghost as he looks forward to the play.

In the third act, which contains the play's crisis and *recognition,* the theatrical stratagems, up to now so carefully rehearsed, are brought to the test of actual performance. Mask confronts mask under conditions of intensified psychological pressure; thus "acting" turns to action, and the faces behind the masks are made (partially, at least) to disclose themselves to each other. After Claudius, with ironic satisfaction, receives from Rosencrantz and Guildenstern the news of Hamlet's interest in the players, the first bout of the "mighty opposites" follows immediately as Polonius and the king withdraw behind the arras to observe Hamlet's behavior towards Ophelia. Polonius gives a last stage-direction to his daughter:

> Read on this book,
> That *show* of such an exercise may *colour*
> Your loneliness. (III, i, 44–46)

Even as he does so, Polonius' recognition of duplicity provides Claudius with a flash of insight into his true self which prepares us for his breakdown later. Characteristically, the first proof of the king's guilt comes in the form of the aside, the usual device (along with the soliloquy) which Shakespeare employs to make it clear that the actor his temporarily dropped his *persona:* "O, 'tis too true!/How smart a lash that speech doth give my conscience!" (III, i, 49–50).

Already the disclosures are beginning. Hamlet's soliloquy intervenes before Polonius' prearranged "act," and the prince (again as commentator) states in more fundamental terms than before the deeply rooted conflicts of being and not being, of appearance and reality. The "nunnery scene" itself reveals to Claudius that "love" is not the cause of Hamlet's madness; his suspicions about the nature of Hamlet's attitude towards him are strengthened, and he therefore determines to send his nephew to England, since "Madness in great ones must not unwatch'd go" (III, i, 196). To Ophelia, who takes the "antic disposition" for genuine lunacy, the scene is also a revelation, though a very partial one. It turns her eyes upon herself, showing her the hopelessness of her love. For the audience in the pit, it portends her eventual collapse. What is pretense for Hamlet will be all too real for her. After the "show" is over, Polonius comes out from behind the arras. But he would pry yet deeper into dangerous secrets, and now he plants what is to be his last theatrical venture—the closet scene.

Hamlet's advice to the players underscores the difference between good and bad acting and states the principle (which we are about to see operating in *The Murder of Gonzago*) of theater as the reflection of inner truth. All the while, Hamlet, like the player he advises, is learning to "Suit the action to the word..." (III, ii, 19). Before the play scene, however, Hamlet has his brief interview with Horatio, who exists outside the world of hypocrisy and symbolizes the kind of human relationship where truth resides divorced from "acting." Now the "mouse-trap" itself begins—the crux of theatrical symbolism in which the two great opponents face each other, each playing the dual role of actor and audience. The relationship is very complex. Claudius, himself, is actor to Hamlet and the others of the court audience, but he is also spectator to the actors of the "mouse-trap." Hamlet is also pretending; he wears his "antic" mask to Claudius and the others, but at the same time he is carefully observing the players' performance and that of Claudius which the play-within-the-play will presumably affect. Audience watches audience. The observed are the observers and the observers are the observed. Meanwhile the theater audience is identifying itself with all these points of view at once. At the crucial moment, Claudius cracks under the strain, revealing his guilt. Ironically he calls for light, as he tries desperately to retreat into his world of moral darkness. This constitutes the major disclosure of the act, and Hamlet has triumphed in a way, for he now *knows* what he had only *suspected* before. But he has also exposed himself, for Claudius is beginning to see through Hamlet's mask too. The player-king has ironically stated the truth of the situation for both segments of the stage audience: "Our wills and fates do so contrary run/That our devices still are overthrown..." (III, ii, 221–222). Hamlet's strategy is defensive—to draw the enemy into his own territory—but after he has done so, pretense alone will no longer suffice. On both sides of the conflict, there is now the necessity *to do.*

The remainder of the third act is devoted to a few lesser skirmishes and Claudius' soliloquy, which manifests his own tragic inner division as a self-aware actor. Hamlet again (more explicitly this time) exposes the hypocrisy of Rosencrantz and Guildenstern by showing them that to play upon him "is as easy as lying" (III, ii, 372), and Polonius, who follows their appearance on the stage, is made the unconscious victim of his own "seeming" through the comic dialogue on camels, weasels, and whales (III, ii, 394–399). Thus the appearance-reality theme is stated throughout the tragedy in almost all of the character relationships and strands of plot, extending in an emotional spectrum which includes a great variety of "serious" and comic colors. Hamlet ends the scene as chorus, stating his willingness to obey the Ghost and analyzing his function as "actor" in the approaching encounter with the queen: "I will speak daggers to her, but use none./My tongue and soul in this be hypocrites..." (III, ii, 414–415).

In Claudius' long and self-searching soliloquy (III, iii, 36–72), we see that the enforced hypocrisy which is destroying Hamlet is also destroying the king. He, too, is caught between the irreconcilable claims of this world and the next. Pretense will only do for this life: "... 'tis not so above./There is no shuffling; there the *action* lies/In his true nature...." But he has chosen his role, and he must act it out to the world, however transparent it may be to heaven. Hamlet enters and faces the problem of whether or not to kill him now. As Claudius struggles vainly to reconcile earthly sin with his consciousness of heavenly judgment, Hamlet struggles to reconcile passion with reason. Deciding for the latter, he moves on to his mother's closet and another "staged" episode, which, like the play-within-the-play, will result in a disclosure of truth.

Polonius has again set up the "scene," and he is ready (once more from behind the arras) to watch Gertrude play her assigned part. Hamlet's entrance, however, suddenly reverses the whole proceeding, and he plays an unexpectedly active performance to them. Polonius cries out in surprise. The wily actor dies ironically as audience to his own play, and the queen has her eyes turned upon her inner self, even as Claudius had been similarly tormented by the "mousetrap." When the Ghost appears in this scene, Gertrude does not see it, continuing to think of Hamlet's madness as real. Thus the queen, too, is involved in the illusion-reality dilemma, and this may be Shakespeare's way of dramatizing the fact that she is so used to corrupt appearances that she still cannot recognize the truth when it is present.[13]

---

[13] To achieve this symbolic effect in modern production, the actor who plays the Ghost should actually appear upon the stage. The audience knows by this time that he is neither a figment of Hamlet's imagination nor a "goblin damned" but a reality—and so does Hamlet himself. To represent the prince as having some kind of special X-ray vision violates the whole intention of the scene, for if the audience does not share the spectacle, they are put most awkwardly in the position of sharing the queen's moral blindness. The multi-consciousness must be able to operate freely.

Hamlet must teach her *dramatically* the difference between true and false illusion by means of the two portraits. The final irony is that Gertrude, when she is made to realize the truth about herself, must immediately reassume her mask. To be sure, she will now "act" for the sake of virtue. But the pretense must go on, and for Claudius she will have to wear the same costume. Gertrude, too (like both Hamlet and Claudius), must continue to live upon the world's stage.

Act IV combines play-acting with real acting. Gertrude relates the events of the closet encounter to Claudius in her new role. Claudius sends Hamlet to England, arranging for a little tragedy there with an actual victim as protagonist, but Hamlet unexpectedly changes the ending and returns to Elsinore. Fortinbras' army moves against Poland, and the innocent go to their deaths "for a fantasy and trick of fame" (IV, iv, 61). The feigned madness of Hamlet produces real madness in Ophelia, and her sad performance seems to the queen "prologue to some great amiss" (IV, v, 18). Laertes returns, prepared in his rage to act openly, but is wooed to the king's side by a masterfully controlled bit of "seeming" and then involved in the plan for another dramatic production (the fencing match) in which the actor is to show himself his "father's son *in deed*/More than in words" (IV, vii, 126–127). Claudius emphasizes the necessity to play the part well:

> If this should fail,
> And that our drift look through our bad performance,
> 'Twere better not assay'd. (IV, vii, 151–153)

The act ends with Gertrude reciting to the stage audience an elegy on Ophelia's death in which artifice and sincerity are one.

In the last act of the play, all the paradoxes of appearance and reality merge and are mysteriously resolved in death. This final harmony is ironically foreshadowed in the graveyard where Hamlet looks upon the skull of Yorick and the court buries Ophelia. In the end, all appearances come to dust; the actors on the world's stage must have exits as well as entrances, and let them paint an inch thick, to this favor they must come. The joking of the clowns gives a tragi-comic emphasis to the contrast between the hypocrisies of life and the realities of death. By a fantastic paradox, Death, the leveler, makes a bid to social appearances and distinctions: "...the more pity that great folk should have count'nance in this world to drown or hang themselves more than their even-Christen" (V, i, 28–30). Hamlet's relation to the grave-digger (the one who remains) is at first that of audience and later, when he engages him in conversation, that of actor, for the clown does not identify him. There is a grim irony on the other side too, since Hamlet does not know that grave before him is to be Ophelia's. The theater audience, again, sees the relationship from both points of view at once. Then Hamlet (in his remarks to Horatio and the address to the skull) performs the choric function, generalizing on death in terms of the dead—Yorick, Caesar, and Alexander (V, i, 202–239).

As the funeral procession enters, Hamlet and Horatio withdraw, playing unseen audience to the ceremony in which the others take parts. Laertes usurps the stage and vents his grief with the passionate diction and exaggerated gesture of the "deep tragedian." Hamlet reacts to the performance as if a bad actor were tearing a passion to tatters, and the reaction in turn impells him to outdo the "actor" in a dramatization of his own grief—to express theatrically the passion that circumstance has heretofore compelled him to repress: "Nay, an thou'lt mouth,/I'll *rant* as well as thou" (V, i, 306–307). The leaping into the grave is symbolic too, for the histrionics point forward to a final "scene" from which neither actor will emerge alive. The king's words are more prophetic than he knows: "This grave shall have a living monument./An hour of quiet shortly shall we see..." (V, i, 320–321).

The following episode discovers Hamlet narrating his sea adventure to Horatio by means of theatrical imagery:

> Being thus benetted round with villanies,
> Or I could make a prologue to my brains,
> They had begun the play. (V, ii, 29–31)

The metaphor summarizes Hamlet's tragic predicament and indicates his progress through the drama—the symbolic advance from thought to action which we have noted. In the soliloquy which concludes Act II, Hamlet had said, we remember: "About, *my brain!* Hum, I have heard/That guilty creatures, sitting at a play,/Have...Been struck so to the soul that presently/They have proclaim'd their malfactions..." (II, ii, 616–620). Preparing for the "mousetrap," Hamlet had been concerned with "playing" in the aesthetic sense and its symbolic relation to his own spiritual conflict. Now, he is caught in a play which he did not begin. He finds himself upon a real stage where the symbols are turning to facts and the actors are making their exits one by one. Polonius and Ophelia have already made theirs, and now Rosencrantz and Guildenstern "go to 't."

Hamlet now expresses regret to Horatio for having forgotten himself to Laertes, for "...by the image of my cause I see/The portraiture of his" (V, ii, 77–78). Both are faced with the problem of avenging a murdered father. As the Pyrrhus speech and the *Murder of Gonzago* had shown the observers their inner selves, so now Hamlet learns to adjust himself to Fortune's role by an increase in imaginative sympathy for the roles of others. This growth is conveyed by his cheerful reception of Laertes' challenge, brought to him by Osric (who ironically says of Laertes that "his semblable is his mirror," [V, ii, 123]), and by his recognition that "to know a man well were to know himself" (V, ii, 145). This is the quietness of mind which allows him to observe that "the readiness is all" (V, ii, 234).

The final episode of the play takes the form of another "show," a sports event in which the stage audience, as well as the performers, unite ironically in the same last "act"[14] which is death. It is noteworthy that the fencing match begins with an attempted reconciliation and that Hamlet, in his speech to Laertes, speaks both truth and falsehood at once. In his apology, Hamlet lies about the cause of his outburst and pleads his madness, for he must continue to "act" so long as the revenge remains unaccomplished. But he also speaks from his heart, for he bears Laertes no enmity. Sincere emotion radiates through the *persona*. Here, then, the actor is seen explicitly as symbol of the man divided against himself, the man who would play one role but is forced by fate to play another. Moreover, Hamlet's "disclaiming from a purpos'd evil" reminds us again of the theatrical terms in which the final spectacle is to be witnessed by his reference to "this *audience*" (V, ii, 251–252). "Audience" here refers to the court, but, by extension, of course, to the theater audience as well.

As the performers "prepare to play," Claudius (now in the double role of actor and audience) announces a ceremonial accompaniment to the bout. He will drink to Hamlet, and the kettles, trumpets, and cannon will echo each other in a chain of cosmic reverberations. Ironically, these are to be a death knell rather than a proclamation of victory, and they therefore point ahead to the final words of the play, "Go, bid the soldiers shoot." The fencing match proceeds, but not according to plan, for "acting" is no protection from the mysterious operations of chance. What begins as "entertainment" ends in a spectacle of death. The illusion becomes reality suddenly and in violence. Gertrude drinks the poisoned cup before Claudius can properly warn her; that he does not snatch it from her hands shows us not only his steel nerves but that he, like Hamlet, must play out his role to the end. Laertes wounds Hamlet with the unbated rapier (as prearranged by the royal stage-manager), but the foils are mistakenly exchanged, and the actor-son, like his actor-father, is justly killed by his own treachery. The masks drop off, and for the first time in the play the characters confront each other without disguise. Laertes lays bare the stratagem; Hamlet immediately carries out his revenge upon the king and exchanges forgiveness with his informant. Shakespeare tells us what our emotional reaction to this holocaust should be by the dramatic terminology in which Hamlet's dying speech is couched, for we are now at one with the stage audience:

> You that look pale and tremble at this chance,
> That are but mutes or audience to this act,
> Had I but time (as this fell sergeant, Death,
> Is strict in his arrest) O, I could tell you—
> But let it be. (V, ii, 345–349)

[14] J. V. Cunningham in *Woe or Wonder* (Denver, 1951), pp. 18–19, points out that the word *act* often has the special significance of "chance" or "fortune" in contexts of tragic catastrophe. The theatrical connotation, however, is present too.

Even in death, Hamlet is eager to speak—to "tell all" like a player, to uncover the truth for those that remain. And so he deputizes Horatio, whom he wears in his heart of hearts, as official epilogue for the drama:

> Absent thee from felicity awhile,
> And in this harsh world draw they breath in pain,
> To *tell my story.* (V, ii, 357–360)

When Fortinbras and the ambassadors enter as audience to the tragic spectacle, Horatio fulfills Hamlet's urgent wish. As Cunningham has noticed (p. 33), it is almost as if Horatio were speaking the *prologue* to the play we have already witnessed:

> ...give order that these bodies
> High on a stage be placed to the view;
> And let me speak to th' yet unknowing world
> How these things came about. So shall you hear
> Of carnal, bloody, and unnatural acts;
> Of accidental judgments, casual slaughters;
> Of deaths put on by cunning and forc'd cause;
> And, in this upshot, purposes mistook
> Fall'n on th' inventors' heads. All this can I
> Truly deliver. (V, ii, 388–397)

Fortinbras answers:

> Let us haste to hear it,
> And call the noblest to the audience. (V, ii, 397–398)

The play ends as it had begun—in terms of the theatrical symbol: "Bear Hamlet like a soldier to the *stage*..." (V, ii, 407). An actor-audience beholds an actor-spectacle upon a scaffold. Through death, the conflicting worlds of "seeming" and "being" coincide; Hamlet and the Ghost are strangely united as we become one with the living actors on the stage. Distinctions are intentionally blurred in the tragic mystery of art. As we are drawn emotionally into this union, we gain a deepened awareness that we, too, are actors playing roles and that our world is a theater. We know that

> ...the great globe itself,
> Yea, all which it inherit, shall dissolve,
> And, like this insubstantial pageant faded,
> Leave not a rack behind. We are such stuff
> As dreams are made on, and our little life
> Is rounded with a sleep. (*The Tempest,* IV, i, 153–158)

# 29

# Justice and Love in *Othello*

*Winifred M. T. Nowottny*

It is a commonplace of criticism of *Othello* that the Moor, entering in Act V to the murder of Desdemona, sees himself as a minister of Justice. It is apparent that this act is full of references to judgment and of images drawn from it. Yet it is usually assumed that this is but an additional turn of the screw, a means of throwing an even more lurid light on Othello's crime against the innocent Desdemona. It is the purpose of this article to put the case that the insistence on justice in Act V of *Othello* is the culmination to which the drama as a whole is designed to lead, and moreover that a fuller perception of the excellence of the dramatic economy will follow upon the recognition that Shakespeare intends in this play an evaluation of justice in its relation to love.

In *Othello* jealousy is treated as a state in which man experiences the opposition of two kinds of belief—belief in "evidence" and belief in the person one loves—and the opposition of the value of justice (as he conceives it) to the value of love. What is tragic in *Othello* derives from these oppositions. The character of Othello serves but to bring them on; jealousy is the stage on which they stand forth. For in jealousy of this nature and magnitude,

*Reprinted from* The University of Toronto Quarterly. *XXI, No. 4 (July 1952) 330–344 by permission of the author and publisher.*

justice and love, which in other situations may be conceived of as parallels, meet. It is therefore no accident that *Othello* is full of allusions to justice and of metaphors drawn from it, since, in the jealousy of Othello, the value of justice and the value of love become openly contestant and reveal their essential incompatibility. The trend of the play becomes clear when one considers the difference between two judgments Othello makes, the one on Cassio:

> Cassio, I love thee;
> But never more be officer of mine,

the other on Desdemona: "I kiss'd thee ere I kill'd thee." The judgment on Cassio can be made, though reluctantly, yet without personal conflict, by subscribing to the idea that justice and love are compatible values; but the judgment on Desdemona is preceded by the personal experience of the conflict of those values and represents a decision between them.

It is possible to argue that the contention of love and justice begins, in this play, with Brabantio's attempt to bring love under the law, from which attempt it follows that the quality of Othello's and Desdemona's love is declared in a kind of trial scene. Brabantio's accusation and the subsequent inquiry might, it is true, be dismissed as being no more than a means of providing for the necessary exposition of what has gone before. Shakespeare's intentions in this matter are debatable: It could be that the excellence of the device for expository purposes was the whole of his reason for adopting it, or it could be that he saw this device as being "fit not only to advance the action of a special plot and to exhibit certain traits in particular characters, but also to prompt in an audience's mind a special vein of semiconscious comment or a special mood of reverie about certain general ideas."[1] But whatever we make of Brabantio, we cannot deny significance to Cassio's part in illuminating Othello's attitude to justice and love, since Shakespeare uses him, in III, iv, to point a clear contrast between Othello's attitude to these two values, and Desdemona's. In this scene Cassio asks Desdemona to intercede for the rescinding of Othello's judgment upon him, and weighs his chances of reinstatement in Othello's love:

> If my offence be of such mortal kind
> That nor my service past, nor present sorrows,
> Nor purposed merit in futurity,
> Can ransom me into his love again....

In contrast to this reference to Othello's hierarchy of values, in which justice stands higher than love, there follows Desdemona's reflection on the "unkind-

[1] C. E. Montague, "The Literary Play," *Essays and Studies by Members of the English Association,* II, 83.

ness" of Othello and then her immediate penetration of her own absurdity in submitting love to the processes of judgment and thereby constituting herself simultaneously plaintiff, witness, suborner, and judge:

> Beshrew me much, Emilia,
> I was, unhandsome warrior as I am,
> Arraigning his unkindness with my soul;
> But now I find I had suborn'd the witness,
> And he's indicted falsely.

The full development of this theme does not come until Act V, but there Othello and Desdemona play exactly the same roles, he as Justice, she as Love:

> *Emil.* O, who hath done this deed?
> *Des.* Nobody; I myself. Farewell:
> Commend me to my kind lord: O, farewell!...
> *Oth.* She's, like a liar, gone to burning hell:
> 'Twas I that kill'd her.
> *Emil.* O, the more angel she,
> And you the blacker devil!

This theme, made explicit in Act V, is implicit in all that leads to Act V. In particular, it shapes the treatment of Iago and Othello in Act III. For the very setting of the stage for conflict, the creation of the situation which brings it about (Iago's temptation of Othello) is done in terms of the differing processes pertaining to judgment and love, and emphasizes the difference between the kind of belief relevant to the forming of judgments and the other kind of belief characteristic of love. Shakespeare chooses to make Iago's success depend upon the fatal interaction between two things: the weakness of testimony as such (which is Iago's strength), and the strength of love (which, fitted into the context of Iago, becomes its weakness). The first dialogue of the temptation falls into two parts, separated by Othello's long speech on jealousy (III, iii, 176–92).[2] In the first part Iago exploits the trickiness of testimony; in the second part he exploits the generosity of love; what is fatal to Othello is the conjunction of the two. It should be stressed that Shakespeare has taken this way of bringing about Othello's mistrust because it allows him to manifest in dramatic terms the pitfalls of reasoning about love and of admitting testimony against it. He shows the process of false testimony succeeding and specifically refers to the reasons why it is impossible to assess it. He posits an Iago entrenched in false opinion; he refers particularly to the impossibility of discriminating between true and false by considering the witness's manner; he shows how the very negatives of testimony can be converted into positives (as Iago, having no proof, makes capital

[2] References are to the Globe Shakespeare.

of a feigned reluctance to speak); further, he points to the element of construction inseparable from testimony (when Iago protests that he "imperfectly conceits" the significance of his "scattering and unsure observance" and in so doing is able to divulge exactly what is in his mind). In short, Iago's testimony is strong in proportion as all testimony is weak; his tricks are possible because of the trickiness of testimony itself. Further, in Othello's speech of protest, Shakespeare adverts to the irony at the root of all these ironies: it is useless for Othello to say "I'll see before I doubt; when I doubt, prove," since infidelity does not necessarily produce evidence of itself and fidelity cannot be put to the proof.

Othello's speech over, the dialogue enters its second phase, in which Iago makes capital of the generosity of love. The characteristic irony of this part of the dialogue is prepared for by Iago's words,

> I would not have your free and noble nature,
> Out of self-bounty, be abused; look to 't.

It is precisely this self-bounty of love (both Desdemona's and Othello's) which he now proceeds to abuse. Desdemona's love had been strong enough to be its own conscience, and is therefore open to another verdict in another context:

> *Iago.* She did deceive her father, marrying you;
> And when she seem'd to shake and fear your looks,
> She loved them most.
> *Oth.* And so she did.

Again, Iago's well-timed "My lord, I see you're moved," makes Othello answer, in loyalty to Desdemona, "I do not think but Desdemona's honest"; he cannot, immediately upon that, challenge Iago for proof. Now, significantly, Othello takes the lead, because it is now the finest part of self-bounty (Iago is not fitted to understand it) which plays him wholly into Iago's hands. Desdemona's love had transcended all obstacles in a magnificent departure from ordinary "nature." It had baffled Brabantio by its unreasonableness. Othello in turn, in self-deprecation, makes the mistake of bringing it to the bar of reason:

> And yet, how nature erring from itself—

He does not complete the thought, but its completion is apparent: nature, having left its course, might no doubt lose that fine exaltation and subside to its course again; it would be quite reasonable to suppose that Desdemona had ceased to love. Here for a moment Iago loses track of Othello and takes this to refer to "foul disproportion, thoughts unnatural," but hastily covers up his mistake and achieves an approximation, though a base one, to Othello's thought:

> Her will, recoiling to her better judgement,
> May...
> happily repent.

Othello dismisses him, but the mischief is done, as his soliloquy shows.

The way in which Shakespeare has directed the dialogue to illuminate the weaknesses of testimony shows that this scene is much more than a device to bring on Othello's conflict. Obviously it was within Shakespeare's power to have manufactured evidence more credible than Iago's bare tale; in *Cymbeline* and *Much Ado about Nothing* he did manufacture it. Here he chooses to make Iago succeed by reason of the gulf between likelihood and love and by reason of the tragic conjunction set up when the nature and processes of love become involved with the utterly different nature and processes of judgment. At this point the audience may, already, feel (to use the words of Shakespeare in another play) that it

> aches
> To know, when two authorities are up,
> Neither supreme, how soon confusion
> May enter 'twixt the gap of both and take
> The one by the other.[3]

It is here, however, that Shakespeare parts company with some of his critics (those who debate whether sufficient reason is made out for Othello's believing Iago). It is not my purpose to join in the critical battle over this ground. It need only be observed, in so far as some critics have laboured the irrationality of Othello, that Shakespeare seems to have taken it for granted that jealousy *is* irrational (to judge from Emilia's comment that men "are not ever jealous for the cause"); on the other hand, in so far as some critics have laboured the inevitability of Othello's believing Iago (as Coleridge did) it seems relevant to observe that such critics seem concerned to defend Othello from the charge of *ignoble* irrationality and that this defence too is foreign to Shakespeare's presentation of the case. Shakespeare's own view may be deduced from the way in which he deliberately draws attention, at this very point in the play, to the fact that immunity from jealousy has as little to do with reason as jealousy itself. For when Desdemona enters, as Othello comes to the end of his soliloquy, Iago's edifice trembles:

> Desdemona comes:
> If she be false, O, then heaven mocks itself!
> I'll not believe 't.

Immunity from jealousy would lie in the continuance of this simple act of faith. Othello cannot maintain this faith, but if he could, it would still be as

3 *Coriolanus,* III, i, 108–12.

non-rational as the jealousy from whose stigma some critics have been anxious to defend him. Shakespeare at this point deliberately forces upon the audience the question, In what strength could Othello reject Iago? The answer would seem to be, By an affirmation of faith which is beyond reason, by the act of choosing to believe in Desdemona. Shakespeare's point is that love is beyond reason. Desdemona's love for Othello has been made "unreasonable" in a way which permits discussion of it in the drama, as when Brabantio tries to bring it to the bar of reason and to punishment by the law, but Othello's race and strangeness (which constitute Brabantio's case) are after all only dramatic heightenings of a simple truism which it is Shakespeare's peculiar excellence to have thought remarkable enough for repeated dramatization: the truism that love, any love, is a miracle. Being a daily miracle, it is not often seen as miraculous; to arrive at that valuation of it costs something, as in *King Lear*; to fail to arrive at it costs more, as in *Othello*. With love, reason and justice have ultimately nothing to do.

There is another play of Shakespeare's in which this idea again takes the dramatic form of jealousy and judgment. Leontes is jealous. He brings his wife to judgment. In the trial scene she describes her helplessness in terms wholly applicable to the situation in *Othello*:

> Since what I am to say must be but that
> Which contradicts my accusation and
> The testimony on my part no other
> But what comes from myself, it shall scarce boot me
> To say "not guilty": mine integrity
> Being counted falsehood, shall, as I express it,
> Be so received. . . .
> You, my lord, best know,
> Who least will seem to do so. . . .

Marital fidelity is the case *par excellence* where the only protection of the accused is that intuitive belief in her integrity which should have precluded accusation, an intuitive belief which is irrelevant to justice, as justice to it. To inquire what Shakespeare takes to be the nature of this intuitive belief will therefore be of importance to the understanding of Othello.

The best commentary on Othello's "I'll not believe 't" is to be found in *Troilus and Cressida*. There Troilus actually sees Cressida's perfidy. He admits the fact:

> *Ulyss.* All's done, my lord.
> *Tro.* It is.

But he finds none the less that his belief in Cressida does not change:

> . . .if I tell how these two did co-act,
> Shall I not lie in publishing a truth?

Sith yet there is a credence in my heart,
An esperance so obstinately strong,
That doth invert the attest of eyes and ears,
As if those organs had deceptious functions,
Created only to calumniate. . . . (V, ii, 118–24)

And again:

O madness of discourse,
That cause sets up with and against itself!
Bi-fold authority! where reason can revolt
Without perdition, and loss assume all reason
Without revolt: this is, and is not, Cressid.
Within my soul there doth conduce a fight
Of this strange nature that a thing inseparate
Divides more wider than the sky and earth. . . .[4] (V, ii, 142–9)

Between the assent of reason to evidence, and the consent of love to a change of belief about its object, there is a great gulf fixed, and to cross it is to experience the terrible passage from one organization of personality to another. Sonnet 138 suggests that it may even seem preferable to descend into the gulf and dwell there:

When my love swears that she is made of truth
I do believe her, though I know she lies. . . .

Othello, incapable of this conscious complexity, wishes that at least he might have been deceived:

What sense had I of her stol'n hours of lust?
I saw 't not, thought it not, it harm'd not me:
I slept the next night well, was free and merry;
I found not Cassio's kisses on her lips. . . . (III, iii, 338–41)

Troilus is aware of the act of choice inherent in ceasing to believe and of the agony that goes with it; Othello, though he understands nothing of this, cannot avoid experiencing it. This is shown in III, iii, 444 ff., where Othello, convinced that Iago's tale is true, acts in gesture the emotional choice:

Now do I see 'tis true. Look here, Iago;
All my fond love thus do I blow to heaven.
'Tis gone.

But it is not. It is impossible to make that choice without a reorientation of personality, and therefore the gesture is followed by the terrible images in

[4] For a fuller treatment of the importance of this scene, see Charles Williams, *The English Poetic Mind* (Oxford, 1932), 58–61.

which he calls upon himself for a reversal in the depth of his nature and the dethroning of the might and dominion of love:

> Arise, black vengeance, from thy hollow cell!
> Yield up, O love, thy crown and hearted throne
> To tyrannous hate! Swell, bosom, with thy fraught. . . .

The poetry, markedly, does not describe this change as taking place of itself; it shows Othello commanding it to take place. For in truth the change of belief which Othello thinks inseparable from his acceptance of Iago's story is not inseparable—it is an emotional *non sequitur*. Othello does not, like Troilus, recognize and define the separateness, but he feels and acts according to its laws: He has to *command* the emotional "effect" to accompany its "cause." The paradox illustrates the truth of Troilus' discovery that there is in the soul a "bi-fold authority"—on the one hand, reason, and on the other the naked will to believe by which the categories of "reasonable" and "unreasonable" are altogether transcended. Othello is not the man to admit the possibility of a "madness of discourse, That cause sets up with and against itself," but this does not alter the fact that his experience, like that of Troilus, involves the conflict between two images of the woman he loves.

Shakespeare has already shown, earlier in the same scene, that what Othello thinks of as uncertainty of mind is in reality an intolerable emotional tension which demands violent expression:

> I think my wife be honest and think she is not;
> I think that thou art just and think thou art not.
> I'll have some proof. Her name, that was as fresh
> As Dian's visage, is now begrimed and black
> As mine own face. If there be cords, or knives,
> Poison, or fire, or suffocating streams,
> I'll not endure it. Would I were satisfied!

Here we have, first, Othello's attempt to interpret his conflict as uncertainty of mind, and his desire to end it (as he thinks he could) by proof. This counterfeit of the problem is followed immediately by the real problem, the two images of Desdemona: "fresh as Dian's visage"; "begrimed and black." From this tension of incompatibles springs the impulse to violence. With "Would I were satisfied!" he reverts to the illusion that proof will quiet that volcano whose raging we have glimpsed. The very form of this speech, enclosing within two patent rationalizations a reality of experience betrayed directly in imagery, shows that the inner conflict between two modes of belief about Desdemona is the heart of the matter and that Othello, in interpreting it to himself as uncertainty of mind, is simply providing the conflict with a surface rationalization. And it is the urgency of the conflict and of the resultant impulse to end it by violent action that explains Othello's snatching at

Iago's lies about Cassio and the handkerchief: by so doing, he can turn the force of his emotions into the current of revenge. It is significant that the image in which he expresses his determination to be revenged (the image of the Pontic sea) contains the promise of release: he promises himself a revenge as "capable and wide" as the Propontic and the Hellespont.

It is one of the finest strokes in the construction of the play that Shakespeare puts the vow of revenge before the test of the handkerchief. By so doing, he makes clear in the action what he has already suggested in the poetry: That the idea of revenge, though it seems to Othello to follow from what he now thinks of Desdemona and offers him the illusion of release from the conflict of his emotions, is not in fact Othello's whole bent. If he could unify himself by revenge, that would be one way out, but he cannot; the test of the handkerchief is a desperate attempt to unify himself in the opposite way—by having Desdemona prove that what Iago has said is false. Othello's description to Desdemona of the mystic nature of the handkerchief—

> A sibyl...
> In her prophetic fury sew'd the work;
> The worms were hallow'd that did breed the silk;
> And it was dyed in mummy which the skilful
> Conserved of maidens' hearts—

is not an irrelevance; he is in reality asking Desdemona to restore to him the sacredness of love.[5] After the failure of this attempt, he is not seen until Act IV, and Act IV concentrates on showing the dreadful interim within Othello when the disjunction of his personality rages for expression and cannot find the means.

It is in Act IV that the nature of the action affords indisputable proof that Shakespeare has in this play a unified design which utterly transcends that concern for immediate theatrical effect which some critics would have us impute to him, for in this act "theatrical effect" is least satisfactory as an explanation of Shakespeare's choice of episodes. Othello falls in a fit; he strikes Desdemona in public; he goes to her as to a prostitute. If these things are chosen only for their immediate effect, the choice is extraordinary, for Act IV is, in itself, hardly to be borne. Its effect is accurately described by the words of De Broglie: "Le spectateur contemple ce tableau, non point avec cette curiosité inquiète qui passe tour à tour de la crainte à l'espoir, mais...avec quelque chose de cette angoisse inexprimable qui s'empare de nous lorsque, dans une cour de justice, nous assistons aux vains efforts de

[5] I am happy to find independent corroboration of this suggestion in R. B. Heilman's essay, "The Lear World" in *English Institute Essays: 1948* (New York, 1949), 49: "Symbolically...[Othello] is in anguish crying for the restoration of the myth of love, for its magic—non-rational, transcendent, mysterious...."

malheureux entraînés vers une condamnation fatale et indubitable."[6] This is not an effect which Shakespeare often risked. The other tragedies increase in illumination as the end approaches; even *Macbeth,* nearest to *Othello* in the increasing denigration of the hero, looks forward in Act IV to a better future—the line of Banquo passes before our eyes, and as the act closes,

> Macbeth
> Is ripe for shaking, and the powers above
> Put on their instruments.

In *Othello* Act IV is well-nigh insupportable. Is not the reason that it is the inescapable outcome of Act III and, more important, the indispensable preparation for Act V, in that the intolerableness of Act IV is the means by which the audience is made to experience, like Othello himself, the necessity for release? The perfection of Shakespeare's art here consists in the economy by which he brings about this participation of the audience in the hero's tragedy: The violence in the action, which creates tension in the audience, is motivated within Othello himself by *his* tension, a tension which is the result of his failure in Act III to unify himself either by the vow of revenge or by making Desdemona restore to him his undesecrated love.

When Act IV opens, it immediately becomes clear that Othello's decision to revenge has in no way touched his real problem. He has even forgotten how he decided: When Iago reminds him of the handkerchief, he says,

> O! it comes o'er my memory,
> As doth the raven o'er the infected house,
> Boding to all.

But though indecision is over, tension is at its greatest; Othello now has the experience as it really is—the tension between two Desdemonas, between two Othellos. (Othello's image in IV, i, 192–4, "my heart is turned to stone, I strike it and it hurts my hand" is the equivalent, in the sphere of the emotions, of Troilus' "madness of discourse, That cause sets up with and against itself"; with Othello as with Troilus "a thing inseparate Divides more wider than the sky and earth.") The episodes of Act IV manifest and communicate this tension by the dreadful spectacle of Othello's attempts to escape from it. The pitch rises as his ways of seeking relief draw, horribly, ever nearer to Desdemona and to the deepest intimacies of love. The falling in a fit is a temporary way of not bearing the tension. That, shocking as it is, affects only himself. The next way is the striking of Desdemona. His striking her in public (for in their private interview there is nothing of this) is a symbolic act: a calling the world's attention to the intolerableness of what he suffers by the intolerableness of what he does. The treating of Emilia as a brothel-keeper is an expression of the division in him at its deepest level: to go to his

[6] Quoted in the New Variorum *Othello* (2nd ed.), 452.

wife as to a prostitute is to try to act out what the situation means to him. Already Othello is driven to symbolize his conflict in act—to seek actions that will express the impossible. But none of these things will serve. Othello is not seen full face again until, in Act V, he finds the perfect symbolic act: to kill, not in hate but in love.

The scene of the murder of Desdemona is a visible demonstration of the laws inherent in the process that led up to it. This is a drama of an error of judgment, the error being in the application of judgment to love. It is not, however, surprising, that the relation of Act V to all that goes before has been imperfectly seen, for the perception of that relation depends upon our recognizing the terrible propositions about human justice which Shakespeare laid down for himself to work by: As, that justice, however it is conceived of, cannot be executed in love; that love and justice differ in their natures, their processes, and their conclusions; that justice, though ideally conceived of as an expiating sacrifice or as the only cure for a wound in the fitness of things, may be, in its human origin and motivation, indistinguishable from man's need to find redress for what he cannot bear to find in human nature; that, finally, the man who accepts justice as the supreme value in life will, if he be wholly consistent, at last execute himself. I believe all these propositions to be implicit in the play. If their starkness should cause us to deny them or simply not to see that such questions arise, then Act V cannot be seen as the logical outcome of Acts I-IV. The fact that Othello perpetrates injustice in no way weakens the significance of Act V, for the play turns upon the conflict between justice and love, not upon the nature of justice itself. No aspect of Othello's experience of that conflict would have been different if Desdemona had in fact been false (though if she had been false, Othello's experience would have been incommunicable to an audience; the audience's participation in his conflict depends upon its having, as he has, two images of her—his image, and the truth).

In Act V, the significance is so entirely fused with the poetry and the action that it is only by faithful attention to these that we can rightly estimate what Shakespeare was about; this is sufficient reason for pondering every phase of the action, and all the meaning that the poetry carries, even at the risk of being thought to consider too closely, or of being accused of attempting to explain, poetry and genius.

First, then, let us consider the opening soliloquy of Act V, scene ii: "It is the cause, it is the cause, my soul. . . ." It is to our great loss that we let these words pass as some oracular utterance not susceptible of commentary. We may begin by inquiring what "cause" meant in Elizabethan English. It meant, first, the accusation or charge against someone, as in *King Lear* (IV, vi, 111–13), "What was thy cause? Adultery?. . .die for adultery! No." Secondly, in an even more specialized sense, it meant the matter about which a person went to law, or the case of one party in a suit. In a third sense, it meant the end in view or the object for which a deed is done. Or again, in a very pregnant sense, it meant good, proper, and adequate ground for action (as Cassio uses the word in "I never gave you cause"). Which of these meanings does Shakespeare intend? He intends the first, the charge against Desdemona; he also intends the second, Othello's case against her; he intends the fourth, in that Othello thinks himself to have good, proper, and adequate ground for action; and indeed he also intends the third, the end to which the action shall be done. The end to which the murder shall be done is, simply, release from the whole agony. In the phrase itself, as in the action it refers to, Othello's complex attitude is unified: Desdemona is guilty and he has a case against her, but what he is about to do is to him an action just in every way, and what he is about to do has a purpose, the making of an atoning sacrifice which shall make all well. The word unites the personal, the social, and the religious aspects of justice, just as the killing is to answer every need of his nature that he recognizes: the need for punishment, for abstract justice, for the restoration of the ideal image of Desdemona by an atoning sacrifice, and, one might add, a need deeper than all these, the need to possess her again—for murder is now the only act of possession open to him.

Knowing how much "cause" means, we can now grasp the whole phrase, "It is the cause." Said thrice, it evidently has depth under depth of meaning for Othello; two ways, at least, in which the phrase has meaning, are apparent. First, it may be taken as the answer to the unspoken question, "What is it that makes me do this?"—"It is the cause." Secondly, the phrase may be interpreted as an utterance of recognition: "It" (the act of killing) "is" (is the same thing as) "the cause" (the whole state of affairs between us). In other words, Othello has found the act which corresponds to all he feels, though what he feels is a complex of opposites, for the act is symbolic; to describe that act he finds the word which means all that the act means, and the syntax which enables him to describe the act as being the same thing as all those opposites he feels, and therefore their expression, and therefore his release. The killing itself is in this sense symbolic: it is an act which stands for all the warring emotions pent up in Othello. These emotions are now fused in a calm of pure concentration on the symbolic act, an act which is the only possible way for Othello to express at once all that Desdemona means and all that he means. He has the exaltation of having struck a perfect equipoise. But what he is about to do would cease to be an all-embracing symbol if he defined its relevance to any one aspect of the problem: If he were to put the act into defining words, they would break up the symbol, for if the act is vengeance, it cannot be justice or atonement, and if it is any of these, it is not passion; and if it is not all of these, it is not release. Hence Othello's refusal to define:

> Let me not name it to you, you chaste stars!—
> It is the cause.

Because of all that "cause" means to Othello, its real emotional meaning is "solution," and because the solution is simply, and as absolute symbol, the act of killing, there is no transition between those words, "It is the cause" and the next, "Yet I'll not shed her blood." It is as though he had said, "The solution is to kill, yet I'll not shed her blood." Then, the moment he looks at Desdemona—at her skin as "smooth as monumental alabaster"—he is forced to give himself a reason why he should destroy her: "Yet she must die, else she'll betray more men." As soon as *one* reason is given, the symbol begins to dissolve, and to stop the dissolution of his symbol, he must cease to see anything but that—and so, "Put out the light, and then put out the light." This again is an act of a purely symbolic nature; again he identifies in one action two entities objectively different but emotionally the same: Desdemona, and the light he extinguishes in order not to see her; indeed, it is as though the parallelism of the two acts constituted their logic. The blackness of the act is matched by the blackness in which alone it can be performed. Othello's state is one in which pattern and relationship take the place of reasoning. As in the parallel, "Put out the light, and then put out the light," so in the whole situation: that an act *fits* is the whole reason for its being done. To kill in love; to revenge by justice; to kill the guilty Desdemona for the honour of the innocent Desdemona, or to sacrifice the innocent Desdemona to atone for her guilt; to torture her because she has tortured him and to torture himself in torturing her—in all this it is the pattern that constitutes the logic, for it is the pattern of his feelings. It is moreover only through pattern and symbol (so tranced is his state) that he can consider the finality of his act:

> If I quench thee, thou flaming minister,
> I can again thy former light restore,
> Should I repent me: but once put out thy light. . . .
> When I have pluck'd the rose,
> I cannot give it vital growth again. . . .

As if this achievement of expressing emotion through form were not sufficient, Shakespeare has all the while developed, within the tranced patterns of Othello's utterances, the great impersonal pattern of Justice and Love. It is in the growing intensity of Othello's realization of his continuing love, counterpointed by the growing compulsiveness of the sanctions of justice which he must allege to outdo it, that Shakespeare expresses the major conflict of the drama. Faced by the fact that love continues, even in this extremity, Othello is driven to urge higher and higher the claims of that justice which shall destroy it. Justice has already been called in under its aspect of safeguard of society: "Yet she must die, else she'll betray more men." Love persists. Justice is then called in as an abstract ideal. Love, still, can almost persuade her to break her sword, and hints that the threatened act of destruction is at heart the act of possession, of plucking the rose. Justice, in a final terrifying aggrandisement, claims the ultimate possible sanction, the sanction of love: "...this sorrow's heavenly; It strikes where it doth love." The process is complete. Justice overrides love by presenting itself as love. In this parallel ascent, where the claims of justice rise with the claims of love, Shakespeare has manifested their tragic contestation, and through the form of the poetry he has shown how the act of killing is related at one level to the tension of opposites in Othello and at a deeper level to the fundamental and eternal opposition of justice and love.

Desdemona wakes. So must Othello. He had thought to strike in heavenly sorrow; he strikes with "Down, strumpet!" From the height of his intention to the depth of the execution the descent is inevitable: At no point in the dialogue could Desdemona's plea for life produce effects other than it does, for the issue of love against justice is settled now; there must inevitably rise up, within Othello's temple of sacrificial justice, the asseverating wrathful self, accusation and self-vindication streaming from its lips:

> O perjured woman! thou dost stone my heart,
> And makest me call what I intend to do
> A murder, which I thought a sacrifice.

It is indeed only the executioner who fully knows the resistance of the sacrificial victim. In human justice as it is commonly ordered the executioner need not question the motive of the judge, nor the judge question his own. With Desdemona, Othello is judge and executioner; he is also plaintiff, and the only possible witness for the defence. In him justice confounds itself by the concentration of all its persons in one, and in being so confounded by unity, throws into relief the indivisible and unconfounded unity of love.

There remains the revelation of the truth. Justice now comes into its own. In *Measure for Measure,* justice pointed to its impartiality:

> When I, that censure him, do so offend,
> Let mine own judgement pattern out my death. . . .   (II, i, 29–30)

Othello has killed Desdemona for betraying their love; he kills himself for the same reason. He surveys his life, judges it, passes sentence, and executes it, as long ago he did in Aleppo:

> Where a malignant and a turban'd Turk
> Beat a Venetian and traduced the state,
> I took by the throat the circumcised dog
> And smote him, thus.

Othello's death is perfectly consistent with his life. From first to last, he is the judge.

# 30

# *Othello:* An Introduction

*Alvin Kernan*

When Shakespeare wrote Othello, about 1604, his knowledge of human nature and his ability to dramatize it in language and action were at their height. The play offers, even in its minor characters, a number of unusually full and profound studies of humanity: Brabantio, the sophisticated, civilized Venetian senator, unable to comprehend that his delicate daughter could love and marry a Moor, speaking excitedly of black magic and spells to account for what his mind cannot understand; Cassio, the gentleman-soldier, polished in manners and gracious in bearing, wildly drunk and revealing a deeply rooted pride in his ramblings about senior officers being saved before their juniors; Emilia, the sensible and conventional waiting woman, making small talk about love and suddenly remarking that though she believes adultery to be wrong, still if the price were high enough she would sell—and so, she believes, would most women. The vision of human nature which the play offers is one of ancient terrors and primal drives—fear of the unknown, pride, greed, lust—underlying smooth, civilized surfaces—

the noble senator, the competent and well-mannered lieutenant, the conventional gentlewoman.

The contrast between surface manner and inner nature is even more pronounced in two of the major characters. "Honest Iago" conceals beneath his exterior of the plain soldier and blunt, practical man of the world a diabolism so intense as to defy rational explanation—it must be taken like lust or pride as simply a given part of human nature, an anti-life spirit which seeks the destruction of everything outside the self. Othello appears in the opening acts as the very personification of self-control, of the man with so secure a sense of his own worth that nothing can ruffle the consequent calmness of mind and manner. But the man who has roamed the wild and savage world unmoved by its terrors, who has not changed countenance when the cannon killed his brother standing beside him, this man is still capable of believing his wife a whore on the slightest of evidence and committing murders to revenge himself. In Desdemona alone do the heart and the hand go together: she is what she seems to be. Ironically, she alone is accused of pretending to be what she is not. Her very openness and honesty make her suspect in a world where few men are what they appear, and her chastity is inevitably brought into question in a world where every other major character is in some degree touched with sexual corruption.

Most criticism of *Othello* has concerned itself with exploring the depths of these characters and tracing the intricate, mysterious operations of their minds. I should like, however, to leave this work to the individual reader and to other critical essays in order to discuss, briefly, what might be called the "gross mechanics" of the play, the larger patterns in which events and characters are arranged. These patterns are the context within which the individual characters are defined, just as the pattern of a sentence is the context which defines the exact meaning of the individual words within it.

*Othello* is probably the most neatly, the most formally constructed of Shakespeare's plays. Every character is, for example, balanced by another similar or contrasting character. Desdemona is balanced by her opposite, Iago; love and concern for others at one end of the scale, hatred and concern for self at the other. The true and loyal soldier Cassio balances the false and traitorous soldier Iago. These balances and contrasts throw into relief the essential qualities of the characters. Desdemona's love, for example, shows up a good deal more clearly in contrast to Iago's hate, and vice versa. The values of contrast are increased and the full range of human nature displayed by extending these simple contrasts into developing series. The essential purity of Desdemona stands in contrast to the more "practical" view of chastity held by Emilia, and her view in turn is illuminated by the workaday view of sensuality held by the courtesan Bianca, who treats love, ordinarily, as a commodity. Or, to take another example, Iago's success in fooling Othello is but the culmination of a series of such betrayals that includes the duping of Roderigo, Brabantio, and Cassio. Each duping is the explanatory image of the other, for in every case Iago's method and end are the same: he plays on and teases to life some hitherto controlled and concealed dark passion in his victim. In each case he seeks in some way the same end, the symbolic murder of Desdemona, the destruction in some form of the life principle of which she is the major embodiment.

These various contrasts and parallelisms ultimately blend into a larger, more general pattern that is the central movement of the play. We can begin to see this pattern in the "symbolic geography" of the play. Every play, or work of art, creates its own particular image of space and time, its own symbolic world. The outer limits of the world of *Othello* are defined by the Turks—the infidels, the unbelievers, the "general enemy" as the play calls them—who, just over the horizon, sail back and forth trying to confuse and trick the Christians in order to invade their dominions and destroy them. Out beyond the horizon, reported but unseen, are also those "anters vast and deserts idle" of which Othello speaks. Out there is a land of "rough quarries, rocks, and hills whose heads touch heaven" inhabited by "cannibals that each other eat" and monstrous forms of men "whose heads grow beneath their shoulders." On the edges of this land is the raging ocean with its "high seas, and howling winds," its "guttered rocks and congregated sands" hidden beneath the waters to "enclog the guiltless keel."

Within the circle formed by barbarism, monstrosity, sterility, and the brute power of nature lie the two Christian strongholds of Venice and Cyprus. Renaissance Venice was known for its wealth acquired by trade, its political cunning, and its courtesans; but Shakespeare, while reminding us of the tradition of the "supersubtle Venetian," makes Venice over into a form of *The City,* the ageless image of government, of reason, of law, and of social concord. Here, when Brabantio's strong passions and irrational fears threaten to create riot and injustice, his grievances are examined by a court of law, judged by reason, and the verdict enforced by civic power. Here, the clear mind of the Senate probes the actions of the Turks, penetrates through their pretenses to their true purposes, makes sense of the frantic and fearful contradictory messages which pour in from the fleet, and arranges the necessary defense. Act I, Scene iii—the Senate scene—focuses on the magnificent speeches of Othello and Desdemona as they declare their love and explain it, but the lovers are surrounded, guarded, by the assembled, ranked governors of Venice, who control passions that otherwise would have led to a bloody street brawl and bring justice out of what otherwise would have been riot. The solemn presence and ordering power of the Senate would be most powerfully realized in a stage production, where the senators would appear in their rich robes, with all their symbols of office, seated in ranks around several excited individuals expressing such primal passions as pride of race, fear of dark powers, and violent love. In a play where so much of the language is magnificent, rich, and of heroic proportions, simpler statements come to seem more forceful; and the meaning of *The City* is perhaps nowhere more completely realized than in Brabantio's brief, secure answer to the first fearful cries of theft and talk of copulating animals that Iago and Roderigo send up from the darkness below his window:

> What tell'st thou me of robbing? This is Venice;
> My house is not a grange. (I, i, 102–03)

Here then are the major reference points on a map of the world of *Othello*: out at the far edge are the Turks, barbarism, disorder, and amoral destructive powers; closer and more familiar is Venice, *The City,* order, law, and reason. Cyprus, standing on the frontier between barbarism and *The City,* is not the secure fortress of civilization that Venice is. It is rather an outpost, weakly defended and far out in the raging ocean, close to the "general enemy" and the immediate object of his attack. It is a "town of war yet wild" where the "people's hearts [are] brimful of fear." Here passions are more explosive and closer to the surface than in Venice, and here, instead of the ancient order and established government of *The City,* there is only one man to control violence and defend civilization—the Moor, Othello, himself of savage origins and a converted Christian.

The movement of the play is from Venice to Cyprus, from *The City* to the outpost, from organized society to a condition much closer to raw nature, and from collective life to the life of the solitary individual. This movement is a characteristic pattern in Shakespeare's plays, both comedies and tragedies: In *A Midsummer Night's Dream* the lovers and players go from the civilized, daylight world of Athens to the irrational, magical wood outside Athens and the primal powers of life represented by the elves and fairies; Lear moves from his palace and secure identity to the savage world of the heath where all values and all identities come into question; and everyone in *The Tempest* is shipwrecked at some time on Prospero's magic island, where life seen from a new perspective assumes strange and fantastic shapes. At the other end of this journey there is always some kind of return to *The City,* to the palace, and to old relationships, but the nature of this return differs widely in Shakespeare's plays. In *Othello* the movement at the end of the play is back toward Venice, the Turk defeated; but Desdemona, Othello, Emilia, and Roderigo do not return. Their deaths are the price paid for the return.

This passage from Venice to Cyprus to fight the Turk and encounter the forces of barbarism is the geographical form of an action that occurs on the social and psychological levels as well. That is, there are social and mental conditions that correspond to Venice and Cyprus, and there are forces at work in society and in man that correspond to the Turks, the raging seas, and "cannibals that each other eat."

The exposure to danger, the breakdown and the ultimate reestablishment of society—the parallel on the social level to the action on the geographical level—is quickly traced. We have already noted that the Venetian Senate embodies order, reason, justice, and concord, the binding forces that hold *The City* together. In Venice the ancient laws and the established customs of society work to control violent men and violent passions to ensure the safety and well-being of the individual and the group. But there are anarchic forces at work in the city, which threaten traditional social forms and relationships, and all these forces center in Iago. His discontent with his own rank and his determination to displace Cassio endanger the orderly military hierarchy in which the junior serves his senior. He endangers marriage, the traditional form for ordering male and female relationships, by his own unfounded suspicions of his wife and by his efforts to destroy Othello's marriage by fanning to life the darker, anarchic passions of Brabantio and Roderigo. He tries to subvert the operation of law and justice by first stirring up Brabantio to gather his followers and seek revenge in the streets; and then when the two warlike forces are met, Iago begins a quarrel with Roderigo in hopes of starting a brawl. The nature of the antisocial forces that Iago represents are focused in the imagery of his advice to Roderigo on how to call out to her father the news of Desdemona's marriage. Call, he says,

> with like timorous [frightening] accent and dire yell
> As when, by night and negligence, the fire
> Is spied in populous cities. (I, i, 72–74)

Fire, panic, darkness, neglect of duty—these are the natural and human forces that destroy great cities and turn their citizens to mobs.

In Venice, Iago's attempts to create civic chaos are frustrated by Othello's calm management of himself and the orderly legal proceedings of the Senate. In Cyprus, however, society is less secure—even as the island is more exposed to the Turks—and Othello alone is responsible for finding truth and maintaining order. Here Iago's poison begins to work, and he succeeds at once in manufacturing the riot that he failed to create in Venice. Seen on stage, the fight on the watch between Cassio and Montano is chaos come again: two drunken officers, charged with the defense of the town, trying to kill each other like savage animals, a bedlam of voices and shouts, broken, disordered furniture, and above all this the discordant clamor of the "dreadful" alarm bell—used to signal attacks and fire. This success is but the prologue for other more serious disruptions of society and of the various human relationships that it fosters. The General is set against his officer, husband against wife, Christian against Christian, servant against master. Justice becomes a travesty of itself as Othello—using legal terms such as "It is the *cause*"—assumes the offices of accuser, judge, jury, and executioner of his wife. Manners disappear as the Moor strikes his wife publicly and treats her maid as a procuress. The brightly lighted Senate chamber is now replaced with a dark Cyprus street where Venetians cut one another down and men are murdered from behind. This anarchy finally gives way in the last scene, when Desdemona's faith is proven, to a restoration of order and an execution of justice on the two major criminals.

What we have followed so far is a movement expressed in geographical and social symbols from Venice to a Cyprus exposed to attack, from *The City* to barbarism, from Christendom to the domain of the Turks, from order to riot, from justice to wild revenge and murder, from truth to falsehood. It now remains to see just what this movement means on the level of the individual in the heart and mind of man. Of the three major characters, Desdemona, Othello, and Iago, the first and the last do not change their natures or their attitudes toward life during the course of the play. These two are polar opposites, the antitheses of each other. To speak in the most general terms, Desdemona expresses in her language and actions an innocent, unselfish love and concern for others. Othello catches her very essence when he speaks of her miraculous love, which transcended their differences in age, color, beauty, and culture:

> She loved me for the dangers I had passed,
> And I loved her that she did pity them. (I, iii, 166–67)

This love in its various forms finds expression not only in her absolute commitment of herself to Othello, but in her gentleness, her kindness to others, her innocent trust in all men, her pleas for Cassio's restoration to Othello's favor; and it endures even past death at her husband's hands, for she comes back to life for a moment to answer Emilia's question, "who hath done this deed?" with the unbelievable words,

> Nobody— I myself. Farewell.
> Commend me to my kind lord. O, farewell! (V, ii, 123–24)

Iago is her opposite in every way. Where she is open and guileless, he is never what he seems to be; where she thinks the best of everyone, he thinks the worst, usually turning to imagery of animals and physical functions to express his low opinion of human nature; where she seeks to serve and love others, he uses others to further his own dark aims and satisfy his hatred of mankind; where she is emotional and idealistic, he is icily logical and cynical. Desdemona and Iago are much more complicated than this, but perhaps enough has been said to suggest the nature of these two moral poles of the play. One is a life force that strives for order, community, growth, and light. The other is an anti-life force that seeks anarchy, death, and darkness. One is the foundation of all that men have built in the world, including *The City;* the other leads back toward ancient chaos and barbarism.

Othello, like most men, is a combination of the forces of love and hate, which are isolated in impossibly pure states in Desdemona and Iago. His psychic voyage from Venice to Cyprus is a passage of the soul and the will from the values of one of these characters to those of the other. This passage is charted by his acceptance and rejection of one or the other. He begins by refusing to have Iago as his lieutenant, choosing the more "theoretical" though less experienced Cassio. He marries Desdemona. Though he is not aware that he does so, he expresses the full meaning of this choice when he speaks of her in such suggestive terms as "my soul's joy" and refers to her even as he is about to kill her, as "Promethean heat," the vital fire that gives life to the world. Similarly, he comes to know that all that is valuable in life depends on her love, and in the magnificent speech beginning, "O now, forever/Farewell the tranquil mind" (III, iii, 344–45), he details the emptiness of all human activity if Desdemona be proved false. But Iago, taking advantage of latent "Iagolike" feelings and thoughts in Othello, persuades him that Desdemona is only common clay. Othello then gives himself over to Iago at the end of III, iii, where they kneel together to plan the revenge, and Othello says, "Now art thou my lieutenant." To which Iago responds with blood-chilling simplicity, "I am your own forever." The full meaning of this choice is expressed, again unconsciously, by Othello when he says of Desdemona,

> Perdition catch my soul
> But I do love thee! and when I love thee not,
> Chaos is come again. (III, iii, 90–92)

The murder of Desdemona acts out the final destruction in Othello himself of all the ordering powers of love, of trust, of the bond between human beings.

Desdemona and Iago then represent two states of mind, two understandings of life, and Othello's movement from one to the other is the movement on the level of character and psychology from Venice to Cyprus, from *The City* to anarchy. His return to *The City* and the defeat of the Turk is effected, at the expense of his own life, when he learns *what* he has killed and executes himself as the only fitting judgment on his act. His willingness to speak of what he has done—in contrast to Iago's sullen silence—is a willingness to recognize the meaning of Desdemona's faith and chastity, to acknowledge that innocence and love do exist, and that therefore *The City* can stand, though his life is required to validate the truth and justice on which it is built.

*Othello* offers a variety of interrelated symbols that locate and define in historical, natural, social, moral, and human terms those qualities of being and universal forces that are forever at war in the universe and between which tragic man is always in movement. On one side there are Turks, cannibals, barbarism, monstrous deformities of nature, the brute force of the sea, riot, mobs, darkness, Iago, hatred, lust, concern for the self only, and cynicism. On the other side there are Venice, *The City,* law, senates, amity, hierarchy, Desdemona, love, concern for others, and innocent trust. As the characters of the play act and speak, they bring together, by means of parallelism and metaphor, the various forms of the different ways of life. There is, for example, a meaningful similarity in the underhanded way Iago works and the ruse by which the Turks try to fool the Venetians into thinking they are bound for Rhodes when their object is Cyprus. Or, there is again a flash of identification when we hear that the reefs and shoals that threaten ships are "ensteeped," that is, hidden under the surface of the sea, as Iago is hidden under the surface of his "honesty." But Shakespeare binds the various levels of being more closely together by the use of imagery that compares things on one level of action with things on another. For example, when Iago swears that his low judgment of all female virtue "is true, or else I am a Turk" (II, i, 113), logic demands, since one woman, Desdemona, *is* true and chaste, that we account him "a Turk." He is thus identified with the unbelievers, the Ottoman Turks, and that Asiatic power, which for centuries threatened Christendom, is shown to have its social and psychological equivalent in Iago's particular attitude toward life. Similarly, when Othello sees the drunken brawl on the watchtower, he exclaims,

> Are we turned Turks, and to ourselves do that
> Which heaven hath forbid the Ottomites? (II, iii, 169–70)

At the very time when the historical enemy has been defeated, his fleet providentially routed by the great storm, his characteristics—drunken loss of control, brawling over honor, disorder—begin to conquer the island only so recently and fortuitously saved. The conquest continues, and the defender of the island, Othello, convinced of Desdemona's guilt, compares his determination to revenge himself to "the Pontic Sea,/Whose icy current and compulsive course/Nev'r keeps retiring ebb" (III, iii, 450–52). The comparison tells us that in his rage and hatred he has become one with the savage seas and the brute, amoral powers of nature that are displayed in the storm scene at the beginning of Act II. But most important is Othello's identification of himself at the end of the play as the "base Judean" who "threw a pearl away richer than all his tribe." The more familiar Quarto reading is "base Indian," but both words point toward the barbarian who fails to recognize value and beauty when he possesses it—the primitive savage who picks up a pearl and throws it away not knowing its worth; or the Jews (Judas may be specifically meant) who denied and crucified another great figure of love, thinking they were dealing with only a troublesome rabble-rouser. A few lines further on Othello proceeds to the final and absolute identification of himself with the infidel. He speaks of a "malignant and a turbaned Turk" who "beat a Venetian and traduced the state," and he then acknowledges that he is that Turk by stabbing himself, even as he once stabbed the other unbeliever. So he ends as both the Turk and the destroyer of the Turk, the infidel and the defender of the faith.

When Iago's schemes are at last exposed, Othello, finding it impossible for a moment to believe that a *man* could have contrived such evil, stares at Iago's feet and then says sadly, "but that's a fable." What he hopes to find when he looks down are the cloven hoofs of the devil, and had they been there he would have been an actor in a morality play, tempted beyond his strength, like many a man before him, by a supernatural power outside himself. In some ways I have schematized *Othello* as just such a morality play, offering an allegorical journey between heaven and hell on a stage filled with purely symbolic figures. This is the kind of abstraction of art toward which criticism inevitably moves, and in this case the allegorical framework is very solidly there. But Othello does not see the cloven hoofs when he looks down; he sees a pair of human feet at the end of a very human body; and he is forced to realize that far from living in some simplified, "fabulous" world where evil is a metaphysical power raiding human life from without, he dwells where evil is somehow inextricably woven with good into man himself. On his stage the good angel does not return to heaven when defeated, but is murdered, and her body remains on the bed, "cold, cold." He lives where good intentions, past services, psychic weaknesses, and an inability to see through evil cannot excuse an act, as they might in some simpler world where more perfect justice existed. In short, Othello is forced to recognize that he lives in a tragic world, and he pays the price for having been great enough to inhabit it.

Here is the essence Shakespeare's art, an ability to create immediate, full, and total life as men actually live and experience it; and yet at the same time to arrange this reality so that it gives substance to and derives shape from a formal vision of all life that comprehends and reaches back from man and nature through society and history to cosmic powers that operate through all time and space. His plays are both allegorical and realistic at once; his characters both recognizable men and at the same time devils, demigods, and forces in nature. I have discussed only the more allegorical elements in *Othello,* the skeleton of ideas and formal patterns within which the characters must necessarily be understood. But it is equally true that the exact qualities of the abstract moral values and ideas, their full reality, exist only in the characters. It is necessary to know that Desdemona represents one particular human value, love or charity, in order to avoid making such mistakes as searching for some tragic flaw in her which would justify her death. But at the same time, if we would know what love and charity *are* in all their fullness, then our definition can only be the actions, the language, the emotions of the character Desdemona. She is Shakespeare's word for love. If we wish to know not just the obvious fact that men choose evil over good, but *why* they do so, then we must look both analytically and feelingly at all the evidence that the world offers for believing that Desdemona is false and at all the biases in Othello's mind that predispose him to believe such evidence. Othello's passage from Venice to Cyprus, from absolute love for Desdemona to extinguishing the light in her bedchamber, and to the execution of himself, these are Shakespeare's words for tragic man.

# 31

# The Fool and Handy-Dandy

*John F. Danby*

I propose in this chapter to isolate one aspect of the Fool. The aim is to see how far Shakespeare's larger theme—the theme of man and his society, of the two Natures and Janus-like Reason*—is reflected in the shivered mirror of the Fool's verse.

The manner of that verse is gnomic and elliptic. It is an ideal idiom for twisting broken fragments into unexpected patterns. On one side it might originate in the medieval nonsense poem. The sixteenth century popular ballad still kept this alive in such scraps and oddments as the Fool sings. On the other it comes down through Shakespeare's own period of Gobbo-like confusion-mongering. It ends, in *King Lear,* as the sort of thing Blake might have taken as a model for his own octosyllables. It is not a carefree or a happy verse, for all its capering and jauntiness. It is taut with anxiety and bafflement, with distress and bitterness. It is abrupt and bewildered. It can juggle with fragments of the two Natures and the two Reasons, and then shrug off the whole business with hideous flippancy. Pain distorts the Fool's grimace, but the pain might equally mask compassion or contempt.

*From* Shakespeare's Doctrine of Nature: A Study of King Lear, *1949, pp. 102–113. Reprinted by permission of Faber & Faber Limited.*

* Two Natures: the visible orderly creation of medieval thought and the malignant nature of Hobbes. Janus-like Reason looks both ways at these. (*Editor's note.*)

A passage from the Fool's first scene in the play provides a fair example of his normal idiom:

*Lear.* When were you wont to be so full of songs, sirrah?
*Fool.* I have used it nuncle, e'er since thou mad'st
thy daughters thy mothers, for when thou gav'st
them the rod, and put'st down thy own breeches,
Then they for sudden joy did weep,
And I for sorrow sung,
That such a King should play bo-peep,
And go the fools among.
Prithee nuncle keep a schoolmaster that can
teach thy fool to lie, I would fain learn to lie.
*Lear.* An you lie, sirrah, we'll have you whipped. (I, iv.)

We might note first that the Fool is under a compulsion to tell the truth, so that what he says has professional reliability. Second, the popular ballad material incorporated into his part is not chosen at random: it matches his own manner, and throws new light on what he has to say. Thirdly, very often his speeches deliberately re-state what has already been given expression in the play elsewhere. "Thou mad'st thy daughters thy mothers," for example, repeats Goneril's outburst of the scene before:

Idle old man
That still would manage those authorities
That he hath given away, now by my life,
Old fools are babes again, and must be us'd
With checks as flatteries, when they are seen abus'd. (I, iii.)

Each of these points is a commonplace of criticism: their combined force is sufficient warrant for treating the whole of the Fool's lines as serious and homogeneous utterance. His statements have as much weight, for interpretation, as those of anyone in the play.

The most significant aspect of the Fool's verse is also illustrated in the passage. This is his habit of translating everything into handy-dandy. (Cp. "When a man is over-lusty at legs, then he shall wear wooden nether-stocks.")

He sees everything as a see-saw. Whichever end of the see-saw anyone chooses, the Fool's job is to be counterweight. The King himself is an instance of this universal handy-dandy. He has made his daughters his mothers. Instead of wielding the rod, he receives correction himself. Instead of remaining a ruler on the throne he has become an irresponsible child playing bo-beep. Handy-dandy is a psychological law, too:

Then they for sudden joy did weep
And I for sorrow sung.

The ballad lines, apart from the *King Lear* context, are merely Launcelot Gobbo silliness. In the *King Lear* context, however, they develop characteristic overtones. There is first the obvious common-sense meaning: excessive joy can make one weep, and hysterical sorrow will sometimes sing. But this in itself shows how the mind rocks perpetually between extremes, with no fixed centre of measure or control. Furthermore there is the meaning that comes from the deliberate switching of the tears and the song. The daughters have stolen the Fool's tears; he is left to sing their song. It might be a profound hypocrisy on the daughters' part—the kind of hypocrisy that steals the good man's weapons and leaves him with none but those the hypocrite has discarded. (This, of course, is Cordelia's plight when she must be dumb because the hypocrites have already made truth seem like a lie.) Hypocrisy can always seize the initiative, put truth in this false position and leave it paralysed and immobile; hypocrisy can force even truth to seem a collaborator. The Fool appears to be as callous as the sisters, they are no more cruel than he. The Fool can see it all happening, and knows exactly how it works. But his knowledge leaves him no better off. It is all an inevitable and miserable handy-dandy.

A striking thing about the Fool is that while his heart makes him belong to the Lear-party, and while his loyalty to Lear himself is unshakeable, his head can only represent to him that meaning for Reason which belongs to the party of Edmund and the Sisters. He is aware of the two common senses in the debate between Goneril and Albany. But his constant recommendation to the King and his following is a counsel of self-interest. Here is his advice to Kent:

> Let go thy hold, when a great wheel runs down a hill, lest it breaks thy neck with following. But the great one that goes upward, let him draw thee after: when a wise man gives thee better council give me mine again: I would have none but Knaves follow it since a Fool gives it:
>
> That Sir, which serves and seeks for gain,
> And follows but for form;
> Will pack, when it begins to rain,
> And leave thee in the storm,
> But I will tarry, the Fool will stay,
> And let the wise man fly:
> The Knave turns Fool that runs away,
> The Fool no Knave perdy. (II, ii.)

It is usual to claim that in instances such as this the Fool is submitting the loyalty of Lear's following to a test. He gives advice which he knows will not be taken by the disinterested; he is a hypocrite in a benevolent sense. This view, I think, makes the Fool less ambiguous than he really is. As I see him, he really does believe that to follow Lear to disaster is foolishness. Absolute loyalty is irrational, and the Fool never suggests that there is a supernatural sanction for such irrationality. Folly is an alternative to knavery, certainly. But that does not make it a virtue. The third term that would rescue him from the counterbalancing negatives is simply missing. Handy-dandy works on the ethical level, too. It is this which separates the Fool from Albany, whom Goneril calls a "moral fool." The Fool can see no sense in the foolish morality Albany would urge his wife to pursue. On the other hand, Goneril's alternative is no more acceptable. The Fool is quite clear on the point that such common sense as hers (such wisdom) is mere knavishness. Wiseman has come to mean for him, as for Bunyan later, worldly-wiseman. Unlike Bunyan thc Fool does not see the wiseman as a candidate for damnation.

Handy-dandy operates in society, too. The "great wheel" runs down the hill and another is drawn upward by its very descent. It is tempting to see behind this image some new device of haulage machinery. (Massinger's image for the great man and his satellites was the great wheel of a mill that makes the lesser wheels go round. In Chapman the wheels are those of a spit.) The wheel is probably, however, the wheel of Fortune. Either way a strong sense pervades the lines of the individual's weakness in the authoritarian setting for human action. The Great Man himself is as insecure as the small man. The tilted plane of society makes tug and scamble inevitable. Under such conditions the panic of save-your-own-skin will be the prevailing mood.

The Fool holds up to Lear a model of cautionary excellence. It is the hypocrite, the canny capitalist, and the self-denying puritan combined:

Mark it, nuncle;
Have more than thou showest,
Speak less than thou knowest,
Lend less than thou owest,
Ride more than thou goest,
Learn more than thou trowest,
Set less than thou throwest;
Leave thy drink and thy whore,
And keep in a door,
And thou shalt have more,
Than two tens to a score. (I, iv.)

Goneril has already charged Lear with the vices of the old regime, riotous "Epicurism and Lust"—the excess of those impulses which, in the mean, are sociability, comradeship, free self-expression, and love. The Fool prescribes the complementary vices of the new dispensation: a riot of acquisitiveness, self-protection, suspicion.

Again, it is impossible to say that the advice is meant only as irony. The model proposed is certainly mean and contemptible, an inversion of the grand image of the King in the scheme of natural theology. It is not one that would be freely espoused if other alternatives were open. However, the Fool doubts whether any alternative does lie open, apart from the permanent alternative of Folly.

We are tempted to think of the Fool as being on the side of some social Utopia, until we see handy-dandy applied to this, too:

> When priests are more in word, than matter;
> When brewers mar their malt with water;
> When nobles are their tailors' tutors,
> No heretics burned, but wenches' suitors;
> When every case in Law, is right;
> No squire in debt, nor no poor knight;
> When slanders do not live in tongues;
> Nor cutpurses come not to throngs;
> When usurers tell their gold i' th' field,
> And bawds, and whores, do churches build,
> Then shall the Realm of Albion,
> Come to great confusion;
> Then comes the time, who lives to see't,
> That going shall be us'd with feet.
> This prophecy Merlin shall make, for I live before his time. (III, ii.)

The first four lines describe the actual state of present corruption. The next four switch without warning to the coming Utopia. The two lines following manage to mix both together:

> When usurers tell their gold i' th' field,
> And bawds, and whores, do churches build.

We can read this either as total conversion or as utter unregeneracy. The confusion is completed by the last four lines. The Golden Age to come will entail the overthrow of Albion, and the last stage will return us to the point from which we start:

> Then comes the time, who lives to see't,
> That going shall be us'd with feet.

There is little hope of enlisting the Fool as a social reformer.

Handy-dandy is even applied to Time: "This prophecy," the Fool explains, "Merlin shall make; for I live before his time." Direction and purpose in history itself are lost. The motion from past to future becomes that of a wheel again.

The wheel is the key to much of the Fool's imagery. The great wheel running up and down the hill is a double wheel-image—a wheel running round in a circle. We used the image of the see-saw to explain the working of the Fool's opposites. A suspended wheel is an endless series of see-saws. The old man and the babe, the moralist and the knave, the wise man and the fool—these are opposites diametrically counterpoised, and then (since the wheel always comes full circle) identified. The mechanism is shown at work in the individual, in society, in the pattern of the moral world, and in history itself. Man is caught in a contraption that bears him up and down, carries him round and round, continually.

Edmund and the Sisters see society as a competition; and Goneril says it is safer to fear than to trust too far. In this competitiveness there is a certain combative courage, and for them fear is an offensive-defensive of caution. Man even as an animal still retains a kind of dignity. He is King of the Beasts. The Fool sees this competitiveness and fear in a different light. "He that has a house to put's head in," he remarks, "has a good head-piece." Or, another occasion:

> *Fool.* Canst tell why an oyster makes his shell?
> *Lear.* No.
> *Fool.* Nor I neither; but I can tell why a snail has a house.
> *Lear.* Why?
> *Fool.* Why, to put's head in, not to give it away to his daughters and leave his horns without a case. (I, v.)

Here he makes the fear, timidity, and the creatures nearest to man in this general respect the close oyster and the fearful snail. Self-interest does not only lead to an aggressive outgoing among one's fellows. It leads also to a self-protective shrinkage within one's shell. Man is a poor, cowering, threatened creature, and will do well to look after himself as best he can.

The shell and the sheltering creature symbolize for the Fool man in the carapace of his society. The compelling factor in the image is the suggestion of the external threat. Man must defend himself in such an environment. His mean shifts are a necessity imposed on him by the sub-humanity of the surrounding universe, a universe constantly threatening to crush the shell men have built for themselves. It is this same sub-humanity (sensed by Kent, as well as by the Fool, as lying behind the Thunder) which amply sanctions man's inhumanity to man. Not all can be equally warm or sheltered. Those like Poor Tom who are pushed outside must blame themselves only—and the elements.

The Fool, like Hobbes, knows that "the passion to be reckoned upon is fear." Fear throbs as a motive through his human world, and beats down from the non-human world of the heavens. It is this underlying feeling which explains the Fool's sincerest piece of advice to the suffering King he accompanies over the heath. It is an example of compassion working to the same effect as cruelty: an unconscious handy-dandy. He is alone with Lear on the heath; the storm is still raging; the King has just called on the "all-shaking thunder" to

> Strike flat the thick rotundity o' th' world,
> Crack Nature's moulds, all germens spill at once
> That makes ingrateful man. (III, ii.)

The Fool says:

> O nuncle, Court holy-water in a dry house, is better than this rain water out o' door. Good nuncle, in, ask thy daughters' blessing; here's a night pities neither wise men, nor fools. (III, iii.)

The heath tests the breaking-points of the human beings wandering over it. This is the Fool's, and a nadir of negated humanity is reached. "Court holy-water" is the sycophancy and corruption of the time-servers that fawn on power. Under the threat of Thunder the Fool's opposition collapses. He will abjectly consent even to playing the hypocritical knave. He urges the king to accept the worst terms society can offer, the blessing of pelican daughters:

> The Knave turns Fool that runs away.

This is an ultimate bankruptcy. And it is the intellect's sincere advice. There is neither bitterness nor irony, only moral panic. We are invited back with Lear into the corrupt world we were glad to have quitted—invited to stand by the same fire with Lady Brach, and stink.

The corrupt world is the final clue to the meaning of the Fool. He is not of tragic scope. He affirms the dignity of man neither as animal nor angelic reason. Nor has he the ennobling weakness of compassion. He remains a figure of pathos because he is so helpless—helplessly immobilized by a handy-dandy of opposites neither of which he can choose. Nor will he admit of any third ground, the possibility that knavishness might not be an ultimate, that wisdom might be redeemable, that society might be capable of re-birth. He does not survive his own grim laughter, and disappears for that reason. He could not survive, without metamorphosis, in the same context as Cordelia. He is fast in the sickening stasis of his handy-dandy.

His summary of the human situation is as follows:

> He that has a house to put's head in, has a good head-piece:
> The codpiece that will house,
> Before the head has any;
> The head, and he shall louse:
> So beggars marry many.
> The man that makes his toe,
> What he his heart should make,
> Shall of a corn cry woe,
> And turn his sleep to wake.
> For there never yet was fair woman, but she made mouths in a glass.
> (III, ii)

This is the closest knot Shakespeare ties in the idiom he invented for the Fool, and is original for both manner and matter.

That the imagery should be both social and sexual is not chance prurience. The idea of sexual love in Shakespeare's time was approaching the end of an interesting career. It had been a relation under which to figure the ideal destiny of man, both as a person and a social agent. In Spenser, for example, love is the consummation of the whole course of virtue in man. It may be that wherever love is more than casual mating it inevitably serves as an allegory of the marriage of the individual to truth. Throughout the Elizabethan period (and in Petrarch and Dante) this liaison seems certainly to have been well established. By 1600 optimism had reached its term (maybe a nemesis for Elizabeth's over-stimulation of the cult of Gloriana). In the Shakespearean breakdown of confidence, extending to most of the human values, love was also involved. *King Lear* reflects moods that are not only anti-authoritarian, and anti-social, but also anti-sexual. Love is left with none of the Spenserian glamour (except in relation to Cordelia), and the revulsion is expressed crudely—as by Lear in his mad speeches, and by the Fool here.

The codpiece is part of the gallant's costume, and also, quite simply, the phallus. The first four lines thus describe how improvident lechering leads to disease, and how this begins a vicious circle: because the head, too (shrewd prudence and cautious provision against all the potential threats of life), becomes lousy. Once the process has started it is increasingly difficult to stop it. This is the explanation of the paradox concerning the Beggarman and his long train of doxies. He "marries" so many because he is poor (the result of an initial imprudence), and not vice versa. The four lines give a kind of condensed Rake's Progress, and the career of proud gallant becoming Abram man conforms to the mechanism of the wheel. This central idea in the lines is repeated, of course, in Poor Tom—the courtier whose vices had just been those that set the wheel turning and who becomes a naked Bedlamite.

The next four lines fuse the images of Beggarman and Courtier after another fashion. The "toe" can belong to either: it might be the Courtier's pinched in his over-tight shoes, or the Beggarman's that has burst through his boot. A sexual symbolism, paralleling "codpiece," accompanies the social reference. The toe is also (*pace* Freud) the phallus. I take the lines to mean: "The man—rich or poor—who makes his "toe" the centre of all his hopes, aspirations, and satisfactions, sacrificing, if he be a courtier, all real human feeling to vanity, or, if he be a beggar, squandering his emotional means in slovenly lust—this man, the composite social creature, will suffer the inevitable pain consequent on his perversity: pangs of guilty remorse that will never let him rest. Thus both extremes in society, acting in opposite ways from opposite motives, come together in the same state—a state of self-torment."

Handy-dandy is doubly exerted in these lines. First, one half of society is neatly folded over the other. The quatrains seem at first sight to be referring only to one, but are in fact applicable to the other, too. The effect is to argue, seemingly, that haves and have-nots are in an identical plight. Secondly, through the intertwining of the social and sexual in the same image, the public world of community and the private world of personal emotional life are shown to interlock.

Yet a third handy-dandy remains to be noted. The poem is about the strife between head and heart, both of them sinning and sinned against. The first quatrain illustrates a sin against the head: Lust flouts prudence, and the unregulated instinct after one's kind leads to disaster. The second depicts a sin against the heart: Either by the vain courtier (cultivating the externals instead of attending to the inward things of the spirit) or through the coney-catching beggarman (exposing and parading his ill-shodness, yet not revealing the design and deceit in his breast). Head and heart, like courtier and beggarman are equally badly off. Neither is a reliable guide. Both are mutually confounding. The eight lines summarize the plight of a fissured society and of a divided man: a severance that is self-perpetuating and self-aggravating. Society and man come together only to make each other worse. This applies to rich as well as poor. At either end of the social scale (and it is a scale with no middle) we see a travesty of human nature—flaunting codpiece, calloused toe, man lacerated in head and heart, in mind and body, by disease or conscience.

To sum up, the Fool can be regarded as the consciousness of a split society Like man, its creator, the society is a twin-headed monster at strife with itself. The Fool consistently uses the imagery of disease and perversity. Complementary ill-healths counterbalance in perpetual handy-dandy. He sees rich man and poor man, head and heart, sympathizes with neither, yet cannot dissociate himself from the conditions of the strife. Harsh as the handy-dandy world of corrupt society is, there is no escape from it: "In, nuncle, in, and ask thy daughters' blessing."

We began by observing the unconscious handy-dandy in the Fool's own behaviour. His head thinks with the Reason of Goneril and Regan, yet what he does is directly counter to the self-interest which for them and for him is the only thing that makes sense. His greatest bit of cruelty is wrung from him by compassion. While he counsels flight, with wiseman and knave, he will not desert the king: because he is a Fool. What he does will not square with what he says, and it is a redeeming insincerity. Wilfully and blindly he holds to the Great Wheel going downhill.

The Fool, I think, stands for the unillumined head—the intellect—as Lear is the soul, and Cordelia the spirit. He can discern in his cold light the alternatives between which he cannot choose. The sort of thing he could desire he will not admit to exist. It would be too good to be true. Nature in him is an arrest of motion. His head will not allow him to descend the scale with Edmund and the Sisters, and yet it shows no sign of rushing into the natural theology of Lear and Cordelia. The Fool is incapable of Goneril's wickedness, of Lear's error and his subsequent growth, of Cordelia's faultless integration. He prefers, however, to walk in a darkness he cannot fathom rather than stay in the light of such reason as he cannot abide. The head would betray him back to Goneril's hearth, with Lady Brach. But for reasons neither he nor the head knows he follows Lear over the heath.

# 32

# *King Lear*

*John Holloway*

*King Lear,* a play set (unlike *Macbeth*) in the legendary pre-history of Britain, depicts a world which is remote and primaeval. This is not to deny that it has life and meaning for all times: Its permanent relevance is what follows from having the quality of legend, and the primaeval as subject. Nor is it a merely trite observation about the play. To apprehend this fact is to be led to a decisive truth. The action of *King Lear* comprises an event which today has largely lost its meaning; though one, indeed, which points back to men's original and deepest fears and convictions, and seems to have been part of their consciousness from primitive times.

This by now largely archaic idea is present elsewhere in the tragedies. It is brought before the mind in the guards' words at the death of Antony:

> *Second Guard.* The star is fall'n.
> *First Guard. And time is at his period.*
>
> (IV, xiv, 106)

*Reprinted from John Holloway,* The Story of the Night, *pp. 75–98 by permission of The University of Nebraska Press and Routledge & Kegan Paul Ltd.*

It is in Macduff's words at Duncan's murder:

> Shake off this downy sleep, Death's counterfeit,
> And look on death itself. Up, up, and see
> *The great doom's image*! Malcolm! Banquo!
> *As from your graves rise up* and walk like sprites
> To countenance this horror! (II, iii, 74)

The point here is that the king's end is like the end of the world: not the Day of Judgement, but the universal cataclysm which was to precede it. Twice, in *Lear*, the idea is mentioned explicitly. Kent, when he sees Lear enter with Cordelia dead in his arms, says:

> Is this the promis'd end?

and Edgar replies:

> Or image of that horror? (V, iii, 263)

The mad Lear and the blinded Gloucester meet:

> *Glou.* O, let me kiss that hand!
> *Lear.* Let me wipe it first, it smells of mortality
> *Glou.* O ruin'd piece of nature! *This great world*
> *Shall so wear out to nought.* (IV, vi, 132)

The idea of a universal deflection of Nature towards evil and disaster (as prelude to final salvation) seems to call forth an echo elsewhere in the play. Gloucester's well-known reference to "these late eclipses of the sun and moon" (I, ii, 99) re-echoes the words of St Luke on the end of the world:

> And there shalbe signes in the Sunne, and in the Moone, & in the starres; and upon the earth trouble among the nations, with perplexitie, the sea and the water roring: And mens hartes fayling them for feare, and for looking after those thinges which are comming on the worlde: for the powers of heaven shalbe shaken. (*Luke* 21: 25–6)

The storm on the heath recalls what the Book of Revelation says of Armageddon:

> And there folowed voyces, thundringes, and lightnynges: and there was a great earthquake, such as was not since men were upon the earth...
> (*Rev.* 16: 18)

For the Elizabethans, the End of the World was a living conviction and even something of a current fear. We touch here on one of the oldest of traditions: that notion of the world's turning upside down which Archilochus already employs when, having unexpectedly seen an eclipse of the sun, he says that the fish might as well now come and feed on land, or wolves feed in the sea. Repeated incessantly,[1] by Shakespeare's time this was a long-established commonplace; but when Hooker (though merely adapting Arnobius) finds his imagination kindled by this thought, and turns from detailed analysis to write with the full range of his eloquence, the idea is present in all its power and solemnity:

> Now if nature should intermit her course...if those principal and mother elements of the world...should lose the qualities which they now have; if the frame of that heavenly arch erected over our heads should loosen and dissolve itself; if celestial spheres should forget their wonted motions... if the moon should wander from her beaten way, the times and seasons of the year blend themselves by disordered and confused mixture, the winds breathe out their last gasp, the clouds yield no rain, the earth be defeated of heavenly influence, the fruits of the earth pine away as children at the withered breasts of their mother no longer able to yield them relief; what then would become of man himself?[2]

The reader of Shakespeare has thus to recognize that the "Elizabethan World Picture" pictured an order quite different from anything which would now come to mind as order. Coherent and providential system as it was, it included within itself a standing potentiality for progressive transformation into chaos. Paradoxically, the more that the world is conceived in religious terms, the easier is it for a potentiality of deflection into chaos to stand as no radical infringement, but a genuine ingredient of order. Further than this, for Shakespeare's time collapse into universal chaos was not merely a permanent possibility in a fallen (though divinely created) Nature: it was a fore-ordained part of created Nature's route to salvation; and to envisage it, to dwell on it, to comprehend what it could be like, was part of what went to make up a comprehension of God's governance of the world.

How *Lear* is in part a rehearsal of this terrible potentiality of Nature becomes plainer, if one bears in mind that what the descent into chaos would be like was delineated by tradition. It already had its familiar contours and features. There is no need here to do more than hint briefly at the length and strength of this tradition. If we go back, for example, to Mark 13, which is the chapter in that gospel corresponding to Luke 21 (the account of the final calamity of the world which was briefly quoted above) we see the major concerns of *Lear* emerge one by one: "There shal nation rise against nation, & kingdome against kingdome: and there shalbe earthquakes...the brother shall betray the brother to death, and the father the sonne: and the children shal rise against their fathers and mothers, and shal put them to death." From this one might turn to Wulfstan's *Sermon*

---

[1] See, e.g., E. Curtius, *European Literature and the Latin Middle Ages* (English ed., 1953), pp. 95 ff.

[2] Hooker, *Laws of Ecclesiastical Polity,* I. iii. 2; Arnobius, *Adversus Gentes,* I. 2 (Anti-Nicene Christian Library, Vol. XIX, p. 5).

*to the English People*, composed in response to the chaos overtaking England when the Danish invasion was at its height: "...the father did not stand by his child, nor the child by the father, nor one brother by another..." and—sign of the traditional combination of ideas from which Lear itself emerged—Wulfstan goes on immediately to speak of how treachery, unlawfulness and infidelity to one's lord have spread everywhere throughout the land.[3]

What must have been a passage familiar to all of Shakespeare's audience, the Homily of 1574 *Against Disobedient and Wilful Rebellion,* also clearly sees dissension between parents and children as the predictable counterpart of dissension in the body politic: "when the subjects unnaturally do rebel against their prince...countrymen to disturb the public peace and quietness of their country, for defence of whose quietness they should spend their lives: the brother to seek, and often to work the death of his brother; the son of the father, the father to seek or procure the death of his sons, being at man's age, and by their faults to disherit their innocent children...."[4] Donne's well-known reference to how "new philosophy calls all in doubt" in the First Anniversary belongs to the same train of thought. These words, so often quoted in bleak and misleading isolation, easily misrepresent the main weight of Donne's argument. This by no means expresses a new-found disquiet resulting from new astronomy or anything like it. All that such things do for Donne is provide mere topical confirmation of that fallen condition which is established on other grounds and by the longest of traditions.

> Then, as mankinde, so is the worlds whole frame
> Quite out of joynt, *almost created lame*:
> For, before God had made up all the rest,
> Corruption entred, and deprav'd the best:
> It seis'd the Angels...
> The noblest part, man, felt it first; and then
> Both beasts and plants, curst in the curse of man.
> *So did the world from the first houre decay....*

Here is the beginning of Donne's discussion. The reference to "new philosophy" has a subordinate place in the middle of it. The poet goes straight on to rehearse the traditional counterparts of chaos in Nature (counterparts, needless to say, having nothing to do with "new philosophy"), and these take us straight back to *Lear*:

---

3 'Forðam on þisan earde waes, swa hit þincan maeg, nu fela geara unrihta fela and tealta getrywða aeghwaer mid mannum. Ne bearh nu foroft gesib gesibban þe ma þe fremdan, ne faeder his bearne, ne hwilum bearn his agenum faeder, ne broðor oðrum....Forðam her syn on lande ungetrywda micle for Gode and for worulde; and eac her syn on earde on mistlice wisan hlafordswican manege...'. Wulfstan, *Sermo ad Anglos.*

4 Homily *Against Disobedience and Wilful Rebellion* (*ed cit.,* p. 574).

'Tis all in peeces, all cohaerence gone;
All just supply, and all Relation:
*Prince, Subject, Father, Sonne are things forgot,*
For every man alone thinkes he hath got
To be a Phoenix, and that then can bee
None of that kinde, of which he is, but hee...

Finally, a passage from Burton's *Anatomy of Melancholy,* resuming the same point, also relates it directly to the twin threads of action which run through the movement of the play: "Great affinity there is betwixt a political and an economic body [i.e. a house or family]; they differ only in magnitude; *as they have both likely the same period*...six or seven hundred years, so many times they have the same means of their vexation and overthrow; as namely riot, a common ruin of both."[5]

Disruption in the kingdom, disruption in the family, linked by tradition, were facets of that universal disruption of Nature, that Descent into Chaos, which for millennia had been a standing dread of mankind and at the same time one of mankind's convictions about providential history in the future.

*King Lear* is an exploration of this potentiality to quite a different degree from, say, *Macbeth.* The nadir of that play, the point at which Macbeth's own evil nature seems to diffuse evil throughout his whole country, falls short of what happens even at the very start of *Lear.* In *Macbeth* the evil emanates from one man (or one couple) quite alone. In *Lear* it seems, from the first, like an infection spreading everywhere, affecting a general change in human nature, even in all nature. Those, like Kent and Cordelia, who stand out against its progress, manifest its influence even in doing so: as if Burton's "riot" could be countered (which may be true, indeed) only by riot of another kind. The disease is general; antidotes are helpless or non-existent; the course must be run.

In its details, the play sometimes displays an extraordinary realism. Lear's hesitation before he demands to see the supposedly sick Duke of Cornwall and his inability to believe that his messenger has been set in the stocks, Edgar's impersonation of the peasant, the whole dialogue in Act V, scene iii between Albany, Edmund, Goneril and Regan, are all instances of unforgettable rightness and richness in catching the complex and individualized movements of minds vehemently working and intently engaged. Yet for a sense of the play as a whole this has less weight than what is almost its opposite: an action deliberately stylized so that its generic quality and its decisive movement should stand out more than its human detail. This is true, notably, of the division of the kingdom with which the play opens. We must see this as stylized not merely in its quality as it takes place on

5 *Anatomy of Melancholy,* 3.2.5.5.

the stage, but in how it points forward. Time and again this kind of event occurs in contemporary drama (*Gorboduc, The Misfortunes of Arthur, Selimus, Woodstock, Locrine* are examples). Its status as decisively misguided or evil is not in doubt; and it is the established sign or first step in a movement which threatens chaos or actually brings it. The direction and nature of what is to happen in *Lear* need not be inferred by the spectator through his detailed response to the behaviour and dialogue of the actors. Richly as it may be confirmed and elaborated in these things, its essence stands starkly before him in the stylization of a known kind of opening event. The intricate complication of the story, the detailed characterization, do nothing to obscure what is clear in the almost folk-tale quality of how the play begins. "*We have seen* the best of our time."

Those words of Gloucester are essentially dynamic words, and this movement and dynamic ought to be seen in an aspect of *King Lear* which has been so much discussed that here it need not be discussed in full: its imagery. That the characters in the play are repeatedly likened to the lower orders of creation, for example, gives no mere general or pervasive tinge to the work, and embodies no merely general idea about humanity at large. It cannot be found in the opening scene. It arrives as the action begins to move, and becomes dominant as the quality of life which it embodies becomes dominant in the play. Just as it is not enough for Professor Muir to say that the plot of Lear "expressed the theme of the parent-child relationship"—for it expressed no mere problem or issue, because it depicts a particular movement which begins when that relationship fails in a definite way—so it is not enough for him to refer to "the prevalence of animal imagery" and to add merely: "This imagery is partly designed to show man's place in the Chain of Being, and to bring out the subhuman nature of the evil characters, partly to show man's weakness compared with the animals, and partly to compare human life to the life of the jungle."[6] The hedge-sparrow that fed the cuckoo, the sea-monster that is less hideous than ingratitude in a child, ingratitude itself sharper than a serpent's tooth, the wolfish visage of Goneril, are not scattered through the play as mere figurative embodiments of those discursive or philosophical interests. They burst upon the audience all together, at the close of Act I. If they throw out some general and discursive suggestion about "human life," that is far less prominent than how they qualify the phase of the action which comes at that point, crowding the audience's imagination, surrounding the human characters with the subhuman creatures whose appearance they are fast and eagerly assuming.

Likewise, when Kent (II, ii, 67–89) speaks of the rats "that bite the holy cords atwain," and the men who follow their masters like ignorant dogs or are no different from cackling geese, we are offered no general com-

---

[6] *King Lear* (Arden ed., by K Muir, 1952, p. lxi).

ment upon human life, but a context in imagery for the conduct of Oswald which preoccupies here and now. The society of the play, in its descent into animality, had reached this point. Edgar, shortly after, underlines the change going on before our eyes:

> I will preserve myself; and am bethought
> To take the basest and most poorest shape
> That ever penury in contempt of man
> *Brought near to beast.* (II, iii, 6)

The descent continues; Regan, Cornwall, Gloucester and Edgar are all drawn in as its ministers or its victims; and now the images gain a new quality. They do indeed become general, for the disease they reflect and stress has become general. The play is indeed coming to depict, in Hooker's phrase, an earth "defeated of heavenly influence"; and the Fool's

> Horses are tied by the heads, dogs and bears by th' neck, monkeys by th' loins, and *men* by the legs... (II, iv, 7)

underlines this. "Man's life is cheap as beast's," Lear adds a moment later (II, iv, 266).

All this is enforced by the progressive transformation, as Act II advances, of the settled society of men, with their fixed abodes, into a confusion of people constantly leaving their homes, constantly on horseback and riding recklessly from place to place. Lear's own words, towards the close of this movement, make the point of it:

> They have travelled all the night! Mere fetches!
> *The images of revolt and flying off.* (II, iv, 87)

Yet Lear himself, quitting Goneril, is the first to break with the settled order:

> ...Darkness and devils!
> Saddle my horses; call my train together.
> ...Prepare my horses.
> ...Go, go, my people.
> ...Away, away! (I, iv, 251–2, 258, 272, 289)

Goneril, in the person of her messengers, is quick to follow his example:

> Take you some company, and away to horse... (I, iv, 337)

Next, it is Cornwall of whom Edmund, at his father's castle, says:

> He's coming hither now, *i' th' night, i' th' haste,*
> And Regan with him. (II, i, 24)

And Kent explains that this hurried journey was the immediate result, like the spreading of an infection, of a letter from Goneril:

> . . . Which presently they read; on whose contents
> They summoned up their meiny, straight took horse,
> Commanded me to follow . . . (II, iv, 33)

Regan has already set the tone of her journey more fully than she intended:

> *Cornwall.* You know not why we came to visit you.
> *Regan.* Thus *out of season, threading dark-eyed night.*
> (II, ii, 118)

The last appearance of this motif of the horse and the homeless rider comes once again from Lear himself:

> *Glo.* The king is in high rage.
> *Corn.* Whither is he going?
> *Glo.* He calls to horse; but will I know not whither . . .
> Alack, the night comes on, and the high winds
> Do sorely ruffle; for many miles about
> There's scarce a bush.

Nothing could lead on more clearly to the idea that the society of men is becoming the chaotic world of the outlaw.

This descent from humanity, however, is something which cannot be envisaged fully through the idea of the brute and its animal life alone. It is a descent, embodied in the action, enriched by imagery, and confirmed by what is said as comment, far below brutality. Lear does not only "choose . . . To be a comrade of with the wolf and owl" (II, iv, 207). He sinks lower still: recreant against Nature and outcast among its creatures:

> This night, wherein the cub-drawn bear would crouch,
> The lion, and the belly-pinched wolf
> Keep their fur dry, unbonneted he runs,
> And *bids what will* take all. (III, i, 12)

Edgar joins him ("What art thou that dost grumble there i' th' straw?" asks Kent, [III, iv, 43]). The spectacle is of man below the animals, since he combines the vices of all of men in his single self:

> Hog in sloth, fox in stealth, wolf in greediness, dog in madness, lion in prey . . . (III, iv, 91)

It is only now, when all left of humanity seems to be a madman, a beggar and a jester surrounded by the storm, that the extreme is reached, and the thought of it put forward at last:

> *Lear.* Why, thou wert better in a grave than to answer with thy uncover'd body this extremity of the skies. Is man no more than this? Consider him well.

[this "him" means Edgar as much as man in general]

> Thou ow'st the worm no silk, the beast no hide, the sheep no wool, the cat no perfume. Here's three on us are sophisticated! Thou are the thing itself: unaccommodated man is no more but such a poor, bare, forked animal as thou art. Come, off, you lendings! Come, unbutton here. (III, iv, 100)

Regan and Goneril also seem to pass down through, and out of, the whole order of Nature; though they are its monsters not its remnants. The word itself, already recurrent in the present discussion, is explicitly used of each of them (III, vii, 101; IV, ii, 62–3); and Albany, in two of the comments which he makes about his wife, draws attention not only to the kind of movement which the play has displayed so far, but also—and it is an important new point—to that further movement with which it will close. He asserts that what has happened so far is bringing his society (again the stress is upon the movement, upon its being *brought*) to the condition of the sea, with its universal war, unlimited in savagery, of all against all:

> If that the heavens do not their visible spirits
> Send quickly down to tame these vile offences,
> *It will come*
> Humanity must perforce prey on itself,
> Like monsters of the deep. (IV, ii, 46)

Besides this, he indicates what may be expected to ensue:

> That nature which condemns it origin
> Cannot be border'd certain in itself;
> She that herself will sliver and disbranch
> From her material sap, perforce must wither
> And come to deadly use... (IV, ii, 32)

The thought is near to that of Cornwall's servants:

> *Second Serv.* I'll never care what wickedness I do
> If this man come to good.
> *Third Serv.* If she live long,
> And in the end meet the old course of death,
> Women will all turn monsters. (III, vii, 98)

Lear's part in this change is a special one. He is not only the "slave" of the elements; he is also the man to whom Kent said "...you have that in your countenance that I would fain call master...authority" (I, iv, 27). But his special part is best understood by dwelling upon something which has seldom received much attention: the clear parallel (though it is also a clearly limited one) between the condition of Lear, and that in the Old Testament of Job. This follows on naturally from how the play brings men down to animals, because Gloucester's "I' th' last night's storm I such a fellow saw/Which made me think a man a worm" (IV, i, 33), recalls Job's "I sayde...to the wormes, You are my mother, and my syster" (17, 14). Again, Albany's "O Goneril!/You art not worth the dust which the rude wind/Blows in your face" sees Goneril as less than the dust, and thus echoes a thought constant in *Job:* "nowe must I sleepe in the dust"; "Thou madest me as the mould of the earth, and shalt bring me into dust agayne"; "our rest together is in the dust"; "one dyeth in his ful strength...another dyeth in the bitternesse of his soule...they shal sleepe both alike in the earth and the wormes shal cover them"; "all fleshe shall come to nought at once, and al men shal turne agayne unto dust" (7, 21; 10, 9; 21, 23–6; 34, 15).

Yet these two points are merely the beginning of a much wider resemblance. Job's patience is something that Lear early claims for himself (II, iv, 229; cf. "I will be the pattern of all patience"; (III, ii, 37), and that Gloucester ultimately acquires:

> henceforth I'll bear
> Affliction till it do cry out itself
> 'Enough, enough,' and die. (IV, vi, 75)

There are many other links in matters, comparatively speaking, of detail. "Thou puttest my fete also in the stockes" (13, 27); "for the vehemencie of sorowe is my garment changed, which compasseth me about as the coller of my coat" (30, 18; cf. "come, unbutton here," [III, iv, 106]; and "pray you undo this button," [V, iii, 309]); "Wherefore do wycked men liue, come to theyr olde age, and encrese in ryches" (21, 7; cf. "Is there any cause in nature that makes these hard hearts," [III, vi, 76], and the servant's "...if she live long,/And in the end meet the old course of death..." [III, vii, 99]).

Besides these sharp if local resemblances, there are passages in *Job* that seem to resume whole sections of the play: "They cause the poore to turne out of the way...they cause the naked to lodge wythout garment and wythout coverying in the colde. They are wet wyth the showres of the mountaynes, and embrace the rocks for want of a covering" (24: 4–8). "Heare then the sound of his voice, & the noyse that goeth out of his mouth. He directeth it under the whole heaven, and his lyght [=lightning] unto the endes of y^e^ world. A roryng voyce foloweth...thundreth marveylously wyth his voyce...He commandeth the snow, and it falleth upon earth: he geueth the rayne a charge, & the shouers have their strength and fal downe"

(37: 2–6). Finally (though it still remains, to discuss exactly what light these parallels throw) in one passage Lear's whole situation is summed up: "Myne owne kinsfolkes haue forsaken me and my best acquaynted haue forgotten me. The seruantes and maydes of myne owne house tooke me for a stranger, and I am become as an aliant [=alien] in theyr sight. I called my seruant, and he gaue me no answere...Al my most familiers abhorred me: and they whome I loued best are turned agaynst me" (19: 14–18).

A resemblance, even a massive resemblance such as exists here, is one thing; light thrown on the exact contour of *King Lear* is another. Yet light is certainly thrown, and abundantly. How this is so may perhaps best be seen through taking note of something both plain and remarkable about the action of the play: what might be called not its *action,* but its *protraction.* In one sense, *Lear* is a much longer play than it need have been—need have been, that is, to have been less ambitiously tragic. By the middle of Act IV (or even the end of Act III) something of an ordinary tragic action has been completed. Lear has fallen from being the minion of Fortune (when the play opens he is presented as in one sense a king of kings) to being its chief victim. Through the ordeal of this fall, his eyes have been opened. From being one who "hath ever but slenderly known himself" (I, i, 292), he has come to say "Here I stand your slave,/A poor infirm, weak and despised old man" (III, ii, 19). He has learnt, moreover, or re-learnt, the central and traditional lessons that good kings must know:

> Poor naked wretches, wheresoe'er you are,
> That bide the pelting of this pitiless storm,
> How shall your houseless heads and unfed sides,
> Your loop'd and window'd raggedness, defend you
> From seasons such as these? O, I have ta'en
> Too little care of this! Take physic, pomp;
> Expose thyself to feel what wretches feel.... (III, iv, 28)

The lines express something of what Piers Plowman learns from Hunger,[7] and the facts to which they point are those explicit in the Wakefield *Second Shepherd's Play,* and implicit indeed in the *Magnificat.* The twin passages which begin:

> Tremble, thou wetch
> That hast within thee undivulged crimes
> Unwhipped of justice... (III, ii, 51)

and

> Thou rascal beadle, hold thy bloody hand.
> Why dost thou lash that whore? Strip thy own back;

[7] *Piers Plowman,* C Text, IX. 203–222, and 229–231.

> Thou hotly lusts to use her in that kind
> For which thou whip'st her... (IV, iv, 160)

are not well seen as philosophical passages about appearance and reality. Their import is moral. They are conventional and traditional, their power lying in this very embodiment of the familiar facts of human hypocrisy in all their brutal force and immediacy; and their point of origin is St Paul: "...Thou therefore which teachest another, teachest thou not thy selfe? thou that preachest, A man should not steale, doest thou steale? Thou that sayest, A man should not commit adulterie, doest thou commit adultery? thou that abhorrest idoles, committest thou sacriledge? Thou that gloriest in the Lawe, through breaking the Law dishonourest thou God...?" (Romans 2: 21–3). Moreover, Lear had learned to repent: "...these things sting/His mind so venomously that burning shame/Detains him from Cordelia" (IV, iv, 45); and by the end of Act IV it partly seems that his madness has ceased: "Be comforted, good madam. The great rage,/You see, is killed in him" (IV, iv, 78).

The completeness of this change must not be insisted on beyond a certain point (though that there is something of the same kind in Gloucester's situation seems clear enough). A transition from blindness and injustice, through suffering, to self-knowledge, responsibility and repentance, is not the final import even of this long central section of the play. Nevertheless, it is there plainly enough. The materials exist for a more conventional and less protracted tragedy which could have ended well before the beginning of Act V. If we ask what extends the play further, the Book of Job reveals the answer.

What makes the situation of Job unique may be brought out by starting from the position of Job's comforters: Eliphaz's "Who ever perished being an innocent? or where were the upright destroyed" (4, 7), and Bildad's "if thou be pure and upright, then surely he wil awake up unto thee" (8, 6). The comforters are orthodox. The men God punishes are sinners. Those who live piously under affliction, he restores; and so far as they are concerned, the sinister implications in Job's case are plain enough. But Job's protracted afflictions are a challenge to this orderly and consoling doctrine. When, despite his miseries, he "holdeth fast to his integrity" ("In all this Job sinned not") his miseries are simply re-doubled. This is the extraordinary event, the terrifying paradox indeed, which begins and demands the discussion that occupies the rest of the work. If there is any order of Nature at all, good must now replace evil; instead, evil returns twofold and is prolonged far beyond its proper span.

The action of Lear is also prolonged by this same conception. Repeatedly, we are made to think that since Nature is an order (though doubtless a stern one) release from suffering is at hand; but instead, the suffering is renewed. Act IV, the act in which the play takes on its second and more remarkable lease of life, conspicuously begins with this very turn of thought and situation. Edgar, seeing himself at the very bottom of Fortune's wheel, finds cause for hope (living as he thinks in a world of order) in that fact alone:

> To be worst,
> The lowest and most dejected thing of fortune,
> Stands still in esperance, lives not in fear.
> The lamentable change is from the best;
> The worst returns to laughter. Welcome, then,
> Thou unsubstantial air that I embrace! (IV, i, 2)

At this very moment, he encounters his father and sees that he has been blinded; and his response is to recognize the very potentiality of life which was embodied in the story of Job:

> O gods! Who is't can say 'I am at the worst'?
> I am worse than e'er I was...
> And worse I may be yet. The worst is not
> So long as we can say 'This is the worst'. (IV, i, 26)

The bitter reversal of events comes again and again. It is less than the full truth to say (as was suggested on p. 88) that Lear recovers from his madness during Act IV. The "great rage" may be killed in him, but among his first words to Cordelia, when he is awakened out of sleep and we hope momentarily for his recovery, are:

> If you have poison for me, I will drink it. (IV, vii, 72)

Cordelia's army, coming to rescue her father, succeeds only in putting her as well as him into the hands of their worst enemies. Later it seems as if Lear and Cordelia are to find a kind of private happiness in prison together. Yet even as this vision forms in our minds, we recall Edmund's threat, and realize that

> The good years shall devour them, flesh and fell,
> Ere they shall make us weep... (V, iii, 24)

is hopeless fantasy on Lear's part, and only too soon to be proved so. Later still, the threat appears to be removed; for as he is dying Edmund confesses to his plot, and the Captain is sent hurrying to save Cordelia from death. But again, we are worse than e'er we were: The only result, the immediate result, is Lear's entry with Cordelia in his arms.

Perhaps this ironic turn in events, this constant intensifying of disaster at the moment when disaster seems to be over, is represented yet once again in the play: in the very moment of Lear's death. Conceivably, Lear is meant to think for a moment that Cordelia is alive; and dies before he realizes his mistake. Certainly, our hopes for Lear himself are, in a limited sense, raised once more by the words of Albany which immediately precede Lear's last speech. On either or both these counts, it seems as if some kind of remission is at hand; but at this moment Lear suffers the last infliction of all. Nor is it possible to accept, as true in anything but an incomplete and strained sense, R. W. Chambers' opinion that both Lear and Gloucester "die of joy."[8] Edgar has already given the audience the exact truth of Gloucester's death:

> But his flaw'd heart—
> Alack, too weak the conflict to support!—
> 'Twixt two extremes of passion, joy and grief,
> Burst smilingly. (V, iii, 196)

The last two words confirm a paradoxical combination of joy and grief, they do not convert it to a state of bliss; and it is a somewhat bold interpretation of the moment of Lear's death, one which without the parallel to Gloucester (and perhaps with it) would be over-bold, to assert that there, joy lies even in equal balance with grief. That Lear's heart breaks is clear from the words of Kent ("Break heart, I prithee break"); and that this is the culmination of an ordeal of torment renewed almost beyond belief, is what we are instructed to see by what this reliable authority says next:

> Vex not his ghost. O, let him pass! He hates him
> That would *upon the rack* of this rough world
> Stretch him out longer. (V, iii, 312)

This in fact is the note sounded throughout the closing scenes. The world can be to mankind, and has been to Lear, a rack: a scene of suffering reiterated past all probability or reason. It can be a place of which Edgar was able to say, at the beginning of Act IV:

> World, world, O world!
> But that thy strange mutations make us hate thee,
> Life would not yield to age. (IV, i, 10)

Later, only a few moments before the play closes, he goes on from the account of his father's death to hint plainly at the coming death of Kent:

> *Edmund.* ...but speak you on;
> You look as you had something more to say.
> *Albany.* If there be more, more woeful, hold it in;
> For I am almost ready to dissolve,
> Hearing of this.
> *Edgar.* This would have seem'd a period
> To such as love not sorrow; but another,

[8] R. W. Chambers, *King Lear* (W. P. Ker Lecture: 1940), p. 44.

> To amplify too much, would make much more,
> And *top extremity.*
> While I was big in clamour, came there in a man...
> ...His grief grew puissant, and the strings of life
> Began to crack.

This is to underline once more the idiom of the play's later movement, its reiteration of suffering, to "top extremely," when it seems that suffering must surely be over.

At this stage in the discussion, one must try to record the note upon which *King Lear* is resolved. It is not easy to do so, and it is less easy than more than one distinguished critic has allowed. One interpretation, certainly, has attracted many readers. We may frame it, with Professor Chambers, as "the victory of Cordelia and of Love"; or with Professor Knights, as the "complete endorsement of love as a quality of being," or with Professor Wilson Knight, as "the primary persons, good and bad, die into love."[9] It is better to see the play thus, than to regard its close as the embodiment only of cynicism, chaos and despair. But one should remind oneself at this point of what, surely, is familiar knowledge: that love (unless that word is taken, as I fear it is often taken, to mean every good thing) is a value with a great but finite place in human life; and that if it is a full description of the affirmation on which the play closes, that affirmation is a limited one; is, indeed, curiously inadequate, curiously out of scale with the range, power and variety of the issues of life on which this incomparable work has touched. Those for whom the word "love" is a talisman will find this suggestion objectionable. That may be an argument in its favour.

With these considerations in mind, one may incline to see the close of *Lear* in another light. The survivors of Cleopatra, say, and of Brutus and Coriolanus, indeed speak as though these characters enjoyed a kind of victory or triumph even in death. When, at the close of *Lear,* Shakespeare characteristically gives those who survive the protagonist lines which suggest what the audience is to see in his end, it is not to any victory or triumph, through love or anything else, that he makes them direct our attention. He causes them to agree that there has never been such a case of a man stretched out on the rack of the world, and released at last. At the close of *Macbeth* there is much emphasis on a movement of regeneration, a restoration of good at the level of the body politic. Lear ends more sombrely. "Our present business...is general woe," says Albany, appealing to Kent and Edgar for nothing more optimistic than to help him rule and "the *gor'd* state *sustain*" —the modest ambition of that last word should not be missed. The last speech of all, that of Edgar, seems peculiarly significant, for all its bald rhyming:

---

[9] R. W. Chambers, *King Lear,* p. 43; L. C. Knights, *Some Shakespearean Themes,* p. 118; *The Wheel of Fire,* p. 206.

> The weight of this sad time we must obey:
> *Speak what we feel, not what we ought to say,*
> The oldest hath borne most; *we that are young*
> *Shall never see so much nor live so long.*

The ordeal has been unique in its protraction of torment, and the note is surely one of refusal to hide that from oneself, refusal to allow the terrible potentialities of life which the action has revealed to be concealed once more behind the veil of orthodoxy and the order of Nature. If there is such an order, it is an order which can accommodate seemingly limitless chaos and evil. The play is a confrontation of that, a refusal to avert one's gaze from that. Its affirmation is as exalted, humane and life-affirming as affirmation can be, for it lies in a noble and unflinching steadiness, where flinching seems inevitable, in the insight of its creator.

To turn to a more intimate awareness of the personal bonds on which the play closes is to extend and amplify this, and still to see something other than what deserves the name of "love" *tout court*. Perhaps there is a clue in the fact that it is Edmund ("Yet Edmund was beloved," [V, iii, 239]) and only Edmund, who speaks of love by itself. We are meant, of course, to see it as embodied always in what Cordelia does; but in her sole reference to this in the later scenes of the play, what she at once goes on to speak of is not her love but, in effect, her duty:

> No blown ambition does both our arms incite,
> But love, dear love, *and our ag'd father's right.* (IV, iv, 26)

This stress, not on loving alone, but on doing and being what it falls to one to do and be, is so insistent that its having been left unregarded is surprising. Cordelia's first speech of any substance to the re-awakened Lear confirms its relevance for both her and him:

> O look upon me, sir,
> And hold your hands in benediction o'er me.
> No, sir, you must not kneel. (IV, vii, 57)

What she wants is for him to do what it is a father's duty to do: not what it is *her* duty to do in return. The same kind of thought is prominent in Lear's first speech after capture:

> When thou dost ask me blessing, I'll kneel down,
> And ask of thee forgiveness. (V, iii, 10)

Each of them is to do what (paradoxically, in Lear's case) it is appropriate for them to do: The idea is of service and duteousness, not love in any simple or emotional sense. In just this light, too, are we invited to see Edgar's bond with his father:

*Albany*. How have you known the miseries of your father?
*Edgar*. By nursing them, my Lord...
...became his guide,
Led him, begg'd for him, sav'd him from despair;
Never—O fault!—reveal'd myself unto him
Until some half-hour past, when I was arm'd;
Not sure, though hoping, of this good success,
I asked his blessing, and from first to last
Told him my pilgrimage. (V, iii, 180–96)

Kent's devotion to Lear is of course one in which feeling means service:

I am the very man...
That from your first of difference and decay
Have followed your sad steps. (V, iii, 285)

I have a journey, sir, shortly to go.
My master calls me; I must not say no. (V, iii, 321)

The bond which remains, at the play's close, among the other (or perhaps only) survivors, is of the same kind:

*Albany*. ...Friends of my soul, you twain
Rule in this realm, and the gor'd state sustain. (V, vii, 319)

With these many pointers in mind, perhaps the final import of the reconciliation of Lear to Cordelia, or Gloucester to Edgar, may also be seen as meaning more than the word "love" can easily mean, at least in our own time; and as being, in the end, one with the whole of what happens at the close of the drama. That the closing phase is one in which the evil in the play proves self-destructive, is well known. Evil has come, it has taken possession of the world of the play, it has brought men below the level of the beasts, it has destroyed itself, and it has passed. Good (I have argued) is far from enjoying a triumphant restoration: we are left with the spectacle of how suffering can renew itself unremittingly until the very moment of death.

If, at the close, some note less despairing than this may be heard, it comes through our apprehending that in an austere and minimal sense, Edmund's words "the wheel has come full circle" extend, despite everything, beyond himself. Below the spectacle of suffering everywhere in possession, is another, inconspicuous but genuine: that the forces of life have been persistently terrible and cruel, but have also brought men back to do the things it is their part to do. Union with Cordelia barely proves Lear's salvation: his salvation is what Kent says, release from a life of torment. But that union is the thing to which he rightly belongs. He deviated from it, and life itself brought him back. So with Gloucester. To follow the master, to sustain the state, to bless one's child, to succour the aged and one's parents—this idea of being brought back to rectitude is what the play ends with. These are the things which it falls to living men to do; and if the play advances a "positive," I think it is that when men turn away from how they should live, there are forces in life which constrain them to return. In this play, love is not a "victory"; it is not that which stands at "the centre of the action," and without which "life is meaningless"; it does not rule creation. If anything rules creation, it is (though only, as it were, by a hairsbreadth) simply rule itself. What order restores, is order. Men tangle their lives; life, at a price, is self-untangling at last.

In view of these things, how fantastic it would be to call *King Lear* a play of intrigue! Yet this idea, immediate though its rejection must be, does indeed suggest the many things going on, and being intricately fitted together, which mark the closing scenes of the play. This very fact is what leads back from the attitudes of the play to what is more intimate with its substance, and with the experience which it offers to us in its sequence. The war with France, the intrigue between Edmund and the sisters, the emergence of Albany, Edmund's plot with the captain and his duel with Edgar, densen into a medium of something like quotidian life, through which and beyond which Lear's own situation stands out in isolation. It is the very variety in the strands of life which brings out how, at the end, life as it were stands back from Lear; and affords him a remoteness, a separation from his fellows, in which his ordeal is completed.

This is the culmination, moreover, of how he begins. As in the tragedies which have been discussed already, at the outset the protagonist is at the focal point of all men's regard. But Lear's progressive isolation does not steal upon him, or his audience, unawares. Relinquishing the kingdom, repudiating Cordelia, banishing Kent, cursing Goneril (I, iv, 275–289), departing wrathfully from Regan:

> He calls to horse, and will I know not whither... (II, iv, 296)

—all these actions set Lear, of his own free will, apart from his fellows; and are the prelude to how he sets himself apart, first from human contact of any kind whatsoever:

> No, rather I abjure all roofs, and choose
> To wage against the enmity o' th' air... (II, iv, 207)

and then from the whole of Nature:

> This night, wherein the cub-drawn bear would crouch,
> The lion, and the belly-pinched wolf
> Keep their fur dry, unbonneted he runs,
> And *bids what will take all.* (III, i, 12)

Yet Lear's position is ambiguous. In his first speech on the heath he is not only the almost satanic enemy of Nature, cursing it in its entirety but also its victim.

> Strike flat the thick rotundity o' th' world
> Crack nature's moulds, all germens spill at once,
> That make ingrateful man. . . . (III, ii, 7)

is followed almost at once by:

> . . .Here I stand, your slave,
> A poor, infirm, weak and despis'd old man.

If the tenor of the first passage is unmistakably like that of Macbeth's giant defiance ("though the treasure/Of nature's germens tumble all together/ Even till destruction sicken—answer me/To what I ask you. . ."), the second has its counterpart in *Macbeth* as well. Macbeth's "They have tied me to a stake; I cannot fly" has its closest parallel, indeed, in Gloucester's "I am tied to the stake, and I must stand the course" (III, vii, 53); but if Gloucester is like Macbeth in that his fate is more of an execution than anything else, so is Lear. Kent's thought of him on the rack is a variant of his own

> I am bound
> Upon a wheel of fire, that mine own tears
> Do scald like molten lead. (IV, vii, 46)

The parallel with Macbeth is a strange and clear one; and the full currency in Shakespeare's own mind of the image through which we see the king in the later part of the play must be brought to attention and life. Today, the direction "enter Lear, fantastically dressed with weeds" can easily seem mere fantasy without a background, or have merely some kind of enrichment in generalized associations with fertility and its converse. For Shakespeare, Lear's status in this scene must have been much more exact and significant. The figure

> Crown'd with rank fumiter and furrow weeds,
> With hardocks, hemlock, nettles, cuckoo-flow'rs,
> Darnel and all the idle weeds that grow
> In our sustaining corn. . . (IV, iv, 3)

whose first words are "I am the King himself," who jests and preaches (IV, vi, 181), who is filled with a conviction that he is soon to be killed ("I will die bravely, like a smug bridegroom," [IV, vi, 200]; "If you have poison for me, I will drink it," [IV, vii, 72]), who can say: "Nay, an you get it, you shall get it by running," and run away dressed in his flowers and pursued by the attendants;—this figure is easily recognizable. He is a Jack-a-Green, at once hero and victim of a popular ceremony. For a moment, he is a hunted man literally, as he is in spirit throughout the play. Nor is such a level of interest in any way out of place for Lear. There is much of the quality of folk thinking or acting, of the folk-tale, about his whole career. This shows in the stylized opening scene, in the formality and symmetry of his break with the three sisters, in his mock court in the outhouse and in this Jack-a-Green spectacle, right through to his final entry,—which cannot but call up the legendary "Come not between the dragon and his wrath" of the opening tableau, and in which Lear and Cordelia must appear not as king and princess, but, beyond normal life, as emblems of the extremes of what is possible in life.

Over the four plays which have been discussed so far there seems by now to emerge, with increasing clarity, a repeated and recognizable pattern. In *Lear* it is surely inescapable. Despite the rich detail and realism of this play, the action and the staging are stylized largely throughout. The protagonist (followed, less fully but in some ways more plainly, by Gloucester) pursues a well-marked rôle. He is the man who begins as centre of his whole world, but who is progressively set, both by the other characters and by himself, apart from it and against it. "Against" means above, in solitary defiance, and below, in an ordeal of protracted suffering which takes on the quality of a hunt. His response to this may indeed be a growing awareness and comprehension of where he stands; but if this makes the onward movement of the action profounder and more impressive, it in no way retards or re-directs it; and its end is a death which, though realistically the outcome of the human situation of the play, has at the same time the quality of stylized and ritual execution. All is foreseen, nothing can be delayed or hastened or mitigated. We are led, in fact, to envisage a new metaphor for the status of the tragic rôle in these plays; to see running through the work, besides its other interests, its detailed representation of life, its flow of ideas, its sense of good and evil, something which might be called the vertebrate structure of its intrinsic design; the developing line, unabridged, of a human sacrifice.

# 33

# *Macbeth* as the Imitation of an Action

*Francis Fergusson*

I propose to attempt to illustrate the view that *Macbeth* may be understood as "the imitation of an action," in approximately Aristotle's sense of this phrase.

The word "action"—*praxis*—as Aristotle uses it in the *Poetics,* does not mean outward deeds or events, but something much more like "purpose" or "aim." Perhaps our word "motive" suggests most of its meaning. Dante (who in this respect is a sophisticated Aristotelian) uses the phrase *moto spirital,* spiritual movement, to indicate praxis. In Aristotle's own writings *praxis* is usually rational, a movement of the will in the light of the mind. But Dante's *moto spirital* refers to all modes of the spirit's life, all of its directions, or focuses, or motives, including those of childhood, dream, drunkenness, or passion, which are hardly rationalized at all. When using Aristotle's definition for the analysis of modern drama it is necessary to generalize his notion of action in this way, to include movements of the spirit in response to sensuous or emotionally charged images, as well as

"Macbeth *as the Imitation of an Action" by Francis Fergusson.* English Institute Essays, 1951 *(New York: Columbia University Press, 1952).* 

consciously willed purpose. But this seems to me a legitimate extension of the basic concept; and I do not think it does real violence to Aristotle's meaning.

Aristotle in his *Psychology* and his *Ethics,* as well as in the *Poetics,* and Dante, in the *Divine Comedy,* seem to imagine the psyche much as an amoeba looks under the microscope: moving toward what attracts it, continually changing direction or aim, and taking its shape and color from the object to which it is attached at the moment. This movement is "action"; and so we see that while the psyche is alive it always has action; and that this changing action in pursuit of real or imagined objects defines its mode of being moment by moment.

When Aristotle says that a tragedy is the imitation of an action, he is thinking of an action, or motive, which governs the psyche's life for a considerable length of time. Such an action is the quest for Laius's slayer in *Oedipus Rex,* which persists through the changing circumstances of the play. In this period of time, it has a beginning, a middle, and an end, which comes when the slayer is at last identified.

I remarked that action is not outward deeds or events; but on the other hand, there can be no action without resulting deeds. We guess at a man's action by way of what he does, his outward and visible deeds. We are aware that our own action, or motive, produces deeds of some sort as soon as it exists. Now the plot of a play is the arrangement of outward deeds or incidents, and the dramatist uses it, as Aristotle tells us, as the first means of imitating the action. He arranges a set of incidents which point to the action or motive from which they spring. You may say that the action is the spiritual content of the tragedy—the playwright's inspiration—and the plot defines its existence as an intelligible *play*. Thus, you cannot have a play without both plot and action; yet the distinction between plot and action is as fundamental as that between form and matter. The action is the matter; the plot is the "first form," or, as Aristotle puts it, the "soul," of the tragedy.

The dramatist imitates the action he has in mind, first by means of the plot, then in the characters, and finally in the media of language, music, and spectacle. In a well-written play, if we understood it thoroughly, we should perceive that plot, character, and diction, and the rest spring from the same source, or, in other words, realize the same action or motive in the forms appropriate to their various media.

You will notice that this is a diagrammatic description of the perfect play, perfectly understood. Therefore one cannot hope to illustrate it perfectly, even in the case of a play like *Macbeth. Macbeth,* however, does impress most of its readers as having a powerful and unmistakable unity of this kind: the plot, characters, and imagery all seem to spring from the one inspiration. It is that strong and immediately felt unity which I rely on—and upon your familiarity with the play. Not that I am so foolish as to suppose I grasp the play completely or that I could persuade you of my view of it in these few minutes. All I can attempt is to suggest the single action which seems to me to be the spiritual content of the play, and illustrate it, in only a few of its metaphors, plot devices, and characterizations.

The action of the play as a whole is best expressed in a phrase which Macbeth himself uses in Act II, scene iii, the aftermath of the murder. Macbeth is trying to appear innocent, but everything he says betrays his clear sense of his own evil motivation, or action. Trying to excuse his murder of Duncan's grooms, he says,

> The expedition of my violent love [for Duncan, he means]
> Outran the pauser, reason.

It is the phrase "to outrun the pauser, reason," which seems to me to describe the action, or motive, of the play as a whole. Macbeth, of course, literally means that his love for Duncan was so strong and swift that it got ahead of his reason, which would have counseled a pause. But in the same way we have seen his greed and ambition outrun his reason when he committed the murder; and in the same way all of the characters, in the irrational darkness of Scotland's evil hour, are compelled in their action to strive beyond what they can see by reason alone. Even Malcolm and Macduff, as we shall see, are compelled to go beyond reason in the action which destroys Macbeth and ends the play.

But let me consider the phrase itself for a moment. To "outrun" reason suggests an impossible stunt, like lifting oneself by one's own bootstraps. It also suggests a competition or race, like those of nightmare, which cannot be won. As for the word "reason," Shakespeare associates it with nature and nature's order, in the individual soul, in society, and in the cosmos. To outrun reason is thus to violate nature itself, to lose the bearings of common sense and of custom, and to move into a spiritual realm bounded by the irrational darkness of Hell one way, and the superrational grace of faith the other way. As the play develops before us, all the modes of this absurd, or evil, or supernatural, action are attempted, the last being Malcolm's and Macduff's acts of faith.

In the first part of the play Shakespeare, as is his custom, gives us the intimate feel of this paradoxical striving beyond reason in a series of echoing tropes and images. I remind you of some of them, as follows.

From the first Witches' scene:

> When the battle's lost and won. . . .
> Fair is foul and foul is fair.

From the "bleeding-sergeant" scene:

Doubtful it stood;
As two spent swimmers that do cling together
And choke their art. . . .
So from that spring whence comfort seem'd to come
Discomfort swells. . . .
Confronted him with self-comparisons
Point against point rebellious, arm 'gainst arm. . . .
What he hath lost noble Macbeth hath won.

From the second Witches' scene:

So fair and foul a day. . . .
Lesser than Macbeth, and greater.
His wonders and his praises do contend
Which should be thine or his. . . .
This supernatural soliciting
Cannot be ill, cannot be good. . . .
. . . nothing is
But what is not.

These are only a few of the figures which suggest the desperate and paradoxical struggle. They are, of course, not identical with each other or with outrunning reason, which seems to me the most general of all. But they all point to the "action" I mean, and I present them as examples of the imitation of action by means of the arts of language.

But notice that though these images themselves suggest the action, they also confirm the actions of the characters as these are shown in the story. The bleeding sergeant, for instance, is striving beyond reason and nature in his effort to report the battle—itself a bewildering mixture of victory and defeat—in spite of his wounds. Even the old King Duncan, mild though he is, is caught in the race and sees his relation to Macbeth competitively. "Thou art so far before," he tells Macbeth in the next scene, "That swiftest wing of recompense is slow/To overtake thee." He then races Macbeth to his castle, whither the Messenger has outrun them both; and when he arrives, he is at once involved in a hollow competition with Lady Macbeth, to outdo her in ceremony.

I do not need to remind you of the great scenes preceding the murder, in which Macbeth and his Lady pull themselves together for their desperate effort. If you think over these scenes, you will notice that the Macbeths understand the action which begins here as a competition and a stunt, against reason and nature. Lady Macbeth fears her husband's human nature, as well as her own female nature, and therefore she fears the light of reason and the common daylight world. As for Macbeth, he knows from the first that he is engaged in an irrational stunt: "I have no spur/To prick the sides of my intent, but only/Vaulting ambition, which o'erleaps itself/And falls on the other." In this sequence there is also the theme of outwitting or transcending time, an aspect of nature's order as we know it: catching up the consequences, jumping the life to come, and the like. But this must suffice to remind you of the Macbeths' actions, which they paradoxically understand so well.

The Porter scene has been less thoroughly studied as a variation on the play's main action. But it is, in fact, a farcical and terrible version of "outrunning reason," a witty and very concentrated epitome of this absurd movement of spirit. The Porter first teases the knockers at the gate with a set of paradoxes, all of which present attempts to outrun reason; and he sees them all as ways into Hell. Henry N. Paul* has explained the contemporary reference: The farmer who hanged himself on the expectation of plenty, the equivocator who swore both ways to commit treason for God's sake. When the Porter has admitted the knockers he ironically offers them lewd physical analogies for outrunning reason: drink as tempting lechery into a hopeless action; himself as wrestling with drink. The relation of the Porter to the knockers is like that of the Witches to Macbeth—he tempts them into Hell with ambiguities. And the inebriation of drink and lust, lewd and laughable as it is, is closely analogous to the more terrible and spiritual intoxication of the Macbeths.

Thus, in the first part of the play both the imagery and the actions of the various characters indicate or "imitate" the main action. Aristotle says the characters are imitated "with a view to the action," and the Porter—who has little importance in the story—is presented to reveal the action of the play as a whole in the unexpected light of farcical analogies, contemporary or lewd and physical.

Before I leave this part of the play I wish to point out that the plot itself—"the arrangement or synthesis of the incidents"—also imitates a desperate race. This is partly a matter of the speed with which the main facts are presented, partly the effect of simultaneous movements like those of a race: Lady Macbeth is reading the letter at the same moment that her husband and Duncan are rushing toward her. And the facts in this part of the play are ambiguous in meaning and even as facts.

These few illustrations must serve to indicate how I understand the imitation of action in language, character, and plot in the first two acts of the play. Macbeth and his Lady are embarked on a race against reason itself; and all Scotland, the "many" whose lives depend upon the monarch, is precipitated into the same darkness and desperate strife. Shakespeare's monarchs do usually color the spiritual life of their realms. And we, who

---

* See *The Royal Play of Macbeth,* Macmillan, 1950.

remember Hitlerite Germany, can understand that, I think. Even Hitler's exiles, like the refugees from Russian or Spanish tyranny, brought the shadow to this country with them.

I now wish to consider the action of the play at a later stage, in Act IV, scene iii. This is the moment which I mentioned before, the beginning of Malcolm's and Macduff's act of faith, which will constitute the final variation on "outrunning reason." The scene is laid in England, whither Malcolm and Macduff have fled, and it immediately follows the murder of Macduff's wife and child. Like the exiles we have known in this country, Macduff and Malcolm, though in England, have brought Scotland's darkness with them. They have lost all faith in reason, human nature, and common sense, and can therefore trust neither themselves nor each other. They are met in the hope of forming an alliance, in order to get rid of Macbeth; and yet under his shadow everything they do seems unreasonable, paradoxical, improbable.

In the first part of the scene, you remember, Malcolm and Macduff fail to find any basis for mutual trust. Malcolm mistrusts Macduff because he has left his wife and child behind; Macduff quickly learns to mistrust Malcolm, because he first protests that he is unworthy of the crown, to test Macduff, and then suddenly reverses himself. The whole exchange is a tissue of falsity and paradox, and it ends in a sort of nightmarish paralysis.

At this point there is the brief interlude with the Doctor. The king's evil and its cure and the graces which hang about the English throne are briefly described. Paul points out that this interlude may have been introduced to flatter James I; but however that may be, it is appropriate in the build of the scene as a whole. It marks the turning point, and it introduces the notion of the appeal by faith to Divine Grace which will reverse the evil course of the action when Malcolm and Macduff learn to outrun reason in that way, instead of by responding to the Witches' supernatural solicitations as Macbeth has done. Moreover, the Doctor in this scene, in whom religious and medical healing are associated, foreshadows the Doctor who will note Lady Macbeth's sleepwalking and describe it as a perturbation in nature which requires a cure beyond nature.

But to return to the scene. After the Doctor's interlude, Ross joins Malcolm and Macduff, bringing the latest news from Scotland. To greet him, Malcolm clearly states the action, or motive, of the scene as a whole: "Good God, betimes remove/Th means that makes us strangers!" he says. Ross's chief news is, of course, Lady Macduff's murder. When he has gradually revealed that, and Macduff and Malcolm have taken it in, accepting some of the guilt, they find that the means that made them strangers has in fact been removed. They recognize themselves and each other once more, in a sober, but not nightmarish, light. And at once they join in faith in their cause and prepare to hazard all upon the ordeal of battle, itself an appeal beyond reason. The scene, which is its opening sections moved very slowly, reflecting the demoralization of Malcolm and Macduff, ends hopefully, with brisk rhythms of speech which prepare the marching scenes to follow.

> This tune goes manly. . . .
> Receive what cheer you may:
> The night is long that never finds the day.

The whole scene is often omitted or drastically cut in production, and many critics have objected to it. They complain of its slowness, of the baroque overelaboration of Malcolm's protests, and of the fact that it is too long for what it tells us about the story. All we learn is that Malcolm and Macduff are joining the English army to attack Macbeth, and this information could have been conveyed much more quickly. In the first part of the play, and again after this scene, everything moves with the speed of a race; and one is tempted to say, at first, that in this scene Shakespeare lost the rhythm of his own play.

Now, one of the reasons I chose this scene to discuss is that it shows, as does the Porter scene, the necessity of distinguishing between plot and action. One cannot understand the function of the scene in the whole plot unless one remembers that the plot itself is there to imitate the action. It is then clear that this scene is the peripeteia, which is brought about by a series of recognitions. It starts with Malcolm and Macduff blind and impotent in Macbeth's shadow and ends when they have gradually learned to recognize themselves and each other even in that situation. "Outrunning reason" looks purely evil in the beginning, and at the end we see how it may be good, an act of faith beyond reason. The scene moves slowly at first because Shakespeare is imitating the action of groping in an atmosphere of the false and unnatural; yet we are aware all the while of continuing speed offstage, where

> each new morn
> New widows howl, new orphans cry, new sorrows
> Strike heaven on the face. . . .

The scene is thus (within the rhythmic scheme of the whole play) like a slow eddy on the edge of a swift current. After this turning, or peripeteia, the actions of Malcolm and Macduff join the rush of the main race, to win. I admit that these effects might be hard to achieve in production, but I believe that good actors could do it.

Shakespeare's tragedies usually have a peripeteia in the fourth act, with scenes of suffering and prophetic or symbolic recognitions and epiphanies. In the fourth act of *Macbeth* the Witches' scene reveals the coming end of the action in symbolic shows; and this scene also, in another way, foretells the end. The last act, then, merely presents the literal facts, the windup of the plot, long felt as inevitable in principle. The fifth act of *Macbeth* shows the expected triumph of Malcolm's and Macduff's super-rational faith. The wood does move; Macbeth does meet a man unborn of woman; and the paradoxical race against reason reaches its paradoxical end. The nightmare of Macbeth's evil version of the action is dissolved, and we are free to return to the familiar world, where reason, nature, and common sense still have their validity.

To sum up: My thesis is that *Macbeth* is the imitation of an action (or motive) which may be indicated by the phrase "to outrun the pauser, reason." I have tried to suggest how this action is presented in the metaphors, characters, and plot of the first two acts; and also in the peripeteia, with pathos and recognitions, the great scene between Malcolm, Macduff, and Ross.

I am painfully aware that these few illustrations are not enough to establish my thesis. Only a detailed analysis of the whole play might do that—and such an analysis would take hours of reading and discussion. But I think it would show that Aristotle was essentially right. He had never read *Macbeth,* and I suppose if he could he would find Shakespeare's Christian, or post-Christian, vision of evil hard to understand. But he saw that the art of drama is the art of imitating action; and this insight, confirmed and deepened by some of Aristotle's heirs, can still show us how to seek the unity of a play, even one which shows modes of the spirit's life undreamed of by Aristotle himself.

# 34

# *Macbeth:* Tense and Mood

*Francis Berry*

The Form of the Verb of *Macbeth,* that which controls the whole plot, is peculiarly striking. It is, of course, the Future Indicative. But the dominant form of the Verb "in" *Macbeth,* that which animates not the main outlines but the detail of passage, is also significant. It is the Subjunctive. The Verb Form "of" *Macbeth* and the Verb Form "in" *Macbeth* struggle against each other, and from this struggle issues the tragedy. It is the struggle which creates the "action," as distinguished from the mere "plot," of *Macbeth.*

Since the Future Indicative is the Tense expressive of future *facts*—of events, things, conditions which *will be,* the main and auxiliary Verbs here equally stressed—it is the necessary Tense of a plot whose substance is a prophecy made to Macbeth "that shalt be King hereafter" (I, iii, 50), a prophecy later followed by other prophecies.

But the Witches, whose function it is to foretell, and who open the play with a question framed in that Tense ("When shall we three meet

*Reprinted from Francis Berry,* The Poet's Grammar: Person, Time and Mood in Poetry *(London: Routledge & Kegan Paul Ltd., 1958) pp. 48–57 by permission of the publisher.*

again?"), are not the only ones who use the Future Indicative. For Macbeth and Banquo, respectively, echo the Witches' words:

> Your Children shall be Kings.
> You shall be King. (I, iii, 86)

and, in so echoing, lean away from the Present they are in, each following his dread, the other's hope, into the Future. Next, Lady Macbeth, when told of the prophecy by letter, cries:

> Glamys thou art, and Cawdor, and shalt be
> What thou art promis'd. (I, v, 16)

Moreover, she not only wills the Future but she goes ahead out of her time into that Tense, experiencing its sensation, as she says to Macbeth:

> Thy Letters have transported me beyond
> This ignorant present, and I feele now
> The future in the instant. (I, v, 57)

Yet even those ignorant of the prophecy express themselves in the Future. If they do not look forward to coming certainties, they have intentions, and these acts of the will require for their expression this Tense. Thus Duncan:

> I have begun to plant thee, and will labour
> To make thee full of growing. (I, iv, 28)

> We will establish our Estate upon
> Our eldest, *Malcome*... (I, iv, 37)

> ...signes of Nobleness, like Starres, shall shine
> On all deservers. (I, iv, 41)

Indeed, the whole play is Future minded, thus →. Unlike *Hamlet* and *Othello* there are in it no temporal flashbacks, no protracted memories of earlier generations, no narrations of past events, but it purely and avidly pursues a Future, and that is why reader and audience derive from it a sensation of rapidity or hurrying.

But if the Future Indicative drives the play as a whole, there is also that other Verb Form which informs the detail of parts, first and particularly in the Speeches of Macbeth himself. Now the Subjunctive is started into life hard upon the Witches' statement of fact that Macbeth "shalt be King hereafter":

> *Macbeth.* ...Present Feares
> Are lesse than horrible Imaginings:
> My thought, whose Murther yet is but fantasticall,

Shakes so my single state of Man,
That Function is smother'd in surmise,
And nothing is, but what is not. (I, iii, 137)

Here we are not in the indicative world of facts (of what is, has been, or will be) but in the subjunctive realm of *possibilities*—the realm of hopes and dreads; of "if's" and phantasies; of what may be and may not be; of what ought to be and what ought not to be. The Subjunctive is a private realm and so Macbeth speaks "aside," for though we may all have to share the world of fact (is-ness), yet each man's subjunctive realm is his alone. In the lines quoted, Macbeth moves over into that realm denoted, we remember by the *recto* pages, where the Verbs are conjugated, in Kennedy's *Latin Primer*. Now the Subjunctive can be the realm of "horrible Imaginings." The Future Indicative of the Witches precipitates Macbeth—as it does not Lady Macbeth who professes scorn for the Mood—into that realm, and habitation therein eventually destroys him. Not that it was perhaps necessary for him to inhabit it at all, as Macbeth himself suspects, since, after the Witches' statement of a simple future fact, he says:

If Chance will have me King,
Why Chance may Crowne me,
Without my stirre. (I, iii, 143)

Yet the two verbs in these three lines belong to different grammatical Moods.

Now Lady Macbeth well knows her husband's disposition to move into the Subjunctive and so brake the wheels of indicative action. She says of him:

Thou would'st be great,
Art not without Ambition, but without
The illnesse should attend it. What thou would'st highly,
That would'st thou holily: would'st not play false,
And yet would'st wrongly winne.
Thould'st have, great Glamys, that which cryes,
Thus thou must doe, if thou have it;
And that which rather thou do'st feare to doe,
Then wishest should be undone. (I, v, 19)

Here two Indicatives stand out: Macbeth *is* ambitious; he *is* without that immunity from qualms of conscience which an ambitious man, to succeed in his ambitions, *ought* to have. Yet conscience, the umpire which distinguishes between moral "ought's" and "ought-not's" operates in the Subjunctive Mood—where its verdicts may well clash with desires which also belong to that Mood. So when Lady Macbeth says her husband *is* without the immunity from conscience which *should* (i.e. ought to) go with ambition she is being curiously casuistical: an ambitious man *ought* not to be concerned with "ought's" and "ought-not's"; Macbeth *ought,* in this case, to make the Future fact a Present fact through "the neerest way" of indicative action. But, in Macbeth's subjunctive realm, his wishes ("thou *would'st* be great...thou *would'st* highly...*would'st* wrongly winne") clash with moral duty ("That *would'st* thou holily: *would'st* not play false").

Until a deed is done it does not exist in time. Desires and duties timelessly exist in a world of "perpetual possibility,"[1] have speculative actuality only, unless and until they are transferred, by a choice of the will resulting in action, on to those left-hand pages of Kennedy's conjugations. But Macbeth would have the *real* goods without experiencing the responsibility for their conversion from subjunctive desire to indicative fact; desires should "materialize" of their own accord without the consent of his will and without his "stirre." Alternatively:

> The Eye winke at the Hand; yet let that bee,
> Which the Eye feares, when it is done to see. (I, iv, 52)

"Let the deed be done without the consent of my will *or* let it be done without my knowing that I do it." The disintegration of Macbeth's personality, to use the fashionable parlance of psychiatrists, concretely conveyed—as here—in terms of one sense (or organ) functioning in dissociation from another or others has been noticed.[2] But the grammatical structure of this condition should be borne in mind. The imagery means that Macbeth hopes that the *instrumental* organ of indicative action (his hand) should perform in isolation from the organ of perception which must "winke" so that his conscience does not have to sanction the deed of his hand. He must both have his cake and eat it. He must translate subjunctive desire into indicative possession and yet keep himself pure and innocent within his subjunctive realm. This is supported by two other grammatical features. Instead of "when I have done it...etc.," we find "yet let that bee,/Which the Eye feares, *when it is done* to see."[3] By employing the Passive Voice, he escapes from having to say "I." He employs grammatical mechanisms whereby he is enabled to *distance* the murder from himself, to reduce or eschew responsibility for it (*it is done: I* don't do it), and to avoid giving the sin and crime its name. This is psychologically true: when people are in misery they can hardly bear to mumble "I"—their "I" lies low; when people are in moral or legal difficulties they try to shield themselves by using the Passive Voice.

The two main Verb Forms, the determining Future Indicative of the

---

[1] T. S. Eliot, *Burnt Norton.*

[2] See, for example, the introduction by Kenneth Muir to his Arden edition of the play.

[3] Italics, here and elsewhere, unless marked in the Folios, are mine.

plot and the Subjunctive of Macbeth, which threatens to—illogically—prevent that which "shalt be," engage each other in the most strenuous conflict in the famous soliloquy of Macbeth in I, vii, 1–28. We should notice the intense and violent activity of the Verbs in this passage. Even numerically, compared with other Parts of Speech, they are of overwhelming importance. Few, if any, other passages of verse of similar length in English can compare with it in this respect. And these Verbs are significant and exciting because of the variety of their inflexional forms, involving contrasts of Tense, Mood and Voice, for Macbeth is contemplating not only alternative states of being; possibilities of action and inaction, of desire, deed and duty; but also Time, that time or tense which takes control once the transference from Mood to Mood is performed. He begins:

> If it were done, when 'tis done, then 'twere well
> It were done quickly; If th' Assassination
> Could trammell up the Consequence, and catch
> With his surcease, Successe: that but this blow
> Might be the be all, and the end all. Heere,
> But heere, upon this Banke and Schoole of time,
> Wee'ld jumpe the life to come. But in these Cases,
> We still have judgement heere, that we but teach
> Bloody Instructions, which being taught, returne
> To plague th' Inventor. . . . (I, vii, 1)

The opening line and a half of the speech consists of a series of Subjunctive Clauses. Since "the deed," which is still merely possible, for the will must choose before the hand strikes, is being contemplated, each of the verbs in each of these clauses is a variant of the one Verb *to do,* and all these clauses are dependent on a speculative, and therefore subjunctively expressed, state of ease and goodness—"'twere well," itself merely contingent. Apart from the connectives and the temporal Adverb "quickly," the only non-verb component is the Subject common to all the clauses. The Subject, if it were named, would be "the deed" which is to be done; but, still not daring to name, he *pro*-names: The Pronoun "it" is a generalizing substitute for something unmentionable. Further, the series of Verbs of which it is the subject are all in the *Passive* Subjunctive: Macbeth will still distance the possible "thing" from himself and conceal from himself his own *active* agency, pretending that the deed did not require a do-er.

Also there are the curious temporal implications of these and the following lines. In a play which, from the premises of its plot, is Future-driven, Macbeth, especially, is one who cannot *be* in his Present. Though Lady Macbeth "feeles the future in the instant," she does not do so as Macbeth does. He projects himself not only into the Future Indicative (Lady Macbeth, believing the prophecy, does this), but also into the possible, the Future Subjunctive, as the soliloquy shows. In this, like all born worriers, he apprehends a Future deed from a future still more remote. He "ore-leapes." Assuming a possible deed done (so that it has entered the time-stream and become Past action) then results *will* be certain: Duncan's Vertues "*will* pleade like Angels" and "teares *shall* drowne the winde." So he chooses not to do. But he is overborne by Lady Macbeth, and the real and the potential fuse at the moment that Duncan's heart ceases to beat.

Now it would be to miss something, significant and in itself beautiful, if one did not also note the one considerable respite from *Macbeth's* ruling Verb Forms in favour of the Present.

Act I, scene vi has long been praised as "charming" and "idyllic," etc. But has it been observed that it owes much of its peacefulness to the fact that Duncan salutes the Castle in the grace, the felicity of his Present?

> This Castle hath a pleasant seat,
> The ayre nimbly and sweetly recommends it selfe
> Unto our gentle sences.

Thus innocents enjoy themselves—in their own good time. Indeed, this contentment in the moment with what the moment brings extends to Banquo in the same scene:

> This Guest of Summer,
> The Temple-haunting Martlet does approve,
> By his loved Mansionry, that the Heavens breath
> Smells wooingly here. . . .

The "martlets" *are showing* their approval and the air is *being* noticed as fragrant. The sense of relaxation which this scene creates is surely as much owing to the Tense, suspending here the play's furious future-drive, as to the lines' soothing melody or delightful imagery.

In Act III, scene i King Macbeth finds that:

> To be thus, is nothing, but to be safely thus.

Shakespeare is again using three contrasting Forms of one and the same Verb—*to be*. Now, *to be* is a simple Verb: simple in the sense that its conjugation is given primary attention in any elementary Grammar of any language. Yet that whole soliloquy of Macbeth (in III, i), which this line initiates, is an essay in the semantics of the two primary Verbs *to be* and *to have,* on a Present-Future Tense axis. For Macbeth is (King) but is not (King) securely. He *has* a "Crowne" but it *will be* "fruitless"; he has a "Scepter," but it *is* barren, and it *will be* "wrencht" away. Macbeth is still at once both chasing and fearing that Future, fixed in the words with which he re-stated the Witches' prophecy, to Banquo: "Your Children shall be Kings." Having arrived at his goal, Macbeth finds that the goal has moved on further into the Future. "Thou shall get Kings, though thou be none" (I, iii), the Witches had told Banquo. But that prophecy was in *Indicative* terms, and so cannot be prevented. This Macbeth should know when he summons "Fate into the Lyst." As a worrier, he is still knocking about in times other than his own, but now in a different kind of time than in I, vii, partly because what was then possible and Subjunctive has *been* enacted, has come into the order of time and is now Past. Moreover, since the Subjunctive counsel of "ought's" and "ought-not's" was neglected, when Macbeth murdered Duncan, this Mood no longer exists for him. Macbeth is, as he tells us, damned. Damnation is a state where the Subjunctive does not exist. So, from Act III, scene i onwards, the Present-Future time-swaying is different, and vainer. Macbeth would, but cannot, prevent a prophecy. His own time-scale of living has altered so much that the only policy left is "hurry and try to overtake"—a sort of vain pursuit, half-known to be vain. He will lean forwards into time to try to snip, at some point, the linked navel cords leading from Banquo to a Future Indicative King of Scotland. But he is made to know final failure when the Witches show him the seed of Banquo, stretching—as Kings—"out to th' Cracke of Doome" (IV, i). Yet he will still try.

So from this Act III, scene i the Poetic-Dramatic Grammar of Time changes rapidly in *Macbeth*. It is a case of the Past catching up with him in league with a Future foreclosing upon him, as the detailed rendering of Tense in the verse shows. Chased by the Past, he *will* attempt to move more quickly than the Future, as in:

> Time, thou anticipat'st my dread exploits:
> The flighty purpose never is o're-tooke
> Unlesse the deed go with it. From this moment,
> The very firstlings of my heart shall be
> The firstlings of my hand. And even now
> To Crown my thoughts with Acts: be it thought and done:
> The Castle of Macduff, I will surprise. (IV, i, 144)

But he cannot succeed, and meanwhile the *overtaking* forces have gathered and pursue.

The Play-Tense and Mood of *Macbeth,* considered as a whole, is that of → or Future/. The → represents the drive from a discounted Present. It is not only Macbeth and Lady Macbeth who discount the Present. Duncan also, as we have seen, is full of "intentions." Banquo, to whom has been said "your Children shall be Kings," is also forward-looking. So is the orphaned Malcolm. So is the widowed and childless man, Macduff. He has a revenge to undertake and a revenge is a future-looking action; for a *revenger* is certainly one who discounts the Present in the expectancy of an end or satisfaction. Finally, and they are most important in serving the

→, in terms of the plot which they thrust, are the Witches, who are "Jugling Fiends"

> That keepe the word of promise to our eare,
> And breake it to our hope. (V, viii, 21)

Which leads us to the bar:/in our formula. The explanation of the bar lies in the two lines just quoted. It is the bar / which makes this play, and much in life, tragic. The Witches prophesy and promise, and Macbeth leans forward in mind to greet in hope more than they verily promise. Macbeth, in hoping for more than is promised, security of tenure and succession by his own line, is irrational; but then hope, from its definition and nature, is irrational.

The hope is broken, not so much because the "Jugling Fiends" "palter...in a double sence," but because they are literal-minded, utter only the literal truth, give literal prophecies which are indicatively fulfilled. The wood of Birnam *does* come to Dunsinane. Before that, Macbeth *has* become King and, in the future, Banquo's descendants *will* become Kings. The tragedy issued from Macbeth for believing in more than the literal.

The "more" he believed in, Shakespeare says, was the "more" of hope. Hope is not the "will be" of the Indicative, but a "may be," or a "might be," sustained in faith until a target-date is reached, or protracted even beyond that, depending on the temper of him who hopes. If the hope is broken in time—elapse of time is needed for defeat, as for fulfilment of hope—then it becomes a "might have been." The Grammatical Mood for the spiritual condition of hope is therefore the Subjunctive. The bar in our Tense formula for *Macbeth* is the simple block of the Indicative fact: namely, Banquo's children "will be Kings." Macbeth, witnessing the show put on for him of the crowned seed of Banquo stretching out in temporal recession to the "Cracke of Doome," sees what indicatively *will be* as an *is*. That is the extreme torment, but the play is a tragedy. The Subjunctive of hope in Macbeth can never become "realized" or Indicative. The cheque always turns out to be post-dated.

After the banquet scene he is "bent to know/By the worst means the worst" (III, iv, 134), but the new knowledge culminated in that "horrible sight" of Banquo's descendants stretching out into a Futurity only limited by doomsday. Yet Macbeth will still try to circumvent the certain facts of a Future although the attempt must necessarily fail. This is paradoxical but so it is. The results also involve a temporal paradox best appreciated at a stage-performance: Birnam wood marches against him at Dunsinane where Macbeth is overtaken by the Future, before he can pre-vent it.

What creates the peculiar → Future /, or Arrow to Future Bar, Play-Tense of *Macbeth*? And by Play-Tense we mean, as we hope will now be apparent, something other than either the time the work takes to act or read, or some time-table of events (e.g. "Act II takes place in the early hours of the following day") on the pattern of P. A. Daniel. All the elements combine to create it, but we especially point to (1) elements in the verse itself, particularly the exceptional frequency of occurrence of the Future Indicative and (2) the plot, or dramatic aspect, which rests on prophecy. Yet verse and plot are not really separable at all. For instance, the line "All haile Macbeth, that *shalt be* King hereafter" is clearly an example of both (1) and (2), and the "hereafter" indicates that temporal qualification, capable of infinite postponement, which signalizes that /, or bar, of the tragedy.

# 35

# *Coriolanus*—and the Delights of Faction

*Kenneth Burke*

## I

This chapter is to involve one of my experiments with the safest and surest kind of prophecy; namely: prophecy after the event. Our job will be to ask how Shakespeare's grotesque tragedy, *Coriolanus,* "ought to be." And we can check on the correctness of our prophecies by consulting the text.

We begin with these assumptions: Since the work is a tragedy, it will require some kind of symbolic action in which some notable form of victimage is imitated, for the purgation, or edification of an audience. The character that is to be sacrificed must be fit for his role as victim; and everything must so fit together that the audience will find the sacrifice plausible and acceptable (thereby furtively participating in the judgment against the victim, and thus even willing the victimage). The expectations and desires of the audience will be shaped by conditions within the play. But the topics exploited for persuasive purposes *within* the play will also have strategic

*Reprinted from "Language as Symbolic Action," originally published in* Hudson Review, *XIX, No. 2 (Summer 1966), by permission of the University of California Press.*

relevance to kinds of "values" and "tensions" that prevail *outside* the play.

There is a benign perversity operating here. In one sense, the aesthetic and the ethical coincide, since a way of life gives rise to a moral code, and the dramatist can exploit this moral code for poetic effects by building up characters that variously exemplify the system of vices and virtues to which the code explicitly or implicitly subscribes. But in another sense the aesthetic and the ethical are at odds, since the dramatist can transform our moral problems into sources of poetic entertainment. Any ethical "thou shalt not" sets up the conditions for an author to engage an audience by depicting characters that variously violate or threaten to violate the "thou shalt not." And many motivational conflicts that might distress us in real life can be transformed into kinds of poetic imitation that engross us. Thus in the realm of the aesthetic we may be delighted by accounts of distress and corruption that would make the moralist quite miserable.

The moral problem, or social tension, that is here to be exploited for the production of the "tragic pleasure" is purely and simply a kind of discord intrinsic to the distinction between upper classes and lower classes. However, a certain "distance" could be got in Shakespeare's day by treating the problem in terms not of contemporary London but of ancient Rome. A somewhat analogous situation is to be seen in Euripides' tragedy of *The Trojan Women,* which appeared some months after the Athenians had destroyed the little island of Melos, though on its face the play was concerned with the Trojan war, the theme of *The Iliad.* When *Coriolanus* appeared there had been considerable rioting due to the Enclosure Acts by which many tenants had been dispossessed of their traditional rights to the land, and were suffering great hardships. Both of these plays may, in their way, have gained strictly contemporary relevance from the allusive exploiting of a "timely topic." But in any case, each was dealing with a distress of much longer duration, in Euripides' case the horrors of war, and in Shakespeare's case the *malaise* of the conflict between the privileged and the underprivileged, as stated in terms of a struggle between the patricians and plebeians of old Rome.

If we are going to "dramatize" such a tension, we shall want first of all a kind of character who in some way helps *intensify* the tension. Where there are any marked differences in social status, in the situation itself there is a kind of "built-in pride," no matter how carefully one might try to mitigate such contrasts. And despite polite attempts to gloss things over, the unresolved situation is intrinsically there. By the nature of the case, it involves *exclusions*.

But for our purposes the main consideration is this: Whereas a hostess, or a diplomat, or an ingratiating politician, or a public relations counsel might go as far as possible towards *toning down* such situations, the dramatist must work his cures by a quite different method. He must find ways to *play them up*. In some respects, therefore, this play will require a kind of character who is designed to help aggravate the uneasiness of the relationship between nobles and commoners.

For this aspect of his role, our chosen victim is obviously a perfect fit. In contrast with the suave Menenius, who has been addressing the mutinous citizens with such a cautious mixture of gravity and humor, our chosen victim's first words to the people are: "What's the matter, you dissentious rogues, / That, rubbing the poor itch of your opinion, / Make yourselves scabs?" Thereafter, again and again, his gruff (or if you will, arrogant) manner of speaking is designed to point up (for the audience) the conflict intrinsic to the class distinctions with which the play is "drastically" concerned. (It's well to recall here that, in earlier medical usage, a "drastic" was the name for the strongest kind of "cathartic." Also, the word derives etymologically from the same root as "drama.")

The Greek word *hubris* sometimes translates best as "pride," sometimes as "excess." And in Athenian law *hubris* was also used to designate a civil offense, an insulting air of superiority, deemed punishable by death. When you note how neatly all three meanings come together in the role of Coriolanus, I think you will realize at least one reason why I find the play so fascinating. The grotesque hero is *excessively* downright, forthright, outright (and even, after his fashion, upright), in his unquestioned assumption that the common people are intrinsically inferior to the nobility. Indeed, though the word "noble" suggests to most of us *either* moral *or* social connotations, Coriolanus takes it for granted that only the *socially* noble can have nobility of any sort. (The word appears about seventy-six times in the play. In half of these contexts it is applied to Coriolanus himself. And, to my knowledge, it is never used ironically, as with Mark Antony's transformations of the word "honourable.") Coriolanus is excessive in ways that prepare the audience to relinquish him for his role as scapegoat, in accentuating a trait that the audience also shares with him, though seldom so avowedly.

More "prophesying after the event" is still to be done. But first, perhaps we should pause to give a generalized outline of the plot, having in mind the kind of tension (or factional malaise) that the drama would transform into terms of purgative appeal:

> After having gained popular acclaim through prowess in war, a courageous but arrogant patrician, who had been left fatherless when young and was raised by his mother, is persuaded by his mother to sue for high political office. In campaigning, he alienates the plebeians who, goaded by his political rivals, condemn him to exile. When in exile, making an alliance with the commander of the armies he had conquered, he leads a force against his own country. But before the decisive battle, during a visit by his closest relatives, his mother persuades him not to attack. In so doing, she unintentionally sets in motion the conditions whereby the allied commander, whom he had formerly vanquished and who envies his fame, successfully plots his assassination.

It is impressive how perfectly the chosen victim's virtues and vices work together, in fitting him for his sacrificial function. The several scenes in the first act that build up his prowess as a soldier not only endow him with a sufficient measure of the heroics necessary for tragic dignification. They also serve to make it clear why, when he returns to Rome and, against his will, consents to seek the office of consul, he is bound to be a misfit. Shakespeare himself usually gives us the formula for such matters. It is stated by the Tribune, Brutus, in Act III, scene iii: Get him angry, for

> ...He hath been us'd
> Ever to conquer, and to have his worth
> Of contradiction. Being once chaf'd, he cannot
> Be rein'd again to temperance; then he speaks
> What's in his heart, and that is there which looks
> With us to break his neck.

He is not the "war games" kind of military man, not the "computer mentality"; thus we spontaneously accept it that his valiant though somewhat swashbuckling ways as a warrior will make him incompetent in the wiles of peaceful persuasion, which the wily Shakespeare so persuasively puts in a bad light, *within* the conditions of the play, by his treatment of the Tribunes. Though Shakespeare's theater is, from start to finish, a masterful enterprise in the arts of persuasion, high among his resources is the building of characters who are weak in such devices. Indeed, considered from this point of view, Coriolanus' bluntness is in the same class with Cordelia's fatal inability to flatter Lear. Later we shall find other reasons to think of Lear in connection with Coriolanus' railings. Meanwhile, note how the Tribunes' skill at petition is portrayed as not much better than mere cunning, even though somewhat justified by our highborn goat's arrogance in his dealings with the commoners. He finds it impossible even to simulate an attitude of deference. And once we have his number, when he sets out to supplicate, armed with the slogan "The word is 'mildly,'" the resources of dramatic irony have already prepared us for the furious outbursts that will get the impetuous war-hero banished from Rome, a climax capped perfectly by his quick rejoinder, "I banish you!" As a fearless fighter, he is trained to give commands and to risk his life, not to supplicate. And the better to build him up, in the role of the Tribunes Shakespeare makes the art of political supplication seem quite unsavory.

All told, Coriolanus' courage and outspokenness make him a sufficiently "noble" character to dignify a play by the sacrificing of him. And excessive ways of constantly reaffirming his assumption that only the *social* nobility can be *morally* noble indicts him for sacrifice. But more than this is needed to make him effectively yieldable.

For one thing, always in drama we encounter a variation on the theme of what I would call the "paradox of substance." A character cannot "be himself" unless many others among the dramatis personae contribute to this end, so that the very essence of a character's nature is in a large measure defined, or determined, by the other characters who variously assist or oppose him. The most obvious instance of what I mean is the role of Aufidius. If it is an integral part of Coriolanus' role to be slain, there must be a slayer. And in this sense Aufidius is "derived from" the character of Coriolanus. The conditions of the play set up Coriolanus as a gerundive, a "to be killed," and Aufidius is to be the primary instrument in the killing. As is typical of a Shakespearean play, just before the close of the first act Aufidius points the arrows of the audience's expectations by announcing to a soldier (and thus to the audience) that he will destroy Coriolanus in whatever way possible. Even so, it's always good if a man speaks with high respect of a slain rival; accordingly, though Aufidius must be plotter enough to fulfill his role in Coriolanus' death, he must be of sufficient dignity so that his final tribute to the "noble memory" of Coriolanus will serve to give the audience a parting reassurance that they have participated in the symbolic sacrifice of a victim worth the killing. The assurance was made doubly necessary by the fact that, just before the slaying, there had been a kind of last-moment revelation, when Aufidius called the bold warrior a "boy of tears," thus propounding a final formula for Coriolanus' relationship to his mother. Aufidius' claims as a worthy opponent (despite his unsavory traits) are established in Coriolanus' first reference to him, such as, "I sin in envying his nobility," and "He is a lion/That I am proud to hunt."

This relationship we should dwell on. For it best illustrates just what we mean by "prophesying after the event" in order to "derive" the play in terms of poetics. If the characters are viewed simply as "people," we should treat the relationship between Coriolanus and Volumnia much as Plutarch did, in the "Life" from which Shakespeare borrowed so much of his plot. Coriolanus would thus be interpreted as the offspring of a bellicose, overbearing mother, who sought to compensate for the death of his father by being both mother and father to him. There is one change worth noting. Whereas Plutarch attributes Coriolanus' resultant irritability to womanishness, Shakespeare seems to have settled for a mere failure to outgrow boyishness. But our main point is this: Along the lines of poetic principles, the derivation should be reversed; and instead of viewing Coriolanus as an offspring of his mother, we view her role as a function contributory to his.

Thus, in an early scene, she is portrayed as a pugnacious virago of whom the son became a responsive masculine copy. This portrait of her prepares us to accept it as "natural" that, when he returns from the battlefields, *she* can persuade him, against his wishes, to stand for consul. And thus, later in the play, we will accept it that *she* can persuade him not to attack Rome—and (quite unintentionally on her part) this decision sets up the conditions responsible for his death. In brief, when using her to account for Coriolanus' character in the first place, Shakespeare is preparing her to serve as plausible explanation for two crucial moments in the *plot*: a non-political man's ventures into politics, and a fighting man's failure to join in battle when success was certain. In brief, her relation to Coriolanus motivates for us two decisions of his that are basically necessary, to make the *turns* in the tragedy seem plausible.

I say "turns," having in mind the Aristotelian word, "peripety," to name the striking moment, near the center of a complex plot, when some significant reversal takes place. But I might here pause to note that this is a play of many such reversals. In Act I, there are the many scenes that might in general be entitled the "Tides of Battle," including the one where Coriolanus—or at that time, Caius Marcius, since he has not yet received his new name from the city he conquered—is thought to be lost, through having single-handedly pursued the enemy within the gate of Corioli, fighting alone where Plutarch less theatrically had reported him as but leader of a small band. At the end of Act II, the commoners are persuaded by the Tribunes to retract their intention of voting for Coriolanus as consul. The big peripety is, as one might expect, in Act III, the hero's fatal bursts of rage having been prepared for ironically by his decision to be mild. In this act, there is a kind of peripety-atop-peripety, when Coriolanus retorts to his banishers, "I banish you!"

In Act IV, scene v, there is a neat turn when Aufidius' servingmen, who would treat Coriolanus shabbily when he first appears, abruptly change their tune after he has talked with Aufidius, and the compact against Rome has been agreed on. Besides being one of the few comic spots in the play, this scene is also useful in preparing for the last fatal reversal, since it brings out the fact that, even if Coriolanus and Aufidius are to become allies, Coriolanus' reputation is a threat to Aufidius. Another reversal, in scene vi, occurs when, just after the Tribunes and citizens have been congratulating themselves on the conditions of peace resulting form Coriolanus' banishment, they are startled by the news that Coriolanus is marching on Rome.

In Act V, there is a fatal peripety, when Coriolanus is persuaded by his mother to give up his intention of attacking Rome. This leads to another peripety, the ironic twist whereby, soon after Menenius has explained to one of the Tribunes that Coriolanus will never yield ("There is no more mercy in him than there is milk in a male tiger"), they learn that Coriolanus has begun to withdraw. And even though the arrows of our expectations were clearly pointing in this direction, there is a final peripety in the hero's slaying.

Coriolanus' wife, Virgilia, is quickly "derivable." In contrast with his continual bluster, she is his "gracious silence." Contrasting with his blood-thirsty mother, she faints at the very mention of blood. In her sensitiveness and devotion, she is by implication a vote for Coriolanus. There's a skillful touch, in Act IV, scene ii, where she flares up for a moment against the Tribunes, and boasts of her husband as a fighter: "He'ld make an end of thy posterity." There's a different twist, but surely conceived in the spirit of the same theater, when the young son (who is a chip off the old block, and loved to rip apart a butterfly) flares up at his father. The most notable thing about Valeria, from the standpoint of Shakespearean dramaturgy, is the fact that, though this friend of the family serves well for handling the relation between mother-in-law and daughter, she has a much less active role in the play than she does in Plutarch. For in Plutarch, *she* suggests that the women go to plead with Coriolanus and dissuade him from attacking Rome, whereas the whole musculature of Shakespeare's play requires maximum stress upon his mother's role in this development. The two Generals (Titus Lartius and Cominius) are "derivable" from Coriolanus in the sense that, both being men of high repute, their constant respect for him speaks for him. Also, his loyalty to them serves to establish that he is not avid for dictatorial power, but genuinely represents an integral conflict between patricians and plebeians. (Shakespeare's formula for Coriolanus' treatment of the commoners had been summed up by a minor character thus: "He seeks their hate with greater devotion than they can render it him.") The citizens have the mixture of distress, resentment, and instability that enables them to help Coriolanus get into the kind of quandaries necessary for him to enact his role. As for the Tribunes, besides their function in making Coriolanus' bluster look admirable in comparison with their scheming, they serve to carry the play forward by goading him into the rage that leads to his banishment, and thus eventually (as one thing leads to another) to his death. All told, in being the kind of characters they are, the other figures help Coriolanus be the kind of character he is; and by their actions at precisely the times when they do act, they help lead the appointed (or stylistically anointed) victim to the decision required, by the logic of the plot, for his downfall. He must turn the army away from Rome, and under conditions that lead step by step to the sacrifice that will permit the purging of the audience.

But we have not yet considered the remarkable function of Menenius. At first glance, one could "derive" him from Coriolanus only in the sense that he serves as the ideal link between the patrician and plebeian factions. In this role, along with his loyalty to Coriolanus, he serves particularly well for shaping the audience's sympathies. For though he is a patrician, and frankly shares the prejudices of his class, the commoners (and the audience) like him. His use in this regard is of crucial importance to the play when, in Act IV, scene vi, a messenger brings the news that Coriolanus is leading an army against Rome. To the extent that Rome allusively stood for England, it was not easy to keep the audience sympathetic with a man whose conduct at this point was so close to out-and-out treason (particularly since at so many points in the play he irritates us). But Menenius picks up Cominius' line, placing the blame upon the Tribunes and the people ("O, you have made good work!")—and when two characters of such high repute take this stand, it helps crowd the audience a bit by shifting the emphasis from the *hero's treason* to his *enemies' provocation* (with the bad effects of the provocation being stressed, while the considerations that would justify it were here left unmentioned). The trick was to show the Tribunes and the people regretting their decision to banish Coriolanus rather than to let them review their grounds for the banishment. This is excellent dramaturgic maneuvering—for Shakespeare, as is typical of him, is here working with more complex motives than an audience's simplest responses to patriot and traitor.

But Menenius' "derivation" as a function of Coriolanus' sacrifice contains other notable ingredients. Despite the great contrast between the diplomatic eloquence of the self-styled "humorous patrician" (who is Coriolanus' godfather) and the heavy-footed, grotesquely heroic mouthings of the formally inevitable victim (for one is mellow where the other is raw), Menenius applies almost the same formula to them both. Of himself he says, "What I think, I utter, and spend my malice in my breath." The same readiness with the word he attributes to Coriolanus thus: "His heart's his mouth./What his breast forges, that his tongue must vent." (War itself, elsewhere in the play, is called "sprightly, waking, audible, and full of vent," an expression that could serve also to describe Coriolanus' invective.)

But whereas Menenius shares Coriolanus' belief in the intrinsic superiority of the patricians, and makes no secret of the fact even when addressing the commoners, his function will be to uphold circumspectly, "reasonably," much the same position that Coriolanus must represent exorbitantly. (I say "must" because his excessiveness is a formal requirement of his role as victim.) Menenius is the only character in the play (except Aufidius' servants) charged with the responsibilities of putting some aspects of this solemn bluster in a comical light.

His early speech likening the body politic to the human body (one of the many themes Shakespeare found in Plutarch, though it was also a standard notion of the times) serves not only to present the attitude of the patricians in the best light (as Coriolanus must present it in the worst). It also sets the conditions for much body imagery throughout the play, particularly images of bodily disease, such as go well with the fact that the body politic is in great disarray. What more relevant than an imagery of bodily diseases in a play dealing with disorders of the body politic? Similarly, since the people are starving, images to do with devouring serve to keep thought of such conditions hovering about the edges of our consciousness. And the many references to animals are so treated as to reinforce the vigorous animality of the underlying situation.

The question of imagery, I submit, should be "derived" thus late in the enterprise. With works of a preponderantly imagistic cast (as in much modern poetry), one might properly *begin* with questions of imagery. But in a drama of this sort, one can most profitably begin with considerations of action and character, afterwards deducing the logic of the imagery from these prior considerations, rather than using imagery as the "way-in."

## II

Fundamentally, then, the play exploits to the ends of dramatic entertainment, with corresponding catharsis, the tension intrinsic to a kind of social division, or divisiveness, particularly characteristic of complex societies, but present to some degree in even the simplest modes of living. (I take it that the presence of a priesthood or similar functionaries dealing with things of this world in terms of a "beyond," is on its face evidence that a society is marked by some degree of social differentiation, with corresponding conflicts of interest. And at the very least, even tribes that come closest to a homogeneous way of life are marked by differentiation between the work of men and women or between youth and age.)

This malaise, which affects us all but which in varying degrees and under varying circumstances we attempt to mitigate, is here made insultingly unforgettable. Coriolanus' *hubris* (whether you choose to translate it as "pride" or as "excessiveness") aggravates the situation constantly. And when he dies (after a change of heart that enables us to pity him even while we resent his exaggerated ways of representing our own less admirable susceptibilities, with their corresponding "bad conscience"), he dies as one who has taken on the responsibility and has been appropriately punished. Thereby we are cleansed, thanks to his overstating of our case.

Along with this tension, which is of long duration in societies, we considered the likelihood that, when the play originally appeared, it also exploited a "timely topic," the unrest caused by the Enclosure Acts, when new men of means took over for sheepraising much land that had traditionally been available to small farmers, and these "legally" dispossessed tenants were in a state of great frustration. Many were starving while the monopolists were being made into patricians. It was a time when many *nouveaux-riches* were being knighted—and as Aristotle points out, it is *new* fortunes that people particularly resent.

An ironic turn of history has endowed this play with a new kind of "timely topic," owing to the vagaries of current dictatorships. But I would incline to contend that this "new immediacy" is more apparent than real. In the first place, Coriolanus isn't a good fit for the contemporary pattern because the frankness of his dislike for the common people would make him wholly incompetent as a rabble-rouser. A modern demagogue might secretly share Coriolanus' prejudices—but he certainly would not advertise the fact as Coriolanus did. His public heart would bleed for the poor, even while he was secretly shipping state funds to a Swiss bank, against the day when his empire would collapse, and he would flee the country, hoping to spend his last years in luxurious retirement on the Riviera. Presumably our nation is always in danger of pouring considerable funds down such rat-holes. Thus, I feel that the attempt to present *Coriolanus* in the light of modern conditions can never quite succeed, since these conditions tend rather to conceal than to point up the cultural trends underlying its purgative use of the tension between upper and lower classes. Or should we call it a "tension behind the tension"? I have in mind a situation of this sort:

The Renaissance was particularly exercised by Machiavelli because he so accurately represented the transvaluation of values involved in the rise of nationalism. A transvaluation was called for, because *religion* aimed at *universal* virtues, whereas the virtues of *nationalism* would necessarily be *factional,* insofar as they pitted nation against nation. Conduct viewed as vice from the standpoint of universal religious values might readily be viewed as admirable if it helped some interests prevail over others. This twist greatly exercised Machiavelli. But though (from the universal point of view) nations confront one another as factions, from the standpoint of any one nation factionalism is conceived in a narrower sense, with nationalism itself taking over the role of the universal.

In Shakespeare's day, as so many of his plays indicate, the kind of *family* factionalism that went with feudal relationships was being transformed into the kind of *class* factionalism that would attain its "perfection" (if we may apply that term to so turbulent a development) in the rise of nationalism, with its drive towards the building of the British Empire. And here Shakespeare tackled this particular tangle of motives in a remarkably direct manner, except of course for the kind of "distance" (with corresponding protection) the play got by treating the subject in terms of ancient Rome rather than his contemporary London.

All told, the motivation split into four overlapping loci: nation, class, family, individual. And in *Coriolanus* we witness a remarkably complex simplification of these issues, dramatically translated into terms of action and character.

Individualism may come and go, but there is a compelling sense in which the individual is always basic. The centrality of the nervous system is such that each of us is unique (each man's steak and his particular toothache being his own and no one else's). And even those who are killed *en masse* nonetheless die one by one. Symbolicity (by assigning proper names and attesting to the rights of private ownership) strongly punctuates this physical kind of individuality. And Shakespeare adds his momentous contribution by building so many plays on the "star" system, with a titular role. I think it is safe to say that *Coriolanus* most thoroughly meets this description. Think of such lines as: "O, me alone! Make you a sword of me?" (I, vi); "Alone I fought in your Corioles walls" (I, vii); "Alone I did it." (V, vi)—or his resolve to stand "As if a man were author of himself" (V, iii) —or a Tribune's grudging tribute to him: "He has no equal" (I, i)—or his own mother's formula: "You are too absolute" (III, ii). And the play backs up such statements by incessantly making him the center of our attention whether he is on the stage or off.

Yet even his name is not his own, but derives from the sacking of a city. And when he is threatening to lead an army against Rome, he does not know himself; and the sympathetic Cominius tells us (V, i) that he "forbade all names./He was a kind of nothing, titleless,/Till he had forged himself a name o' th' fire / of burning Rome"—and that's precisely what, in obedience to his mother's pleadings he did not do.[1] Incidentally, the longer one works with this text, the more ingenious Shakespeare's invention seems when, just before Coriolanus is killed, he *apologizes* because he had fallen into a rage: "Pardon me, lords, 'tis the first time ever/I was forced to scold." But he is addressing the *lords* of Antium, not the commoners. Shortly thereafter the Conspirators will shout, "Kill, kill, kill, kill, kill him!" thereby as they slay modifying poor impotent Lear's line, "Then, kill, kill, kill, kill, kill, kill!" (IV, vi, 192).

But such considerations bring us to the next locus of motives, the *familial,* which the play brings to a focus in the "mother, wife, child" formula, used variously by Menenius (V, i, 28–29), himself (V, ii, 78), and Volumnia (V, iii, 101), hers being the most effective, when she bewails the sight of him for "Making the mother, wife, and child to see/The son, the husband, and the father tearing/His country's bowels out." Yet to say as much is to move us almost as quickly into the realm of *class* and *nation,* since his family identity was so intensely that of a *patrician,* and his individualistic ways of being a patrician had brought him into conflict with all Rome.

Here you confront the true poignancy of his predicament, the formula being: individualistic prowess, made haughty towards the people by mother's training, and naturally unfit for the ways of peaceful persuasion with regard to the citizenry as a whole. The *class* motive comes to a focus terministically in the manipulations that have to do with the key word, "noble." But the *nation* as motive gets its forceful poignancy when the play so sets things up that Coriolanus maneuvers himself and is maneuvered into a situation whereby this individualistic mother-motivated patrician patriot is all set to attack his own country, which at the beginning of the play he had defended

[1] If he had got a new name from the destruction of Rome as he got the name of "Coriolanus" from his victory over Corioli, the preservation of the pattern would have ironically required that in his new identity he be called "Romanus."

with such signal valor, despite his invective against the commoners. As Granville-Barker has well said: "Play and character become truly tragic only when Marcius, to be traitor to Rome, must turn traitor to himself."

Yet, so far as I can see, the treatment of this motivational tangle (individual-family-class-nation) is not in itself "cathartic," unless one uses the term in the Crocean sense rather than the Aristotelian. (That is, I have in mind the kind of relief that results purely from the well-ordered presentation of an entanglement. Such a complexity just *is*. But Shakespeare transforms this motionless knot into terms of an irreversible narrative sequence, the "cure" here residing not in a sacrifice as such, but rather in the feeling of "getting somewhere" by the sheer act of expression, even though the scene centered in conditions when Coriolanus was totally immobilized, a quite unusual state for so outgoing a character.) My soundest evidence for catharsis of this sort (whereby the sheer unfolding of expression can impart a kind of relief to our kind of animal, that lives by locomotion) is the nursery rhyme:

The grand old Duke of York
He had ten thousand men
He marched them up to the top of the hill
Then he marched them down again.
And when they were up they were up
And when they were down they were down
And when they were only halfway up
They were neither up nor down.

## III

I'm among the company of those who would call *Coriolanus* a "grotesque" tragedy. So our final problem is to make clear just wherein its grotesqueness resides, and how this quality might also contribute to its nature as medicinal.

Obviously, in contrast with the typical sacrificial victims of Greek tragedy, Coriolanus rather resembles a character in a satyr play. He is almost like a throwback to the kind of scurrilities that Aristotle associates with the origins of the tragic iamb, in relation to the traditional meter of lampoons. (See Poetics IV) So some critics have called it a "satiric" tragedy. But "grotesque" seems closer, since Coriolanus is *not* being satirized. The clearest evidence that he is being presented as a *bona fide* hero is the fact that *every* person of good standing in the play admires him or loves him and is loyal to him, despite his excesses. What does all this mean?

Still considering the problem from the standpoint of *tensions* and their exploitation for dramatic effects (that is to say, poetic delight), can we not find another kind of tension exploited here for medicinal purposes? It concerns the function of Coriolanus as a "railer," a master of vituperation.

Dramaturgically, such a figure is, at the very least, of service in the sense that, by keeping things stirred up, he enables the dramatist to fish in troubled waters. When a cantankerous character like Coriolanus is on the stage (and Shakespeare turns up many such), there is a categorical guaranty that things will keep on the move. Yet, beyond that sheerly technical convenience (whereby Coriolanus does in one way what Iago does in another, towards keeping a play in motion), there is the possibility that such a role in itself may be curative, as a symbolic remedy for one particular kind of repression typical of most societies.

I might best make my point by quoting some remarks I made elsewhere about another scurrilous tragic victim, Shakespeare's Timon of Athens. There, however, the cut is different. Coriolanus throughout is respectful to the patricians and directs his insults only to the plebeians. But Timon, beginning as a great lover of mankind, ends as a total misanthrope. These paragraphs from my essay on *Timon of Athens* bear upon Timon's possible appeal as vilifier in the absolute.

> *Invective,* I submit, is a primary "freedom of speech," rooted extralinguistically in the helpless rage of an infant that states its attitude by utterances wholly unbridled. In this sense, no mode of expression could be more "radical," unless it be the closely allied motive of sheer *lamentation,* undirected wailing. And perhaps the sounds of contentment which an infant makes, when nursing or when being bedded or fondled, mark the pre-articulate origins of a third basic "freedom," *praise.*
>
> Among these three, if rage is the infantile prototype of invective, it is a kind of "freedom" that must soon be subjected to control, once articulacy develops. For though even praise can get one into trouble (for instance, when one happens to praise A's enemy in the presence of A, who happens also to be both powerful and rancorous); and though lamentation can on occasion be equally embarrassing (if one is heard to lament a situation among persons who favor it), invective most directly invites pugnacity, since it is itself a species of pugnacity.
>
> Obviously, the Shakespearean theater lends itself perfectly to the effects of invective. Coriolanus is an excellent case in point. Even a reader who might loathe his politics cannot but be engrossed by this man's mouthings. Lear also has a strong measure of such appeal, with his impotent senile maledictions that come quite close to the state of man's equally powerless infantile beginnings. . . . And that delightfully run-down aristocrat, Falstaff, delights us by making a game of such exercises.

Though one has heard much about the repression of sexual motives, in our average dealings invective is the mode of expression most thoroughly repressed. This state of affairs probably contributes considerably to such "cultural" manifestations as the excessive violence on television, and the popular consumption of crude political oratory. Some primitive tribes set aside a special place where an aggrieved party can go and curse the king without fear of punishment (though if our society had such an accommodation, I'm sure there'd be a secret agent hiding behind every bush). In earlier days the gifted railer was considered invaluable by reason of his expert skill at cursing the forces deemed dangerous to the welfare of the tribe (see on this point some interesting data in Robert C. Elliott's book, *The Power of Satire: Magic, Ritual, Art,* and above all his suggestive and entertaining Appendix on "The Curse"). At the very least, in figures such as Coriolanus we get much of such expressiveness, without the rationale of magic, but under the "controlled conditions" of a drama about political unrest. And if he dies of being so forthright, downright and outright (if not exactly upright), it's what he "deserved." For as regards the *categorical* appeal of invective, it resides not so much in the particular objects inveighed against, but in the sheer process of inveighing. And Coriolanus, like Timon, has given vent with fatal overthoroughness to untoward tendencies which, in our "second nature," we have "naturally" learned to repress.

## IV

In conclusion, then, where are we? We have been considering Coriolanus' qualifications as a scapegoat, whose symbolic sacrifice is designed to afford an audience pleasure. We have suggested: (1) His primary role as a cathartic vessel resides in the excessiveness with which he forces us to confront the discriminatory motives intrinsic to society as we know it. (2) There is a sheerly "expressive" kind of catharsis in his way of giving form to the complexities of *family, class,* and *national* motives as they come to a focus in the self-conflicts of an *individual.* (3) There is the "curative" function of invective as such, when thus released under controlled conditions that transform the repressed into the expressed, yet do us no damage. (4) The attempt has been made to consider the "paradox of substance" whereby the chosen scapegoat can "be himself" and arrive at the end "proper to his nature" only if many events and other persons "conspire" to this end, the persons by being exactly the kind of persons they are, and the events by developing in the exact order in which they do develop. To sum it all up, then, in a final formula for tragic catharsis: (a formula I wrote with such a play as *Coriolanus* in mind, though it could be applied *mutatis mutandis* to other texts):

> Take some pervasive unresolved tension typical of a given social order (or of life in general). While maintaining the "thought" of it in its overall importance, reduce it to terms of personal conflict (conflict between friends, or members of the same family). Feature some prominent figure who, in keeping with his character, though possessing admirable qualities, carries

this conflict to excess. Put him in a situation that points up the conflict. Surround him with a cluster of characters whose relations to him and to one another help motivate and accentuate his excesses. So arrange the plot that, after a logically motivated turn, his excesses lead necessarily to his downfall. Finally, suggest that his misfortune will be followed by a promise of general peace.

## Comments

Our reference to the Enclosure Acts requires a gloss. Though the private enclosing of public lands ("commons") had begun in the thirteenth century, its effects were still being felt at the time when Shakespeare wrote, and indeed much later (as cf. Goldsmith). Indeed, when we read of one churchman's lament, "Where there have been many householders and inhabitants, there is now but a shepherd and his dog," we suddenly get a closer glimpse into the aristocratic connotations of pastoral poetry. It is the shepherd who, among the lowly, would be identified with the big new landowners (who made their money by "legally" dispossessing small farmers of their traditional rights and turning over the land to sheepgrazing, connected with the higher profits in wood).

Professor William Frost, at the University of California, Santa Barbara, has suggested that the tension should be located rather as anticipatory of the later Civil Wars than as reminiscent of earlier disturbances (that had their epitomizing in the Wars of the Roses). Thus he would see a symbol of crown vs. parliament rather than of landowners vs. peasants. I think that both interpretations would fit here. In its possible relation to a "timely topic" (recent rioting) it could be reflecting the result of enclosures that were still "progressively" driving dispossessed peasants to the towns. It would also be reflecting emergent disorders that would come to a focus in Cromwell's time. But essentially, over the long stretch, it would be exploiting the tension intrinsic to differences of status.

As for the food imagery (talk of devouring, etc.): Though its relation to the theme of starving rioters obviously accounts for its presence, students who approach the play from an overly psychoanalytic point of view are likely to become so interested in food imagery as the possible deflection of a sexual motive they completely neglect the primary rational explanation, in terms of the people's economic distress.

Most often, perhaps, the tragic principle operates as follows: The hero acts; in the course of acting, he organizes an opposition; then, in the course of suffering the opposition (or seeing "in terms of" it) he transcends his earlier position—and the audience, by identification with him, undergoes a similar "cathartic" transformation.

But in the case of *Coriolanus* the process seems somewhat different.

The hero never really matures. His killer formulates the victim's plight in the formula, "thou boy of tears" (a summarizing "revelation," we might say, which the audience is prepared to receive just before the end of the play). And the ultimate insight is in the audience's own developments rather than in their sympathetic duplication of a higher vision on the part of sacrificed hero.

Many kinds of works involve variants of this process. In the case of Richard Wright's *Native Son,* for instance, Bigger was not the sort of character who could (while remaining in character) arrive at a conceptually mature statement of his difficulties. But such a statement could properly be made by a lawyer who, in defending him, could present the sheer *theory* of the case. This is probably one reason why, where plots hinge about characters of limited insight, the device of a concluding court trial is especially serviceable. Another resource is the use of an emotionally imagistic solution, as in James Baldwin's *Go Tell It On the Mountain,* where the Negro problem is merged with a religious conversion that ambiguously suggests homosexual connotations.

Coriolanus is to Menenius as raw adolescence is to ripe old age. Lear is sick old age that falls into infantile tantrums, a Coriolanus without the physical power. And I dare repeat: It is tremendously interesting to see how, for all their superficial differences, Cordelia and Coriolanus both exemplify variants of a forthrightness that is essential to the advancing of the plot. If Lear, Cordelia, and Coriolanus were like Menenius, neither of these tragedies would be possible.

Though the names are taken over literally from Plutarch, it is remarkable how tonally suggestive some of them are, from the standpoint of their roles in this English play. "Volumnia" suggests the voluminous—and often, on students' papers, I have seen the name spelled "Volumina." "Virgilia" suggests "virginal." "Aufidius" suggests "perfidious." And in the light of Freudian theories concerning the fecal nature of invective, the last two syllables of the hero's name are so "right," people now often seek to dodge the issue by altering the traditional pronunciation (making the *a* broad instead of long).

This article should be a summing-up in three ways:

First, its stress upon the Dramatistic principle of victimage (the "sacrificial" motive) provides a logological analogue of the issue at which Friedrich Nietzsche grew wroth in his *Birth of Tragedy*. Its concern with dramatic catharsis modifies the version of dialectical (Platonic) transcendence featured in the third of these essays.

Second, it is designed to show by specific example how our theory of symbolic action in general can be tied down to considerations of poetics in particular.

Third, it should serve to point up the difference between an approach to a text in terms of poetics ("intrinsically") and an approach to it ("extrinsically") from the sociological point of view. And above all, the distinction should be made in a *nonindividious way,* both approaches being needed for the full treatment of symbolic action. Besides using beliefs (what Aristotle's *Rhetoric* would call "topics," or "places") to give characters and situations the appeal of verisimilitude (to make an imitation seem "natural" or "lifelike" even while we remain aware that it is an artifact), a work uses beliefs to arouse states of tension, by pitting some beliefs (or "equations") against others. Or, to put the case in sociological terms, we could say that a given society is characterized by a scheme of "values" that variously reinforce one another or conflict with one another in given situations and that authors variously embody such "values" in constructing characters and plots. In this sense, the *Rhetoric* can serve as a bridge between sociology and literary criticism (except insofar as sociologists and literary critics fail to ask how the *Rhetoric* can be applied even to their own field).

Thinking along such lines, in lectures I have at times placed more emphasis upon this area of overlap. For instance, Talcott Parsons' collection of essays, *Social Structure and Personality,* serves as a convenient point of entry for a treatment of the play in terms of "Social Structure and Poetics." But his concern with the interweaving of sociological and psychological coordinates is paralleled by a different but analogous interweaving of poetics and the sociological-psychological.

After noting the recurrence of the term "expectation" in the Parsons volume, one can discuss the similarity between the role of expectation in classical form and the place of expectations in men's notions of current reality and in threats and promises regarding the future. The kind of "values" and "expectations" that a sociologist deals with can be shown to figure also in the structure of a literary work, as enjoyed for its own sake (so that practical problems are transcended by being transformed into sources of artistic enjoyment). And by the same token, the role of "values" can be shown to figure prominently in the "equations" that are either implicit or explicit in a given work. But, of course, the reverse kind of "derivation" which we would consider central to Poetics (as when "deriving" Volumnia from Coriolanus) would be wholly alien to either sociology or psychology. And whereas Plutarch, viewed as biography, would be judged by tests of "truth," or "factuality," the play should be judged by tests of "verisimilitude," or "plausibility." However, the symmetry of the case is impaired by the fact that Plutarch was not by any means a biographer in the sheerly "factual" sense; and his method of writing encouraged kinds of "identification" that go with poetic appeal.

Finally, though I dare hope that one can distinguish between dialectical transcendence and dramatic catharsis at their extremes (as illustrated by my third and fifth essays), I must admit that the realms covered by the two terms considerably overlap. And both in previous works and later in essays included here, I have sometimes used one of the terms where I might as well have used the other.

We might discern the rudiments of transcendence when an individual dons a uniform. For now he is seen in terms of this "more inclusive whole" (that can also be called *less* inclusive, insofar as it eliminates many of the individual's personal possibilities); and it could be called "cathartic" in the sense that the identification indicated by the uniform is in effect the "sacrifice," or symbolic "slaying," of the individual's nonuniformed identity. In story, as in history, a situation can undergo a rudimentary kind of transcendence by the sheer process of moving on to other matters.

The rudiments of catharsis are present in that most readily available resource of symbolism: substitution. For implicit in the possibilities of substitution there is the possibility of vicarious victimage.

There is a further process not reducible to terms of either "transcendence" or "catharsis," as considered in the third and fifth chapters respectively. It involves analogues of unburdening or cleansing, in the sheerly physiological sense (as with the *explicit* use of fecal imagery in Aristophanic comedy or Swiftian satire, and the "dignified" devices for *implicitly* transforming bathos into pathos).

The relation to victimage is revealed in the "fecal" nature of invective. But this "problematic" element can also impinge upon a realm of motives that, while honorifically related in one respect to the hierarchal mysteries of courtliness, in another respect would seem to be rooted in infantile "equations" that *precede* the notions of "propriety" inculcated by toilet training. In his *Psychology of the Unconscious,* Jung offers some excellent instances of "reverence" as so conceived. For related stylistic "miracles," see my chapter on "The Thinking of the Body," or the comments on *"scoriae,"* in my discussion of Emerson's "Nature."

# 36

# *Coriolanus:* Wordless Meanings and Meaningless Words

*James L. Calderwood*

Standing inspection before the plebeians as a candidate for the consulship, Coriolanus asks himself why he is compelled to endure what is to him a degrading experience, and answers:

> Custom calls me to't.
> What custom wills, in all things should we do't,
> The dust on antique time would lie unswept,
> And mountainous error be too highly heapt
> For truth to o'er-peer. Rather than fool it so,
> Let the high office and the honor go
> To one that would do thus. (II, iii, 124–130)[1]

Coriolanus's indictment of "custom" as the means through which society perpetuates error and obscures truth expresses verbally what is visually evident to the audience, for in the present situation "error" is equivalent to the gown of humility which Coriolanus wears over the "truth" of a proud and

*Reprinted from* Studies in English Literature, *VI, No. 2 (Spring 1966), 211–224 by permission of The Rice University Press.*

[1] All references are to the text in *The Complete Plays and Poems of William Shakespeare,* ed. William A. Neilson and Charles J. Hill (Cambridge, Mass., 1942).

unbending spirit. In the world of *Coriolanus* there is no traffic between "custom" and "truth." The sense of community needed for the ritual custom of inspection to be "truth"—for the ritual to stand as a reference point of values shared by both Coriolanus and the plebeians—simply does not exist. The ritual form, which should be a symbol of social order and harmony, has become meaningless because it is invested with false content. And in becoming meaningless in this fashion the ritual ironically becomes a true symbol of the social and political disorder into which Rome has fallen.

It is not only customs or rituals that have become meaningless symbols in Rome; symbols themselves have become meaningless, and, most important, words have become meaningless. As Sigurd Burckhardt has argued,[2] it is the logical corollary to the dissolution of a stable social order that language should become flaccid, words semantically irresolute, and truth itself hard to come by. The bond between what is meant and what is understood by words, the common ground between speaker and listener which makes dialogue possible, is the whole social structure from which language issues. If this structure breaks down, as it does in *Coriolanus,* language breaks down with it. In what follows I shall suggest that examining the breakdown of language in *Coriolanus* will provide us with a useful and, hopefully, an illuminating perspective from which to view the play. In particular, we will find in Coriolanus's attempts to defend himself against linguistic chaos a reflection of his more general problem of establishing a sense of personal identity and worth in terms of the concept of honor.

The play opens with the cacophany of the plebeians' speech, all of them speaking at once. We quickly learn that the plebeians have no good words for Coriolanus, that they will not "give him good report" for his actions in the field since he "pays himself with being proud" (I, i, 32–34). "In hunger for bread," the plebeians have mutinied in hopes of obtaining a more equable distribution of grain. But when they encounter Menenius, instead of bread or grain they are given a banquet of words, the Fable of the Belly. "What say you to't?" Menenius asks complacently, referring to the belly's answer to the complaining members of the body, and Second Citizen replies tersely, "It was an answer"—a string of words in response to another but, so far as the citizen is concerned, devoid of substance and bearing no recognizable relation to the present case. Voicing vituperations as he enters, Coriolanus replies to Second Citizen's sarcastic "We have ever your good word" with "He that will give good words to thee will flatter/Beneath abhorring" (I, i, 170–172). There are, it becomes evident, no "good" words available, in the sense of their arising from a common ground of values and facts and so having a generally acknowledged meaning. To the plebeians "hunger" is a word filled with meaning and force—"They said...That hunger broke stone walls"

[2] Sigurd Burckhardt, "The King's Language: Shakespeare's Drama as Social Discovery," *Antioch Review,* XXI (1961), 369–387.

(209–210)—but to Coriolanus all the plebeians' words of complaint are merely "shreds" of air "vented" through the vulgar mouth (212–213). The rebellion itself, as he and Menenius perceive, is mostly verbal, full of sound and fury but lacking the substance of firm intent and action, "For though abundantly they lack discretion,/Yet are they passing cowardly" (206–207). And so far as Coriolanus is concerned, the plebeians themselves are like so many unreliable words: "He that trusts to you,/ Where he should find you lions, finds you hares;/ Where foxes, geese" (174–176). They will not answer to the right names nor mean what they should.

Lacking a common set of values, feelings, allegiances, principles, and knowledge, and hence lacking a viable language, Coriolanus and the plebeians can have no real dialogue. It is not that Shakespeare is making out a case against either of them in the interests of a political philosophy; perhaps too much has been made of that. But he is—while presenting the issue in a spirit of "negative capability," distributing good and ill to both parties without aspiring to the dubious exactitude of right or wrong, true or false—he is, among other things, exploring what happens to language when mere "opinion" encroaches upon authority. At the opening of the play the plebeians have already been granted increased authority in the affairs of state, have been given the tribunes, the "tongues o' th' common mouth" (III, i, 22). With the addition of a tongue the common mouth acquires a voice; but it is an unreliable voice. William Rosen has argued convincingly that the plebeians are presented in the play as the embodiment of unstable "opinion"[3]—phonic chameleons echoing the words of the tribunes, a "multitudinous tongue" (III, i, 156) giving voice now to one thing, now to another. Fickle, vacillating, mutable, constant only in capriciousness, the plebeians exercise a corrosive influence upon language. "With every minute," Coriolanus says to them, "you do change a mind,/ And call him noble that was now your hate,/ Him vile that was your garland" (I, i, 186–188). Used thus language falls apart. The symbol "noble" as applied to a man is emptied of meaning, in the sense of having an identifiable referent, if the same referent is in the next instant symbolized by "hateful." Words lose their substance, drift free of meanings, and become merely noises or breath. Full of sound, the plebeians' words have no stable point of reference, cannot be relied upon at any given moment to mean what they literally say, and hence come dangerously close to signifying nothing.

If the popular language is unacceptable, its words corrupt, its relation to truth shifting and elusive, then one must, or at least Coriolanus must, create a language of his own in which the validity and reliability of words are restored. And in his ruthless devotion to his own conception of truth we may see an attempt on Coriolanus's part to fashion a private language whose

---

3 William Rosen, *Shakespeare's Craft of Tragedy* (Cambridge, Mass.: 1960), pp. 167–171.

words, unlike those of the plebeians, are cemented to their meanings and incapable of distortion. He invests his words with meaning in one sense by being "constant" to his word, to his promise (I, i, 242–243). Again, when given the name "Coriolanus" he dedicates himself to keeping the meaning of the word intact and unambiguous, intending, as he tells Cominius "at all times/ To undercrest your good addition/ To th' fairness of my power" (I, ix, 71–73). The name and the thing united inseparably, "Coriolanus" will have one meaning only, at all times and in all situations, and so in his person it does. This singleness and unchangeableness of meaning that he aspires to is suggested again in the same scene. Cominius has had the drums and trumpets sounded in honor of Coriolanus's achievements in battle. Coriolanus responds with adolescent truculence, speaking of the instruments as though of misused words:

> May these instruments, which you profane,
> Never sound more! When drums and trumpets shall
> I' th' field prove flatterers let courts and cities be
> Made all of false-fac'd soothing! (I, ix, 41–44)

We shall return to this scene later, but for the moment it is enough to observe that drums and trumpets have for him one use only, the military use that is now being "profaned," just as words have, or should have, he feels, one meaning only. Divorced from its use or meaning, each becomes corrupt, its truth falsified.

Compared with that of the plebeians, Coriolanus's is a stereotyped language—even, in its emphasis upon the exactness and reliability of meanings for all occasions, a form of scientific language; and insofar as this can be suggested by the language of poetic drama, his speech reflects such a conception of language. In the first place Coriolanus is highly distrustful of speech generally, preferring to use instead of words the unambiguous expressive power of his sword—"When blows have made me stay, I fled from words" (II, ii, 76). Lacking the verbal resources and the confidence in language required for effective argument, he remains taciturn whenever possible, and in the two major scenes where his family appeals to him (III, ii and V, iii) he locks himself in silence, neither acknowledging nor attempting to refute the arguments pressed upon him. Insensitive to the tone or connotative qualities of words, he is, as Menenius says, "ill-school'd/ In bolted language; meal and bran together/ He throws without distinction" (III, i, 321–323). If for him language is not subject to modification by the requirements of different social situations, not flexible enough to respond in tone and style to the demands of decorum—if it is not a social instrument, neither is it an instrument with which to probe and express the workings of consciousness. Coriolanus has only three rather abbreviated soliloquies in the play (II, ii, 119–131; IV, iv, 12–26; V, iii, 22–37), and in none of them does he turn the focus of language upon himself. Thus it is characteristic that the most penetrating exploration of what may lie within him must come from the outside, in the speech by Aufidius at the end of Act IV. In line with his general distrust of words, there is very little of the lyric in his speech. His address to Valeria in V, iii, for instance—

> The noble sister of Publicola,
> The moon of Rome, chaste as the icicle
> That's curded by the frost from purest snow
> And hang's on Dian's temple (64–67)

—stands in unexpected contrast with the "meal and bran" of his typical language. He rarely calls upon the full evocative power of language; there is none of the richness and depth of expression in his speech that we take for granted in Hamlet's, and none of the "Othello music." Nor does he engage in wordplay: of all Shakespeare's tragic heroes, he must be the least given to punning. In short, then, he is preoccupied with the meanings of words rather than with words themselves, and though Shakespeare speaks superb poetry through him, Coriolanus is not, as Richard II is usually said to be, a poet himself.

We might even argue that Coriolanus's general imperceptiveness—his rigidity of mind, his lack of self-awareness, his failure to see issues or people in their full reality (his inability, for instance, to view the plebeians in a way that does justice to their mixed character)—owes something to the inflexibility of his language and to his indifference to nuances of meaning governed by tone and style. Devoted to truth, he cannot grasp the full truth about either himself or others because truth, especially in qualitative matters of human values or character, will not yield itself fully to a language oriented to exact but blunt meanings. In his single-minded concern that words mean precisely what they say, for example, he is unable to distinguish between "false-fac'd soothing" and genuine admiration, and hence he misses the truth of Cominius's feelings when he rejects his praise after Corioli: "Too modest are you," Cominius admonishes him, "More cruel to your good report than grateful/ To us that give you truly" (I, ix, 53–55). Shakespeare elsewhere pointedly relates Coriolanus's use of language to his cast of mind. In the passage cited earlier, Menenius says that Coriolanus is "ill-school'd/ In bolted language; meal and bran together/ He throws without distinction" (II, i, 321–323). Later, when Coriolanus has led the Volscian army to the gates of Rome and is preparing to burn the city, Cominius reports on the ill success of his attempt to intercede with Coriolanus:

> I offered to awaken his regard
> For's private friends; his answer to me was,
> He could not stay to pick them in a pile
> Of noisome musty chaff. He said 'twas folly,

> For one poor grain or two, to leave unburnt
> And still to nose th' offence. (V, i, 23–28)

An insensitivity to distinctions in words, it would seem, reflects, and perhaps helps create, a general insensitivity of feeling and a lack of discrimination in matters of human worth. The man who in some degree brutalizes language may well come to brutalize justice. However, to avoid adopting Coriolanus's own pseudo-precise, black or white view of things, we should observe that his devotion to meaning is a source of strength as well as of weakness in him. It is to his credit, for instance, that he is ultimately unable to divorce language from meaning in the way Volumnia advocates when she asks him

> to speak
> To th' people; not by your own instruction,
> Nor by the matter which your heart prompts you,
> But with such words that are but roted in
> Your tongue, though but bastards and syllables
> Of no allowance to your bosom's truth. (III, ii, 52–57)

The Machiavellian technique with words that Volumnia argues for here is no less destructive of the stability of language than the plebeians' verbal capriciousness. When words are "but roted in" the tongue, when they are no longer a reliable bridge between purport and understanding, they become truly "bastards and syllables of no allowance."

## II

In an unstable society whose verbal currency is fluctuating back and forth between inflationary and deflationary levels, one can never know at any time what words are worth. Coriolanus's response is to revert to a private verbal standard in which he gives his own value to words and, refusing to accept outside currency, good or bad, "pays himself with being proud" (I, i, 33–34). Dismissing the plebeians' words as illegal tender, he will neither take payment from them nor give any to them. "Answer to us," Sicinius says, and Coriolanus replies that "'tis true, I ought so" (III, iii, 61–62); but he cannot answer as Volumnia, the patricians, and the plebeians want—can reply only in his own language because his "heart's his mouth" (III, i, 257) and "Being once chaf'd. . .he speaks what's in his heart" (III, iii, 27–29). But to construct a "private language" is of course a futile venture since language, to be language, must be public. Hence no genuine verbal transactions are possible between him and the plebeians. In accord with Gresham's Law of verbal currency, the plebeians' bad words have driven out of circulation Coriolanus's good words—"good" in terms of his own verbal standard.

Unless he can be forced to put his words back into circulation, he must be held a menace to society—and he cannot be so forced:

> Let them pronounce the steep Tarpeian death,
> Vagabond exile, flaying, pent to linger
> But with a grain a day, I would not buy
> Their mercy at the price of one fair word. (III, iii, 88–91)

Thus the people banish him, though he defiantly insists upon giving the word his own meaning: "I banish you!" (III, iii, 123).

The difficulties Coriolanus encounters with language are closely related to those he encounters in forming a sense of personal identity and worth. As he distrusts words in general and is preoccupied with the private meanings he invests them with, so he distrusts public estimations of himself and is preoccupied with his own inner integrity, his nobility. To be fully authentic, inner worth or nobility needs to be based upon personal convictions firmly held but also identified with something external to self—God, office, cause, social class, political movement, etc. In the Renaissance concept of honor, for instance, authentic honor involved a harmonious merger of self-esteem and public esteem, inner nobility publicly recognized as such. On this view self-worth does not fully exist until it has achieved a station in the public consciousness as represented by fame, glory, good name, reputation. Thus Volumnia tells Virgilia that when Coriolanus was still a comely and promising youth she, "considering how honour would become such a person, that it [i.e., his noble person] was no better than picture-like to hang by th' wall, if renown made it not stir, was pleas'd to let him seek danger where he was like to find fame" (I, iii, 10–14). However, if the social order has became corrupt and there is nothing external to self with which nobility can be identified, then nobility itself becomes susceptible to corruption. It may turn into the blind idealism of Troilus or the misanthropy of Timon, or, in trying to sustain itself in isolation, it may petrify into pride, as it does in Coriolanus. For although Brutus may say that Coriolanus seeks "fame" (I, i, 28 ff.), Coriolanus himself seems only too aware that fame is meaningless unless it is received from a society worthy of rendering it. The value of the plebeians' "good report" is as dubious as the value of their words in general, for, as he says, "With every minute you do change a mind,/ And call him noble that was now your hate,/ Him vile that was your garland" (I, i, 186–188). If the identity and value of the self are made dependent upon public interpretations, then the whole structure of the self is in danger of collapsing as the social order collapses. Coriolanus's response to this problem is to render himself independent of public judgment by withdrawing into the fortress of his own nobility where he can be himself alone, as within the walls of Corioli "He is himself alone,/ To answer all the city" (I, iv, 51–52). He will answer the Volscians with his sword, but he refuses to be answerable to the plebeians', and ultimately to Rome's, judgments of him. It is not that he rejects unfavorable views of himself only; he rejects favorable views as well. For to accept praise would be to relinquish his right to total self-definition by acknowledging that his nobility is at least partly dependent upon the interpretations of others, even his mother (I, ix, 13–15). Thus his pseudo-modesty is prompted less by self-effacing than by self-aggrandizing motives; it is actually an assertion of the autonomy of self.

Coriolanus's attitudes toward both words and nobility come into dramatic focus in terms of the motif of "name." In I, ix, he both receives a name and forgets one. For his accomplishments at Corioli he is honored with the name "Coriolanus." It is a public honor, a symbol of the repute in which he is held, and the value of the name is supplied by the good opinion which prompts its bestowal. However, as we have said, Coriolanus is reluctant to accept others' judgments of him, even when the judgment is favorable. He accepts the name here and says that he will keep it meaningful, that he intends "at all times/ To undercrest your good addition/ To th' fairness of my power" (I, ix, 71–73), which should mean that he will so conduct himself that "Coriolanus" remains publicly accepted as a symbol of nobility. But as his subsequent conduct reveals, he has not accepted an obligation to the public so much as an obligation to self. He invests the name with his own private meaning and remains true to that, to his own conception of nobility, despite the fact that as he does so "Coriolanus" becomes increasingly a public symbol of pride instead of nobility. The name as a public symbol, as a negotiable word, is of less importance to him than the meaning which he himself injects into it. This leads to difficulties, of course, and in the same scene (I, ix) Shakespeare forecasts these difficulties when he has Coriolanus forget the name of the poor man of Corioli who had treated him hospitably.

In this minor incident with the man from Corioli, what Shakespeare is doing, it seems evident, is illustrating the futility of private meanings that cannot be translated into a public language. To Cominius and the others, the man from Corioli is meaningless, an anonymous Volscian prisoner; but to Coriolanus the man has a private significance that distinguishes him from all the other Volscian prisoners and makes him worthy of release. However, the private meaning of the man cannot be expressed by a publicly recognized symbol, the name Coriolanus has forgotten, and hence the kindness Coriolanus would do him cannot be effected. Unless meanings find their way into the public language and become subjects of general agreement, they are as doomed to anonymity as the Volscian prisoner.[4] Coriolanus could be well instructed by the plight of the man from Corioli, since he refuses to allow his

[4] Coriolanus's inability to give a name to the "meaning" of the man from Corioli here parallels Bottom's difficulties in *AMND* when he awakens in Act IV, scene i. The fairy reality experienced by fools like Bottom evaporates into "airy nothing," becoming a wordless "dream past the wit of man to say what dream it was," because Bottom lacks not only the wit but also the power over language to "say what dream it was." See *"A Midsummer Night's Dream:* The Illusion of Drama," *MLQ,* XXVI (1965), 506–522.

private identity, his "meaning," to enter and conform to, or in any way to be affected by, the mainstream of public opinion. Typically, however, he learns nothing from the incident, and hence he, like the Volscian, is finally banished into obscurity—"I' th' people's name" (III, iii, 104)—losing his "good name" publicly, though for him it remains privately and unalterably "good."

Thus we may see in the conflict between Coriolanus and the plebeians a conflict between a stationary meaning and drifting words, between private meanings incapable of fitting into a public language and a public language that has become meaningless, or, as we have said in our title, between wordless meanings and meaningless words. Isolated from one another in this fashion, both meanings and words become self-destructive as well as destructive of language generally. It is one of the major ironies of the play that Coriolanus, resolute, unyielding, shackled to his own verbal and moral integrity, becomes by virtue of these qualities every bit as manipulable by the tribunes as are the plebeians by virtue of their fickle irresolution (see, e.g., II, i, 269–275, II, iii, 266–268). Until the stable meaning can be linked reliably to the right word, language in Rome remains as chaotic as Rome's social and political order.

After his banishment from Rome Coriolanus appears without warning in Antium, where he seeks Aufidius. His situation when he faces Aufidius in IV, v, is analogous to that of the man of Corioli earlier. "Whence com'st thou?" Aufidius asks him, "What wouldst thou? Thy name? Why speak'st not? Speak, man: what's thy name?" (58–59) Coriolanus's reluctance to give his name can hardly be attributed to fear of consequences; fear, and most of all fear of physical punishment, is simply alien to him. Rather it would seem that he is attempting to impose his private identity upon Aufidius, his own individual "meaning" apart from his public name, as though despite the "mean apparel" he wears and the fact that his face is muffled the force of his unique nature could make him recognizable. Hence he then unmuffles himself, saying, "If, Tullus, not yet thou know'st me, and, seeing me, dost not think me the man I am, necessity commands me name myself." That Aufidius must ask for the name five times is a measure of Coriolanus's commitment to his private identity, to "the man I am" as distinct from the man he is publicly regarded as being. But at the same time, Aufidius's inability to identify him without the name reveals the futility of so exclusive a commitment to private meaning. For without name, honor, a public identity, Coriolanus becomes, not the autonomous individual he has striven to be, but a blank. Unable to acquire recognition on his own terms—"Know'st thou me yet?" he asks, and Aufidius replies "I know thee not. Thy name?" (69–70)—he is commanded by necessity to name himself:

> My name is Caius Marcius, who hath done
> To thee particularly and to all the Volsces
> Great hurt and mischief; thereto witness may

My surname, Coriolanus. The painful service,
The extreme dangers, and the drops of blood
Shed for my thankless country are requited
But with that surname; a good memory
And witness of the malice and displeasure
Which thou shouldst bear me. Only that name remains.
(IV, v, 71–79)

His private identity unrecognizable without the name, Coriolanus seems here for the first time to realize that his public identity is gone too, and that it matters. "Only that name remains": but the honorable surname has become merely breath, a word from which Rome has siphoned all meaning. Deprived of private and public meaning, and with little else to lose, Coriolanus can thus offer himself to Aufidius: "then, in a word, I also am/ Longer to live most weary, and present/ My throat to thee and to thy ancient malice" (100–102). It is not too farfetched to suggest that the phrase "in a word" here should be read literally. To live only "in a word," a sound void of significance, which is what "Coriolanus" has become, is worse than death.

By shifting his allegiance to the Volscians, Coriolanus trades in his identity as "Coriolanus." "Coriolanus" is no symbol of honor in Corioli—Aufidius accepts him not as "Coriolanus" but as "Marcius" (IV, v, 107, 112, 132, 153); nor is it any longer a symbol of honor in Rome, where "Coriolanus" has reverted to "Marcius" (IV, vi, 29, 43, 65, 70, 75). Its reserves of good opinion depleted, the name has become mere breath, an inadmissible sound; and Coriolanus has become "a kind of nothing" operating only on the borrowed capital of hatred. Reporting upon his attempt to intercede with Coriolanus, Cominius says:

Yet one time he did call me by my name,
I urg'd our old acquaintance, and the drops
That we have bled together. Coriolanus
He would not answer to; forbade all names;
He was a kind of nothing, titleless
Till he had forg'd himself a name o' th' fire
Of burning Rome. (V, i, 9–15)

If Coriolanus has himself become nothing, he now has the power to reduce Rome to nothing also, and in the process to forge for himself a new identity. When he was in Rome, the name of the people was dominant, and his own private meaning could find no adequate expression in their "voices" or language. Now he is the controller of language, and Rome must come to him to discover its own identity and meaning, whether it will remain "Rome" or be reduced to rubble. Roman words no longer have any power of definition. Thus when Menenius makes his bid for Coriolanus's mercy, he is told by the watchman, "The virtue of your name/ Is not here passable" (V, ii, 12–13); is silenced by Coriolanus, "Another word, Menenius,/ I will not hear thee speak" (V, ii, 97–98); and is mocked by the watchmen again as he leaves:

"Now, sir, is your name Menenius?"—"'Tis a spell, you see, of much power" (V, ii, 101–103).

However, if Coriolanus has cashed in his identity as "Coriolanus" by becoming the Volscians' general, he seems at some level of awareness to realize that a new identity forged in the fires of burning Rome is no more admissible than "Coriolanus" in Corioli. Though his conduct as Volscian general looks good on the surface, Aufidius observes, "yet he hath left undone/ That which shall break his neck or hazard mine/ Whene'er we come to our account" (IV, vii, 24–26). He has given his "word" to the Volscians that he will serve their cause, but this verbal commitment is not backed by a full psychic commitment, as Aufidius perceives. Thus his nascent identity as Volscian general collapses when in V, iii, his family bring their combined verbal and emotional pressures to bear upon him. The name that he would forge in the fires of burning Rome is revealed in its true nature for him by Volumnia:

> ...if thou conquer Rome, the benefit
> Which thou shalt thereby reap is such a name
> Whose repetition will be dogg'd with curses,
> Whose chronicle thus writ: "The man was noble,
> But with his last attempt he wip'd it out,
> Destroy'd his country, and his name remains
> To th' ensuing age abhorr'd." (V, iii, 142–148)

That name and the meaning that goes with it he rejects. As a result, "Coriolanus" becomes again a symbol of honor in Rome, and Coriolanus himself regains in the consciousness of the Romans his former identity: "Unshout the noise that banish'd Marcius!" one of the senators cries as Volumnia and the others make their triumphant entrance to Rome, "Repeal him with the welcome of his mother" (V, v, 4–5).

Coriolanus, however, returns not to Rome but to Corioli, knowing perfectly well what the cost of his betrayal will be: "Most dangerously you have with [your son] prevail'd," he tells Volumnia, "If not most mortal to him," adding, however, "But let it come" (V, iii, 188–189). In a speech hopelessly out of character with his former self (V, vi, 71–84), he attempts to reinstate himself with the Volscians, defending himself in his public role as Volscian general. But Aufidius, in attacking him as Volscian general, also attacks him personally as "Marcius" and "boy." " 'Marcius!' " Coriolanus repeats angrily. "Ay, Marcius, Caius Marcius! Dost thou think I'll grace thee with that robbery, thy stol'n name,/ Coriolanus, in Corioli?" (88–90) Coriolanus's violent repetition, " 'Marcius!' " indicates that he is now identifying himself with "Coriolanus." But what does "Coriolanus" mean to him now? Does he realize that by saving Rome he has earned the right to "Coriolanus" again, that the word has again become a symbol of honor in Rome, and that in accepting the name for himself he is asserting not merely an individual identity but also his public identity as a Roman? If so, then it would seem that the wordless meaning and the meaningless word have finally achieved the synthesis required for language to be viable. However, if such a synthesis is suggested, it is so only briefly, as though Shakespeare momentarily flashed into view an ideal possibility which must remain dramatically unrealized. For in his last assertion of identity it is not an image of himself as Rome's soldier that Coriolanus capitalizes upon:

> Cut me to pieces, Volsces; men and lads,
> Stain all your edges on me. "Boy!" False hound!
> If you have writ your annals true, 'tis there
> That, like an eagle in a dove-cote, I
> Flutter'd your Volscians in Corioli;
> Alone I did it. "Boy!"

He is attempting of course to create an image of self superior to the occasion, invoking death not for the man who saved Rome and betrayed the Volscians, but for the man who stormed Corioli single-handed. There is a certain limited grandeur in his assertion of a self transcendently isolated and autonomous, answerable to nothing but its own conception of nobility; it has meaning and force, but it is still the old meaning, unmodified by experience, untouched by understanding. Coriolanus never learns what Aufidius knows, that "our virtues/ Lie in th' interpretation of the time" (IV, vii, 49–50), that the private meaning becomes fully meaningful only when it submits itself to the discipline of language. Yet he does impose his meaning upon language, or, perhaps more accurately, language and the "interpretation of the time" are sufficiently flexible at the end to accept the Coriolanus meaning under the head of "noble"—"Yet he shall have a noble memory" (155)—although the last word of the play, "Assist," suggests a relation between meanings and words, and between individuals and societies, that he could never grasp.

# 37

# The Image of Antony: Lyric and Tragic Imagination

*Arnold Stein*

Antony is no explorer of consciousness. He has very little Hamlet or Macbeth in him. Nor does he, like a Lear, come into his tragic self by the eloquence of suffering. But he has, like everyone, his images of himself, and these he expresses, not directly in soul-searching, but indirectly in imaginative gestures that project the self he has in his mind's eye. That self, being an object of expression, and Antony being Antony, is, it follows, a public self. The play, however, will not grant Antony exclusive control of the public image, various though the contributions of its author are. There must be other contributions, which supplement, and qualify, and assert their claim to describe the public image. Somewhere, we must assume, the real self of Antony does exist among these images. What is the process, we must ask ourselves, which finally permits Antony, against great odds, to project an authentic tragic self which is the image that emerges triumphantly from all the others?

The landmark to start from is that defiant assertion:

> Let Rome in Tiber melt, and the wide arch
> Of the rang'd empire fall! Here is my space.

It is an imagined world, that space—like Hamlet's nut-shell. "The nobleness of life" there asserted comes as an act of the transcendent will, defying the ordinary world to say otherwise. It is a view much mocked by the play, beginning with the very first lines of the preceding scene and followed at once with Cleopatra's "Excellent falsehood!" Rome refuses to melt, and the world of clay and dung has its own energy of will to command men's efforts against a world the lovers assert.

The early play gives us other gestures to note. There is Antony as the man's man, the soldier's soldier. His life in Egypt makes explicit for his men one perennial dream of the soldier. But back of that lies an opposite ideal—opposite, yet to a soldier not contradictory. Caesar is invoking the absent Antony:

Antony,
Leave thy lascivious wassails. When thou once
Was beaten from Modena, where thou slewst
Hirtius and Pansa, consuls, at thy heel
Did famine follow; whom thou fought'st against,
Though daintily brought up, with patience more
Than savages could suffer. Thou didst drink
The stale of horses, and the gilded puddle
Which beasts would cough at; thy palate then did deign
The roughest berry on the rudest hedge;
Yea, like the stag, when snow the pasture sheets,
The barks of trees thou brows'd; on the Alps
It is reported thou didst eat strange flesh,
Which some did die to look on; and all this—
It wounds thine honour that I speak it now—
Was borne so like a soldier, that thy cheek
So much as lank'd not.

This is a "nobleness of life," a transcendence of will, to which Caesar can give single-minded admiration. (He would rather fast for four days than feast for one.) What he is not interested in seeing is that the same high energy of will can be applied to a feast as to a famine.

The public image of a man's man must represent not only the kinds of unattainable strength which all admire, but also the kinds of humanizing weakness in which all may fraternally participate. "As for my wife," says Antony to Caesar, turning against himself the common, endearing joke, while managing the deft apology which makes all mankind, past and present, support a share in the loss of dignity:

As for my wife,
I would you had her spirit in such another.
The third o' th' world is yours, which with a snaffle
You may pace easy, but not such a wife.

Or again, in answer to Pompey's polite surprise at his unexpected presence, Antony can reply with a characteristically masculine grace:

> The beds i' th' East are soft; and thanks to you,
> That called me timelier than my purpose hither...

Some of Antony's range of charm is caught up in these few words. First, there is the easy admission of the known manly weakness, the universal joke he is confident enough to share with others. At the same time there is the candid acknowledgement, as man to man, of the opponent's effective power to draw him hence. Implicit and utterly itself is the fact—standing against all common rumors and predictions—of his being where he now is.

Antony may be considered Shakespeare's manliest man. This is not a category for which any certain criteria exist; but one may assume that what will be most important is not the degree of muscular development, or any other single, extreme specialization of manliness. The manliest man will be most admired by other men, not only for his virtues but for his faults. (The play does not neglect this puzzle in Antony's character.) Nor will the judgment of men, however ungrudging, suffice without the complementary judgment of women. Cleopatra, a connoisseur of some masculine virtues and the choicest masculine faults, may testify here. And not least important, such a man must exhibit a discriminating but strong weakness for women. If he is a great conqueror, it will help that Cleopatra gets him drunk the morning after a night before, and puts him to bed decked in her clothes while she wears "his sword Philippan." It will help if his response to Cleopatra's first gorgeous display of herself is that of the simple, shy, awkward male:

> Our courteous Antony,
> Whom ne'er the word of "No" woman heard speak,
> Being barber'd ten times o'er, goes to the feast.

Antony loves women and all *their* womanly weaknesses. He can act like a lyric poet rejoicing in the full sensibility of the moment (and ignoring time) when Octavia takes her sisterly farewell of Caesar:

> The April's in her eyes; it is love's spring,
> And these the showers to bring it on....
> Her tongue will not obey her heart, nor can
> Her heart inform her tongue,—the swan's down-feather,
> That stands upon the swell at the full of tide,
> And neither way inclines.

Antony savors moments, can put himself wholly into a moment; and this would appear to be a major source of both strength and weakness. But a source of this ability, to push matters a little further back, must be located in the man's heroic self-confidence. It is a rich and complex confidence. At the worst it may seem to approach petulance at one extreme and megalomania at another. Or it may seem as concentrated on short time and as evasive of long time as the gambler's *fiducia*. But it is a real and unquestionable base of strength, from which he can freely admit real weakness, which is always complicated in effect; and though he can also extravagantly display the shallow forms of weakness to which strength and confidence are conventionally subject, no superficial extravagance on his part quite counters the steady presence of an essential confidence. Gesture after gesture reaffirms the rich resource he draws upon, and proves—whether or not in the main assertion at least moment by moment—a "nobleness of life." The old term, which does not simplify the problem in its context, is "magnanimity"—that authentic generosity of imagination that shapes with spontaneous grace the superior response to ordinary and immediate concerns. We shall see better examples later, but let us for the moment draw again on the scene of parting from Caesar. When it is Antony's turn to act, and to separate the farewell embrace of brother and sister, he does it thus, with a magnificence that elevates the honest sentiment of the scene, and—the caustic remarks of Enobarbus notwithstanding—endows the moment with the personal style of Antony:

> Come, sir, come;
> I'll wrestle with you in my strength of love.
> Look, here I have you; thus I let you go,
> And give you to the gods.

In defeat the confidence of Antony is subjected to intensified pressures and revelations. He wilfully elects to fight by sea, "For that he dares us to 't." If we fail, he adds, "We then can do 't at land." But this is true, he forgets, only if it is the hero of Modena speaking, and absolutely sure of his discipline, and of his own effective belief in his leadership. When the blow falls he faces an anguished image of self under the shadow of a transformed opponent and a terrible change of circumstances and time. He must imagine, and perform, the "shifts of lowness," the gestures of diplomacy not backed by any confidence in his power over the moment. The mature hero who played as he pleased with half the world must now humble himself before "the young man." Antony says all the bitter things.

But the sudden decline in the material basis of his greatness is not accompanied by any simple and equivalent decline in his grandeur of gesture. The external report we hear is that he "violated" himself, that he followed Cleopatra "like a doting mallard." Antony's own version elevates the metaphors from a sub-human to a superhuman level: "Thy beck might from the bidding of the gods/Command me." And soon there comes a shift of mood—Shakespeare's great device for shaping an inner conflict between the chills and fevers of imagination, a device already present in success but accelerated and heightened in defeat:

> Fall not a tear, I say; one of them rates
> All that is won and lost: give me a kiss.
> Even this repays me.

It is the lyric imagination asserting itself against brute fact, and proclaiming the human value of earthly love over other earthly values, indeed, over "the bidding of the gods" as well. It is an impressive gesture, but it will be matched and bettered many times, and especially because in the present context the assertiveness of the gesture leaves itself a little exposed. The grandeur once launched, Antony's mind creeps back to its immersion in prose fact. Has the schoolmaster-ambassador returned? "Love, I am full of lead." He shouts an order for wine "and our viands." And then another piece of grandeur, that consciously picks itself up again, as it were, from the unpleasant surroundings among which it has fallen back: "Fortune knows/We scorn her most when most she offers blows." It is a dubious aphorism; it may even strike one as desperate, but that is to underestimate Antony. Still, we cannot ignore the pattern, or process, which Antony has revealed. It reminds us, inevitably, of that grand assertion with which the drama began—that "nobleness of life" which flaunted the world, and at the time could. But even more important, we are being alerted to a development implicit in that first assertion, and now in part released: a development that points toward a tragic center of the human mind creating its own reality.

At this point we need a group of comments which come in rapid succession from Enobarbus. The fault, he tells Cleopatra, was Antony's alone, and the shame equalled the loss. Antony "would make his will/Lord of his Reason." That is a comment which cannot be separated from the behavior subsequent to the battle, for it coldly confronts Antony's lyric efforts to outface the shame and loss. And at the end of the scene, as Antony's confidence rises and the feast is proclaimed, we have the harsh analysis that he has been "frighted out of fear": "A diminution in our captain's brain/Restores his heart." Magnanimity, always hard to separate from courage, is here associated with the ancient flaw to which courage is most subject: ignorance and reckless delusion. It is also one line of development possible for manly weakness.

In between these two detached and unsympathetic comments are two statements of far greater resonance, for they intensify attitudes at the heart of the play. First there is the penetrating summary:

> I see men's judgements are
> A parcel of their fortunes; and things outward
> Do draw the inward quality after them,
> To suffer all alike.

In tone this is like the preceding remarks, and the context is the desperate "dream" that Caesar would entertain a challenge to single combat, and "Against a sworder!" But the statement is resonant because it is central; and the larger terms of the judgment here pronounced concern the truth of the imagination itself and the abiding issue of the "real" Antony. Enobarbus is passing the hardheaded, shrewd judgment; he is impressed with the immediate power and effective reality of "things outward." And he has the dominating support of the bulk of the play, and certainly of the plot, which has consciously maneuvered Antony into this pass—but, as certainly, not in order to read the simple lesson upon him. We must return to the issue involved here, for we cannot engage it fully at this point. But Enobarbus himself in part returns, and almost in the next breath. It is to imagine profoundly the complexities of genuine weakness and to raise again the claims of imaginative truth:

> Mine honesty and I begin to square.
> The loyalty well held to fools does make
> Our faith mere folly; yet he that can endure
> To follow with allegiance a fallen lord
> Does conquer him that did his master conquer,
> And earns a place i' th' story.

As foreground to the comments of Enobarbus we have Antony's indecorous whipping of the messenger and his vulgar quarrel with Cleopatra—beautifully timed to *follow* the lovely "Fall not a tear" and the scene that demonstrates Caesar's unblinking awareness of his advantage. Furthermore, for a while Antony's image of himself threatens to lose all dignity and power. He can muster no more than irritation at Caesar, and a kind of merely peevish imagination:

> He makes me angry with him; for he seems
> Proud and disdainful, harping on what I am,
> Not what he knew I was. He makes me angry.

But such an image fades almost at once, and he draws another breath, more authentically his own, in the very next line:

> And at this time most easy 'tis to do 't,
> When my good stars, that were my former guides,
> Have empty left their orbs, and shot their fires
> Into th' abysm of hell.

With another violent upswing the old Antony returns to make a characteristic gesture:

> Let's have one other gaudy night. Call to me
> All my sad captains. . . .

tonight I'll force
The wine peep through their scars. Come on, my queen;
There's sap in 't yet.

We have heard Enobarbus on the brain and the heart. Caesar adds his comment by also ordering a feast:

And feast the army; we have store to do 't.
And they have earn'd the waste. Poor Antony!

We never see the feast that is going to "drown consideration," though we do not doubt what it will be like, more or less. It begins like a last supper, with Antony exchanging his reckless grandeur of gesture for the humbler gestures of manly weakness. It is a weakness that evokes deep human feeling in men who have shared his fortunes, and even Enobarbus is "onion-ey'd." We have had some insight into the kinds of weakness which were a source of Antonys' power over men at the height of his heroic confidence. Now that it is real weakness ringing its changes, and making its claims on the spontaneous generosity of manly hearts, we have some further insight into a source of Antony's genuine power. The answer still must be referred to *confidence* and *magnanimity*. It is a humble magnanimity, producing gestures which allow his followers to share the grief: "I wish I could be made so many men. . . that I might do you service/So good as you have done." It revives their old association, and their *sense* of that: which is a mysterious thing and a power of leadership. And the memory of that depends upon what he was. Which brings us back to the confidence: his confidence, which he can make good, in a real Antony who *was*.

Looked at narrowly, the generous feelings he can express and create derive from an image he has of himself. But the effects cannot be limited to, or explained away by, any simple exposure of source. In spite of all that the play unsparingly reveals, Antony is the inscrutable master of spontaneous and generous honesty. (This may not be so admirable as a "free" and disciplined honesty, but our subject is a man and not a monumental idea.) He can greet the old soldier: "Would thou and those thy scars had once prevail'd/To make me fight at land!" And there is the crowning

Say that I wish he never find more cause
To change a master. O, my fortunes have
Corrupted honest men!

It is a gesture that overwhelms Enobarbus. Even before the messenger and his treasure arrive, he has united rational analysis with moral imagination and consciously acknowledged his "ill." Now he loses his conscious place "i' th' story," but in his defeat he lends authority to the story. The last wish of the tough-minded Enobarbus subscribes to the reality of the image of Antony, and to the "story," and to the earning of "a place."

Who is the Antony who has evoked this great gesture of defeated loyalty, the private tragedy in a ditch? Not the demigod of Cleopatra's lyrical "dream"—not to Enobarbus. Nor the extended figure of Antony's own heroic imagination. Nor just the titular leader to whom Enobarbus owes loyalty, in spite of the many faults clearly seen in all their comic undress. Nor just the ruined leader, as recklessly generous in defeat as in victory. We are made to see many Antonies by Enobarbus. No one is "real," and all together they are a composite of the play's imagination; but a symbol of commanding power, more real to Enobarbus than the world or his own life. (The world is real to him only as a place in which to register his shame, but forgiveness lies only in Antony.) The symbol is more real, one wants to say, than Antony's life, or Antony the mere man without an image. Rome will not melt into Tiber; it has to be there for Caesar to return to. And Enobarbus, that casual lover of the world's body, offers only the private testimony of one converted man. But Enobarbus is no ordinary convert. He stands midway between Antony and Caesar, and he tries to stand as the detached, witty observer. But his wit is defeated by tragedy. And this, we may recognize, is one authentic rhythm of human fate.

The central statement of what Antony is not, the full denial of the imaginative illusion, we get from Antony. It is part of the agony of "greatness going off." Charmian compares it to the agony of the soul and body which "rive not more in parting." But it is also the agony of a world coming apart, a world which is inextricably compounded of the real and the imagined, a world centered on Antony but reaching out far beyond him. Antony provides a great, clear statement against what is imaginary in that world; but even he, with all his tragic authority of vision upon him, cannot dismiss, cannot cancel out, that compound world, neither for himself nor for others. There will be further statements to follow. Here is Antony's:

> Sometime we see a cloud that's dragonish;
> A vapour sometime like a bear or lion,
> A tower'd citadel, a pendent rock,
> A forked mountain, or blue promontory
> With trees upon 't, that nod unto the world,
> And mock our eyes with air. Thou hast seen these signs;
> They are black vesper's pageants. . . .
> That which is now a horse, even with a thought
> The rack dislimns, and makes it indistinct,
> As water is in water. . . .
> My good knave Eros, now thy captain is
> Even such a body: here I am Antony;
> Yet cannot hold this visible shape, my knave.

The central counterstatement is by Cleopatra, whose tragic commission it is to proclaim the truth of Antony's image, and to be herself drawn up into it. Her audience is, according to Shakespeare's unflinching dramatic tact, an unsympathetic one. It is Dolabella, Caesar's friend. Cleopatra describes him before she begins:

> You laugh when boys or women tell their dreams;
> Is't not your trick?

And then her statement:

> I dream'd there was an Emperor Antony.
> O, such another sleep, that I might see
> But such another man!...
> His legs bestrid the ocean; his rear'd arm
> Crested the world; his voice was propertied
> As all the tuned spheres, and that to friends;
> But when he meant to quail and shake the orb,
> He was as rattling thunder. For his bounty,
> There was no winter in 't; an autumn 'twas
> That grew the more by reaping: his delights
> Were dolphin-like, they show'd his back above
> The element they liv'd in: in his livery
> Walk'd crowns and crownets; realms and islands were
> As plates dropp'd from his pocket....
> Think you there was or might be such a man
> As this I dream'd of?

"Gentle madam, no," he answers. But if he will not subscribe to the literal truth of the dream, he will subscribe to the authenticity of the grief and its dimensions. And no object-in-itself, we must pause to remember, ever causes grief by its loss. It is always the object-and-its-image in the mind and heart of the loser. In no other human experience, perhaps, is the imagination so incontestably and essentially inseparable from the fact. Dercetas has already demonstrated one familiar human response to loss: he has run hopefully to Caesar with Antony's self-bloodied sword. Dolabella demonstrates another familiar response. It includes, properly enough, but is not limited by, his own allegiance to practical truth, the practical truth of success:

> Hear me, good madam.
> Your loss is as yourself, great; and you bear it
> As answering to the weight. Would I might never
> O'ertake pursu'd success, but I do feel,
> By the rebound of yours, a grief that smites
> My very heart at root.

And he reveals the necessary fact to make the tragedy possible, that Caesar will lead her in triumph to Rome. A little later he reveals the precise timing.

However reluctantly, he joins Enobarbus in disloyalty to a leader; and so also earns his place "i' th' story," helps create the story; and like Enobarbus, unwillingly and indirectly testifies to an authenticity in the "dream."

In between these two central statements of what Antony is we have a renewal of the great gestures of confident imagination. Caesar briefly joins the chorus of high feeling, against the bent of self and the forces he represents in the play. He enters the moment with the proper credentials of adequate Roman eloquence. As Maecenas says,

> When such a spacious mirror's set before him,
> He needs must see himself.

Antony has the spendthrift generosity of a master of moments, but Caesar is in partnership with time, and is neither master of nor subject to the moment. He interrupts his eloquence, properly, when his alert eye notices that the "business" of an entering messenger "looks out of him." And when he returns to the subject the moment has been assimilated into time. Come to my tent, the victor says, aware that the past must be brought into workable public relations with present and future. Read over the evidence, "How hardly I was drawn into this war."

But Caesar is an unwilling witness, and we have Antony himself, with a renewed confidence of imagination rising to meet his end. A falsehood, not to be dignified with the word imagination, reports Cleopatra's death, and he resolves to die.

> Eros!—I come, my queen!—Eros!—Stay for me!
> Where souls do couch on flowers, we'll hand in hand,
> And with our sprightly port make the ghosts gaze.
> Dido and her Aeneas shall want troops,
> And all the haunt be ours.

It is a magnificent gesture. The grandeur no longer available to the imagination on earth invades the world of death and reestablishes its kingdom. It is the kingdom of lyric poetry, subject neither to time nor Caesar, and defiantly invulnerable to, because indifferent to, fact. The nobleness of life, or death, receives another external testimony by Eros, in word and deed.

> Turn from me, then, that noble countenance,
> Wherein the worship of the whole world lies,

he says, and then kills himself rather than kill Antony, and so out-gestures the master, and by "brave instruction" gains upon him "A nobleness in record." Antony pays his usual generous tribute, and then imagines that he will be

A bridegroom in my death, and run into 't
As to a lover's bed.

But he botches a little: which is another comment on what he is; but it is also a grand dramatic opportunity for a little postponement and a full death-scene, with a full, confident restatement of what he was, as an image that dominates what he is, and offers to the present mind the nourishment of that past image, now reasserted in triumph over the last moment, when the dignity of human death suspends all usual debate and rebuttal, and a man is under the greatest pressure either to embrace the image he holds of himself or to reject it.

The miserable change now at my end
Lament nor sorrow at; but please your thoughts
In feeding them with those my former fortunes
Wherein I liv'd, the greatest prince o' the world,
The noblest.

Cleopatra is left to carry on, with a story far more difficult to tell in the world than the assignment Hamlet leaves Horatio. I have had to neglect Cleopatra, and I shall want to return finally to Shakespeare's brilliant invention in giving her an independent tragic development. But first let us follow up her contribution to the lyrical statement of the imagination:

O, see, my women,
The crown o' the earth doth melt. My lord!
O, wither'd is the garland of the war,
The soldier's pole is fall'n! Young boys and girls
Are level now with men; the odds is gone,
And there is nothing left remarkable
Beneath the visiting moon.

What is the effect of this great poeticism? It is made of the same stuff, and partly of the same language, as Macbeth's lament for the death of Duncan. But that is a different scene, and language always imagines its reality in a scene, though some of its energy, one would want to admit, can escape from its local place and speak to willing ears in other places. Cleopatra is convincing in the moment's passion. It is lyric and not subject to fact, but subject only to the truth and the energy of the feelings, and to the audience's willingness to believe in the truth of the feelings and to respond to that truth, which is a truth created by the imagined object of the loss. The audience will not be more sternly sceptical than Dolabella. And yet the poeticism radiates out from this scene to meet the contradiction, not only outside this scene but partly built into it too.

Lyric, I say, is indifferent to fact. Lyric is the authorized human expression of the unapologetic imagination. For lyric must be true only to the truth of the feelings. Its right is to express its rightness rightly. It can be wrong only by reference to what lies outside itself; and even here, when caught in the very flagrance of the error it advertizes, it may gain strength in our recognition, a redoubled confirmation of its rightness. We have the case of Dolabella, but let me refer to another more famous incident, Lear's recovery of consciousness to see Cordelia bending over him:

> You do me wrong to take me out o' th' grave.
> Thou art a soul in bliss; but I am bound
> Upon a wheel of fire, that mine own tears
> Do scald like molten lead.

The feelings are so extreme and brief here that only a literal mind of prodigious consistency would want to examine the probable accuracy of the details. But there is another scene in which the illusion is more consciously separated from reality. Lear, who has suffered through all illusion, and paid almost all the full price of his tragic progress, can still return to a fabricated lyric illusion, a lovely impossible paradise that seems to contradict his hard-earned tragic vision.

> Come, let's away to prison;
> We two alone will sing like birds i' th' cage.
> When thou dost ask me blessing, I'll kneel down
> And ask of thee forgiveness. So we'll live,
> And pray, and sing, and tell old tales, and laugh
> At gilded butterflies, and hear poor rogues
> Talk of court news; and we'll talk with them too,
> Who loses and who wins; who's in, who's out;
> And take upon 's the mystery of things
> As if we were gods' spies; and we'll wear out,
> In a wall'd prison, packs and sects of great ones,
> That ebb and flow by the moon.

Even after we have noted the pathetic admission of guilt, and the qualitative changes that echo the process of Lear's tragic transformation, still we shall not subscribe to that dream. And if we should take a severe and measured view of human affairs, we might have to deny the rightness of the feelings and declare that there has been a relapse from the tragic height—one that brings Lear perilously close to the senility that characterizes him at the beginning of the play. But one thing he has most securely earned already, the right that we not judge him; we have lost that right, we have disqualified ourselves. All we can have left to apply to him is pity. And the lyric levels directly at that now, and teaches us its own human lesson.

To return to Cleopatra. She follows her lyric lament for Antony by turning directly to herself and her own feelings. It is not rhapsodic, no high assertion of fancy. In one respect it may seem to deny the whole order of the preceding image.

No more but e'en a woman, and commanded
By such poor passion as the maid that milks
And does the meanest chores.

But it is only, we may see, another kind of lyric, an imaginative acknowledgement of the most un-empress-like common humanity, one which verifies the truth of the high feelings by admitting the personal failure, the imaginative inability to maintain the high point of feeling.

It were for me
To throw my sceptre at the injurious gods;
To tell them than this world did equal theirs
Till they had stolen our jewel.

But the lyric imagination fails, and this is part of its inevitable course when it participates in the tragic imagination. (This is too simple a description of a complex relationship, and I shall want to add another word at least.)

The final wonderful focus of the play is all on Cleopatra. But who is Cleopatra? The play has not neglected to provide rich and varied images of her, both images of her own making and those supplied by others, friend or foe or friend-and-foe. We have to take shortcuts, so let us deal with the last big image, the one that contains all the others. This is the "story" of Antony's grandeur, his "nobleness of life," in which her own image participates, both by proclaiming his and by proclaiming and acting out her own in his. Not without some famous embarrassment, of course. She does not choose tragedy, but who does? She is not even ground into it, like Antony, by immediate and long-range error, by external forces showing their hand steadily from afar and gaining momentum in spite of the fine living shifts and starts in the long day's dying. She is backed into it, and though on a throne and not in a ditch like Enobarbus, she has less real freedom of choice than he. But it is on a grand scale, in spite of all the play's counter-statements and the presence of hard-eyed sordid necessity. She is not a new but a specialized Cleopatra; the potential in her is elevated by external circumstances. The grandeur of her past (however qualified, or challenged, or illusory), and the image that she holds of Antony, faced by the squalor of the future—these push her into a present grandeur of gesture that is authentically tragic, though few tragic figures can rival this full presentation of the contradictory elements out of which the tragic is made. But whether the tragic now comes clearly from character or not, whether earned in advance or borrowed on human credit and then deserved, the results come from the authentic human resources of tragedy. Her boldest expression of faith in the greatness of Antony expresses a greatness that she must share:

But, if there be or ever were one such,
It's past the size of dreaming: nature wants stuff
To vie strange forms with fancy; yet, t' imagine

An Antony, were nature's piece 'gainst fancy,
Condemning shadows quite.

She speaks, and causes those around her to speak, the bonafide high tragic feelings, and we recognize the language, which even skilful actresses will find hard to conjure up for any occasion.

My desolation does begin to make
A better life. 'Tis paltry to be Caesar;
Not being Fortune, he's but Fortune's knave,
A minister of her will: and it is great
To do that thing that ends all other deeds;
Which shackles accidents and bolts up change;
Which sleeps, and never palates more the dung,
The beggar's nurse and Caesar's.

She is made to weather one final great self-created scene for self-humiliation, her being caught out cold, her white fingers and swarthy cheeks most red with unqueenly embarrassment, when her treasurer reveals that she has juggled the books and held out "some lady trifles" on Caesar. But that is not the real issue; it is only incidental to her sifting of Caesar's intentions. She does not need ordinary dignity any more, and she has the language to show that. She says, of Caesar's polite eloquence:

He words me, girls, he words me, that I should not
Be noble to myself.

And she endures the clown's fine clowning, and adds her own, wishing the asp could speak, "That I might hear thee call great Caesar ass/Unpolicied." A fine insult to the image of Caesar. And all the final lyrics are equal to the nobility of the feelings:

Show me, my women, like a queen: go fetch
My best attires; I am again for Cydnus
To meet Mark Antony. . . .
Methinks I hear
Antony call; I see him rouse himself
To praise my noble act; I hear him mock
The luck of Caesar, which the gods give men
To excuse their after wrath. Husband, I come!
Now to that name my courage prove my title!
The stroke of death is as a lover's pinch,
Which hurts, and is desir'd. . . .
If she first meet the curled Antony,
He'll make demand of her, and spend that kiss
Which is my heaven to have. . . .
Peace, peace!
Dost thou not see my baby at my breast,
That sucks the nurse asleep?

Now for some final considerations. We have a tragedy that bodies forth dramatically all the evidence against itself, against tragedy, against the life of the imagination. The final failure of the imagination—and it is a failure, we had better admit it, but we had also better recognize that the subject of tragedy is failure, and the failure is always complex—the final failure of imagination is not entirely unlike failure in other great human assignments. It is not literal or self-contained failure, except to the literal. It is resonant in the imagination: where it means and feels, where it reveals human nature in an essential condition. The fire that proves the tragic truth finally is not so much the world and its unattractive material concerns (or the countering effects of Enobarbus and Dolabella), but the follies of the protagonists and their central illusion of greatness, their checkered dream of "nobleness of life" that cannot destroy the dream. "Nobleness of life" is submitted to the most outrageous and humiliating domestic revelations, as well as to a full range of external comic exhibition. But it is powerful to assert itself; if not to persuade us, at least to baffle our judgments with a brilliant mixing of dramatic arguments. Then finally, as the destruction of the dream closes in, the protagonists separately escape the destruction. The victor possesses the prosaic world, and its business, to which he is subject in order to be master; but the defeated possess their dream, even if the question of the dream still remains an open one. Antony and Cleopatra are subject to their dream, it is true; they give in to it, but not in order to achieve any relationship of mastery, like Caesar's: but in order to be one with their dream, to become it, to be it. They refuse to admit their absurdity, though they would willingly take a convenient way out—Antony as a private citizen in Athens, and Cleopatra her ordinary legal throne in Egypt. They would accept the fate of ordinary rational folk. But if denied this opportunity they will not recant and recite the elementary human lesson. The dream that in its bad moments looks like ordinary self-infatuated egocentricity, by persevering, by refusing to come to terms with the world, survives, and defies the world from beyond the grave. And the world, even Caesar, will admire them. But the world cannot afford such everyday luxuries, though it can afford to admire, as a "story" someone else lives. Do we go too far if we say the world *must* admire—perhaps to endure the world's business? Caesar has the last word; it is not one of scorn, though time, as usual, is pressing:

High events as these
Strike those that make them; and their story is
No less in pity than his glory which
Brought them to be lamented. Our army shall
In solemn show attend this funeral;
And then to Rome.

One final note on the lyric order. It is indifferent to fact; but in a tragedy, which is no self-contained lyric world, the lyric is not exempt from the force of fact, and must pay the price for its rightness of feeling. What we finally approve in our tragic wisdom may not be the rightness of the feeling, perhaps not even the imaginative rightness: but the right—proved and paid for, however reluctantly—of a man to feel what he feels. When we are reduced by tragedy to the basic question, we have passed righteousness (most easily), and rightness. We are left only with right, and the question, What is man? The tragic wins over the lyric; but it is benevolent and tolerant—lessons learned from the familiar imagination of human defeat. It does not repeal the lyric, or scorn it, but allows its voice to be heard even in the final chorus, and to make its mingled claim in the memory of the listener.

# 38

# The Time Sense of *Antony and Cleopatra*

*David Kaula*

*Antony and Cleopatra* opens with one Roman commenting to another on what is, to them, the deplorable change that has come over their general: the Mars-like warrior of the past has become the "strumpet's fool" of the present. A little later, Antony, after refusing to hear the latest news from Rome, insists to Cleopatra that nothing matters but the immediate "now":

> Now for the love of Love and her soft hours,
> Let's not confound the time with conference harsh.
> There's not a minute of our lives should stretch
> Without some pleasure now. (I, i, 44–47)

In scene ii, Charmian and Iras hear the Soothsayer obscurely prophesy approaching misfortune for them and their mistress, but instead of taking his words seriously they blithely anticipate a future of unlimited sensual gratification. When Antony next appears, he is listening with alarm to the messengers' reports of the rapidly worsening situation in Italy and other parts of the Empire. No longer finding the present moment all-sufficient—

*Reprinted from* Shakespeare Quarterly, *XV (1964) by permission of the author and of The Shakespeare Association of America, Inc.*

The present pleasure,
By revolution low'ring, does become
The opposite of itself— (I, ii, 120–122)

he rebukes himself for his idleness and resolves to return to Rome with all possible speed. When Cleopatra caustically reminds him of his earlier vows of eternal fidelity he pleads the "strong necessity of time."

These few instances, all coming in the first three scenes, are enough to alert us to the special importance of time in the play as a whole. The sharp fluctuations of awareness between past, present, and future, the sudden turnabouts of attitude in response to the pressure of events, the emphatic contrasts between loyalty and expedience, idleness and activity—these continue through the play, complementing the equally free and versatile handling of geographical space. Much of the action is infused with that sense of temporal urgency which was felt so strongly by Shakespeare and his contemporaries, to whom time very often appeared in the guise of the insidious destroyer, the ever-active opponent of the human need for continuity. But the play also reveals another, more distinctly Shakespearian awareness of time, one which was gradually deepened and subtilized as Shakespeare's powers as a dramatist increased. It shows the intimate relationship the sense of time bears to the basic contours of the dramatic action, and its significance as one of the principal media through which the characters reveal their governing attitudes and thereby locate themselves within the moral universe of the play.

Although it embraces a historical period of ten years, the action of the play does not proceed in chronicle fashion through a series of virtually independent episodes. It rather gives the impression of rapid, continuous movement. Especially in the first three acts, beginning with Antony's hasty departure from Egypt and culminating in his defeat at Actium, the complexion of affairs in the political realm is constantly shifting as one development follows another with almost confusing speed. Shakespeare fortifies this impression by resorting to a device he had used more perfunctorily in the earlier history plays, that of frequently introducing messengers bearing the "news" which time has brought forth in other places. When Antony refuses to hear the messenger from Rome in the first scene he is trying, as it were, to erect a barrier against the irresistible pressure of time, so that when in the next scene he does receive the news—now conveyed by two messengers instead of one—it is as though a dam were bursting. Things happen so quickly that in some instances the news is already stale in the telling, rendered obsolete by the events of preceding scenes. At the beginning of Act I, scene iv, for instance, Caesar speaks of Antony as still idling in Alexandria when in fact he is already on his way to Rome; and in Act II, scene v Cleopatra learns of Antony's marriage to Octavia after he has privately made up his mind to return to Egypt. Through his abrupt shifts of locale Shakespeare also creates the impression that time moves at different velocities in different places. The last-mentioned scene is followed by four scenes of complex activity which take place in various parts of the Empire: Misenum, Pompey's galley, Syria, and Rome. Act III, scene iii returns us to Cleopatra, showing her listening to the messenger's description of Octavia after she had received the original report five scenes earlier. Thus if time in the world of political affairs moves with relentless speed, in Alexandria, while Cleopatra has nothing to do but wait for Antony, it is almost static.

During those periods in the action when the pressure of events is felt with particular urgency, the sense of time is conveyed through images which suggest a ceaseless fertility ever threatening to run out of control. Smarting under the shame of his idleness, Antony declares:

> O, then we bring forth weeds
> When our quick minds lie still, and our ills told us
> Is as our earing. (I, ii, 105–107)

Again:

> Much is breeding,
> Which, like the courser's hair, hath yet but life
> And not a serpent's poison. (I, ii, 188–190)

The quickening of events before Actium prompts Canidius to remark:

> With news the time's with labor and throws forth
> Each minute some. (III, vii, 81–82)

But if time for the slow-mover breeds with dangerous rapidity, for the agile opportunist it is capable of being cultivated or "eared." When Pompey is riding the full tide of fortune, commanding both the sea and the hearts of the commoners, his confederates, Menecrates and Menas,

> Make the sea serve them, which they ear and wound
> With keels of every kind. (I, iv, 49–50)

Caesar later "cuts" the Ionian Sea toward Actium with such speed that time for him seems a more fluid medium than it is for others, especially the slower, heavier Antony, whose own efforts at naval maneuvering are shortly to prove so ill-advised.

The turbulent flux of events is matched, on the human side, by the instability of desire. The play repeatedly dramatizes a sharp discrepancy between judgment and loyalty, between the apparent demands of the moment and the deeper, more abiding needs of the heart. What is scorned in the present becomes appreciated once it is past and beyond recovery. Antony, on hearing of Fulvia's death, discovers "she's good, being gone"

(I, ii, 122); and when he is told of Cleopatra's pretended death, bitter rejection turns in a flash into fervent devotion. Enobarbus learns too late that what reason recommends has little to do with his true emotional interests, and even the phlegmatic Caesar, after hunting down Antony to his death, is moved to weep. As Agrippa remarks:

And strange it is
That nature must compel us to lament
Our most persisted deeds. (V, i, 27–29)

These sudden reversals of sentiment are observable not only in the principal characters but also in the anonymous *hoi polloi.* Commenting on the "slippery" Roman people's enthusiasm for Pompey, Antony says their love "is never linked to the deserver Till his deserts are past" (I, ii, 181–183). Caesar amplifies the idea:

It hath been taught us from the primal state
That he which is was wished until he were;
And the ebbed man, ne'er loved till ne'er worth love,
Comes deared by being lacked. This common body,
Like to a vagabond flag upon the stream,
Goes to and back, lackeying the varying tide,
To rot itself with motion. (I, iv, 41–47)

In the play, as G. Wilson Knight observes, "there is continually this wavering, ebb and flow, of the spirit, a shifting, varying psychology."[1] Fundamental to the play's sense of time is the perception that the human heart, in ceaselessly riding the undulations of time, is unable to find a locus of commitment in the enduring present, and so is forced to vacillate continually between future and past, anticipation and memory.

Beneath the sharp oscillations of time and desire, however, there runs through the play a deeper, longer undercurrent of time, one which in its furthest extension into the past begins with the first Caesar and culminates in the triumph of the second. What might be called the memory of the play goes back to Caesar's murder and Philippi, the events which lie behind the Triumvirate and the political conflicts of the present, and to Cleopatra's old love affairs, which cast such an ambiguous light on her relationship with Antony. From the audience's viewpoint the future of the play, since it belongs to the historical past, is already set, predetermined. Caesar's pronouncements about "destiny" (III, vi, 84–85) and the coming "time of universal peace" (IV, vi, 5–7) are therefore to be taken literally as indications of the shape of things to come. Yet the more emphatic intimations of the future have to do not with Caesar's triumph and the reunification of the Empire but, under-

[1] *The Imperial Theme* (London, 1931), p. 275.

standably enough, with the downfalls of the two protagonists, their destinies being dramatically the more important. The Soothsayer is introduced at two points, once to foretell the doom of Cleopatra (I, ii), and once (II, iii) to warn Antony that he will lose in any competition with Caesar simply because Caesar is more fortunate, because time and the stars are working in his favor. The ominous music of Act IV, scene iii, which carries the implication that Antony's ancestor and guardian spirit, Hercules, has deserted him on the eve of the decisive battle, suggests obscurely but potently that supernatural processes are involved in Antony's downfall. The following scenes, covering Antony's preparation for battle and initial victory, are marked by an uncustomary retardation of pace, a momentary suspension of the onward rush of time which permits a slower, more ceremonious showing forth of the hero's final acts of generosity and prowess; as though here, just before the foredoomed end, he were once more returning to the Antony of old. The final outcome of the battle is anticipated in the ominous reports of the Egyptian augurers (IV, xii, 3–6). One effect of these foreshadowings is to indicate that the protagonists are opposed by time not only because they are forced to cope with the continually shifting demands of the present, but also, in a deeper sense, because their downfalls are implicated in the evolving, preestablished plan of history. But it is largely through their resistance to this plan and their ultimate transcendence of it that they gain a tragic supremacy, moving into the timeless dimensions of "their story" (V, ii, 359).

All these factors together produce the impression that time in this play is, except for Caesar, an unsalutary force, a medium against which rather than through which man must work to achieve his highest aims. Nevertheless, it is not invested with the same destructive potency it has in other Shakespeare plays and the Sonnets. It is envisioned neither as the implacable enemy of youth, beauty, and sensuous delight (the hero and heroine may be well on in years but they do not complain of it), nor as the "monster of ingratitude" which ruthlessly assigns all human worth and achievement to oblivion (Antony's former triumphs *are* vividly remembered). Nor does the play include the dilemma suffered by several of Shakespeare's tragic heroes, that of experiencing time as nothing but a painful monotony, without direction or purpose, merely sifting away into dust and nothingness. Such does it become at various moments for Richard II, Hamlet, Macbeth, and Lear, but here no character is driven to the point of seeing all human activity as meaningless: there is always at least the possibility of a Roman death. Conversely, time in *Antony* also lacks the positive, beneficent connotations that it has for those Shakespearian characters, mainly heroines, who learn to respond to it with a patient fortitude or "readiness." To Cordelia, Imogen, and, eventually, Hamlet, patience signifies a recognition that time, because it is under providential governance, ultimately heals and restores; but to Cleopatra patience is "sottish." While Caesar's vision of the evolving Empire does imply a kind of providential design, Caesar himself is hardly presented as the faithful and benevolent agent of higher powers.

If the world of the play is generally dominated by a heightened sense of temporal change, among the major characters sharply differing responses to this condition may be distinguished. It is in this area that time takes on a more refined, elusive significance, for here it becomes closely associated with the particular modes of expression and conduct created for each character. The subject may only be properly examined if first another, related element in the play is taken into account. This is the persistent emphasis given to the public images of Caesar, Antony, and Cleopatra. One of the accepted conditions of their milieu is that their essential worth is determined not by those hidden qualities which in a Christian context are visible only to the all-seeing eye of God, but rather by the way they appear outwardly to the world. The implied metaphor for this is that of the stage: The rulers of the earth, emperors and queens, are obliged to perform their roles before the world's audience in such a way as to imitate the established qualities of greatness. Honor, reverence, and loyalty are apportioned according to the success of their performance. In this the play illustrates the "high mimetic" mode attributed by Northrop Frye to Renaissance literature, insofar as the central theme of this mode is that of "cynosure or centripetal gaze, which... seems to have something about it of the court gazing upon its sovereign, the court-room gazing upon the orator, or the audience gazing upon the actor."[2] Appropriately, when Cleopatra displayed herself on the Cydnus, the very air would, but for a vacuum, have gone to "gaze" on her too (II, ii, 218); and Antony, resolving to join Cleopatra beyond the grave, envisions their ultimate bliss as being "gazed" upon by so many ghosts that Dido and Aeneas will want admirers (IV, xiv, 52). Other expressions which often recur are those of seeing, showing, and acting. Soon after the play begins the audience is pointedly enjoined to observe the queen and her paramour: "Look where they come: Take but good note, and you shall see..." (I, i, 10–11). Antony prepares for his death by asking Eros whether he would "see" him in the shameful posture of captivity (IV, xiv, 72–77); Cleopatra for hers by commanding Charmian and Iras: "Show me, my women, like a queen" (V, ii, 226). The play ends with Caesar's announcement: "Our army shall In solemn show attend this funeral..." (V, ii, 361–362).

One result of this emphasis on the public image is that revelations of inner experience are held to a minimum, receiving decidedly less attention than they do in Shakespeare's earlier tragedies. As acutely conscious as they are of how they appear to others, the characters show relatively little awareness of the private, isolated self. Caesar is never alone to soliloquize; indeed, only twice does he display a spontaneous attitude undetermined by calculated

---

[2] *Anatomy of Criticism: Four Essays* (Princeton, 1957), p. 58.

impression or political expedience—when he praises Antony for his Spartan demeanor during the retreat from Modena, and when he laments Antony's death. With Cleopatra there is no clear distinction between private and public attitude. All her moods and utterances are—not necessarily in a pejorative sense—theatrical. When more important personages are unavailable, she uses her retainers as an everpresent audience whose main function is to witness and appreciate. Antony does soliloquize—six times; but only one of his soliloquies, the first, in which he registers the impact of Fulvia's death, shows the kind of analytic self-awareness which follows upon abrupt disillusionment or reversal of expectation. The others are as though spoken to an audience which does not happen to be present at the moment. The one character whose private experience becomes in the end of paramount significance is Enobarbus. Through his disloyalty he dissociates himself from a human audience, from anyone like the Roman staff officers with whom he can share an immediate camaraderie and mutual respect. Hence he is forced to suffer his agony of self-reproach in isolation, having only the moon to call upon as witness to his guilt and repentance.

The kinds of public image the characters strive to create or preserve in the face of universal mutability is closely related to their sense of time; and both public image and sense of time are bound up with the implicit moral valuation Shakespeare places on each of them. While within the dominant time sense of each character there are obvious fluctuations, generally it may be said that for Caesar the most meaningful aspect of time is the future; for Antony, the past; for Cleopatra, the present.

For Caesar time in its broader movement is progressive, pointing ahead to the final goal of "universal landlordship." Not that he clearly envisions this goal from the start; rather it emerges gradually as he recognizes and seizes upon the opportunities which time engenders. His progress is facilitated by an acute time-consciousness which appears both in the frequency with which the word "time" itself occurs in his discourse—more often than in any other character's—and in his aversion to wasting time in the pleasures of the moment. In his first scene he complains of Antony's "confounding the time" in Alexandria (I, iv, 28), emphasizing the latter's flagrant violation of the normal diurnal routine through his wasting "The lamps of night in revel" and reeling about "the streets at noon" (I, iv, 5, 20). During the debauched symposium on Pompey's galley Caesar refuses to be "a child o' th' time," claiming that "our graver business Frowns at this levity" (II, vii, 119–120). When it comes to military and political tactics, he knows the value of an efficient spy system ("I have eyes upon him, And his affairs come to me on the wind" [III, vi, 62–63]) and can dispense with the advice of his subordinates because he has already anticipated what has to be done and has done it (" 'Tis done already, and the messenger gone" [III, vi, 31]). Caesar's efficiency is supported by another attitude, an unillusioned acceptance of the slipperiness of human desire. Since he regards human nature, especially the feminine part of it (III, xii, 29–31), as gullible and unsteadfast, he is never caught off balance by betrayed expectations. Hence he is unsurprised by the Roman people's flocking to the support of Pompey, experience having led him to expect as much. When the jilted Octavia returns from Athens—already the victim of her brother's practice of subordinating personal feeling to policy—he offers her the consolation that it is no use regretting things that could not have happened otherwise:

> Cheer your heart:
> Be you untroubled with the time, which drives
> O'er your content these strong necessities;
> But let determined things to destiny
> Hold unbewailed their way. (III, vi, 81–85)

The public image Caesar consistently tries to present is that of the just, conscientious ruler. Already in his opening words he is showing Lepidus how fair-minded he can be about Antony, and whenever he takes action against an opponent he carefully provides self-exonerating reasons, as though his action were provoked. Greeting Octavia, he is disturbed that her unexpected arrival has prevented the "ostentation" of his love, "which, left unshown, Is often left unloved" (III, vi, 50–53). After defeating Antony he proposes to "show" his officers how reluctant he was to make war against him (V, i, 73–77). His dealings with Cleopatra amount to an elaborate exercise in letting "the world see / His nobleness well acted" (V, ii, 44–45). In these deliberately theatrical gestures Caesar is observing the Machiavellian principle that the ruler should strive always to *appear,* not necessarily be, just and virtuous. For all his talk of bonds, oaths, and justice, in the course of the play he deceives, or tries to deceive, every other character of political consequence: Pompey, Lepidus, Antony, and Cleopatra. His public image therefore seems unrelated to any consistent personal ideal. Owing to his concentration on the future he neither commits himself to anything beyond the "strong necessities" of his program nor inspires genuine commitment in return. Only twice, as we have seen, does he avert his attention from the future and indulge in retrospection, on both occasions eulogizing Antony. Politically speaking, Shakespeare no doubt means to suggest that the consolidation of the Empire under one ruler and the resulting "universal peace" are desirable achievements, insofar as they reestablish the order which was disrupted by the murder of Julius Caesar. But in terms of the deeper moral values asserted in the play—in Enobarbus' observations on loyalty, for instance (III, xiii, 43–46)—Caesar gains his success at the expense of an unedifying compromise with the ways of the world. By regarding time as instrumental, solely in its aspect of emergent opportunity, he himself becomes, in a sense, time's instrument.

> Not being Fortune, he's but Fortune's knave,
> A minister of her will. (V, ii, 3–4)

Antony plainly lacks Caesar's facility for adapting himself to the changing demands of time. Much of his behavior is characterized by a persistent strain. He is rarely able to meet with ease and assurance the circumstances confronting him. His shifts in strategy and allegiance arise not like Caesar's from clear-sighted calculation, but rather from sudden, unreflective impulse —in Enobarbus' terms, not from judgment but from will. Beginning with his revulsion from the "present pleasure" and quick retreat from Egypt, the strain, the radical fluctuations of temper, continue, except for rare interludes of equilibrium, until he is told of Cleopatra's death. Then, at the line

> Unarm, Eros. The long day's task is done,
> And we must sleep, (IV, xiv, 35–36)

there is a sudden loosening, a grateful relinquishment of effort. Now that "All length is torture" (IV, xiv, 46), death appears to Antony as a welcome liberation.

The source of the strain seems to be a self-dividedness in Antony which goes deeper than the surface conflict between Love and Honor, Egypt and Rome. At several points the name Antony ("That magical name of war") is invoked both by himself and others in almost incantational fashion, as though it signified a fixed concept of Antony; and this concept, or "true" self, is often seen as dangerously contradicted by the visible Antony. This appears at the outset of the play in Philo's contrast between what Antony was and what he has become, and again at the end of the first scene:

> Sir, sometimes when he is not Antony
> He comes too short of that great property
> Which still should go with Antony. (I, i, 57–59)

What propels Antony back to Rome is his fear of "losing himself" in dotage (I, ii, 113), and once there he admits to Caesar that in Alexandria "poisoned hours had bound me up From mine own knowledge" (II, ii, 90–91). To Octavia he declares: "If I lose mine honor, I lose myself" (III, iv, 22–23). After Actium, a battle he would have won had he "Been what he knew himself" (III, x, 27), he is bitterly conscious of self-betrayal:

> I have fled myself. . . .
> My very hairs do mutiny: for the white
> Reprove the brown for rashness, and they them
> For fear and doting.
> Let that be left
> Which leaves itself. (III, xi, 7, 13–15, 19–20)

In the throes of defeat, Antony viciously reasserts his authority by having Thidias whipped ("I am Antony yet" [III, xiii, 92–93]) and by sending an angry message to Caesar:

For he seems
Proud and disdainful, harping on what I am,
Not what he knew I was. (III, xiii, 141–143)

Fully aware of Antony's self-conflict, Caesar exploits it by arranging the final battle in such a way "That Antony may seem to spend his fury Upon himself" (IV, vi, 10–11).

Unmistakable emphasis is given, then, to a cleavage in Antony which can be expressed in temporal terms, a cleavage between what he is in the present and what he has been in the past, prior to the time of the play. Since most of his efforts are directed toward perpetuating or revivifying his self-image against the constant threat of temporal change, his vision of time is essentially retrospective. The past he tries to preserve is not the kind which is recreated through active personal reminiscence (Antony himself actually does very little recalling of former exploits, only doing so when chafing under the shame of losing a battle to the "boy" Octavius); rather it is the kind which is enshrined in the public memory as an image of incomparable greatness. And this image is based, in turn, not on the discreet political virtues cultivated by Caesar, but on those qualities of military prowess and munificence which inspire intense awe and devotion in the observer. Caesar's relationships with others are contractual, regulated by bonds and oaths; Antony's, on the other hand, are at their best chivalric, based on close personal commitment between leader and follower. Hence Antony's efforts to perpetuate his image, to "be himself," are closely linked with his ability to command the loyalty of his devotees, Cleopatra before all others. Their loyalty is the mirror in which he sees his greatness reflected.

Many of Antony's movements in the play result, then, from his impulsive attempts to retrieve that eminence which he regards as virtually synonymous with his being. Such is the reason for his hasty return to Rome, and again for his return to Egypt. During the prolonged process of his downfall, however, there is one sequence of scenes in which he momentarily conquers his characteristic oscillations of attitude and succeeds in becoming one with his image, in making it authentically present. These are the scenes just before and during the final battle which, as noted earlier, show a marked retardation in the usual accelerated pace of the action (IV, iv-v, vii-viii). No longer obsessed with the undeserved prosperity of the younger, luckier Caesar, Antony does not resort to the desperate bravado of challenging him to single combat, but instead, feeling the morning imbued with the "spirit of youth," regards the coming battle with buoyant anticipation. With uncommon humility he acknowledges his past errors of strategy and assumes some of the blame for Enobarbus' defection. Towards Cleopatra and his followers he displays a spirited comradeship, showing no anxiety over the fidelity of the one, and freely praising the others for their deeds with none of that finicky concern for his own honor earlier ascribed to him by Ventidius. His speech is filled with the terms and attitudes of chivalry ("our gests," "this great fairy," "promises royal peril," [IV, xiii, 2, 12, 35]), as though for him the battle were purely a matter of old-style heroism, uncontaminated by Caesarian Realpolitik. Antony's momentary triumph in the dual role of lover and warrior makes this the one point in the play, as Knight observes,[3] where the two hitherto antagonistic values of Love and War converge and support one another.

But the scenes are already ironically undercut by the premonitions of doom conveyed through the mysterious music just preceding. The battle lost, Antony is thrust once again into his quandary of self-division by what he supposes to be the betrayal of Cleopatra and the thousands she draws after her. Owing to the "discandying" of their loyalty, he feels that his image has become as illusory as the evanescent forms of clouds at sunset: "here I am Antony, Yet cannot hold this visible shape..." (IV, xiv, 13–14). Upon recovering himself in response to Cleopatra's supposed suicide, Antony looks upon death at first with joyful anticipation, as a means of escaping the entanglements of temporal existence into a realm of idyllic freedom, where he and Cleopatra will be the sole objects of "gazing" admiration (IV, xiv, 44–54). But when he is actually dying and learns that Cleopatra is not waiting to meet him in the Elysian Fields, this attitude gives way to another: He comes to look upon death instead in its aspect of finality, as a means of fixing unalterably the "visible shape" he will hold in memory. Although Eros, his soldiers, and Cleopatra show that their devotion is as firm as ever, his main satisfaction is that in his suicide he has performed an entirely autonymous act of honor, "conquering" that self which had proved so difficult to hold intact at the latter end of his career.

> Not Caesar's valor hath o'erthrown Antony,
> But Antony's hath triumphed on itself. (IV, xx, 14–15)

As Antony approaches his end, the falling rhythms of his lines betray an enervation not merely physical but spiritual, a final loosening of the strain. The kiss he begs of Cleopatra is not the prelude to future voluptuousness beyond the grave—he assumes she will live after him—but simply the "poor last." At the end he makes a final effort to fix himself in the memory of his audience, directing their attention away from the ignominious present to the resplendent past:

> The miserable change now at my end
> Lament nor sorrow at; but please your thoughts
> In feeding them with those my former fortunes,

[3] *The Imperial Theme,* pp. 280, 305–306.

> Wherein I lived the greatest prince o' th' world,
> The noblest. . . . (IV, xv, 51–55)

After Antony's death, the task of perpetuating his image falls to Cleopatra and her volatile imagination, fired into intense activity by her devotion. Through the imagery of her lamentation (IV, xv, 59–68) he becomes the world's central symbol of excellence whose absence makes the world no longer worth abiding in. Cleopatra's "dream" of Antony (V, ii, 76–92) magnifies the image even further: It virtually deifies him, assimilating him to the larger controlling processes of nature—the spheres, seasons, and elements—so that like them he appears permanent and inexhaustible, above mortal limitation. Thus if the living Antony must forever struggle to preserve his image against the pressures of time, once he is bodily removed from the scene his image is liberated into a visionary realm where "fancy outworks nature," and those pressures no longer prevail.

The significance of time for Cleopatra is not quite so easy to decide as it is for Caesar and Antony, her attitudes being more rapid and mutable, more imbued with "variety," than theirs. Much of the ambiguity about her, reflected in the widely differing views of her offered by modern criticism, arises from Shakespeare's deliberate failure to distinguish clearly between what she really feels and what she merely pretends. To those who judge her with the sobriety of a Caesar, nearly all her actions are tainted with coquetry or self-interest until she resolves, or rather carries out her resolution, to die for Antony. But perhaps the kind of "truth" implied in such a judgment, a kind exemplified by the "holy, cold, and still" Octavia, is not one that can be meaningfully applied to Cleopatra. She eludes the sharp distinction between sincerity and pretense because her nature is intrinsically histrionic. It is impossible to conceive her as having an unobserved existence, apart from an audience. At every moment she forces her onlookers to recognize and appreciate the fact of her being. If she is not indulging in such more obvious forms of play-acting as dressing up as Isis, wearing Antony's sword Philippan, or wandering the streets of Alexandria in disguise, then she is testing her power to captivate on a Thidias, Dolabella, or Caesar. She is morally naive in the sense that she is incapable of regretting what she has done in the past or of disciplining her desires in the present. She regards all her moods and impulses as equally valid, equally worthy of revelation:

> Whom every thing becomes—to chide, to laugh,
> To weep; whose every passion fully strives
> To make itself, in thee, fair and admired. (I, i, 49–51)

This means in effect that time for Cleopatra is not a rationally demarcated sequence of past, present, and future, but consists of a flexible, continuous present. Since every moment offers an opportunity for self-disclosure, then every moment has its own particular authority. From the efficient Roman viewpoint Cleopatra is a creature of "idleness" for whom time means nothing in a moral or practical sense; but actually her kind of idleness involves a full emotional commitment quite incompatible with mere sensual indulgence. As she tells the unsympathetic Antony:

> 'Tis sweating labor
> To bear such idleness so near the heart
> As Cleopatra this. (I, iii, 93–95)

Her idleness also involves an incessant imaginative activity which carries her freely beyond the immediate here and now, enriching even the "great gap of time" when she has nothing to do but wait passively for Antony. In his absence, her thoughts reach out to him in the present moment:

> Where think'st thou he is now? Stands he, or sits he?
> Or does he walk? or is he on his horse? (I, v, 19–20)

Then comes a quick movement of empathy:

> O happy horse, to bear the weight of Antony! (I, v, 23)

Cleopatra's "freer thoughts" proceed to dwell appreciatively on her irrepressible seductive powers, and in so doing move into the past:

> Now I feed myself
> With most delicious poison. Think on me,
> That am with Phoebus' amorous pinches black
> And wrinkled deep in time. Broad-fronted Caesar,
> When thou wast here above the ground, I was
> A morsel for a monarch; and great Pompey
> Would stand and make his eyes grow in my brow;
> There would he anchor his aspect, and die
> With looking on his life. (I, v, 26–34)

However dark and wrinkled she may be, "age cannot wither her." Time has a ripening effect on Cleopatra, bringing her to a plenitude of vitality through the sun's gradual action. She prides herself not only on having fascinated the great ones of the earth but also on having outlived them: they pass on but she endures. So strong in her is the sense of vital continuity that she can hardly be imagined as ever having been essentially different from what she is—as once having been "green in judgment, cold in blood" (I, v, 74). When she refers to her "salad days" she is sharing a joke with Charmian.

The paradoxical linking of life and death at the end of the last quotation suggests that extensive range of images with which Cleopatra is associated throughout the play—images, such as those of the ebb and flow of the Nile, having to do with the cyclical processes of nature, the endless round of growth and decay; also with the two kinds of "death"—mortal and erotic—represented ambiguously in Cleopatra's "celerity in dying" (I, ii, 141) and the immortal worm that "kills and pains not" (V, ii, 244). These oxymora recur so often that they seem inseparable from Cleopatra and her milieu. As her barge floats rhythmically on the waters of the Cydnus (not cutting through them purposefully like the ships of Pompey and Caesar), she holds her gazers rapt, simultaneously raising and allaying appetite, making "hungry Where most she satisfies" (II, ii, 238–239). Again in Enobarbus' description: "she did make defect perfection And, breathless, pow'r breathe forth" (II, ii, 232–233). Cleopatra is further identified with the animating forces of nature through her association with Isis, and her declaration to Antony that if she is ever "cold-hearted," then not only she but also the "memory" of her womb and her "brave Egyptians all" will perish (III, xiii, 158–167). The import of these images is that Cleopatra inhabits a sphere where time is natural rather than historical, where instead of moving in linear progression as it does for Caesar, or with perilous unpredictability as it does for Antony, it forever undulates through the mingled revolutions of depletion and renewal, life and death.

As Cleopatra prepares for her own death she does not undergo complete regeneration so much as a refinement of qualities she has shown all along, a sublimation into "fire and air" (V, ii, 288). This can be expressed as a movement from a present rather haphazard in its fluctuations to one which through ceremonious deliberateness gains a definitive clarity, or "shackles accidents and bolts up change" (V, i, 6). Her actions are more consciously histrionic than before, partly stemming as they do from her desire to "show" herself in the posture of invincible queenliness so as to escape the unthinkable fate of being exhibited to the shouting *hoi polloi* of Rome. But the image she creates, in contrast to the exhausted finality of Antony's dying gestures, fully preserves her sense of vital continuity. Death to her means "liberty" (V, ii, 237), a chance to rejoin Antony in all the triumphant splendor of their first meeting on the Cydnus. She hastens towards it with the impatience of "immortal longings" (V, ii, 280), and the commands she gives are crisp and energetic:

> Yare, yare, good Iras; quick. Methinks I hear
> Antony call: I see him rouse himself
> To praise my noble act. (V, ii, 282–284)

The closer to death Cleopatra draws, the more actively her histrionic imagination works as she rehearses in rapid succession the multiple roles of queen, wife, mistress, cunning victor over Caesar, and nursing mother. The quick change of mood in her final lines, from swooning rapture to alert impatience, shows her "variety" undampened to the end. Even in death she sustains the impression of a vitality not extinguished but merely dormant:

> She looks like sleep,
> As she would catch another Antony
> In her strong toil of grace. (V, ii, 344–346)

In the end, the realm of disordered and directionless time, the realm under the sway of the "false huswife Fortune," is met and overcome in two sharply opposed ways. Caesar has gained his grand objective: the "three-nooked world" is at peace. The confidence with which he wears his new hegemony appears in his refusal to be annoyed by the deception worked on him by his prize captive. If he is aware of having been made an "ass Unpolicied," he does not show it. Unimpeded in his forward progress, he is looking ahead once again in his next to last word: "And then to Rome"—words which even in their parenthetical brevity evoke the coming Augustan grandeur. But Caesar also pauses to commemorate in choric fashion the "story" of his two opponents, and it is this story which dramatically represents the more impressive and enduring victory. Through his dedication to an impersonal historical destiny, his concentration on the possibilities of the future, Caesar, as we have seen, suffers an impoverishment of self, an inability to regard any impractical activity as more than a wasteful indulgence or "confounding" of time. Antony's obsession with a static image of former greatness leads to another kind of self-dislocation, an inability to exist fully and consistently in the present. His is necessarily a post-mortem success, achieved through the releasing of his image from the complexities of time into uninhibited fantasy. The "story" of the play, its final dramatic impact, therefore, depends on Cleopatra. Her last scene is tragic in an especially exalted sense because more than any other figure in Shakespeare she consciously and ceremoniously fashions the style of her death. She treats it as a kind of inspired play—play in the sense of free histrionic activity and the full enjoyment of one's faculties in the present, without a deflection of energy into either the recapturing of the past or the conquering of the future. She demonstrates the paradox familiar in modern psychoanalytic literature, that to live fully one must accept the actuality of death, be able to die with "celerity." In her readiness to "play till doomsday" she asserts the supremacy of being over becoming, and illuminates the meaning of one of the key Shakespearian terms: "ripeness."